The Routledge International Handbook of Walking

Walking is an essentially human activity. From a basic means of transport and opportunity for leisure through to being a religious act, walking has served as a significant philosophical, literary and historical subject. Thoreau's 1851 lecture on *Walking* or the Romantic walks of the Wordsworths at Grasmere in the early nineteenth century, for example, helped create a philosophical foundation for the importance of the act of walking as an act of engagement with nature. Similarly, and sometimes inseparable from secular appreciation, pilgrimage trails provide opportunities for finding self and others in the travails of the walk. More recently, walking has been embraced as a means of encouraging greater health and well-being, community improvement and more sustainable means of travel. Yet despite the significance of the subject of walking there is as yet no integrated treatment of the subject in the social science literature.

This handbook therefore brings together a number of the main themes on the study of walking from different disciplines and literatures into a single volume that can be accessed from across the social sciences. It is divided into five main sections: culture, society and historical context; social practices, perceptions and behaviours; hiking trails and pilgrimage routes; health, well-being and psychology; and method, planning and design. Each of these highlights current approaches and major themes in research on walking in a range of different environments.

This book carves out a unique niche in the study of walking. The international and cross-disciplinary nature of the contributions are expected to be of interest to numerous academic fields in the social and health sciences, as well as to urban and regional planners and those in charge of the management of outdoor recreation and tourism globally.

C. Michael Hall is Professor of Marketing, University of Canterbury, New Zealand; Docent in Geography, Oulu University, Finland; Visiting Professor, Linnaeus University, Sweden; and Senior Research Fellow, University of Johannesburg, South Africa. Author and editor of over 80 books, he has published widely on tourism, sustainability, governance and food issues.

Yael Ram is Senior Lecturer at the Department of Tourism Studies, Ashkelon Academic College, Israel.

Noam Shoval is Professor of Geography at the Hebrew University of Jerusalem, Israel.

The Routledge International Handbook of Walking

*Edited by C. Michael Hall, Yael Ram
and Noam Shoval*

Routledge
Taylor & Francis Group

LONDON AND NEW YORK

First published 2018 by Routledge

2 Park Square, Milton Park, Abingdon, Oxon OX14 4RN

605 Third Avenue, New York, NY 10017

Routledge is an imprint of the Taylor & Francis Group, an informa business

First issued in paperback 2022

British Library Cataloguing-in-Publication Data
A catalogue record for this book is available from the British Library

Library of Congress Cataloging-in-Publication Data
Names: Hall, Colin Michael, 1961– editor. | Ram, Yael, editor. | Shoval, Noam, editor.
Title: The Routledge international handbook of walking / edited by C. Michael Hall, Yael Ram & Noam Shoval.
Other titles: International handbook of walking
Description: Abingdon, Oxon ; New York, NY : Routledge, 2017. |
    Includes bibliographical references and index.
Identifiers: LCCN 2017004098 | ISBN 9781138195349 (hardback : alk. paper) |
    ISBN 9781317271116 (web pdf) | ISBN 9781317271109 (epub3) |
    ISBN 9781317271093 (mobipocket) | ISBN 9781315638461 (ebk)
Subjects: LCSH: Walking. | Fitness walking. | Hiking. | Pedestrian areas. |
    Pedestrian facilities design
Classification: LCC GV199.5 .R68 2017 | DDC 796.51—dc23
LC record available at https://lccn.loc.gov/2017004098

ISBN: 978-1-138-19534-9 (hbk)
ISBN: 978-1-03-233954-2 (pbk)
DOI: 10.4324/9781315638461

Typeset in Bembo
by Apex CoVantage, LLC

This book is dedicated to the memory of Anja Hälg Bieri and John Clarke

Contents

Contents

Contents

Figures

Tables

Contributors

Giovanna Bertella, School of Business and Economics, UiT The Arctic University of Norway, N-9037 Tromsø, Norway.

Anja Hälg Bieri, formerly School of Performing Arts, Virginia Tech, Blacksburg, Virginia, USA.

Ray Boland, Breda University of Applied Science, NHTV, Breda, The Netherlands.

María Laura Borla, Asociación Profesionales en Turismo de Tierra del Fuego, Las Margaritas 38 (9410) Ushuaia, Tierra del Fuego, Argentina.

Heriberto Cairo, Facultad de Ciencias Politicas y Sociologia, Campus de Somosaguas, Universidad Complutense de Madrid, 28223 Pozuelo de Alarcon, Madrid, Spain.

Derek P.T.H. Christie, Ecole polytechnique fédérale de Lausanne (EPFL), Station 16, 1015 Lausanne, Switzerland.

Annika Dahlberg, Department of Physical Geography, Stockholm University, Sweden.

Subhajit Das, Department of Geography, Presidency University, Kolkata 700073, India.

Adele Doran, Department of Service Sector Management, Sheffield Business School, Sheffield Hallam University, Sheffield S1 1WB, UK.

Hélène Ducros, University of Leicester, Department of Geography, Bennett Building, University Road, Leicester LE1 7RH, UK.

Merete Kvamme Fabritius, Nordland Research Institute, Postboks 1490, N-8049 Bodø, Norway.

Kirsty Finnie, MSc Occupational Therapy, University of Brighton, Cockcroft, Lewes Road, Brighton BN4 2GJ, UK.

Peter Fredman, European Tourism Research Institute (ETOUR), Mid Sweden University, Östersund, Sweden and Department of Ecology and Natural Resource Management (INA), Norwegian University of Life Sciences, Norway.

Warwick Frost, Department of Management and Marketing, La Trobe University, Melbourne, VIC 3086, Australia.

Karein K. Goertz, University of Michigan's Residential College, Ann Arbor, Michigan, USA.

Rubén Camilo Lois González, Grupo de Investigación de Análisis Territorial, Instituto Universitario de Estudos e Desenvolvemento de Galicia, Avenida das Ciencias, University of Santiago de Compostela, E-15782 Santiago de Compostela, Galicia, Spain.

Miia Grénman, Marketing and International Business, Turku School of Economics at University of Turku, 20014 University of Turku, Finland.

Sven Gross, Professor of Transport Carrier Management, Harz University of Applied Sciences, Faculty of Business Management, Institute for Tourism Research (ITF), Friedrichstrasse 57–59, 38855 Wernigerode, Germany.

C. Michael Hall, Department of Management, Marketing and Entrepreneurship, University of Canterbury, Christchurch, New Zealand; Department of Geography, University of Oulu, Finland; and School of Business and Economics, Linnaeus University, Kalmar, Sweden.

Kevin Hannam, The Business School, Edinburgh Napier University, Edinburgh, Scotland, UK.

Debbie Hopkins, Transport Studies Unit, School of Geography and the Environment, University of Oxford, UK.

Rami K. Isaac, Academy for Tourism, NHTV Breda University of Applied Sciences, Breda, The Netherlands.

Manirul Islam, Department of English, Asannagar Madan Mohan Tarkalankar College, Nadia, India.

Yoshitaka Iwasaki, Professor and Associate Dean, Research, Faculty of Extension, 2–252 Enterprise Square, 10230 Jasper Avenue, University of Alberta, Edmonton, Alberta, Canada T5J 4P6.

Vanessa Jansen-Meinen, Rhine-Waal University of Applied Sciences, Marie-Curie-Strasse 1, 47533 Kleve, Germany.

Kumi Kato, Faculty of Tourism, Wakayama University and Graduate School of Tourism, Center for Tourism Research, Wakayama University, Japan.

Vincent Kaufmann, Ecole polytechnique fédérale de Lausanne (EPFL), Station 16, 1015 Lausanne, Switzerland.

Jennifer Laing, Department of Management and Marketing, La Trobe University, Melbourne, VIC 3086, Australia.

María Lois, Facultad de Ciencias Politicas y Sociologia, Campus de Somosaguas, Universidad Complutense de Madrid, 28223 Pozuelo de Alarcon, Madrid, Spain.

Sandra Mandic, Active Living Laboratory, School of Physical Education, Sport and Exercise Sciences, University of Otago, New Zealand.

Ron McCarville, Department of Recreation & Leisure Studies, University of Waterloo, Waterloo, Ontario, Canada N2L 3G1.

Xosé Somoza Medina, Departmento de Geografía y Geología, University of León, Campus de Vegazana, León, 24071 Spain.

Stephen Miles, Affiliate Research Fellow, School of Interdisciplinary Studies, University of Glasgow, Rutherford/McCowan Building, Crichton University Campus, Dumfries DG1 4ZL Scotland UK.

Andrew Mondschein, Department of Urban and Environmental Planning, University of Virginia School of Architecture, Campbell Hall, PO Box 400122, Charlottesville VA 22904–4122.

Diana Müller, Ostfalia University Of Applied Science, Faculty of Transport-Sports-Tourism-Media, Institute for Tourism and Regional Research, Karl-Scharfenberg-Str. 55/57, D-38229 Salzgitter, Germany.

Ray Nolan, Department of Service Sector Management, Sheffield Business School, Sheffield Hallam University, Sheffield S1 1WB, UK.

Ingeborg M. Nordbø, University College of Southeast Norway, Department of Business, Administration and Computer Science, University College of Southeast Norway.

Wan Rabiah Wan Omar, Faculty of Architecture, Planning and Surveying, Universiti Teknologi MARA, Seri Iskandar Campus, Perak, Malaysia.

Ian Patterson, School of Business (Tourism Cluster), The University of Queensland, St Lucia campus, Queensland, Australia.

Shane Pegg, School of Business (Tourism Cluster), The University of Queensland, St Lucia campus, Queensland, Australia.

Chantel Pilon, Department of Recreation & Leisure Studies, University of Waterloo, Waterloo, Ontario, Canada N2L 3G1.

Monika Popp, LMU Munich, Department of Geography, Luisenstraße 37, 80333 Munich, Germany.

Heinz-Dieter Quack, Ostfalia University of Applied Science, Faculty of Transport-Sports-Tourism-Media, Institute for Tourism and Regional Research, Karl-Scharfenberg-Str. 55/57, D-38229 Salzgitter, Germany.

Juulia Räikkönen, Marketing and International Business, Turku School of Economics at University of Turku, 20014 University of Turku, Finland.

Yael Ram, Department of Tourism and Leisure Studies, Ashkelon College, Yitshak Ben Zvi St 12, Ashkelon, Israel.

Outi Rantala, Multidimensional Tourism Institute, University of Lapland, P.O. Box 122, FI-96101 Rovaniemi, Finland, and Tourism & Northern Studies, Faculty of Sports, Tourism and Social Work, UiT – the Arctic University of Norway, Follumsvei 31, 9509 Alta, Norway.

Emmanuel Ravalet, Ecole polytechnique fédérale de Lausanne (EPFL), Station 16, 1015 Lausanne, Switzerland.

Neil Ravenscroft, Brighton Doctoral College, University of Brighton, Cockcroft, Lewes Road, Brighton BN4 2GJ, UK.

Dirk Reiser, Rhine-Waal University of Applied Sciences, Marie-Curie-Strasse 1, 47533 Kleve, Germany.

Anna Dóra Sæþórsdóttir, School of Engineering and Natural Sciences, Faculty of Life and Environmental Sciences, University of Iceland, Reykjavik, Iceland.

Robert Saunders, Department of Management, Monash University, Melbourne, Victoria, Australia.

Hannelene Schilar, Department of Geography and Economic History, Umeå University, Umeå, 90187 Sweden.

Peter Schofield, Department of Service Sector Management, Sheffield Business School, Sheffield Hallam University, Sheffield S1 1WB, UK.

Kathrin Schumacher, Ostfalia University of Applied Science, Faculty of Transport-Sports-Tourism-Media, Institute for Tourism and Regional Research, Karl-Scharfenberg-Str. 55/57, D-38229 Salzgitter, Germany.

Noam Shoval, Department of Geography and the Institute for Urban and Regional Studies, Faculty of Social Sciences, Hebrew University of Jerusalem, Israel.

Phil Smith, Plymouth University Koduke, Taddyforde Court, Exeter EX4 4AR, UK.

Sverker Sörlin, Division of History of Science, Technology and Environment, KTH Royal Institute of Technology, Stockholm.

Þorkell Stefánsson, School of Engineering and Natural Sciences, Faculty of Life and Environmental Sciences, University of Iceland, Iceland.

Daniel Svensson, Division of History of Science, Technology and Environment, KTH Royal Institute of Technology, Stockholm, Sweden.

Contributors

Franziska Thiele, Ostfalia University of Applied Science, Faculty of Transport-Sports-Tourism-Media, Institute for Tourism and Regional Research, Karl-Scharfenberg-Str. 55/57, D-38229 Salzgitter, Germany.

Seija Tuulentie, Natural Resources institute Finland, Eteläranta 55, 96100 Rovaniemi, Finland.

Marisol Vereda, Universidad Nacional de Tierra del Fuego, Onas 450 (9410) Ushuaia, Tierra del Fuego, Argentina.

Sandra Wall-Reinius, European Tourism Research Institute (ETOUR), Mid Sweden University, Östersund, Sweden.

Betty Weiler, School of Business and Tourism, Southern Cross University, Lismore, New South Wales, Australia.

Kim Werner, Business Management (Tourism & Event Management), Hochschule Osnabrück, University of Applied Sciences, Faculty of Business Management and Social Sciences, PO Box 1940, 49009 Osnabrück, Germany.

Brian Wheeller, Breda University of Applied Science, NHTV, Breda, The Netherlands.

Tania Wiseman, Senior Lecturer Occupational Therapy, University of Brighton, Cockcroft, Lewes Road, Brighton BN4 2GJ, UK.

Alexandra Witte, Leeds Beckett University, ICRETH, Carnegie Faculty, Cavendish 111, Leeds LS6 3QU, UK.

Preface and acknowledgements

Walking is an essentially human activity. From a basic means of transport and opportunity for leisure through to being a religious act, walking has served as a significant philosophical, literary and historical subject. Thoreau's 1851 lecture on *Walking* or the Romantic walks of the Wordsworths at Grasmere in the early nineteenth century, for example, helped create a philosophical foundation for the importance of the act of walking as an act of engagement with nature. Similarly, and sometimes inseparable from secular appreciation, pilgrimage trails provide opportunities for finding self and others in the travails of the walk. More recently, walking has been embraced as a means of encouraging greater health and well-being, community improvement and more sustainable means of travel. The subject of walking, perhaps understandably given its importance for the human condition, cuts across a wide number of disciplines but especially in the social sciences and humanities. The purpose of this book is therefore to bring together a number of the main themes on the study of walking from different disciplines and literatures into a single volume that can be easily accessed by readers from different fields and which clearly encourages stronger multi-disciplinary and post-disciplinary appreciation of an essential topic.

This volume, like many, also arises out of the particular combinations of our private and academic lives. We are, after all, walkers. The opportunity for walks and discussion in various parts of the world, but particularly in Germany, Israel, Mauritius and Sweden, have contributed greatly to the development of this and other projects. We also want to give thanks to our families. Yael especially thanks Eyal, Niv, Yoav and Yuval for the support, inspiration and long walks. Michael would like to thank Nicole Aignier, Tim Baird, Dorothee Bohn, Tim and Vanessa Coles, David and Melissa Duval, Martin Gren, Stefan Gössling, Johan Hultman, Michael James, John Jenkins, Dieter Müller, Helena Power, Girish Prayag, Jarkko Saarinen, Anna Dóra Sæþórsdóttir, Dan Scott, Dallen Timothy, and Maria-Jose Zapata Campos, who have all recently contributed in various ways to some of the ideas contained within, although the interpretation of their thoughts is, of course, my own. Beirut, Ane Brun, Paul Buchanan, Nick Cave, Bruce Cockburn, Elvis Costello, Ebba Forsberg, Fountains of Wayne, Lotte Kestner, Yael Naim, Agnes Obei, Vini Reilly, Glenn Tilbrook, Loudon Wainwright, BBC Radio 6 and KCRW were also essential to the writing and editing process. Finally, Michael would like to thank the many people who have supported his work over the years, and especially to the Js and the Cs who stay at home and mind the farm, and with whom he is always happy to go walking.

We would all like to extend our grateful thanks to Jody Cowper-James for her assistance with editing as well as to our editor Emma Travis at Routledge and to Carlotta Fanton and Pippa Mullins for their shepherding as well as to the rest of the Routledge team who have supported us over the course of the project.

1

Introduction

Walking – more than pedestrian

C. Michael Hall, Yael Ram and Noam Shoval

In one sense, it may seem strange to have an introduction to walking. After all, walks are something that almost every able-bodied person is able to experience, and every journey begins and ends with a walk. However, like many taken-for-granted everyday experiences, there are (sometimes unseen) influences and factors that affect how, where and why we do what we do, many of which we are unaware of until they are pointed out to us. So it is with the present volume, in which we bring together a range of perspectives on the histories, cultures, psychology, geography and planning of walking. The range of academic approaches is no accident; walking is an inherently cross-disciplinary topic, it

> trespasses through everybody else's field . . . and doesn't stop in any of them on its long route . . . If a field of expertise can be imagined as a real field . . . yielding a specific crop – then the subject of walking resembles walking itself in its lack of confines.
>
> *(Solnit 2000: 4)*

The purpose of the volume is therefore to highlight current research approaches, encourage further conversation between different fields on the subject of walking and contribute to walking as an important area of study in its own right.

Walking is a good thing. Walking encourages good public and private health, interaction between neighbours, contributes to feeling of community and positive sense of place, and, importantly in a time of concerns over climate and environmental change, contributes to reductions in traffic congestion, air pollution and emissions, and resource use (Leyden 2003; Forsyth and Southworth 2008; Ewing and Handy 2009; C3 Collaborating for Health 2012; Forsyth 2015). Furthermore, walkable places are increasingly being positioned as a positive in terms of economic performance and desirable from a real-estate perspective (Leinberger and Alfonzo 2012; Trowbridge *et al.* 2014) (see Box 1.1). However, in many cases, walking, especially in terms of where and when you can walk, is also constrained by social practices shaped by gender, culture, religion and economics. Furthermore, despite all the perceived benefits of walking, in many parts of the world the extent to which people engage in walking as a daily activity appears to have been in decline, as a result of new lifestyles and forms of personal mobility, as well as changes in planning and design of the built environment, that have often led to a decline in public space.

Walking is about being outside, in public space, and public space is also being abandoned and eroded in older cities, eclipsed by technologies and services that don't require leaving home, and shadowed by fear in many places . . . In many new places, public space isn't even in the design: what was once public space is designed to accommodate the privacy of automobiles; malls replace main streets, streets have no sidewalks; buildings are entered through their garages . . . Fear has created a whole style of architecture and urban design, notably in Southern California, where to be a pedestrian is to be under suspicion in many of the subdivisions and gated communities.

(Short 1991: 10)

Simultaneously with the transformation of public space, and arguably a part of the same processes of neoliberal capitalism and a reduction of the public sphere, walking has developed more as a commodity with associated development of commercial products such as specialist clothing, walking and fitness aids, as well as walking holidays and walking trails. Walking therefore represents some of the major themes of our age with respect to the marketization of what was previous private activities; indeed, the clash between notions of public and private is an important theme in much of the walking literature, relating as it does not only to the act of walking as an activity but where, when and how it can be conducted. As Macauley (2000) observed, walking

might be re-rooted in and re-routed through the urban and suburban landscape so as to pose a challenge to social tendencies that accentuate forms of domestication or domination. By understanding the dynamic and democratic dimensions of walking, we can also begin to interrogate and critically contest the opaque and authoritarian features of urban architecture, private property and public space. If we follow walkers through city and suburban placescapes, we might begin to observe the implicit cultural politics at work in various orders of ambulation. The control and maintenance of space and place, the organization of speed and pace, and the erection or transgression of community ideas of citizenship or race are instances of such phenomena. Further, the similarities become noticeable between pedestrian activity and linguistic speech acts in terms of a rhetoric of walking – a trail of 'foot notes' so to speak – within the processual setting and mobile text of the city. In short, an examination of walking in the city and suburbs shows us the many particular and overlapping 'walks of life'.

(Macauley 2000: 4)

The book is divided into five main sections: culture, society and historical context; social practices, perceptions and behaviours; hiking trails and pilgrimage routes; health, well-being and psychology; and method, planning and design. Each of these highlights current approaches and major themes in research on walking in a range of different environments. This first chapter looks to broadly introduce the reader to the topic of walking.

Walking

Although almost everyone walks, data on walking is highly variable. Table 1.1 provides a range of data on walking and related factors, such as obesity and perceived safety, for a range of countries. As the table illustrates, there are substantial variations between countries regarding the extent to which individuals engage in active transportation (bicycling and walking) as a percentage of all transport. However, of equal importance is the number of able-bodied people who do not go walking at all. For example, between April 2008 and April 2009, the US National Household Travel Survey (NHTS) asked respondents: 'In the past week, how many times did you take a walk outside including walking the dog and walks for exercise?' Remarkably, for this one-week time period nearly

---

Box 1.1   The economic promise of walkable places in Metropolitan Washington, DC

An economic analysis of a sample of neighborhoods in the Washington, DC metropolitan area in the United States using four metrics (Walk Score walkability measures, regional serving, economic performance and social equity) and a modified stratified random sampling scheme of 201 places found the following.

- More walkable places perform better economically. For neighborhoods within metropolitan Washington, as the number of environmental features that facilitate walkability and attract pedestrians increases, so do office, residential, and retail rents, retail revenues and for-sale residential values.
- Walkable places benefit value-wise from being near other walkable places. On average, walkable neighborhoods in metropolitan Washington that cluster and form walkable districts exhibit higher rents and home values than stand-alone walkable places.
- Residents of more walkable places have lower transportation costs and higher transit access, but higher housing costs. Residents of more walkable neighborhoods in metropolitan Washington generally spend around 12 per cent of their income on transportation and 30 per cent on housing. In comparison, residents of places with fewer environmental features that encourage walkability spend around 15 per cent on transportation and 18 per cent on housing.
- Residents of places with poor walkability are generally less affluent and have lower educational attainment than places with good walkability. Places with more walkability features have also become more gentrified over the past decade. However, there is no significant difference in terms of transit access to jobs between poor and good walkable places.

(Leinberger and Alfonzo 2012: 1)

According to Leinberger and Alfonzo (2012) the study's findings offer useful insights for a number of interests, including lenders, developers, investors, planning agencies and government agencies and private foundations.

Lenders . . . should find cause to integrate walkability into their underwriting standards. Developers and investors should consider walkability when assessing prospects for the region and acquiring property. Local and regional planning agencies should incorporate assessments of walkability into their strategic economic development plans and eliminate barriers to walkable development. Finally, private foundations and government agencies that provide funding to further sustainability practices should consider walkability (especially as it relates to social equity) when allocating funds and incorporate such measures into their accountability standards.

(Leinberger and Alfonzo 2012: 1)

Table 1.1 Data on walking and related factors for select countries

Country	% Active transportation (bikes and walking)[1]	% Walking trips[2]	Km of walking per capita per day[2]	% Walking from physical activity[3]	% Walking trips from daily trips[4]	Ave. length of walking trips (in km)[5]	% Obesity[6,7]	% Children aged 5–17 who are overweight or obese[8]	% Self-reported health[9]	Life satisfaction (1–10 scale)[9]	% Feeling safe to walk at night[9]
Australia	4.7	5		27	5		27.9[6]	23	85	7.3	62.6
Austria		21	419		21	0.9	12.5[7]	18	69	7.1	81.2
Belgium		16	380	25	16	1	18.6[6]	15.5	74	6.9	69.6
Brazil	11.9			25			13.5[7]	15	70	6.5	39.5
Canada		7		33	11		25.8[6]	24.5	89	7.4	81.7
China	46.1			57			2[7]	20	60	6.6	
Czech Republic				68			21[6]	15.5			70.1
Denmark		16	431		16		11.5[7]	18	72	7.5	85.2
Finland	19.5	22			22	1.8	24.8[6]	21.5	65	7.4	85.8
France	34.9	19	404	15	22	0.8	16.9[6]	15	67	6.4	70.6
Germany	32	23	372		24	1.6	23.6[6]	20	65	7	74.6
India				32			1[7]	20			
Ireland	12.8	13			11		23[6]	22	82	6.8	77
Italy			410				10[7]	35	66	5.8	59.3
Japan				43			3.9[7]	20	35	5.9	70.2
Netherlands	37.9	22	377		25	1.2	11.5[7]	16	76	7.3	80.5

Country										
New Zealand			26		0.85	29.9[6]	34	90	7.4	64.4
Norway	22		33	22	1.7	9.5[7]	14.5	76	7.6	89.6
Portugal			21			15.5[7]	28	46	5.1	69.2
Spain	35[est]		42			17.5[7]	25	72	6.4	81.6
Sweden	27.6[est]	383	33	23	2	10[7]	17	81	7.3	76.8
Switzerland	2.5				0.9	8.5[7]	18	81	7.6	87.4
UK	14.5	355		22		25.6[6]	24	74	6.5	77.8
USA	4	141	29	7	1.2	38.2[7]	30	88	6.9	73.9

Key

1 Hallal *et al.* 2012

2 Bassett *et al.* 2008

3 Bauman *et al.* 2009

4 Pucher and Buehler 2010

5 International Transport Forum 2012

6 OECD 2016b

7 Sassi 2010

8 OECD 2014

9 OECD 2016a

est = estimated

37% of Americans reported taking no walking trips at all. About 25% of children (5–15 years old) reported taking no walks or bike rides outside for any reason. Nearly one-third of younger people (16–65), and almost half of older Americans (65 and over) reported taking no walks outside for any purpose in the previous week (Department of Transportation 2010), while the average amount of time spent in active travel each day for all respondents was just 10 minutes per capita.

There was also substantial variation between different demographics in the US NHTS. For example, with respect to children, middle-income African-American families (household incomes of $40–$80,000 per year) and higher-income White families (household incomes of over $80,000 per year) were more likely to report taking any walks. Thirty per cent of Asian children reported taking no walking trips at all in the previous week, regardless of income (Department of Transportation 2010).

In the United States, the number of US workers who travelled to work by bicycle increased from about 488,000 in 2000 (approximately 0.4% of total commuting to work) to about 786,000 (0.6%) in 2008–2012, a larger percentage increase than that of any other commuting mode. However, the proportion of people walking to work over the same period dropped from 3.9% to 2.8%, indicating that fewer people that ever were engaged in an active mode of travel to work (5.0% took public transport). Indeed, in the 1980 US Census, 5.6% of travel to work consisted of walking and 0.5% cycling (McKenzie 2014). Also of interest is that several "university towns" showed high rates of walking to work, including Ithaca, New York, and Athens, Ohio, where about 42.0% and 37.0% of workers walked to work, respectively. Those aged 16 to 24 reported the highest rate of walking to work at 6.8% (McKenzie 2014).

The American situation with respect to lack of active travel and health problems is not occurring in isolation and highlights the global epidemics of cardiovascular disease and obesity and their relationships to diet and exercise regimes, including walking (Sallis et al. 2012; Hall et al. 2017). For example, if present trends continue, half of the UK's adult population is expected to be clinically obese by 2050 (Barton 2009). Nevertheless, walking practices do not occur in isolation from the environments within which people are situated, and such issues as the availability of public space, the walkability of where people live and work, and the extent to which mobility practices have been designed and encouraged not to be car-dependent (Feng et al. 2010; Durand et al. 2011; Sallis et al. 2012; Strandell and Hall 2015). Health and well-being has therefore become a major driver in trying to encourage people to walk more, as well as a factor in rethinking urban design and transport (Wolf and Wohlfarth 2014; Hall et al. 2017).

Walking is a fundamental means of transport for everyone. Clearly, there are physical limitations, with medically or physically impaired individuals regarded as pedestrians with reduced mobility. Nevertheless, the human body is well designed for a range of terrain characteristics – it can manage stairs, irregular surfaces, slopes and various weather conditions (Allan 2001). Therefore, constraints to engaging in walking may take a number of other forms. This may include physical, e.g. distance, built environment and weather; and social dimensions, e.g. motivations and perceptions, lifestyles, social norms and practices, and cost; and the interplay between the two (Mehta 2008; Ewing and Handy 2009). In addition, the purpose of walking, i.e. for transport, exercise and/or leisure, may be an influential factor, as well as whether or not you are a visitor to a location (Le-Klähn et al. 2015).

The broad urban design qualities of the built environment that have been suggested as more relevant to walking include the following (Ewing and Handy 2009; see also Southworth 2005; Moura et al. 2014, 2017).

- Imageability: the quality of a place that makes it distinct, recognizable and memorable.
- Legibility: the ease with which the spatial structure can be understood and navigated as a whole.

- Enclosure: the degree to which streets and other public spaces are visually defined by buildings, trees, walls and other elements.
- Human scale: the size, texture and articulation of physical elements that match the size and proportions of humans and, equally important, the speed at which humans walk.
- Transparency: the degree to which people can perceive or see what lies beyond the edge of a street or other public space and, more specifically, the degree to which people can see or perceive human activity beyond the edge of a street or other public space.
- Linkage: physical and visual connections between building and street, building to building, space to space, as well as one side of the street to the other.
- Complexity: the visual richness of a place.
- Coherence: the sense of visual order a place provides.

Much attention has therefore gone into understanding the way in which the built and natural environment provides opportunities for people to walk (Wang *et al.* 2016). Ding (2012) examined a series of potential moderators of the associations between neighbourhood environments and physical activity with the selection of moderators being based on ecological models (Giles-Conti *et al.* 2005). The analysis of the Neighborhood Quality of Life Study (NQLS) of 2,199 adults from selected neighbourhoods in two US regions found that psychosocial attributes (self-efficacy, social support, enjoyment, benefits and barriers) were moderators of neighbourhood environments with leisure walking as the outcome, but not with transport walking or accelerometer-based physical activity as the outcome. All interactions consistently supported stronger neighbourhood environment–leisure walking associations among those with less favourable psychosocial attributes. Similarly, using data from an international prevalence study collected in 11 countries, Ding (2012) found that the associations of physical activity/walking with land-use mix, sidewalks and bicycle facilities were consistent across different countries, suggesting a degree of generalizability. Associations involving other neighbourhood attributes were more variable. Similarly, a systematic review of the relationship between the built environment and physical activity among adults by McCormack and Shiell (2011) found that land-use mix, connectivity and population density, and overall neighbourhood design were important determinants of physical activity. However, the built environment was more likely to be associated with transportation walking compared with other types of physical activity, including recreational walking.

However, the concept of walkability has a number of different layers relating to the field and purpose for which it is used. Forsyth (2015), for example, suggest that the various definitions of walkable places and walkability could be categorized according to the extent they focused on means, e.g. traversible, compact, physically enticing and safe; outcomes, e.g. exercise-inducing, sustainable transportation, and lively and sociable; and where the terms were being used as a proxy for holistic or multi-dimensional urban design.

Walking and safety

Safety, in the context of walking, has multiple aspects and can refer to safety from traffic, safety from other people (i.e. from crime), and physical safety (i.e. from falls or animal attacks) (Southworth 2005; Forsyth 2015). The nature of the built environment, e.g. the provision of lighting at nighttime and good sidewalks, can have a significant impact of perceived safety. Safety has both real and perceived dimensions. In the US NHTS for children living close to their schools (within two miles/3.21 km), half of the parents thought the amount or speed of traffic was a serious issue in letting their kids walk to school, while less than a quarter thought crime or weather was a serious issue (Department of Transportation 2010). Safety from traffic depends, among other things, on the conditions of infrastructure, traffic laws and driving cultures. Consequently, pedestrian in countries with poor infrastructure are exposed to higher risk. Table 1.2 presents the rates of mortality of pedestrians from all traffic road deaths in 61 countries. The data shows that in non-OECD countries there is, on average, a higher mortality rate among pedestrians compared to OECD countries. The share of death of pedestrians is 26.06% (SD=10.269%) from all road death cases in non-OECD countries, and it is significantly higher than the share of deaths of pedestrians in OECD countries (mean 20.77%, SD=8.149%), the significant t-test value is $t(59) = 2.213, p = 0.031$.

Table 1.2 Mortality rates of pedestrians from all traffic road deaths in 61 countries

Country	Year	Road traffic deaths among pedestrians (% of all traffic death cases)
OECD Countries		
Australia	2013	13.2%
Austria	2013	18.0%
Belgium	2013	13.7%
Canada	2012	15.7%
Chile	2013	38.9%
Czech Republic	2013	24.8%
Estonia	2013	28.4%
Finland	2013	13.2%
France	2013	14.2%
Germany	2013	16.7%
Greece	2012	17.2%
Hungary	2013	24.9%
Ireland	2013	16.5%
Israel	2013	32.9%
Italy	2013	16.2%
Japan	2013	36.2%
Mexico	2012	30.3%
Netherlands	2013	9.8%
New Zealand	2013	11.8%
Norway	2013	9.6%
Poland	2013	34.0%
Portugal	2013	22.6%
Slovenia	2013	16.0%
Spain	2013	22.5%
Sweden	2013	16.2%
Switzerland	2013	25.7%
Turkey	2013	26.2%
United Kingdom	2013	22.9%
United States of America	2012	14.1%
Average rate OECD countries		20.77%

Country	Year	Road traffic deaths among pedestrians (% of all traffic death cases)
Non-OECD Countries		
Argentina	2013	10.1%
Armenia	2013	35.8%
Belarus	2013	41.6%
Bolivia	2013	32.5%
Bosnia and Herzegovina	2013	27.3%
Brazil	2012	19.7%
Bulgaria	2013	18.1%
China	2013	26.1%
Colombia	2013	29.3%
Croatia	2013	18.8%
Cyprus	2013	18.2%
Ecuador	2012	30.0%
Egypt	2013	29.2%
Georgia	2013	24.3%
India	2013	9.1%
Indonesia	2010	21.0%
Iran (Islamic Republic of)	2013–14	23.2%
Jordan	2013	35.7%
Kazakhstan	2012	22.5%
Kenya	2013	46.4%
Lebanon	2013	43.3%
Lithuania	2013	37.5%
Malaysia	2013	6.6%
Mongolia	2013	30.6%
Philippines	2013	19.0%
Romania	2013	39.0%
Russian Federation	2013	28.9%
Serbia	2013	26.9%
South Africa	2010–11	33.4%
Thailand	2012	8.1%
United Arab Emirates	2013	26.1%
Uruguay	2013	15.7%
Average rate non-OECD countries		**26.06%**

Source: WHO 2015

In all EU countries, pedestrians over 65 years are the most vulnerable group, with 28 death cases to a million population over 65 (Adminaite *et al.* 2015). As a group, elderly people tend to participate less in walking and physical activity outside their house than other age groups (Nelson *et al.* 2007; Department of Transport Statistics 2014/15). This makes their relative vulnerability even more disproportional to other age groups. Children, on the other hand, are the safest age group in the EU, with an average of 3.4 children killed as pedestrians per million population under 15. Exceptions are Romania and Lithuania, with 16 and 11 death cases respectively per million population under 15 (Adminaite *et al.* 2015).

Urban settings are the most dangerous to European pedestrians, with 69% of all pedestrian deaths. Given the high urbanization of Europe, this figure is not surprising. The lowest proportion of pedestrian deaths in urban areas was found in Lithuania (44%) and Latvia (50%). Most of the deaths were caused by an impact with a car (68%), followed by 22% due to impact with goods vehicles or buses, and around 4% in collisions with motorcycles. Naturally, cyclists and pedestrians do not endanger other road users as much as car drivers do. Accordingly, a modal shift to walking and cycling (as well as public transport overall) can potentially increase overall road safety (Adminaite *et al.* 2015). The presence of sidewalks is potentially an important factor for safety while walking as well as encouraging walking in general (Parra *et al.* 2010). Although it should be noted that while Reed *et al.* (2006) found a significant association between the perceived presence of sidewalks and walking, it was not statistically significant for sufficient physical activity for maintaining health.

Safety from falls may sound like an issue that mainly applies to the elderly. However, the texting-while-walking phenomenon turns it into a problem for all ages. According to the US Consumer Product Safety Commission (cited in Fowler 2016), more than 2,500 injured distracted pedestrians visited an emergency room in the United States in 2014 after using their cellphones while walking. The number was almost doubled in the two years since 2012.

Previous studies indicated that people who walk and use their phones pay less attention to situations, a phenomenon that was titled 'inattentional blindness'. They walk more slowly, changed directions more frequently, and were less likely to recognize other people (Nasar and Troyer 2013) as well as unusual situations on their routes such as a clown on a unicycle (Hyman *et al.* 2010) or a giant Wookiee (Fowler 2016). In 2010, more self-distracted cellphone-user pedestrians were injured in the United States compared to self-distracted cellphone-user drivers: 1,506 injured pedestrians (3.67% of all injured pedestrians) and 1,162 drivers (2.32% of all injured drivers). People younger than 25 were found as the most vulnerable age group (Nasar and Troyer 2013).

Nasar and Troyer (2013) called for legislation against texting while walking that would be followed by a deep change of norms, using parents as a role model. This recommendation is based on the assumption that this change is welcomed, but laws banning texting while walking failed in Toronto (Ward 2016), Arkansas, Illinois, Nevada, New Jersey and New York (Giancaspro 2016). Meanwhile, high-tech firms are developing technological solutions to the problem, offering a transparent screen that allows the pedestrians to see what is going on in front of them while texting (by using the back camera). Another direction for adaptation to the problem was provided by city councils via better urban planning and interventions to generate awareness. Fowler (2016) noted that some towns and college campuses have put 'look up' signs in dangerous stairwells and intersections. Hong Kong added announcements in its subway system recommending passengers to look around; New York City reduced speeds for cars, and San Francisco fosters pedestrian-only corridors.

Walking and gender

Walking in public spaces is often perceived as different experiences for men and women. Perceptions of safety can significantly affect access to public space and participation in leisure activities, such as walking, especially for women (Beebeejaun 2009; Oh *et al.* 2010; Hall and Page 2014). A worldwide Gallup survey in 143 countries with more than 180,000 participants (Crabtree and Nsubuga 2012), found an average gap of 10% between the share of men and women who answered 'Yes, feel safe' to the question: 'In the city or area where you live, do you feel safe walking

Table 1.3 Perception of feeling safe when walking alone at night

Region	Female	Male
Worldwide	62%	72%
Low-income countries	59%	67%
Lower middle-income countries	70%	75%
Upper middle-income countries	40%	54%
High-income countries	59%	82%

Source: Crabtree and Nsubuga 2012

alone at night, or not?' (Table 1.3). The gap was found to be larger in high-income countries (23%) than in lower- or middle-income countries (5%).

The Gallup survey indicated that only 60% of women in the UK feel safe walking at night, compared to 82% of men (Crabtree and Nsubuga 2012). However, the official data from the UK Department of Transport Statistics (2014/15) indicates that equal numbers of men and women walk for utility and recreational use. Of UK men, 86.2% walked at least 10 minutes in the previous month, compared to 85.8% of UK women. The data suggest that women, at least in the UK, are walking the same amount as men, but worry more. However, location as well as culture are very important factors in influencing whether or not places are regarded as safe for women, as well as whether they are perceived differently between men and women (Lee and Cho 2009; Velasquez *et al.* 2009).

Technologies

The walking experience is changing due to the impact of technology. Obviously, walking has always been affected by changes in transport technology as both alternatives to walking and as means for people to walk more easily outside of their home environment. However, of far more direct impact on walking is the use of mobile phones and, increasingly, wearable ICT and augmented reality.

An example of the way that technology interacts with walking is with the adoption of technology that helps walkers to count how many steps they have taken. The origins of this trend are linked to the 1964 Tokyo Summer Olympic Games. The Japanese wanted to support the physical activity of their population and developed the first electronic pedometer, called a *manpo-kei*, meaning '10,000 steps meter'. The goal of 10,000 steps/day (equivalent to 8 km) appears to be a reasonable key of daily activity for healthy adults (Kang *et al.* 2009). For 2016, 50 years after the first attempts at measuring steps, it is estimated that there are that 20 million people around the world using Fitbit devices (Fitbit is a popular step tracker, launched in 2009) (Ballard 2016) and one in five Americans use some form of technology to measure steps (Graham 2016). Even the fast-food company McDonald's joined the step-tracking trend, and began to include a step-tracker in its happy meals (only to remove it shortly afterwards, due to skin irritations among children) (Chen 2016).

Google and Nintendo have taken the gamification of steps even further and launched the augmented reality version on the Pokémon world. Their Pokémon GO app broke the record of 100 million downloads in its first month (Crider 2016), potentially enhancing physical activity and contributing an additional dimension to the link between physical activity and technology. Yet walking does not require augmented reality games and advanced devices. Beyond questions about the accuracy of devices and advantages and disadvantages of smartphone apps versus wearable devices (Ballard 2016), it seems that there is a rare consensus about the importance of steps, although the number of 10,000 steps-per-day goal is not universally appropriate across all populations and purposes. Yet the 10,000-steps goal is associated with weight loss, improved glucose tolerance and reduced blood pressure (Rosenkranz *et al.* 2015), and people over 55 who take more steps are reported to be happier and healthier (Ballard 2016). Ballard (2016) noted that increasing the number of steps taken per day, e.g. by taking stairs instead of an elevator, parking not so close to destination, walking with the dog and daily errands, will benefit anyone. Furthermore, Jakicic *et al.* (2016) found that the addition of a wearable technology device to a standard behavioural intervention did not produce more weight loss among overweight and obese participants. On the contrary, participants who self-monitored their physical activities and diet lost more weight than the participants who were given wearable technology

The impact of carryable and wearable augmented technologies on walking is likely to be profound. As Horvat (2016) noted:

> What makes Pokémon Go novel is that [augmented reality] has gone mainstream for the first time. And it has to be understood as a historical break, which will profoundly change the way we perceive and experience reality. It will change reality itself.

Augmented reality (AR) is does not replace the real world with a simulated one, but is rather a sophisticated combination of the two. Instead, AR integrates the digital into the real (by using your smartphone camera to transfer the digital Pokémon into the physical world) and the real into the digital (your physical body becomes part of a simulated reality). Even though Google Glass was subject to legislative actions and privacy concerns, the success of such technologies points the way forward for greater use of augmentation in the walking experience, whether it is to receive further information on places, products or people. These may have potential for improved behavioural interventions (Schlossberg *et al.* 2012) as well as data collection for improved design, planning, and public health (see Box 1.2), though of course they also raise huge concerns about privacy and surveillance. Nevertheless, the intersection of walkability and mobility with the "Internet of Things", "smart cities", social networks, transport networks, Google, and augmented and virtual realities does suggest that, perhaps in only ten years' time, the social practices of walking for many will be profoundly different.

Box 1.2 Tracking tourists

Most of the activities of tourists in destinations whether urban, rural or in resorts (ski or seaside) are taking place without the use of motorized vehicles once tourists reach the destination. There is a contradiction between the speed and efforts invested in reaching the destination versus the relatively slow speed exploration of the destination, mainly by walking and public transport (Le-Klähn and Hall 2015). In fact. it seems that as tourists we are walking much more than in our regular lives, since tourists tend to stay in the centre of towns, right near attractions or right on the beach in order to avoid the hassle of spending time in traffic in order to pursue their touristic consumption (Shoval 2006). Even new types of environments for tourism consumption, such as cruise ships, are characterized by being walking environments for tourists who visit them.

Although activities such as walking appear to be relatively set in time and space, so far, when comparing to other areas of research, relatively little attention has been paid to visitor mobility as opposed to the mobility of permanent residents (Dietvorst 1995; Thornton *et al.* 1997; Shaw *et al.* 2000). The dearth of research on this subject can, in part, be attributed to the methodological complexity involved in studies of this kind (Shoval and Isaacson 2010). First, it is often difficult to locate the tourist when he or she enters and leaves a city or region, due to the absence of defined entry and exit points. Second, the term "tourist" includes a wide variety of different types of tourists that are distinguishable from one another by their interests, the purpose of their visits and their time budgets, among other factors, so that in order to illustrate *the tourist's* spatial behaviour, the different types of tourists in a destination must first be identified. Third, the funding requirements for such surveys have restricted the wide implementation of empirical research on tourists' time–space activities (Forer 2002).

Traditional methods for investigating tourism spatial behaviour

Until the turn of the century, the two primary methods used to collect data on the spatial and temporal activity of tourists in a destination were direct observation and non-observational techniques, such as time–space budgets. The method of direct observation can be summed up in the words 'identify, follow, observe and map' (Thornton *et al.* 1997: 1851). In practical terms, the participant-observer method involves the observer accompanying the individual under scrutiny in person. Alternatively, the observer may follow the subject(s) at a distance, recording the pattern of their activities over time and space. This technique is known as "non-participatory observation". When studying the spatial and temporal behaviour of American tourists in Munich, Hartmann (1988) used both techniques, but was happy with neither, which were, he noted, incredibly time-consuming. Nor were these the only problems Hartmann encountered. While the non-participatory technique yielded a mine of information, it failed to unveil the purpose and meaning underlying the subjects' decisions and activities. It also posed various ethical questions, particularly when pursued in covert form (Hartmann 1988). While these were less of a problem when it came to the participant-observer procedure – the observer, thanks to his or her intimate contact with the subjects was constantly aware not only of what the subjects were doing but also, possibly, why – there was in this case the risk of the subjects tailoring their behaviour and explanations, albeit subconsciously, to the presumed expectations of their observer-companion.

Keul and Küheberger (1997) used the non-participatory technique in order to analyse the spatial behaviour of tourists in Salzburg, Austria. Hoping to resolve the problem of motivation, as well as to fill in some spatial gaps, the two followed up their non-participatory observations with a series of interviews of the tourists observed. However, as the non-participatory technique can be applied only for very short time periods, they limited their observations to 15 minutes out of what were, on average, four-hour-long walks.

Aware of the technique's restrictions, Murphy (1992), who conducted a similar non-participatory type observation study in the city of Victoria, British Columbia, put his subjects under surveillance for an average of 23 minutes, the longest surveillance period lasting 87 minutes and the shortest four minutes. Another drawback to this technique is that beyond a simple visual estimate as to the subjects' socio-economic background, it cannot, in those cases where interviews are not used, render non-visual data such as the total length of visit or the subject's next destination, for example. It is also a hugely expensive, time-consuming and labour-intensive procedure.

A less expensive non-participatory technique is remote observation, which is used to record and analyse aggregate tourist flows. Hartmann (1988) used this technique in Munich, where he positioned a camera on top of the city hall's 80-metre-high spire and took aerial pictures of the crowds gathering below to watch the Glockenspiel in the old city's main square. He then used the pictures to estimate the percentage of young North American tourists among the total number of people watching the 10-minute display. Some several years earlier, the same technique was used to track the routes selected by pedestrians through a busy office parking lot, in this instance, by setting up an observation point in a tall building overlooking the lot (Garbrecht 1971). However, as Hill (1984) has noted, these 'eye in the sky' techniques, though effective for studying the behaviour of individuals within a restricted spatial setting, are of little use once the pedestrians step beyond the observation point's line of sight. This is true of most other fixed-point observation studies, whether using time-lapse photography, video recorders or the increasingly ubiquitous closed-circuit television (Hill 1984). Moreover, as Hartmann commented, remote observation techniques, though providing an objective snapshot of the subjects' behaviour, cannot, by their very nature, reveal the motivations underlying the activities thus documented (1988). This, he claims, is the technique's principal drawback, one it shares with other non-participatory procedures.

A more commonly used non-observational method for gathering information on human time–space patterns is the time–space budgets technique. A time–space budget is the

> Systematic record of a person's use of time over a given period. It describes the sequence, timing, and duration of the person's activities, typically for a short period ranging from a single day to a week. As a logical extension of this type of record, a space–time budget includes the spatial coordinates of activity location.
>
> *(Anderson 1971: 353)*

Based mostly on time–space diaries, the time–space budget technique records behavioural patterns, which, owing to their spatial and/or temporal nature, are impossible to observe directly (Thornton *et al.* 1997). Other than this all-important asset, the technique has all the advantages of questionnaire type surveys: it is relatively cheap, provides relatively large samples and affords the speedy collection of data and therefore prompt analysis.

In practice, the time–space budget procedure utilizes several techniques. The first involves recall diaries, usually in the form of a questionnaire or interview, which the subjects complete *post factum*. Both Cooper (1981) and Debbage (1991) employed recall diaries during their work. The principal problem with recall diaries is that the amount and quality of information gathered depends on the subjects' ability to recollect past events with any degree of precision and detail. Furthermore, most questionnaires are, of necessity, phrased rather succinctly, lest the subject lose patience, which inevitably limits the amount of information obtained. Face-to-face interviews, on the other hand, while allowing for more detailed questioning, are again dependent on the subjects' memory, and however good that might be, most people will have only the haziest notion, or at best an approximate idea, of the frequency, sequencing and duration of their activities. The result is that reliable and accurate information about the activities of tourists at destinations, of which walking is a major part, is not available.

Self-administered diaries, to be filled by the subject in real time, make up another time–space budget technique. Researchers used such diaries when studying the spatial and temporal behaviour of tourists (Fennell 1996). However, while resolving the question of memory lapses, these diaries have several problems of their own. Above all, they demand a considerable effort on the part of the subjects, who are required to record in detail their spatial activities while busy enjoying themselves touring the city or countryside. It is a distracting, disruptive, tiring as well as time-consuming process, which goes far to explain why so few are willing to take part in such studies. Yet, even among those ready to volunteer their services, there will be distinct differences in terms of their commitment and enthusiasm, and so, consequently, considerable variations in the quality of the information thus garnered. Moreover, the longer a project goes on, the less keen and so cooperative most subjects will become (Pearce 1988), leading to a sharp fall in the amount and quality of the data recorded.

New digital methods for tracking tourists' walking and spatial activity

Since 2000, we have witnessed unprecedented advances in the collection and utilization of high-resolution digital data on tourist mobility. This is a result of a variety of technological developments, as well as the widespread availability of tracking technologies such as GPS, mobile positioning, geocoded social media messages and Bluetooth (Shoval et al. 2014). Most recently, researchers have also benefited greatly from the development and widespread use of smart-phones, which incorporate several tracking abilities in one device and can transmit obtained locations easily and cheaply (Birenboim and Shoval 2015).

Early efforts to apply tracking technologies to scientific research began in the mid-1990s, when transport studies used advanced technologies to track the paths of motorized vehicles (Zito et al. 1995). The fact that cars have a constant power supply and that the size and weight of the tracking device did not affect the nature of the data collected allowed transport researchers to use tracking technologies at a relatively early stage. Research on pedestrians, such as tourist time–space activities using advanced technologies, followed about a decade later, when tracking devices became smaller and cheaper (Shoval and Isaacson 2006).

The development of mobile technologies that can be used for tracking, such as GPS and mobile phones, has been very dynamic (Shoval and Ahas 2016). These devices present researchers with several advantages, giving them the opportunity to collect higher-quality data: in the case of GPS receivers, the data is continuous, thorough and of a high resolution in time (seconds) and space (metres), which has not previously been possible in tourism research. Mobile tracking technologies hold clear advantages over traditional methods such as surveys and self-report diaries; they are more accurate, reduce the burden on participants, and are not dependent on respondents' enthusiasm and/or memory. As a result, these technologies have become in recent years a central data-collection tool in human mobility studies.

Digital tracking technologies represent a revolution in terms of the accuracy of time/spatial information regarding the whereabouts of tourists in destinations on different scales, from the tourist attraction to the regional, national and even global scales. Figure 1.1 represents an example of GPS tracking from Heidelberg, one of Germany's most popular tourist destinations. In May

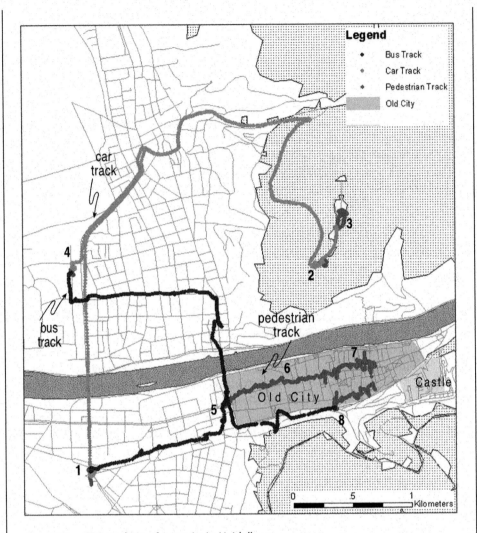

Figure 1.1   GPS tracking of a tourist in Heidelberg

2005, a visitor carried with him, in a specially designed harness, an Emtac Crux II Bluetooth GPS receiver and pocket PC. The receiver, set to record one tracking point per second, was secured by a strap situated just below the shoulder, thus saving the subject not only from having to hold it in his hands, but also from having to constantly manipulate it in order to ensure that it was exposed to the sky. Using wireless Bluetooth technology, the data from this essentially passive receiver was transferred instantly to the pocket PC.

The tracked tour of Heidelberg lasted four hours, during which the subject covered 19.3 kilometres (Figure 1.1). The subject began his journey, accompanied by his host, at the Ibis hotel, situated alongside the town's main train station (1). Leaving the hotel, the two drove to the Heiligenberg Mountain, where they disembarked and climbed an observation tower for a panoramic view of the Old Town's skyline (2). Returning to their car, they took a short trip up the mountain, parked and climbed a further 65 metres to the Heiligenberg's summit (3). They then travelled back to town to the Neuenheim Feld district and the University of Heidelberg's new campus. They parked the car on campus, and took a bus to the Old Town (4). Getting off at Bismarckplatz, the subject and his host entered Heidelberg's Old Town through its main gateway (5). From this point onwards, they continued their tour on foot. Having strolled along the Hauptstrasse, the Old Town's main commercial street, the two made their way along several of its smaller side streets (6). After 28 minutes of wandering around, they stopped at the Café Burkardt for one hour and 27 minutes (7). At the end of their walk, they boarded a bus (8) back to the Ibis hotel and the trip's starting point (1).

The fact that in the course of his expedition in and around Heidelberg the subject used three different modes of transport – car, bus and on foot – is clearly marked on the track obtained using the GPS device (Figure 1.1). The fact that the subject in this experiment switched his means of transportation in mid-journey underlines the importance of tracking the tourist and not the vehicle he or she might use. Because Heidelberg has many narrow streets and alleyways, it was ideally suited for testing the GPS receiver's ability to provide a clear and accurate track in dense urban environments. As the results of the experiment show, the GPS receiver remained fully functional throughout the test, and was able to pin down its position with remarkable accuracy. Indeed, neither Heidelberg's dense, maze-like streets nor the roofs of the bus or car used by the subject were sufficient to render it inoperative. One point worth mentioning is that the density of the tracking points obtained varied according to the type of transportation used. This is not unexpected, as it is the speed at which the subject moves that determines the density of the tracking points. Accordingly, if, as was the case here, the sampling rate (e.g. one point per second) remains the same, the more closely packed the points the slower the motion and vice versa. This allows one to establish whether the subject is travelling by car or moving on foot (for a further discussion, see Shoval and Isaacson 2007).

A second example is that of tracking a visitor to Jerusalem during summer 2016 (Figure 1.2). The individual began the day by leaving the Abraham Hostel, where he was staying, and walking down Jaffa Street. He entered the Old City through Jaffa Gate, continued through the Christian Quarter visiting the Church of the Holy Sepulchre. Then he continued towards the Jewish Quarter and visited the Western Wall. He left the Old City and went back to the hostel, then later he boarded a tram to visit the Yad Vashem World Holocaust Remembrance Center. Note that is it possible to distinguish walking from tram travel due to the distances between the points recorded by the receiver (GPS samples in this case taken at intervals of one minute). He finished the day back at the Abraham Hostel.

Recently researchers started to collect real-time information about tourists' subjective and objective feelings while walking around the destination. Loiterton and Bishop (2008) used GPS and personal digital assistant devices (PDAs) in the Royal Botanic Gardens in Melbourne in order to track visitors. Using the PDAs, they generated location-sensitive questionnaires in specific places in the gardens, which included questions about subjective feelings such as boredom, fatigue and hunger. They implemented this data in their agent-based model and used it to predict the movement of visitors in the garden. Pettersson and Zillinger (2011) utilized tracking technologies in order to study the immediate experiences of visitors to a sport event. They supplied participants with GPS devices during the Biathlon World Championships of 2008 that took

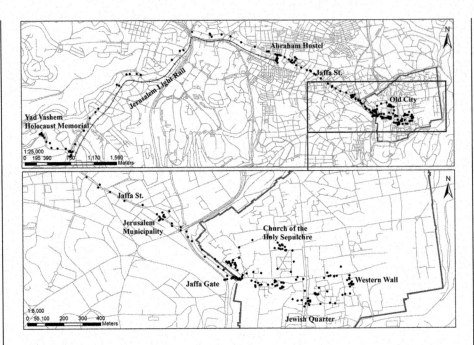

Figure 1.2 GPS tracking of a tourist in Jerusalem

place in Östersund, Sweden. Half of their participants were instructed to geotag their location whenever they experienced positive feelings and the second half were instructed to record their location when experiencing negative feelings. However, the researchers could only obtain a more detailed textual report on the factors that led to the negative and positive experiences from additional questionnaires that were delivered to the respondents. Birenboim *et al.* (2015) used a combination of SMS messages and GPS devices to understand visitor's emotion during their visit to the Aalborg Zoo in Denmark. Kim and Fesenmaier (2015, 2016) present the feasibility of investigating 'objective' emotions of visitors during their visit to a destination by tracking changes in Electro Dermal Activity (EDA) over time and space. However, their ground-breaking work did not fully couple GPS and SCL data, but rather showed SCL over time and the participants' routes. This is a new dimension in the ability to monitor visitors at a destination, not only in geographic space but also in emotional space. These advances in research are not just theoretical; tourist movement has profound implications for infrastructure and transport development, tourism product development, marketing strategies, the commercial viability of the tourism industry and the management of the social, environmental and cultural impacts of tourism. Thus, highly accurate and reliable information in real time represents a major advance in applied and theoretical research.

Conclusion

There is a growing body of research regarding the implementation of tracking technologies in visitor studies. Many of the early publications were occupied with presenting the feasibility of the different methods in a variety of contexts and with developing methods to analyse and visualize the data. A second generation of papers in this field used new data to discover or measure spatial and temporal phenomena of tourist movement. Some papers deal with research questions per se, using the new technologies and their advantages over traditional tools. The outcome of these methodological developments is that today we have accurate and efficient tools to investigate the paths that tourists are using to reach the destination and to understand their paths within the destination itself.

There can be no doubt that tracking technologies are giving us new avenues for the advancement of tourism research, but it is not only about tracking time–space activities. Thanks to the wide use of smartphones and sensors that can be connected to them, information can be received in real time and location-triggered questionnaires can be sent out to participants. Meaning that, as a result, it can be possible to better match different data sets that might better explain tourist activity, as well as the tourist experience while walking in the destination. In addition, it is possible to expand the range of sensors to make it possible to understand a wider range of subjective feelings and consumption experiences in relation to objective factors. We predict that smartphones and Google Glass (or similar) that can connect to various external sensors will facilitate this line of inquiry in a very short period of time.

Summary and conclusions

This chapter has provided a brief introduction to the subject of walking. It has tried to give particular attention to the significance of walking, as well as issues of safety, gender and the role of the built environment. In addition, it has highlighted the way in which technology is affecting, not only the walking experience, but how walking is researched. Although walking is significant as an embodied way of knowing and producing scholarly narrative (Butler 2006; Pink *et al.* 2010), and as both a means and subject of ethnographic and cognate methods (Kusenbach 2003; Ingold and Vergunst 2008; Hall 2011), advances in mobile, augmented, virtual and sensory technologies will radically change the way in which walking and walkability is studied spatially and experientially. Indeed, new technologies are potentially serving to break down methodological barriers between qualitative ethnographic and quantitative observational methods. Undoubtedly, like much of the recent advance in ICT, such developments will create new opportunities for marketization, the furthering of capital and the closing of the informational commons. However, simultaneously they hold considerable promise for better design of built environments and the enhancement of walkability. Nevertheless, the extent to which such methods and the people who adopt them contribute to the public rather than the private good will depend as much on political and ethical decisions as it will the availability of technologies.

The various chapters in this volume intersect with technology in various ways; however, their focus is clearly much wider. The first Part deals with various cultural and political dimensions of walking in a range of different historical, national, media and even educational spaces. The second Part provides an account of walking as a social practice in different contexts. The third Part examines social practices in the specific domain of hiking and pilgrimage, highlighting not only management dimensions but also the search for meaning, whether sacred or profane, by the act of walking. Indeed, the relational significance of walking is an important component of the fourth Part of the book, which examines issues of health and well-being.

An important assumption of a number of chapters in this and other sections is that behavioural and environmental interventions can encourage walking and/or improve the overall walking experience. These issues come to the fore in the final Part, which looks at the way planning, design and the application of particular research methods are used to encourage walking. Interestingly, many of these chapters also have a strong underlying economic dimension in that the attraction and satisfaction of walkers is increasingly regarded as an important element of regional development strategies in the same way that walkability in the built environment is perceived as important for real-estate values and urban economic development and regeneration (Leinberger and Alfonzo 2012). Of course, whether such strategies are socially inclusive remains to be seen.

Walking is a democratic act. All can potentially share in it. However, as this and the other chapters in this book demonstrate, there are a wide range of constraints that limit where, when and even how people can walk. Nevertheless, the slowness of walking enables linkages and connectivity to people and place that other forms of transport do not provide. It is hard to gain a sense of place or community from inside an automated vehicle. Walking contributes to personal and public well-being in a myriad of ways. We hope that, even if only in a small way, this volume sheds further light on the importance of something so basic, yet which says so much about who we are and the society we live in.

References

Adminaite, D., Allsop, R. and Jost, G. (2015) *Making Walking and Cycling on Europe's Roads Safer*, PIN Flash Report 29, Brussels: European Transport Safety Council.

Allan, A. (2001) 'Walking as a local transport modal choice in Adelaide', *World Transport Policy and Practice*, 7(2): 44–51.

Anderson, J. (1971) 'Space–time budgets and activity studies in urban geography and planning', *Environment and Planning*, 3(4): 353–368.

Ballard, D. (2016) 'Medically clear: counting steps: fit or fad?', *Emergency Medicine News*, 38(3B). DOI: 10.1097/01.EEM.0000481859.43313.72.

Barton, H. (2009) 'Land use planning and health and well-being', *Land Use Policy*, 26: S115–S123.

Bassett, D.R., Pucher, J., Buehler, R., Thompson, D.L. and Crouter, S.E. (2008) 'Walking, cycling, and obesity rates in Europe, North America, and Australia', *Journal of Physical Activity and Health*, 5(6): 795–814.

Bauman, A., Bull, F., Chey, T., Craig, C.L., Ainsworth, B.E., Sallis, J.F., Bowles, H.R., Hagstromer, M., Sjostrom, M., Pratt, M. and the I PS Group (2009) 'The international prevalence study on physical activity: results from 20 countries', *International Journal of Behavioral Nutrition and Physical Activity*, 6(21). DOI: 10.1186/1479–5868–6–21.

Beebeejaun, Y. (2009) 'Making safer places: gender and the right to the city', *Security Journal*, 22(3): 219–229.

Birenboim, A. and Shoval, N. (2015) 'Mobility research in the age of the smartphone', *Annals of the Association of American Geographers*, 106(2): 283–291.

Birenboim, A., Reinau, K.H., Shoval, N. and Harder, H. (2015) 'High resolution measurement and analysis of visitor experiences in time and space: the case of Aalborg Zoo in Denmark', *The Professional Geographer*, 67(4): 620–629.

Butler, T. (2006) 'A walk of art: the potential of the sound walk as practice in cultural geography', *Social and Cultural Geography*, 7(6): 889–908.

C3 Collaborating for Health (2012) *The Benefits of Regular Walking for Health, Well-being and the Environment*. London: C3 Collaborating for Health.

Chen, A.H. (2016) 'McDonald's removes fitness tracker from Happy Meals', CNN.com, 19 August. Available at: http://edition.cnn.com/2016/08/17/health/mcdonalds-removes-fitness-tracker-happy-meal-step-it.

Cooper, C. P. (1981) 'Spatial and temporal patterns of tourist behavior', *Regional Studies*, 15: 359–371.

Crabtree, S. and Nsubuga, F. (2012) 'Women feel less safe than men in many developed countries', Gallup. Available at: www.gallup.com/poll/155402/women-feel-less-safe-men-developed-countries.aspx.

Crider, M. (2016) 'Pokémon GO passes 100 millions Play Store downloads in just a month', 8 August. Available at: www.androidpolice.com/2016/08/08/pokmon-go-passes-100-million-play-store-down loads-just-month (accessed 4 September 2016).

Debbage, K. (1991) 'Spatial behavior in a Bahamian resort', *Annals of Tourism Research*, 18: 251–268.

Department of Transport Statistics (2014/15) Walking and cycling levels demographic breakdown: England, 2014/15. Available at: www.gov.uk/government/organisations/department-for-transport/series/ walking-and-cycling-statistics (accessed 30 September 2016).

Department of Transportation (2010) *NHTS Brief National Household Travel Survey: Active Travel. December.* Washington, DC: Department of Transportation.

Dietvorst, A.G.J. (1995) 'Tourist behavior and the importance of time–space analysis', in G. Ashworth and A.G.J. Dietvorst (eds), *Tourism and Spatial Transformations*, Wallingford: CAB International, pp. 163–181.

Ding, D. (2012) 'Built environments and physical activity: improving understanding of the moderators'. PhD, University of California, San Diego.

Durand, C. P., Andalib, M., Dunton, G.F., Wolch, J. and Pentz, M.A. (2011) 'A systematic review of built environment factors related to physical activity and obesity risk: implications for smart growth urban planning', *Obesity Reviews*, 12(5): e173–e182.

Ewing, R. and Handy, S. (2009) 'Measuring the unmeasurable: urban design qualities related to walkability', *Journal of Urban Design*, 14(1): 65–84.

Feng, J., Glass, T.A., Curriero, F.C., Stewart, W.F. and Schwartz, B.S. (2010) 'The built environment and obesity: a systematic review of the epidemiologic evidence', *Health & Place*, 16(2): 175–190.

Fennell, D.A. (1996) 'A tourist space–time budget in the Shetland islands', *Annals of Tourism Research*, 23(4): 811–829.

Forer, P. (2002) 'Tourist flows and dynamic geographies', in D.G. Simmons and J. Fairweather (eds), *Understanding the Tourism Host–Guest Encounter in New Zealand: Foundations for Adaptive Planning and Management*, Christchurch, New Zealand: EOS Ecology, pp. 21–56.

Forsyth, A. (2015) 'What is a walkable place? The walkability debate in urban design', *Urban Design International*, 20(4): 274–292.

Forsyth, A. and Southworth, M. (2008) 'Cities afoot – pedestrians, walkability and urban design', *Journal of Urban Design*, 13(1): 1–3.

Fowler, G.A. (2016) 'Texting while walking isn't funny anymore: as pedestrian injuries rise, what responsibility do tech companies have to address our addiction?' *The Wall Street Journal*, 17 February. Available at: www.wsj.com/articles/texting-while-walking-isnt-funny-anymore-1455734501.

Garbrecht, D. (1971) 'Pedestrian paths through a uniform environment', *Town Planning Review*, 41: 71–84.

Giancasprom, M. (2016) 'Should using your mobile phone while walking be outlawed?' *The Conversation*, 12 April. Available at: http://theconversation.com/should-using-your-mobile-phone-while-walking-be-outlawed-57542.

Giles-Conti, B., Timperio, A.F., Bull F.C. and Pikora, T. (2005) 'Understanding physical activity environmental correlates: increased specificity for ecological models', *Exercise and Sport Sciences Reviews*, 33(4): 175–181.

Graham, G. (2016) 'Wearable technology creates cult around 10,000 steps', *Oklahoma News*, 11 August. Available at: http://newsok.com/article/5513368.

Hall, C.M. (ed.) (2011) *Fieldwork in Tourism: Methods, Issues and Reflections*, Abingdon, Oxon: Routledge.

Hall, C.M. and Page, S. (2014) *The Geography of Tourism and Recreation* (4th edn). Abingdon, Oxon: Routledge.

Hall, C.M., Le-Klähn, D.-T. and Ram, Y. (2017) *Tourism, Public Transport and Sustainable Mobility*. Bristol: Channel View.

Hallal, P.C., Andersen, L.B., Bull, F.C., Guthold, R., Haskell, W., Ekelund, U. and Lancet Physical Activity Series Working Group (2012) 'Global physical activity levels: surveillance progress, pitfalls, and prospects', *The Lancet*, 380(9838): 247–257.

Hartmann, R. (1988) 'Combining field methods in tourism research', *Annals of Tourism Research*, 15: 88–105.

Hill, M. (1984) 'Stalking the urban pedestrian: a comparison of questionnaire and tracking methodologies for behavioral mapping in large-scale environments', *Environment and Behavior*, 16: 539–550.

Horvat, S. (2016) 'Pokémon Go is just the start – Silicon Valley is taking over our reality', *The Guardian*, 25 July.

Hyman, I.E., Boss, S.M., Wise, B.M., McKenzie, K.E. and Caggiano, J.M. (2010) 'Did you see the unicycling clown? Inattentional blindness while walking and talking on a cell phone', *Applied Cognitive Psychology*, 24(5): 597–607.

Ingold, T. and Vergunst, J.L. (eds) (2008) *Ways of Walking: Ethnography and Practice on Foot.* Aldershot, Hants: Ashgate.

International Transport Forum (2012) *Pedestrian Safety, Urban Space and Health.* Paris: OECD publishing.

Jakicic, J.M., Davis K.K., Rogers R.J., King, W.C., Marcus, M.D., Helsel, D., Rickman, A.D., Wahed, A.S. and Belle, S.H. (2016) 'Effect of wearable technology combined with a lifestyle on long-term weight loss: the IDEA randomized clinical trial', *Journal of the American Medical Association*, 316(11): 1161–1171.

Kang, M., Marshall, S.J., Barreira, T.V. and Lee, J.O. (2009) 'Effect of pedometer-based physical activity interventions: a meta-analysis', *Research Quarterly for Exercise and Sport*, 80(3): 648–655.

Keul, A. and Küheberger, A. (1997) 'Tracking the Salzburg tourist', *Annals of Tourism Research*, 24(4): 1008–1012.

Kim, J. and Fesenmaier, D.R. (2015) 'Measuring emotions in real time: implications for tourism experience design', *Journal of Travel Research*, 54(4), 419–429.

Kim, J.J. and Fesenmaier, D.R. (2016) 'Tourism experience and tourism design', in D.R. Fesenmaier and Z. Xiang (eds), *Design Science in Tourism: Foundations of Destination Management.* Cham, Switzerland: Springer International, pp. 17–29.

Kusenbach, M. (2003) 'Street phenomenology: the Go-Along as ethnographic research tool', *Ethnography*, 4: 455–485.

Lee, C.G. and Cho, Y. (2009) 'Relationship between perceived neighbourhood characteristics and vigorous physical activity among adult Seoul residents', *Journal of Preventative Medicine and Public Health*, 42(4): 215–222.

Leinberger, C.B. and Alfonzo, M. (2012) *Walk this Way: The Economic Promise of Walkable Places in Metropolitan Washington, D.C.* Washington, DC: The Brookings Institution.

Le-Klähn, D-T. and Hall, C.M. (2015) 'Tourist use of public transport at destinations – a review', *Current Issues in Tourism*, 18: 785–803.

Le-Klähn, D.-T., Roosen, J., Gerike, R. and Hall, C.M. (2015) 'Factors affecting tourists' public transport use and areas visited at destinations', *Tourism Geographies*, 17: 738–757.

Leyden, K.M. (2003) 'Social capital and the built environment: the importance of walkable neighborhoods', *American Journal of Public Health*, 93(9): 1546–1551.

Loiterton, D. and Bishop, I. (2008) 'Simulation, calibration and validation of recreational agents in an urban park environment', in R. Gimblett and H. Skov-Petersen (eds), *Monitoring, Simulation, and Management of Visitor Landscapes.* Tuscon, AZ: University of Arizona Press, pp. 107–122.

Macauley, D. (2000) 'Walking the city: an essay on peripatetic practices and politics', *Capitalism Nature Socialism*, 11(4): 3–43.

McCormack, G.R. and Shiell, A. (2011) 'In search of causality: a systematic review of the relationship between the built environment and physical activity among adults', *International Journal of Behavioral Nutrition and Physical Activity*, 8(1): 125.

McKenzie, B. (2014) *Modes Less Traveled – Bicycling and Walking to Work in the United States: 2008–2012 American Community Survey Reports.* Washington DC: US Department of Commerce Economics and Statistics Administration, US Census Bureau.

Mehta, V. (2008) 'Walkable streets: pedestrian behavior, perceptions and attitudes', *Journal of Urbanism: International Research on Placemaking and Urban Sustainability*, 1(3): 217–245.

Moura, F., Cambra P. and Gonçalves, A. (2014) 'IAAPE – pedestrian accessibility and attractiveness assessment tool when planning for walkability', in *Bridging the Implementation Gap of Accessibility Instruments and Planning Support Systems*, Joint Conference CITTA 7th Annual Conference and COST TU1002 Final Conference, Porto, Portugal.

Moura, F., Cambra, P. and Gonçalves, A.B. (2017) 'Measuring walkability for distinct pedestrian groups with a participatory assessment method: a case study in Lisbon', *Landscape and Urban Planning*, 157: 282–296.

Murphy, P.E. (1992) 'Urban tourism and visitor behavior', *American Behavioral Scientist*, 36(2), 200–211.

Nasar, J.L. and Troyer, D. (2013) 'Pedestrian injuries due to mobile phone use in public places', *Accident Analysis and Prevention*, 57, 91–95.

Nelson, M.E., Rejeski, W.J., Blair, S.N., Duncan, P.W., Judge, J.O., King, A.C., Macera, C.A. and Castaneda-Sceppa, C. (2007) 'Physical activity and public health in older adults: recommendation from the American College of Sports Medicine and the American Heart Association', *Circulation*, 116(9): 1094–1105.

OECD (2014) *Obesity Update.* Paris: OECD Directorate for Employment, Labour and Social Affairs. Available at: www.oecd.org/els/health-systems/Obesity-Update-2014.pdf.

OECD (2016a) Health Statistics. Available at: www.oecd.org/els/health-systems/health-data.htm.

OECD (2016b) Better Life Index. Available at: www.oecdbetterlifeindex.org/#/11111111111.

Oh, A.Y., Zenk, S.N., Wilbur, J., Block, R., McDevitt, J. and Wang, E. (2010) 'Effects of perceived and objective neighbourhood crime on walking frequency among midlife African American women in a home-based walking intervention', *Journal of Physical Activity and Health*, 7(4): 432–441.

Parra, D.C., Hoegner, C.M., Hallal, P.C., Ribeiro, I.C., Reis, R., Brownson, R.C., Pratt, M. and Simoes, E.J. (2010) 'Perceived environmental correlates of physical activity for leisure and transportation in Curitiba, Brazil', *Preventative Medicine*, 52(3–4): 234–238.

Pearce, D.G. (1988) 'Tourist time-budgets', *Annals of Tourism Research*, 15: 106–121.

Pettersson, R. and Zillinger, M. (2011) 'Time and space in event behavior: tracking visitors by GPS', *Tourism Geographies*, 13: 1–20.

Pink, S., Hubbard, P., O'Neill, M. and Radley, A. (2010) 'Walking across disciplines: from ethnography to arts practice', *Visual Studies*, 25(1): 1–7.

Pucher, J. and Buehler, R. (2010) 'Walking and cycling for healthy cities', *Built Environment*, 36(4), 391–414.

Reed, J.A., Wilson, D.K., Ainsworth, B.E., Bowles, H. and Mixon, G. (2006) 'Perceptions of neighbourhood sidewalks on walking and physical activity patterns in a Southeastern community in the US', *Journal of Physical Activity and Health*, 3(2): 243–253.

Rosenkranz, R.R., Duncan, M.J., Caperchione, C.M., Kolt, G.S., Vandelanotte, C., Maeder, A.J., Savage, T.N. and Mummery, W.K. (2015) 'Validity of the stages of change in steps instrument (SoC-Step) for achieving the physical activity goal of 10,000 steps per day', *BMC Public Health*, 15: 1197.

Sallis, J.F., Floyd, M.F., Rodríguez, D.A. and Saelens, B.E. (2012) 'Role of built environments in physical activity, obesity, and cardiovascular disease', *Circulation*, 125(5): 729–737.

Sassi, F. (2010) *Obesity and the Economics of Prevention: Fit not Fat*. Paris: OECD Publishing.

Schlossberg, M., Evers, C., Kato, K. and Brehm, C. (2012) 'Active transportation, citizen engagement and livability: coupling citizens and smartphones to make the change', *URISA Journal*, 25(2): 61–70.

Shaw, G., Agarwal, S. and Bull, P. (2000) 'Tourism consumption and tourism behavior: a British perspective', *Tourism Geographies*, 2: 264–289.

Short, J.R. (1991) *Imagined Country: Society, Culture and Environment*. London: Routledge.

Solnit, R. (2000) *Wanderlust: A History of Walking*. London: Penguin Books.

Shoval, N. (2006) 'The geography of hotels in cities: an empirical validation of a forgotten theory', *Tourism Geographies*, 8: 56–75.

Shoval, N. and Ahas, R. (2016) 'The use of tracking technologies in tourism research: the first decade', *Tourism Geographies*, 18: 587–606.

Shoval, N. and Isaacson, M. (2006) 'The application of tracking technologies to the study of pedestrian spatial behaviour', *The Professional Geographer*, 58(2): 172–183.

Shoval, N. and Isaacson, M. (2007) 'Tracking tourists in the digital age', *Annals of Tourism Research*, 34(1): 141–159.

Shoval, N. and Isaacson, M. (2010) *Tourist Mobility and Advanced Tracking Technologies*. London: Routledge.

Shoval, N., Kwan, M-P., Reinau, K.H. and Harder, H. (2014) 'The shoemaker's son always goes barefoot: implementations of GPS and other tracking technologies for geographic research', *Geoforum*, 51(1): 1–5.

Southworth, M. (2005) 'Designing the walkable city', *Journal of Urban Planning and Development*, 131(4): 246–257.

Strandell, A. and Hall, C.M. (2015) 'Impact of the residential environment on second home use in Finland – testing the compensation hypothesis', *Landscape and Urban Planning*, 133: 12–33.

Thornton, P.R., Williams, A.M. and Shaw, G. (1997) 'Revisiting time–space diaries: an exploratory case study of tourist behaviour in Cornwall, England', *Environment and Planning A*, 29: 1847–1867.

Trowbridge, M.J., Pickell, S.G., Pyke, C.R. and Jutte, D.P. (2014) 'Building healthy communities: establishing health and wellness metrics for use within the real estate industry', *Health Affairs*, 33(11): 1923–1929.

Velasquez, K.S., Holahan, C.K. and You, X. (2009) 'Relationship of perceived environmental characteristics to leisure-time physical activity and meeting recommendations for physical activity in Texas', *Preventing Chronic Disease*, 6(1): A24.

Wang, Y., Chau, C.K., Ng, W.Y. and Leung, T.M. (2016) 'A review on the effects of physical built environment attributes on enhancing walking and cycling activity levels within residential neighborhoods', *Cities*, 50: 1–15.

Ward, L. (2016) 'Ontario quickly turns down Toronto's request to ban pedestrian texting on roads', *CBC News* Toronto. Available at: www.cbc.ca/news/canada/toronto/text-crossing-street-ticket-1.3680311

WHO (2015) Distribution of road traffic deaths by type of road user, World Health Organization Global Health Observatory Data. Available at: www.who.int/gho/road_safety/mortality/traffic_deaths_distri bution/en (accessed 30 September 2016).

Wolf, I.D. and Wohlfarth, T. (2014) 'Walking, hiking and running in parks: a multidisciplinary assessment of health and well-being benefits', *Landscape and Urban Planning*, 130: 89-103.

Zito, R., d'Este, G. and Taylor, M.A.P. (1995) 'Global positioning in the time domain: how useful a tool for intelligent vehicle-highway systems?', *Transportation Research C*, 3(4): 193-209.

Part I
Culture, Society and Historical Context

2

Walking in the capitalist city
On the socio-economic origins of walkable urbanism

Anja Hälg Bieri

Introduction

Walking has become a trend in the USA. In recent years, the desire to walk has brought forth specific urban design for walkable places. Whence this trend? In order to understand this phenomenon, this chapter suggests we view walking not simply as a human form of locomotion or a transportation mode, but identify it as a social phenomenon. Offering a way of theorizing walking anthropologically as a social practice that takes on different forms in different historical and spatial contexts, and drawing a genealogy of the walking trend and theorizing its underlying logic with the help of critical theory is the aim of this chapter. A dialectic of aestheticization and commodification runs through modernity that generates aestheticized forms of walking today. While the desire to walk is initially a form of aesthetic struggle against the rational principles of modernity and the forces of capitalism, this struggle is co-opted by the logic of capital in a continuous interlacing of the processes of aestheticization and commodification. The social and spatial consequences of capitalism together with the process of aestheticization of society produce new spatial forms of capitalism, new commodified forms of social interaction, and new forms of walking. What became of the yearning for agency through walking? With walkable urbanism, capital returns to the city centre and creates new markets for a budding walkable lifestyle which is fed through conspicuous consumption.

Theorizing contemporary forms of walking

Walking is a social practice. Anthropologically speaking, walking is a human invariant, a universal phenomenon, but it takes on different forms in different cultures, times and places. Those forms, in turn, are subject to change. We need to understand walking not simply as a human kind of locomotion or a form of transportation. Walking is a cultural invariant – apart from specific exceptions, every human can walk. But how, when, why, where and who walks change with time and space. Moreover, walking is a performative act, in the sense that it co-creates social distinction and social identity. Walking and the social possibilities of walking represent the spatial organization of a given society and its subjects. It is both a physical and a social practice.

This chapter seeks to explore the genealogy of contemporary aestheticized and commodified forms of walking, in particular walking in the context of walkable urbanism. Walkable urbanism is a trend in urban design and planning, which promotes urban space that is more walkable than the traditional car-centred spaces. I suggest that we understand the notion both in its urban design dimension and in its social dimension. Walkable urbanism creates a new form of built environment; it also and possibly to an even greater extent creates a social environment, an ecology, and even a lifestyle. Urban design and architecture styles are not isolated, but they need to be conceived in their social, historical and spatial context: 'Architecture is a subject which demands to be understood in context: that is, within the context of its production (society, economics, politics, culture) and the context of its consumption, representation and interpretation (different academic disciplines, interest groups, institutions, users)' (Rendell *et al.* 2000: xi).

In a dialectical approach, I identify contemporary forms of walking as a product of the aestheticization of society and capitalism's continuous quest for new markets. These processes interweave and generate the society we live in. The trend for walking needs to be seen in this context. In this view, the social imaginaries and the material manifestations of walkable urbanism are places of spectacle. The form of walking in these spaces is an aestheticized form, contributing to the spectacle. Since Debord's publication of *La Société du spectacle* in 1967, technological progress and the growing emphasis on the visual and the iconic have pushed the spectacular even further. In this context, the spectacle is a social relation between people mediated by images (Debord 1967). The misleading impression is that the human-scale, somewhat analogue character of making America more walkable seems to go against the grain of a spectacular society of simulacra and pastiche. Indeed, the desire to walk is a desire for more spatial, physical and ultimately political agency, for more creativity. But the answer to this yearning is yet another stage of commodification, using the growing aestheticization of society to appropriate the yearning for more creativity and agency. Adorno (1969, 1991) has shown how the culture industry works hand in hand with capital's need for sufficiently entertained and docile masses. First, consumption became the mantra to live by, economically and culturally. Today, we are experiencing a new phase of the suave domination through the culture industry. As the postmodern 'aesthetic subject' (Reckwitz 2012) is yearning for creative expression and physical capacity in this technologically assisted and alienated culture, it is therefore prone to fall prey to the false promises of happiness. The trend is shifting from consumption to production, or rather pseudo-production, as we observe it in various phenomena involving making and creativity. The visual predominance in our society helps further these trends through a specific aesthetics and aestheticization in the omnipresent image: the tip of the iceberg probably being the consumer goods one can buy which allude to hands-on creativity, such as new-made-old furniture, blog themes that look like a paper-and-pencil journal, quick-fix creativity apps. The aesthetic rebellion is commodified; the yearning remains unfulfilled.

The postmodern yearnings are also reflected in architecture (Ellin 1999). The various new serialized urban designs ranging from Bohème-inspired to vernacular and neo-traditional are used in walkable urbanism and revitalization projects. Walkable urbanism and the trend for creativity find their aesthetic and commodified realization in creative cities and their creative economy. The urban creativity hype has been termed 'creativity fix', emphasising the economic intention behind it (Peck 2007). In other words, and in terms of walking, the tender aesthetic rebellion against the car-centred, isolating landscape and culture of post-war America through initiatives to further walking has been co-opted by capital's interest in finding new markets, aided by the aestheticization of society, thereby deceptively combining the economic and political needs of capital. Furthermore, the continuous aestheticization and commodification of practices and spaces formerly untouched by the logic of the market adapts and continues the suave oppression through the culture industry. Walkable urbanism was appropriated from its very beginnings and has been developing along those lines. I identify this development as part and parcel of postmodernity, which I understand as an operational notion for culture and society in late capitalism (Jameson 1984, 2015). The dialectic of aestheticization and commodification throughout modernity and into postmodernity is the underlying and driving dialectic of the phenomenon of walkable urbanism (Bieri 2015).

In critical theory's framework, to understand modern Western society, alienation and cultural domination play a crucial role in explaining the continuity of the capitalist mode of production and rule. Today, alienation might come from a mixture of allegedly creative jobs in the creative economy and the suave repression through the expanding culture industry. Postmodern scientists and artists turned to everyday phenomena with an interest in breaking this domination and reclaiming life and thought from the bottom up – or from the everyday up. Walking as art, walking as research method, and walkable urbanism can all be understood as an attempt to reclaim an everyday practice – walking. It is striking, however, that the predominant forms that emerge from this endeavour are not everyday forms of walking but performative forms of walking – art walking, research walking, and walking in walkable spaces that are spaces of spectacle. The alienation from walking, from a direct use of the body for locomotion, is so advanced that all the postmodern reclaimations of walking result in these performative forms of walking. An everyday activity is elevated to something extraordinary. It is aestheticized. Thereby, walking (or the relationship to walking and the use of the body) goes through another stage of alienation through creating even more spectacle. It reproduces late capitalism's logic and cannot unwind the postmodern spiral. It cannot fulfil the yearning still attached to the modern promise of happiness, it only aggrandizes the yearning by creating images of idealized walking and the silent realization of failure to live up to this image without understanding the reasons for this failure. Adorno (1991: 106) described the non-awareness within the culture industry like this:

> In so far as the culture industry arouses a feeling of well-being that the world is precisely in that order suggested by the culture industry, the substitute gratification which it prepares for human beings cheats them out of the same happiness which it deceitfully projects.

In reference to the mechanisms of the culture industry in the context of postmodernism some decades later, Bernstein (1991: 25) writes: 'The culture industry's response is the production of works, typified in the new architecture, that, through a mimesis of aestheticization, indict the spectator for failing to find gratification where there is none'. Soft domination through culture transformed into a heightened sense of individual experience in which simulacra (Baudrillard 1994) and pastiche (Jameson 1998) create the deceitful gratification critical theory speaks of. Walking's subversive potential is appropriated. Postmodernism devours its offspring.

Postmodern attempts to refocus on walking come out of a set of postmodern contexts: be it out of frustration with a car-based society and landscape, a yearning for human-scale and human-speed mobility, a desire to reclaim the body's capacities in a technologically assisted world, or any other postmodern reason for refocusing on the subjective and the everyday. This happens for a set of reasons, led on by the force of the image, social imaginary and the spectacular in the maelstrom of late capitalism's alienation and domination through the channels of culture. It also happens through the aestheticization of society, art and science, which create a pseudo-individuality, style or lifestyle, instead of what Adorno called the

29

'non-identical'. Thereby, the political force is taken out of the movement towards more walking, more physical capacity, imaginary freedom and ultimately happiness, as there is a qualitative and political difference between 'pseudo-individuality and individuality, pleasure and happiness, consensus and freedom, pseudo-activity and activity, illusory otherness and non-identical otherness' (Bernstein 1991: 26).

Imaginaries of urbanity

The landscapes and buildings we live in are more than a combination of material, form and function. Indeed, the environment created by architects, planners, designers, developers, homeowners and many more are both a reflection of our society, our culture, and actively producing that society (Knox and Ozolins 2000; Delitz 2009). Architectural construction is social construction. The landscaped and built environments tell us how a society spatially organizes its subjects, but they also tell us how subjects might reorganize that spatial order. Architecture and society are in a dialectical relation to each other, therefore, urban design is highly political – this is how I suggest walkable urbanism and walking should be read. Landscape and built environment also inform us about a society's imaginaries, the socially constructed representations and ideas transported by images such as photographs, but also buildings, streetscapes and ideas. Imaginaries are what a society can imagine and what it strives for. Quite obviously, the creation, definition and reproduction of social imaginaries, this indisputable common sense that defines what and how things are, is highly political and disputable (Castoriadis 1975).

Already aesthetic disciplines per se, urban design and architecture are further aestheticized through the growing importance of the visual and the iconic. Two influential works have contributed to this phenomenon. Venturi *et al.* (1988) pioneered an 'instant ethnography' and photographic aesthetics for architecture in *Learning from Las Vegas*, and, with *The Image of the City*, Kevin Lynch (1960) established guidelines for urban designers and planners that are still applied today. While the architect went with the postmodern urge to experience and value the simple, the urban planner tried to standardize the 'legibility' of cities through a behaviourist model that measured the relation between urban material and individuals. Both leave out the cultural context of their built environment and thereby depoliticize architecture and urban design. Venturi *et al.*'s (1988) work laid the foundation for a highly aestheticized and iconic culture of American urban landscape in these disciplines and beyond. Lynch's (1960) contribution has been taken up by various urban designers and planners in their handbooks and manuals for revitalizing or developing urban space with walkability in mind (e.g. Campoli 2012; Duany and Speck 2010; Ewing and Bartholomew 2013; Ewing and Handy 2009). His approach has been further reduced to the behaviourist stimulus–reaction model between urban material and persons, mediated by the concept of 'imageability', leading to standardized, serialized, highly codified urban walkable design: 'Imageability is the quality of a place that makes it distinct, recognizable, and memorable. A place has high imageability when specific physical elements and their arrangement capture attention, evoke feelings, and create a lasting impression' (Ewing and Bartholomew 2013: 11).

The tendency to reduce cultural phenomena to quantitative evidence has a couple of strings attached to it, since it factually voids the built environment of its social and political dimensions. This model is deeply drenched in the methodological individualism that has dominated the social sciences in America (Adorno 1969; Bourdieu 1975), to the detriment of a more contextual and political understanding of the built environment and its dialectical relation with the people who build, transform and move in them. Designing walkable urbanism like a theme park with a set of supposedly evidence-based arguments, ranging from health benefits to tourism attractions to economic uplift, creates places of spectacle that only further our state of alienation. They build on an anachronistic imaginary of vernacular dwelling, obvious in the mix-and-match architecture of such developments (Ellin 1999; Hirt 2009), where the historical and political references are blurred into a Disneyesque set design. The idea of legibility posits the high dependency on conveying and confirming imaginaries so that both the obvious and the underlying actions in a given space are defined and clear to the visitor – if not stated on a board of rules. Indeed, walkable spaces, often private, treat people like visitors rather than as co-creators of the space; the co-creation merely happens in terms of social reproduction, and this is not only the case in homogenous gated communities. Imaginaries of class differences are reproduced in walkable urbanism, as consumption is a means for social distinction. Genders are performed in relation to other established categories of difference, such as class, ethnicity and sexual orientation. Indeed, women carry out class distinction through the extensive need for shopping and consumption in most of the walkable urban environments. Elsewhere, I distinguish women's bodies in walkable urbanism as "walkable bodies" rather than walking bodies, a highly aestheticized and commodified body, a body needed by walkable urban design (Bieri 2015).

Moreover, the quest for producing imageability is probably one of the main reasons why urban design and architecture in globalized capitalism have started to design in a context of commercial competition, combining aestheticization and commodification. Sklair (2006) points out the changed context of architectural production in globalized capitalism, urging architects to create different, unique and outstanding buildings in what has been termed "iconic architecture" (Sklair 2006), "decotecture" (Boyer 1988) or "architainment" (Saunders 2005). The belief in the importance of such imageable icons and the icons' photographic presence in the media co-create the spectacular dimension of walkable urbanism. Visiting rather than living in these spaces, mediated by smartphones and the staging of one's being part of this spectacle, is what replaces the civic and political bloodstream of a city with an intravenous flow of images and imaginaries of a "walkable body". Leinberger (2009), promoter and developer of walkable urbanism, genuinely calls for a 'New American Dream' with more human-scale landscapes and less dependency on oil. But the dream is turning into what Benjamin (1999) referred to as something similar as the false consciousness created in capitalism's culture industry. That dream state is constructed. And, in an all-too-literal metaphor, urban design and planning co-construct the late capitalist dream state through walkable urbanisms' spaces of spectacle.

The walkability fix

Indeed, the New American Dream, the promise of happiness through walkable urbanism has stirred up the real-estate market, which shows a tendency for walkable neighbourhoods to be more expensive than others because of their walkability (Pivo and Fisher 2011). It appears that there are some real implications for the dream, and Walter Benjamin reminded us of having to wake up from the dream state that capitalism has put everyone in. Ehrenreich (2009) uncovered the imaginaries of happiness and positive thinking that depoliticize social phenomena and put them back exclusively on the shoulders of individuals by stimulating a sense of failure to be happy and successful rather than also understanding the socio-economic relations at work when things go wrong.

So, today are people unhappy with their suburban landscapes and lives? They need a new lifestyle that promises happiness and continues the dream. The dream, with false consciousness as part and parcel of alienation, is generated through the capitalist mode of production and through the suave repression in a happiness-promising entertainment society. The culture industry satisfies just as much as is needed to keep people at bay, and to keep capitalism running. The new developments for pedestrian-friendly lifestyles will keep entertainment and the pursuit of happiness going, while at the same time offering capitalism new profitable markets. The dialectic between the needs of capitalism and the yearnings of people create new landscapes and spatial forms, not without consequences for society.

Architecturally and culturally, walkable urbanism is an expression of capitalism's continuous quest for new markets. Leaning on Harvey's (2001) notion of 'spatial fix' and the idea that capital continuously searches new markets and is in a constant state of adaptation bringing forth temporary but consequential fixes, I suggest that walkable urbanism is another spatial fix, the "walkability fix". This quest and the solutions applied have consequences for the landscape and for life within that built environment, the result being the spatial form of capitalism. While the suburb was the spatial form of capitalism during much of the twentieth century, today we observe a return to the city. City centres are revitalized. Main streets all over America are revitalized. Urban infill is constructed. Even suburbs receive new "urban" walkable centres. New and revitalized buildings and developments appear; condos, town houses, loft apartments, entire communities or villages in the city or the very close suburban ring; the same happens in towns that urbanize or try to revitalize. This re-urbanization is inspired by a general image of European dense city life and finds its American adaptation following key words such as walkability and sustainability. Innovation districts are declared, special zoning allows for mixed-use that combines home, work and leisure/entertainment time. Art districts are introduced to attract artists with the idea of having them revitalize abandoned buildings and create a bohemian buzz, which is intended to attract tourists and potential residents and businesses to return to the city. The young and trendy move out of their parents' suburban homes and into the city for a walkable lifestyle. Retirees move to the city to be more mobile and socially connected than in the suburbs. Forbes even suggests pre-retirement in a city: 'Move there now, retire there later' (Anonymous 2015). Businesses are moving back to the city, job opportunities grow, shops and restaurants appear. Moving suburban-trained people back to the city in what has been called the new "white infill" or "back-to-the-city" movement (Piiparinen 2013), to continue their suburban life in higher density is constructing a new kind of urbanity: high-density living with a suburban culture. Suburban big box stores open smaller city versions such as City Target and Target Express, Walmart Express or Tesco Express. Yet, suburban anonymity is not the same as urban anonymity. Urbanity breathes in the rhythms of people's activities through the seasons, through the months, the weeks, days and even hours (Knox 2005). Urbanity is not a theme park you can visit to experience urbanity; it means people living in a city, having urban lives, and above all, having and developing urban skills.

Nevertheless, the image of the quality of life in the city is definitely changing into this positive image of a buzzing place of entertainment, al-fresco dining and constant interaction; the image of the suburb, in turn, is crumbling for many. Several decades of critique have pointed out the limits of suburban life, such as the wastefulness of the suburban construction, the disappointed dream of the bucolic suburb, the corroboration of the patriarchal system: in the 1960s, Friedan (1963) famously described the one-dimensionality of life with pseudo-choices of lifestyle, and the numbing effect of commuting by car. The car was the prolongation of capitalism's arm in times of suburbanization. Building the suburbs inscribed capitalism into the landscape. The car-centred, low-density suburb became capitalism's vast spatial form. The image of the American city centre from the mid-twentieth century was one of crime and disorder, and that image contributed to further suburbanization (Beauregard 2006). The suburban landscape was initially started with tramways fingering out from the city business centre, followed by trains. Later the "railroad suburb" was replaced by the car and its highways to access the further and further outward-reaching suburbs. Suburbia is a crumbling spatial fix with lasting and costly effects on the landscape. Capital has to find new profitable markets. And people want a different lifestyle that has a more human-scale dimension, with time and space being manageable without having to spend too much time in the car: a rebellion against capitalist space and its restricted lifestyles, away from the outdated styles of suburbia and back into the city, where an aestheticized and commodified lifestyle is at the end of a mobile phone. Moving back to the city appears as a liberating step, an answer to the postmodern yearning for community, creativity and self-realization. An educated choice for whomever can afford it. In this sense, walkable urbanism conveys an alleged agency.

With capital's inward movement to create new markets, specifically its return to the city, social spaces, which were to a certain extent only proto-capitalist and functioned not through the rule of money but through urban and civic rules of cohabitation, are now being colonized by capital. Limits are stretched, since the entertaining and gratifying aspects of what money can buy outweigh the old-fashioned benefits of more complex interactions of public life. Here's an example: Starbucks introduced a smartphone app that lets you 'skip the line next time'. With technology and money, the first-come-first-served rule of a queue is brought to a virtual level. Is there still a queue when waiting for your app order? What are the rules of that queue? The machine will decide who is next and which name the barista calls out. No queue. No reference point of a rule to start a conversation. New reference points maybe – while the machine decides, we gratefully wait and enjoy the time Starbucks gives us. It works well; after all, it is efficient. As we are constantly adapting together with technology, Marcuse described this new matter-of-factness as early as the 1940s, and it is poignant still, as culture, technology and capitalism are getting more and more tightly interwoven.

> And all this is indeed for his benefit, safety and comfort; he receives what he wants. Business, technics, human needs and nature are welded together into one rational and expedient mechanism. He will fare best who follows its directions, subordinating his spontaneity to the anonymous wisdom which ordered everything for him. The decisive point is that this attitude – which dissolves all actions into a sequence of semi-spontaneous reactions to prescribed mechanical norms – is not only perfectly rational but also perfectly reasonable. All protest is senseless, and the individual who would insist on his freedom of action would become a crank. There is no personal escape from the apparatus which has mechanized and standardized the world. It is a rational apparatus, combining utmost expediency with utmost convenience, saving time and energy, removing waste, adapting all means to the end, anticipating consequences, sustaining calculability and security.
>
> *(Marcuse 1941: 143)*

In this manner, with the help of technology, capital conquers spaces that had functioned on a socially and culturally defined basis, not on a money-defined basis. Philosopher Michael Sandel (2012) has an entire chapter on 'Jumping the Queue' in his reflections on how the moral limits of markets are transgressed. But capital needs new markets to continue, and the city with its many human nooks and crannies is a great place to conquer and colonize, now that walkable urbanism is bringing back wealthy people to the city. They are supported by a variety of apps that have been published to promote walkable urbanism through an algorithmic calculation of the walkability of a place. They try to become more and more extensive in their consideration of factors, while at the same time they define walkability for us. The people at Walkonomics, for instance, want to define what a walkable street actually is. For them, trees are most important, as they follow a study which found that trees make people happy (behaviourism, anyone?). Their app serves only a handful of cities in the UK and the US so far and its claim is to 'find the most beautiful walking route to anywhere in your city' (Davies 2015).

The pioneering Walk Score app has upgraded from the simple Walk Score algorithm, which included proximity to shops, restaurants, entertainment and a bank, to the Street Smart Walk Score algorithm, which is advertised as including much more local data, such as pedestrian friendliness, zoning and range of choice. The old version offered a description of their method, but the new version does not explain how pedestrian friendliness is defined or what exactly the local data is composed of. It pops up in the app simply as a category to choose from. There is also a "choice map" feature, which one can subscribe to in order to find restaurants or whatever is needed at the moment, and a Bike Score. Most interestingly, shortly after appearing on the web, Walk Score became a real-estate search engine – Leinberger's (2012) vision is apparent. The Walk Score site states their wish to see each real-estate advertisement to feature the number of bedrooms, the number of bathrooms, and the score number achieved on Walk Score. Three numbers of social distinction. It is not about walking; it is about social distinction, through being able to afford the new markets that capital is creating with walkable urbanism. 'Walking isn't just good for you. It has become an indicator of your socioeconomic status' (Leinberger 2012). The taken-for-granted technology and its prescribing force contribute to standardizing and reifying walkable urbanism in its most profitable way.

Walking co-opted

The desire to make American towns and cities, even suburbs, more walkable and to sell walkability to real-estate clients and tourists has led to the quest for a repeatable scenario, a tendency already present in the beginnings of this urban design trend (Boyer 1988) and which established itself over time. A recipe for mass-produced walkability design emerged, which might not have been in some of the pioneers' spirit of "pedestrian pockets" and which will gradually link more and more "transit-oriented development" pockets to mass transit networks, nor in the spirit of the possible 'life between buildings' that allows civic interaction to happen (Calthorpe and Kelbaugh 1989; Gehl 1987).

My aim is not to denounce the various initiatives to further walking. I don't want to offer yet another attack on New Urbanism either. Indeed, the efforts that reflect on our transportation practices and our built environment can only be welcomed. Rather, I would like to point out the complex evolution of rebellious initiatives in the postmodern setting. As with any "rebellious" or innovative initiative, there lies the danger of it being recuperated by the dominating forces in ways that we might not notice right away. I seek to analyse the social phenomenon of walkable urbanism as it plays on the level of power relations in the socio-economic and spatial organization of our society. In this sense, it is necessary to understand walkable urbanism in its economic and social-political context: as a spatial form of capitalism with social consequences. The fact that walkability is becoming a sales pitch for real-estate premiums, that a whole spectrum of gear, clothes and even cars go with a walkable lifestyle, that walkable neighbourhoods are becoming an exclusive place of social distinction through consumption rather than through civic activity, all point to the necessity to try and understand this phenomenon in its economic and social context.

References

Adorno, T.W. (1969) 'Scientific experiences of a European scholar in America', in D. Fleming and B. Bailyn (eds), *The Intellectual Migration. Europe and America 1930–1960*, Cambridge, MA: Belknap Press of Harvard University Press, pp. 338–370.

Adorno, T.W. (1991) *The Culture Industry*, ed. J.M. Bernstein, London: Routledge.

Anonymous (2015) 'The 10 best cities to pre-retire: move there now, retire there later', *Forbes Magazine*. Available at: www.forbes.com/pictures/fgmi45fjil/move-there-now-retire-there-later.

Baudrillard, J. (1994) *Simulacra and Simulation*, Ann Arbor: University of Michigan Press.

Beauregard, R.A. (2006) *When America Became Suburban*, Minneapolis: University of Minnesota Press.

Benjamin, W. (1999) *The Arcades Project*, Cambridge MA: The Belknap Press of Harvard University Press.

Bernstein, J.M. (1991) 'Introduction', in J.M. Bernstein (ed.), *The Culture Industry*, London: Routledge, pp. 1–28.

Bieri, A.H. (2015) 'Walking in late capitalism: dialectic of aestheticization and commodification'. Unpublished doctoral dissertation, Virginia Tech, Blacksburg.

Bourdieu, P. (1975) 'La spécificité du champ scientifique et les conditions sociales du progrès de la raison', *Sociologie et sociétés*, 7(1): 91–118.

Boyer, M.C. (1988) 'The return of aesthetics to city planning', *Society*, 25(4): 49–56.

Calthorpe, P. and Kelbaugh, D. (eds) (1989) *The Pedestrian Pocket Book: A New Suburban Design Strategy*, New York: Princeton Architectural Press.

Campoli, J. (2012) *Made for Walking. Density and Neighboorhood Form*, Cambridge, MA: Lincoln Institute of Land Policy.

Castoriadis, C. (1975) *L'institution imaginaire de la société*, Paris: Seuil.

Davies, A. (2015) 'Find the most beautiful walking route to anywhere in your city', Walkonomics, 26 June. Available at: http://walkonomics.com/blog/2015/06/find-the-most-beautiful-walking-route-to-anywhere-in-your-city

Debord, G. (1967) *La Société du spectacle* [Society of the Spectacle], Paris: Buchet/Chastel.

Delitz, H. (2009) *Architektursoziologie*, Bielefeld, Germany: Transcript Verlag.

Duany, A. and Speck, J. (2010) *The Smart Growth Manual*, Toronto: McGraw-Hill.

Ehrenreich, B. (2009) *Bright-Sided: How Positive Thinking is Undermining America*, New York: Metropolitan Books, Henry Holt.

Ellin, N. (1999) *Postmodern Urbanism*, Revised Edition, New York: Princeton Architectural Press.

Ewing, R. and Bartholomew, K. (2013) *Pedestrian- and Transit-Oriented Design*, Washington, DC: Urban Land Institute, American Planning Association.

Ewing, R. and Handy, S. (2009) 'Measuring the unmeasurable: urban design qualities related to walkability', *Journal of Urban Design*, 14(1): 65–84.

Friedan, B. (1963) *The Feminine Mystique*, New York: W.W. Norton & Company.

Gehl, J. (1987) *Life Between Buildings*, New York: Van Nostrand Reinhold.

Harvey, D. (2001) 'Globalization and the "spatial fix"', *Geographische Revue*, 2(3): 23–30.

Hirt, S. (2009) 'Premodern, modern, postmodern? Placing new urbanism into a historical perspective', *Journal of Planning History*, 8(3): 248–273.

Jameson, F. (1984) 'Postmodernism, or the cultural logic of late capitalism', *New Left Review*, 1(146): 53–92.

Jameson, F. (1998) *The Cultural Turn. Selected Writings on the Postmodern, 1983–1998*, London: Verso.

Jameson, F. (2015) 'The aesthetics of singularity', *New Left Review*, 92 (March–April): 101–132.

Knox, P. (2005) 'Creating ordinary places: slow cities in a fast world', *Journal of Urban Design*, 10(1): 1–11.

Knox, P. and Ozolins, P. (eds) (2000) *Design Professionals and the Built Environment*, Chichester, UK: John Wiley & Sons.

Leinberger, C.B. (2009) *The Option of Urbanism – Investing in a New American Dream*, Washington, DC: Island Press.

Leinberger, C.B. (2012) 'Now coveted: a walkable, convenient place', *New York Times*, 25 May. Available at: www.nytimes.com/2012/05/27/opinion/sunday/now-coveted-a-walkable-convenient-place.html?_r=0.

Lynch, K. (1960) *The Image of the City*, Cambridge, MA: The Technology Press & Harvard University Press.

Marcuse, H. (1941) 'Some social implications of modern technology', *Studies in Philosophy and Social Sciences*, 9(3): 414–439.

Peck, J. (2007) 'The creativity fix', *Eurozine*, June: 1–12.

Piiparinen, R. (2013) 'The persistence of failed history: "white infill" as the new "white flight"?', *New Geography*. Available at: www.newgeography.com/content/003812-the-persistence-failed-history-white-infill-new-white-flight.

Pivo, G. and Fisher, J.D. (2011) 'The walkability premium in commercial real estate investments', *Real Estate Economics*, 39(2): 185–219.

Reckwitz, A. (2012) 'Gesellschaftliche Moderne und ästhetische Moderne', *Internationales Archiv für Sozialgeschichte der deutschen Literatur*, 37: 89–98.

Rendell, J., Penner, B. and Borden, I. (eds) (2000) *Gender Space Architecture*, London: Routledge.

Sandel, M.J. (2012) *What Money Can't Buy: The Moral Limits of Markets*, New York: Farrar, Straus, Giroux.

Saunders, W.S. (ed.) (2005) *Commodification and Spectacle in Architecture: A Harvard Design Magazine Reader*, Minneapolis: University of Minnesota Press.

Sklair, L. (2006) 'Iconic architecture and capitalist globalization', *City*, 10(1): 21–47.

Venturi, R., Scott Brown, D. and Izenour, S. (1988) *Learning from Las Vegas*, Cambridge, MA: MIT Press.

3

Radical twenty-first-century walkers and the Romantic qualities of leisure walking

Phil Smith

Introduction

In Jiro Taniguchi's 1992 manga, *The Walking Man*, the everyday walks of a conservative white-collar worker are diverted by chance and curiosity into an ambiguous zone between leisurely strolls and hyper-sensitised exploration, trespass, stalking and pilgrimage. The "walking man" breaks into a swimming pool to swim naked, climbs Mount Fuji symbolically and obsessively follows an elderly man. At the end of each disruption, he returns home and normativity is re-made.

Taniguchi's manga maps the territory for this chapter, which examines examples of UK-based walking arts practitioners who work around the boundaries of everyday or leisure walking; part of an identifiable "meshwork" with unevenly shared principles, aesthetics and narratives. The chapter then examines representations of the "why" of conventional recreational walking (hiking and rambling) as expressed in popular walking publications, and concludes by identifying philosophical affordances in leisure and radical walking for mutual engagement.

The practices

Jess Allen practises "tractivism". She walks footpaths, mostly rural, and engages those she meets in dialogues about ecology and climate change. As prompts for conversation she carries props or gifts (low-energy light bulbs) or uses costume (carrying a yoke and pails). Elspeth Owen is a long-distance walking artist who makes "epic" durational walks, during which she is often uncertain of destination and must usually find a space for camping at night. One of her walking artworks, *Grandmother's Footsteps* (2009), passed through fifteen of the UK's counties and marked her becoming a grandmother; it involved taking messages between other first-time grandparents. On the delivery of each message, she acquired a new message and a new, previously unknown, destination. For Owen, now 77, one

> motivator is her acute sense of fear when walking in unknown places – a fear that she acknowledges, confronts and overcomes . . . all the bad things that she imagined might happen . . . placed beside all the good things that did: 'somebody has probably done something fantastic for me, or shown me the way or taken me in'.
>
> *(Heddon and Turner 2010: 18–19)*

While Allen and Owen generally walk alone, their practices are sociable and relational (unlike the epic solo journeys of earlier male walking artists, such as Richard Long); not only challenged by terrain and duration, but ecologically woven into that environment (Owen making 'blue moon' actions where she stays outside for the 28 days of a two-moon month and takes night walks (Heddon and Turner 2010) and reflexively confronting the social in their own bodies).

Emma Bush's art event, *Village Walk* (2008), in Harbertonford (Devon, UK) was led at different times by different residents; they narrated the history of individual houses, discussed residents' paintings, told autobiographical and fantastic stories (channelling a Samurai warrior). There were collective actions of planting, singing and witnessing a newly engaged couple dancing. Somewhere between a community and an aesthetic event, the walk wove together public spaces with private gardens and rooms, entangling local historiography with subjective fantasies, challenging the valorisation of authenticity and dismantling each narrative as it established itself.

Lucy Furlong's *Amniotic City* (2011) maps a space as defined as any village, close to the City of London; a poem-map covering a similar area to "Jack the Ripper" tours. Rather than make morbid space, she offers choices around passion, corporeality and female agency, ranging widely across roles and discourses: fictional, independent, maternal, affectionate, exploratory, loving, marking and supernatural. Furlong's poems are recognisably sited; potential liturgies for re-enactment. They are proposals, less bent on cutting passages than on following clues to alignments of desire in patterns immersed in the terrain; an interweaving of intimacy and otherness reminiscent of Janet Cardiff's projection of herself in audio works: '[M]y surrogate body starts to infiltrate their consciousness while in reverse their remembered dreams, triggered by phrases and sounds, invade and add to the artwork' (Cardiff 1999: 15).

The zines collected in *dériviste* Laura Oldfield Ford's *Savage Messiah* (2011) share a raw anger with older punk publications like *Sniffin' Glue* (1976–1977) at the alienation of communities and individuals, but without their pessimism. Ford's work is fuelled by emotions, rushes, love, desiring, dreaming and an erotic urge to fight back. Inspired by her "drifts" through the brutalist architecture of the emptying housing estates she has lived in, they speak of the spontaneity of parties, squatting and protests, of self-questioning and heightened states. Ford uses everyday materials such as biros, yet deploys literary and philosophical references. Her hybrid images defy any single reading, her presence is always ambiguous. She comments passionately, she refuses to comment; she protects her interiority while exercising her self-determination. Her drift from authenticity is a retreat from the state, from the threat of dependency on anything other than her own agency.

These are just five of the hundreds of self-designating "walking artists" or artists and activists using walking in the UK. The London-based Walking Artists Network, which informally networks among walking artists, has over 500 members. While they are distinctive practitioners, there is much common ground in immersive and reflexive subjectivities, the deferral of synthesis and the sustenance of multiplicities, placing oneself at the mercy of the world, shifts between solitude and sociability, use of everyday materials, distance from a recognised art market and playing around common forms of walking such as strolling, tourist visiting, rural rambling and guided walks.

The genealogies

Despite growing numbers and a meshwork of practices, these walkers are still mostly absent from the "canonical" narratives of Western European walking arts repeated and finessed in accounts by Rebecca Solnit (2000) (the only account of the "canon" to appropriately feature women walkers), Rachael Antony and Joël Henry (2005), Merlin Coverley (2006), Tomas Espedal (2010), Frédéric Gros (2014) and others. This narrative extends back to Romanticism and was first articulated as mass participatory recreational walking groups proliferated and a self-consciously aesthetic, critical practice of walking in its own right emerged from iconoclastic movements like the Dadaists, Surrealists, International Lettristes/situationists and Fluxus. In the UK, the canon includes Richard Long and Hamish Fulton's emergence from the broader context of Land Art and literary psychogeographers like Iain Sinclair (1998, 2003), Alan Moore (2000), and Peter Ackroyd (1993). The more obscure Psychogeographical Associations of the 1990s (Home 1997; Bonnett 2014; Smith 2015) are sometimes footnoted.

The "canonical" narrative places twentieth-century radical walkers and movements in a genealogical relation to Romanticism, implying continuity despite their explicit breaks from it. Contemporary mainstream literary walkers, like "new nature writer" Robert Macfarlane (2012), philosopher-hiker Frédéric Gros (2014) and journalist Sinclair McKay (2013), write, often appreciatively, of these iconoclasts, even adopting some of their tactics, only to fold these practices back into Romanticist walking. However, when I conducted an email questionnaire among "new walkers" (18 responses from a range of activists, art-walkers and psychogeographers, over 9,000 words of response to seven "open" and yes/no questions) over half (11) rejected any influence from the Romanticist tradition and/or saw their work as a break from Romanticism (7); five of the walkers identified with Romanticism and three saw their walking as a critical extension of, or in a continuum with, it.

Recent accounts of the latest generations of radical walkers (Evans 2012; Collier 2013; Richardson 2015a) have begun to uncouple them from the Romantic "canon". The ambulatory practices of this "new movement" (Smith 2015) of walkers, made up partly by what Richardson (2015b) calls 'the new psychogeography' shift across sharply different relations to both Romanticism and recreational walking, with over half (11) of my questionnaire respondents identifying their walks with either recreational or everyday ambulation. The 'new' walkers are taking advantage of earlier movements' breaks from functional and ideal walking to make their work increasingly in the ruptures and margins of everyday and recreational walking.

The many "whys"

'Why Walk?' Colin Speakman (2011) titles a chapter of his *Walk!* His answers are more philosophical than corporeal or geographical; and this holds good for the general introductions to recreational walking surveyed for this chapter. No matter how technical or anecdotal they become, they usually begin by citing aesthetic, philosophical or spiritual motivation.

S. P. B. Mais opens *We Wander in the West* (1950) with a rich conflation of metaphors from colonialism, serial monogamy, the idea of *genius loci*, female Christian pilgrimage and sexual conquest: walking 'in the company of Egeria, not always the same Egeria. I have gone through life in search of Egeria and Egeria and I together have gone through life in search of the West Country. Both are elusive' (Mais 1950: 13). In Mais's construct, walking the landscape is an exploration/exploitation of eternally renewable territory with 'always something fresh to discover' (Mais 1950: 13). His corporeal/spiritual/geographical assemblage is echoed in later books on hiking and rambling that equally valorise a 'spiritual sense . . . planting our feet on grass . . . asserting our true, organic natures' (McKay 2013: 4), 'becom[ing] part of your surroundings, at one with the environment' (Speakman 2011: 16), 'an opportunity for mental and spiritual renewal' (Lawrence *et al.* 2009: 9), 'the land makes mystics of some of us' (Evans 1998: iv), '[T]he impulse to go walking . . . [is] a religious one' (Murray 1939: 2).

For some writers, recreational walking constitutes an extreme nostalgia: 'able to rediscover the instinctive simplicity of our cavemen ancestors . . . on foot' (Marais 2009: 8); the more literary express such ideas very personally: 'love and landscape were all that I needed . . . "It is eternity now. I am in the midst of it'" (Parker 2011: 120), '[T]ramping brings one to reality' (Graham 1936: 1), '[W]alking unlocks the treasures' (Cracknell 2014: 30). Even the more "down-to-earth" volumes suggest a psycho-physical motive: 'nothing more therapeutic than roaming' (Bradbury 2010: 13).

Frédéric Gros (2014: 181) historicises such sentiments, associating them with 'the great roman-tic walker' for whom walking is 'a ceremony of mystic union, the walker being co-present with the Presence . . . [and] testimony to . . . mystical fusion'. In the intensity of such "at-oneness" with the Romantic sublime, the walker can experience diminution (a 'real sense of the . . . massiveness of the hill compared with your minute sense of self'), 'tranquillity', 'emptiness' and 'near silent activity' (Speakman 2011: 15–16). These are parts of a common narrative of the hiker walking themselves into anonymous symbiosis with the landscape, significantly under-representing the impact of the walker on their environment, a directly localised and site-specific spirituality served by parallel and contradictory narratives in which rural pedestrianism is either a near universal 'form of religious practice in itself' (McKay 2013: 4) or disappearing; either way, an essentialist resistance to the evolution of 'Homo automobiliensis' (Speakman 2011: 10).

It is far rarer to find an acknowledgement, like Morris Marples', that 'mankind . . . has seldom regarded walking as a pleasure' (Marples 1960: xiii), though some of the more recent guides note that walking remains an economic necessity for the world's majority. Colin Speakman begins his 'Why Walk?' chapter: '[W]alking is what we all do. To walk is to be a human' (Speakman 2011: 9). Babies are not human? Those with disabilities preventing them from moving bipedally are not human? Of course, the writer has no intention of implying any such things, but such is the enthusiasm for loading the 'gentle art' of walking with universal meanings and virtues that such excesses blurt out. Yet competition, property accumulation, normativity and colonialism are among the roots of recreational walking, from sports 'originated in the seventeenth and eighteenth centuries by upper class gentlemen who . . . placed wagers on their footmen' (Speakman 2011: 14), in mass-based, often anti-establishment, walking clubs originating in Central and Western Europe, in mountaineering clubs with principles of risk and conquest, and in an ecological strain of walking initiated by the Sierra Club in a Yosemite almost entirely cleared of its indigenous inhabitants (Solnit 2000).

Representations of landscape, ramblers and rambling – valorised in the idea that 'cultural significance . . . lies not so much in the movement of one's legs but in what such movement symbolises' (Coverley 2012: 11) – explicitly and implicitly express contradictions that inhibit the fusion to which romanticist walking aspires. A footpath, when represented as a 'pretty, but pointless, thing in itself, a truncated chuff from nowhere to nowhere, and connected at either end . . . by the inevitable car', becomes a separation from the "real world" (Parker 2011: 101). A walking defined by moralism (a 'love of plain living and high thinking which permeates the rambling fraternity to the present day' (Speakman 2011: 58), aversion to risk ('I would rather die walking than die of boredom reading about how to walk safely' (Gooley 2014: 3)), or restriction ('a gloriously middle-aged pastime' (Parker 2011: 320)), undoes the "base" transgressive and sen-sual work of Romantic fusion articulated by Mais (1950) and Gros (2014). Describing Rights of Way Improvement Plans as 'beat[ing] themselves up about the lack of disabled people . . . young people . . . ethnic minorities' (Parker 2011: 292), unintentionally reveals how the "wild and unconstructed" landscapes with which the Romantic walker is to fuse elementally, are, in fact, cluttered with obstructive and constructed representations.

Other tensions emerge within these publications, between walking as a righteous but func-tionalist exertion (the countryside as "Green Gym"; walkers' hands cluttered with Nordic poles, reducing sensual contact with the terrain), a corporeal re-statement of common rights over property, and an inward-looking ambulation relegating the landscape to a visual background for contemplation. Entanglements of such conservative and radical, appropriative and ecological, romantic and materialist views are complexly manifest within individual walking groups, and within and between memberships and leaderships of walking organisations (Parker 2011).

The anthropologist Tim Ingold (2012), who has written widely on walking, has attempted to distil, personify and resolve some of the above contradictions (rather than transcend them, as Gros attempts) through "opposing" understandings of landscape perception. Ingold reveals deep structural and philosophical differences at work in seemingly minor characteristics of rambling. Ingold sets historian Simon Schama, who privileges the imagination in relation to the terrain – 'landscape is the work of the mind . . . built as much from strata of memory as from layers of rock' (Schama 1995: 6–7) – against the perceptual scientist James J. Gibson who champions a whole-organism immersion in a material world indifferent to representations, interpretations and imagination (in Speakman's *Walk!*, both positions appear, without apparent contradiction, on the same page: 15!). Ingold (2012) favours a Gibsonian, interwoven, active sensing over the abstracted mental processes of 'culture, convention and cognition' (Schama 1995: 12), but he baulks at Gibson's 'clos[ing] the gap between the reality of the world and our perception of it . . . by opening up a chasm between perception and imagination' (Ingold 2012: 3).

Seeking to 'find a way beyond these alternatives', Ingold (2012: 3) performs a very peculiar, but revealing, act of wishful thinking. Perhaps lacking a detailed knowledge of the latest generation of walkers, he turns to the photographs of walking artist Richard Long, despite their 'conforming in every respect to the romantic ideal of the scenic panorama' and their collection in books 'designed to appeal to an aesthetic sensibility that perceives beauty in finished forms, and not in the processes that give rise to them' (Ingold 2012: 16). Ingold proposes that we re-imagine these commodified images, encouraging passive consumption, as the mere slough of Schama's (1995) viewpoint and as 'bait to feed the market in fine art', and as somehow releasing the reader to apprehend landscape 'not in the unification of memory and rock . . . but in the never-ending, contrapuntal interweaving of material flows and sensory awareness' (Ingold 2012: 16). Ingold suggests an aggressive *détournement* (a situationist-originated process in which moribund art products and ideologically constrained materials are broken and redeployed for unintended hybrid purposes, critiquing and destroying their original purpose) of both the products and sensibilities of Long's practice, (including the latter's parallels and similarities to the "whys" of Romanticism-inflected leisure walking). Ingold (2012: 16) urges the walker/reader to 'leave this [Long's] view . . . at the roadside' and to walk 'in an alternating movement of casting forward and drawing up'. Published in a collection of academic papers, Ingold's strategy is bold, but yet to find its audience; a more receptive field awaits somewhere between the contradictions of recreational walking and the reparative practices of the new generation of walking artists and psychogeographers.

Rural and urban

Despite Stephen Graham's (1936: 192–207) urban "zig-zag" walks of the 1920s and Geoffrey Murray's 1939 prediction, inspired by Graham, of 'walks undertaken in pursuit of the "Natural History of Streets"' (Murray 1939: 305), recreational urban walking remains something of a novelty in recreational walking. So, while Speakman (2011) salutes The Ramblers' (UK) diversification into urban walking, he still characterises urban paths as conduits to the rural hinterland and demonises outer-urban areas as monstrous labyrinths 'with no pavement and poor signage . . . a bleak and forbidding environment especially in the hours of darkness . . .

dangerous, unpleasant and threatening . . . no-go areas for pedestrians' (Speakman 2011: 118–119). Such a representation is contradicted in the UK's larger cities by regular expeditions of psychogeographers (Richardson 2015a), walking artists and urban explorers across derelict wastelands (Edensor 2005), into retail sites (Richardson 2013), along routes of culverted rivers, through sewerage and other concealed systems (Garrett 2013) and around abject traffic structures (Sinclair 2003; Davies 2007).

In sharp contrast to the 15 (of 18) questionnaire respondents who regard urban and rural spaces as entangled, Frédéric Gros (2014) elevates recreational walking's rural/urban walking binary to the level of philosophical category. In his account of Pedestrian Romanticism, the 'urban stroller doesn't put in an appearance at the fullness of Essence, he just lays himself open to scattered visual impact', while the rural rambler in 'the pure bosom of a maternal Nature . . . is fulfilled in an abyss of fusion' (Gros 2014: 181). Gros might be thinking here of Richard Long, walking in 'places where nothing seems to have broken the connection to the ancient past' (Solnit 2000: 272), though, in the case of his much-favoured Dartmoor, Long must be ignoring the extensive nineteenth-century quarrying and the more venerable deforestation of the moor, or, perhaps, hikers imagining that 'walking ancient paths . . . not only are we on exactly the same routes as our forefathers, we are also travelling in precisely the same way' (Parker 2011: 115).

Yet, if any one group of walkers has truly explored an "abyss of fusion" it is the oft-maligned, urban, occult, late-twentieth-century literary psychogeographers (Ackroyd 1993; Sinclair 1998; Moore 2000), who have sought out and described cryptic patterns in the urban fabric and invoked an intensity of presence equivalent to anything in the literature of rural waking. This is acknowledged, if imprecisely and backhandedly, in McKay's (2013: 180) description of 'a cult enthusiasm among younger urban walkers . . . [for] divining the old spirit of each street . . . seeing the invisible lines of historical – even occult – energy that connect them'. When McKay (2013: 180) seeks to belittle these new 'younger' walkers as 'actually romantics, in the old-fashioned poetic sense', he not only misses the ambiguous relation between the latest generation of psychogeographers and art walkers (of which he seems to know very little) and Romanticism, but misidentifies the new generation of walkers with the ideas of a previous literary one. For while the same immersion as with both Romantics and occult psychogeographers is at work in the practices of "new" urban, suburban and edgeland walkers like Morag Rose (2015) and the Loiterers Resistance Movement, Gareth E. Rees (2013) and Nick Papadimitriou (2012), all of whom know either the members or writings of the older occult generation, they are peculiar in embracing difference and ambiguity (of signs detached from dominant discourses, occult or otherwise), the fracture of subjectivity (stepping back from the heroic), and clinging to the rim of the abyss not as an extreme moment on a mountain pass but as the *modus vivendi* of late capitalist psychic precarity (Smith 2010), to which Clive Austin devotes a full-length movie (*The Great Walk* (2013)), the walk of uncertainty in uncertain times done anywhere.

This diversity and hybridity of tradition is reflected by the 18 questionnaire respondents (all of whom knew of the situationists, seven acknowledging profound influence), citing as influential 30 walking artists/activists (individuals or groups), 29 theorists, 25 theories, 10 artists/writers and five practices (with only the situationists mentioned more than three times). To take one of many possible examples: the reflexivity of the "new movement" is represented by the many "new" walkers adopting neo-vitalist 'thing-power' (Bennett 2010), even animist tendencies and a new phenomenology (Trigg 2014); walking artists drawing chalk and mud into their paintings, dragging ambulant architectures along footpaths. Terrain becomes meaningful, not just by the walker's immersion in it, but by the terrain's percept of the walker; something pre-empted by "tramper" Stephen Graham (1936: 207): '[Y]ou are not choosing what you see in the world, but are giving the world an even chance to see you'.

The new movement

Tina Richardson's (2015a, 2015b) 'new psychogeography' has much in common with contemporary walking artists: the intense instability of its grounding on a public terrain under incremental threat from private property, its 'focus on the affective', 'archaeological critique that excavates the signs contained in the terrain that might be contrary to the dominant discourse', 'physical enactment of placing one's body in the terrain in order to read the signs therein', and a resistance to binaries of 'inside/outside, mind/matter and natural/manmade . . . bring[ing] these oppositions into a different focus whereby they become constructs that are overridden through one's very movement through the space itself' (Richardson 2015b: 241, 247).

Unlike the neo-psychogeographers of the 1990s, pulled between Marxian materialism, tedious algorithmic drifting and 'mystical fusion' with occult patterns, the 'new psychogeography', in common with the new movement of contemporary art walking, is reflexive, 'you become part of the very landscape you are scrutinizing' (Richardson 2015b: 247), and reparative, its *dérives* tailored for deconstructing binaries and repairing the outfall in pedestrian scores and "texts" that are 'open and heterogenous . . . [characterised by] what might be called the *stereographic plurality* of its weave of signifiers' (Richardson 2015b: 248, original emphasis).

As well as providing the entanglement (necessary for the second, reparative part of *détournement*) required by Tim Ingold's proposal for re-making walking, Richardson's (2014: 45) phrase, 'physical enactment of placing one's body', reveals the gap that separates these kinds of walking from both Romantic and occult psychogeographical walking; their reflexive sensitivity to the performed nature of everyday life, their deconstruction of their own materials and forms of representation (as they use them), their postmodern sensibility to the mediation of aesthetics and iconoclasm, and their privileging of multiplicity ('first and foremost . . . heterogeneity' (Richardson 2015b: 250)) over the distillation of Essence or Presence. Their product is praxis, democratic but also provocative, in the positive sense of 'encourage[ing] people to participate . . . anyone can do it' (Richardson 2015b: 250–251).

Conclusion

Richard Long and Hamish Fulton, members of the first generation of UK walking artists, continue to make representations that cite a functionality recognisable to conventional hikers: journey duration, start and end points, route maps. Anyone meeting them by chance might easily mistake them for hikers. Immersed in the hiker's terrain of choice (moors, long trails, mountain regions), they walk in the commanding tradition of Caspar David Friedrich's *Wanderer*, evoking the apotheosis of the walker's presence and fusion with spectacular place to which recreational walking, at various stages of dilution, aspires. Nevertheless, their intense solitude (Fulton's artwork, *No Talking for Seven Days*, 1993), epic journeys at "heroic" pace (Fulton walking 120 miles of the Pilgrim's Way without sleep, 1991) and Long's physical interventions in and extractions from the landscape put a considerable distance between them and anything like leisure.

More significantly, perhaps, while Fulton has recently made choreographed walks with community participation, their art products do not "bait", but successfully circulate within, the conventional art market and generate a passive, mentally appropriative consumption rather than provoke trespass. Equally, though probably less well known to recreational walkers, the first generation of UK literary psychogeographers continue a Romanticist line (to re-direct McKay's (2013) misguided characterisation) inherited more from the often occult Neo-Romanticism of Arthur Machen, John Cowper Powys and Paul Nash than Wordsworth and Keats (Woodcock 2000); their literary and fictional output just as likely as Long to encourage passive consumption (though Iain Sinclair's walk-based books like *Lights Out for the Territory* (1997) are probably, in their inspiring effect, at odds with this).

The latest generation of performative, postmodern walkers (artists, activists and psycho-geographers) has more in common with the iconoclastic break of the International Lettristes/situationists; but without their retreat from engagement. Where there is product, other than walking itself, it often takes the form of documentation, handbooks and exemplary objects designed to encourage others to further exploratory walking rather than of commodities for new markets.

This 'new movement' of walkers places itself in ambiguous and critical, but not dismissive, proximity to the gaze and ethos of the leisurely stroll, at times borrowing from the practices of recreational walking. Rather than confrontation, this ablative, 'just to the side' of the ramble, is not 'absorbed within a wider perspective' (Speakman 2011: 16) of nature, implacable time, massive space, emptiness and near silence, but proposes a sociability, ordinariness and intense relation to the terrain (built and natural, rural and urban) that is both an abolition and an extension, an *aufhebung*, of Romantic "fusion".

So, when writers on rambling describe their experiences of 'different sorts of emotional resonance that each individual area has' (McKay 2013: 9) or how

> various sensory perceptions blend . . . elusive qualities that gave a place its own identity . . . subtle changes and moods of light, sounds, scent and smells, the lie of the land and texture of path or soil . . . a sense of history or of personal associations.
>
> *(Speakman 2011: 15)*

then they come close to describing new walking's multiple layering (Hodge *et al.* 2013) and archaeological engagement (Pearson and Shanks 2001) with space; evidence of a potential ground for "new walking" within hiking and rambling's territories.

Given their strategic positioning, valorising the everyday and the 'to the side' of the aesthetic, the 'new movement' and 'new psychogeographers' are well placed to gain leverage within the multiple contradictions of recreational walking; to embrace and redeploy immersive, sensual, ritualistic, contemplative and interpretative elements of Romantic, recreational walking. To expose, accentuate and challenge the contradictions of the appropriative, neo-colonialist products of Romanticist walking arts and 'new nature writers' and persuade leisure walkers to take a small step to the side of the conventions of their strolling/hiking/rambling to an agentive, non-appropriative walking; to walk in the gaps (both in the sense of ideological contradictions and affordances for trespass) rather than 'in fusion'. To re-invoke recreational walking's origins in rebellion: 'Walking is protest' (Speakman 2011: 151), 'walking . . . . will always be subversive' (Deakin 2000: 4), 'the walker . . . represents pure anarchy' (McKay 2013: 214).

References

Ackroyd, P. (1993) *Hawksmoor*, Harmondsworth: Penguin.
Antony, R. and Henry, J. (2005) *The Lonely Planet Guide to Experimental Travel*, Footscray, Victoria, Australia: Lonely Planet Publications.
Bennett, J. (2010) *Vibrant Matter*, Durham, NC: Duke University Press.
Bonnett, A. (2014) *Off the Map*, London: Aurum Press.
Bradbury, J. (2010) *Railway Walks*, London: Francis Lincoln.
Cardiff, J. (1999) *The Missing Voice*, London: Artangel.
Collier, M. (2013) *Walk On: 40 Years of Art Walking*, Sunderland, UK: Art Editions North.
Coverley, M. (2006) *Psychogeography*, Harpenden, Herts: Pocket Essentials.
Coverley, M. (2012) *The Art of Wandering*, Harpenden, Herts: Oldcastle Books.
Cracknell, L. (2014) *Doubling Back: Ten Paths Trodden in Memory*, Glasgow: Freight Books.

Davis, J. (2007) *Walking the M62* (self-published).

Deakin, R. (2000) *Waterlog*, London: Vintage.

Edensor, T. (2005) *Industrial Ruins*, Oxford, UK: Berg.

Espedal, T. (2010) *Tramp or the Art of Living a Wild and Poetic Life*, trans. James Anderson, London: Seagull.

Evans, D. (ed.) (2012) *The Art of Walking: A Field Guide*, London: Black Dog.

Evans, V.S. (1998) *The Celtic Way*, Wilmslow, Cheshire: Sigma Press.

Ford, L.O. (2011) *Savage Messiah*, London: Verso.

Furlong, L. (2011) *Amniotic City* (self-published).

Garrett, B.L. (2013) *Explore Everything: Place-hacking the City*, London: Verso.

Gooley, T. (2014) *The Walker's Guide to Outdoor Clues and Signs*, London: Sceptre.

Graham, S. (1936) *The Gentle Art of Tramping*, London: Thomas Nelson.

Gros, F. (2014) *A Philosophy of Walking*, New York and London: Verso.

Heddon, D. and Turner, C. (2010) 'Walking women: interviews with artists on the move', *Performance Research*, 15(4): 14–22.

Hodge, S., Persighetti, S., Turner, C. and Smith, P. (2013) 'Performance and the stratigraphy of place', in P. Graves-Brown, R. Harrison and A. Piccini (eds), *The Archaeology of the Contemporary World*, Oxford: Oxford University Press, pp. 149–165.

Home, S. (ed.) (1997) *Mind Invaders*, London: Serpent's Tail.

Ingold, T. (2012) 'Introduction', in M. Janowski and T. Ingold (eds), *Imagining Landscapes*, Farnham, Surrey: Ashgate, pp. 1–18.

Lawrence, P., Maple, L. and Sparshatt, J. (eds) (2009) *The UK Trailwalker's Handbook*, Milnthorpe, Cumbria: Cicerone.

Macfarlane, R. (2012) *The Old Ways: A Journey on Foot*, London: Hamish Hamilton.

Mais, S. P. B. (1950) *We Wander in the West*, London: Ward, Lock & Co.

Marais, J. (2009) *Hiking*, London: New Holland Publishers.

Marples, M. (1960) *Shanks's Pony: A Study of Walking*, London: The Country Book Club.

McKay, S. (2013) *Ramble On*, London: Fourth Estate.

Moore, A. (2000) *From Hell*, London: Knockabout Comics.

Murray, G. (1939) *The Gentle Art of Walking*, London: Blackie & Son.

Papadimitriou, N. (2012) *Scarp*, London: Sceptre.

Parker, M. (2011) *The Wild Rover*, London: HarperCollins.

Pearson, M. and Shanks, M. (2001) *Theatre/Archaeology*, London: Routledge.

Rees, G.E. (2013) *Marshland*, London: Influx.

Richardson, T. (2013) *Concrete, Crows and Calluses*, Leeds: Particulations Press.

Richardson, T. (2014) 'The unseen university: a schizocartography of the redbrick university campus'. PhD thesis, University of Leeds, School of Fine Art, History of Art and Cultural Studies.

Richardson, T. (2015a) 'Introduction', in T. Richardson (ed.), *Walking Inside Out: Contemporary British Psychogeography*, London: Rowman & Littlefield, pp. 1–30.

Richardson, T. (2015b) 'Conclusion: the new psychogeography', in T. Richardson (ed.), *Walking Inside Out: Contemporary British Psychogeography*, London: Rowman & Littlefield, pp. 241–254.

Rose, M. (2015) 'Confessions of an anarcho-flâneuse', in T. Richardson (ed.), *Walking Inside Out: Contemporary British Psychogeography*, London: Rowman & Littlefield, pp. 147–162.

Schama, S. (1995) *Landscape and Memory*, London: HarperCollins.

Sinclair, I. (1997) *Lights Out for the Territory*, Harmondsworth: Penguin.

Sinclair, I. (1998) *Lud Heat*, London: Granta.

Sinclair, I. (2003) *London Orbital*, Harmondsworth: Penguin.

Smith, P. (2010) *Mythogeography*, Axminster, Devon: Triarchy.

Smith, P. (2015) *Walking's New Movement*, Axminster, Devon: Triarchy.

Solnit, R. (2000) *Wanderlust: A History of Walking*, New York: Viking.

Speakman, C. (2011) *Walk! A Celebration of Striding Out*, Ilkley, West Yorks: Great Northern Books.

Taniguchi, J. (2006) *The Walking Man*, Tarragons, Spain: Fanfare.

Trigg, D. (2014) *The Thing*, Alresford, Hants: Zero Books.

Woodcock, P. (2000) *This Enchanted Isle*, Glastonbury, Somerset: Gothic Image.

4

Long-distance walking in films

Promises of healing and redemption on the trail

Warwick Frost and Jennifer Laing

Introduction

In 2015, we interviewed Luke Mills, a schoolteacher who had developed a 230-kilometre walking trail through national parks and farmland in south-eastern Australia. It is themed on St Mary MacKillop, linking two towns in which she had been active during the nineteenth century, and the walk has been branded as the "Aussie Camino". Luke explained to us how the idea had originated:

> I share a large office, as you do in schools. There was a bloke who sat around the corner from me and I said 'Have you seen this video'? He said 'I can't believe you're asking me that, I saw it last night'. It was *The Way* with Martin Sheen and Emilio Estevez and I said 'Oh, I just love that'. He said 'Yeah, so do I'. We both sort of lamented the fact that we had children who are teenagers and that our trips to Santiago [Spain] were going to be a long time away . . . some people that we had known had been to Santiago and told us what a wonderful thing it was and had done the journey . . . it's 800 kilometres over the Pyrenees and through Northern Spain and they had told us stories, But it hadn't really been made real. When we saw this film – oh fascinating, this is good. Then we both sort of sagged our shoulders and said 'We're never going to get there'. In a short period, just over a period of one or two conversations, we said, 'Well let's do something here . . . in Australia'. We tried to draw some parallels between what they do in Spain and here. Santiago, Sant Iago . . . Saint James. We thought, well we've got our own saint. Why don't we do something about her?

Books and films can play an important role as a source of inspiration to travel and imaginings about travel, as well as where and how people travel (Laing and Frost 2012). More recent work illustrates the way that the media frames our travel imaginings through different contexts, including crime fiction and television shows (Reijnders 2011), films about the Australian Outback (Frost 2010), films about the American West (Frost and Laing 2015) and books and films about exploration and adventure travel (Laing and Frost 2014). The influence of the media on imaginings of long-distance walking is another potentially fruitful area of research, given its popularity both as a plot device in books and films and as a leisure activity more generally.

This chapter explores the depiction of walking in two recent films, *The Way* (dir. Estevez 2010), which focuses on pilgrims on the Camino Way in Spain, and *Wild* (dir. Vallée 2014), based on a memoir by Cheryl Strayed (2012), in which a young woman comes to term with loss by walking the Pacific Crest Trail. Through these two cinematic narratives, we examine how these books and films present common tropes of walking as an activity that promotes healing and redemption. Even though the protagonist generally begins the journey with the intention of walking solo, it is the encounters with various people along the way that shape the experience and ultimately provide them with a renewed sense of purpose and meaning in their lives. We conclude with a consideration of the implications of these findings, both in a practical and theoretical sense.

Walking as a therapeutic pursuit

The potentially therapeutic benefits of travel have long been acknowledged. Graburn (1983) refers to the phenomenon of *rite of passage* tourism, where a traveller is typically going through a major life transition. The idea of a *transition* has been described by Bridges (2004: 186) as 'the psychological process of disengagement from the old, going through the nowhere between old and new, and then embracing and identifying with the new'. Common life transitions include a divorce or the ending of a relationship, attempting to solve or change problematic personal or work situations, or dealing with grief over the loss of a loved one such as a parent, child or partner (Ross 1994). These situations need to be worked through and processed psychologically, so that individuals can move on with their lives. In a travel context, the tourist has to 'prove to themselves that they can make the life changes' (Graburn 1983: 13), often through some arduous or testing form of travel (Laing and Frost 2014).

Long-distance walking might offer its adherents the potential to successfully negotiate life transitions. A number of studies have examined experiences of walkers on famous routes such as the Appalachian Trail and the West Highland Way (e.g. Collins-Kreiner and Kliot 2016; den Breejen 2007; Fondren 2015). A sub-set of this work focuses on the role that this activity plays in *personal transformation* or *self-directed change*. Recent work by Saunders *et al.* (2014: 143) suggests that long-distance walking can 'facilitate processes of relief and disengagement from common stresses and problems in life and can help people find ways to resolve their issues'. It allows time to mull over problems or reflect on the past, as well as looking ahead to a potentially brighter future. It may also boost self-esteem and help to instil a sense of meaning or purpose in one's life, which assists with dealing with change (Saunders 2014; Saunders *et al.* 2014).

In addition, there is an extensive body of research that examines pilgrimages, which are often performed as a walk over long distances and periods of time. The pilgrimage is therefore a useful frame for considering the experience of a long-distance walk. There is no single accepted definition of a pilgrimage (Coleman 2002), although traditionally, it has been 'associated with a religious journey, faith or devout seekers' (Frey 1998: 4). Devereux and Carnegie (2006: 50) see the pilgrimage in post-modern/hyper-modern times more in terms of a spiritual process, which might not necessarily be connected to a formal religion: 'The physical and emotional and spiritual challenges the individual encounters whilst on the journey offer time for reflection and renewal, and recognition of both the immanent and the transcendent in the course of the journey.'

Others focus on the mobility involved, both in a physical and psychological sense, and describe pilgrimages as 'movements towards new identities, new selves and hopefully a more fulfilling way of being-in-the-world' (Nilsson and Tesfahuney 2016: 23). People come and go 'at will . . . [forming] a mobile assemblage' (Nilsson and Tesfahuney 2016: 24). They note that the sacredness of the route might be 'a social construction' (Nilsson and Tesfahuney 2016: 25), often assisted by the pilgrim narrative being handed down through a variety of media, including travel books, travel guides, films and documentaries. This may result in common tropes, including that of *communitas*, the idea that people within a liminal space bond with those with whom they share the experience (Turner 1969; Turner and Turner 1978). This trope has been criticised as 'just one [more] idealizing discourse about pilgrimage' (Coleman 2002: 357).

The focus on transformation or change as an outcome of undertaking a long-distance walk has led to allied concepts being under-researched and thus not fully understood. In this chapter, we use the motif of *redemption* as a means to understand travel narratives about long-distance walking. It is the third pillar of 'the Christian eschatological narratives of sin, sacrifice and redemption' (Taylor 2001: 10), where the sinner atones for what they have done and is released from or cleansed of their sin. However, it dates back further than this, to 'the myths of ancient Greece and in sacred stories in all the world's major religions' (McAdams *et al.* 2001). It is one of two narrative sequences that are commonly used when people attempt to 'make narrative sense of personal experiences that entail significant transformation in affect' (McAdams *et al.* 2001: 474). The *redemption sequence* depicts something positive resulting from adversity and is thus a story of hope. In contrast, the *contamination sequence* is based on the idea that negative things occur that spoil the good that preceed them (McAdams *et al.* 2001). The redemption narrative can take a variety of forms, ranging from 'tales of personal recovery and conversion to accounts of healing, growth and self-fulfillment' (McAdams *et al.* 2001: 483). Use of this narrative may, of course, be a faithful representation of what has actually happened to an individual. However, it may also be a construction, chosen because the individual wishes their story to be seen in this more optimistic light. We consider how the redemption narrative is used in two recent films in order to explore the transformative benefits of long-distance walking. A cinematic analysis of the films was conducted by both authors, working together, following the approach we used in Frost and Laing (2015).

The Way (2010)

Tom (Martin Sheen) receives a phone call informing him that his son Daniel (Emilio Estevez) has died while walking the Camino de Santiago in France. He travels from California to St Jean Pied de Port in France to identify the body and arrange a funeral. Through a series of flashbacks, we find out that Tom is a widower and Daniel his only son. Though Tom loves his son, their relationship has been fraught and what he remembers are the arguments they have had. Tom is a successful ophthalmologist and has aspirations of a professional career for his boy. Daniel, on the other hand, does not want to settle down, even though he is now in his forties. He wants to travel the world. When Tom admonishes him saying 'What sort of life are you choosing?', Daniel snaps back 'You don't choose a life, you live it'. Adding to this exchange is the audience's knowledge that the actors are really father and son and that this is a highly personal project for the Sheen/Estevez family.

Captain Henri of the French police explains to Tom that Daniel died when caught in a storm on the first day of walking the Camino. When Henri asks whether Daniel was religious, the bewildered Tom realises that not only did he not know that his son was undertaking the pilgrimage, he has no real idea of why he was doing it. After looking through his son's photographs, Tom decides that he will walk the Camino, honouring his son's memory and spreading his ashes at various places.

Captain Henri warns him that it will be difficult at his age (Sheen was 70 at the time the film was made). However, Henri also gives Tom – and the audience – some background on the trail and states that having walked it three times previously, he plans to undertake it again when he turns 70. The trail from St Jean Pied de Port to Santiago de Compostela is 770 kilometres long, and is only one of multiple pilgrimage routes that end in the Spanish town (Frey 1998). Various traditions are explained to Tom, such as the *compostela* – the certificate given to those who have completed the pilgrimage 'with a religious motive' (Frey 1998: 67) and who have travelled by foot or horseback (at least 100 kilometres) or by bicycle (at least 200 kilometres).

Tom sets out alone using Daniel's gear and guidebook. On the first day, he passes the spot where Daniel died. He is shocked at how short the distance out of town was. The next day, Tom almost drowns when his backpack falls in a river. Both incidents serve to emphasise how fragile life is. Furthermore, it demonstrates that while the trail through the rural countryside appears idyllic and benign, there are potential dangers for the unwary.

As Tom walks, he has a series of encounters with people and they all have a part in his emotional journey. They notice how he scatters ashes throughout the route and this leads to discovering Tom's back story and the tragedy of his son's death. Tom's intention when he sets out is to walk by himself; he sees it as a solitary endeavour, although he mentions to the policeman that 'we' are making the journey, 'both of us', referring to his son. Nevertheless, he must interact with others, whether they be fellow pilgrims or locals. Tom's journey fits the conventions of Campbell's Hero. As conceptualised by Campbell (1949), many cultures have stories of heroic journeys and in the modern world it is a staple of literature and cinema. Following the conventions of Campbell's Hero, Tom is initially unwilling, but is eventually and unwittingly transformed by his experiences. Significantly, his encounters with people along the way all come in groups of three. Such an emphasis has religious connotations, suggesting the Holy Trinity.

The father who has lost his way, Tom gains guidance from three fathers. The first is Captain Henri, who provides advice and directions. Tom is puzzled as to why a police officer is so concerned. Without specifying any details, Henri replies that he too has lost a son. The second is Father Frank, an old Catholic priest from New York who is walking the trail. Tom is drawn to him and they have some enjoyable conversations. When the priest asks Tom whether he is a practising Catholic, Tom's response is that he only goes to church at Easter and Christmas. The priest chuckles in reply that there 'are a lot of lapsed Catholics out here on the Camino, kid'. The third is Ishmael, a gypsy. When his young son steals Tom's backpack, Ishmael is ashamed and makes him return it. Having asked for forgiveness, he takes Tom aside and tells him that once he gets to Santiago his quest will not be over. Instead, Tom must continue on to the ocean at Muxia. It is there on the wild Atlantic coast that Tom will empty the last of Daniel's ashes.

It is, however, three fellow walkers that are the most influential on Tom. These are the Dutch Joost (played by Yorick van Wageningen), the Canadian Sarah (Deborah Kara Unger), and the Irish Jack (James Nesbitt). IMDb (2010) argues that they are based on Dorothy's companions in the *Wizard of Oz* (1939). The rationale for this is that Joost lacks courage, Sarah does not have a heart and Jack is missing a brain. While cute, such an analysis does not take us too far, for it is hard to link Tom with Dorothy. Instead, our interpretation is that these three characters are crucial as they represent elements of Daniel and, through walking with them, Tom gains a better understanding of his son.

All three characters are played by actors in their early to mid-forties and Emilio Estevez is a similar age to them. Tom finds his initial encounters with the walkers to be negative, seeing them as rude, argumentative or shallow. This parallels his early flashbacks to his son, which are full of conflict and disappointment. However, as he walks along with them, their relationship starts to change. They help him. They form a walking community and enjoy the benefits of *communitas*, including sharing, conversation, working together and supporting each other. We start to see the complexity of the companions. Like Tom, they all have some deep personal issue which they try to keep hidden, but which is shared along the walk. And as Tom walks with them, they become surrogates for the son he has lost, providing him with an unexpected way to process his grief.

Joost is the first companion encountered by Tom. While Tom wants to be alone, Joost sits down at his cafe table. Joost is a constant talker and his prattle annoys Tom. Far worse, Joost tries to tell Tom about how a walker died a few days earlier. Once on the trail, Joost sticks with Tom, constantly talking. Joost's explanation for taking the walk is that he needs to lose weight to fit into his suit for his brother's wedding. Accordingly, Tom is appalled when he finds Joost in a cafe eating *cordero asado* (roast lamb). Joost counters 'That's part of the Camino experience, no? You can't come to Spain without having the roast lamb'. This is a curious scene, reflecting American cultural concerns. Walking all day would dramatically raise Joost's calorie needs, so that such a protein-rich dish would be quickly burnt off. In the same cafe scene, Tom makes a fool of himself, insisting that his American guidebook is superior to Joost's Dutch one. Tom quickly gets his comeuppance when corrected by the waiter, but Joost has the good grace to say nothing. Seemingly the most open of the companions, Joost is the most complex and functions as the emotional glue for the group. He never gives a full explanation of his problems, though there are hints that his wife has left him.

At their initial meeting, Sarah is obnoxious and criticises Tom for being a shallow Baby Boomer. His reply is: 'You sound angry', and it is Sarah's anger that defines her throughout the walk. At one stage, she asks Joost: 'Why does something that should be inspirational make me so angry?' She tells the others that she is undertaking the Camino to quit smoking, but all sense that there is far more to her story. Eventually, she tells Tom that when she was younger she was married to a man who often hit her. When she fell pregnant, she decided to have an abortion. It is the guilt about her unborn baby that is her motivation. Unlike much of what is discussed on the walk, this confession is kept secret by Tom. Having unburdened herself, Sarah's anger is greatly diminished, though she never gives up smoking.

Jack is a travel writer suffering from writer's block. He tells the others that 'the idea of a pilgrim's journey on the road is a metaphor bonanza', but while he is constantly talking about the Camino, he can't find anything worth writing. At first, Tom finds the garrulous Jack to be banal and annoying, especially when he lectures them on the concept of the true pilgrim. When Tom gets drunk, he shouts at Jack that he is 'an arrogant bore . . . a jackass, you are a true fraud'. After a night in gaol, Tom is chagrined to find that it is Jack who bailed him out.

Walking with the group, Jack overcomes his writer's block. He is drawn to the story of Tom and his son and wants to write about it. He asks Tom: 'What was your son like?' Tom replies 'Daniel was a lot like you, smart, confident,' and then he pauses and continues 'stubborn, he pissed me off a lot'. As they walk and talk, Jack opens up, explaining his disappointments: 'After I left college I wrote for travel mags. Thought I'd do that for a while, put some money away and then get down to *the novel*. Ten years later, here I am, still writing for the travel magazines'. When he then continues 'I'm not feeling sorry for myself, it's the life I chose', Tom is stunned, for those words echo the argument he had with Daniel. At this point, he gives his blessing to Jack to include his story in his book.

Eventually Tom will complete his journey. He has come to understand his son through the people he has met, and possibly to understand himself better as well. Perhaps his grief was not just for his son, but for the years he had wasted until this point. He has realised that his everyday life is introspective and lonely, as opposed to the rich tapestry of life as a traveller, meeting people and experiencing different cultures. Tom is now drawn to travel the world like his son extolled him to do and his life appears immeasurably enriched as a result.

Wild (2014)

We first encounter Cheryl Strayed (Reese Witherspoon) sitting on a rocky outcrop above a river, taking off her hiking boots. She is part-way through her walk on the Pacific Crest Trail, one of the toughest walking trails in the world, and it has left her frustrated, exhausted and suffering from bruises and blisters. The film's audience feel an empathetic flash of pain as she rips off her big toe nail with a scream.

Far longer than the Camino Way, the Pacific Crest Trail is 4,279 km long and runs from the US/Mexican border to the US/Canadian border, through the states of California, Oregon and Washington. According to the official website, about 200 people each season attempt to walk the trail (United States Department of Agriculture Forest Service 2016). This is much lower than the average number of people walking the Camino Way each year, and means that a walker is likely to be more isolated unless they start off with a companion or partner. There are also fewer towns and thus less access to supplies than on the Camino Way, and the terrain is more extreme: 'The trail traverses through some of the most extreme wilderness in the continental USA' (United States Department of Agriculture Forest Service 2016). Most of the walkers must camp on the trail, as there are few huts available and certainly not the well-established system of *albergues* or *refugios* to be found along the Camino Way. Another difference is that bicycles and motorised vehicles are not allowed on the Pacific Crest Trail. While horses are allowed, 'only a few equestrians have ever ridden the entire trail' (United States Department of Agriculture Forest Service 2016).

As Cheryl sits on the rock, one boot falls into the ravine below. In a fit of rage, she sends the other one flying to join it, and screams 'F**k you bitch!' If we are in doubt who or what she is referring to, the rest of the film makes it clear. Flashbacks during the film establish her back story and reason for undertaking this route. Cheryl Strayed lost her mother Bobbi (Laura Dern) to cancer when the latter was just 45 years old. Her death is swift and unexpected – neither child is present, though they are on their way to see her. Cheryl later says 'She was the love of my life'. But there is also guilt at her failure to understand her mother's relentless optimism in the face of adversity – the classic redemption narrative. When her daughter mocks this, Bobbi replies: 'Cheryl, if there's one thing I can teach you, it's how to find your best self. And when you do, hang on to it for dear life'. Bobbi's life with an 'abusive alcoholic husband' (in Cheryl's words), though traumatic, gave her two beloved children.

As the film progresses, we realise that her mother's death has been a catalyst for Cheryl to go off the rails. She starts taking heroin, both ingested and intravenously, and has casual sex with a series of random men. Unable to stand this self-destructive behaviour, her husband Paul initiates a divorce. Cheryl reaches her lowest ebb the day she realises that she might be pregnant by one of the men she has slept with. She spies a copy of the Pacific Crest Trail guide in a shop. It is her last chance. As she says to her friend: 'I don't know when I became such a piece of s**t . . . I was *good*, you know. I've gotta go back to the start. I'm going to walk myself back to the woman my mother thought I was'. She seeks to become 'good' again, and to wipe the slate clean, through an activity that is audacious in its challenges. The Robert Frost quote she writes in the log book at one of the waypoints sums up this goal: 'But I have promises to keep and miles to go before I sleep'.

For most of the film, Cheryl is walking by herself. There are many panoramic shots of her in the midst of vast wilderness, including one memorable scene of her tiny translucent tent lit up in an ocean of blackness, emphasising her vulnerability. She is, however, genuinely pleased to see another woman on the trail, and this provides the opportunity for her to reflect on her experiences and let her guard down. She tells Stacey stories about her beloved mother, which is part of the grieving process, as they watch a sunset together: 'My mother used to say something that drove me nuts. There is a sunrise and a sunset every day and you can choose to be there for it. You can put yourself in the way of beauty.' Stacey is empathetic ('My kind of woman'). On the other hand, the men Cheryl meets on the trail are more inclined to give her practical advice, such as the man in the roadside stop who tells her that her pack is too heavy and her boots are too small. The pack here can be seen as a metaphor for the burden of grief that is weighing her down (Kam 2015). An exception is the man who tells her: 'Don't beat yourself up. You strike me as someone who has done plenty of that already'. She is mostly wary of the men along the trail, sometimes with good reason. Some are potentially menacing, particularly the two men she encounters on a hunting trip ('Here's a young girl all alone in the woods'). This is the underbelly of isolation for a woman in the wild – it is not just nature that is potentially threatening to life and limb.

Yet for Cheryl, walking alone through nature is empowering, and it 'allows for introspection, forgiveness and acceptance' (Kam 2015: 12). Stacey asks whether she is lonely. Cheryl replies: 'Honestly? I'm lonelier in my real life than I am out here. I miss my friends, of course, but it's not as if I have anybody waiting for me at home.' The time on her own gives her the space she needs to work through her despair, both in relation to her marriage and her mother. She also has to accept herself, flaws and all. As she writes in one log book on the trail, using a quote from Joni Mitchell: 'Will you take me as I am?' A scene with a young boy shows how far she has come. She tells him: 'Problems don't stay problems. They turn into something.' This is her mother's philosophy on life, and it is now her own. Cheryl cries after the boy and his grandmother leave her. This is raw and visceral grief, on her knees, great tearing sobs that represent the catharsis of the journey.

The motif of redemption is thus strong in this film. There are recurring references to the scientist Marie Curie, who died of radiation poisoning, and her mother, both women whose 'wounds . . . came from the same source as [their] power', turning adversity into their own personal triumph. Cheryl later begins to understand that she could have done this herself, and perhaps has already done so, even before she started to do the walk. Did her journey towards redemption start when she hit rock bottom in order to get to her present state of acceptance of the past? As she muses:

> What if I forgive myself? What if I was sorry? But if I could go back in time, I wouldn't do a single thing differently. What if I wanted to sleep with every single one of those men? What if heroin taught me something? What if all those things I did were the things that got me here? What if I was never redeemed? What if I already was?

The ending of the film sees Cheryl continue to try to make sense of her walk, something which she found difficult to articulate at the beginning. When her ex-husband says on the phone to her before she departs: 'I'm sorry that you have to walk 1000 miles just to . . . ', tailing off in embarrassment, she replies: 'Finish that sentence. Why do I have to walk 1000 miles?' Cheryl knows deep down that it is to save herself from the depths to which she has descended, but she wants her ex-husband to be the one to put this into words; admitting the hard truth without dressing it up. He doesn't answer her – he knows that she has to be the one to face up to her history, if she is to achieve closure and healing. As she finishes the walk, she does just that:

> It took me years to be the woman my mother raised. It took me four years, seven months and three days to do it, without her. After I lost myself in the wilderness of my grief, I found my

own way out of the woods. And I didn't even know where I was going until I got there, on the last day of my hike. Thank you, I thought over and over again, for everything the trail had taught me and everything I couldn't yet know . . . Now in four years, I'd cross this very bridge. I'll marry a man in a spot almost visible from where I was standing. Now in nine years, that man and I would have a son named Carver and a year later, a daughter named after my mother, Bobbi . . . My life, like all lives, mysterious, irrevocable, sacred, so very close, so very present, so very belonging to me. How wild it was, to let it be.

Author's own transcription

Discussion and conclusion

The two films we have chosen for analysis both feature long-distance walking as the central plot device, but involve protagonists of different genders and different (but equally iconic) walking routes or trails. In each case, the protagonist is dealing with the grief of losing a loved one, but also with a measure of guilt over their relationship with the deceased. We felt that the comparison of the two films would be interesting, both in terms of how the redemption narrative played out in the context of long-distance walking, but also how it was constructed.

The plots of *The Way* and *Wild* essentially deliver the same central message – 'the liberating potential of solitude in nature to re-examine one's life' (Kam 2015: 18). Time in nature, particularly walking, is thus a form of *ecotherapy*, which heals through its ability 'to relieve emotional congestion and restore equilibrium to the soul' (Kam 2015: 19). The difference lies in the role that other people play in the therapeutic process. In *The Way*, Tom cannot help but be surrounded by people. That is the nature of the Camino Way. Prickly and reluctant to open up, he eventually learns that he has helped others as much as they have helped him through his journey. The trope of *communitas* is at play here, and underpins the redemption narrative, where Tom learns to trust others and to understand what he really wants out of life. This is the gift that his son's death has given him. Cheryl Strayed, on the other hand, is largely alone on her journey and this isolation is liberating, especially for a woman. There is a joy in not giving in to the voices that tell her to give up, and a peace that comes from acceptance of the past. She has found a meaning in life, through her mother's example, but it took the loss for Cheryl to see it.

This study has a number of practical and theoretical implications. First, it suggests that the media promotes tropes or narratives centred on the therapeutic role of travel, which might play a role in framing travel imaginings and expectations about the travel experience. In particular, the study examines the redemption narrative, which emphasises the beneficial outcomes that can arise from negative or difficult situations. Second, it highlights the recurrent cinematic narrative of transformation through long-distance walking, that reflects the real-life experiences of some walkers (e.g. see Saunders 2014; Saunders *et al.* 2014). Further research could analyse other recent examples of long-distance walking in films, such as *The Road* (2009) and *A Walk in the Woods* (2015). Third, it points the way towards the utility of walking as therapy, particularly for those dealing with life transitions. This again might be a fruitful area for future studies, with consideration given to how these pursuits might be opened up to more people, in more places.

References

Bridges, W. (2004) *Transitions: Making Sense of Life's Changes*, 2nd edn, Cambridge, MA: Da Capo Press.

Campbell, J. (1949) *The Hero with a Thousand Faces* (1993 reprint), London: Fontana.

Coleman, S. (2002) 'Do you believe in pilgrimage? *Communitas*, contestation and beyond', *Anthropological Theory*, 2(3): 355–368.

Collins-Kreiner, N. and Kliot, N. (2016) 'Particularism vs. universalism in hiking tourism', *Annals of Tourism Research*, 56: 132–137.

den Breejen, L. (2007) 'The experiences of long distance walking: a case study of the West Highland Way in Scotland', *Tourism Management*, 28(6): 1417–1427.

Devereux, C. and Carnegie, E. (2006) 'Pilgrimage: journeying beyond self', *Tourism Recreation Research*, 31(1): 47–56.

Estevez, E. (dir.) (2010) *The Way* (motion picture), prod. D. Alexanian and E. Estevez, US: Icon Entertainment International.

Fondren, K.M. (2015). *Walking on the Wild Side: Long-Distance Hiking on the Appalachian Trail*, New Brunswick, NJ: Rutgers University Press.

Frey, N.L. (1998) *Pilgrim Stories: On and Off the Road to Santiago*, Berkeley, CA: University of California Press.

Frost, W. (2010) 'Life changing experiences: film and tourists in the Australian Outback', *Annals of Tourism Research*, 37(3): 707–726.

Frost, W. and Laing, J. (2015) *Imagining the American West Through Film and Tourism*, Abingdon, Oxon: Routledge.

Graburn, N.H.H. (1983) 'The anthropology of tourism', *Annals of Tourism Research*, 10(1): 9–33.

IMDb (Internet Movie Database) (2010) *The Way* Available at: www.imdb.com/title/tt1441912/?ref_=nv_sr_4 (accessed 6 June 2016).

Kam, T.Y. (2015) 'Forests of the self: life writing and "wild" wanderings', *Life Writing*, 13(3): 351–371.

Laing, J. and Frost, W. (2012) *Books and Travel: Inspiration, Quests and Transformation,* Bristol: Channel View.

Laing, J. and Frost, W. (2014) *Explorer Travellers and Adventure Tourism*, Bristol: Channel View.

McAdams, D.P., Reynolds, J., Lewis, M., Patten, A.H. and Bowman, P.J. (2001) 'When bad things turn good and good things turn bad: sequences of redemption and contamination in life narrative and their relation to psychosocial adaptation in midlife adults and in students', *Personality and Social Psychology Bulletin*, 27(4): 474–485.

Nilsson, M. and Tesfahuney, M. (2016) 'Performing the "post-secular" in Santiago de Compostela', *Annals of Tourism Research*, 57: 18–30.

Reijnders, S. (2011). *Places of the Imagination: Media, Tourism, Culture.* Farnham, Surrey: Ashgate.

Ross, G. (1994) *The Psychology of Tourism*, Melbourne: Hospitality Press.

Saunders, R.E. (2014) 'Steps towards change: personal transformation through long-distance walking'. Unpublished PhD thesis, Monash University, Melbourne, Australia.

Saunders, R., Laing, J. and Weiler, B. (2014) 'Personal transformation through long-distance walking', in P. Pearce and S. Filep (eds), *Tourist Experience and Fulfilment: Insights from Positive Psychology*, London: Routledge, pp. 127–146.

Strayed, C. (2012) *Wild: From Lost to Found on the Pacific Crest Trail* (2013 edn), New York: Vintage.

Taylor, J.P. (2001) 'Authenticity and sincerity in tourism', *Annals of Tourism Research*, 28(1): 7–26.

Turner, V. (1969) *The Ritual Process*, Harmondsworth: Penguin.

Turner, V. and Turner, E. (1978) *Image and Pilgrimage in Christian Culture: Anthropological Perspectives*, Oxford: Basil Blackwell.

United States Department of Agriculture Forest Service (2016) *Pacific Crest Trail, Frequently Asked Questions.* Available at: www.fs.usda.gov/detail/pct/home/?cid=stelprdb5310782 (accessed 5 June 2016).

Vallée, J.-M. (dir.) (2014) *Wild* (motion picture), prod. B. Papandrea, B. Pohlad and R. Witherspoon, US: Fox Searchlight.

5

Walking as pedagogy

Karein K. Goertz

Introduction

For a variety of economic, ideological and quality-of-life reasons, so-called millennials (born between the early 1980s and 2000) are rejecting cars and choosing to live in walkable urban communities. This cultural shift is so pronounced among this cohort of young adults that they can justifiably be described as a 'walking generation' (Speck 2012: 19). The resurgence of walking is fuelled by a "great reset" in attitudes towards cars (Florida 2010). Millennials, who now outnumber Baby Boomers as America's largest living population group, no longer buy into the mythology of the car as symbol of freedom, fashion and social status. Instead, they are attracted to the considerable financial savings and personal autonomy of *not* owning a car. Living without a car also embodies values and a conscious choice to be more sustainable, less consumerist, and to leave a smaller carbon footprint. Being freed from the car gives them agency and a sense of moral authority in a world plagued by global warming and fossil-fuelled wars. When millennials think about where they want to live, many envision pedestrian-friendly communities with good public transportation that makes car ownership obsolete. Increasingly, walkability factors into the decision-making process about viable colleges. Prospective students consult online resources such as walkscore.com or do searches for campuses listed as the "most walkable". Colleges should capitalize on this generational shift by designing campuses that are safe, comfortable and convenient for walking and by more deliberately mobilizing walking within and beyond the curriculum.

As intentionally built environments, college campuses are well positioned to make walking an integral part of their ethos and identity. In fact, when the US Surgeon General issued his 2015 Step It Up! Call to Action to promote walking, he specifically identified colleges as one of the sectors to help implement community-based walking strategies. If walking is to become a public health priority in the fight against chronic disease, institutions of learning must lead the way. Campuses can do so by explicitly encouraging "active living behaviours" and training students across the curriculum to 'recognize their role in promoting walking and walkable communities' (US Department of Health and Human Services 2015). Some universities have already begun 'stepping up' their walking initiatives (Stevens 2015). The University of Kentucky, for example, is collaborating with the *Walk [your city]* civic startup to install signs across campus that can be

scanned by phone to determine walking distances in minutes to destinations. People often over-estimate distances and find that walking is, in fact, quite doable. This project is exemplary as it signals an institutional commitment to walkability, cultivates awareness about personal walking attitudes and habits, and allows participants to be part of a larger national conversation on walking.

For many American students, the transition into a daily routine without a car and with a lot more walking marks a radical departure from their past experience. After all, unlike their European counterparts, most communities in the United States are still predominantly car-centric and, unlike their parents, few millennials will actually have grown up walking to school. It is likely that they will have spent years being shuttled in cars to schools, play-dates and after-school programmes. Thus, for the average incoming American student, college often marks the first sustained introduction to a lifestyle that involves more walking than ever before. These forma-tive, typically car-free college years can and should play a significant role in initiating and shaping them as walkers. Colleges have an incentive to examine and promote this transformation more explicitly on campus. There are compelling health, public policy, financial and ethical reasons to do so, but also a resounding pedagogical rationale for walking as means to facilitate experiential learning that engages the whole student. Walking can have a profound impact on student lives and their academic performance: it orients and connects them to their new community, bolsters creative thinking and intellectual productivity, balances their emotional lives, and provides an accessible form of exercise. This chapter examines data from science and the humanities on the mental, emotional and physical impact of walking and proposes pedagogical applications to enhance student learning and wellness.

The student as walker

Freshmen must get used to many things: from living in dorms to meeting the demands of col-lege courses and finding their own social niche. They have to learn to manage the exhilarating, sometimes overwhelming, freedom of living without parents and navigating their way through the challenges of stress, anxiety and homesickness. The first year is a time of exploration and experimentation, adaptation and transformation. Students have the opportunity to discover their intellectual aspirations and to forge a more mature identity. This new identity takes shape against the backdrop of a lifestyle change that may not be readily apparent to them unless, of course, they already came to campus as self-aware walkers. For many, becoming a student coincides with becoming a daily walker out of necessity. The "student as walker" holds true on both literal and figurative levels. In one way, walking is usually the primary mode of transportation in a student's campus-centric routine, a way to transition between the dorm, classroom and extra-curricular locations. For many, this will be the extent of their walking experience. Even so, these small daily walks add up. Pedometers and apps can help translate cumulative steps into tangible numbers to teach students how much walking they are actually doing.

Perhaps more interestingly, walking can be seen as a metaphor for change and dynamism: just as the walker is on the move, not stuck to one place or perspective, so too, the student is in a particularly fluid time of life when, ideally, old patterns are broken, ideas are approached anew and self-identity undergoes transformation. College is meant to challenge and stimulate the student's mind with new ideas. Analogously, walking gets us away from our desks to chang-ing scenery, unplanned encounters and surprising thoughts that engage the mind. The nexus of physical and mental activation is supported by medical research that warns against the hazards of prolonged sitting and recommends that, at the very least, we get up every half hour and walk. Organ damage, muscle degeneration, obesity, back pain and depression are all measurable consequences of excessive sitting. There is also a long lineage of thinkers who write about the dangers of inactivity in a less medically quantifiable way. Nietzsche (1954) advised that we sit as little as possible because *Sitzfleisch* (the ability to sit still), perhaps deemed virtuous in the traditional classroom, produces static, predictable and formulaic thinking. All 'true great thoughts' (Nietzsche 1954: 947) he aphorized, are *ergangen* (conceived while walking). His coinage lends itself to a more layered interpretation than the translation suggests: thoughts have to be walked, enacted, and endured in order to become something of value. This generative power of walking is a recurrent theme in the canon of walking literature: Montaigne (1987 [1595]) describes his thoughts as falling asleep if he seats them and that his legs need to be moving for his spirit to move. Likewise, Thoreau (1994 [1862]) observes how his thoughts begin to flow the moment his legs start moving. Physical movement and mental activity are complimentary, and walking, in particular, fosters the very kind of original, inquisitive and creative thinking that is the hallmark of a college education.

Getting oriented

Often a student's first visit to a new university will involve a walking tour of the campus. Walking the terrain is the best way to get spatially oriented, to figure out how to coordinate time and distance with a tight schedule, and to discover special places off the beaten track. In small seminars, one might ask freshmen to design a thematically oriented walking tour (e.g. "Quiet Places to Study" or "Greenspaces and Gardens"), with the goal of cultivating navigational skills and encouraging exploration of the campus and beyond. This ice-breaking activity fosters a sense of community and belonging, for walking 'establishes intimate contact with place' (Amato 2004: 276). As urbanists such as William Whyte (1980) and Jane Jacobs (1961) have long observed, pedestrian street life is integral to making a place great. Likewise, students walking across campus create the social space between buildings. Admittedly, most of the time, students walk goal-oriented with their eyes or ears tuned into their smartphones instead of the surrounding environment. But walking, more than any other form of movement, invites occasional dwelling, observing and partaking. The slow pace of walking encourages a sociability that is less likely while biking, driving or jogging. Thus, on one level, walking provides a means for students to ground themselves and to feel invested in their new home, both physically and socially: 'The walker makes and becomes the city he or she walks' (Amato 2004: 273).

Mental health and wellness

American colleges are reporting record numbers of mental health problems among students including depression, anxiety, eating and sleep disorders (Gruttadaro 2012). A combination of individual and societal factors may explain this crisis: economic uncertainty, greater financial and academic pressures to succeed, overprotective parenting, generational narcissism, existential confusion, technology addiction and information overload, flaws in the education and health care systems, over-medicalization and over-diagnosis, environmental toxins. There now appear to be greater levels of stress and psychopathology than any time in the nation's history (Henriques 2014a, 2014b). The first year of college, in particular, can take a significant toll on students as they get acclimatized to academic and social pressures that are exacerbated by lapses in sleep, nutrition and exercise. The impacts are physical, as the proverbial, though exaggerated, "freshman 15" indicates, and psychological. Most alarming, of course, is the prevalence and severity of depression, anxiety and suicidal thoughts. While walking should not replace the work of mental health practitioners in crisis situations, it can help on the level of preventive care. Many people with mental illness have found that walking helps them manage their inner anguish.

Kierkegaard (2000 [1847]), who described himself as someone afflicted with a 'suffering bordering on madness', believed in the therapeutic value of walking. He regularly walked the streets of Copenhagen to stoke his creativity, but also to prevent his depression from descending into the paralysis and hopelessness of despair. In a letter to his eighteen-year-old niece, Kierkegaard urged her to do the same: 'Above all, do not lose your desire to walk: every day I walk myself into a state of well-being and away from every illness . . . Health and salvation can only be found in motion' (Kierkegaard 2000 [1847]: 6). Similarly, British historian George Macaulay Trevelyan spoke of the close connection of mind and body, and how the legs he called his 'two doctors' helped maintain a healthy balance when he became melancholic: 'When body and mind are out of gear . . . I know that I have only to call in my doctors and I shall be well again' (Trevelyan 1928: 19).

The literature extolling the many health benefits of walking often cites the ancient wisdom of Hippocrates, who reputedly said that 'walking is man's best medicine'. Recent empirical findings in (neuro)physiology validate the curative properties of walking with variables relative to duration, intensity and frequency: it clears the body of stress hormones, boosts endorphins, strengthens the immune system, increases energy, elevates mood and promotes restful sleep. It burns fat, helps in weight reduction and controlling appetite. The flow of oxygen to the brain heightens mental alertness, concentration and memory. Walking enhances connectivity of brain circuits and boosts performance on cognitive tasks. Brisk walking is on par with running for lowering the risk of high blood pressure, high cholesterol, diabetes, heart disease and some cancers. Activity recommendations are age-dependent, but for adults to be in good health, the Center for Disease Control advises 30 minutes a day of "moderate intensity" exercise five times a week (C3 Collaborating for Health 2012). Barring physical disability or other barriers to walking (such as safety, pollution, traffic, weather, lack of paths and walkable places), walking allows for physical activity without having to think much about it. This kind of 'natural exercise' that is woven into the fabric of everyday life is a habit worth cultivating. In his study of the best health practices in the so-called 'blue zones' of the world, Dan Buettner (2008: 220) notes that 'longevity all-stars . . . engage in regular, low-intensity physical activity, often as part of a daily work routine'. In other words, special gear, gym memberships and intense physical exertion are not needed to maintain effective and sustainable wellness habits. Walking is an accessible, low-cost and effective form of exercise. As such, colleges should explicitly encourage and support it as basic preventive care for mental and physical health.

Academic skills

The cognitive benefits of walking support the college mandate of teaching students how to think critically, analytically and creatively. The connection between walking, thinking and teaching is not new: many of the ancient philosophers, famously reimagined and memorialized in Raphael's painting *The School of Athens*, walked while teaching. Socrates, the "street-corner philosopher", was known to walk through Athens engaging in informal conversations that 'planted the seeds from which his philosophical schools were to grow' (Wycherly 1961: 161). The image of the wandering philosopher was so commonplace that when Crantor, a follower of Plato, was out simply taking a walk, people gathered around him assuming he would hold a discussion. After morning lessons in the Lyceum, Aristotle strolled the grounds, walking along the colonnades (*peripatoi*) and into the groves while lecturing to students. His followers later founded the so-called Peripatetic school, which some have, perhaps mistakenly, linked to the philosopher's walking habit, instead of the colonnaded locale. By contrast, the Stoics sat on porches (*stoa*), from where their founder, Zeno, lectured.

Centuries later, Thoreau envisioned an experiential, personal and transformative educational practice that alternated classroom learning with regular walks in nature, bringing an appreciation for discovery, the unexpected and 'the wild'. When he and his brother opened a private boys' school in Concord, weekly exploratory walks into the woods were an important part of the curriculum. During these walks, Thoreau was at his most effective and authentic. He could be the kind of teacher he felt was most productive, 'a fellow student with the pupil . . . who should learn of, as well as with him' (Wycherly 1961: 60). These walks are what former students remember the best. It is said that students learned more in a month there than they did in a year at other local schools. For Thoreau, a "liberal" education must engage the student in experiences that create active, inquisitive minds. It must live up to its name to be 'worthy of freeman' (Ryan 1969: 56) and not merely serve as training in servility. This emancipatory view of education echoes Thoreau's description of walking as a means to 'shake off the village' (Thoreau 1994 [1862]: 78) – work, routine, convention – to become a free man.

The German expression *Gedankengang* (train of thought, reasoning) beautifully captures the connection between thinking and walking. In its typical usage, the word refers to the actual process or sequencing of thoughts, both of which involve a number of *Gedankenschritte* (steps in a thought process). The literal translation is far more suggestive: 'thought walkway' or 'the pace/gait of thought(s)' draw a link between thinking, movement and space. Walking shapes our thoughts into ideas. Interestingly, the word *spazierengehen* (to take a walk) also contains within its Latin root *spatium* (space) the notion of spatial expansion. Thoughts need the space afforded by walking to grow, or as Virginia Woolf so elegantly put it: 'I like to have space to spread my mind out' (Woolf 1981 [1925]: 107). Experimental psychologists have begun measuring the impact of walking on our thought processes, observing a reciprocal relationship between mind and body. The pace of our steps influences the pace of our thoughts, so by adjusting the speed of our walk we can change the rhythm of our thoughts. There is also a direct connection, or 'bodily and cognitive feedback loop', between the way we walk and our mood. Our emotions are embodied: 'emotional states affect somato-visceral and motoric systems . . . [and] bodily states have effects on how emotional information is processed' (Michalak *et al.* 2009: 580). Walking in an upright position, with long strides and at a vigorous pace boosts the energy level and lowers depression and fatigue. The inverse also holds: walking in a shuffling and slouched manner with short strides is associated with sadness and lack of vigour. In fact, one study found that 'changing the walking style of depressed people might help de-escalate pathological vicious circles between bodily and emotional processes that maintain depression' (Michalak *et al.* 2015: 125).

Walking as embodiment of thought resonates in descriptions of walking as the 'ambulation of the mind' (Gretel Ehrlich in DeMarco-Barrett 2004: 69), 'thinking made concrete' (Solnit 2000: 6) and the 'externalization of an interior seeking' (Ammons 1968: 116). Rousseau's (2011 [1782]) *Reveries of the Solitary Walker* provides a literary illustration of this interplay between the concrete and the abstract. Walking allows him to let go and his thoughts to become animate: his mind '*wanders* quite freely' and his ideas '*follow* their own course unhindered and untroubled' (Rousseau 2011 [1782]: 11). Rousseau decides to concretize the ambulation of his mind in the form of essays, which are, in turn, as unstructured, associative and digressive as walking thoughts themselves. The wisdoms culled from his walks, too, bear the imprint of walking: 'Everything on earth is in a state of constant flux' (Rousseau 2011 [1782]: 55) and 'without movement life is lethargy' (Rousseau 2011 [1782]: 56). Rousseau claims that we are most likely to attain peace and contentment when there is 'neither total calm nor too much agitation, but a steady and moderate movement with neither jolts nor pauses' (Rousseau 2011 [1782]: 56). Indeed, the regular pace of our footsteps calms and stabilizes the 'oscillatory system' (Crovitz 1970: 36) that is our mind.

When we get into a sustained walking groove, the pace of our thinking starts matching up with our steps. This attunement of mind and body allows the mind to calm down, to absorb information, to process and store it into long-term memory. These are the ideal prerequisites to deep, sustainable learning and quite the opposite of distracted multi-tasking.

In addition to facilitating the assimilation of information, walking is useful as an analytical tool to break a problem down into its component parts. It may even provide the actual solution: *solvitur ambulando* (the problem is solved by walking), as Greek philosopher Diogenes claimed in response to Zeno's paradox that motion is impossible. The simple act of getting up and walking away, rather than reasoning, resolved the debate. The phrase can also be taken literally: instead of proverbially sleeping on a problem, one must walk it through or through it. Solving a problem requires mental agility and the ability to approach an issue from different angles, in other words, movement and space. Physical movement generates mental movement: the vitality of walking, changing external stimuli, unplanned and unexpected encounters discourage circular or stagnant thinking. Walking may not necessarily involve movement towards a set goal, but it is movement in and across a space. Solnit evocatively collapses the physical and mental into a mindscape through which we walk: 'A passage through a landscape echoes the passage through a series of thoughts . . . The mind is a landscape of sorts and walking is one way to traverse it' (Solnit 2000: 6). The metaphor may be extended to describe a problem as a difficult terrain to cross and problem-solving as a "mapping out" of the best route to take (Nezu *et al.* 2007). As we wind our way through a problem, the different components become points along the path that are connected through our walking. The ancients developed a powerful mnemonic device that involved creating a mental map and placing images to be remembered at locations on it. Likewise, one might associate different parts of an argument with different topographical features, thereby reconstructing the thought process by retracing steps across a landscape.

Finally, walking has been shown to considerably promote creative thinking and the generation of new ideas (Jabr 2014). After filling up with information and letting it incubate, students need to transform the pieces of received knowledge into something new. This crucial phase of illumination occurs when the mind is given the opportunity to make different kinds of connections. Walking is an excellent facilitator of original, innovative thinking because the physical act of left-right steps simulates the integration of the two halves of the brain, the logical and the intuitive. The rhythmic alternation of steps can put the walker into a relaxed, but fully aware alpha state that is conducive to creative thinking. Oppezzo and Schwartz (2014) found that walking significantly boosts creativity: 'After people walked, their subsequent seated creativity was much higher than those who had not walked' (Oppezzo and Schwartz 2014: 1144). The study pinpointed divergent thinking, i.e. the ability to generate many possible solutions to a problem, as the cognitive process most positively affected by walking. By contrast, walking does not promote convergent thinking, i.e. the ability to come up with single, correct answers. In other words, walking has a selectively beneficial effect on creativity and may be most useful for the initial phase of brainstorming ideas. The implementation of walking would be most strategic as a technique to generate ideas, to contemplate different approaches to an issue, and to overcome writer's block. In *Thinkertoys: A Handbook of Creative-Thinking Techniques*, aimed at business professionals, creativity expert Michael Michalko (2006) presents an application of such divergent or analogical thinking: in his 'thought walk', participants walk around the grounds, looking for objects that relate metaphorically to a particular subject or problem at hand. Returning from the walk, they discuss how these metaphors provide new ways of thinking about or solving the problem (Michalko 2006). Coming up with metaphors is analogous to the shifting of perspective that is a trademark of creative thinking

Integrating walking into the college curriculum

Throughout the corporate world, walking meetings have caught on as a useful strategy for companies to encourage physical and mental wellness among employees and as a way to foster creative ideas, collaboration and discussion. President Obama, Facebook co-founder Mark Zuckerberg, Twitter co-founder Jack Dorsey and the company LinkedIn are some of the more well-known practitioners of 'Walk and Talks'. In her TED talk about this phenomenon, CEO Nilofer Merchant (2013) notes that 'getting out of the box leads to out-of-the-box thinking', so that, instead of thinking about a problem as an either-or dilemma, we can reframe it to consider both solutions as possible or true (Merchant 2013). Walking increases talkativeness, supports the flow of conversation, and walking side-by-side, in particular, allows for more openness and comfort than face-to-face conversations. An academic advisor at Virginia Tech who uses 'peripatetic advising' to great effect, observes that eye contact can inhibit students when they talk about uncomfortable topics and that the walking terrain can fill in for awkward gaps in conversation (McIntyre 2011). Walking hours may thus be a useful alternative when students come to discuss academic or personal matters.

Walking is, of course, not always practical when students need access to computers, whiteboards, desks, etc., but there are a number of curricular applications that would enhance the learning experience. In the flipped classroom, students are less reliant on frontal instruction and traditional amenities, and are presumably ready to discuss and implement the new material. Small walking groups could help brainstorm ideas, break up habituated seating arrangements, change the scenery and energy level, and shift attention away from the instructor. The 'gallery walk' discussion technique, in which students walk to rotating stations to engage with different problems or activities, offers a contained application of walking within the classroom. Getting out of the classroom and going for a walk can be very freeing and productive for writing. As part of a First Year Seminar entitled 'The Art of Walking' (taught at the University of Michigan's Residential College Fall 2013 and Fall 2015), students regularly spent twenty class-time minutes walking outside and then sitting down afterwards to free-write with or without a prompt. The profound impact of walking on their state of mind was evident in these representative responses:

> As I walk, I think about the tranquility in the cool air that consoles me. I no longer have an endless to-do list running circles in my brain. Instead, I am aware of my surrounding. I feel the soft ground as I take each step. Walking gives me the comfort of home. It reminds me of the security of my family and hometown. I feel warm because I have left our never-resting world and I have allowed myself to be free; to explore my mind.

For this student, walking heightens awareness and creates the stable emotional and mental conditions to allow her to attend to her thoughts. Another student commented on the reciprocal connection between walking and writing, using the transition from body to pen as a launchpad to think about the relationship between image and text in poetry: 'Sitting still inside the body, with the pen moving across the paper like feet across the earth, consider the visual quality of words – Mallarmé.' One student demonstrates how walking heightens our lateral thinking:

> I tried to notice how I felt and thought while walking. My thoughts moved more easily from one subject to another, leading me to the analogy of water. I began thinking of physics and how it applied to my thought process, specifically hydrodynamics. I thought about the mind as a pipe and whether there is a limit to how much or how fast I can think.

Kernels of analytical and creative ideas that could, if necessary, be expanded into theses lie in these spontaneously written, anonymously submitted post-walk responses. They reflect a freeing of the mind that is crucial to any intellectual project.

In light of the many benefits of walking for mental and physical health, academic skills and creativity, it makes sense that colleges actively promote walking. The 'Art of Walking' seminar students came up with the following ideas after taking a partner walk to brainstorm ideas on incentivizing campus walking: grab attention by citing health statistics; create a punch-card reward programme for miles walked in exchange for campus currency or vouchers; launch rec-reational walking clubs; hold competitions between colleges for the most steps walked; organize more cause-related walk-a-thons; design slogans or icons to brand walking as a lifestyle choice; make colleges more pedestrian-friendly; podcast lectures for students to listen to while walk-ing; design curricular activities that require students to walk around their campus community. Students were surprised to discover how such a seemingly ordinary, self-evident activity as walking had relevance across the curriculum. They proposed lecture series and course clusters that highlight the relevance of walking in disciplines from literature, art and philosophy to urban planning, anthropology and medicine. Walking is an inherently cross-disciplinary topic: it

> trespasses through everybody else's field . . . and doesn't stop in any of them on its long route . . . If a field of expertise can be imagined as a real field . . . yielding a specific crop— then the subject of walking resembles walking itself in its lack of confines.
>
> *(Solnit 2000: 4)*

This description might sum up the goal of the freshman year in a liberal arts curriculum: to yield students who are active and curious about learning, and who are not yet confined to one discipline.

Conclusion: walking as counter-strategy and critique

Every year since 1998, the Beloit College's *Mindset* List (see http://themindsetlist.com) has been tracking cultural milestones that have shaped the attitudes of each generation of incoming First Year students. Ubiquitous technology predominates again in the 2016 list for the class of 2019 (born in 1997): Google has always existed for them, they treat Wi-Fi as an entitlement, texting and tweeting are the medium of casual conversation, parents have switched from encouraging internet use to begging them to get off it, teachers have to remind them to use sources beyond the internet for research papers, texting while walking through a crowd allows them to avoid eye contact with passers-by. While the list does not explicitly focus on walking, it does imply that the communication, experience and intellectual exploration of this freshman generation are facilitated by technology rather than actual physical means. While technology is unavoidable and certainly a great asset to education, it should not completely supplant hands-on experience and face-to-face encounters. Our teaching and learning should reflect the fact that the body and the mind are connected; that neglecting one over the other will ultimately lead to an imbalanced whole. The resurgent interest in experiential learning signals a desire for more actively engaged educational practices.

As technology becomes more ubiquitous, there is a growing cultural backlash and awareness that electronic gadgets often distract us from having real experiences and making genuine per-sonal connections. A provocative article in *The Atlantic* pointed to the paradox of social media creating more network connectivity, but also more loneliness (Marche 2012). The amount of information and the speed at which it comes to us can also be overwhelming and alienating.

Honoré (2004: 3) observes a cultural shift away from the 'cult of speed' towards a more decelerated lifestyle, first epitomized by the 'Slow Food' movement and now spreading to other fields such as schooling and parenting. Walking is part of this trend to slow down, to be more mindful and connected, to better align our modern lives with the slower pace of our thoughts and emotions. Walking culture has long been a reaction against speed and the alienating effects of industrialization and mass society. It continues to function as a counterpoint to the status quo: 'Walking has assumed a powerful symbolic role as a means of protest and develops an enhanced potential to evoke alternative worlds and experiences' (Amato 2004: 18). As such, it serves as a compelling model and vehicle for students to assert their own position as active, aware and engaged participants in this world – and to step towards it.

Acknowledgments

I would like to thank the students in my 'The Art of Walking' First Year Seminars for allowing me to test out the curricular application of walking and to witness first-hand its impact on their thinking, writing and general well-being. I would also like to dedicate this essay to my friend Sue Finley (1953–2015) with whom I shared many walks.

References

Amato, J. (2004) *On Foot: A History of Walking*, New York: New York University Press.

Ammons, A.R. (1968) 'A poem is a walk', *Epoch*, 18(1): 114–119.

Buettner, D. (2008) *The Blues Zones: Lessons for Living Longer from the People Who've Lived Longest*, Washington, DC: National Geographic Society.

C3 Collaborating for Health (2012) *Review: The Benefits of Regular Walking for Health, Well-Being and the Environment*. Available at: www.c3health.org/wp-content/uploads/2009/09/C3-report-on-walking-v-1-20120911.pdf (accessed 15 May 2016).

Crovitz, H. (1970) *Galton's Walk: Methods for the Analysis of Thinking, Intelligence and Creativity*, New York: Joanna Cotler Books.

DeMarco-Barrett, B. (2004) *Pen on Fire*, Orlando, FL: Harcourt.

Florida, R. (2010) 'The great car reset', *The Atlantic*, 3 June. Available at: www.theatlantic.com/national/archive/2010/06/the-great-car-reset/57606/ (accessed 1 May 2016).

Gruttadaro, D. (2012) *College Students Speak: A Survey Report on Mental Health*, Arlington, VA: National Alliance on Mental Health.

Henriques, G. (2014a) 'What is causing the college student mental health crisis?', *Psychology Today*, 21 February. Available at: www.psychologytoday.com/blog/theory-knowledge/201402/what-is-causing-the-college-student-mental-health-crisis (accessed 11 May 2016).

Henriques, G. (2014b) 'The college student mental health crisis', *Psychology Today*, 15 February. Available at: www.psychologytoday.com/blog/theory-knowledge/201402/the-college-student-mental-health-crisis (accessed 11 May 2016).

Honore, C. (2004) *In Praise of Slowness: Challenging the Cult of Speed*, New York: HarperCollins.

Jabr, F. (2014) 'Why walking helps us think', *The New Yorker*, 3 September. Available at: www.newyorker.com/tech/elements/walking-helps-us-think (accessed 15 May 2016).

Jacobs, J. (1961) *The Death and Life of Great American Cities*, New York: Vintage.

Kierkegaard, S. (2000 [1847]) 'Letter to Henrietta Lund', in D. Minshull (ed.), *The Vintage Book of Walking*, London: Random House, pp. 6–7.

Marche, S. (2012) 'Is Facebook making us lonely?', *The Atlantic*, May. Available at: www.theatlantic.com/magazine/archive/2012/05/is-facebook-making-us-lonely/308930 (accessed 10 August 2014).

McIntyre, C.M. (2011) 'Peripatetic advising: how Socrates, advising and running shoes influence student success, *Academic Advising Today*. Available at: www.nacada.ksu.edu/Resources/Academic-Advising-Today/View-Articles/Peripatetic-Advising-How-Socrates-Advising-and-Running-Shoes-Influence-Student-Success.aspx (accessed 10 April 2016).

Merchant, N. (2013) 'Got a meeting? Take a walk', *TED Talk*, April. Available at: www.ted.com/talks/nilofer_merchant_got_a_meeting_take_a_walk/transcript?language=en (accessed 5 April 2016).

Michalak, J., Troje, N.F., Fischer, J., Vollmar, P., Heidenreich, T. and Schulte, D. (2009) 'Embodiment of sadness and depression – gait patterns associated with dysphoric mood', *Psychosomatic Medicine*, 71(5): 580–587.

Michalak, J., Rohde, K. and Troje, N. (2015) 'How we walk affects what we remember: gait modifications through biofeedback change negative affective memory bias', *Journal of Behavior Therapy and Experimental Psychiatry*, 46: 121–125.

Michalko, M. (2006) *Thinkertoys: A Handbook of Creative-Thinking Techniques*, 2nd edn, Berkeley, CA: Ten Speed Press.

Montaigne, M. (1987 [1595]) *Michel de Montaigne: The Complete Essays*, vol. 3, ch. 2, trans. M.A. Screech, London: Penguin.

Nezu, A.M., Nezu, C.M. and D'Zurilla, T.J. (2007) 'Problem-solving skills training', in G. Fink (ed.), *Encyclopedia of Stress*, 2nd edn, Atlanta, GA: Elsevier, pp. 227–231.

Nietzsche, F. (1954) *Friedrich Nietzsche: Werke in drei Bänden*, vol. 2, Munich: Hanser Verlag.

Oppezzo, M. and Schwartz, D. (2014) 'Give your ideas some legs: the positive effect of walking on creative thinking', *Journal of Experimental Psychology: Learning, Memory, and Cognition*, 40(4): 1142–1152.

Rousseau, J. (2011 [1782]) *Reveries of the Solitary Walker*, trans. R. Goulbourne, New York: Oxford University Press.

Ryan, K. (1969) 'Henry David Thoreau: critic, theorist, and practitioner of education', *The School Review*, 77(1): 54–63.

Solnit, R. (2000) *Wanderlust: A History of Walking*, New York: Penguin Books.

Speck, J. (2012) *Walkable City*, New York: Farrar, Straus, Giroux.

Stevens, A. (2015) 'How colleges are stepping up campus walkability', *The Atlantic*, 10 December. Available at: www.theatlantic.com/education/archive/2015/12/college-campus-walkable/419553 (accessed 1 May 2016).

Thoreau, H.D. (1994 [1862]) 'Walking', in J. Elder (ed.), *Nature Walking*, Boston, MA: Beacon Press, pp. 69–122.

Trevelyan, G. (1928) *Walking*, Hartford, CT: Edwin Valentine Mitchell.

US Department of Health and Human Services (2015) *Step It Up! The Surgeon General's Call to Action to Promote Walking and Walkable Communities: Executive Summary*. Available at: www.surgeongeneral.gov/library/calls/walking-and-walkable-communities/exec-summary.html (accessed 14 April 2016).

Whyte, W.H. (1980). *The Social Life of Small Urban Spaces*, Washington, DC: Conservation Foundation.

Woolf, V. (1981) *The Diary of Virginia Woolf 1925–30*, vol. 3, ed. A. Bell, London: Harcourt Brace and Company.

Wycherly, R.E. (1961) 'Peripatos: the Athenian philosophical scene', *Greece and Rome*, 8(2): 152–163.

6

Walking in Germany

Between recreation and ideology

Dirk Reiser and Vanessa Jansen-Meinen

> Walking is one of the first things an infant wants to do and one of the last things anyone of us wants to give up doing.
>
> (Sussmann and Goode 1967)

Introduction

In Germany, the recent trend to walking started with novels such as Wolfgang Buescher's *Reise zu Fuß* (Journey by Foot, 2003) from Berlin to Moscow, followed by the novel *Ich bin dann mal weg* (I'm off then, 2006) from the German actor Hape Kerkeling, describing his pilgrimage on the Camino de Santiago, leading to a run on this trail and, accompanied by Manuel Andrack, *Du musst wandern: Ohne Stock und Hut im deutschen Mittelgebirge* (You have to hike: without hiking stick and hat in the German Central Uplands, 2005), who walked through the German low mountain range. This is remarkable, as walking itself is no new invention, but had an outmoded image until the late 1990s (Kouchner *et al.* 2000). For centuries, merchants and travelling journeymen, like pilgrims, walked from village to village. The reasons for that are manifold.

In his book *Vom Wandern: Neue Wege zu einer alten Kunst* (On walking: new ways to an ancient art), Ulrich Grober (2011: i) states that 'walking replies directly to the impertinent increase in velocity', which is currently attractive due to the concept of "flow", the condition in which someone is so immersed in an activity that nothing else seems to be important. It is not an issue only in sports science and the tourism industry, but offers a general high suitability. The "new art of walking" has developed since the late 1990s from an occupation for retired people to a fashionable activity (Grober 2010, 2011). According to Brämer (2009), there are now more than 40 million Germans who walk regularly, which means that walking is currently the most favoured outdoor leisure activity (BMWi 2010).

This is supported by a study from the German rambling club and the Federal Ministry for Economic Affairs and Energy conducted in 2010, which showed that 56 per cent of the German population belongs to the group of active walkers (Deutscher Wanderverband 2010). However, the walking intensity differs widely: every fifth German claims to walk at least five to six times every six months. An additional 20 per cent indicate that they walk at least "several times per year"

(Deutscher Wanderverband 2010). Over 75 per cent of people in Germany under 30 regard themselves as active walkers, which is, according to Brämer (2009) and Opaschowski (2008), due to the fact that this gentle form of mobility fits in with a growth in health-conscious behaviour and a movement towards sustainability. This positive image change during the last decade is due to the possibility of an outdoor experience with low entry barriers that is consistent with a sustainable, environment-conscious and nature-responsible lifestyle – although walking has a long history as a vital part of tourism and recreational activities in Germany.

In the past, people did not walk long distances for leisure reasons (Kaschuba 1991), but to transport and sell goods, to guide animals to meadows or for military purposes (Deutscher Wanderverband 2010). However, walking as a popular leisure time activity developed in parallel with tourism in general (Deutscher Wanderverband 2010). Nevertheless, while travelling for recreation, cultural exchange or education became motivational drivers for the public that were only valid for the privileged before, walking went through a variety of changes. It developed from the main mode of recreational travel before the industrialisation of transport to the principal way of travel for the under-privileged and then to one of the favourite transport modes for environmentally conscious persons (Kouchner et al. 2000). Today, walking as part of the outdoor market is a growing sector, often attracting many tourists to destinations and is a 'tradition sport transformed to a trend sport' (Deck and Teves 2015).

Forms of walking

The term "wander" (walking) in general comes from the middle high German word *wanderen* that originates again from the old high German *wanton*. This is synonymous with the word to stroll, to turn repeatedly and going back and forth. However, the terms to stroll and to walk have different connotations in German. Therefore, there needs to be a differentiation between walking and strolling around, which is difficult, but nevertheless important for the demarcation of the market. Boundaries between the concepts are fluid. Strolling around is regarded as being more spontaneous, without special equipment or preparation, in contrast to what is required for walking (e.g. planning of route and equipment, shoes, checking of weather and maps). Fluid boundaries are shown in the classification of different activities to the area of walking: every second German considers strolling around as a form of walking, whereas activities such as bouldering, climbing and geocaching are not regarded as directly connected.

Due to linguistic and cultural differences, hiking is the walking term most often used in English-speaking countries, especially in the USA, pointing to longer walks and trails in the countryside. Here, walking is instead used for shorter walks (Kouchner et al. 2000). Trekking, in contrast, is used for walks that last several days (Vogt 2010). Besides these forms, there are several sub-forms, including hillwalking, mountaineering, long-distance hiking, height hikes, scouting, hut hikes, with the differences between them deriving from the place of accommodation, seasonal nature of walking, and the use of fixed rope routes. Different modes of allied transport can also be used (Hall et al. 2017), as for example travelling by canoe, bike or horse, which may help attract younger people to walking (Stumpf 2001).

Every year, German walkers collectively walk 3.6 billion km on their 378 million domestic and international hikes. Every active walker undertakes more than nine walks per year with an average length of 10 kilometres. This high volume can only develop when the walking season is spread over the year and focuses not only on the summer months, although the high season can be still identified as August and September.

There are also differences between day activities and the chosen form of vacation. Sixteen per cent of Germans conduct a pure walking holiday, whereas others combine some walks with their usual vacation programme. Different motivations for walking are, for example, the desire to spend time in natural surroundings, as a form of travel, as a form of fitness, and some, like the estimated 40 million Germans who regularly enjoy a summer's day stroll, walk for the pure pleasure of being in nature and outside (Laws 2007). Several studies (Brämer 2008, 2009; Statista 2016; Project M 2014) suggest that a focus on one's own body and health is the second most important motivation. Brämer (2008, 2009) found that the main reasons for walking were: getting back to nature; less focus on technology and achievability; and a concentration on oneself. It is important to note that the last issue is not about walking as many kilometres as possible, but focuses on health and relaxation, especially as a response to daily stress. Also of significance is the shared experience of walking with a partner and/or friends; walking in large groups is not favoured. At the same time, Brämer (2008) also suggests that many walkers have become individualists.

This view is supported by Grober (2011: i), who argues that

> an old passion is re-discovered. The old art of walking is nowadays the protest against the dictate of the increasing velocity . . . the walker walks new ways. He is searching for the exotic of the nearby surroundings – and is finding himself.

Grober's observation underlines the notion that contemporary walkers are sense-seekers, connecting to a new target group of younger people focusing on themselves and their body and soul during walking.

When it comes to target groups for walking, Project M (2014) found out that the biggest group are the so-called "best ager" (27 per cent), directly followed by singles and couples without children (26 per cent). This is followed by elderly people as well as families with at least one child below 14 years of age (both 17 per cent). But also young persons under 30 without children form a huge group of 3.2 million walkers, which is about 13 per cent of the total group. Walking is also an important activity for international tourists. The German Quality monitor (Deutsche Zentrale für Tourismus (DZT) 2014) found out that walking is the favourite sporting activity of foreign visitors (17 per cent), especially with visitors from the Netherlands, Poland, Switzerland and Belgium. The next section discusses the history of walking in Germany.

History of walking in Germany

Enlightenment and Romanticism

Trampers were some of the original walkers in Germany. Travelling journeymen were graduates from craft apprenticeships who walked from region to region in order to learn new techniques or perspectives in their field of interest. Only after that were they allowed to start their examination for the master craftsman's certificate, for example, as a carpenter. The famous walking song *Das Wandern ist des Müllers Lust* (walking is the miller's delight) or the fairy tale of *Hans im Glück* (Hans in luck) report how returning journeymen felt with their wages and their life tramping (Naturpark Südeifel n.d.; Lemke 2002).

Historically, walking is closely connected with pilgrimage, walking for religious motives, and with the travels of merchants, traders, vagrants and scholars in the Middle Ages. However, until the seventeenth and eighteenth centuries, landscapes such as the mountains were seen as dangerous and wild and therefore not attractive for walking. This was changed by the impact of Romantic scholars, landscape painters and travelling writers; for example, Albrecht von Haller with his poem *Die Alpen* (The alps) in 1729 or the travels of Johann Wolfgang von Goethe to Switzerland in 1775 and 1779 (BMWi 2010).

In the late eighteenth century, walking was linked to the emancipatory movement of the bourgeoisie from nobility (Amato 2004). Many of those bourgeois walkers journeyed through Europe and wrote down their experiences. Their particular focus was thereby on the social, economic and political situation in the countries they passed. For example, in 1802, Johann Gottfried Seume wrote *Spaziergang nach Syrakus* (walk to Syracuse) after walking for nine months from his hometown Leipzig to Syracuse in Sicily and back (Seume 1803; Krüger 2010). This is an important event because such authors began to give nature a more positive aesthetic dimension, describing it as beautiful for the first time (Knoll 2016).

In the Romantic era, the idea of walking changed from looking at the social, economic and political circumstances of the visited people to primarily looking at the landscape as a mirror of the inner self (Dick 2010). Favourite destinations and motives for landscape paintings were the Harz, the island of Rugen and Saxon Switzerland. Romantic walkers searched for solitude to find their place in the universe. This still remains an important motivation today.

Another change came about around 150 years ago. The development of the railway in the middle of the nineteenth century enabled a wider part of the population to travel further and faster than ever before. Suddenly, people were not forced to do things only by walking – the way to leisure walking was open, especially for the inhabitants of the rapidly growing cities. Many people at this time responded to the nature of the rapidly industrialising cities by using the new railway systems to discover new destinations that were previously out of reach.

Modern times: the institutionalisation of walking

In general, the institutionalisation of walking is closely linked with industrialisation and urbanisation, in particular, the development of the steam engine (train) and later, the internal combustion engine (automobile) (Smolka 2009). Changed mobilities made it possible for the citizens of the cities to travel comfortably to the mountains and the ocean, with corresponding shifts in identity, connectivity and notions of place (Coles *et al.* 2004). Consequently, mountaineering and walking clubs started to appear, to cater for the increased demand for walking (Ferienwandern 2008). This led to an increasing institutionalisation of walking through walking and alpine organisations. The German Alpine Association (DAV) was established in 1869 in order to create walking ways, leading to the development of good-value inns of mountain farmers (Deck and Teves 2015).

Numerous terms were used to describe the great success of walking as a leisure activity at that time. The BMWi (2010), for example, describes the time after 1850 as the 'Golden Age of Mountaineering', while Peters (2001) argues that the time between 1860 and 1903 can be called the 'Pedestrian Age', when walking was the leading physical leisure activity in Europe and the United States. During this time, walking changed from being a necessity to a pleasurable activity and an experience (BMWi 2010). Solnit (2000: 156) describes the time as a golden age of organisations that 'provided social cohesion for the displaced of a rapidly changing world, others offered resistance to industrialisation's inhuman appetite for the time, health, energy and rights of workers'. Consequently, organisation such as walking and mountaineering clubs became popular.

In the mid-nineteenth century, walking began to be institutionalised by walking and mountaineering clubs. These clubs developed walking trails, signposting, produced maps of walking trails, built shelters and viewing towers, and thereby pioneered the opening-up of nature. In 1900, clubs included the protection of natural beauties and the promotion of the knowledge of the German landscape in their statutes (Ferienwandern 2008). The first mountaineering club, the Baden Black Forest Club (*Badischer Schwarzwaldverein*), was founded in 1864. This club also created the first walking trail (*Höhenweg*) in 1900 (Knoll 2016). The German Walking Association

(*Deutscher Wanderverband*), an umbrella organisation for the mountaineering and walking clubs in Germany, was founded in Fulda in 1883. The 58 clubs and their 600,000 members voluntarily signposted and looked after 200,000 km of walkways (Deutscher Wanderverband 2016). The German Walking Association, together with the Sauerland Mountaineering Club, also founded the German Youth Hostel Association in 1909 to provide cheap accommodation to democratise walking and travelling (BMWi 2010).

The German Youth Hotel Association opened its first youth hostel in Altena (Sauerland) in 1909. The general idea of cheap accommodation fitted well with other movements of the time, such as the Wandervögel, or the developing idea of walking as an important leisure activity (Hafeneger 2009). Additionally, the association had the goal to attract youth to walking. Its predecessors were the so-called student hostels that started to appear in 1884 (Hachtmann 2007). It was not just a pedagogic reform movement, but also the result of an idea of a simple, healthy lifestyle close to nature. The founding fathers saw themselves as fighters for youth walking, public health, home care (*Heimatpflege*) and against the dangers of alcohol and addiction, and for the protection of nature and promoting a natural lifestyle (Hafeneger 2009). The rapid increase of hostels mainly as a consequence of governmental support in the Weimarer Republic was particularly strong, when the overnight stays rose from 60,000 in 1919 to 4 million in 1929/30 (Hachtmann 2007). A further important factor was the increasing holiday entitlements for workers, for example, during the Weimarer Republic workers were able to take 8–12 days of holiday leave (Kaufmann 2016).

Another institution that was formed during this period was the *Naturefreunde* (nature friends), established in Vienna in 1895 by the teacher and socialist Georg Schmiedl (Naturfreunde 2016). The purpose was to facilitate walking for the proletarians. The organisation opened a number of houses to allow members and guests a cheap overnight stay and therefore a holiday. It had the goals to enforce the right of free access to nature against the interests of the big landowners, to explore nature as a source for recreation, to get together, to organise activities and to learn about nature (Knoll 2016).

A further movement was the so-called *Wandervögel* youth movement, founded in 1901. *Wandervögel* is a term taken from a poem, meaning a magical bird. It originated from students in a school in Berlin as a 'reaction against the authoritarianism of the German family and government' (Solnit 2000: 157). Their members were mainly students who fled the cities into nature to rebel against the lifestyle of the Kaiser Wilhelm period. Its main intention was political, as a critic of society and its norms (BMWi 2010). Nevertheless, this middle-class organisation was also exclusive, had initiation rituals, wore semi-formal uniforms and the structure was hierarchical, asking for obedience to a leader. Moreover, most of the members were ethnic nationalists, meaning that Jewish people (Hachtmann 2007) and Catholics were generally not welcome. The movement collapsed after the First World War, but it was at least partly replaced by the German Boy Scouts, who rebelled against their adult leaders (Solnit 2000). However, walking and tourism nearly stopped completely for the duration of the First World War from 1914 to 1918, before continuing in the 1920s, when it included all layers of society (BMWi 2010). But it was not long before there was a monumental change in walking in Germany, which made it possible for the Nazi regime to exploit walking for their own purposes.

Walking in Nazi Germany

Walking changed dramatically after the Nazis got into power in 1933. It was their goal to return Germany to supposedly traditional "German" and "Nordic" values, and shape a racial community after their principles in which family and race and the *Volk* represented the highest German

69

values. According to these, the most important virtues were living in harmony with the homeland and nature, loyalty, struggle, self-sacrifice (putting the *Volk* and nation above its individual members), and discipline. Culture was the main tool to disseminate the Nazi worldview. Consequently, one of the first steps after taking power was the synchronisation of all professional and social organisations, such as the walking and mountaineering clubs in the German Labour Front in 1933 (United States Holocaust Museum 2016). As a compensation for the political disfranchisement of the working class, the Nazi regime introduced the "Strength through Joy" (*KdF, Kraft durch Freude*) programme. This was meant to symbolise the destruction of class privileges, especially the holiday privileges of the bourgeoisie and was a central point in the image policies of the Hitler regime (Hachtmann 2007).

The Strength through Joy programme was based on the Italian Fascist *Opera Nazionale Dopolavoro* (National Recreational Club), and introduced on 27 November 1933. It was the largest sub-organisation of the German Labour Front (*DAF, Deutsche Arbeiterfront*) and included the Office for Travel, Walking, Holiday (*Amt für Reisen, Wandern, Urlaub*) (Hachtmann 2007). Every member of the German Labour Front was also a member of the Strength through Joy Programme, paying at least the equivalent of 50 cents per month membership fee to participate in their activities (Gußmann and Stegemann 2014). Between 1933 and 1939 the programme organised the majority of short trips and walks (an estimated 80–90 per cent) (Hachtmann 2007), but also holidays and cruises, before abandoning those last two activities with the start of the Second World War (Kaufmann 2016).

The main aim was to establish control over leisure time and to indoctrinate Germans with Nazi ideology (Ferienwandern 2008), or, as Mosse (2003) puts it, to create total culture. This was part of the socio-cultural re-organisation of the German society. In Nazi ideology, leisure was a tool that had to serve the country and the people to create a new German people and a new social order in Germany, but also to prepare for war. There was, therefore, no place for so-called non-Aryan people or Marxists; all youth groups were integrated into the Hitler Youth and walking and mountaineering clubs became part of the Reich Sports Federation (*Reichssportbund*) (Ferienwandern 2008). The cultural goals of those organisations were to strengthen the sense of home, community and national socialism (Gußmann and Stegemann 2014). It was supported by an increase in holiday entitlements for workers from the 8–12 days in the Weimarer Republic to 14–21 days during the period of Nazi government (Kaufmann 2016).

All of the above-mentioned walking and mountaineering clubs were synchronised. For political reasons, the Naturfreunde, for example, were banned in 1933, and its 428 huts and houses confiscated (Knoll 2016). A similar fate met the Youth Hostel Association, which was integrated into the national educational system, despite the fact that it officially remained an independent organisation until 1941 (Hafeneger 2009). The German Walking Association was put under the control of the Nazi regime in 1933 (Ferienwandern 2008). Under this highly controlled leisure regime, leisure time and leisure space changed accordingly and walking became marching (Hafeneger 2009).

Walking in Germany after the Second World War

For the first few years after the end of the Second World War, Germans were mainly occupied with rebuilding their lives. It was not until the early 1950s that walking and travelling became prominent again. However, walking lost its importance somewhat to holidaying, in particular in the economic "miracle times" (*Wirtschaftswunder*) of the 1960s. This development was driven by greater personal car and motorbike ownership, growing disposable time and income, and the construction of a tourist infrastructure (Hachtmann 2007).

However, the evolution of walking was different in the Russian-occupied zone in the east from that in the Western zone. In the east, walking clubs were not allowed. Nevertheless, walking became one of the favourite leisure activities there. In the west, the Allies did not consider the walking clubs as a national socialist organisation and allowed their re-establishment (BMWi 2010). In West Germany, the walking clubs and the Youth Hostel Association were again somewhat institutionalised by the occupying forces to re-educate Germans with regards to their democratic understanding and for international understanding between nations (Hafeneger 2009). But it took up to the end of the 1990s before walking experienced a renaissance (BMWi 2010), because until then walking was often seen as a popular activity for older members of society. But since 2000, walking clubs and walking associations have experienced a substantial growth in membership. This has been supported by the increase of self-organised walking as part of an outdoor trend that some describe as a "walking boom" (Dreyer *et al.* 2010).

Today, every second German enjoys nature walking (34–40 million citizens). It is often perceived as a counterbalance to urban life, the urge to move outside asphalt and concrete (Hohenester 2009). Walking is also linked to a sustainable lifestyle because it is environmentally sustainable (it is a soft nature sport, strengthens the relationship with nature, needs only minimal technical infrastructure, is possible in many places, creates an awareness of the speed of nature), is economically sustainable (it facilitates regional development, secures a sustainable livelihood, offers a high value ratio, creates synergistic effects, and is healthy) and socially sustainable (it is an ideal sport for small groups, is relatively cheap, is possible outside holiday times, connects people and allows a view into different life circumstances) (Smolka 2009).

Conclusion

Over the history of Germany, walking has become an important leisure time activity, with access to it moving from privileged aristocrats and artists to the great majority of Germans. Its development is thereby closely linked to the development of tourism, but also to the different political systems at various times.

Walking in Germany has a long history. Its earliest forms were connected to pilgrimage, walkers on the tramp or trade. For those walkers, walking was a necessity. The view of walking as a leisure activity "arrived" with the enlightenment period. Suddenly the once-feared mountains and oceans were seen as having an aesthetic quality worth being visited. This was a consequence of the Romantic movement, when walking as a leisure activity became a spiritual movement, while remaining a privilege for a minority of Germans. However, this was to change with the institutionalisation of walking in the mid-nineteenth century, when industrialisation and urbanisation made people hold nature in very high esteem. The formation of walking and mountaineering clubs, the youth hostel movement and the *Wandervögel* youth movement bear witness to the new organisation of walking. These organisational structures were, however, utilised by the Nazis to organise leisure activities in their Strength through Joy programme in order to indoctrinate people with the Nazi ideology and to prepare them for war. After the end of the Second World War, walking decreased in importance due to mass motorisation, an increase in disposable income and time, and the urge to travel further for holidays. However, walking experienced a renaissance in the late 1990s. Today, more than half of all Germans enjoy walking on a regular basis.

References

Amato, J.R. (2004) *On Foot: A History of Walking*, New York: New York University Press.
Andrack, M. (2005) *Du musst wandern: Ohne Stock und Hut im deutschen Mittelgebirge* (You have to hike: without hiking stick and hat in the German Central Uplands), Cologne: Verlag Kiepenheuer and Witsch.

BMWi (*Bundesministerium für Wirtschaft und Technologie*) (2010) 'Forschungsbericht Nr. 591: Grundlagenuntersuchung Freizeit- und Urlaubsmarkt Wandern', *Langfassung*. Available at: www.bmwi.de/BMWi/Redaktion/PDF/Publikationen/Studien/grundlagenuntersuchung-freizeit-und-urlaubsmarkt-wandern,property=pdf,bereich=bmwi,sprache=de,rwb=true.pdf (accessed 26 June 2016).

Brämer, R. (2008) 'Warum wandern? Neues aus der Wanderforschung von Dr. Rainer Brämer', *Wandermagazin*, 142 (Sept/Oct). Available at: www.wandermagazin.de/heft-abo/heftarchiv/artikel/2008/142/warum-wandern-neues-aus-der-wanderforschung-von-dr-rainer-braemer (accessed 23 May 2016).

Brämer, R. (2009) *Profilstudie Wandern 2008*. Available at: www.wanderforschung.de/files/prostu081124 9833531.pdf (accessed 20 May 2016).

Buescher, W. (2003) *Reise zu Fuß* (Journey by Foot), Reinbek bei Hamburg: Rowohlt Verlag.

Coles, T.E., Duval, D. and Hall, C.M. (2004) 'Tourism, mobility and global communities: new approaches to theorising tourism and tourist spaces', in W. Theobold (ed.), *Global Tourism*, Oxford: Heinemann, pp. 463–481.

Deck, Y. and Teves, C. (2015) *Sport: Wandern*. Available at: www.planet-wissen.de/gesellschaft/sport/wandern/index.html (accessed 22 May 2016).

Deutscher Wanderverband (2010) *Grundlagenuntersuchung Freizeit- und Urlaubsmarkt Wandern*, Kassel, Germany: Deutscher Wanderverband.

Deutscher Wanderverband (2016) *Die Geschichte des Deutschen Wanderverbandes*. Available at: www.wanderverband.de/conpresso/_rubric/index.php?rubric=Verband+Die-Geschichte (accessed 25 June 2016).

Dick, A. (2010) 'Die romantische Wander-Metapher in Literatur und Musik', *Badische Zeitung*, 7 August. Available at: www.badische-zeitung.de/kultur-sonstige/die-romantische-wander-metapher-in-literatur-und-musik—33961642.html (accessed 26 February 2016).

Dreyer, A., Menzel, A. and Endreß, M. (2010) *Wandertourismus. Kundengruppen, Destinationsmarketing, Gesundheitsaspekte*, Munich: Oldenbourg Verlag.

DZT (*Deutsche Zentrale für Tourismus*) (2014) *Qualitätsmonitor Deutschland-Tourismus*. Available at: www.germany.travel/media/pdf/dzt_marktforschung/dzt_qualitaetsmonitor_2012_web.pdf (accessed 24 May 2016).

Ferienwandern (2008) *1883–2008: 125 Jahre Deutscher Wanderverband*. Available at: www.wanderverband.de/conpresso/_data/Geschichte_des_DeutschenWanderverbandes.pdf (accessed 26 June 2016).

Grober, U. (2010) *Die Entdeckung der Nachhaltigkeit. Kulturgeschichte eines Begriffs*, Munich: Kunstmann.

Grober, U. (2011) *Vom Wandern: Neue Wege zu einer alten Kunst*, 2nd edn, Frankfurt am Main: Zweitausendeins.

Gußmann, O. and Stegemann, W. (2014) *'Kraft durch Freude' – Urlaube sollten die volkswirtschaftliche Produktion ankurbeln und dienten dem inneren Arbeitsfrieden – ideologisierter Massentourismus und 'KdF-Wagen' fürs Volk*. Available at: www.rothenburg-unterm-hakenkreuz.de/kraft-durch-freude-urlaube-sollten-die-volkswirtschaftliche-produktion-ankurbeln-und-dienten-dem-inneren-arbeitsfrieden-ideologisierter-massentourismus-und-geplanter (accessed 27 June 2016).

Hachtmann, R. (2007) *Tourismus-Geschichte*, Göttingen, Germany: Vandenhoeck & Ruprecht GmbH & Co. KG.

Hafeneger, B. (2009) '100 Jahre Deutsches Jugendherbergswerk. Zur Geschichte einer jugendpädagogischen Idee', *Sozial Extra*, 33(5): 9–13.

Hall, C.M., Le-Klähn, D-T. and Ram, Y. (2017) *Tourism, Public Transport and Sustainable Mobility*, Bristol: Channel View.

Hohenester, G. (2009) 'Wandern – jetzt ein Trendsport. Die neue Lust am Wandern', *DAV Panorama*, 3: 20–21.

Kaschuba, W. (1991) 'Erkundung der Moderne. Bürgerliches Reisen nach 1800', *Zeitschrift für Volkskunde*, 87(1): 29–52.

Kaufmann, S. (2016) *Geschichte des Reisens: Kraft durch Freude*. Available at: www.planet-wissen.de/gesellschaft/reisen/geschichte_des_reisens/pwiekraftdurchfreude100.html (accessed 27 June 2016).

Kerkeling, H. (2006) *Ich bin dann mal weg: meine Reise auf dem Jakobsweg* (I'm off then: my journey along the Camino de Santiago), Munich: Malik.

Knoll, G.M. (2016) *Handbuch Wandertourismus*, Konstanz, Germany: UVK.

Kouchner, F., Lyard, J.-P., Zimmer, P. and Grassmann, S. (2000) *Developing Walking Holidays in Rural Areas. Guide on How to Design and Implement a Walking Holiday Project*, Parma: LEADER European Observatory.

Krüger, A. (2010) 'Historie des Wanderns', in A. Dreyer, A. Menzel and M. Endreß (eds), *Wandertourismus*, Munich: Oldenbourg, pp. 15–21.

Laws, B. (2007) *Byways, Boots and Blisters: A History of Walks and Walking*, Stroud, Glos: Sutton Publishing.

Lemke, G. (2002) *Wir waren hier, wir waren dort. Zur Kulturgeschichte der modernen Gesellenwanderns*, Cologne: PapyRossa Verlag.

Mosse, G.L. (2003) *Nazi Culture: Intellectual, Cultural, and Social Life in the Third Reich*, Madison, WI: University of Wisconsin Press.

Naturfreunde (2016) *Chronik der Naturfreunde.* Available at: www.naturfreunde.de/chronik-der-natur-freunde (accessed 25 June 2016).

Naturpark Südeifel (n.d.) *Das Wandern ist des Müllers Lust.* Available at: www.naturpark-suedeifel.de/our-zeit/pdfs-arbeitsblaetter/ab-natour-08_muellers-lust.pdf, (accessed 22 May 2016).

Opaschowski, H.W. (2008) *Einführung in die Freizeitwissenschaft*, Wiesbaden, Germany: VS Verlag für Sozialwissenschaften.

Peters, E. (2001) *The Complete Idiot's Guide to Walking for Health*, Indianapolis, IN: Penguin Group.

Project M (2014) *Wanderstudie. Der deutsche Wandermarkt 2014*, Berlin: Project M.

Seume, J.G. (1803) 'Spaziergang nach Syrakus im Jahre 1802', *Braunschweig und Leipzig*. Available at: www.deutschestextarchiv.de/book/view/seume_syrakus_1803?p=11 (accessed 25 June 2016).

Smolka, H. (2009) Wandern und Nachhaltigkeit- eine Positionsbestimmung. Available at: www.wanderforschung.de/files/wandern-und-nahhaltigkeit-21242219697.pdf (accessed 26 June 2016).

Solnit, R. (2000) *Wanderlust. A History of Walking*, New York: Penguin Books.

Statista (2016) *Was sind Ihre Motive zum Wandern? (im Jahr 2013)*. Available at: http://de.statista.com/statistik/daten/studie/301176/umfrage/motive-zum-wandern-im-ueberblick (accessed 26 May 2016).

Stumpf, N. (2001) *Abenteuer im Schulsport. Was Kinder sich wünschen und wie man diese Wünsche realisieren kann*, Wissenschaftliche Examensarbeit, Karlsruhe, Germany: GHS.

Sussmann, A. and Goode, R. (1967) *The Magic of Walking*, New York: Simon & Schuster.

United States Holocaust Museum (2016) *Culture in the Third Reich: Dissemanating the Nazi Worldview*. Available at: www.ushmm.org/wlc/en/article.php?ModuleId=10007519 (accessed 27 June 2016).

Vogt, L. (2010) '"Megatrend" Wandern und Trekking? – Eine narrative Synopse von Marktforschungsdaten, Medienberichten und anderen, vermeintlichen Indikatoren', *Mitteilungen der Österreichischen Geographischen Gesellschaft*, 152: 276–304.

7

Walking and art
Perambulating pleasures

Ray Boland and Brian Wheeller

Introduction

We weren't sure, without stepping on each other's toes, how best to overcome the inherent problem of writing something individual/personal in a jointly authored paper, so we had a chat . . . a sort of preamble ramble . . . about how best to tackle this conundrum and decided that we should write the piece as a dialogue. Beginning with Plato's dialogues nearly 2,500 years ago, featuring in novels such as *Pride and Prejudice* (Austen 2003), and continuing to the present day, the combination of walking and dialogue has been a continuous feature of philosophy and literature in the West. Coleridge's discussions with Wordsworth while they walked the Quantocks helped formulate the embryonic *Ancient Mariner*. Furthermore, it can be argued that all communication is dialogic, in that it takes place in response to what has already been said and written and stimulates what will be said and written in the future (Volosinov 1986). While obviously not claiming to be the equals of such literary giants, we nevertheless hope that the ensuing text reveals something of our take on the joys of walking and art. We'll try to reflect on walking in the countryside and in the city, and on walking before and after sundown.

There are many good reasons to walk: it is good for our health, it helps make us happy, it helps us to think clearly and resolve problems, and it is low on carbon emissions. However, these are all extrinsic to the act of walking itself, and they are all associated with the relatively modern obsession with utility – everything should have a purpose or goal. Here, we are also interested in the intrinsic pleasures of walking itself and the simple enjoyment of putting one foot forward and then the next and moving freely through space. We hope to show how a sympathetic engagement with art can alert individuals to their environment and to themselves during their walks. 'Walking is the celebration of being alive, alone or with friends, epic expeditions or easy rambles, as long as it is outside . . . where the perspective on life is longer and clearer and higher' (Maconie 2012: 2).

Brian: As background I've been reading some of the standard texts on walking, but Wilde provided inspiration: 'There is nothing that art cannot express' (Wilde 2001: 11). As you well know, Ray, subjective, rather than objective, in perspective I always draw heavily on the anecdotal, "the personal" (and some might say random) and on "experience" – a personal journey reflected in the thoughts aired and examples proffered by way of illustration.

Ray: Well, Brian, whether subjective or objective, art and walking afford moments of pleasure, opportunities for reflection and sometimes a reason to think about things anew. That's all there is to it.

Brian: I can make some sense of that. You can't beat the coast path or a stroll along the prom for clearing those cobwebs! Many writers such as Wordsworth and Thoreau were great walkers. By all accounts, Dickens was also something of a walker.

> At one point in his life he believed he had a moral duty to spend as many hours walking as he did writing. I'm not sure whether he used walking as a way of meditating on his feelings or as a way of escaping from them. Certainly he must have thought about his work and his characters as he walked, maybe he even found material he could use, so it wasn't wasted time, but more than that he seems to have used walking as a way of driving away melancholy.
>
> *(Nicholson 1997: 153)*

Ray: Yes, but Wordsworth's and Thoreau's encounters with the sublime and its awe-inspiring power arises from a Christian worldview, in which nature is the sign of an original creator. In Buddhism, for example, there is much more of a continuum, so nature still has a significance, but this arises from within the individual and does not originate from God. The numinous quality of nature is largely absent in the East (Lemaire 2011). Certainly, if we examine Chinese landscape painting, for example, it becomes clear that aesthetically the focus is on how the dynamic of nature itself has been represented and not on how this nature manifests the work of a Creator (Turner 2009).

However, walking does have an ethical dimension. 'Foot transects [repeated data gathering walks through the same terrain over an extended period of time] . . . make possible an otherwise unattainable acquaintance with a region' (Macfarlane 2012: 264). This attention to specific detail and a felicity with the language necessary to recognize and describe it accurately, means that we see nature as a unique phenomenon and not as a bland nothingness waiting to be used by humans.

British hedgerows, for example, contain an incredible diversity of animal and plant life (Wright 2016). Cycling or driving past a hedgerow does not allow sufficient time to see the prodigious variety there. However, walking does, and is perhaps a way to transcend what Weber (cited in Macfarlane 2015: 24) refers to as *Entzauberung* – the modern process by which nature has lost its magic and enchantment. If we are aware of the diversity and charm of nature, we may well become more attached to it and less willing to allow it to be harmed. We will certainly enjoy it more. Wordsworth, as you mentioned earlier, is one of the artists who sensitizes us to what is actually out there. Reading his poetry can be a step on the road to appreciating nature more fully. (See de Botton 2003 for a more detailed explanation of how art can help open our eyes to the world.)

Brian: And, of course, there's the "You're never alone with a phone" syndrome. But if technology in itself can be classed as an art form then, surely, the impact of the aptly labelled Walkman . . . and the multitude of variants it spawned . . . shouldn't be underestimated. Walking is synonymous with accompanying "sounds" for today's gilded youth.

Now, of course, there's Google . . . One further step away from reality, you can don headphones, listen to sounds, while, in front of the computer, embarking on, and vicariously enjoying, the delights of the outdoors with the recent appearance of some of England's and Wales's finest long-distance footpaths now available "online" . . . "the Google Effect". An "online" walk?

Ray: Yes, but I prefer reality to its enhanced version on a walk. The aimlessness of a walk is a form of pure freedom. To Chatwin (1998), for example, walking is humanity's natural state and one of the activities that is guaranteed to make us happy. We are free and independent while walking and not subject to some corporate environment such as in an airplane and the injunction to "sit back, relax and enjoy the flight", usually made at the end of the safety briefing. Incidentally, I read a great description of flying economy class while I was waiting in the departure lounge at an airport quite a few years ago, so maybe that is why it stayed with me, but it's still true and funny. 'Crammed into a ridiculously tiny space from which it's impossible to move without disturbing an entire row of fellow passengers, you are greeted from the onset with a series of embargos announced by stewardesses sporting fake smiles' (Houllebecq 2003: 30). Flying for me has never been the same since. I now enjoy it much more.

Brian: Not so sure about this, Ray . . . Free and Independent? Maybe? But do we walk 'aimlessly'? I doubt it. Free and independent tourists don't, generally, walk aimlessly . . . and, certainly, not if they are on a guided tour, anyway. They may well be sightseeing . . . and maybe that only involves a walk from the coach to the requisite photo opportunity, but it does have a purpose.

Anyway, this wandering aimlessly and all this abstract, philosophical meandering may be all well and good. But what about The Four Seasons' didactic 'Walk Like a Man?' (Crewe and Gaudio 1963). Admittedly, there's also Lou Reed's lugubriously suggestive '(Take a) Walk on the Wild Side' (Reed 1972b).

Ray: Don't forget, Lou also had a flip, Romantic (actually b-) side, as in 'Perfect Day' (Reed 1972a). But Lou was able to take the cliché out of the seedy side of life. Urban walking has never had 'the high moral tone of nature appreciation' (Solnit 2014: 174), but has always been more enjoyable for me – partly because it's easy. As Self (2015) remarks '[T]here's no Gore-Tex necessarily involved'. Urban walkers don't need to lug food and drink around either, as 'In the city we have places called cafes – and some serve excellent coffee' (Self 2015).

Brian: Depending on the weather, wherever you are, you can either be 'Walking on Sunshine' (Rew 1985), courtesy of Katrina, or 'Walking in the Rain' (Mann et al. 1964) with the Ronettes (or David Cassidy, if you'd prefer). Actually, Walking (or Singin') in the rain seems a particularly prevalent pastime in song . . .

Ray: Yes, but irrespective of rain or sunshine, walking in the city does not have to be, and indeed should not be, through the scenic, the dramatic or the memorable. Sinclair (2003) shows how the suburbs and the edges of cities can be where the action is. Apollinaire's 1913 poem *Zone* (2015) is a great celebration of the modern city and an articulate rejection of heritage. Just as with Wordsworth and the countryside, reading Apollinaire can show us how to see the beauty in our urban walks. And don't forget, Wordsworth himself wasn't averse to the "splendours" of the city; witness 'Composed upon Westminster Bridge' (Wordsworth 1802). I walk the same route to work and back home every weekday, and have done so for the last twelve years, and every day it's different, every day it's new.

Brian: You'll never get a starring role in *Groundhog Day* (Ramis 1993): *The Sequel* then. Or would that just be a re-issue, anyway?

Ray: Given its content, there should probably be an infinite number of sequels. Anyway, returning to the aural, Brian, Chatwin's (1998) exploration of how the sounds of the songs of the original inhabitants of Australia communicated as much about the topography of the places they described as did words, is indicative of the way in which art can transcend the limitations of language. Music often has a much greater emotional impact on us than words – avoiding the rationalizing drive of the spoken and the written and going straight to our hearts.

Furthermore, a walk in the mundane can in itself be spectacular and epic. One need only consider Bloom and his walk through Dublin on 16 June 1904 (Joyce 2010), to see the heroic potential of "the everyday" (O'Connor 2013) and be aware of, and acknowledge, how interesting our own imagination and daydreams can be. By walking through space, we also create it through a process of 'cosmogenesis' (Augoyard 2007) – actually, quite similar to Chatwin's (1998) account of the dreamtime, now I think of it – and if we have a large library of sounds, images and words (garnered to a large extent from art) at our disposal, this bringing into existence can be so much more fulfilling.

Much traditional social research concentrates on the abstract and the general. However, Joyce (2010), through literature, and Augoyard (2007: 14), through academic study, distille 'the lived practices of the inhabitants' – practices which are usually sidelined in academia and elsewhere. It is essential that we consider these different and multiple stories (Adichie 2009), and that we can live with complexity and contradiction (Sinclair 2011) if we want an interesting life.

The Russian Formalists believed that the function of art was to reflect our everyday life back to us and make it strange. Our walks and encounters, and the thoughts and dreams we have during and after them, contribute to this life of the imagination. As Eliot in 1943 (2001) so eloquently put it after our explorations, both physical and metaphysical, we can return home and see it as if it was for the first time.

Brian: At the other end of the walking spectrum, aimless meandering would get short shrift from the swaggering, focused John Travolta strutting along the streets of Brooklyn in the opening frames of *Saturday Night Fever* (Badham 1977). It is so macho, so testosterone-driven . . . despite the rather incongruous falsetto Bee Gees soundtrack – medallion-man incarnate. However, I suppose, on the other foot, Nancy Sinatra's boots (Hazlewood 1966) provides a striking strident alternative.

Ray: Sinatra or Travolta, Hoboken or Brooklyn, though, cities at night are different than during the day (Osborne 2010), and walking after sundown is unlike walking in the daylight.

Brian: Alexandre Privat d'Anglemont – a Parisian Bohemian in the first half of the nineteenth century – used his nighttime rambles as the basis of a series of sympathetic newspaper articles about the poor and dispossessed in Paris published in the 1850s (Seigel 1999). He spent so much time walking that, according to Delvot (as cited in Sante 2016), 'he wrote his books with his legs'. He was interested in the city dwellers, 'for whom the streets are paved with cold', as Arlidge (2016: 49) so sympathetically describes the contemporary beggars on London's streets, and to refer to your earlier point about "foot transects" and the countryside, his 'botanizing on the asphalt' (Taylor 2016) unlocked the diverse stories there.

D'Anglemont (Sante 2016) said:

[Y]es our literature is etched in acid. Yes we use blood and fire as others employ tears and warmth. But we were nursed on alcohol not milk. We have seen on our streets things more terrible and more awful (than we could ever describe). If we deal in the terrible, it is because everything around us is terrible.

Graphic material garnered by walking the streets.

Ray: Willemsen's (2012) *Bangkok Noir* and Ralf Tooten's accompanying photos also provide a more contemporary and sympathetic account of the night workers, the poor and the dispossessed in Bangkok without seeing things through rose-tinted glasses. They spent three months walking around Bangkok at night, and through their words and eyes we visit the sleeping haunts of urban elephants and their mahouts, encounter other night walkers and enter various hidden spaces.

Film noir, of course, is the pinnacle of the artistic representation of the city at night. Many film noir feature cars and trains as the chief mode of mobility, but *He Walked by Night* (Werker 1948) provides a brilliantly bleak and nail-bitingly nihilistic exploration of the underside of the city streets, as the Richard Basehart character escapes into the LA sewers to evade capture. Although he is on the run, he attempts to walk to freedom.

Brian: Shades, then, of Chandler's (1988: 18) noble 'But down these mean streets a man must go who is not himself mean, who is neither tarnished nor afraid'. For 'go' read 'walk'. So none of this meandering 'off the beaten track/trek' nonsense? Stick to the straight and narrow. The road to redemption. *Walk Tall* (Wayne 1964) as (even the usually mild-mannered) Doonican would say.

Actually, there is often a macho theme to some "walking music". Besides the aforementioned, Dion's *The Wanderer* (Maresca 1961) is a classic . . . though Caspar David Friedrich's painting of the same name is a different matter all together, isn't it? One of contemplative reflection on Nature, whereas Dion's all about sexual prowess.

Ray: Sorry to interrupt, Brian, but I always felt Dion subverted his own bravado in the song when he ends by admitting that he isn't going anywhere. Then again, maybe I was too influenced by my post-modern youth and still try to find ways to read texts against themselves, as we used to say in the 1980s.

Brian: True . . . but the 1980s? Not wishing to steal a march on you, Ray, but you're 20 years too late . . . With walking and music, sometimes it's place-specific . . . *Walking to New Orleans* (Charles 1960), sometimes "directional" – *Walk on By* (Bacharach and David 1964).

Ray: I think maybe we've walked and talked enough for now. However, before we stop, I think we should reflect on Li Po's (n.d.) 'Visiting the Taoist Priest Dai Tianshan but not finding him' and just enjoy the inherent pointlessness in much of what we do . . . including walking. There's no direction, no goal; just movement.

Brian: Yeah . . . Geoff Dyer's (2016) answer to his own question 'Why are we here? – 'We are here to go somewhere else' seems sort of apposite.

References

Adichie, C. (2009) 'The danger of a single story', TED talk. Available at: www.ted.com/talks/chimamanda_adichie_the_danger_of_a_single_story?language=en.

Apollinaire, G. (2015) *Zone: Selected Poems*, trans. R. Podgett, New York: New York Review of Books.

Arlidge, J. (2016) 'London's dark underside', *The Sunday Times Culture International*, 24 January: 49.

Augoyard, J-F. (2007) *Step by Step: Everyday Walks in a French Urban Housing Project*, trans. D.A. Curtis, Minneapolis: University of Minnesota Press.

Austen, J. (2003) *Pride and Prejudice*, London: Penguin.

Bacharach, B. and David, H. (1964) *Walk on By*. Performed by Dionne Warwick. New York: Scepter Records.

Badham, J. (dir.) (1977) *Saturday Night Fever* (motion picture), Los Angeles: Robert Stigwood Productions.

Chandler, R. (1988) *The Simple Art of Murder*, London: Vintage Books.

Charles, B. (1960) *Walking to New Orleans*. Performed by Fats Domino. New Orleans: Imperial Records.

Chatwin, B. (1998) *The Songlines*, London: Vintage Books.

Crewe, B. and Gaudio, B. (1963) *Walk Like a Man*. Performed by The Four Seasons. Gary, IN: Vee-Jay Records.

de Botton, A. (2003) *The Art of Travel*, London: Penguin Books.

Dyer, G. (2016) *White Sands: Experiences from the Outside World*, Edinburgh: Canongate.

Eliot, T.S. (2001) *Four Quartets*, London: Faber and Faber.

Hazlewood, L. (1966) *These Boots Are Made for Walking*. Performed by Nancy Sinatra. New York: Reprise Records.

Houllebecq, M. (2003) *Platform*, trans. F. Wynne, London: Vintage Books.

Joyce, J. (2010) *Ulysses*, Ware, Herts: Wordsworth Classics.

Lemaire, T. (2011) *Filosofie van het Landschap*, Amsterdam: Ambo.

Macfarlane, R. (2012) *The Old Ways: A Journey on Foot*, London: Hamish Hamilton.

Macfarlane, R. (2015) *Landmarks*, London: Hamish Hamilton.

Maconie, S. (2012) *Never Mind the Quantocks*, Newton Abbot, Devon: David & Charles.

Mann, B., Spector, P. and Weil, C. (1964) *Walkin' in the Rain*. Performed by The Ronettes. Philadelphia, PA: Philles Records.

Maresca, E. (1961) *The Wanderer*. Performed by Dion. New York: Laurie Records.

Nicholson, G. (1997) *Bleeding London*, Chelmsford, Essex: Harbour.

O'Connor, J. (2013) *Reimagining the City: Dublin* (radio broadcast). London: BBC Radio 4, 12 January.

Osborne, L. (2010) *Bangkok Days,* London: Vintage Books.

Po, L. (n.d.) 'Visiting the Taoist Priest Dai Tianshan but not finding him', Personal Tao. Available at: http://personaltao.com/gallery/poetry/poetry-of-li-po.

Ramis, H. (dir.) (1993) *Groundhog Day* (motion picture), Los Angeles: Columbia Pictures Corporation.

Reed, L. (1972a) *Perfect Day*. Performed by Lou Reed. New York: RCA Music.

Reed, L. (1972b) *Walk on the Wild Side*. Performed by Lou Reed. New York: RCA Music.

Rew, K. (1985) *Walking on Sunshine*. Performed by Katrina and the Waves. London: EMI Music.

Sante, L. (2016) *Book of the Week: The Other Paris* (radio broadcast). BBC Radio 4, 24 February.

Seigel, J. (1999) *Bohemian Paris: Culture, Politics, and the Boundaries of Bourgeois Life, 1830–1930*, Baltimore, MD: Johns Hopkins University Press.

Self, W. (2015) 'Take to the city streets for a walking adventure', *The Guardian*, 1 February. Available at: www.theguardian.com/travel/2015/feb/01/great-city-walks-will-self-take-to-the-streets (accessed 5 February 2016).

Sinclair, I. (2003) *London Orbital*, London: Penguin Books.

Sinclair, I. (2011) *The Culture Show* (television broadcast). London: BBC2 Television, 2 June.

Solnit, R. (2014) *Wanderlust: A History of Walking*, London: Granta.

Taylor, L. (2016) *Thinking Allowed* (radio broadcast). London: BBC Radio 4, 27 April.

Turner, M. (2009) 'Classical Chinese landscape painting and the aesthetic appreciation of nature', *The Journal of Aesthetic Education*, 43(1): 106–121.

Volosinov, V. (1986) *Marxism and the Philosophy of Language*, trans. L. Matejka and I. Titunik, Cambridge MA: Harvard University Press.

Wayne, D. (1964) *Walk Tall*. Performed by Val Doonican. London: Decca Records.

Werker, A. (dir) (1948) *He Walked by Night* (motion picture), Los Angeles: Bryan Foy Productions.

Wilde, O. (2001) *The Picture of Dorian Gray,* London: Wordsworth Classics.

Willemsen, R. (2012) *Bangkok Noir,* Frankfurt am Main: Fischer Taschenbuch Verlag.

Wordsworth, W. (1802) 'Composed upon Westminster Bridge, September 3, 1802', *Poetry Foundation*. Available at: www.poetryfoundation.org/poems-and-poets/poems/detail/45514#poem.

Wright, J. (2016) *Natural History of the Hedgerow and Ditches and Dykes and Stone Walls*, London: Profile Books.

Part II
Social Practices, Perceptions and Behaviours

8

Dog walking as a leisure activity

Yoshitaka Iwasaki

Introduction

Dog walking is one of the most popular leisure activities worldwide (Banks and Bryant 2007; Brown and Rhodes 2006; Christian *et al.* 2012, 2013; Reeves *et al.* 2011). Guided by the current literature on dog walking, this chapter critically examines opportunities and challenges of dog walking as a leisure activity. Besides the health benefits of dog walking (Hoerster *et al.* 2011; Utz 2014), the chapter addresses intrapersonal, social and environmental factors that contextualize dog walking. Examples for such exploration include the effects of socio-demographic factors and urban design (e.g. street pattern, proximity to a park area including access to an off-leash park; McCormack *et al.* 2011), a sense of attachment to dogs as companions, and social support of dog walkers (Netting *et al.* 2013). Attention is given to the dog–owner relationship (e.g. practice of caring), the dog's positive effects on an owner's cognitive beliefs about and motivation towards walking (Degeling and Rock 2012; Westgarth *et al.* 2014), and the provision of dog-supportive physical environment for dog walking (Christian *et al.* 2010). In addition, dog walking as a leisure activity can provide opportunities to promote meaning-making as another benefit of this potentially meaningful leisure engagement (Greenebaum 2010; Swall *et al.* 2015), as humans naturally seek the pursuit of a meaningful, enriching life (Baumeister and Vohs 2002; Frankl 1985; Hicks and Routledge 2013). Finally, the chapter highlights research-informed knowledge that has practical implications for tourism and recreation managers and professionals. Overall, this chapter addresses: (a) dog walking as a leisure-time physical activity; (b) social and ecological perspectives of dog walking; (c) dog walking as a leisure activity to promote meaning-making; and (d) practical implications of dog walking as a leisure/recreation activity.

Dog walking as a leisure-time physical activity

It has been shown that dog walking can be a means of promoting leisure-time physical activity among family members (Reeves *et al.* 2011; Christian *et al.* 2012, 2013). For example, Christian *et al.*'s (2012) study with 1,218 Australian children aged 10–12 years highlights the potential for dog ownership to significantly impact children's physical activity levels. Specifically, their findings suggest that within dog-owning families, the promotion of walking and active play with a dog (e.g. switching from sedentary screen play) can be a strategy to increase children's physical activity and curb obesity. According to Gretebeck et al.'s (2013) study with community-dwelling older adults in the Midwestern US, dog owner/dog walkers (n = 77) reported significantly more total walking, walking frequency, leisure and total physical activity, and higher total functional ability than dog owner/non-dog walkers (n = 83) and non-dog owners (n = 931).

Generally, walking a dog can contribute to a physically active lifestyle (Giaquinto and Valentini 2009). Thus, dog walking as a leisure activity is seen as a method of promoting a healthy lifestyle within communities (Lentino et al. 2012; Rhodes et al. 2012). Oka and Shibata's (2012) internet-based study with Japanese dog owners (n = 930) found that dog walking significantly helps dog owners meet physical activity recommendations for health and that dog-specific factors, such as dog attachment, appear to be stronger correlates of dog walking than socio-demographic factors. Enhancing the owner's interaction with the dog through playing, feeding and grooming seems to promote the attachment with the dog, which can help increase dog walking (Cutt et al. 2008; Zasloff 1996). Baumann et al. (2001, 2011) have calculated that increases in physical activities from dog walking would curb 5–9% of the incidence of chronic diseases, estimating annual healthcare savings of AU$175 million, should Australian dog owners walk their dogs on a regular basis.

Degeling and Rock's (2012) in-depth qualitative study of 11 Canadian dog owners showed heterogeneity in a caring practice both for personal health promotion and broader community-wide health promotion. Specifically, such heterogeneity was characterized by the practical (e.g. when and where dog walking takes place and by whom) and emotional (e.g. canine care, networks of care) dimensions of dog walking as a caring practice for personal health promotion among owners and families, as well as by implications of the presence of dogs within neighbourhoods for overall health promotion at population and community levels. In particular, Degeling and Rock (2012) found that the dogs figure as active participants in shaping ties between people, and between people and places in different ways, and that care is central to decisions surrounding dog walking. In general, dog owners appear to be more physically active than those without dogs, but dog ownership does not guarantee that owners will regularly walk with their dogs (Cutt et al. 2008). Christian et al.'s (2013) meta-analysis (n = 29 studies) showed that dog owners engage in more walking and physical activity than non-dog owners, but the effect sizes are small to moderate.

Social and ecological perspectives of dog walking

Besides the health benefits of dog walking (Hoerster et al. 2011; Utz 2014), it is important to address intrapersonal, social and environmental factors that contextualize dog walking. From a social ecological perspective, it is essential to explore whether and how dog ownership and neighbourhood characteristics are associated with sense of community and neighbourhood-based recreational walking. For example, Toohey et al.'s (2013) study showed that older adults who walk dogs often in their neighbourhoods can benefit from both increased physical activity and heightened sense of community, to an extent that supports healthy ageing. Specifically, older adults who are frequent dog walkers reported more positive feelings about their neighbourhoods (i.e. sense of community). Similar to these findings, sense of community, linked to perceptions of one's neighbourhood (McMillan and Chavis 1986), has also been positively correlated with neighbourhood-based walking (Du Toit et al. 2007; Wood et al. 2010). Thus, regular dog walking in neighbourhoods may bolster sense of community (Wood et al. 2005; Wood et al. 2007). On the other hand, creating neighbourhood environments that facilitate positive social interactions to support sense of community would also lead to more walking among community residents, e.g. appropriate walking pathways/layouts and amenities for dog walkers (Toohey *et al.* 2013).

Understanding the factors that facilitate or discourage owners to walk with their dogs is another key area of research. For example, Cutt *et al.* (2008) conducted a study with new dog owners (i.e. non-owners who had acquired a dog by the time of follow-up; n = 92) and continuing non-owners (non-owners at both baseline and follow-up, 12 months later; n = 681) in Perth, Australia. They found that the most likely mechanism through which dog acquisition facilitates increased physical activity is through behavioural intention, via the dog's positive effect on owner's cognitive beliefs about walking, and through the provision of motivation and social support for walking. McCormack *et al.*'s (2011) telephone survey with 506 adults in Calgary, Canada found that adjusting for all other correlates, the frequency of dog walking was higher among respondents who resided within 1.6 km of an off-leash area, women, university-educated owners, those with a dependent under 18 years living at home, and those living in attached housing. The finding that a less-walkable street pattern was negatively associated with usual participation in dog walking also lends support to a previous study, which showed that dog owners who walk their dogs were more likely than dog owners who do not walk their dogs to reside in more walkable neighbourhoods (Coleman *et al.* 2008).

In line with these findings, current evidence suggests that dog walking may be most effectively encouraged through targeting the dog-owner relationship and by providing dog-supportive physical environments (Christian *et al.* 2010; Herzog 2011; Westgarth *et al.* 2014). Specifically, there is good evidence that the strength of the dog–owner relationship, through a sense of obligation to walk the dog, and the perceived support and motivation a dog provides for walking, are strongly associated with increased walking (Herzog 2011; McNicholas *et al.* 2005). The other key environmental factors to facilitate dog walking include access to suitable walking areas with dog-supportive features that fulfil dog needs such as off-leash exercise, and that also encourage human social interactions (Christian *et al.* 2010; Cutt *et al.* 2008; Westgarth *et al.* 2014).

Netting *et al.*'s (2013) study on dog walking as a physical activity intervention found that while it is not surprising that all participants in their study (i.e. dog owners presenting for care at a tertiary-care veterinary hospital) are highly attached to their dogs, younger owners had stronger attachments to their dogs and less social support. Their study suggests the importance of companion animals for social support, particularly for those without close friends/relatives. For younger owners, the study reveals vulnerabilities in support networks that have implications for an intervention. Overall, Netting *et al.*'s study emphasizes the importance of including companion animals (in this case, a dog) as part of the human social convoy, especially in terms of providing affectionate and interactional social support.

Accordingly, dog walking is considered as a social activity whereby an individual gets to know other dog owners, performs an outdoor physical activity, and engages in communication and information sharing (Netting *et al.* 2013; Wood *et al.* 2005). Wood *et al.* (2005: 1162) suggested that dog ownership can be 'a protective factor for mental health, which in turn may influence attitudes toward, and participation in, the local community and relationships with people in the community'. Consequently, 'dog walkers become part of a larger community of interactions as they move along sidewalks, exercise within parks, and traverse their neighbourhoods and local environments' (Netting *et al.* 2013: 264). Based on these observations, companion animals including dogs are considered important conduits of social capital (Netting *et al.* 2013), which can be defined as the features of social life – 'networks, norms, and social trust – that facilitate coordination and cooperation for mutual benefit' (Putnam 1993: 35).

As noted earlier, Degeling and Rock's (2012) qualitative in-depth study with Canadian dog owners suggests heterogeneity, not only in the practical and emotional dimensions of what dog care involves for health among owners and families, but also for what the presence of dogs implies for overall health in communities, neighbourhoods and populations. In particular, their study findings illustrate that caring for a dog tends to promote physical activity and social interactions with family members, friends and neighbours. In foregrounding networks of care, inclusive of pets and public spaces, a relational conceptualization of dog walking as a practice of caring, from a social ecological perspective, helps to make sense of heterogeneity in patterns of physical activity among dog owners (Degeling and Rock 2012).

Finally, using focus groups and interviews, Higgins *et al.* (2013) explored dog guardians' walking practices and relationships with their dogs. Specifically, four themes were identified, including: (a) transcending the human–animal distinction (e.g. dogs as sentient family members); (b) dogs as walking "sole mates" (good companions and motivators for walking); (c) activity/ health benefits; and (d) dogs as social conduits (e.g. "third party" facilitator of social support networks in the community). Higgins *et al.* (2013: 237) suggest that 'an empathetic stance benefits dog guardians because, as valued family members whose health and happiness they are responsible for, their canine companions serve to motivate, enable, and sustain walking behaviors'.

Dog walking as a leisure activity to promote meaning-making

The concept of *meaning-making* seems applicable and relevant to dog walking as a leisure activity, which appears to have important implications for elaborating the benefits of this potentially meaningful leisure engagement. Generally, the perception of dogs as a subjective being and one's connectedness with them seem to provide opportunities for meaning-making within one's life through actively engaging with dogs (Greenebaum 2010). Specifically, some research suggests that animals such as dogs are often given "personhood status", as they are perceived as mindful, active participants who engage in meaning-making with their caretakers and other animals through symbolic interactions and communications (Alger and Alger 2003; Brandt 2004; Greenebaum 2010). Meaning-making refers to the ways in which and how people gain meanings within life that are important for personal, spiritual, social and cultural reasons (Lancaster and Carlson 2015; Markman *et al.* 2013). It has been shown that leisure provides opportunities or spaces for people to seek and find meanings of life (Hutchinson and Nimrod 2012; Iwasaki 2008; Iwasaki *et al.* 2013, 2015; Mata-Codesal *et al.* 2015; Shaw and Henderson 2005).

In particular, Sanders' (1999: 108) groundbreaking work on dogs and their caretakers identified this meaning-making process that involves an 'authentic social relationship' through developing a 'shared emotional bond' (Sanders 1999: 149) between caretakers and their dogs. His examination based on detailed ethnographic data showed how dogs serve not only as social facilitators, but also as adornments to social identity through a meaningful human–dog relationship. In addition, Edminster's (2012) ethnographic study with assistance-dog agency staff and their clients illustrated the ways that shared and embodied relational meaning emerges as they make meaningful lives together. In search of the good life, Marcus (2010) identified humans' relations with dogs as a primary way to give greater meaning and purpose to their personal lives.

Cline's (2008) study used role strain and role enhancement theories to explore the role of dog ownership in well-being, with a focus on the conditions under which dog ownership is most strongly related to well-being, and the meaning of dogs within the owners' lives. Findings revealed gender and marital status differences in the relationship between dog ownership and well-being and in the way that respondents speak about their relationship with their dogs. Interestingly, women and single adults were more likely to benefit from dog ownership and to focus more on the expressive dimensions of dog ownership in a meaningful way.

More recently, Swall *et al.* (2015) explored the meaning of the lived experience of encounters with a therapy dog for persons with Alzheimer's disease, using a phenomenological hermeneutical approach. The results identified a main theme, 'being aware of one's past and present existence', that involves meaningfully connecting with one's senses and memories and to reflect upon these with the dog. The time spent with the dog provided the persons with opportunities to recount their memories and feelings, and to reach them on a cognitive level that can increase quality of life and well-being in persons with dementia (Swall *et al.* 2015). It appears that the notion of dog walking as a leisure activity to promote meaning-making is applicable and relevant to almost all humans, regardless of differences in human characteristics, including people with disabilities, as shown by Swall *et al.*'s (2015) study.

Furthermore, Maharaj *et al.*'s (2016) qualitative study with 27 dog owners aged 17–74 years in British Columbia, Canada explored the relational significance of the human–animal bond as a way of finding meaning in one's everyday life. Their thematic analysis of focus group data revealed three themes: (a) *this is a sacred relationship*; (b) *all we have is today*; and (c) *I'm going to fix you, hang on*. These themes, named after dog-owners' language, addressed a sacred, spiritual and meaningful human–canine relationship based on the depth of the emotional bond, including calming, stress-coping and healing effects of such meaningful relationship through promoting happiness, levity and companionship. Overall, Maharaj *et al.*'s (2016) study gave insights into the ways people perceive and relate to their companion dogs and how this affects their sense of meaning in life. Their study showed that 'along with enriching their own life, some participants found it particularly meaningful to see their dogs bring joy and levity to other people in need of comfort' (Maharaj *et al.* 2016: 84).

Practical implications of dog walking as a leisure/recreation activity

Finally, this area of research has practical implications for tourism and recreation managers. For example, Lee and Shen's (2013) study explored the influence of leisure involvement and place attachment on destination loyalty among recreationists walking their dogs (n = 526) in dog-friendly urban parks in Taiwan. Their findings imply that urban park managers could consider developing programmes that increase activity involvement, such as by providing dog-friendly opportunities for dog owners, which can strengthen destination loyalty in recreationists walking their dogs in urban parks.

Using leisure constraints and negotiation frameworks, Hung *et al.* (2012) examined the constraints imposed by the pet (i.e. dog), the owner's motivation to take the pet to leisure activities (e.g. nature-related sightseeing, outdoor sports, visiting cultural sites, participating in events), and the owner's ability to negotiate this issue. The findings highlight a recreation and tourism management issue of providing necessary assistances/resources to address the constraints that pet owners face. Examples include providing facilities (e.g. pet shops, fenced-in/shaded areas designed for pets, and washrooms for visitors who walk their pets) and a signage that welcomes dogs and other companions. According to Hung *et al.* (2012: 489) 'through these steps, not only pet owners will be benefited, but operators can encourage others not with a pet to accept the normalisation of having pets accompany their companions and participate in activities'. Given the renewed focus on the health effects of the social and physical environment, the way that public spaces are used as a resource for dog care has implications for urban planning and management (Degeling and Rock 2012).

Furthermore, dog walking is considered as a method for therapy (O'Conner-Von 2014), for instance, with older adults and/or those living with disabilities to promote human–animal bonds/companionship and physical and mental health (Giaquinto and Valentini 2009; Cangelosi and Sorrell 2010). A broad range of investigations strongly suggest that animal–human interactions reduce anxiety, depression and loneliness as they enhance social support and well-being (Hooker *et al.* 2002; Walsh 2009). For example, Souter and Miller's (2007) meta-analysis of five studies using animal-assisted activities to treat depression indicate that animal-assisted interventions may be associated with fewer symptoms of depression, thus contributing to the patient's mental health. Not only dogs, but cats, horses, birds and a variety of other animals have been used in animal-assisted therapy – as emotional support, animals or psychiatric service animals can provide therapeutic interactions and reduce suffering for a variety of psychological and medical disorders (Mangan 2016).

At present, there is consistent evidence of the protective effect against cardiovascular risk, mainly through the moderate exercise prompted by walking a dog (Allen *et al.* 2002; Giaquinto and Valentini 2009). Moreover, patients suffering from chronic illness are likely to benefit from pet companionship (Giaquinto and Valentini 2009; Thorpe *et al.* 2006), for example, through helping alleviate the stress and alienation of old age and illness (Giaquinto and Valentini 2009). For another example, LaFrance *et al.* (2007) noted the potential effect of a therapy dog on stimulating communicative abilities of patients with aphasia. In addition, Silver (2005) showed that animal-assisted therapy with a dog might contribute to the psychosocial rehabilitation and life quality of patients with schizophrenia, especially, through an improvement in the hedonic tone and the use of leisure time. As stressed by Degeling and Rock (2012: 406) 'focusing on networks of care and care practices through relational approaches promises to open up new avenues for responding compassionately to sickness and promoting health, in both canine and human populations'.

Conclusion

Currently, we are witnessing a growing popularity in dog walking worldwide (Banks and Bryant 2007; Brown and Rhodes 2006; Christian *et al.* 2013; Reeves *et al.* 2011). Guided by the emerging literature on this topical area, the chapter addressed: (a) dog walking as a leisure-time physical activity; (b) social and ecological perspectives of dog walking; (c) dog walking as a leisure activity to promote meaning-making; and (d) practical implications of dog walking as a leisure/ recreation activity.

Specifically, beyond health benefits of dog walking, the chapter addressed personal, social and environmental factors that contextualize dog walking, including the effects of socio-demographic factors and urban design (e.g. street pattern, proximity to a park area including access to an off-leash park), a sense of attachment to dogs as companions, and social support of dog walkers. Through such examination, the chapter gave attention to the dog–owner relationship (e.g. practice of caring), the dog's positive effects on an owner's cognitive beliefs about and motivation toward walking, and the provision of dog-supportive physical environment for dog walking. Another key idea addressed in this chapter includes the role of dog walking in promoting meaning-making. Finally, the chapter gave insights into practical implications of dog walking as a leisure activity for tourism and recreation managers and professionals.

Besides the benefits of dog walking and human–dog relationships for humans, acknowledging dogs as 'thinking and active agents in communication and the socialization process' (Greenebaum 2010: 140) is important. Indeed, Sanders' (1999) classic book showed how everyday dog owners come to know their animal companions as thinking, emotional and responsive individuals.

In addition, as emphasized by Degeling and Rock (2012: 404), dogs are 'active participants in shaping ties between people and between people and places'. More specifically, it seems that the effects of relationships between people, dogs and places are mediated by the characteristics of individuals (both humans and dogs), their interactions with each other, and the resources available to them through their shared social and physical environments (Cummins *et al.* 2007; Degeling and Rock 2012). Considering such complexity, more holistic inquiries on dog walking as a meaningful leisure activity are needed from both conceptual and practical perspectives. For example, exploring the various ways in which humans and dogs find meanings of life through their communications and interactions at personal, social and environmental levels seems to be an important area of research, while considering the diversity in human and dog populations.

References

Alger, J. and Alger, S. (2003) *Cat Culture: The Social World of a Cat Shelter*, Philadelphia, PA: Temple University Press.

Allen, K., Blascovich, J. and Mendes, W.B. (2002) 'Cardiovascular reactivity and the presence of pets, friends, and spouses: the truth about cats and dogs', *Psychosomatic Medicine*, 64: 227–239.

Banks, P.B. and Bryant, J.V. (2007) 'Four-legged friend or foe? Dog walking displaces native birds from natural area', *Biology Letters*, 3: 611–613.

Bauman, A.E., Schroeder, J.R., Furber, S.E. and Dobson, A.J. (2001) 'The epidemiology of dog walking: an unmet need for human and canine health', *Medical Journal of Australia*, 175: 632–634.

Bauman, A.E., Christian, H., Thorpe, R.J. and Macniven, R. (2011) 'International perspectives on the epidemiology of dog walking', in R.A. Johnson, A.M. Beck and S. McCune (eds), *The Health Benefits of Dog Walking for Pets and People*, West Lafayette, IN: Purdue University Press, pp. 25–49.

Baumeister, R.F. and Vohs, K.D. (2002) 'The pursuit of meaningfulness in life', in C.R. Snyder and S.J. Lopez (eds), *Handbook of Positive Psychology*, New York: Oxford University Press, pp. 608–618.

Brandt, K. (2004) 'A language of their own: an interactionist approach to human–horse communication', *Society and Animals*, 12(4): 299–316.

Brown S.G. and Rhodes, R.E. (2006) 'Relationships among dog ownership and leisure-time walking in Western Canadian adults', *American Journal of Preventive Medicine*, 30: 131–136.

Cangelosi, P.R. and Sorrell, J.M. (2010) 'Walking for therapy with man's best friend', *Journal of Psychosocial Nursing and Mental Health Services*, 48(3): 19–22.

Christian, H., Giles-Corti, B. and Knuiman, M. (2010) '"I'm just a'-walking the dog": correlates of regular dog walking', *Family & Community Health*, 33(1): 44–52.

Christian, H., Trapp, G., Lauritsen, C., Wright, K. and Giles-Corti, B. (2012) 'Understanding the relationship between dog ownership and children's physical activity and sedentary behaviour', *Pediatric Obesity*, 8(5): 392–403.

Christian, H., Westgarth, C., Bauman, A., Richards, E.A., Rhodes, R.E., Evenson, K.R., Mayer, J.A. and Thorpe Jr, R.J. (2013) 'Dog ownership and physical activity: a review of the evidence', *Journal of Physical Activity & Health*, 10(5): 750–759.

Cline, K.M.C. (2008) 'Dogs and people: using role strain and role enhancement theories to predict dog owners' well-being', *Dissertation Abstracts International Section A: Humanities and Social Sciences*, 68(12-A): 5219.

Coleman, K.J., Rosenberg, D.E., Conway, T.L., Sallis, J.F., Saelens, B.E., Frank, L.D. and Cain, K. (2008) 'Physical activity, weight status, and neighborhood characteristics of dog walkers', *Preventive Medicine*, 47: 309–312.

Cummins, S., Curtis, S., Diez-Roux, A.V. and Macintyre, S. (2007) 'Understanding and representing "place" in health research: a relational approach', *Social Science and Medicine*, 65: 1825–1838.

Cutt, H.E., Giles-Corti, B., Wood, L.J., Knuiman, M.W. and Burke, V. (2008) 'Barriers and motivators for owners walking their dog: results from qualitative research', *Health Promotion Journal of Australia*, 19: 118–124.

Degeling, C. and Rock, M. (2012) '"It was not just a walking experience": reflections on the role of care in dog-walking', *Health Promotion International*, 28(3): 397–406.

Du Toit, L., Cerin, E., Leslie, E. and Owen, N. (2007) 'Does walking in the neighbourhood enhance local sociability?', *Urban Dictionary*, 44: 1677–1695.

Edminster, A. (2012) '"This dog means life": making interspecies relations at an assistance dog agency', *Dissertation Abstracts International Section A: Humanities and Social Sciences*, 72(8-A): 2869.

Frankl, V. (1985) *Man's Search for Meaning*, New York: Washington Square Press.

Giaquinto, S. and Valentini, F. (2009) 'Is there a scientific basis for pet therapy?', *Disability and Rehabilitation: An International, Multidisciplinary Journal*, 31(7): 595–598.

Greenebaum, J.B. (2010) 'Training dogs and training humans: symbolic interaction and dog training', *Anthrozoos*, 23(2): 129–141.

Gretebeck, K.A., Radius, K., Black, D.R., Gretebeck, R.J., Ziemba, R. and Glickman, L.T. (2013) 'Dog ownership, functional ability, and walking in community-dwelling older adults', *Journal of Physical Activity & Health*, 10(5): 646–655.

Herzog, H. (2011) 'The impact of pets on human health and psychological wellbeing: fact, fiction, or hypothesis?', *Current Directions in Psychological Science*, 20: 236–239.

Hicks, J.A. and Routledge, C. (eds) (2013) *The Experience of Meaning in Life: Classical Perspectives, Emerging Themes, and Controversies*, New York: Springer Science & Business Media.

Higgins, J.W., Temple, V., Murray, H., Kumm, E. and Rhodes, R. (2013) 'Walking sole mates: dogs motivating, enabling and supporting guardians' physical activity', *Anthrozoos*, 26(2): 237–252.

Hoerster, K.D., Mayer, J.A., Sallis, J.F., Pizzi, N., Talley, S., Pichon, L.C. and Butler, D.A. (2011) 'Dog walking: its association with physical activity guideline adherence and its correlates', *Preventive Medicine*, 52: 33–38.

Hooker, S.D., Freeman, L.H. and Stewart, P. (2002) 'Pet therapy research: a historical review', *Holistic Nursing Practice*, 16(5): 17–23.

Hung, K.P., Chen, A. and Peng, N. (2012) 'The constraints for taking pets to leisure activities', *Annals of Tourism Research*, 39(1): 487–495.

Hutchinson, S.L. and Nimrod, G. (2012) 'Leisure as a resource for successful aging by older adults with chronic health conditions', *The International Journal of Aging & Human Development*, 74(1): 41–65.

Iwasaki, Y. (2008) 'Pathways to meaning-making through leisure-like pursuits in global contexts', *Journal of Leisure Research*, 40(2): 231–249.

Iwasaki, Y., Coyle, C., Shank, J., Messina, E. and Porter, H. (2013) 'Leisure-generated meanings and active living for persons with mental illness', *Rehabilitation Counseling Bulletin*, 57(1): 46–56.

Iwasaki, Y., Messina, E., Coyle, C. and Shank, J. (2015) 'Role of leisure in meaning-making for community-dwelling adults with mental illness: inspiration for engaged life', *Journal of Leisure Research*, 47(5): 538–555.

LaFrance, C., Garcia, L.J. and Labreche, J. (2007) 'The effect of a therapy dog on the communication skills on an adult with aphasia', *Journal of Communication Disorders*, 40: 215–224.

Lancaster, S.L. and Carlson, G.C. (2015) 'Meaning made, distress, and growth: an examination of the integration of stressful life experiences scale', *International Journal of Stress Management*, 22(1): 92–110.

Lee, T.H. and Shen, Y.L. (2013) 'The influence of leisure involvement and place attachment on destination loyalty: evidence from recreationists walking their dogs in urban parks', *Journal of Environmental Psychology*, 33: 76–85.

Lentino, C., Visek, A.J., McDonnell, K. and Di Pietro, L. (2012) 'Dog walking is associated with a favorable risk profile independent of a moderate to high volume of physical activity', *Journal of Physical Activity & Health*, 9(3): 414–420.

Maharaj, N., Kazanjian, A. and Haney, C.J. (2016) 'The human–canine bond: a sacred relationship', *Journal of Spirituality in Mental Health*, 18(1): 76–89.

Mangan, T. (2016) *Animals that Help People with Depression*. Available at: www.livestrong.com/article/40421-animals-people-depression (accessed 1 April 2016).

Marcus, P. (2010) *In Search of the Good Life: Emmanuel Levinas, Psychoanalysis, and the Art of Living*, London: Karnac Books.

Markman, K.D., Proulx, T. and Lindberg, M.J. (eds) (2013) *The Psychology of Meaning*, Washington, DC: American Psychological Association.

Mata-Codesal, D., Peperkamp, E. and Tiesler, N.C. (2015) 'Migration, migrants and leisure: meaningful leisure?', *Leisure Studies*, 34(1): 1–4.

McCormack, G.R., Rock, M., Sandalack, B. and Uribe, F.A. (2011) 'Access to off-leash parks, street pattern and dog walking among adults', *Public Health*, 125(8): 540–546.

McMillan, D.W. and Chavis, D.M. (1986) 'Sense of community: a definition and theory', *Journal of Community Psychology*, 14: 6–23.

McNicholas, J., Gilbey, A., Rennie, A., Ahmedzai, S., Dono, J.A. and Ormerod, E. (2005) 'Pet ownership and human health: a brief review of evidence and issues', *BMJ*, 331: 1252–1254.

Netting, F.E., Wilson, C.C., Goodie, J.L., Stephens, M.B., Byers, C.G. and Olsen, C.H. (2013) 'Attachment, social support, and perceived mental health of adult dog walkers: what does age have to do with it?', *Journal of Sociology and Social Welfare,* 40(4): 261–283.

O'Conner-Von, S. (2014) 'Animal-assisted therapy', in: R. Lindquist, M. Snyder and M.F. Tracy (eds), *Complementary and Alternative Therapies in Nursing,* 7th edn, New York: Springer, pp. 229–251.

Oka, K. and Shibata, A. (2012) 'Prevalence and correlates of dog walking among Japanese dog owners', *Journal of Physical Activity & Health,* 10(1): 122–131.

Putnam, R.D. (1993) *Making Democracy Work: Civic Traditions in Modern Italy.* Princeton, NJ: Princeton University Press.

Reeves, M.J., Rafferty, A. P., Miller, C.E. and Lyon-Callo, S.K. (2011) 'The impact of dog walking on leisure-time physical activity: results from a population-based survey of Michigan adults', *Journal of Physical Activity & Health,* 8(3): 436–444.

Rhodes, R.E., Murray, H., Temple, V.A., Tuokko, H. and Higgins, J.W. (2012) 'Pilot study of a dog walking randomized intervention: effects of a focus on canine exercise', *Preventive Medicine,* 54(5): 309–312.

Sanders, C. (1999) *Understanding Dogs: Living and Working with Canine Companions,* Philadelphia, PA: Temple University Press.

Shaw, S.M. and Henderson, K. (2005) 'Gender analysis and leisure constraints: an uneasy alliance', in E.L. Jackson (ed.), *Constraints to Leisure,* State College: Venture Publishing, pp. 23–34.

Silver, H. (2005) 'Animal-assisted therapy ameliorates anhedonia in schizophrenia patients', *Psychotherapy and Psychosomatics,* 74(1): 31–35.

Souter, M.A. and Miller, M.D. (2007) 'Do animal-assisted activities effectively treat depression? A meta-analysis', *Anthrozoos,* 20(2): 167–180.

Swall, A., Ebbeskog, B., Hagelin, C.L. and Fagerberg, I. (2015) 'Can therapy dogs evoke awareness of one's past and present life in persons with Alzheimer's disease?', *International Journal of Older People Nursing,* 10(2): 84–93.

Thorpe Jr, R.J., Simonsick, E.M., Brach, J.S., Ayonayon, H., Satterfield, S., Harris, T.B., Garcia, M. and Kritchevsky, S.B. (2006) Dog ownership, walking behavior, and maintained mobility in late life (Health, aging and body composition study), *Journal of the American Geriatrics Society,* 54: 1419–1424.

Toohey, A.M., McCormack, G.R., Doyle-Baker, P.K., Adams, C.L. and Rock, M.J. (2013) 'Dog-walking and sense of community in neighborhoods: implications for promoting regular physical activity in adults 50 years and older', *Health & Place,* 22: 75–81.

Utz, R.L. (2014) 'Walking the dog: the effect of pet ownership on human health and health behaviors', *Social Indicators Research,* 116(2): 327–339.

Walsh, F. (2009) 'Human-animal bonds I: the relational significance of companion animals', *Family Process,* 48: 462–480.

Westgarth, C., Christley, R.M. and Christian, H.E. (2014) 'How might we increase physical activity through dog walking?: A comprehensive review of dog walking correlates', *The International Journal of Behavioral Nutrition and Physical Activity,* 11: 83.

Wood, L.J., Giles-Corti, B. and Bulsara, M.K. (2005) 'The pet connection: pets as a conduit for social capital?', *Social Science & Medicine,* 61: 1159–1173.

Wood, L.J., Giles-Corti, B., Bulsara, M.K. and Bosch, D.A. (2007) 'More than a furry companion: the ripple effect of companion animals on neighborhood interactions and sense of community', *Society & Animals,* 15: 43–56.

Wood, L.J., Frank, L.D. and Giles-Corti, B. (2010) 'Sense of community and its relationship with walking and neighborhood design', *Social Science & Medicine,* 70: 1381–1390.

Zasloff, R.L. (1996) 'Measuring attachment to companion animals: a dog is not a cat is not a bird', *Applied Animal Behaviour Science,* 47(1/2): 43–48.

9

Walking in Switzerland

Urban and not so leisurely

Derek P.T.H. Christie, Emmanuel Ravalet and Vincent Kaufmann

Introduction

Walking is the most easily accessible form of physical activity. Regular physical activity has significant health benefits and can help prevent numerous chronic diseases, as well as improving well-being and quality of life. Physical inactivity is a modifiable causal factor contributing to the current global epidemic of overweight and obesity (Millward *et al.* 2013).

Despite the evidence that physical inactivity is driving the epidemic of overweight and obesity, many campaigns still focus on diet rather than daily physical activity activities such as walking. It should, however, be borne in mind that unhealthy behaviours such as sedentariness and bad eating habits are often correlated with each other. Indeed, with respect to non-communicable diseases, the World Health Organization pinpoints daily physical activity as one of four important prevention areas globally, along with nutrition, tobacco and alcohol control (WHO 2016).

Across the world, various health, environmental or transport policies encourage people to walk. In order to monitor such policies, data are required at national, regional and municipal levels. But walking can be difficult to investigate at an aggregate level, because it may be combined with other modes – often motorised – within a transport chain or used as a transport mode it its own right.

Methods

The Swiss transport micro-census (MRMT2010) is a complex database with data from 62,686 individuals aged 6–99 interviewed by telephone, in a representative stratified sample covering the whole of Switzerland (SFSO 2012). It is made up of 13 interlinked databases, each with between 4 and 214 variables, and between 8,000 and 1 million data lines. It contains all transport movements in excess of 25 metres which are not entirely within a single entity, such as a train station, university campus or shopping mall. The MRMT2010 database therefore allows the detailed analysis of walking at national level, whether it is associated with other transport modes or not (see Table 9.1).

The MRMT database is able to divide trips by their destination and motive, with the trips themselves being subdivided into stages. If there is a single stage (e.g. a person walks to work), then the trip and the stage are identical. However, it is common for trips to have several stages and at least one of them is likely to be walking (walking to or from the bus stop, to or from the

Table 9.1 The seven most used datasets within the MRMT2010 database

Data	Observations	Variables
Households / Ménages / Haushalte	59,971	99
Target people / Personnes-cibles / Zielpersonen	62,868	214
Home trips / Boucles / Ausgänge	85,436	36
Trips / Déplacements / Wege	211,359	87
Stages / Etapes / Etappen	310,193	116
Routes / Routen	285,529	4
Segments / Segmente	10,064,058	2

car park). For example, each home trip (trips that start and finish at home) is subdivided into trips, which in turn are composed of stages that each have a single transport mode. This organisation has an important consequence, as the mode share of walking is likely to be very different if one looks at trips or at stages. If a person walks 100 metres to his or her car and then drives off to work or another location, this will count as one walking stage plus one car driving stage, but only a single trip, which will be attributed automatically to car driving.

Limitations of the data

There are limitations associated with the MRMT data. The first is self-declaration, since all interviews were carried out by telephone. Another is that trips of under 25 metres are not taken into account, nor are trips within buildings or facilities. So a person going three times round a shopping mall or university campus would register no movement at all. The most important limitation is that there is data only for a single day, for each survey participant. MRMT2010 therefore yields very good data at population level, but results for individuals need to be interpreted with caution. Indeed, a person who walks 5 km on a given day may well walk twice that amount – or not at all – on any other day of the same week. Each respondent has her own reference day, which is usually the day before the telephone interview. The reference days are spread out through the week and the year: the first interviews took place in January 2010 and the last in December 2010.

Distribution of walking in the population

Despite research interest for walking, little is known about the distribution of this activity in the general population. In Switzerland, an average (mean) walking distance of 1.9 km per person and per day was estimated by the Swiss Federal Office of Statistics (based on MRMT2010 data). But information was lacking about the distribution of walking within the population.

Our preliminary analysis of MRMT2010 shows that each resident of Switzerland covered around 37 km on the reference day (without counting trips abroad). This corresponds to a travel time of 83 minutes. There are substantial differences between socio-demographic groups. No doubt due to the large size of the database, all differences tend to be statistically significant (any non-significant differences would be labelled as such).

Men cover 11 km more per day than women. People living in households with a monthly income over CHF 14,000 cover distances 2.5 times greater than people living in households with incomes under CHF 2,000 (at the time of writing a Swiss franc (CHF) was approximately equivalent to a US dollar).

People with only compulsory education walk more than those with a qualification, whatever that qualification may be: apprenticeship, vocational education, university, etc. (respectively 36% vs 29% mode share for walking). In a similar vein, people at the lowest salary level walk a great deal more (41%) than those at the highest salary level (28%). Despite recent changes in urban lifestyles, basic economic power still appears to exert a "traditional" effect on mode choice. Furthermore, walking is negatively linked to the availability of a car. This is particularly relevant in cities such as Zurich or Geneva, where around half of all residents do not own a car.

Looking at mode shares

Walking represents around 44.5% of all stages of trips (Table 9.2). Of course, many of these stages will be combined with stages using other modes. While walking and car driving account for a majority of all transport stages, cycling and motorbike riding are marginal, and public transport only accounts for 13.2% of transport stages.

The situation regarding trips is very different from the analysis of the stages, because if a person walks 100 metres to his or her car, then the trip will only register as a car trip. This analysis of trips rests on the examination of the variable *Hauptverkehrsmittel* (main transport mode), which, as its name suggests, involves discounting the walking element usually included in the trip. Nevertheless, as Table 9.3 indicates, walking remains at a high level in Switzerland, at over 30% of all trips. Cycling increases slightly, from 4.8% of stages to 6.2% of trips, while personal motorised vehicles increase their share from around 36% to around 49%. The share of public transport remains essentially the same, at around 13%.

Table 9.2 Mode shares for transport stages (MRMT2010)

Mode	Frequency	Percentage
Walking	143,330	44.5
Cycling	15,420	4.8
Motorbike	4,051	1.3
Car	112,592	34.9
Public transport	42,489	13.2
Other	4,340	1.3
System	68	0.0
Total	322,292	100.0

Table 9.3 Mode shares for transport trips (MRMT2010)

Mode	Frequency	Percentage
Walking	66,091	30.4
Cycling	13,468	6.2
Motorised vehicle	106,807	49.1
Public transport	27,921	12.8
Other	2,994	1.4
Missing	68	0.0
Total	217,349	100.0

An explanation is that almost all people who take public transport have to walk more than 25 metres to get to the bus stop or train station. So it appears the 14% of so of walking that disappeared between the stages analysis and the trips analysis has been channelled into a slight increase in cycling and above all an increase in the use of motorised vehicles. It should not come as a surprise that many people need to walk more than 25 metres to get to their car. What is surprising, however, is that many people are able to use their car without having to walk in order to get to it.

Looking at distances

Table 9.4 shows the average distances for trips for each of the main transport modes. It can be seen that the average distance for walking is 900 metres. Unsurprisingly, this is a shorter distance than for other modes. However, looking at the average does not yield a precise indication of what most trips look like. This is because the distribution of distances covered does not follow a normal (Gaussian) distribution at all (Christie *et al.* 2015a). For walking, an indication of this skewed distribution can be obtained by looking at the median and at the standard deviation (SD), as illustrated in Table 9.5.

It can be seen that although the average distance covered while walking is 900 metres, the median distance is only 430 metres. This indicates that most walking distances are significantly shorter than 900 metres, but that a limited number are a lot greater, going up to a maximum of 60 km. Furthermore, computed values in SPSS for skewness and kurtosis were found to be very high. The main features of the distribution of walking distances are summed up in Table 9.5.

When investigating total distances covered each day, it makes more sense to use the stages rather than the trips data. This is because a Trip done by car might contain, for example, 200 metres of walking (to the car park), 9.5 km of car driving, then a further 300 metres of walking to the final destination. If the data used were from the Trip file, then the whole trip would merely register as 10 km of "car" and the information about the 500 metres of walking would be lost (as well as the distance covered by car being overestimated).

However, just looking at the average Stage gives a skewed vision of how much walking people do, because the data contains many small bouts of walking, some of them connected with other modes. For example, a typical day might involve a person walking to the tram stop in the morning, taking the tram, then walking to her office; then she might walk to a restaurant

Table 9.4 Average distance (km) per trip, per mode (MRMT2010)

On foot	Cycling	Motorbike	Car as a driver	Car as a passenger	Train	Bus/tram	Other
0.90	3.25	8.88	13.79	17.93	29.78	3.74	146.37

Table 9.5 Total distances (km) covered each day (Stages, Etappen, Etapes) in 2010

	N	Min.	Max.	Mean	SD	Median	Skewness	Kurtosis
Distance in km	143 330	0.03	60.00	0.9021	1.696	0.43	7.390	104.38

for lunch before walking back to work; then in the evening she may walk to the tram stop, take the tram and walk home; but then she may walk to the car park later in the evening to pick up her car.

Looking at individuals

Mode shares are interesting in their own right, and they form the basis of many decisions in the field of transportation research. However, they have drawbacks. Focusing on individuals is rare in the literature: often, while much is known about the proportion of trips done with different modes, nothing is known about the people who have done them. This is surprising, because if, say, five trips were done by a single person with four people staying at home, it is clearly not the same as if the five trips were done by five different people.

As has been described elsewhere (Ravalet *et al.* 2014; Christie *et al.* 2015a), walking is not normally distributed within the population of Switzerland. The curve representing kilometres walked on the reference day is strongly skewed towards the left, because a substantial proportion of the population walks very little or not at all on any given day. Indeed, by aggregating all walking trips onto the individuals present in a different part of the database, we found that around 12% of the sample stayed at home on the reference day. Perhaps more surprising, we also discovered that some 23% of the sample managed to drive a mechanised vehicle (usually a car), without doing any walking in a public space (it should be reminded that transport within buildings or facilities is not covered in MRMT2010, nor are any trips of under 25 metres).

Looking at conurbations

Because Switzerland is – among other things – a rather urban country, it is therefore interesting to look at the mode share of walking in the five largest urban areas in the country. In Table 9.6, it can be seen that Lausanne and Geneva have shares of walking that are comparable to those found in Basel, Bern and Zürich. This is an important finding, because many people believe that people in French-speaking areas walk less than in the German-speaking part of the country. A word of caution, however: levels of public transport use remain higher in the three Swiss-German cities than in Lausanne or Geneva.

Interestingly, levels of walking are slightly higher in Geneva than in Lausanne. This may be due to more efficient public transportation in Lausanne, which has two metro lines, whereas Geneva relies on a network of slow-moving trams. Another interesting comparison is the choice of walking when a car may be available as an alternative. The following table shows the

Table 9.6 Mode shares for walking in the five largest conurbations (MRMT2010)

Conurbation	Men	Women	All
Zurich	28%	33%	30%
Geneva	34%	40%	37%
Basel	29%	35%	32%
Bern	29%	34%	32%
Lausanne	28%	34%	31%
Average	30%	35%	32%

Table 9.7 Walking in relation to access to a car (MRMT2010)

Conurbation	Car always available	Car available after discussion	No car available	Average
Zurich	23%	29%	37%	25%
Geneva	29%	39%	55%	32%
Basel	25%	32%	44%	28%
Bern	26%	31%	37%	28%
Lausanne	23%	33%	49%	26%
Average	25%	31%	44%	27%

mode shares of walking, in relation to availability of a car. It can be seen in Table 9.7 that, above any difference between conurbations, it is access to a car that is associated with the likelihood of walking. There is a clear dose-response relationship between "Car always available" (25% mode share of walking") and "No car available" (44%) with "Car available after discussion" occupying an intermediate position. However, association does not mean causation. People tend to walk less if they have access to a car, but they do not necessarily walk less on a given day *because* they have access to a car. Indeed, they may have access to a car *because* they would rather not walk.

Where and why do people walk?

Some 85% of Switzerland's 8.5 million people live within the 50 statistically recognised conurbations, which, together, cover only 8% of the surface area of this nation. At the same time, it should not be forgotten that around two-thirds of Switzerland is mountainous. Given this unique concentration of adjacent mountainous and urban regions, we found it of interest to investigate whether the population of Switzerland does most of its walking in mountain regions (which include not only the Alps but also the Jura mountain range) or in the conurbations. A related question is whether most of the walking is motivated by leisure or other pursuits such as commuting or shopping.

Using the MRMT2010 database, we found that people living in city centres or in mountain resorts reported significantly more walking (approximately 2.4 km per day) than those living elsewhere: only 1.7 km per day in rural areas, for example (Christie *et al.* 2015b). Furthermore, people who walked more than 5 km on their reference day tended to live in city centres or mountain resorts, rather than suburban or rural areas.

Walking is common in all types of setting in Switzerland. The highest values are reached for mountain resorts (51% mode share for walking) and city centres (52%) (Table 9.8). Almost half of all walking trips take place in city centres and a further one-third in suburbs; only 3.6% are found in mountain resorts, even if this definition is stretched to include all peripheral rural communities.

The data suggest that less than a quarter of walking trips are motivated by leisure. The most common reasons given for walking are to access another transport mode (28%) or to return home (22%). Work and education together account for 13% of the walking trips, and shopping for a further 9%, as can be seen in Table 9.9. Less than a quarter of all walking trips in Switzerland are declared to be for leisure. Commuting, whether to work or to a place of study, accounted for 36%

Table 9.8 Proportions of walking trips in seven statistical regions (MRMT2010)

	City centre	Inner suburb	Outer suburb	Isolated town	Peri-urban rural	Peripheral rural	Alpine resort
% of all walking trips that occur in these areas	49.7	12.8	19.8	1.0	13.0	2.7	0.9
% of trips in this area attributable to walking (mode share)	52.0	41.0	39.3	43.4	35.8	43.2	50.9

Table 9.9 Given reasons for walking trips (MRMT2010)

	Access another transport mode	Commute to work	Commute to study	To shop	Access services	Return home	Leisure	Other
% of all walking trips	28.0	8.1	4.5	8.9	3.1	22.4	22.6	2.4

Table 9.10 Leisure activity at destination, among walking trips and walking trips identified as being related to leisure (MRMT2010)

	Visit friends or family	Bar, café, restaurant	Sport (jogging, football, etc.)	Dog walking	Hiking	Attend a match or event	Other
% of all walking trips	2.9	5.6	2.0	7.0	1.1	1.3	2.7
% of leisure walking trips	12.7	24.8	8.8	30.8	4.7	5.9	12.3

of walking trips. Mundane descriptions, such as accessing another transport mode (e.g. walking to a bus stop or car park) or returning home after an errand, accounted for over half of the walking trips.

A role for dog walking

Dog walking plays a role, albeit a minor one, in the walking scenario playing out in Switzerland (see Table 9.10). In MRMT2010, the precise description of this item is: "Non-sport outdoor activity (e.g. walking with the dog)", so it is possible that the data described here actually over-estimates the importance of dog walking within walking as a whole.

Conclusions

The fact that dog walking is only a minor contributor to walking in this country can be taken to mean one of two things. First, that walking from A to B is far more important than walking for leisure (including dog walking) and therefore public authorities should concentrate on helping people get to and from where they live, where they work and where they use public transport. Second, some thought should be given to promoting dog walking (and other leisure pursuits involving walking) by setting aside walking trails within urban and suburban areas.

Finally, there is nothing wrong in writing that both types of measure need to be pushed firmly up the political agenda, especially because walking for transport, walking for leisure – and also walking for exercise – are all worthwhile political goals from the public health, environmental and transportation policy points of view.

References

Christie, D., Ravalet, E. and Kaufmann, V. (2015a) 'Analysing the distribution of walking in the Swiss population'. Swiss Transport Research Conference, Ascona, Switzerland, April.

Christie, D., Ravalet, E. and Kaufmann, V. (2015b) 'Transport mode choice in alpine resorts in Switzerland'. Mountains of Our Future Earth, Perth, Scotland, October.

Millward, H., Spinney, J. and Scott, D. (2013) 'Active-transport walking behavior: destinations, durations, distances', *Journal of Transport Geography*, 28: 101–110.

Ravalet, E., Christie, D., Munafò, S. and Kaufmann, V. (2014) 'Analysis of walking in five Swiss cities: a quantitative and spatial approach'. Swiss Transport Research Conference, Ascona, Switzerland, May.

SFSO (2012) *Mobility and Transport Micro-census 2010* (MRMT2010), Neuchâtel and Bern, Switzerland: Swiss Federal Statistical Office and Swiss Federal Office for Spatial Development.

World Health Organization (WHO) (2016) *Physical Activity*. Available at: www.who.int/topics/physical_activity/en (accessed 1 April 2016).

10

Purposeful leisure mobilities

Reframing the walk to school

Debbie Hopkins and Sandra Mandic

Introduction

Walking is promoted as a low-carbon, active transport mode, contributing to positive environmental, social and health-related outcomes (Ogilvie *et al.* 2012). For this reason, walking is often a key element of health and exercise interventions, with varying degrees of success (Chillón *et al.* 2011). Walking has also been identified as an opportunity to increase physical activity among school students through "incidental exercise", frequently coupled with cycling under the banner of "active-transport-to-school" (ATS) (Stewart 2011). In this context, walking is framed as a mobility practice that requires fewer competencies in order to participate (e.g. compared to cycle skills or a driver's licence) and is without the requirement for mobility-enabling artefacts (e.g. bikes, helmets).

However, research has also suggested that walking can be constrained by distance (McDonald 2008; Stewart 2011). For instance, the likelihood of a student walking to school declines substantially when the distance between home and school is greater than 1.6 km (1 mile) (McDonald 2008). In recent decades, there have been well-documented declines in walking to school in the UK and the USA (McDonald 2008; Pooley *et al.* 2005). In New Zealand, average time spent walking per day has decreased from 10 minutes to 8 minutes, and walking to school has reduced from over 40% mode share in 1990, to less than 30% by 2014 for primary school students, and remained relatively stable at just over 25% for high school students (Ministry of Transport 2015). Distance to school is the most significant correlate of walking to school among New Zealand adolescents (Mandic *et al.* 2015a).

With an imperative to address transport-related carbon emissions (Sims *et al.* 2014), and rising levels of childhood obesity (Nishtar *et al.* 2016), walking to school has been identified as a powerful policy objective. Yet this chapter will argue that walking to school is usually framed as a transport mode, putting walking in competition with other motorised and non-motorised forms of transport and measured by traditional transportation metrics, including distance and travel time. We argue that this framing overlooks the additional opportunities and benefits that arise from walking, and that reframing the walk to school may contribute to greater success in ATS interventions. Thus we explore *purposeful leisure mobilities*; a conceptualisation of the co-benefits of walking, as both an objective (i.e. to travel between home and school) and a leisure space (e.g. for individual reflection and socialising). We develop our argument by presenting empirical material gathered through focus groups with high school students in Dunedin, New Zealand.

Framing is of interest to a range of academic disciplines, and is of particular significance where behaviour change is a core focus of the research. For instance, Avineri and Waygood (2013) examined the framing of information on transport-related carbon dioxide emissions, and found that the way information is framed and communicated impacts how the information is received, and subsequent behavioural choices. In the current chapter, framing is defined as the semantic restructuring of identical problems (Hallahan 1999). While we are not testing the way different frames are received, we propose that new framings of walking to school are required, that better align with insights from the mobilities literatures (e.g. Kellerman 2006; Cresswell 2006), and the articulation of walking to school found in the current research.

Research has suggested that perceptions of the physical and social environment may differ between people who walk for leisure and those who walk for transport (Cleland et al. 2008). For example, the accessibility of public transport, along with trust of many people in the neighbourhood, predicted increases in walking for leisure. Yet physical environment features (such as connectivity, pedestrian crossings and local traffic speed) predicted increases in walking for transport (Cleland et al. 2008). However, we question whether framing walking as diametrically opposed to "leisure" or "transport" is a useful distinction, particularly given the complexity and variability of everyday social activities (Sheller and Urry 2006).

The promotion of "walking for transport" is relatively well established (e.g. Giles-Corti et al. 2008; Hall et al. 2017), particularly in the health field (Cooper et al. 2003). Yet research has suggested that, for young adults, walking is not always perceived to be a transport mode, but rather an everyday activity (Hopkins and Stephenson 2015). Nevertheless, Hanson (2015) argues that traditional approaches to transport planning focus on saving time, which can mean that

> [The idea] that simply walking to a neighbourhood store might also be considered transportation and might even be considered more pleasurable than driving to a supermarket, can get lost in a fixation on speed and technologies that support and promote it.
>
> *(Hanson 2015: 3)*

And while we support this view, there still appears to be an underlying assumption that it is necessary to frame walking as transport to increased uptake, by identifying walking as a viable alternative to other transport modes (e.g. cycling, driving). This frame often results in walking being understood through quantifiable, automobility-derived terms of speed, geographic proximity of A to B, and derived demand.

In many ways, walking is the antithesis of the dominant, pace-driven mobility system. Walking, it has been suggested, 'is the best way to go more slowly than any other method that has ever been found' (Gros 2014). Similarly, walking has become intertwined with concepts of mindfulness, with claims that for children and young adults, the best practices of mindfulness are done in movement (Willard 2016). Furthermore, following the 'mobilities turn' within the social sciences (Sheller and Urry 2006), walking is about more than getting from A to B, it is about 'the political, cultural and aesthetic implications and resonance of these movements, the meanings ascribed to these movements, and the embodied experiences of mobility' (Cresswell and Merriman 2011: 11). From this point of departure, we now introduce the research methods used to examine practices of walking, before situating "purposeful leisure mobilities" as a frame to incentivise walking among high school students.

Methodology and methods

The research presented in this chapter adopts a moderate social constructionist position (Milton 1996), which 'acknowledges the power of individual, social and cultural forces, without denying the reality and power of external, physical and environmental forces' (Weber 2010: 332), and recognises the socially and culturally embedded values, meanings and definitions of the discourse as social constructs. This positionality is significant, as meanings (i.e. the meanings attached to walking) are constructed by human interactions and interpretations (Robson 2011). Moreover, this positionality is valuable when considering the role of framing, which has been identified as 'a critical activity in the construction of social reality because it helps shape the perspectives through which people see the world' (Hallahan 1999: 207).

This chapter uses the findings of an interdisciplinary, multi-method study on transport to school behaviours in Dunedin high schools; the Built Environment and Active Transport to School (BEATS) study (Mandic *et al.* 2015b, 2016), to explore alternative framings of walking to school as purposeful leisure. It draws from ten focus group sessions with high school students. The focus groups were used to elicit in-depth, nuanced social perceptions of walking to school. The focus group sessions allow the participants to interact with one another (Ritchie *et al.* 2014) and to develop lines of communication without researcher input. In this way, focus groups can be more closely related to real life, as 'participants are influencing, and influenced by others' (Krueger and Casey 2009: 7).

The research was undertaken in Dunedin, a small, coastal city on the lower South Island of New Zealand with a population of approximately 130,000 people. Dunedin is the seventh-largest New Zealand city by population, and second largest by territorial land area. Dunedin has a generally temperate climate, characterised by mild summers and cool winters, but with a range of microclimates across Dunedin suburbs. Much of Dunedin is built on the hills surrounding the harbour, and this topography represents a particular challenge for the promotion of walking.

Student focus groups

Students were recruited for the focus groups through their high school, as part of the Built Environment and Active Transport to School (BEATS) Study. High school students (age 13 to 18 years; school year 9 to 13) enrolled in any of Dunedin's 12 high schools were eligible to take part in this study. Gender and year group balance was sought but not always achieved, for the focus group sessions (Table 10.1). Five of the schools that participated were co-educational and another five were single-single sex (three girls' schools and two boys' schools). The focus groups were conducted on site at each of the ten schools, at a mutually agreeable time, and lasted for 60 minutes. Students received a reward for participation. Across the ten student focus groups, 54 students participated (Table 10.1). Full details of the BEATS Study research protocol, including the focus group research methodology is published elsewhere (Mandic *et al.* 2016).

Key themes for the student focus groups included: travel practices, motivations, barriers to alternative practices, perceptions of transport modes, stereotypes of transport users, and influences on travel behaviours (e.g. parents, teachers, peers). Sticky-note diagrams were also used to explore perceptions of transport modes and types of transport mode users. This activity gave voice to less confident participants of the student focus groups. It also provided a tangible focus for the participants to direct conversations and to stimulate discussion. Sticky-note activities can provide an additional data source and are a particularly valuable accompaniment to focus group sessions, especially with school-aged children and teenagers (e.g. Pawlowski *et al.* 2014).

Table 10.1 Student focus group details

Focus group code	Co-educational status of the school	Number of participants	Year groups included in session
SFG #01	Girls' school	2	9
SFG #02	Boys' school	6	9, 10, 12
SFG #03	Co-ed	11	9, 10, 11, 12,
SFG #04	Girls' school	5	9, 13
SFG #05	Boys' school	4	9
SFG #06	Co-ed	3	9, 11, 13
SFG #07	Co-ed	5	9, 13
SFG #08	Co-ed	5	9, 10, 13
SFG #09	Girls' school	9	9
SFG #10	Co-ed	4	9, 10, 13

The focus groups were digitally audio-recorded, fully transcribed into text documents and uploaded to Nvivo 10 qualitative analysis software. The transcriptions were explicitly explored for discussions relating to walking. A process of abstraction and interpretation was adopted, through which the researchers categorised the empirical material looking across and within key themes. The use of an iterative coding process allowed the researchers to gain a deeper, more nuanced view of the empirical material. Each focus group was examined collectively through 'whole group analysis' (Ritchie *et al.* 2014) then similarities and differences between the focus group sessions were examined.

In this chapter, we purposefully point to a traditional framing of walking, centred on timeliness and distance, contrasted with alternative conceptualisations of walking, that appear to be distinct from a "transport" lens, and instead prioritise alternative co-benefits from walking.

Research limitations

This chapter presents the findings of a small number of focus groups with a non-representative sample of high school students specific to the city of Dunedin, New Zealand. The findings are therefore illustrative of this specific context (e.g. people, time, place). While these findings provide a depth of insight into perceptions of walking among students, they cannot be interpreted as generalisable beyond the specific sample.

Findings

A traditional "transportation" framing of walking

A traditional framing of walking as transportation was evident through the focus groups, and the sticky-note activity. In particular, it became clear that walking was largely viewed to be viable only for students who live in close proximity to school. The quote below, from student focus group #1, underscores the perception of proximity as a measure for walkability to school. This traditional, and constraining, lens was articulated by many of the focus group participants and links together notions of proximity and time, which could be interpreted as perceptions of walking as a slow mode of transport.

B: Well, if they live close to the school [they might walk].

A: Somebody [who walks will] generally [be someone] who has enough time in the mornings to walk to school.

(Student Focus Group #1)

Time to walk to school featured prominently in the focus group sessions, and time was contingent on either by living close enough to the school, or by waking up early enough to have sufficient time to walk to school. An additional dimension for Dunedin is topography, where hills became a barrier to active modes of transport, often with greater influence than distance. This contrasts with other walking activities such as "walking for exercise". One participant was able to wake up early to walk for exercise with her mother, but was driven to school by car. This can signal the different meanings and expectations associated with types of walking: 'I usually go for walks in the mornings with my mum. It's like the time thing; it would take too long to get here if I did my exercise in the morning already' (Student Focus Group #4, Participant D). Many students spoke of concern for their physical appearance, which may contribute to an unwillingness to combine exercise with walking to school, or to perceive walking to school as a multi-functional activity.

The socio-economical contingency of proximity to school was also highlighted in some focus groups, particularly in schools located in wealthy suburbs. In some schools, participants stated that "rich people" will walk to school, as they can afford housing in high-cost suburbs. Thus, the ability to walk to school is predicated by house prices in suburbs close to the school. With rising house prices in cities across the globe, this could become more common, which could result in walking to school being associated with wealth and privilege.

INTERVIEWER: What sort of person walks to school?

D: A rich person.

A: You don't need to be, why?

D: Because if they live in [neighbourhood near school], they're probably rich.

B: True.

INTERVIEWER: So who else do you think might walk?

C: Pretty much people that live close by.

(Student Focus Group #5)

Walking was contrasted with the features of different transport modes. For instance, one participant compared walking to school with being driven to school. It was argued that, while being driven to school is more timely, there are exercise benefits from walking to school. 'Well, walking gives you exercise. But coming by car, yeah it gives you more time, but you won't do any exercise in school' (Student Focus Group #10, Participant A). This type of cost–benefit analysis between transport modes can often favour motorised forms of transport, due to deeply embedded social norms, particularly in industrialised countries, prioritising efficiency and speed over health benefits of exercise (Hanson 2015).

"Walking as leisure" framings

From the focus groups we found evidence of multiple, often competing "walking as leisure" framings, which, to varying degrees, challenge or complement the traditional transport frame of walking. Participants provided evidence of specific places for walking and the experience of walking through places within the city. These places were often viewed as pleasant environments to be enjoyed and experienced, for instance: 'I usually walk through the botanical gardens on the way home, because it's just nice to walk through the gardens, I quite like that' (Student Focus Group #8, Participant C). Or alternatively, these spaces were viewed as inaccessible to other transport modes; special places that opened access to different parts of the city: 'You can go through places that aren't accessible to cars, like alleyways and stuff for a short cut' (Student Focus Group #7, Participant D).

The experience of walking to school was discussed, with students identifying that 'there might be interesting things to look at on the way' (Student Focus Group #1, Participant A). This was also highlighted in another student focus group, who suggested that from walking 'You get a good awareness of your surroundings' (Student Focus Group #3, Participant B). This could suggest that there can be values to walking to school that go beyond health benefits and reduced carbon emissions, whereby walking enables students to learn about and experience the local environment. This type of enjoyment and experiential learning might be overlooked through the traditional transport framing.

Similarly, a perceived value of walking that moves beyond functional transport was articulated by participants: 'time to think' (Student Focus Group #5, Participant C), 'thinking time to prepare for the day' (Student Focus Group #7, Participant A) and 'quiet [time]' (Student Focus Group #4, Participant A) were all discussed by participants. These attributes underscore the leisurely values of walking that can be neglected by a speed/pace-focus. For these students, the speed of travel is less important than reflective opportunities enabled through time spent walking.

When asked why they enjoy walking, one student stated that walking is good 'because . . . you get yourself a good feeling and [after] you sit down or from here going to school, you feel happy' (Student Focus Group #6, Participant A). To extend this point further, another participant who regularly walks to school stated that he enjoys the walk. When pressed on this, he positioned the period of time that he spent walking as a transition between school and home; the demands on his attention and the stresses of home life and school life are temporarily suspended, and he says 'you've just got to walk':

It's just kind of a break from . . . [pause] kind of the transition between [being] at home. In the mornings things can be a little frantic, the organisation of everything. And then school, then when you actually have to start to knuckle down and get working. So it's quite nice [to walk]. There is nothing else really to do, you know what I mean? You've just got to walk.

(Student Focus Group #2, Participant C)

The independence and freedom of walking for high school students was also articulated in this research: 'You can also stop [at] places, like go to your friend's places or the supermarket while you're walking to school' (Student Focus Group #7, Participant B). This was reiterated by another student who stated that: '[Walking] might mean a bit of freedom. If you're earlier in the morning you can meet a friend on the way. On the way back you can stop at the dairy or whatever' (Student Focus Group #1, Participant A). And walking was identified as a social activity, undertaken in groups. While this is somewhat at odds with some earlier findings, it highlights the way walking interacts with individual or collective processes and norms: 'I normally find that when people walk to school they normally don't walk by themselves. If they have a long distance, they normally do it with a couple of friends' (Student Focus Group #2, Participant A).

Of the participants who currently walk to school, a range of benefits and opportunities were highlighted through the focus groups, which are listed below. These experiences identify more nuanced meanings of walking, which go beyond the function of travel from A to B:

- It's just nice in the morning, I just like it. (Student Focus Group #3, Participant F)
- Not relying on your parents to take you to school. (Student Focus Group #3, Participant D)
- It [walking] saves other people going around after you. And it passes time. It's a good time-killer if you are bored. I think it's quite rewarding knowing that you've been out. It's quite nice. (Student Focus Group #6, Participant B)
- The endorphins, they make you happy . . . people might enjoy the fresh air. (Student Focus Group #6, Participant B)
- I quite like walking, and seeing everything. Sometimes, if I have some money, I might buy something from the Four Square [a local food store]. (Student Focus Group #6, Participant A)
- You can do things like listen to music on your iPod. (Student Focus Group #7, Participant C)

Purposeful leisure mobilities

In this chapter, we have presented empirical research examining the travel to school practices of high school students in Dunedin, New Zealand. Our findings suggest that traditional framings of walking construct spatial and temporal barriers to walking to school, often through comparisons with other, motorised, transport modes. Thus, we suggest that barriers to walking are framed within traditional transport discourses. However, we also highlight the articulated benefits of walking that transition away from this perspective, and present a conceptualisation of walking to school that relates more closely to leisure mobilities. The purposeful nature of these mobilities lies in the directed travel between places (i.e. from home to school). We therefore propose that "purposeful leisure" could present a new framing that could be beneficial for the promotion of walking as part of an active transport promotion intervention.

The traditional focus of transport researchers on specific categories of travel (e.g. commuting, leisure, business), or spheres (e.g. walking, driving, or travelling virtually) treats these movements as separate and self-contained (Sheller and Urry 2006). Instead, Sheller and Urry (2006: 213) argue that 'the complex patterning of people's varied and changing social activities' should be the starting point. While the research presented in this chapter focuses on the purpose of travel to school, it illuminates the range of ways that walking is experienced by high school students and suggests that reframing the walk as purposeful leisure rather than transport, could expose more nuanced ways that mobility is performed.

Prioritised, hegemonic conceptualisations of "speed" can mean that walking will be adopted when it is perceived to be a viable alternative to other, usually motorised, modes. Yet in this research, it is clear that for some high school students, negotiating the urban space, using short cuts and accessing new parts of the city, contributes to the attractiveness of walking and experiences of the city. This finding aligns with Cresswell, who states; 'the urban landscape provides a vast labyrinth of streets, sidewalks, parks, short cuts and alleyways, which we inhabit by walking, by getting lost, by idling away the hours', and through which the walker has the freedom 'to pick and choose the spaces he or she crosses, the ability to take short cuts and to refuse the directions offered by the text of the city' (Cresswell 2006: 213). Our participants clearly articulated experiences of Dunedin city that were gained through walking to school; routes of particular meaning, taking short cuts, and enjoying nature, that would be missed if other modes were used. The *experiences* of moving between A and B are often neglected (Middleton 2011), and this is also true of children's experiences of travelling to school. This research exposes both experiences of walking as space for quiet, reflection and preparation, but it also highlights the sustained physical and emotional sensations, feelings of happiness and positivity, after walking.

Interestingly, we found that the sticky-note exercise tended to reflect traditional framings of walking, through which the participants identified people who would walk as primarily living close to school, or having no other option. This could be due to the group norms reflecting this perspective, but also due to the need to more fully articulate the "walking as leisure" framing through oral communication. However, a financial lens on walking to school was identified through the sticky notes that had not emerged through the focus group; the notion that walking is a transport mode for those unable to afford bus or car transport costs. This contradicts earlier discussions of house prices and wealth, which can be associated to close proximity to school in some areas. This thereby highlights the nuanced, place-based and localised perceptions that will draw from specific geographic, socio-cultural and socio-economic contexts in determining perceptions of walking to school. Nevertheless, a "walking as purposeful leisure" framing may help to overcome any stigma attached to these perception, and could contribute to interventions to increase walking to school among high school students.

These findings present a new lens through which to view the benefits of walking to school; benefits that could inform future interventions. By talking in relative terms across transport modes, and through discourses of speediness, walking may be conceptually demoted, as a socially constructed 'slow' and/or 'inconvenient' transportation mode. Future research should examine alternative framings for ATS interventions and promotional activities that adopt the spectrum of co-benefits gained from walking to school. We argue that framing walking for transport as "purposeful leisure" may overcome some barriers. Further empirical studies are required to test this proposition.

References

Avineri, E. and Waygood, E.O.D. (2013) 'Applying valence framing to enhance the effect of information on transport-related carbon dioxide emissions', *Transportation Research Part A: Policy and Practice*, 48: 31–38.

Chillón, P., Evenson, K.R., Vaughn, A. and Ward, D.S. (2011) 'A systematic review of interventions for promoting active transportation to school', *International Journal of Behavioral Nutrition and Physical Activity*, 8(10). DOI: 10.1186/1479–5868–8–10.

Cleland, V.J., Timperio, A. and Crawford, D. (2008) 'Are perceptions of the physical and social environment associated with mothers' walking for leisure and for transport? A longitudinal study', *Preventive Medicine*, 47(2): 188–193.

Cooper, A.R., Page, A.S., Fister, L.J. and Qahwaji, D. (2003) 'Commuting to school: are children who walk more physically active?', *American Journal of Preventive Medicine*, 25(4): 273–276.

Cresswell, T. (2006) *On the Move: Mobility in the Modern Western World*, New York: Routledge.

Cresswell, T. and Merriman, P. (2011) *Geographies of Mobilities: Practices, Spaces, Subjects*, Farnham, Surrey: Ashgate Publishing.

Giles-Corti, B., Knuiman, M., Timperio, A., Van Niel, K., Pikora, T.J., Bull, F., Shilton T. and Bulsara M. (2008) 'Evaluation of the implementation of a state government community design policy aimed at increasing local walking: design issues and baseline results from RESIDE, Perth Western Australia', *Preventive Medicine*, 46(1): 46–54.

Gros, F. (2014) *A Philosophy of Walking*, London: Verso.

Hall, C.M., Le-Klähn, D.-T. and Ram, Y. (2017) *Tourism, Public Transport and Sustainable Mobility*. Bristol: Channel View.

Hallahan, K. (1999) 'Seven models of framing: implications for public relations', *Journal of Public Relations Research*, 11(3): 205–242.

Hanson, S. (2015) 'Foreword 1: Transportation geographies and mobilities studies: towards collaboration', in J. Cidell and D. Prytherch (eds), *Transport, Mobility and the Production of Urban Space*, New York: Routledge, pp. 3–11.

Hopkins, D. and Stephenson, J. (2015) *Generation Y Mobilities: Full Report*, Centre for Sustainability, University of Otago, New Zealand. Available at: https://ourarchive.otago.ac.nz/bitstream/handle/10523/5641/Hopkins%26Stephenson_2015_GenYMobilities_FullReport.pdf?sequence=1&isAllowed=y.

Kellerman, A. (2006) *Personal Mobilities*, Abingdon, Oxon: Routledge.

Krueger, R.A. and Casey, M.A. (2009) *Focus Groups: A Practical Guide for Applied Research*, 4th edn, London: Sage Publications.

Mandic, S., Leon de la Barra, S., García Bengoechea, E., Moore, T., Middlemiss, M., Stevens, E., Flaherty, C., Williams, J. and Skidmore, P. (2015a) 'Personal, social and environmental correlates of active transport to school among adolescents in Otago, New Zealand', *Journal of Science and Medicine in Sport*, 18(4): 432–437.

Mandic, S., Mountfort, A., Hopkins, D., Flaherty, C., Williams, J., Brook, E., Wilson, G. and Moore, A. (2015b) 'Built environment and active transport to school (BEATS) Study: multidisciplinary and multi-sector collaboration for physical activity promotion', *Retos*, 28: 197–202.

Mandic, S., Williams, J., Moore, A., Hopkins, D., Flaherty, C., Wilson, G. García Bengoechea, E. and Spence, J.C. (2016) 'Built environment and active transport to school (BEATS) study: protocol for a cross-sectional study', *BMJ Open*. Available at: http://bmjopen.bmj.com/content/6/5/e011196.full.

McDonald, N.C. (2008) 'Children's mode choice for the school trip: the role of distance and school location in walking to school', *Transportation*, 35: 23–35.

Middleton, J. (2011) 'Walking in the city: the geographies of everyday pedestrian practices', *Geography Compass*, 5(2): 90–105.

Milton, K. (1996) *Environmentalism and Cultural Theory: Exploring the Role of Anthropology in Environmental Discourse*, New York: Routledge.

Ministry of Transport (2015) '25 years of New Zealand travel: New Zealand household travel 1989–2014', *Wellington: Ministry of Transport*. Available at: www.transport.govt.nz/assets/Uploads/Research/Documents/25yrs-of-how-NZers-Travel.pdf.

Nishtar, S., Gluckman, P. and Armstrong, T. (2016) 'Ending childhood obesity – a time for action', *The Lancet*, 387(10021): 825–827.

Ogilvie, D., Bull, F., Cooper, A., Rutter, H., Adams, E., Brand, C., Ghali, K., Jones, T., Mutrie, N., Powell, J., Preston, J., Sahlqvist, S. and Song, Y. (2012) 'Evaluating the travel, physical activity and carbon impacts of a "natural experiment" in the provision of new walking and cycling infrastructure: methods for the core module of the iConnect study', *BMJ Open*, 2: 1–13.

Pawlowski, C.S., Tjørnhøj-Thomsen, T., Schipperijn, J. and Troelsen, J. (2014) 'Barriers for recess physical activity: a gender specific qualitative focus group exploration', *BMC Public Health*, 14: 639.

Pooley, C.G., Turnbull, J. and Adams, M., (2005) 'The journey to school in Britain since the 1940s: continuity and change', *Area*, 37(1): 43–53.

Ritchie, J., Lewis, J., McNaughton Nicholls, C. and Ormston, R. (2014) *Qualitative Research Practice: A Guide for Social Science Students and Researchers*, 2nd edn, London: Sage.

Robson, C. (2011) *Real World Research*, Chichester, West Sussex: John Wiley & Sons.

Sheller, M. and Urry, J. (2006) 'The new mobilities paradigm', *Environment and Planning A*, 38(2): 207–226.

Sims, R., Schaeffer, R., Creutzig, F., Cruz-Núñez, X., D'Agosto, M., Dimitriu, D., Figueroa Meza, M.J., Fulton, L., Kobayashi, S., Lah, O., Mckinnon, A., Newman, P., Ouyang, M., Schauer, J.J., Sperling, D. and Tiwari, G. (2014) 'Transport', in O. Edenhofer, R. Pichs-Madruga, Y. Sokona, E. Farahani, S. Kadner, K. Seyboth, A. Adler, I. Baum, S. Brunner, P. Eickemeier, B. Kriemann, J. Savolainen, S. Schlömer, C. Von Stechow, T. Zwickel and J.C. Minx (eds), *Climate Change 2014: Mitigation of Climate Change. Contribution of Working Group III to the Fifth Assessment Report of the Intergovernmental Panel on Climate Change*, Cambridge: Cambridge University Press.

Stewart, O. (2011) 'Findings from research on active transportation to school and implications for safe routes to school programs', *Journal of Planning Literature*, 26(2): 127–150.

Weber, E.U. (2010) 'What shapes perceptions of climate change?', *Wiley Interdisciplinary Reviews: Climate Change*, 1: 332–342.

Willard, C. (2016). *Growing Up Mindful: Essential Practices to Help Children, Teens and Families Find Balance, Calm and Resilience*, Louisville, CO: Sounds True Inc.

11

Spiking

The quest for challenge and meaning among hikers

Ron McCarville and Chantel Pilon

Introduction: the appeal of walking

Walking represents one of our most beloved outdoor recreational activities. This is not surprising. It offers the opportunity to disconnect and reflect; to experience beauty; to focus on the task that walking represents. Thoreau, an unapologetic walking advocate, once observed: 'I cannot preserve my health and spirits, unless I spend four hours a day at least, – and it is commonly more than that, – sauntering through the woods and over the hills and fields, absolutely free from all worldly engagements' (Thoreau 1910 [1862]: para 6).

Thoreau's view very much represents the "reflection and repose" model of hiking behaviour. Consistent with Thoreau's musings, a recent study found, that walkers 'reported feeling detached from more complex problems that exist in other areas of life and tended to contrast the experience of walking . . . to describe a much reduced level of cognitive effort, and a release from responsibilities' (Crust *et al.* 2011: 253).

This detachment may be enhanced when the walking takes place in natural settings. As Thoreau reminded us, there exists often profound connection between the walker and nature (Chhetri *et al.* 2002; Hull and Stewart 1995; Korpela and Kinnunen 2011). From the early primitivists, like Rousseau and Lord Byron, or transcendentalists, like Thoreau and Emerson, we have celebrated the unique bond between walking and the natural environment. It seems that interaction with the nature can be profoundly positive for the walker. As Emerson (1995: 6–7) once confided, 'in wilderness I find something more dear and connate than in streets or villages . . . Its effect is like that of a higher thought or a better emotion coming over me'.

Choosing a path

The popularity of walking may also be enhanced by its inherent flexibility. An extensive constraint literature suggests that leisure participation often requires negotiation on the part of hopeful participants. Participants must negotiate any number of constraints (e.g. lack of time, fitness levels or suitable companions) in order to engage in most leisure activities (Coble *et al.* 2003; Little 2002; Walker and Virden 2005). One of the great appeals of walking is the flexibility it offers. Walkers may choose from an array of distances, terrains and conditions. They may explore their own back yard or may travel the globe to experience hikes organized and coordinated by others. Their journeys may take place over several months on iconic routes like the Appalachian Trail, El Camino or the Milford Track, or may be completed before lunch.

Flexibility offered by walking is noteworthy for two reasons. First, we know that walkers and hikers will self-select settings that best meet their own particular requirements (Backlund and Stewart 2012). There is a profoundly "do-it-yourself" aspect to walking and hiking, enabling participants to choose those activities and locations that match their own interests and capacities. They can, both literally and figuratively, select the path that best suits them. Second, this flexibility helps participants explore, express and develop sense of self. They can choose from activities, challenges and locations that meet their own interests and capabilities. They may pursue familiarity or novelty. They may seek out or avoid crowds. They may focus on exertion or relaxation. These choices help hikers, the focus of this chapter, to discover and express their own particular sense of self (Kelly 1983). As their preferences are expressed, notions of self are challenged or affirmed.

Hikers' exploration of self and settings may play out in a variety of intriguing ways. For example, we tend to think of hiking in ways consistent with the pensive image promoted by proponents like Emerson and Thoreau. For them, hiking was very much the pursuit of tranquility and reflection. But what about when reduced stress is not what motivates the hiker? What if the intended goal is one of inducing rather than reducing stress?

The practice of spiking

We use the term "spiking" here to describe the phenomenon in which traditionally non-competitive activities (like hiking) are approached with a competitive spirit. Spiking, a term derived from "sport hiking" exists when: 1) the primary motive is overcoming a challenge; 2) the degree of difficulty is enhanced by self-imposed conditions; and 3) specific goals are set such that these conditions render goal attainment uncertain. While all hikes may be challenging, the goal of spiking is to enhance and even celebrate that challenge.

The venue offered by the Grand Canyon offers a case in point. It is becoming increasingly popular for hikers to traverse iconic portions of the canyon. The challenge emerges from establishing, in advance, a goal distance especially over difficult terrain. For example, the "rim to rim" challenge is being widely promoted within the hiking community at the Canyon. Typically hikers arrange being dropped off at the north rim then hike back to the south rim. This rim-to-rim effort covers approximately 24 miles and the vertical drop/climb is about 9,000 feet. It represents considerable challenge. A recent magazine article devoted to this rim-to-rim hike asked 'Looking for a hike that'll kick your a★★ and demand months of training?' (Yeomans 2015). This title speaks eloquently of the spiking perspective. It is one that promises and inherently celebrates discomfort and even pain.

Not surprisingly, many sources recommend that hikers allocate two to three days to complete this very difficult hike. However, the spiking spirit is both ingenious and diabolical. Enthusiasts continue to add to the challenge. Much of the rim-to-rim coverage is highlighting ever more aggressive time limits for completing this route. Many of those who complete the challenge report doing so in a single day. But the challenge continues to grow. Recently, a small group has begun to toy with the idea of hiking rim to rim to rim. They hike from one rim to the other, then return to their starting point. This is twice the rim-to-rim distance.

In an issue of *Outside* magazine, Arnold (2013) described how she and friends undertook the rim-to-rim-to-rim hike. In doing so, the challenge posed by the hike was very much on her mind. She noted that the canyon hike was selected because it promised 'tough climbs and descents, and bragging rights' (Arnold 2013: para. 7). She understood and welcomed the challenge the terrain at the canyon offered. Indeed, she actively sought that challenge. Most noteworthy, she and her friends set aside only a single day to traverse the Canyon. Not only had they selected a difficult route and a gruelling distance, they had added the additional constraint of time. Their efforts to manipulate and increase the difficulty of the task seemed very much an exercise in spiking. It is through such stories that the spiking goals and limits are set and extended.

Spiking as a tourism opportunity

Spikers, as a tourism sub-group, represent considerable potential for tourism sites now struggling for attention. We typically think of tourists being drawn to sites that are noteworthy for their positive attributes. Scenic beauty, calm weather patterns, favourable terrain – all can render a site compelling for the tourist. While this is helpful for providers blessed with idyllic settings, it is problematic for those who hope to promote "lesser sites". Not all locations have obvious appeal to the visitor.

However, spiking excursions may seek anything but the ideal. The goal is to seek out challenge; and (perhaps) to rejoice in the discomfort that the challenge might bring. Spiking routes and settings garner popularity, at least partly, as a result of their inhospitality. This seems an important insight for tourism providers.

For the spiker, any site can be rendered desirable. Any supposed (setting-based) vice can be rendered virtuous. For the purposes of spiking, sites can be promoted for the adverse conditions they offer. No site is too hot, cold, dry, wet, flat or mountainous. All may be prized for the challenge they offer. Any location will do, as will any time of year.

Death Valley, as its name implies, is a region known for its inhospitable terrain and weather. Yet it now hosts world-famous foot races ranging from 10 km events to a 135-mile-long ultra-marathon. The challenging conditions found there have been used to promote the area to tourists, from around the world, seeking a challenge. It isn't a coincidence that they promote one of their events as the 'world's toughest foot race' (Kostman 2014). In these ways, truly difficult and inhospitable regions can become iconic. As a result, tourism providers may benefit from the aggressive promotion of "less than ideal" locations as spiking destinations. Those destinations can benefit from promoting site characteristics that are traditionally ignored or even avoided.

In order to capitalize on the opportunity that spiking represents, providers might first consider some of the dynamics that guide and direct spiking behaviours. These dynamics can then inform subsequent planning and promotional efforts. We begin with the importance of challenge. Hiking is inherently challenge-based. Spiking simply makes that challenge more explicit.

The role played by challenge

Challenge is at the heart of all spiking pursuits. There may be variations in levels of difficulty, formality, uncertainty, and/or risk within these pursuits, but the appeal of challenge is constant. Spiking can be as simple as walking to the corner store faster than was the case the day before. It can be as complex as climbing Mount Everest without supplemental oxygen. Although variations in the characteristics of the pursuit exist, each individual's motivations to engage in a pursuit are the same. Each individual seeks to overcome a challenge.

There exists, in the hiking community, a profound and longstanding appreciation of challenge and adversity. For some, at least, there seems an implicit understanding that demanding challenges are more noteworthy. A "thru hike" (a continuous effort extending from the beginning to the end of a long-distance trail) might garner more prestige than would a day hike. A hike over difficult terrain is more memorable than one completed with ease. Many hikers already embrace and even celebrate challenge and hardship.

It is important to note that it is the notion of challenge, not hardship per se, that is the essence of spiking. Hardship may be an attribute of certain spiking activities, but overcoming a challenge seems the more central interest. Organizers understand the importance of challenge as they design and label events intended to appeal to the hiking and running communities (Prahalad and Ramaswamy 2004).

Another event hopes to attract participants by labelling its stages as "The Blood", a vertical kilometre (5 km with 1,000 m of elevation gain); "The Sweat", (a 55-km ultramarathon with 2,500 m of elevation gain); and "The Tears", (a 20-km jaunt on beautiful, rolling single track) (Trail Maniacs 2015). Note how names are selected to highlight the challenge the event represents.

The appeal of achieving balance

Challenge alone seems insufficient in creating meaning for the spiker. If that were the case, all spikers would set impossible goals that offered challenge after challenge. Instead challenge is best enjoyed when the participant is able to overcome that challenge. Consequently, spiking might best be represented by what Csikszentmihalyi (1990) labelled a "flow" experience. Flow is an immersive experience in which the participant becomes one with the activity. Attention is focused and the participant may even become unaware of the passage of time.

In Csikszentmihalyi's (1990) terms, spiking is a quest for balance. The participant is seeking a balance between challenge and skill. The more difficult it is to negotiate the balance, the more profound and meaningful the experience. As one high-altitude mountain climber observed,

> The climber likes difficult pitches, even those which tax him to the utmost, but in such cases, it is as pleasant for him to feel safe, in his heart of hearts, as it is unpleasant to go beyond his resources, to run a risk, or to incur some climbing hazard.
>
> *(Mitchell 1983: 157)*

The goal is one of overcoming, through the application of skill and effort, whatever challenge awaits.

The do-it-yourself nature of spiking permits hikers to choose challenges/parameters that best meet their personal skills and goals. The hiker may manipulate distance, time, terrain, time of year, or even equipment used. Travellers may use only self-generated power to move forward or ultra-light hikers may choose travel with only the bare minimum of equipment in order to reduce pack weight. In this way, hikers can best express their own values, abilities and skill sets.

Observations and suggestions

Challenge and the potential to overcome that challenge stir the heart of the spiking community. This represents considerable opportunity for tourism providers. Locations and venues that can promise challenge will gain the attention of the spiking community. In preparing this chapter, we identified activities and campaigns that have become popular with spikers. We offer a few resulting insights here to aid tourism providers in promoting events and locations to the spiking community.

Become collectable

Tourism activities, events and places are not unlike crockery or spoons in that they are imminently collectable. They often appear on lists that people seek to undertake. Spiking choices seem to lend themselves to such lists (often referred to as "bucket lists"). Bucket lists represent checklists of experiences or achievements that hikers hope to accomplish during their lifetime. While these lists are highly individual in nature, they often emerge from the input from the media. *Backpacker Magazine*, for example, promoted on its cover 'The 101 places to go . . . before you die' (Backpacker Magazine 2015). Such coverage places both a sense of importance and urgency to visiting those locations. *National Geographic* published an 'Ultimate Adventure Bucket List' containing twenty trips from twenty of the world's most fit individuals (Siber 2012). Such lists inevitably generate interest among hikers generally, and spikers in particular.

Consider one of the *National Geographic* "Ultimate Lists" provided by Jennifer Pharr Davis. Pharr Davis is the current record holder for the fastest completion of the Appalachian Trail. Her biography in the article also notes that she has completed the Pacific Crest Trail (2,663 miles). Her "to do" list includes the Continental Divide Trail, referring to it as one of the most scenic and memorable routes on earth. This characterization will undoubtedly encourage others to sample or complete that same trail.

Of even greater importance to spikers, we suspect, is that Pharr Davis's plan to complete the Continental Divide Trail is motivated by an express desire to become a 'triple crowner' (Siber 2012: para. 2). This third hike is primarily intended to "complete the set". The completed set is much coveted among long-distance hikers because of the challenge it represents. Lists and suggestions such as these are noteworthy, because they not only suggest the importance of activities and places, but they also add credibility to the notion of these challenges. They acknowledge and even celebrate the importance of undertaking these endeavours. In the *National Geographic* example, they even suggest where and how the challenge might be undertaken. In these ways, media can create and maintain demand for an event or location. They help the places and activities become collectable.

While these examples point out the obvious power of mainstream media, for many tourism providers, media can also be problematic. It is often difficult to earn the gaze of mainstream media. Lesser locations may be neglected by traditional outlets and fail to share in the spotlight compared to their more iconic counterparts. In the case of spiking, however, the influence of mainstream media seems to pale beside the power of the blog.

Leverage the blog

When hikers engage in activities that offer meaningful challenge, where skill can be applied, where balance can be "earned", they often wish to share that experience. The internet has enabled hikers to tell the story of their adventures. We were particularly interested in blogging activities in our exploration of spiking behaviours. The term blog, a shortened form of "weblog" (Blood 2002), describes a web-based journal that is available to the public. A blog constitutes a 'compilation and construction of lists of relative links, personal commentary, observations and filtering of pertinent web content by the website author' (Blood 2002: 39). Blogs tend to offer first-hand accounts of those activities that the participants found meaningful and worthwhile. They represent a helpful and unvarnished record of many spiking endeavours, often providing testimonial support for locations and events.

Spikers seem very much interested in telling their stories. Participants may seek validity from other adherents and storytelling is one way to do that. Atkinson (2008) observed that many feel compelled to tell their story to help garner distinction within what he called the "community of suffering". By telling their story, participants may feel both recognized and valued.

These testimonials are all the more important because of the types and amount of information they can provide. Kaye (2010) notes that bloggers bring together information from the traditional media, insider knowledge, and the blogger's own expertise to create their blogs. Blogs provide access to various websites, news and events pages, and social media outlets related to the leisure activity of interest. Furthermore, these resources are becoming increasingly interactive. Individuals are encouraged to share their own stories on websites, or post photos of their adventures on Facebook, Twitter and/or Instagram. Thus, connections are built, stories are told and behaviours are influenced.

Within the context of tourism-related blogs, the bloggers bring activities, sites, events and even hosts to life. Readers from all over the world can engage in meaningful interactions with others who might enjoy the same activities, who might enjoy visiting the same locations. More than that, bloggers can provide first-hand knowledge of both the activity and the location in which it took place. Their comments can celebrate and extol the virtues of the place and the people. In this way, storytelling within the spiking community may breed awareness and even iconic status for a wide variety of tourism locations. Such notoriety may in turn attract more mainstream media outlets.

In these ways, spiking enthusiasts may promote, guide and direct the spiking efforts of others. For the tourism provider, such blogging represents an opportunity. These blogs may serve a "self-perpetuating" role in that they highlight both the activity and its various merits. Tourism providers and locations can also guide and direct spiking and tourism activities by becoming part of the online community. We have noted how spiking represents participants' own efforts to enhance the experience. Providers are increasingly accepting that same role. In doing so, they are taking on an active role in supporting and perpetuating spiking efforts. The example of Grouse Mountain, described below, offers a case in point.

Make it social – the Grouse Mountain example

Grouse Mountain in Vancouver, British Columbia, Canada, often referred to as "Mother Nature's Stairmaster", offers a 2.9-km hiking trail straight up its face. Called the "Grouse Grind", the trail boasts an elevation gain of 2,800 feet (853 m). The trail is known for the demands it places on the hiker, yet, despite the hardship the trail offers, hikers travel from around the world in order to take on that challenge.

Organizers have been very intentional in promoting this location for hikers. They have, for example, embraced the difficulty of the trail by creating the "Grind Timer". The Timer, a device that times each individual run, adds a degree of difficulty to the pursuit. In this sense, they are adding a spiking component to hiking the trail. They are adding the pressure of time to the activity.

It is important to note that, not only have organizers provided a way to time each run, but they have made these times visible to others. Individual run results are available online and in print, and the name and time of each finisher appears on the monitor at the chalet on the mountain. Further, Grouse Grind course records are visible on the main page of the Grouse Mountain website. The public display of one's performance adds an even greater sporting atmosphere to the endeavour. Records are set, performance is noted, and goals are pursued. In this way, participant engagement is enhanced and social connections are developed.

Grouse Mountain organizers also maintain an easy-access, user-friendly website keeping this community of hikers connected. They provide a hub for community member blogs, an up-to-date news and events page, and even a live feed that shows members what is happening on the mountain in that moment (Grouse Mountain 2015). They unite their members using social media outlets; their Twitter page – @grousemountain (with an impressive 16,000+ followers), Instagram page – GrouseMountain (6,000+ followers), and Facebook page – Grouse Mountain Resort (30,000+ likes). The Facebook page provides hikers with a discussion board, and a place to post photo albums and attach uploads to share information.

Ameliorate risk

Any discussion of spiking activity must acknowledge the dark shadow posed by risk and personal injury. Recall the Arnold (2013) example offered above. The author and two friends travelled rim to rim to rim at the Grand Canyon in a single day. This self-described bucket-list adventure covered 42 miles, including a combined ascent/descent of just over 9,000 feet. This spiking activity was undertaken despite warnings from the US Park Service, caretakers of the trails over which the trio travelled. It is noteworthy that current Park Service literature advises hikers like Arnold not to attempt completing that journey in a single day. Yet that is exactly what they sought to do.

The challenge undertaken by these hikers can be dangerous to the point of being life-threatening, yet their story is being promoted in a popular outdoor magazine. This seems problematic. It is all the more problematic when it is only one of perhaps thousands of typical efforts that populate the internet and media of all sorts. Currently, there exist dozens of websites, blogs, YouTube videos, and articles highlighting hikers' efforts to complete the same task each year. They each share how they were able to create then negotiate a challenge worth celebrating.

We note, though, that while many of the posted blogs and stories fuel interest in potentially dangerous activities, the hiking community also offers guidance to its members as they seek out spiking opportunities. For example, the official Grouse Grind website bluntly states 'Keep in mind that there is a wide range of mountaintop trails that might better suit the average hiker' (Grouse Mountain 2015).

Providers must ponder how spikers might be encouraged to operate within safe parameters; to seek the trails and challenges that best suit their skill set. Protection motivation theory suggests that choices are influenced by the hikers' appraisal of the threat and their own capacity to handle that threat. The greatest danger exists when hikers believe the threat is lower than is actually the case *and* that their capacity to meet the threat is greater than is actually the case.

Virtual and media-based communities seem to represent an excellent opportunity to reduce this mismatch. Those reporting these experiences often focus on the difficulty of the event, the hardship they endured, the means used to overcome those hardships. All seem useful in helping hikers assess both the threat involved and the skills required to successfully negotiate those threats. As suggested above, they may also provide guidance on levels and types of preparation required to successfully negotiate the challenge created by the task they have set for themselves. For example, the authors have noted that efforts to report experiences like hiking the canyon are also filled with advice and guidance for the reader. There seems considerable mentorship capacity in these various blogs and posts. Tourism efforts to encourage spiking might benefit from parallel efforts to aid in the safe completion of the activities.

Points to ponder

Spiking efforts may emerge in any setting. While the term "spiking" is derived from a particular sub set of activities (sport hiking), it can occur when any traditionally non-competitive activity is approached with a competitive spirit. This spirit has been with us for a very long time. Indeed, it has been an integral part of leisure activities for centuries. One notable example is that of the traditional sport of fox hunting. In rural Britain, foxes were routinely "controlled" because of the threat they posed to small farming operations. Through the years, farmers had trapped and killed foxes efficiently and without much fanfare. For them, the control of foxes was a necessity and not an object of sport.

However, privileged fox hunters applied a spiking spirit to the hunt for the fox. They intentionally applied rules to render fox hunting more sporting/difficult. They actively sought to render the outcome (capture of the fox) more uncertain and infinitely more challenging in order to enhance the hunt's leisure potential.

> In foxhunting, humans do not engage the fox quietly, efficiently, and unobtrusively . . . they announce their presence to the countryside, they expect (and require) the fox to flee, to be difficult to find and capture. They willingly obey rules that limit the possibilities [of success] . . . they expect that foxes will often escape.
>
> *(Marvin 2007: 93)*

This seems a striking example of spiking. The fox hunters sought and created challenge and uncertainty, where farmers, by comparison, sought to reduce both. In spiking, the goal is one of challenge and even disruption to predictable and manageable activity patterns. While it may be an essentially unsettling process, we know that such disruption can 'paradoxically provide greater meaning and a sense of personal achievement' to participants (Crust *et al.* 2011: 15).

Even profoundly non-competitive pursuits like birding have spiking potential. For example, birders might set a goal for new sightings on a given outing. They might wish to identify new species, numbers of birds or hear specific songs. By way of example, the birding community has organized an annual 'World Series of Birding', in which participants set and seek to achieve a variety of 'bests' (World Series of Birding 2015). Created in 1984, the annual World Series of Birding is now the oldest and longest-running bird competition in the world (World Series of Birding 2015). Starting with 13 teams in its first year, this prestigious event currently attracts thousands of participants, ranging from novice birders to experts with decades of experience in the field (World Series of Birding 2015). Held on the second Saturday in May each year, teams (with a minimum of three members) are required to tally as many species of birds by sight or sound in a 24-hour period throughout the state of New Jersey. In other words, participants are constrained by time and location in their pursuit of very specific goals.

Spiking seems an apt term for the series and its many elements. If the spiking spirit can be applied to birding or the culling of foxes, we suspect it can be applied to almost any setting. We acknowledge that spiking adds an element of competition that, at first, might seem unnatural and even unseemly to any traditionally non-competitive activity (like birding). In a documentary on the birding World Series, one participant complains 'this isn't even birding' (Kessler 2008). His point is noteworthy. When the basic goals of a non-competitive activity are subverted in order to seek other, more competitive goals, is the essence of the original activity retained? This is a philosophical question that should create lively debate by the avid followers of any sport where spiking occurs.

Concluding comments

Walking and hiking may offer the tourist more than a contemplative opportunity. Many hikers seek more than repose and reflection. Indeed, their primary goal may be one of inducing rather than reducing stress. Where some hikers seek solitude and ease of movement in the outdoors, others seek and embrace challenge and even suffering. We explore this search in this chapter. In particular, we explore hikes chosen and organized for their capacity to inflict hardship on the hiker. Fuelled by a media that constantly promotes the notion of "bucket list sites and activities" and endless virtual references to optimal experience, spiking seems a worthwhile area of interest for the tourism community.

We want to stress the do-it-yourself nature of most spiking. While many events offer the opportunity to hike in competitive settings (adventure races offer a case in point), we refer here primarily to tourists' efforts to create their own experiences in personally meaningful settings. Each day, hikers seek opportunities to test themselves in natural settings. Many travel the globe to experience challenging hikes they themselves have selected and organized. Travel agencies may find opportunities in the spiking environment.

References

Arnold, K. (2013) 'Running rim-to-rim-to-rim', *Outside*. Available at: www.outsideonline.com/1919911/running-rim-rim-rim (accessed 20 June 2015).

Atkinson, M. (2008) 'Triathlon, suffering and exciting significance', *Leisure Studies*, 27(2): 165–180.

Backlund, E.A. and Stewart, W. P. (2012) 'Effects of setting-based management on visitor experience outcomes: differences across a management continuum', *Journal of Leisure Research*, 44(3): 392–415.

Backpacker Magazine (2015) 'The outdoors at your doorstep', *Backpacker Magazine* (front cover). Available: www.backpacker.com.

Blood, R. (2002) 'Weblogs: a history and perspective', in J. Rodzvilla (ed.), *We've Got Blog: How Weblogs Are Changing Our Culture*, Cambridge, MA: Perseus Publishing, pp. 7–16.

Chhetri, P., Arrowsmith, C. and Jackson, M. (2002) 'Determining hiking experiences in nature-based tourist destinations', *Tourism Management*, 25: 31–43.

Coble, T.G., Selin, S.W. and Erickson, B.B. (2003) 'Hiking alone: understanding fear, negotiation strategies and leisure experience', *Journal of Leisure Research*, 35(1): 1–22.

Crust, L., Keegan, R., Piggott, D. and Swann, C. (2011) 'Walking the walk: a phenomenological study of long distance walking', *Journal of Applied Sport Psychology*, 23(3): 243–262.

Csikszentmihalyi, M. (1990) *Flow: The Psychology of Optimal Experience*, New York: Harper Perennial.

Emerson, R.W. (1995) *Nature*, London: Penguin Books.

Grouse Mountain (2015) *Grouse Mountain*. Available at: www.grousemountain.com (accessed 7 July 2015).

Hull, R.B. and Stewart, W.P. (1995) 'The landscape encountered and experienced while hiking', *Environment and Behavior*, 27(3): 404–426.

Kaye, B.K. (2010) 'It's a blog, blog, blog world: users and uses of weblogs', *Atlantic Journal of Communication*, 13(2): 73–95.

Kelly, J.R. (1983) *Leisure Identities and Interactions*, London: George Allen & Unwin.

Kessler, J. (dir.) (2008) *Opposable Chums: Guts & Glory at the World Series of Birding* (motion picture), prod. J. Kessler, US: Boulder Oak Films.

Korpela, K. and Kinnunen, U. (2011) 'How is leisure time interacting with nature related to the need for recovery from work demands? Testing multiple mediators', *Leisure Sciences*, 33: 1–14.

Kostman, C. (2014) *Badwater*. Available at: www.badwater.com (accessed 10 July 2015).

Little, D. (2002) 'Women and adventure recreation: reconstructing leisure constraints and adventure experiences to negotiate continuing participation', *Journal of Leisure Research*, 34(2): 157–177.

Marvin, G. (2007) 'Animal and human bodies in the landscapes of English foxhunting', in S. Coleman and T. Kohn (eds), *The Discipline of Leisure: Embodying Cultures of 'Recreation'*, New York: Berghahn Books, pp. 91–107.

Mitchell Jr, R.G. (1983) *Mountain Experience: The Psychology and Sociology of Adventure*, Chicago: University of Chicago Press.

Prahalad, C.K. and Ramaswamy, V. (2004) 'Co-creation experiences: the next practice in value creation', *Journal of Interactive Marketing*, 18(3): 5–14.

Siber, K. (2012) 'Ultimate adventure bucket list 2012', *National Geographic*. Available at: http://adventure.nationalgeographic.com/adventure/trips/ bucket-list/hike-continental-divide-trail (accessed 4 July 2015).

Thoreau, H.D. (1910 [1862]) 'Walking', in C.W. Eliot (ed.), *Essays English and American*, Harvard Classics, vol. 28, New York: P.F. Collier and Son. Available at: www.bartleby.com/28/15.html (accessed 20 June 2015).

Trail Maniacs (2015) *Golden Ultra*. Available at: http://trailmaniacs.com/sps/ultra/golden-ultra (accessed 10 July 2015).

Walker, G.J. and Virden, R.J. (2005) 'Constraints on outdoor recreation', in E.L. Jackson (ed.), *Constraints to Leisure*, State College, PA: Venture Publishing, pp. 201–209.

World Series of Birding (2015) *World Series of Birding*. Available at: www.worldseriesofbirding.org/wsb/default.asp (accessed 12 July 2015).

Yeomans, N. (2015) *Fit Travel: Hiking the Grand Canyon Rim to Rim*. Available at: www.mensfitness.com/life/travel/fit-travel-hiking-the-grand-canyon-rim-to-rim (accessed 12 July 2015).

12

On the beaten track

How do narratives from organised hiking differ from "real" hiking narratives?

Outi Rantala and Seija Tuulentie

Introduction

The ideal figure of a hiker in Finnish Lapland is a Jack-London-type lonely wolf surviving easily in wilderness. In reality, however, there is an emerging market for soft adventure holidays offering convenient, risk-assessed and quality-assured hiking experiences for people with little wilderness experience. Since busy city dwellers are seen to be accustomed to walking paved urban streets during their everyday life and seem to prefer participation in easily accessed holidays, current commercial hiking holidays are described in terms of easiness of accessing beautiful scenery, convenience, and no-need-for-previous-experience. Besides busy international city dwellers, who seem to be the primary market of these holidays, elderly people find the commercial hiking holidays highly attractive. For example, according to Patterson and Pegg (2009), "Baby Boomers" have demonstrated that they are willing participants in new and adventurous forms of leisure and are opting for more physically challenging and "adrenalin-driven" experiences.

Traditional, independently arranged hiking in Finnish Lapland means walking fairly long distances, carrying quite heavy backpacks with equipment for camping out, and having some orienteering and fire-making skills. On the other hand, infrastructure such as open huts and fireplaces are available easily for everyone, Everyman's rights permit walking almost everywhere, and nature can be regarded as safe. Despite the relative easiness of hiking terrain, good infrastructure and well-marked trails, demand exists for organised hiking trips. Thus, in our chapter, we ask: how do the experiences of hiking differ between the two groups of hikers?

The concept of hiking refers here to trips that include long-distance walks across mountain areas or woods, and at least one overnight stay. By organised hikes, we refer to trips that have been arranged by tourism companies or outdoor and other associations, and which have a participation fee. Organised hikes also differ from independent hikes in that the group members usually do not know each other beforehand, and the group has a guide or a leader. In addition, luggage transportation may be arranged and accommodation provided by local enterprises. These arrangements make the organised hikes naturally more costly, but also more safe and easy, than the independent hiking trips. However, both types of hiking include a lot of walking along paths or terrain, which requires good physical condition and appropriate clothing and shoes.

An example of organised hiking is the "Lapland Classic", a series of organised hikes arranged every autumn in Pallas-Ylläs National Park in northwest Finnish Lapland. It serves also as an example of the increased interest in organised hikes: it started in 2012 with 23 participants and one departure, and already by 2013 there were more almost 400 participants divided into groups of 15 hikers. The groups start their hikes at intervals of several days and are accommodated in villages and hotels that are situated near the national park. The initiator of this organised hiking trip describes the participants as belonging to one of two types of hikers: first, there are those who have previously hiked independently, carrying their own backpacks, but due to old age or decreased physical condition are no longer able to do this; and, second, those first-timers who are inexperienced and do not dare to go alone (personal communication, 20 May 2016). Here, we use online hiking narratives related to the Lapland Classic and other organised hikes, together with narratives from independent hikes, as our data.

General online hiking narratives talk about the accessibility of the route, the (in)convenience of the hike, the equipment, time management, weather conditions, and the quality of the views. However, when reading the narratives more closely, it is the slow pace of life and the embeddedness in the landscape that matters in the end. And, as Ingold and Vergunst (2008) noticed, walking is a profoundly social activity – even when walking is practised in the wilderness, interaction with other people seems to be important.

Narrative analysis of online diaries

In order to compare the narratives from organised hiking holidays with those of the independent and more adventurous hikers, we have applied narrative analysis on data gathered from online diaries and discussions. Online diaries refer here to various types of blogs or published diaries related to hiking trips. Thus, we define online hiking diaries in a similar way to Banyai and Glover's (2012) definition of travel blogs: the various forms of online writing are meant to provide information and engage the reader in the hiking experience. The diaries have been collected from personal blogs, Facebook pages and virtual discussion groups. Commonly, a narrative is more than a statement; it means that an event is reportable and calls for accounting as a specific event (Labov 2006). However, it does not have to be extremely rare: in Finland, it is quite common to report in a personal blog about outdoor life or hiking trips, even if they are not special year-long projects. In addition, several online magazines (e.g. outa.fi), online outdoor groups (e.g. retkipaikka.fi) and online discussion groups (e.g. relaa.com and vaellus.net) share stories about hiking.

While producing our data, we found out that there is a difference between online diaries produced by "real" hikers and those produced by persons participating in organised hiking trips. Organised hiking trip narratives were more often published on the organisers' websites instead of independent blogs or diaries. This is also due to the fact that organised hiking trips are a more rare and recent phenomenon than independently arranged trips.

Our data concerning diaries on organised hiking consists of one personal blog (referred to as O1), two visual diaries (O2, O3) and four online discussions (O4–O7), where hikers have commented about requests related to organised hiking. The visual part of the diaries consists of two sets of pictures from the hikes (24 and 108), which the hikers themselves have uploaded on the Facebook pages of the company arranging the hike, and which have been commented on by the hikers themselves, by co-hikers and by guides. The personal blog writings typically include both text and pictures. However, in our data regarding the independent hikes (seven blogs; referred to as IB1–IB7), there seems to be a clear change in the style of keeping the blog. When choosing the representatives from the vast material available regarding "real" hiking, we could see that the recent blogs consist mainly of pictures, whereas the older ones have more textual narration.

Since we analyse narratives that have been shared both in textual and visual form, we apply two methods of narrative inquiry. According to Smith (2007), there are two ways to conduct narrative inquiry: formulaic and playful. The formulaic inquiry is based on using standardised transcription procedures and conducting analysis with mechanical and formal methods, whereas the playful inquiry is applied to data with limited detail – with or without systematic analytical methods. Interpretations within the playful inquiry are represented in a fashion similar to creative analytic practice (Smith 2007; see also Sparkes 2002). Here we move between the two ways of conducting narrative inquiry.

Within tourism research, narrative analyses have been used mainly to gain insight into tourist-constructed identities or meaning making in relation to tourist experiences – and often for marketing purposes (Banyai and Glover 2012; Elsrud 2001; Noy 2004). Narrative analysis has provided an opportunity to identify, for example, key events related to travel and details related to these events. We are more fundamentally interested in what is seen as reportable and what kind of expectations relate to hiking narratives. To analyse the evaluation in detail, we track down several evidences of expectation (Tannen 1993) in our data, and in addition we apply a visual approach in a more "playful" manner to imagine ourselves within other peoples' worlds – to empathise with their physical and emotional emplacement (Pink 2008).

The key events of a narrative are often not reported in a chronological order, but instead the narrator reacts to the expectations by telling about events that somehow did not meet expectations or were different from what was expected (Hyvärinen 2010). In addition, the main episodes of a narrative are often full of expectation and therefore a narrative is not only a report of what happened but also a narration of things that did not happen (Hyvärinen 2010). First, we read the narratives from the point of view of their core rhetoric and the plot. Second, we utilised a list of different evidences of expectation such as *repetition, modalities* or *hedges* that clarify and define the expectations introduced by Tannen (1993; see also Katisko 2011; Kietäväinen 2009) to analyse what kind of expectations relate to different hiking narratives.

Narrating adventures on and off the beaten track

In this section, we analyse the most important features of the narratives from the point of view of what is left out in an organised hike but is worth reporting in "real" adventure. The topics raised here are the ones that can be regarded as forming the plot or the core rhetoric of the narratives. The combination of the two ways of analysing the data has led us to distinguish the following practices that seem to differentiate the "real" hikers from commercial ones in Finnish Lapland: finding the way, setting up the camping area, and adventuring. Lastly, we focus on the issues that are common to the walking experiences of both types of hikers' narratives.

Way-finding

Orienteering, or simply finding one's way, in the wilderness dominates the narratives of independent hikers. For example, in one of the narratives, the entire plot has been constructed around the theme of getting lost: the title of the blog-writing is 'Being lost' (IB2) and it starts by getting lost by car along the road north and continues with getting lost in the fells. One of the reasons for getting lost is said to be that the person who usually does map-reading for the group was not participating that trip. Similar to this blog, evaluations such as 'we got a little lost but eventually found our way' are common by other independent hikers. The only exception is an older and very experienced hiker (IB7), who starts his hikes with a small plane ride straight into the wilderness – instead of hiking through the landscape, as he has been doing during the previous thirty years.

In his narratives, the thickness of description is present, especially in the detailed description of the practice of hiking itself, of fishing, cooking and camp life.

The practice of way-finding is also illustrated in the visual images as pictures of paths and wooden sticks marking the way – or as pictures of rocky ground, where it is hard to find one's way. Through the pictures, one can feel the wind and tiredness of the legs and the kilometres ahead before reaching the next hut or setting up camp. The practice of finding one's way thus brings together the previous embodied experience of hiking in the wilderness and the hours spent preparing for the trip by reading maps, counting kilometres, evaluating the fitness of each hiking companion, learning about the spots to find fresh water, and checking the weather forecast. In addition to exemplifying the importance of previous knowledge and planning, the descriptions of way-finding often refer to the process of learning – learning the best route, learning how to walk on rocky ground, or learning not to trust other people's advice. The last one is especially important, since a lot of information about way-finding is shared between hikers. Sometimes the advice is regarded as useful, but some blogs warn not to trust the 'so-called experiences of others' (IB2).

Furthermore, the need to be ready to change plans while hiking is also reported. Careful consideration is demanded at all times, and the situation is thoroughly discussed in the narratives: 'In the evening we made a decision that we'll keep our original route plan' (IB1). A lot of repetition and self-assuring is included in the way-finding stories. For example, one hiker tells: 'We trusted that many others had walked the way from Pältsa to Gappo and the path helped us not to panic' (IB1). She continues with an educational notion that 'You only have to make sure that the river bed is on your left. If you manage to get lost, the level of panic must be significant' (IB1).

Independent hikers also comment that way-finding often goes without problems; such evaluations as 'good trail, easy and safe' or 'we got a little lost but eventually found our way' are common. Also, when giving advice to those first-timers who are planning to take a guided trip, the more experienced argue that safe and well-marked trails can be found and there is no fear of getting lost (O4). Still, as a generalisation, orienteering skills, such as the ability to read a map and to use a compass, are emphasised.

Way-finding is also present in the narratives of participants from organised hiking in visual form: paths show the way, but they also give perspective to the pictures of open landscape. In addition, the expectations used in narrating the hiking experience differ between the two groups: independent hikers use way-finding as a plot in their narrative or fill the narration of way-finding with thick description, whereas the participants from organised hiking use pictures related to way-finding more as proof of being in a certain spot and as marking where the path next takes them. Thus, the expectations are not forwarded towards the embodied knowledge of not getting lost.

Setting up the camp

Similar to way-finding, the parts of narratives that describe setting up the camp for a night and sleeping in the wilderness are thick with expectations and modalities. For example, one hiker (IB1) tells how they – in spite of the mosquitoes – do not stay in the pre-paid hut, but set their tent in the vicinity of the hut. By using hedge words such as 'yet' and 'in spite of' and referring to modalities related to expectations of getting along in the wilderness without built infrastructure, the hiker wants to highlight both the fact that they are experienced enough to carry their own tent and that they do not pay the expensive fee for the huts (there are both huts requiring a fee and huts that are open for everyone). Thus, for the independent hikers, the practice of setting up the camp is very much intertwined with the practice of walking – both because the longer it takes to find a good spot to set up the camp, the longer one needs to walk and carry their heavy backpack with all the gear related to sleeping, and because the rhythms of walking and sleeping impact each other. Sleeping out in the wilderness does not form a break from the day's activities for independent hikers, but is rather an integral part of the experience where the walking body is in a lying position on the same ground that is trodden by feet during the hike (Ingold 2004; Rantala and Valtonen 2014).

The narratives related to setting up a camp are intertwined with narratives on weather. The challenge of weather – facing a storm or hard rain – brings out strong emotions such as fear. One hiker tells how they had to check after the storm that everyone was alive in their tents and that she has never been so afraid in her life (IB1). Another hiker describes their struggle while hiking the rocky ground and how she does not raise the tent to the maximum height because she is so afraid of the strong winds (IB5). Storms and strong winds are not part of everyday life in Finland, where the weather conditions are typically quite regular. Furthermore, the weather can force hikers to set up their camp earlier than planned or may tempt hikers to walk longer days than planned. One group of hikers reported deciding to change their daily rhythm of walking due to the hot weather – they walked shorter distances, set up a more permanent camp, slept during the hottest part of the day, and walked during the light summer nights (IB5).

In the narratives of the independent bloggers, the freedom of setting up camp anywhere in the wilderness and freedom to change plans is apparent throughout the stories. This freedom is often pointed out and used as a reference point for expectations. For example, one mother hiking with her teenage son reflects throughout her narrative on her own expectations, related to sleeping in the open huts and walking on the marked trails, and on her positive surprises when her son wants to walk in the wilderness instead of the trail and to sleep in the open wooden shelters instead of the huts (IB4). It is the freedom of choosing the place to set up camp, but also the embodied skill needed to be able to do so, that differentiates the narratives between the two groups of hikers.

The expected adventure

The pictures taken by both independent hikers and participants from organised hikes resemble each other surprisingly. It is usually the open landscape as seen from the top of the fells and the rocky ground that has been photographed. The repetition of open landscapes and rocky fell grounds refers to the expectation of difference – adventure is constructed through hiking in a special and prestigious destination, in a fell landscape (Kane and Tucker 2004). However, the independent hikers add another layer of adventure to the narration by describing when something unexpected happens in this landscape – when the vastness of the wilderness or hardness of the rocky ground causes changes to the planned hike. The unexpectedness refers to risks that are apparent in hiking in the (relatively safe) wilderness and mastery of the risky conditions. Outdoor adventure tourism is, however, as much about mastering the risks as about communion with nature (e.g. Varley 2006) and therefore various methods can be used to construct expectations related to adventure in the narratives of hikers.

The communion with nature is referred to when the rhythm of walking and sleeping is changed to match better the rhythm of nature (IB5), when a child starts to live a healthier life due to the practice of walking long distances daily outside and being exposed to fresh air (IB4) or when describing in detail the joy of fishing (IB7). The communion of nature is also present in the thick descriptions of the 'tactile, feet-first, engagement with the world' (Ingold and Vergunst 2008: 3). It is the continuous embodied and sensuous engagement with the outdoors that constructs the adventure and that defines the experience. The engagement is constructed through the rhythm of walking, alternating with the rhythm of making one's food and setting up camp on the unsteady ground.

Shared narratives of sociability and achievement

Although nature and being in the wilderness are the most important issues, sociability is also a significant focus of the narratives. This applies both to the independent hikers and to the participants of organised trips. Independent hikers often report being with friends and meeting other hikers, while the participants of the arranged trips have to adjust their walking to that of the group of previously unknown participants and the guide.

Very few hike alone, since it is regarded as dangerous; thus, also the independently arranged hiking trips consist usually of a group of two or more participants. Comments on the group are common: 'This was the fourth trip with the same group'. And the writer evaluates: 'It seems that we have done something right since we always start to wait for the next trip when one ends. Together we have roamed around Halti, Kevo and Kebnekaise' (IB1).

In arranged trips, sociability is even more related to safety, since the group is not otherwise familiar. It is emphasised that being in a group with a guide is a safe and easy way to start a hiking hobby (O4). In the discussion comments, there are also moralistic tones that one should go to Lapland in order to find solitude and avoid social interaction. Because of these expectations related to the wilderness experience, it is not surprising that some of the participants of the organised hikes want to emphasise that it is possible to be alone in a group; to walk alone and only have pauses and nights together, or the notion of the group being so small that it is possible to feel the wilderness (O4).

Social relations are, however, strained when something goes wrong. In the narrative about getting lost (IB2), a thick description is given of how the silence fell among the members of the group, and as an evaluation is the realisation that 'we learned the hard way that one should never fully trust so-called experienced others'.

Another important part of the narratives, which is common to both independent and organised hikers, is the expression of surviving and exceeding oneself. The idea that "we made it" relates to many kinds of achievements. It may be a tens-of-kilometres-long hike in hot weather reflected upon by the notion 'we survived as winners' (IB1), or a climb to the height of 1,500 metres and "after a rocky slope and hot weather" they made it (O1). Such small problems as swollen feet make the achievement even better. A participant from an organised trip sums this up as 'yes, my legs were unfortunately swollen, but no need to complain since the trip otherwise succeeded well' (O1). This applies to a wide body of narratives: difficulties make the experience more memorable (Tuulentie 2003; Vergunst 2008).

Achievement means different things to different people. For some, it can be a topographical collection of visits to all the summits over 1,000 metres, as in our narratives of a father-and-son hiking trip through 20 summits, which were carefully examined and measured beforehand on a map (IB3). The most comprehensive description in this kind of narrative is related to the planning of the route: it is an integral part of the trip. Collecting visits also leads to a specific type of narrative; it is a precise and scientific-style description of the terrain, distances and altitudes. In a less exact manner, a poetic narrative of a female hiker comes to the conclusion that 'after this trip I have summited all the mythical fells from the song Halti Wedding [a famous Finnish song]' (IB5). Although being enchanted by all she sees, achieving the summits is important: she titled her narrative with the following wordplay: 'A top trip to the tops' (IB5). In a visual narrative, the summits become even more important: if someone reaches the summit, a photo is taken and presented.

Lorimer and Lund (2008), who have analysed the experiences on collecting among summit-oriented walkers in Scotland, came to the conclusion that collection is, however, not the ordering mechanism for walking; it does not determine the action of walking. This applies to our narrative data as well: despite the very declarative and passive guidebook style, the father's narrative focuses more on the walking itself than on the summits (IB3).

Discussion

Similarly to Vergunst's (2008) description of the narratives of hill walkers in Scotland, the Finnish narratives convey an intensity of experience, when something "really happened" during the journey. When the route is lost, the weather gets worse or some small injury happens, the narrative gets more layered. Vergunst (2008) has interpreted these as the meaningfulness of the walking itself and the presence of the body.

Bodily experience and the purpose of doing one's best in a difficult environment (Vergunst 2008) become also the most important aspect in the narratives of our data. The Romantic idea of Nature as a view seen from afar is different than the nature encountered via walking and trying to find one's way – even in an arranged trip without "real" dangers or extreme challenges. Still, there is a difference if the route is improvised in the course of walk, or if it is pre-planned by other people (cf. Vergunst 2008). Thick description emerges when decisions about the change of route or place to set up camp have to be made, or when there is hesitation if the hikers have lost their way.

Hiking in a group is generally a sociable experience. This is obvious both in independently arranged hikes and in organised hikes. "Lonely wolves" are rare, especially due to security reasons – and even if someone hikes alone, they usually meet other people, since the wilderness in Lapland is not empty. However, the emphasis on the *possibility* of solitude is strong.

In a study from the Appalachian Trail, the most important benefits of hiking have been recognised as being self-fulfilment, self-reliance, affinity with nature, and interaction and warm relationships with others (Hill *et al.* 2009; Robertson and Babic 2009). All these aspects are present in the narratives analysed here. The social side of hiking, especially, seems to be important in various studies (Hill *et al.* 2009; Lorimer and Lund 2008; Robertson and Babic 2009; Vergunst 2008), and walking as a social practice was also highlighted in our study for both kinds of hikers.

Conclusion

In this chapter, we set out to study the experiences of traditional, independently arranged hiking trip participants, in comparison to those participating in organised hikes with a guide or a leader. The main difference between the two groups of hikers relates to making decisions related to way-finding and setting up the camp. The narratives of either deciding to continue the trip as planned or to take a step away from the planned route and rhythm were full of expectations. The continuous decision making, based on embodied knowledge and sensory perception of weather, is an important part of independent hikers' experiences, but is not apparent in participating in an organised hike.

However, even the most devoted hikers today have a less traditional approach to hiking: the lonely hiker and fisherman (IB7) has started to fly to the wilderness – over the lands that he had walked for thirty years. Another hiker (IB5) tells that they decided to order a car ride earlier than they had planned because of the hot weather.

Narratives consist of several narrative styles: some have a guidebook-like declarative style; some use many exclamation marks and report their enhancement openly. Still, the styles get mixed. The technical style of reporting the length of the trip and time spent is interrupted with exclamation marks and, on the other hand, the entranced style is interrupted with technical information.

A diversity of story types exist within blogs. There are those story types that are constructed around conquering summits and reporting technical facts and using passive and generalised forms of narrating the experience. On the other hand, there are narrative types that are overwhelmed with emotions, reflections and evaluations, but still include the attribute referring to the length of the hike. In addition, there are stories constructed afterwards, such as a holistic story about getting lost. Finally, there is a story about a mother–son relationship that exemplifies the deep sociality of the hiking practice. Hence, we suggest that the diversity within story types, as well as the importance of facing (un)expected interruptions, should be taken into account when developing organised hiking experiences.

References

Banyai, M. and Glover, T. (2012) 'Evaluating research methods on travel blogs', *Journal of Travel Research*, 51: 267–277.

Elsrud, T. (2001) 'Risk creation in traveling: backpacker adventure narration', *Annals of Tourism Research*, 28: 597–617.

Hill, E., Goldenberg, M. and Freidt, B. (2009) 'Benefits of hiking: a means-end approach on the Appalachian trail', *Journal of Unconventional Parks, Tourism & Recreation Research*, 2: 19–27.

Hyvärinen, M. (2010) 'Haastattelukertomuksen analyysi', in J. Ruusuvuori, P. Nikander and M. Hyvärinen (eds), *Haastattelun analyysi*, Tampere: Vastapaino, pp. 90–118.

Ingold, T. (2004) 'Culture on the ground: the world perceived through the feet', *Journal of Material Culture*, 9: 315–340.

Ingold, T. and Vergunst, J.L. (2008) 'Introduction', in T. Ingold and J.L. Vergunst (eds), *Ways of Walking: Ethnography and Practice on Foot*, Aldershot, Hants: Ashgate, pp. 1–20.

Kane, M. and Tucker, H. (2004) 'Adventure tourism: the freedom to play with reality', *Tourist Studies*, 4: 217–234.

Katisko, M. (2011) *Kansalaisuus työyhteisön arjessa. Maahanmuuttajien kertomuksia työelämästä*, Helsinki, Finland: Sosiaalitieteiden laitoksen julkaisuja.

Kietäväinen, A. (2009) *Metsään raivatut elämänpolut. Toimijuus ja identiteetti asutustilallisten elämänkertomuksissa*, Rovaniemi, Finland: Lapland University Press.

Labov, W. (2006) 'Narrative pre-construction', *Narrative Inquiry*, 16: 37–45.

Lorimer, H. and Lund, K. (2008) 'A collectable topography: walking, remembering and recording mountains', in T. Ingold and J.L. Vergunst (eds), *Ways of Walking. Ethnography and Practice on Foot*, Aldershot, Hants: Ashgate, pp. 185–200.

Noy, C. (2004) 'This trip really changed me. Backpackers' narratives of self-change', *Annals of Tourism Research*, 31: 78–102.

Patterson, I. and Pegg, S. (2009) 'Marketing the leisure experience to baby boomers and older tourists', *Journal of Hospitality Marketing & Management*, 18: 2–3.

Pink, S. (2008) 'Mobilising visual ethnography: making routes, making place and making image', *Forum: Qualitative Social Research*, 9: 1–17.

Rantala, O and Valtonen, A. (2014) 'A rhythmanalysis of touristic sleep in nature', *Annals of Tourism Research*, 47: 18–30.

Robertson, D.N. and Babic, V. (2009) 'Remedy for modernity: experiences of walkers and hikers on Medvednica Mountain', *Leisure Studies*, 28: 105–112.

Smith, B. (2007) 'The state of art in narrative inquiry. Some reflections', *Narrative Inquiry*, 17: 391–398.

Sparkes, A.C. (2002) *Telling tales in sport and physical activity: a qualitative journey*, Champaign, IL: Human Kinetics Press.

Tannen, D. (1993) *Framing in Discourse*, Oxford: Oxford University Press.

Tuulentie, S. (2003) 'Lapin hullujen luontoelämykset [Nature experiences of Lapland enthusiasts]', *Muuttuva Matkailu*, 3: 14–21.

Varley, P. (2006) 'Confecting adventure and playing with meaning: the adventure commodification continuum', *Journal of Sport & Tourism*, 11: 173–194.

Vergunst, J.L. (2008) 'Taking a trip and taking care in everyday life', in T. Ingold and J.L. Vergunst (eds), *Ways of Walking: Ethnography and Practice on Foot*, Aldershot, Hants: Ashgate, pp. 105–121.

13

Comparisons between hikers and non-hikers in Iceland

Attitudes, behaviours and perceptions

Anna Dóra Sæþórsdóttir, C. Michael Hall and Þorkell Stefánsson

Introduction

Often portrayed in both tourism and the popular imagination as a wild land of fire and ice (Sæþórsdóttir *et al.* 2011; Witze and Kanipe 2014), Iceland has become a nature-based tourism destination that has experienced extremely rapid growth in visitor arrivals since 2007. The tourist industry is economically significant and provided 12–13% of total exports between 1995 and 2009. However, since then, it has become a core economic sector and now earns over 25% of foreign exchange earnings (Statistics Iceland 2015).

The growth in export earnings from tourism has mainly been the result of increased numbers of international tourists coming to Iceland, which increased on average by about 9% per year from 1980 to 2010 (Jóhannesson and Huijbens 2010). However, since 2010, growth rates have been of the order of 20% per year, with 1.3 million international tourist arrivals in 2015, as well as more than 200,000 cruise ship visitors, whose numbers are not included in the official tourist numbers for overnight stays (Statistics Iceland 2015). Although these extraordinary high growth numbers are not expected to be maintained, tourism is nevertheless expected to grow well into the future.

Yet Iceland is not a large country. An island in the North Atlantic Ocean, between 63° and 66° northern latitudes, it has an area of 103,000 km², almost 60% of which lies at altitudes above 400 m with 24% lying below 200 m. The population of the country is about 330,000 and almost all settlement is below 200 m. About 64% of the population lives in the capital region (Reykjavik), and the rest in towns and villages scattered along the coast and on farms on plateaus along the coast and in valleys that penetrate the country (Statistics Iceland 2015). This human geography, especially when combined with the island's volcanic, geothermal and hydrological resources, creates a landscape that has proven to be a major attraction for tourism, with the nature-based tourism market (Sæþórsdóttir and Saarinen 2016) contributing around four in every five visitors to the country (Icelandic Tourist Board 2014). Yet this is also an increasingly contested terrain.

Iceland's cheap renewable energy is a major driver for attracting energy-intensive industry, such as smelters, to the country. At the same time, geothermal and hydro-electricity developments, together with the construction of transmission lines and associated energy infrastructure, are starting to have an impact on the landscape, creating significant spatial planning issues between tourism and energy development (Thórhallsdóttir 2007; Sæþórsdóttir 2010a; Sæþórsdóttir and

Ólafsson 2010a, 2010b). Research among travellers in the Highland wilderness areas has shown that the majority of tourists feel negatively towards power plants in the destination where they are travelling and these are considered to have a negative effect on the wilderness experience (Sæþórsdóttir 2010b; Sæþórsdóttir and Saarinen 2016). Furthermore, there is substantial debate within communities as to the potential trajectories that economic development will take and the relative employment and environmental advantages of energy development and tourism, especially given the potential for lock-in to a trajectory that cannot be easily reversed.

In general, the public has a negative attitude towards energy infrastructure and transmission lines, especially issues such as visual pollution, although these may be influenced to a degree by the nature of public participation processes (Cotton and Devine-Wright 2011; Cain and Nelson 2013; Tempesta *et al.* 2014) and, for visitors, comparisons between the destination and the visitor environment (Coles *et al.* 2005; Hall and Page 2014). Even when the public are in favour of sustainable renewable energy sources, such as wind power and geothermal energy, they are usually against the erection of the relevant structures in their local communities, or in areas to which there is a significant degree of place attachment (Wolsink 2000; Zoellner *et al.* 2008). Consideration therefore needs to be given as to how developments fit with the symbolic and socially constructed ideas about the area in which they occur (Devine-Wright 2009; Devine-Wright and Howes 2010). Infrastructure, such as roads, factories, power plants and transmission lines, that are considered out of place in the landscape, are often felt to detract from an area's attractiveness (Tveit *et al.* 2006), while also lowering an area's wilderness values by negatively affecting naturalness and remoteness (Hall 1992; Hall and MacArthur 1993; Olafsdottir and Runnström 2011). Moreover, this is a significant issue for tourism, not only because visitor and walking experiences can be factors in perceptions of attractiveness and forming attachments to place, but also because the extent of tourism activity itself, and associated infrastructures and developments, can also influence tourist perceptions of landscapes and experiences.

In Iceland, hiking and walking opportunities are an integral component of the tourist experience. Active involvement in an environment, for example from hiking, has been shown to be related to strength of place attachment (Kyle *et al.* 2003, 2004; Brooks *et al.* 2007; Kil *et al.* 2012), and influence environmental attitudes and return visitation (Kil *et al.* 2014). Given the potential for some landscapes of high natural quality to be affected by energy-related developments, an understanding of hikers is significant from a spatial planning perspective (Sæþórsdóttir and Ólafsson 2010a, 2010b), as well as for a broader understanding of wilderness tourism in the Icelandic context (Thórhallsdóttir 2007; Sæþórsdóttir and Saarinen 2016). This chapter therefore examines hikers and non-hikers in Iceland and analyses differences in their characteristics and behaviours, as well as comparing their satisfaction levels, preferences with respect to infrastructure, and experiences of crowding and of the environment.

Methods and data

This research builds on an empirical case study methodology, which uses questionnaire surveys that have been gathered at 24 nature destinations in Iceland, 11 of them in the Highlands (wilderness areas/areas with a high degree of naturalness) and 13 in the Lowlands (rural areas). They were collected in various research projects steered by one of the authors in the years 2011, 2013, 2014 and 2015 (Table 13.1), including research undertaken for the Workgroup 2 of the third phase of the Master Plan for Nature Protection and Energy Utilization, which is an Iceland government project that aims to categorize power plant proposals (hydro, geothermal areas and wind power) for protection or energy utilization. Most of the questions are identical and can be compared. Many of the questions are on a five-point Likert scale, e.g. the visitors' opinions

Table 13.1 Research areas and data

	Year	N	Non-hikers	Hikers	% Hikers	Highlands
Aldeyjarfoss	2015	324	283	41	12.7	
Álftavatn	2011	202	35	167	82.7	✓
Djúpalónssandur	2014	746	708	38	5.1	
Eldgjá	2011	398	320	78	19.6	✓
Geysir	2014	2763	2502	261	9.4	
Hagavatn	2015	80	75	5	6.3	✓
Hólaskjól	2015	422	345	77	18.2	✓
Hrafntinnusker	2011	345	87	258	74.8	✓
Hraunfossar	2014	1316	1284	32	2.4	
Jökulsárgljúfur	2013	953	914	39	4.1	
Jökulsárlón	2014	1969	1831	138	7.0	
Landmannahellir	2011	172	154	18	10.5	✓
Langisjór	2013	135	81	54	40.0	✓
Lónsöræfi	2013	56	6	50	89.3	✓
Mývatn	2013	1619	1578	41	2.5	
Nýidalur	2015	78	64	14	17.9	✓
Seltún	2015	653	625	28	4.3	
Skaftafell	2013	1400	1335	65	4.6	
Skagafjörður	2015	223	199	24	10.8	
Sólheimajökull	2014	488	459	29	5.9	
Trölladyngja	2015	122	108	14	11.5	
Þingvellir	2014	3435	3197	238	6.9	
Þórsmörk	2014	426	213	213	50.0	✓
Öldufell	2011	50	43	7	14.0	✓
Total		18375	16446	1929	10.5	11/24

regarding the desirability of various facilities, such as hotels, roads and visitor centres, where the respondents could mark options from 1 = very much against to 5 = very much in favour. Those answers were used to analyse the opinions of respondents; for instance, by calculating the average and doing a significance test to explore whether the average between groups varied according to gender, nationality, area of residence in Iceland (capital area or rural areas), mode of transportation, length of hike, location, overnight stay or day trip, whether the respondents had previously visited the area, whether they were visiting in order to experience wilderness, and the categories of the purist scale (urbanists, neutralists, purists, strong purists) (Stankey 1973), in which attitudes towards elements of recreational settings in natural areas are used to separate visitors into a range between "purists", who look for pure wilderness, and "urbanists", who accept certain human impacts (see Stankey 1973; Sæþórsdóttir 2010a). If there were two groups, t-tests were employed, and ANOVA tests if there were three or more. Additionally, the difference between groups was analysed further with a multilateral comparison, either with a Games–Howell test or a Hochbergs GT2, depending on whether the Levene test demonstrated an equal variance between groups.

The research areas represent a spectrum of nature tourist destinations in the Highlands, taking into account the number of visitors, the level of development of the infrastructure, environment types and difficulty of access. Data collection was carried out at the main entrance point at each destination, either at parking places at main attractions, in mountain huts, or on campsites.

A. Sæþórsdóttir *et al.*

Data were collected by one to four interviewers, who asked as many tourists as possible to answer the questionnaire. Interviewers stayed at each destination for a week during the peak tourist season in the summer. The visitors filled out the questionnaire after they had been in the area for a while and before they left the area, in order for their experience, knowledge and opinion of the area to be as thorough as possible. However, since many tourists on organized guided group tours are on a very tight schedule, some tourists answered the questionnaire inside the bus after they had left the area. Tour guides were given a pre-paid envelope and they were asked to gather the completed questionnaires and send the envelope back to the researcher. In that way, an attempt was made to avoid a biased sample containing a lower-than-actual ratio of answers from organized group tourists. The data collection in Skagafjörður differed from the others, as there is no specific place where most tourists stop, e.g. at a waterfall or a certain sightseeing destination. Therefore, the data had to be collected at more than one specific location, including in conjunction with tourist service providers.

Completed questionnaires were received from more than 18,000 visitors, of which almost 2,000 were defined as hikers, as they marked hiking as their mode of travel, sometimes along with other modes of travel, mostly by bus. There was a tremendous difference between the research areas in the percentage of hikers: up to as much as 89%, and as few as 2%, used hiking as their mode of travel in the areas. Overall, hikers comprised 11% of tourists in the areas where interviews were conducted. Hikers were generally more common in the Highlands, at 40% of visitors, than in the Lowlands, where they constituted only 6%.

Results

Male hikers are slightly more common (51%) than female hikers (49%), while more non-hikers are female (54%) (Table 13.2). The French are the most common nationality among hikers, amounting to 21% of the group. Germans, Icelanders and North Americans are also prevalent nationalities within the hiker group. About 30% of hikers are professionals (doctors, lawyers,

Table 13.2 Tourist characteristics

	Non-hikers		Hikers	
	N	%	N	%
Gender				
Female	8634	53.7	933	48.9
Male	7458	46.3	975	51.1
Nationality				
German	3435	22.0	304	16.5
USA/Canadian	2079	13.3	211	11.4
French	1845	11.8	386	20.9
Icelandic	1807	11.5	241	13.1
Swiss/Austrian	1282	8.2	140	7.6
British/Irish	1058	6.8	140	7.6
Beneluxian	1011	6.5	130	7.0
Nordic	932	6.0	94	5.1
Italian/Spanish	791	5.1	48	2.6
Others	1409	9.0	152	8.2

	Non-hikers		Hikers	
	N	%	N	%
Profession				
Professional (doctor, teacher, lawyer, etc.)	4441	29.6	406	30.8
Retired	3118	20.8	51	3.9
Students	1630	10.9	361	27.4
Managerial	1567	10.4	133	10.1
Vocational/technical	1424	9.5	131	9.9
Clerical/service	1071	7.1	72	5.5
Other	1749	11.7	165	12.5
Purist Scale				
Urbanist	1203	29.1	167	16.5
Neutralists	2205	53.4	541	53.4
Purists	638	15.5	258	25.4
Strong purists	82	2.0	48	4.7
Geographical Location				
Lowlands	15023	91.3	988	51.2
Highlands	1423	8.7	941	48.8
Wilderness part of site's attraction	5742	93.0	1115	95.7

teachers) and 27% are students, while only 4% of hikers are retirees. On the purism scale, non-hikers (29%) tend more to be urbanists than hikers (17%), and a higher proportion of hikers are purists and strong purists (25%; 16%) then non-hikers (16%; 2%). Most of the non-hikers (91%) are visiting Lowland areas, while the hikers are more equally distributed between the Highlands and the Lowlands. Over 90% of both groups think that wilderness is a part of the attraction of the areas they are travelling in.

Behaviours

Almost 60% of hikers stay overnight in the area they are travelling in, and 40% are on a day trip. Among non-hikers this is the opposite, as 67% of them are daytrippers (Table 13.3). Over 83% of both groups are first-time visitors. About one-quarter of hikers are on an organized tour, compared to about one-third of non-hikers. Over 60% of hikers camp, about 23% stay in hotels, and 28% in hostels. Over 42% of hikers use mountain huts, where they are available. About 59% of non-hikers, on the other hand, use hotels, 38% mountain huts, where they are available, and only 17% camp.

Hikers are younger, or a little over 35.4 years, than non-hikers, who are a bit over 46 years (Table 13.4). There is a statistical significant difference regarding how appropriate hikers and non-hikers perceive various infrastructure and services to be. Hikers consider all kinds of roads, bridges across rivers, hotels, cooked food for sale, gas stations, visitor centres and power plants less appropriate than non-hikers. Hikers are also more in favour of mountain huts and campsites than non-hikers. Designed footpaths, walkways, picnic places and markings on places of interest are more important to non-hikers than hikers. However, enjoying peace and unspoilt nature,

Table 13.3 Tourist behaviour

	Non-hikers		Hikers	
	N	%	N	%
Type of visitor				
Day trippers	10048	67.1	747	41.3
Overnight visitors	4919	32.9	1061	58.7
Repeat visitors	2606	16.4	255	15.1
First-time visitors	13259	83.6	1435	84.9
Travel partners				
Family members	6724	42.4	627	33.3
Organized tour	5112	32.2	464	24.6
Relatives/ friends	4222	26.6	734	38.9
By myself	672	4.2	202	10.7
Work or club mates	416	2.6	113	6.0
Accommodation				
Hotel	5745	59.0	326	22.9
Mountain hut	233	38.3	223	42.6
Camping	1647	16.9	873	61.3
Hostel	1395	15.3	249	27.6
Farm accommodation	1050	10.8	81	5.7
At friend's	563	5.8	66	4.6
In the car	384	3.9	56	3.9

Table 13.4 A comparison between hikers' and non-hikers' characteristics, attitudes and perceptions

	Hikers			Non-hikers			T-test	
	N	Mean	SD	N	Mean	SD	t-value	p-value
Age	1868	35.41	14.54	15535	46.19	21.61	−28.493	<0.001
Purist score	1014	46.36	7.17	4128	43.27	7.04	12.476	<0.001
Day visitors' length of stay (hours)	741	3.26	4.30	9852	3.01	3.88	1.515	0.130
Overnight visitors' length of stay (nights)	1215	3.42	7.39	6480	2.48	4.70	4.276	<0.001
Appropriateness of infrastructure	1 = very inappropriate → 5 = very appropriate							
Campsites	590	4.05	0.98	4031	3.68	1.07	8.603	<0.001
Mountain huts	1008	4.04	1.06	4383	3.80	1.02	6.731	<0.001
Gravel roads	748	2.88	1.24	4774	3.36	1.04	−10.128	<0.001
Cooked food for sale	542	2.81	1.29	4377	3.25	1.18	−7.616	<0.001
Bridges across rivers	1027	2.70	1.40	5354	3.37	1.27	−14.398	<0.001
Gestastofa (visitor centre)	861	2.61	1.30	2252	2.89	1.26	−5.483	<0.001
Shops/restaurants	1068	2.19	1.21	5535	3.01	1.23	−20.055	<0.001
Built-up gravel roads	1005	2.49	1.26	5144	3.27	1.11	−18.344	<0.001

	Hikers			Non-hikers			T-test	
	N	Mean	SD	N	Mean	SD	t-value	p-value
Roads passable year round	768	2.18	1.21	2125	2.78	1.28	−11.241	<0.001
Asphalt roads	1041	2.03	1.25	5550	3.19	1.39	−27.060	<0.001
Gas stations	1028	1.90	1.15	4925	2.94	1.31	−25.653	<0.001
Power plants	984	1.86	1.12	4697	2.47	1.23	−15.291	<0.001
Hotels	994	1.85	1.12	5054	2.74	1.33	−22.065	<0.001

Importance to visitor	1 = not important at all → 5 = very important							
Enjoying unspoilt nature	1165	4.71	0.66	6131	4.54	0.81	7.986	<0.001
Enjoying peace	1172	4.52	0.79	6060	4.31	0.93	8.285	<0.001
Marked walking routes	1170	4.05	1.16	6022	3.86	1.12	5.294	<0.001
Walking without seeing structures	1168	3.89	1.16	5721	3.44	1.27	11.702	<0.001
Seeing no trace of off-road driving	1148	3.82	1.20	5626	3.68	1.30	3.387	0.001
Campsites with facilities	1173	3.66	1.20	5534	3.47	1.31	4.648	<0.001
Having few other tourists around	1150	3.50	1.14	5811	3.22	1.25	7.510	<0.001
Special markings on places of interest	1170	3.49	1.12	6121	3.91	1.03	−11.864	<0.001
Seeing no trace of others having been there	1155	3.48	1.19	5572	3.18	1.29	7.636	<0.001
Designed footpaths	1161	3.16	1.33	5949	3.38	1.20	−5.220	<0.001
Walkways (footbridge)	1155	3.16	1.27	5750	3.36	1.16	−4.893	<0.001
Camping where you don't hear or see others	1147	3.05	1.31	5134	2.54	1.29	11.840	<0.001
Camping wherever you want in the area	1156	3.03	1.37	5208	2.50	1.32	12.069	<0.001
Picnic places (benches and tables)	1161	2.17	1.17	5840	2.74	1.18	−15.055	<0.001

Contribution to satisfaction	1 = very dissatisfied → 5 = very satisfied							
Nature	1125	4.60	0.84	11654	4.61	0.83	−0.748	0.455
The stay	1830	4.33	0.84	15580	4.28	0.89	2.635	0.008
Hiking trails	897	4.18	0.90	9325	4.17	0.88	0.225	0.822
Service	893	3.97	0.88	9153	3.88	0.89	2.909	0.004
Parking space	813	3.82	0.89	9281	4.04	0.91	−6.577	<0.001
Toilets	873	3.81	0.98	9053	3.69	1.04	3.633	<0.001
Markings on interesting places	902	3.79	0.95	9599	3.91	0.95	−3.418	0.001
Signs	904	3.76	0.96	9441	3.84	0.93	−2.304	0.021

Perceptions of crowding	1 = too few → 5 = too many							
Icelandic tourists	1088	2.67	0.83	11862	2.76	0.75	−3.200	0.001
Hikers	943	3.10	0.64	4195	2.88	0.63	9.568	<0.001
Buses	1602	3.25	0.81	13444	3.27	0.78	−1.402	0.161
Cars	1596	3.26	0.76	13246	3.17	0.63	4.984	<0.001
Foreign tourists	1099	3.33	0.73	12427	3.22	0.65	5.068	<0.001
Tourists in general	1660	3.37	0.73	13858	3.25	0.67	6.355	<0.001
Tourist groups	890	3.48	0.84	9283	3.36	0.78	4.185	<0.001

(Continued)

Table 13.4 (Continued)

	Hikers			Non-hikers			T-test	
	N	Mean	SD	N	Mean	SD	t-value	p-value
Perceptions of environmental degradation			1 = not at all → 5 = very much					
Trampling by horses	718	1.50	0.86	4092	1.49	0.81	0.420	0.675
Damage to geological formations	1560	1.52	0.79	12734	1.55	0.84	−1.681	0.093
Garbage	1595	1.62	0.82	13085	1.59	0.83	1.677	0.094
Damaged vegetation	1579	1.83	0.99	12972	1.76	0.98	2.792	0.005
Traces of off-road driving	722	2.05	1.09	4111	1.90	1.00	3.415	0.001
Erosion of footpaths	1579	2.25	1.10	12730	1.99	1.04	8.810	0.000
Overall perceptions of areas								
1 Beautiful → 5 Ugly	1125	1.31	0.63	11417	1.29	0.66	0.964	0.335
1 Clean → 5 Dirty	935	1.41	0.70	9791	1.40	0.74	0.105	0.916
1 Safe → 5 Unsafe	928	1.45	0.73	9708	1.51	0.81	−2.363	0.018
1 Natural → 5 Developed	1116	1.66	0.95	11388	1.58	0.91	2.728	0.006
1 Accessible → 5 Inaccessible	1106	1.79	0.96	11238	1.62	0.85	5.794	<0.001
1 Quiet → 5 Loud	1120	1.99	1.09	11236	1.94	1.08	1.422	0.155

walking without seeing structures, having few other tourists around, seeing no trace of off-road driving, and no trace of others having been there, of marked walking routes and campsites with facilities, and to be able to camp wherever they want and where they do not hear or see others, are all more important to hikers than non-hikers. Interestingly, in the 2015 survey, which, in part, examined attitudes towards transmission lines, it was noted that those who walked for less than an hour ($\bar{x}$ = 2.44) were less negative towards power lines in the Lowlands than those who walked for longer periods ($\bar{x}$ = 1.91–2.02). Tourists who visited the 2015 study areas (see Table 13.1) in their own cars ($\bar{x}$ = 2.00) were more against power lines than those who travelled by bus ($\bar{x}$ = 2.27) and rental car ($\bar{x}$ = 2.31). Hikers ($\bar{x}$ = 1.71), and those who travelled on motorcycles or quad bikes ($\bar{x}$ = 1.83) were very strongly opposed to transmission lines.

There is no significant difference between how satisfied hikers and non–hikers are with nature and hiking trails. Hikers are, on the one hand, more satisfied than non–hikers with the stay in the area, the service and toilets, while non–hikers are more satisfied with the parking spaces, signs and markings on interesting places. There is also no significant difference between hiker and non-hiker satisfaction regarding the number of buses in the areas. Nevertheless, hikers are more sensitive to the numbers of tourists and cars than non-hikers.

There is no significant difference between hikers' and non–hikers' perception as to whether the areas are beautiful or ugly, clean or dirty, quiet or loud. However, hikers tend to perceive the areas as safer, more natural and more accessible than non–hikers. Similarly, there is no significant difference as to whether hikers and non-hikers notice tramping by horses, damage to geological formations or garbage, although hikers notice more damaged vegetation, traces of off-road driving and erosion of footpaths.

Conclusions

The rapid growth of tourism and energy generation in Iceland in recent years is having a substantial affect on how natural resources are perceived and how they need to be managed if they are to continue being utilized. Around 80% of international tourists visit Iceland because of its nature, which makes it a resource for the tourism industry, as well as for energy generation and low-cost, energy-dependent businesses such as smelters. Nevertheless, the capacity to reconcile infrastructure development with tourism is substantially limited from a visitor perspective, if the results of the series of surveys presented here remain constant in the future. The situation is only further complicated by the significance of hiking as a domestic and international tourism activity in Iceland.

Approximately 10% of respondents engaged in hiking as an activity, although higher results were found for some markets (German, North American, French and Icelandic). However, spatially, hiking was much more prevalent as an activity in the Highlands. This is important, not only because of the potential implications for tourist perceptions of infrastructure, but also because the peripherality of the area means that the hiking market is a significant source of localized expenditure, which has important economic and employment impacts. As the results of visitor surveys in rural and wilderness areas of Iceland indicate, hikers perceive and understand the landscape in a different way from non-hikers. Their willingness to tolerate certain infrastructure or evidence of environmental disturbance is more limited than non-hikers, and only reinforces the results of Devine-Wright and Howes (2010), who note that antagonism towards power-plant structures is higher in relatively unspoilt nature. However, hiking may also have other implications for how the Icelandic landscape is understood.

Walking, and therefore hiking, is a highly embodied experiential activity (Lund 2012) that potentially creates connections to place. As Devine-Wright (2009) has pointed out, an emotional attachment often makes it difficult for people to imagine, or be reconciled with, changes in areas they feel a relationship to. From a tourism industry perspective, this is a significant issue for generating positive word-of-mouth and repeat visitation. However, it also has implications for understanding the relationalities that exist between the walker and the places they visit and how these extend over time, an area of research that has not been well examined previously but which will have potentially major consequences for individual and place identity.

References

Brooks, J.J., Wallace, G.N. and Williams, D.R. (2007) 'Is this a one-night stand or the start of something meaningful? Developing relationships to place in national park backcountry', in A. Watson, J. Sproull and L. Dean (eds), *Science and Stewardship to Protect and Sustain Wilderness Values: Eighth World Wilderness Congress symposium, September 30–October 6, 2005, Anchorage, Alaska.* Proceedings RMRS-P-49. Fort Collins, CO: US Department of Agriculture, Forest Service, Rocky Mountain Research Station, pp. 451–459.
Cain, N.L. and Nelson, H.T. (2013) 'What drives opposition to high-voltage transmission lines?' *Land Use Policy*, 33: 204–213.
Coles, T.E., Duval, D. and Hall, C.M. (2005) 'Tourism, mobility and global communities: new approaches to theorising tourism and tourist spaces', in W. Theobold (ed.), *Global Tourism,* 3rd edn, Burlington, MA: Elsevier, pp. 463–481.
Cotton, M. and Devine-Wright, P. (2011) 'Discourses of energy infrastructure development: a q-method study of electricity transmission line siting in the UK', *Environment and Planning A,* 43(4): 942–960.
Devine-Wright, P. (2009) 'Rethinking NIMBYism: the role of place attachment and place identity in explaining place-protective action', *Journal of Community & Applied Social Psychology*, 19(6): 426–441.
Devine-Wright, P. and Howes, Y. (2010) 'Disruption to place attachment and the protection of restorative environments: a wind energy case study', *Journal of Environmental Psychology*, 30(3): 271–280.
Hall, C.M. (1992) *Wasteland to World Heritage: Preserving Australia's Wilderness*, Melbourne: Melbourne University Press.

Hall, C.M. and MacArthur, S. (eds) (1993) *Heritage Management in New Zealand and Australia: Visitor Management, Interpretation and Marketing*, Auckland: Oxford University Press.

Hall, C.M. and Page, S. (2014) *The Geography of Tourism and Recreation*, 4th edn, Abingdon, Oxon: Routledge.

Icelandic Tourist Board (2014) *Erlendir ferðamenn á Íslandi. Sumar 2014*, Reykjavík: Icelandic Tourist Board.

Jóhannesson, G.T. and Huijbens, E.H. (2010) 'Tourism in times of crisis: exploring the discourse of tourism development in Iceland', *Current Issues in Tourism*, 13: 419–434.

Kil, N., Holland, S.M. and Stein, T.V. (2014) 'Structural relationships between environmental attitudes, recreation motivations, and environmentally responsible behaviors', *Journal of Outdoor Recreation and Tourism*, 7: 16–25.

Kil, N., Stein, T.V., Holland, S.M. and Anderson, D.H. (2012) 'Understanding place meanings in planning and managing the wildland–urban interface: the case of Florida trail hikers', *Landscape and Urban Planning*, 107(4): 370–379.

Kyle, G., Graefe, A., Manning, R. and Bacon, J. (2003) 'An examination of the relationship between leisure activity and place attachment among hikers along the Appalachian Trail', *Journal of Leisure Research*, 35(3): 249.

Kyle, G.T., Mowen, A.J. and Tarrant, M. (2004) 'Linking place preferences with place meaning: an examination of the relationship between place motivation and place attachment', *Journal of Environmental Psychology*, 24(4): 439–454.

Lund, K. (2012) 'Landscapes and narratives: compositions and the walking body', *Landscape Research*, 37(2): 225–237.

Olafsdottir, R. and Runnström, M.C. (2011) 'How wild is Iceland? Wilderness quality with respect to nature-based tourism', *Tourism Geographies*, 13(2): 280–298.

Sæþórsdóttir, A.D. (2010a) 'Planning nature tourism in Iceland based on tourist attitudes', *Tourism Geographies*, 12(1): 25–52.

Sæþórsdóttir, A.D. (2010b) 'Tourism struggling as the wilderness is developed', *Scandinavian Journal of Hospitality and Tourism*, 10(3): 334–357.

Sæþórsdóttir, A.D. and Ólafsson, R. (2010a) 'Nature tourism assessment in the Icelandic master plan for geothermal and hydropower development. Part I: Rapid evaluation of nature tourism resources', *Journal of Heritage Tourism*, 5(4): 311–331.

Sæþórsdóttir, A.D. and Ólafsson, R. (2010b) 'Nature tourism assessment in the Icelandic Master Plan for geothermal and hydropower development. Part II: assessing the impact of proposed power plants on tourism and recreation', *Journal of Heritage Tourism*, 5: 333–349.

Sæþórsdóttir, A.D. and Saarinen, J. (2016) 'Challenges due to changing ideas of natural resources: tourism and power plant development in the Icelandic wilderness', *Polar Record*, 52(1): 82–91.

Sæþórsdóttir, A.D., Hall, C.M. and Saarinen, J. (2011) 'Making wilderness: tourism and the history of the wilderness idea in Iceland', *Polar Geography*, 34(4): 249–273.

Stankey, G.H. (1973) *Visitor Perception of Wilderness Recreation Carrying Capacity*, Ogden, UT: Intermountain Forest & Range Experiment Station, Forest Service, US Department of Agriculture.

Statistics Iceland (2015) *Landshagir – Statistical Yearbook of Iceland – 2015*, vol. 25, Reykjavík: Statistics Iceland.

Tempesta, T., Vecchiato, D. and Girardi, P. (2014) 'The landscape benefits of the burial of high voltage power lines: a study in rural areas of Italy', *Landscape and Urban Planning*, 126: 53–64.

Thórhallsdóttir, T.E. (2007) 'Environment and energy in Iceland: a comparative analysis of values and impacts', *Environmental Impact Assessment Review*, 27(6): 522–544.

Tveit, M.S., Sang, Å.O. and Fry, G. (2006) 'Key concepts in a framework for analysing visual landscape character', *Landscape Research*, 31(3): 229–255.

Witze, A. and Kanipe, J. (2014) *Island on Fire: The Extraordinary Story of a Forgotten Volcano That Changed the World*, New York: Pegasus Books.

Wolsink, M. (2000) 'Wind power and the NIMBY-myth: institutional capacity and the limited significance of public support', *Renewable Energy*, 21(1): 49–64.

Zoellner, J., Schweizer-Reis, P. and Wemheuer, C. (2008) 'Public acceptance of renewable energies: results from case studies in Germany', *Energy Policy*, 36(11): 4136–4141.

14

Passeggiata nuova
Social travel in the era of the smartphone

Andrew Mondschein

Introduction

Italians have engaged in the tradition of the "passeggiata" for centuries. In villages and neighbourhoods, residents come out each evening to stroll. On these strolls, they see and are seen, and they exchange pleasantries, gossip and news. During the passeggiata, social ties are reinforced and the link between place and community is deepened (Del Negro 2004). Similar traditions of social travel exist throughout the world, but the essentiality of the passeggiata to the life of an Italian community is exceptional. In part, what makes the passeggiata work is the relatively small scale of Italian villages and neighbourhoods. An entire community can be seen and heard during a night's walk. In contemporary large cities, a significant proportion of daily travel is accomplished by car or transit (train/subway), and social ties can be scattered across cities. Teens may cruise and neighbours may chat across the fence, but a true citywide passeggiata would be an impossibility. Still, does the passeggiata persist, inasmuch as we can observe a pedestrianized social life in major cities? Furthermore, what role, if any, might new technologies of communication and mobility play in socially oriented walking?

This chapter examines whether the passeggiata endures and is even emergent in this technological urban era. Drawing on inquiry from several disciplines, supplemented with findings from a San Francisco area travel survey, I assess interactions among social activities, walking, and information and communication technologies (ICTs). Previous research and recent data suggest a distinctive relationship between the adoption of ICTs and social activity. Broad agreement across disciplines accepts that technology can facilitate increased social interactions in urban settings. However, the nature of those interactions, particularly how and where they are accomplished, is less well understood. Do ICTs facilitate more or less walking? Where do we go when we use ICTs? The breadth and changing nature of available technologies means that effects on social behaviours are likely to be quite varied. However, in the aggregate, we can make several notable empirical observations. In particular, looking at the San Francisco Bay Area, use of mobility-enhancing ICTs is associated with increased social activity on foot, clustered in some of the most urban and diverse parts of that region.

The phenomena explored in this chapter may represent a further evolution in urban social life, where technologies facilitate more complex and flexible patterns of walkability through the urban milieu. However, whether the increased, technology-supported sociable walking observed in contemporary big cities can actually serve to reinforce ties among communities at any scale remains unproven. From one point of view, the expansion of social walking through technology presents city planners and designers with opportunities to energize and pedestrianize marginal and potentially neglected parts of a region, even while introducing additional challenges for sustainably and equitably addressing the impacts of this "new passeggiata".

Rewiring urban social walking

The literature on social activity, travel patterns and technology spans several fields, including urban planning and geography, sociology, economics and tourism studies. While the broad outlines of ICT's effects on social activity and travel have been well addressed, theorization and empirical research have yet to describe how ICTs may influence the spatial patterns of social activity and sociable walking in particular. Beginning at the passeggiata, I construct a framework linking social activity, walking and technology that suggests why emergent technologies may facilitate clustered social walking.

From the passeggiata to the middle ring

The passeggiata is a venerable tradition of Italian cities and towns (Del Negro 2004). This ritual urban stroll, which occurs nightly in many towns, is an opportunity for residents to interact both directly and indirectly through observation. The truism that the social life of Italians goes on in public is borne out in the case of the passeggiata, where Italians reinforce ties at the personal and broader social scales. Del Negro emphasizes the physicality of the passeggiata, and to see and be seen is an essential part of the ritual. Thus, being on foot, exposed to others, is critical to the embodied experience. It is also a function of place, carried out in a central location, such as the village square. The passeggiata perseveres in Italy today, a distinctive part of asserting a local identity in a globalizing society (Castellanos 2011).

While this ritual may be most distinct and reified in Italy, the importance of place to socialization is certainly not limited to the passeggiata. Sociologists have noted the role of urban spaces and neighbourhoods in social ties worldwide, as well as the possibility that lifestyles in large urban regions may or may not be conducive to reinforcing localized social ties (Guest and Wierzbicki 1999; Putnam 2000; Gans 1965). Significant debate continues on how place impacts socialization, but it is worth noting that evidence of concentrated social activities occurs in both urban and suburban settings. Some activities occur on foot, others are motorized, or function as a hybrid of the two: consider urban dwellers meeting on the stoops of their apartment buildings, teenagers cruising in cars down the main street, or suburbanites strolling and shopping at the mall or (Ides 2009; Mehta 2013; Vanderbeck and Johnson 2000).

Regardless of name, all of these experiences are spatially focused and comprised of face-to-face interactions with companions. as well as generalized access to a broader social group. Dunkelman (2014) postulates a hierarchy of relationships defined by social distance, termed as "inner ring", "middle ring" or "outer ring". The traditional passeggiata arguably facilitates a distinctive type of "middle ring" interaction, facilitating affinity for neighbours even in the absence of direct interactions with all participants. Importantly, Dunkelman critiques sprawling contemporary cities – as well as ICT-based social networks – as responsible for eroding the "middle ring" relationships that he associates with a stronger local sense of belonging as citizenship.

Social travel on foot

Researchers have sought to understand the motivations and patterns of social activity and travel, with findings underscoring that social travel behaviour is distinct from more utilitarian travel, such as work and household errands (Carrasco *et al.* 2008; Axhausen 2005). All else being equal, social activities cluster most densely around the home and then disperse from them (Kwan 1999). However, people engage in social activities with other members of their social network, so the geography of social activities and trips is highly correlated with a person's social network, even as it expands due to ICT adoption (Kwan 2007).

In general, research on social travel is unspecific with regard to travel modes such as walking, biking, transit and driving. However, some inquiry emphasizes that particular modes can possess characteristics that increase their utility for social travel. Notably, walking can be understood as a social activity in itself, with utility for social interaction not just at the destination but along the way (Mokhtarian *et al.* 2015). Walking – with its slow pace, more direct sensory connection to one's surroundings, and being fully "on display" to others in a way that the car does not allow, have the potential to increase the utility of walking for social and recreational activities, beyond its utility in getting to a particular destination (Bean *et al.* 2008; du Toit *et al.* 2007; Csikszentmihalyi 2000).

Sociological mobilities research contributes additional insight into the nature of social travel. In particular, tourism and spectator-like "flaneurism" is presented as a paradigm for understanding how individuals interact with much of the contemporary city on a day-to-day basis, beyond the confines of home and work (Urry 1992; Shortell and Brown 2016). In the case of social travel, the literature highlights individuals' desire to "consume" social experiences throughout the city (Schroeder 2002). Urban economics frames contemporary cities as "centres of consumption", where high densities of amenities lead to faster growth rates (Glaeser *et al.* 2001). Further, density is correlated specifically with consumer amenities (Glaeser and Gottlieb 2006). Thus, dense, high-amenity cities may be more likely to conflate the consumption of amenities as a form social activity and travel. Such observational, consumption-oriented walkability may possess the physical characteristics of the passeggiata but still lack the civic value of authentic "middle ring" relationships.

Despite the possibility that contemporary walking sets walkers at a remove from their setting, including other walkers, economic geography has reinforced the value of face-to-face contacts in transactional activities (Storper and Venables 2004; McCann 2007). Face-to-face contact also enables participants to assess competitors, display one's strengths and reinforce network ties, echoing the motivations of the traditional passeggiata. Imperatives for face-to-face contact hold even more strongly for social interactions, where "to see and be seen" is an essential component of human behaviour (Csikszentmihalyi 2000). Walking can provide this quality of social interaction in a way that no other travel mode can.

The role of information technologies in social travel

Much of the research into the impact of technologies on travel behaviour has sought to determine whether ICTs replace trips, increase travel, or have little impact (Salomon 1985; Golob and Regan 2001; Janelle 2004). In principle, ICT was first understood as a travel replacement, reducing the need for physical proximity. Telecommuting, in particular, was seen as a means to reduce work trips (Nilles 1988). Others disagreed and argued that information technologies are not substitutes for face-to-face interactions, but complement them (Gaspar and Glaeser 1996). In fact, subsequent research found that telecommuting, despite its increasing adoption by workers, had relatively little effect on overall traffic patterns (Mokhtarian 1998). In this view, ICT is not a substitute for travel but a complement to it, increasing total interactions and thus the need or desire for face-to-face meetings. More recently, technology has been seen as a possible means of reducing household-serving trips, such as errands and shopping (Zhai *et al.* 2016). Again, however, evidence suggests that online shopping may actually stimulate in-store shopping as well (Lee *et al.* 2016).

Like telecommuting and online shopping, networked social activities such as gaming, online social networks such as Facebook, and instant communication modes such as texting and Twitter, could be construed as replacements for face-to-face social interaction. However, the idea that ICTs increase travel has held true for social travel as well. Not only is increased communication a lubricant for embodied interaction, but the flexibility in scheduling afforded by ICTs facilitates increased social interaction (Mokhtarian *et al.* 2006). Wang and Law (2007), for example find that ICT generates additional time use for out-of-home recreation activities and travel and increases trip-making propensity, particularly among younger or higher-income individuals, and a study in Melbourne, Australia finds that ICT use is associated with more frequent in-person contact with friends (Delbosc and Currie 2015).

Beyond the emerging consensus that it can increase the quantity of social travel, how ICTs effect the spatial and temporary organization of social travel remains little understood. Certainly, ICTs can change the timing and location of activities, increasing flexibility with regard to location and their timing (Kwan 2002). Furthermore, cognitive mapping and wayfinding research has reinforced the importance of having accurate spatial information to access destinations in a complex built environment such as a contemporary large city (Golledge and Stimson 1997; Mondschein *et al.* 2010). Traditionally, such information was gleaned through the experience of travel and secondarily through social networks. ICT provides a new source for information both about potential destinations and the routes to reach them. Technologies like GPS navigation, internet mapping, and recommendation services such as Yelp can allow individuals to go beyond the information constraints of their cognitive maps and circumvent the spatial constraints of previous experience and existing social networks (Vautin and Walker 2011; Mondschein 2015). Relief of these constraints changes where individuals travel, as these ICT services provide choices and routes assembled from the entire city.

The peripatetic passeggiata

Taking both the informational and behavioural effects of ICTs into account, a distinct tension arises between spatially extensive knowledge of social activity destinations and an increased demand for embodied, face-to-face interactions. Increased contact via ICT increases the utility of face-to-face social activities, but information technologies reduce time–space constraints, enhance coordination among individuals, and increase knowledge of opportunities and the means to reach them across the entire city. Taken together, these effects may facilitate social activities occurring outside familiar neighbourhood confines. However, the embodied quality of social activity should still apply. Social activities are "in person" activities. They are not just tied to a person's social network, but are more reliant upon physical and emotional cues that require embodied presence.

If urban dwellers are able to select social destinations from a broader set of choices enabled by ICTs, what will they choose? Will they stay closer to home, go further, or select for specific qualities of place? The wherewithal afforded by ICTs to be more selective about locations may facilitate social activities in locations that maximize the benefits of social experiences. Insofar as ICT users opt for locations that provide access to embodied human contact coupled with the amenities touted by urban theorists, ICT users may be more likely to engage in social activities in some of the most walkable places in a city, relative to others. This pattern, even across a large urban region, may in some ways recreate some part of the traditional passeggiata and other forms of social mobility: something done on foot and in the presence of a community engaging in similar activities. Despite the potential for clustered social walking, the question remains whether such patterns reinforce social ties, strengthening civic, "middle ring" relationships.

Looking at California

Current research on how ICTs may affect the location and travel modes of social activities is limited. However, a 2010–2012 travel survey in the state of California, US, can begin to illuminate how ICT use, social activity, and location may interact in large cities. Though the breadth of ICTs available to travellers has continued to expand, this recent survey captures data on ICT use across multiple relevant dimensions, including internet usage for personal use or work and the adoption of new ICT-enabled mobility technologies such as car sharing and road-toll transponders (Transportation Secure Data Center 2015). The analysis of the San Francisco Bay Area presented here shows that the social activities of ICT users do vary across neighbourhoods and by travel mode, as compared to the typical traveller. This pattern of social activity is noteworthy, not just because of its incidence in walkable places, but because of demographic differences between the residents of neighbourhoods hosting social activities and the visitors engaging in those activities.

Defining terms: ICT usage and the passeggiata

To observe the phenomena discussed in this chapter through empirical analysis, ICT usage and "the passeggiata" have been operationalized using the variables collected for San Francisco Bay Area adults (eighteen and over). Two types of information about ICT usage are provided for each individual: (1) time using the internet for personal and work reasons; and (2) use of specific mobility-related information technologies: car sharing, toll-road transponders, and transit smart cards. By 2010, cellphone penetration had become nearly ubiquitous among adults, and even smartphone ownership was estimated to be over 95% in most of the Bay Area and Southern California by 2013 (Environmental Systems Research Institute (ESRI) 2013). Thus, the use of mobility-focused ICTs such as car sharing and "smart" payment devices may be representative of an emergent class of travel-focused ICTs, with particular relevance to spatial activity and travel choices.

While each type of ICT usage is likely to have its own effect on activity and travel, we can also examine combined effects. For this spatial exploratory analysis, I estimate an "ICT usage score" for each individual in the survey, using principal components analysis (PCA), a standard method for exploring shared variability latent in a set of variables (Dunteman 1989). This analysis identifies common variability among daily internet usage (in minutes), car sharing membership, toll transponder possession, and transit smart card usage, defining the resulting measure as a generalized ICT usage score. PCA diagnostics show that the score is comprised relatively equally of variability from individual ICT measures, facilitating a "modally agnostic" approach to transportation technologies that is dominated neither by auto- or transit-oriented ICTs.

In addition to the ICT score, the analysis characterizes the passeggiata as social activity during non-working hours in a walkable place. The California travel survey supplies information about each activity along those measures. In addition to standard social activities such as visiting friends and family, the analysis includes meals taken outside the home. Content analysis of "restaurant reviews" on services such as Yelp and TripAdvisor confirms the significant social component of many restaurant experiences in urban neighbourhoods (Mondschein 2015). The passeggiata occurs in the evening, but many other social activities are likely to occur on weekends (Bhat and Misra 1999). This analysis therefore includes both evenings and weekends, times when coordinated social activities among adults are most likely to occur.

The final relevant dimension of the "passeggiata" concept is whether it occurred on foot in a central place. Unlike in a small village, however, many activities in large cities may be accomplished first by driving or taking transport to a walkable place, where the activity is finally effectuated. Travel surveys often privilege the longest trip involved in completing an activity, meaning that walking, even if critical to an activity, can often be left out of the dataset. Thus, the analysis emphasizes whether an activity was taken in a walkable place, defined by the walking rate for activities as a whole in a given neighbourhood. Neighbourhoods in the travel survey are represented by postal "zip" codes, which cover relatively small urban areas. Put another way, this analysis captures social activity in a walkable place, no matter the mode people use to arrive – on foot, by bike, transit or car. This may not be the traditional passeggiata, where arrival and the activity itself occur on foot, but is hopefully expressive of the likely scenario in a large contemporary city, where people travel by any means to access walkability.

ICT and social activity in the San Francisco Bay area

Figure 14.1 illustrates neighbourhoods in San Francisco and surrounding cities in terms of social activity patterns. The "social activity ICT score" represents how important ICT use is to a neighbourhood's social life. The score is the sum of each social activity, weighted by the socializer's ICT usage score, divided by the total number of social activities occurring in the neighbourhood, to provide a neighbourhood-level score on a scale from 0 to 1. A score of 0 would mean that every social activity occurring in a neighbourhood was undertaken by people with a personal ICT score of 0, and a neighbourhood score of 1 would mean that every social activity was completed by those with a personal score of 1. A higher score effectively means that relatively more ICT users go to that neighbourhood for their social activities, compared to other neighbourhoods.

The pattern in San Francisco is revealing. The City of San Francisco, in the centre left of the map (Figure 14.1), demonstrates a higher preponderance of ICT users coming to many of its neighbourhoods for social activities, but not uniformly so. While central neighbourhoods such as Nob Hill and the Financial District score highly, so do more peripheral neighbourhoods such as the Mission and Bayview. Importantly, these places in the southern parts of the city, are also known to be changing, with the term "gentrifying" frequently applied (Stehlin 2015). The pattern across the bay in Berkeley and Oakland is similar, with high ICT scores not just in core areas, but also those that are changing rapidly.

Table 14.1 expands upon the spatial patterns in Figure 14.1, with a comparison among neighbourhoods. Dividing Bay Area neighbourhoods into four ordered groups based on their social ICT scores, we see that, indeed, there is a very strong relationship between ICT score and walking. The higher the score, the more social trips, or trips of any type, are taken on foot. Note that while this is an aggregate ICT measure, which includes ICTs such as car sharing and transit smart cards that may be commonest in dense walkable neighbourhoods, the patterns here also hold for single ICT measures, including toll transponder usage and minutes of internet use.

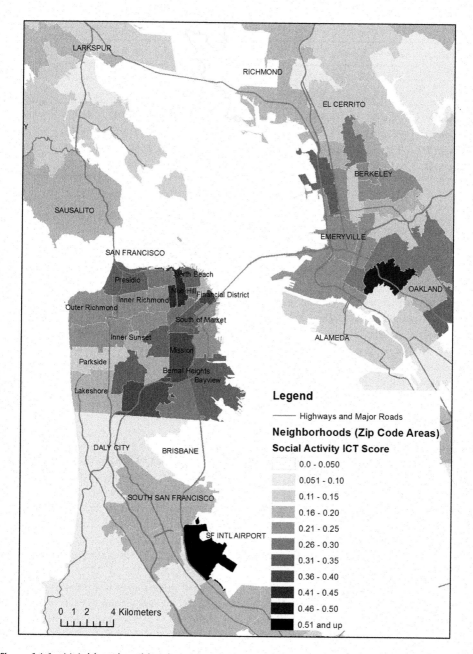

Figure 14.1 Neighbourhood-level social activity ICT Scores

Social walking and ICT usage may be closely correlated in neighbourhoods, but is that evidence of some kind of passeggiata in these neighbourhoods? Inasmuch as the passeggiata is a phenomenon not just of social walking with family and friends, but walking to reinforce broader community ties, the answer may be discouraging. Table 14.1 shows differences among those engaging in social activities – the "actors" – and those hosting that activity in their neighbourhoods – the "locals". The data reveal that neighbourhoods with more ICT users

Table 14.1 Walkability and demographic differences by local social activity ICT scores

Social activity ICT Score[1]	Local walkability		Education score[2]			% Non-Hispanic White		
	% All trips on foot	% Social trips on Foot	Actors	Locals	Diff.	Actors	Locals	Diff.
1st Quartile	8.6%	6.9%	3.95	3.80	0.15	47.0%	48.0%	–1.0%
2nd Quartile	10.2%	13.0%	4.34	4.00	0.34	61.4%	54.4%	7.0%
3rd Quartile	13.7%	10.4%	4.63	4.27	0.36	60.8%	49.8%	11.0%
4th Quartile	33.4%	37.7%	4.79	4.26	0.53	57.6%	47.7%	9.9%

Key

1 The score is the sum of each social activity, weighted by each actor's ICT usage score, divided by the total number of social activities occurring in the neighbourhood, providing a neighbourhood-level score on a scale from 0 to 1. Neighbourhoods are grouped into quartiles by their scores.

2 The average education level of "actors" engaging in social activities in the neighbourhood and "locals" living in the neighbourhood on an ordinal education scale, where: 1= Not a high school graduate; 2 = High school graduate; 3 = Some college; 4 = Associate or technical school degree; 5 = Bachelor's or undergraduate degree; 6 = Graduate degree

arriving to socialize are substantially more bifurcated among residents and visitors with regard to both education and race/ethnicity. Using the education scale from the travel survey, differences between actors and locals increase to more than half a step in neighbourhoods where ICT users are most likely to go. Similarly, the difference in ethnicity between social actors and locals increases substantially as ICT score increases. Non-Hispanic whites are more prevalent as actors by 10 percentage points than locals in high-ICT neighbourhoods.

Conclusions

The passeggiata is an appealing concept, because it not only ascribes personal utility to walking, whether cardiovascular health or mental well-being, but also social value in reinforcing both "inner ring" and more civic "middle ring" relationships. While these values may persist in small towns and less mobile cities, we do not yet understand how, if at all, this plays out in big contemporary cities. Empirical research has largely borne out the claim that ICTs increase social activity overall and may increase the demand for embodied social activity on foot, if only to facilitate the consummation of networked relationships and the consumption of urban amenities. What, though, does this new type of social walking, stimulated by ICTs, mean for the communities in which it occurs?

The examination of the Bay Area presented here is for a single city at one point in time, but the strength of the pattern merits further consideration. ICT users accomplish relatively more of their social activity in walkable neighbourhoods, often on foot. However, this social walking occurs in neighbourhoods that are demographically different – less educated and ethnically homogeneous – than the visiting walkers. Certainly, these results do not indicate whether these visitors either engage with or overlook neighbourhood residents as they meet their own social objectives. Nevertheless, concern that ICTs actually reinforce differences among urban populations, and contribute to social detachment rather than attachment, is growing among researchers as well as community members (Dal Fiore *et al.* 2014; Kelley 2014).

While travel behaviour patterns are part of the story, ultimately, further qualitative research must refine our understanding of how ICTs do not just shape behaviour, but modify our connections to the people we encounter near our homes or elsewhere, as part of a social experience. The "new passeggiata", inasmuch as we observe increased walking for social purposes, represents a change in how people make use of cities. Planners and other urban policy makers should consider how we can facilitate those changes. Exploration becomes easier and less risky with many new technologies, and a potential positive outcome, as the Bay Area data demonstrate, is increased activity in traditionally neglected or "under-the-radar" neighbourhoods. However, today, one of the most critical concerns for urban policy worldwide is gentrification and displacement, and the positive of economic development takes on negative implications as well (Hyde 2014; Zuk *et al.* 2015). Without suggesting that social activities on foot equate to displacement, at a minimum, advocates for walking and walkability should remain cognizant that where we walk can be just as important as how much.

References

Axhausen, K.W. (2005) 'Social networks and travel: some hypotheses', in K. Donaghy, S. Poppelreuter and G. Rudinger (eds), *Social Dimensions of Sustainable Transport: Transatlantic Perspectives*, Aldershot: Ashgate, pp. 90–108.

Bean, C.E., Kearns, R. and Collins, D. (2008) 'Exploring social mobilities: narratives of walking and driving in Auckland, New Zealand', *Urban Studies*, 45(13): 2829–2848.

Bhat, C.R. and Misra, R. (1999) 'Discretionary activity time allocation of individuals between in-home and out-of-home and between weekdays and weekends', *Transportation*, 26(2): 193–229.

Carrasco, J.A., Hogan, B., Wellman, B. and Miller, E.J. (2008) 'Collecting social network data to study social activity-travel behavior: an egocentric approach', *Environment and Planning B: Planning and Design*, 35(6): 961–980.

Castellanos, E. (2011) 'The symbolic construction of community in Italy', *Ethnology: An International Journal of Cultural and Social Anthropology*, 49(1): 61–78.

Csikszentmihalyi, M. (2000) 'The costs and benefits of consuming', *Journal of Consumer Research*, 27(2): 267–272.

Dal Fiore, F., Mokhtarian, P.L., Salomon, I. and Singer, M.E. (2014) '"Nomads at last"? A set of perspectives on how mobile technology may affect travel', *Journal of Transport Geography*, 41: 97–106.

Del Negro, G.P. (2004) *The Passeggiata and Popular Culture in an Italian Town*, Montreal: McGill-Queen's University Press.

Delbosc, A. and Currie, G. (2015) 'Does information and communication technology complement or replace social travel among young adults?', *Transportation Research Record: Journal of the Transportation Research Board*, 2531: 76–82.

du Toit, L., Cerin, E., Leslie, E. and Owen, N. (2007) 'Does walking in the neighbourhood enhance local sociability?', *Urban Studies*, 44(9): 1677–1695.

Dunkelman, M.J. (2014) *The Vanishing Neighbor: The Transformation of American Community*, New York: W.W. Norton & Company.

Dunteman, G.H. (1989) *Principal Components Analysis*, Newbury Park, CA: Sage.

ESRI (2013) *Joy to the Smartphone*, Redlands, CA: Environmental Systems Research Institute.

Gans, H.J. (1965) *The Levittowners: Ways of Life and Politics in a New Suburban Community*, New York: Institute of Urban Studies, Teachers College, Columbia University.

Gaspar, J. and Glaeser, E. (1996) 'Information technology and the future of cities', *National Bureau of Economic Research Working Paper Series*: 5562. Washington, DC: NBER.

Glaeser, E.L. and Gottlieb, J.D. (2006) 'Urban resurgence and the consumer city', *Urban Studies*, 43(8): 1275–1299.

Glaeser, E.L., Kolko, J. and Saiz, A. (2001) 'Consumer city', *Journal of Economic Geography*, 1(1): 27–50.

Golledge, R.G. and Stimson, R.J. (1997) *Spatial Behavior: A Geographic Perspective*, New York: The Guilford Press.

Golob, T.F. and Regan, A.C. (2001) 'Impacts of information technology on personal travel and commercial vehicle operations: research challenges and opportunities', *Transportation Research Part C: Emerging Technologies*, 9(2): 87–121.

Guest, A.M. and Wierzbicki, S.K. (1999) 'Social ties at the neighborhood level', *Urban Affairs Review*, 35(1): 92–111.

Hyde, Z. (2014) 'Omnivorous gentrification: restaurant reviews and neighborhood change in the downtown eastside of Vancouver', *City & Community*, 13(4): 341–359.

Ides, M.A. (2009) 'Cruising for community: youth culture and politics in Los Angeles, 1910–1970'. PhD thesis, University of Michigan, Ann Arbor.

Janelle, D.G. (2004) 'Impact of information technologies', in S. Hanson and G. Giuliano (eds), *The Geography of Urban Transportation*, 3rd edn, New York: The Guilford Press, pp. 86–112.

Kelley, M. (2014) 'Urban experience takes an informational turn: mobile internet usage and the unevenness of geosocial activity', *GeoJournal*, 79(1): 15–29.

Kwan, M.-P. (1999) 'Gender, the home–work link, and space–time patterns of nonemployment activities', *Economic Geography*, 75(4): 370–394.

Kwan, M.-P. (2002) 'Time, information technologies, and the geographies of everyday life', *Urban Geography*, 23(5): 471–482.

Kwan, M.-P. (2007) 'Mobile communications, social networks, and urban travel: hypertext as a new metaphor for conceptualizing spatial interaction', *The Professional Geographer*, 59(4): 434–446.

Lee, R.J., Sener, I.N., Mokhtarian, P.L. and Handy, S.L. (2016) 'Relationships between the online and in-store shopping frequency of Davis, California Residents'. Paper presented at Transportation Research Board 95th Annual Meeting. in Washington, DC, 10–14 January.

McCann, P. (2007) 'Sketching out a model of innovation, face-to-face interaction and economic geography', *Spatial Economic Analysis*, 2(2): 117–134.

Mehta, V. (2013) *The Street: A Quintessential Social Public Space*, London: Routledge.

Mokhtarian, P.L. (1998) 'A synthetic approach to estimating the impacts of telecommuting on travel', *Urban Studies*, 35(2): 215–241.

Mokhtarian, P., Salomon, I. and Handy, S. (2006) 'The impacts of ICT on leisure activities and travel: a conceptual exploration', *Transportation*, 33(3): 263–289.

Mokhtarian, P.L., Salomon, I. and Singer, M.E. (2015) 'What moves us? An interdisciplinary exploration of reasons for traveling', *Transport Reviews*, 35(3): 250–274.

Mondschein, A. (2015) 'Five-star transportation: using online activity reviews to examine mode choice to non-work destinations', *Transportation*: 42(4): 707–722.

Mondschein, A., Blumenberg, E. and Taylor, B.D. (2010) 'Accessibility and cognition: the effect of transport mode on spatial knowledge', *Urban Studies*, 47(4): 845–866.

Nilles, J.M. (1988) 'Traffic reduction by telecommuting: a status review and selected bibliography', *Transportation Research Part A: General*, 22(4): 301–317.

Putnam, R.D. (2000) *Bowling Alone: The Collapse and Revival of American Community*, New York: Simon & Schuster.

Salomon, I. (1985) 'Telecommunications and travel: substitution or modified mobility?', *Journal of Transport Economics and Policy*, 19(3): 219–235.

Schroeder, J.E. (2002) *Visual Consumption*, London: Routledge.

Shortell, T. and Brown, E. (eds) (2016) *Walking in the European City: Quotidian Mobility and Urban Ethnography*, London: Routledge.

Stehlin, J. (2015) 'Cycles of investment: bicycle infrastructure, gentrification, and the restructuring of the San Francisco Bay Area', *Environment and Planning A*, 47(1): 121–137.

Storper, M. and Venables, A.J. (2004) 'Buzz: face-to-face contact and the urban economy', *Journal of Economic Geography*, 4(4): 351–370.

Transportation Secure Data Center (2015) 2010–2012 California Household Travel Survey.

Urry, J. (1992) 'The tourist gaze "revisited"', *American Behavioral Scientist*, 36(2): 172–186.

Vanderbeck, R.M. and Johnson Jr, J.H. (2000) '"That's the only place where you can hang out": urban young people and the space of the mall', *Urban Geography*, 21(1): 5–25.

Vautin, D.A. and Walker, J.L. (2011) 'Transportation impacts of information provision and data collection via smartphones'. Paper presented at 2011 Annual Meeting of the Transportation Research Board 90th Annual Meeting, Washington, DC, 23–27 January.

Wang, D. and Law, F.Y.T. (2007) 'Impacts of information and communication technologies (ICT) on time use and travel behavior: a structural equations analysis', *Transportation*, 34(4): 513–527.

Zhai, Q., Cao, X., Mokhtarian, P.L. and Zhen, F. (2016) 'The interactions between e-shopping and store shopping in the shopping process for search goods and experience goods', *Transportation*: 1–20. DOI: 10.1007/s11116-016-9683-9.

Zuk, M., Bierbaum, A., Chapple, K., Gorska, K., Loukaitou-Sideris, A., Ong, P. and Thomas, T. (2015) *Gentrification, Displacement, and the Role of Public Investment: A Literature Review*, Berkeley, CA: University of California.

15

Walking online

A netnography of China's emerging hiking communities

Alexandra Witte and Kevin Hannam

Introduction

Walking practices and perceptions of nature and wilderness are socially and culturally determined and encoded. Edensor (2010) argues that movement in general is governed by rules, habits and conventions that are implicit forms of social knowing. This is a basic acknowledgement that where, how and why we move is dependent on a multitude of social, cultural, political and economic dimensions. Walking, as a most fundamental way of moving, is an easily accessible example of a mundane activity that yet holds within it a complicated array of codes of behaviour. Although the majority of the world's population walks, walking for leisure and as touristic activity, such as hiking, trekking, rambling and other related walking practices, are commonly associated with Western culture, finding its roots as an acceptable leisure pastime in the Romantic era as a individualistic as well as socially rewarding leisure activity (Ingold 2004). Research has thus been focused on Western tourists' motivation and experiences of walking, for example, on the Inca trail (Arellano 2004; Cutler *et al.* 2014), an autoethnographic narrative of walking the South West Coast Path (Wylie 2005), and the development of the Appalachian Trail community (Berg 2015; Hill *et al.* 2014; Littlefield and Suidzinski 2012), to name a few examples. While there is some research available looking at walking practices in non-Western contexts, these tend to not be focused on walking as recreational (e.g. Simbao 2013; Middleton 2009, 2011; Vaughan 2009; Legat 2008; Tuck-Po 2008; Collier and Hannam 2016).

However, leisure and tourism is no more an exclusively Western pursuit. With economic growth, generations of increasingly urbanised populations with emerging middle classes, in countries such as China, India and Brazil, now have more disposable income and leisure time, and increased mobility opportunities. Moreover, the diversification of the leisure and tourism markets in non-Western economies are bringing with them the potential for growing outdoor markets, including those dedicated to recreational walking practices, such as hiking, trekking, rambling and others. China, specifically, has become a new powerhouse in terms of tourism, its domestic market by far surpassing both outbound and inbound markets (Arlt 2013). Tourism in China had for a long time meant mainly travelling in a tour group, being shuffled from one scenic spot to the next. China's domestic tourism and leisure communities are thus not usually associated with the kind of walking communities found in the Western hemisphere, such as the

Ramblers in the UK or the US-based Sierra Club. In fact, spatial control measures within the People's Republic have for a long time made free movement, even for leisure purposes, impossible for the vast majority of Chinese citizens, a serious impediment for any leisure pursuit that depends on at least a certain amount of free movement. Relaxation of these restrictions and the increased mobility, easing of legislation to increase personal autonomy, and the rise of a new, predominantly urban, Chinese middle class that is highly consumption-driven, have meant that China's citizens are now increasingly on the move, pursuing various forms of travel and leisure activities (Shepherd 2008).

Leisure and tourism has become an individual and social activity within which people pursue activities that express their individual lifestyles (Yue-Fang *et al.* 2015). This process has been aided by the decentralisation and privatisation of areas such as sports, exercise and leisure and the emergence of concepts of individual health, pleasure and well-being, as well as increased leisure time (Xiong 2007). The internet has additionally made it possible for Chinese citizens to form communities dedicated to specific activities online that move outside the restrictions of "real-world" societies that are subjected to heavy state control in China (Zhang 2014). One of the specialised communities that have evolved as a result are China's online hiking communities. This chapter thus presents findings from a netnographic study of five such online communities, which focus on recreational walking practices, aiming to offer insight into the peculiarities of these communities and how online walking narratives are present performances of community, self and nature that are informed by both Chinese and seemingly imported Western narratives, which then merge into unique interpretations and representations of community identity and walking in nature as self-transformative experiences.

Methodological note

The research for this chapter is based on a netnographic approach that was chosen due to the development of Chinese online communities dedicated to specific leisure and tourism pursuits. Netnography is where the researchers immerse themselves in a range of related websites, blogs and/or other social media in order to explore and understand virtual communities (Mkono 2012). Kozinets (2002: 61) argues that "netnography" is ethnography adapted to the study of online communities: 'As a method, "netnography" is faster, simpler, and less expensive than traditional ethnography, and more naturalistic and unobtrusive than focus groups or interviews. It provides information on the symbolism, meanings, and consumption patterns of online consumer groups'.

In China, the development of online communities has allowed the formation of new hybrid worlds in which people interact among each other in combination of both the physical and digital worlds, allowing spatially and socially more stretched social networks (Jordan 2009; Larsen *et al.* 2006). In China, these new relational spaces for community building have opened opportunities to form networks outside of more traditional Chinese relational spaces of work and family environments. As Zhang (2014) has argued, this has given middle-class Chinese citizens the opportunity to diverge from the often formal and hierarchical conformity in traditional associational spaces in China, in which offline organisations, regardless of orientation, are highly controlled due to the legal requirement to be associated with an official sponsor (e.g. ministries) that overviews day-to-day activities. These new associational spaces allow for a more decentralised approach to community action and collaboration, which may foster democratic engagement and social networking (Zhang 2014) and also allow detachment from habitual situations and social spheres. Immersion within these non-traditional communal activities enables Chinese people to experience transformation and exploration of a personal nature, a way of stepping outside normative frameworks and building community identities and personal identities, which do not have to overlap with other their identities created offline (Scriven 2014).

For this research, five communities dedicated to recreational and touristic walking, ranging from speed hiking over wilderness trekking to mountain hiking, have been observed and engaged in over a time period of six months. These communities used recreational walking activities in nature to build community and individual identities centred on narratives of transformative journeys in nature against the "pampered" self, and a strong sense of community that in its structure challenges traditional vertical social hierarchies in China.

Discussion

Chinese society is often seen as of a highly collectivist nature in which identities are constructed around community and social networks rather than personal achievements and individual traits (Goodman 2014). This idea of a more collectivist orientation appears to hold true to an extent within online hiking communities in China as well. Community discussions, planning and evaluation of trips tended to strongly emphasise the communal and social aspect of the walking experience. One community member expressed their experience of participating in a three-day trek in the Gobi as follows.

Post after a hiking trip in Online Community 1

To be under the starry sky of the Gobi
To be in front of a warm campfire
And small exchanges and learning between partners
To share knowledge and comprehension
Not to seek fame and fortune
Not to deceive each other
Just beer
And barbecue
In the middle of laughter and cheerful voices
Enjoying rare satisfying days
A three-day long arduous trip
Working hard unhesitatingly
But everyone from this process
Receives unexpected rewards
And unforgettable memories

The experience of going on a walking trip together is presented as an opportunity for the members to connect through the companionship of the physical journey and the shared experience of the efforts involved, in which the walk allows for more interaction and a sense of "shared understanding" (Coleman and Collins 2006:79). For these communities, the organisation of group walks offers the opportunity to practise the identities formed in the online space of discussion forums and news bulletins in the offline space, connecting with the normally absent other in a physical form and affirm companionship and community identity during these outings. The sense of companionship on the trail is integral to the overall experience underlining all other experiences of challenge, escape and enjoyment, which has also been found to feature more strongly for

Chinese backpackers than for their Western counterparts (Luo *et al.* 2015; Zhang 2014), pointing to the traditionally strong cultural emphasis on interpersonal relations in Chinese society.

Frequently, posts evaluating and discussing walking and hiking trips afterwards would mention the cohesiveness of the team, the group atmosphere, and team members who made specific contributions during the experience (frequently the original organiser).

Posted after a bushwalking hike in Community 2

MEMBER A: A super fun bushwhacking full of dramatic surprise of dead snake and monkey encounter. Thanks Marc to move away the snake carcass and lead the screaming team to scare the monkeys away. Relished so much of Aiai's icy pineapple that served us the best energy booster for the second half of the walk, and the juicy pear from Sam. Thanks to the great team of joining me to tackle the incline of 800m under the early summer heat and humidity. Hope you like the reward of the shaded bamboo tunnel, light breeze at the top of Sze Fong Shan, cold dip at Tai Shing and the forestry trails that wrapped up the adventure.

MEMBER B: Amazing trail with full lot of energy well done everyone. Thank you Xiaohui. It's so lovely to have frozen pineapple on trail thank you Aiai.

MEMBER C: Thanks Xiaohui, it's a good underbrush hike. Also much thank for Aiai's pineapple as well =)

MEMBER D: Thanks Xiaohui, really appreciate this hike.

MEMBER E: Thanks Xiaohui, very enjoyable hike for pre summer! Nice to meet you all. Thank you Aiai ice pineapple!!

This emphasis on the social and sociable aspect of the hiking trips within the observed communities is based on an ethos of a supportive value system that engenders an emphasis on the team achievement practised in these outings, with a shared understanding of what it is to hike, trek or ramble together, belonging to one community.

Much of this creation of a community identity embodied in communal walking practices is happening in the online spaces, however. Specific markers of belonging to these communities are the common understanding and use of specific language. People engaging in outdoor walking practices such as hiking or trekking, as well as, more generally, Chinese backpackers, are widely known as "donkey friends" in China. The term donkey friend itself is not one given by academia, marketing or others outside these communities, but has developed in online forums, just as the ones observed here, as a play on the Chinese word for travel (旅游 lü3you2), which is pronounced similarly to the Chinese word for donkey friend (驴友 lü2you3), alluding to an emphasis on respecting nature, as well as the physical challenge of travelling on foot. Some of the communities engaged in here used their own specific language to describe themselves, always alluding to the kind of physical skills needed for the kind of leisure walking pursued, such as mountain goat (山羊 shan1yang2) for hill walking, hiking wolf (徒步狼 tu2bu4lang2) for long-distance trekking, and camel (骆驼 luo4tuo2) for desert hiking. These communities are therefore developing an insider language that symbolises their ideas of recreational walking practices in the outdoors as ways of being closer to nature, like the animal "avatars" they are using to describe themselves, and also as clear markers of belonging to their respective community.

A further marker of community identity is the subscription to a common code or community ethos that is the basis for being accepted as a member. This practice is reminiscent of original walking clubs such as the Sierra Club or *der Wandervogel* (Sonit 2001), that organise people around the common activity of walking. The existence of a community ethos that lays the basis for a common understanding of walking practices and associated codes of conduct is an aspect also commonly associated with forms of serious leisure, in which a community identity allows members serious about the particular leisure pursuit to acquire a sense of belonging to this community and identify with a specific value and belief system (Liu *et al.* 2016). They are common among outdoor-related recreation styles, such as climbing or hiking, that beyond the recreational activity in itself offer a form of lifestyle. The adoption of such a community ethos represents a degree of dedication that has the potential to move the individual from casual to serious leisure participants (Littlefield and Siudzinski 2012). It has to be acknowledged, however, that the simple subscription to such online communities as presented here does not necessitate a regular and intense engagement with it. Rather, these communities offer a platform for serious leisure participants, but members will be on a wide continuum from completely inactive to those who have made a career out of this leisure pursuit.

Beyond the adoption of a community ethos, a further aspect of these online communities points towards commonalities with the serious leisure discourse: skill and knowledge as markers of status and hierarchy. As Richmond *et al.* (2015) state, all communities have inherent power structures, hierarchies and rules of engagement that are created and assessed by formal and informal means. Status in Chinese society is strongly influenced by the concept of guanxi (关系 guan1xi), i.e. the individual's status is assessed and furthered strongly (though not exclusively) by networks of family, friends and work, which are based on a highly vertical hierarchy (Goodman 2014). In contrast, structures within the observed communities were not only much more horizontal and fluid, but also primarily based on personal skill and knowledge within the field of recreational walking practices. It was notable that usual social markers, such as occupation or family status, were absent from discussion forums, news bulletins and even member profiles. Instead, knowledge, skill and expertise in the kind of recreational walking activity the community was dedicated to, for example, speed hiking or mountain hiking were determinants of status of individual members, in many cases marked by titles such as, in one forum *Kid Goat, Nanny Goat* and *Mountain Goat* or *Sparrow, Seagull* and *Eagle* in another. These hierarchies are not, however, static, but open to reassessment at times, even initiated by the communities themselves. Challenges through which members can attain a certain status officially were common in the communities:

Hiking Challenge launched in Online Community 3

The Mountain Goat Challenge

reaching minimum 50 hills as a Kid Goat before June 2017 – honoured by facebook mention

reaching minimum 75 hills as a Nanny Goat before March 2018 – honoured by facebook mention

finishing 100 top hills and being certified as a Mountain Goat before Dec 2018 – honoured by certificate/trophy

Training Hikes offered by Online Community 2

To recognise your commitment to fitness, we will award you a title to a Sparrow, a Seagull or an Eagle if you attend more than 10, 30 or 50 training hikes respectively. All you need to do is to declare your intention to the coordinator who will check the records. If you don't declare it, there is no change!

This sense of experience and knowledge as status markers has been identified as a characteristic of serious leisure in the literature (Littlefield and Suidzinski 2012; Wheaton 2000). Skill and knowledge as basis for status within the community hierarchy allows for these hierarchies to be fluent, for the individual to gain recognition through a stronger dedication to their activity, regardless of "whom they know". In fact, the emphasis on expertise gained through experience engendered a strong sense of social learning within the communities. Forums and posts dedicated to issues such as proper equipment for specific types of outdoor and wilderness walking pursuits, information on health and safety and advice on walking techniques were common.

A series of discussion forum headings in Discussion Forum in Online Community 4 (Forum posts and discussions were both in Chinese and English. Chinese posts have been translated by one of the authors.)

- The need to train your muscles before going on a long-distance hike.
- Do you want to know a method for never getting tired during mountain hiking?
- Do you know the difference between walking sticks and trekking poles?
- Choosing an appropriate summer mountain hike.
- Teaching you the most comfortable outdoor walking technique.
- Principles to be followed by outdoor hikers.

In some communities, walks were marked by difficulty level and training walks were offered to members who wanted to achieve these levels of expertise.

Training Hikes offered by Online Community 1

Note: The primary objective to all our training is to build stamina through cardio hiking. In order to achieve the result of better fitness, not only you need to hike regularly but over time you need to go for faster, longer and higher altitude hikes.

We name our training – Sparrow for basic, Seagull for moderate and Eagle for hard and will try to schedule these hikes all year round if we find hosts. Since all hikes are host-driven, there will no hike if there is no host and host will have the final say whether to accept you into his or her hike.

This creation of a site for social learning between less and more experienced members of a community has also been observed as defining for outdoor walking practices in the Western context, e.g. for the Appalachian trail hiking community (Littlefield and Siudzinski 2012). It reaffirms social hierarchies within these communities that are dynamic and constantly under reassessment.

A further important characteristic in which these online hiking communities have shown themselves to differ from the normalised attitudes in Chinese society is their perception of nature and the place of humanity within the natural world. Notions of "proper" walking practices in nature and perceptions of nature itself as the site for these practices seem to draw on discourses of walking in nature as escape from, or even a protest against, urbanised lifestyles – drawing upon wider 'anti-urban' Romanticised ideologies (Whiting and Hannam 2014; Collier and Hannam 2016). Research on hiking in different contexts has emphasised the escape from city life as a common motivation (Cutler *et al.* 2014; Arellano 2004; Edensor 2000; Neumann 1992). For these communities too, exploring nature on foot is strongly linked to ideas of freedom, escape and reconnecting with a more natural state of being, a central theme in their walking experiences documented online.

Post of a Member of Online Community 1 (Author's transation)

Ultimately it is because I like nature, like the dense jungles, the crystal clear waters and the free fish within, I like the quiet rather than the hustle and bustle. So I am filled with love for nature. And thus I naturally love hiking. Measuring the world with both my feet, I can go to places where wheels cannot reach. [. . .] When you go hiking you are free, you go where you want to go.

Proposed trips often emphasise the beauty of nature as an escape from everyday life. It mirrors discourses of nature as a counterweight to modern urban life, a way to recharge or possibly even critique modern ways of living (Svarstad 2010) that are frequently argued to desensitise and undermine the human body (Edensor 2000; Lewis 2000). In a country with rapid urban development, nature and walking in nature in particular is now viewed increasingly by the Chinese middle classes, who live in the major urban centres, as a way of slowing down and moving differently from the dominant logic of speed (Vannini 2014).

Nature itself is also a culturally constructed concept. Any visitor to well-known nature destinations in China, such as Huangshan Mountain or Jiuzhaigou National Park, will have been confronted with very visible evidence of human intervention, whether in the form of inscriptions in stones, small shrines or cable cars. These underline a distinct tourist gaze in regards to nature-based recreation and tourism present in Chinese society, such that nature is appreciated in terms of its meaning and significance for local and national history and culture, thus signs of human intervention add rather than detract from the Chinese tourism experience (Winter 2009; Packer *et al.* 2014). However, this perception of nature as only being valuable within the framework of its historical, cultural or economic utility for humanity does not seem to hold true for the hiking communities here. Notably, many posts on planned or already finished outings singled out the fact that these hikes, walks and treks happened away from human intervention as much as possible, emphasising ideas of remoteness, lack of development and wilderness.

Conversation with member of Online Community 1 (Author's translation)

Hiking lovers enjoy and prefer pristine and quiet environments, not the spots with oceans of people. Donkey friends continuously explore and find new, previously untouched areas. One maybe has never heard of these places before but there the landscapes are unique.

These representations underscore a strive for quietness, a way of doing nature that is counter to built and controlled environments, in which speed and material gain hold pre-eminence. Implicitly and, at times, explicitly human-imposed boundaries are refuted.

Conversation in Discussion Forum in Online Community 2

USER 1: The hill top of Mt Kellett is a radio station. It is a restricted area. One needs to walk along the fence following ribbons and scramble inside to reach a flat roof with radio stations at corners.

USER 3: The nearby luxurious flats will be hemmed by different bunch of MG soon. The owners might need to recruit more security guards to keep an eye on the curious goats☺

Research on donkey friends with regards to backpacking has similarly found that many donkey friends will try to circumvent government-imposed entrance fees for entering old towns or mountains, and that not paying these fees may be seen as a badge of honour in the creation of a travel identity (Luo *et al.* 2015; Zhang 20014).

However, while antithetical to more traditional ideas of nature and human intervention, walking in nature is still regulated by certain types of 'expert' knowledge and body discipline that are communicated by certain values and attitudes (Edensor 2000). A theme common across all five online communities observed and strongly linked to ideas of remote nature and wilderness was that of challenge and accomplishment, a narrative that Edensor calls 'Spartan Endeavours', that produce superior physical conditions and more intense bodily experiences as a counterweight to the over-socialised urban body (Edensor 2000). Solnit (2001) refers to this form of walking as movement at the body's limit, an equally valid if less culturally hallowed experience of nature (Solnit 2001). It is a way of walking in nature that is most commonly associated with the body aestheticised as goal-driven, overcoming its limits, in long-distance hiking such as the West Highland Way, Pacific Crest Trail or the Appalachian Trail. Interestingly, however, there is relatively little opportunity for this type of long-distance hiking, as China does not have a single long-distance trail and geographical and cultural barriers are relatively high for those wishing to engage in this kind of hiking. As one community member expressed in a conversation:

> The type of long-distance hiking typified by the Appalachian, Pacific Crest, and Continental Divide trails [. . .] is rarely undertaken in China by the domestic population. [. . .] the relative lack of economic freedom as compared to the West, allows relatively few people to under- take such trips. Work scheduling is a significant barrier. [. . .] Moreover, this is a country which, outside of Western borderlands such as Yunnan, Sichuan, Tibet and Xinjiang, lacks significant areas of true wilderness.

Nevertheless, many accounts of walking experiences in the communities spoke of overcoming challenges, mental and physical, enduring physical hardship and developing endurance, strength and skill through more strenuous outdoor walking practices. These accounts ranged from com- pleting a pre-given trail in a certain amount of time, to several days of potentially dangerous and physically and mentally harrowing long-distance treks through unmarked mountains and deserts in the aforementioned Western borderlands.

Member Post in Online Community 1 (Author's translation)

If there is no backup during the Gobi desert crossing, then there is a considerable risk; just recently there were reports of two students crossing the Gobi who had run into danger: one died one was injured – this is not a joking natter. The Gobi is arid, in the daytime you get sunburned, at night it is freezing, the lack of referencing points disorients, coming across wild animals – these are all problems encountered. For people without professional training and preparation, it should not be attempted lightly.

Member Post in Online Community 1 (Author's translation)

Looking down from our flight home, I realise in these brief few minutes, we have surpassed this four-day long arduous trail. We smile at each other. This was a free choice – facing the wind, depending on each other, because we believe: your spirit exists in a distant place waiting for your footsteps. [. . .] On this trail you experience physical and mental hardship, putting some things aside and retrieving others – this is the purpose of our trip.

These accounts of facing and passing challenges posed by nature and one's own body also link back to the previously discussed emphasis on community – 'depending on each other' – and the development of expert knowledge as status markers – 'for people without professional training and preparation, it should not be attempted lightly'. They emphasise the struggle with the self, the pain of sore muscles and blistered feet and the conquering of one's own perceived limitations.

Conclusions

The stories discussed in this chapter are testimonies of walking practices that are embodied both off- and online, in which quests for nature, self-transformation through challenge and community belongingness are alternately at play. For the Chinese hikers, finding the real "mountain goat, donkey friend or hiking wolf" leads to a conceptualisation of recreational walking practices that adapt and merge Western ideas of nature walking practices with normative Chinese society. Within these hybrid worlds, the online hiking communities challenge traditional Chinese attitudes to nature, as well as social conventions of community formation and hierarchies, by showing little concern for family, work units, gender, class, geography or ethnic belonging as defining aspects of their identities. Instead, they develop online a sense of 'individuality' within the overall community identity that is based upon their individual experiences, knowledge and skills in walking. These narratives are informed by and contest the urban roots of these communities, in which nature and walking in nature are seen as escapes, ways of critiquing modern lifestyles driven by the logic of speed and commercialisation. Walking for leisure and tourism and online clubs dedicated to these practices are a relatively new phenomenon in China, and seem likely to continue drawing on existing Western discourses, such as the anti-urban, especially those that valorise the physical and mental challenges of long-distance hiking.

References

Arellano, A. (2004) 'Bodies, spirits and Incas: performing Machu Picchu', in M. Sheller and J. Urry (eds), *Tourism Mobilities: Places to Play, Places in Play*, London: Routledge, pp. 67–77.

Arlt, W.G. (2013) 'The second wave of Chinese outbound tourism', *Tourism Planning and Development*, 10(2): 126–133.

Berg, A. (2015) '"To conquer myself": the new strenuosity and emergence of "thru-hiking" on the Appalachian Trail in the 1970s', *Journal of Sport History*, 42(1): 1–19.

Coleman, S. and Collins, P. (eds) (2006) *Locating the Field: Space, Place and Context in Anthropology*, Oxford: Berg.

Collier, M. and Hannam, K. (2016) '(Re)envisioning the anti-urban: artistic responses in the walking with Wordsworth and Bashō exhibition', in A. Kjærulff, K. Hannam, S. Kesselring and P. Peters (eds), *Envisioning Networked Urban Mobilities*, London: Routledge.

Cutler, S., Carmichael, B. and Doherty, S. (2014) 'The Inca Trail experience: does the journey matter?', *Annals of Tourism Research*, 45: 152–166.

Edensor, T. (2000) 'Walking in the British countryside: reflexivity, embodied practices and ways to escape', *Body and Society*, 6(3–4): 81–106.

Edensor, T. (2010) 'Walking in rhythms: place, regulation, style and the flow of experience', *Visual Studies*, 25(1): 69–79.

Goodman, D. (2014) *Class in Contemporary China*, Cambridge: Polity Press.

Hill, E., Gómez, E., Goldenberg, M., Freidt, B., Fellows, S. and Hill, L. (2014) 'Appalachian and Pacific Crest trail hikers: a comparison of benefits and motivations', *Journal of Unconventional Parks, Tourism and Recreation Research*, 5(1): 9–16.

Ingold, T. (2004) 'Culture on the ground: the world perceived through the feet', *Journal of Material Culture*, 9(3): 315–340.

Jordan, B. (2009) 'Blurring boundaries: the "real" and the "virtual" in hybrid spaces', *Human Organization*, 68(2): 181–193.

Kozinets, R.V. (2002) 'The field behind the screen: using netnography for marketing research in online communities', *Journal of Marketing Research*, 39: 61–72.

Larsen, J., Axhausen, K. and Urry, J. (2006) 'Geographies of social networks: meetings, travel and communications', *Mobilities*, 1(2): 261–283.

Legat, A. (2008) 'Walking stories; leaving footprints', in T. Ingold and J. Vergunst (eds), *Ways of Walking: Ethnography and Practice on Foot*, Aldershot, Hants: Ashgate, pp. 35–50.

Lewis, N. (2000) 'The climbing body, nature and the experience of modernity', *Body and Society*, 6(3–4): 58–80.

Littlefield, J. and Siudzinski, R. (2012) 'Hiking your own hike': equipment and serious leisure along the Appalachian Trail', *Leisure Studies*, 31(4): 465–486.

Liu, H., Bradley, M. and Burk, B. (2016) 'I am roller derby: the serious leisure and leisure identity of roller derby participants', *World Leisure Journal*, 58(1): 28–43.

Luo, X., Huang, S. and Brown, G. (2015) 'Backpacking in China: a netnographic analysis of donkey friends' travel behaviour', *Journal of China Tourism Research*, 11: 67–84.

Middleton, J. (2009) '"Stepping in time"': walking, time, and space in the city', *Environment and Planning A*, 41: 1943–1961.

Middleton, J. (2011) 'Walking in the city: the geographies of everyday pedestrian practices', *Geography Compass*, 5(2): 90–105.

Mkono, M. (2012) 'Netnographic tourist research: the internet as a virtual fieldwork site', *Tourism Analysis*, 17(4): 553–555.

Neumann, M. (1992) 'The trail through experience: finding self in the recollection of travel', in C. Ellis and M.G. Flaherty (eds), *Investigating Subjectivity*, London: Sage, pp.176–201.

Packer, J., Ballantyne, R. and Hughes, K. (2014) 'Chinese and Australian tourists' attitudes to nature, animals and environmental issues: implications for the design of nature-based tourism experiences', *Tourism Management*, 44: 101–107.

Richmond, D., Sibthorp, J., Jostad, J. and Pohja, M. (2015) 'Social dynamics in outdoor adventure groups: factors determining peer status', *Journal of Outdoor Recreation, Education, and Leadership*, 7(2): 180–183.

Scriven, R. (2014) 'Geographies of pilgrimage: meaningful movements and embodied mobilities', *Geography Compass*, 8(4): 249–261.

Shepherd, R. (2008) 'Cultural preservation, tourism and "donkey travel" on China's frontier', in T. Winter, T. Peggy and C. Tou (eds), *Asia on Tour: Exploring the Rise of Asian Tourism*, London: Routledge, pp. 253–263.

Simbao, R. (2013) 'Walking the other side: Doung Anwar Jahangeer', *Third Text*, 27(3): 407–414.

Solnit, R. (2001) *Wanderlust: A History of Walking*, New York: Penguin Books.

Svarstad, H. (2010) 'Why hiking? Rationality and reflexivity within three categories of meaning construction', *Journal of Leisure Research*, 42(1): 91–110.

Tuck-Po, L. (2008) 'Before a step too far: walking with Batek hunter-gatherers in the forests of Pahang, Malaysia', in T. Ingold and J. Vergunst (eds), *Ways of Walking: Ethnography and Practice on Foot*, Aldershot, Hants: Ashgate, pp. 21–34.

Vannini, P. (2014) 'Slowness and deceleration', in P. Adey, D. Bissell, K. Hannam, P. Merriman and M. Sheller (eds), *The Routledge Handbook of Mobilities*, Abingdon, Oxon: Routledge, pp. 116–124.

Vaughan, L. (2009) 'Walking the line: affectively understanding and communicating the complexity of place', *The Cartographic Journal*, 46(4): 316–322.

Wheaton, B. (2000) '"Just do it": consumption, commitment, and identity in the windsurfing subculture', *Sociology of Sport Journal*, 17(3): 254–274.

Whiting, J. and Hannam, K. (2014) 'Journeys of inspiration: working artists' reflections on tourism', *Annals of Tourism Research*, 49: 65–75.

Winter, T. (2009) 'The modernities of heritage and tourism: interpretation of an Asian future', *Journal of Heritage Tourism*, 4(2): 105–115.

Wylie, J. (2005) 'A single day's walking: narrating self and landscape on the South West Coast Path', *Transactions of the Institute of British Geographers*, 30(2): 234–247.

Xiong, H. (2007) 'The evolution of urban society and social changes in sports participation at the grassroots in China', *International Review for the Sociology of Sport*, 42(4): 441–471.

Yue-Fang, W., Xu, H.-G. and Lew, A. (2015) 'Consumption-led mobilized urbanism: socio-spatial separation in the second-home city of Sanya', *Mobilities*, 10(1): 136–154.

Zhang, N. (2014) 'Web-based backpacking communities and online activism in China: movement without marching', *China Information*, 28(2): 276–296.

Part III
Hiking Trails and Pilgrimage Routes

16

Hut-to-hut-hiking trails

A comparative analysis of popular hiking destinations

Sven Gross and Kim Werner

Introduction

Hiking, as demonstrated by many contributions in this volume, is one of the most popular leisure and holiday activities across the world. While a multitude of different definitions exists, hiking in its simplest form can be defined as 'walking for recreational purposes' (Taylor 2015: 263). Related terms include rambling, tramping, hill-walking, bushwalking, yomping, trail-walking and trekking (Taylor 2015; Werner *et al.* 2009). The current chapter will treat these terms as being for the most part synonymous and will use *hiking* as the preferred term.

Several forms of hiking can be distinguished, dependent on different criteria. According to the duration of the hike, half-day, day and multi-day hikes are differentiated. Depending on the elevation, lowland, upland and mountain walks exist (Menzel *et al.* 2008). A further differentiation is the geographic spread: here, international/European long-distance trails, national long-distance trails, regional trails and local trails (including themed and heritage trails) can be distinguished (Dreyer *et al.* 2010).

The so-called "hut-to-hut hiking" can be found in more than a dozen countries and at different spatial levels. A "hut" is the common term used for overnight accommodation associated with hiking. These facilities are typically basic and often include shared cooking facilities, sometimes cold water, composting toilets and bunk beds in shared sleeping rooms (Werner *et al.* 2009). After an extensive online research, (hiking) huts could be identified in Australia, Austria, Canada, Finland, France, Germany, Iceland, Ireland, Italy, Japan, Kenya, New Zealand, Norway, Peru, Scotland, South Africa, Sweden, Switzerland and the USA. Due to space limitations, four countries on four different continents (excluding Africa, since hut-to-hut-hiking options are rather limited on the African continent) have been selected for this chapter. As such, hut-to-hut-hiking offerings in Germany, Canada, New Zealand and Japan are described and compared.

Methods

For the comparative analysis of the four hiking destinations, an extensive review of relevant literature on hut-to-hut hiking and related terms was conducted. This included peer-reviewed research papers (e.g. Chhetri *et al.* 2004; Beedie and Hudson 2003), textbooks (e.g. Dreyer

159

et al. 2010; Musa *et al.* 2015), conference proceedings (e.g. Gross and Menzel 2012; Lumma and Gross 2010) tourism research and statistics (e.g. Canadian Tourism Commission 2003; TNZ 2016a), internal management reports (e.g. DoC 2015), promotional literature (e.g. DoC 2013), press articles (e.g. Cook 2016), hiking magazines (e.g. *Backcountry Magazine* 2016) and guide books (e.g. McLachlan *et al.* 2009) and formed the basis for a strengths and weaknesses analysis of the selected destinations.

Comparative analysis of popular hiking destinations

Germany

Hiking is a preferred leisure and/or holiday activity for Germans. Approximately 40 million Germans hike and spend up to 7.5 billion euros annually for 370 million one-day hiking tours. The typical German hiker is between 40 and 60 years old, has an educational level above average and there is a slight bias toward male (52 per cent). Germany has numerous interesting and well-signposted hiking tracks in all the federal states and almost one-third of the total area is covered with forests. The most popular mountain regions for hiking (holidays) are the low mountain ranges and the Alps (Dreyer *et al.* 2010; Dreyer and Menzel 2016; Gross and Menzel 2012; Project M *et al.* 2014). Hut-to-hut hiking can be found in the Alps and in various low mountain ranges in Germany. Examples are the Black Forest, the Bavarian Forest, the Harz Mountains, the Palatinate Forest, as well as the Eifel, the Röhn Mountains, the Rennsteig and the Rothaarsteig.

Part of the Alps are located in the southern part of Germany, which is regarded as one of the largest and most important hiking areas in Europe and well known for hut accommodation. The huts are mostly used in summer by mountaineers and hikers. However, winter rooms also exist and provide protection and accommodation outside the management period of the mountain huts, thus enabling hiking experiences during all four seasons (DAV 2016). There are 325 huts, all managed by the German Alpine Association, Deutschen Alpenverband (DAV), located not only in Germany, but also in Austria and Switzerland. Most of the huts (around 200 of the 325 huts) are managed and leased by a section of the DAV and operated by refuge managers (DAV n.d.a).

The DAV offers three hut categories. Category I-huts are located in regions well known for alpine mountaineering and should retain their character as a base for climbers and hikers. They are simply equipped and either managed, unmanaged, maintained or can be a bivouac. Category II-huts are usually in highly frequented tourist areas and offer better facilities and catering, making them especially suitable for active summer and winter breaks, such as family holidays, cross-country skiing or hiking. They are managed all year round and can be reached by car or lift. Category III-huts are primarily for day visitors, offering typical regional food and accessibility by lifts. Overnight stays are offered infrequently. In addition to the huts there are also self-catering chalets. These are often only available for members of the respective section (DAV n.d.b).

In May 2013, a hut and tariff regulation was introduced which stipulates that a maximum of 75 per cent of beds may be booked in advance and that the use of a special hut sleeping bag is mandatory. Also, at least one warm meal must be offered between 12 noon and 8 pm. Hut prices depend on the cabin categories, discounts are available for Alpine Club members. Further regulations cover aspects such as security, behaviour in the cabin and in the environment, complaints as well as compulsory registration. Adequate first aid kits must be provided in each hut and each overnight guest has to sign into the hut book on arrival (DAV n.d.c).

The issue of environmental protection is important, since most huts are located in protected natural areas such as nature parks, national parks and nature reserves. Consequently, a sustainable operation and modernisation of the huts is important and recent technological developments (e.g. sustainable energy supply or wastewater treatment) assist in this matter. Huts that are particularly environmentally friendly and energy-efficient (52 in Germany in 2014) are awarded an environmental seal of quality (AVS/DAV/oeAV 2006).

Rather than offering fixed tracks, the Alps provide route suggestions, e.g. suggestions from alpine clubs or on tour portals such as www.alpenvereinaktiv.com. About 50 suggestions for hut-to-hut hikes can be found here (mid-2016), mostly for the summer season. Besides these suggested individual tours, various package deals are also available.

For individual tours, the huts can be booked on the website of the DAV or via the online platform www.alpenvereinaktiv.com. On both websites, each hut is presented in conjunction with tour suggestions. Package tours can be booked via websites from tour operators, tourism organisations or mountain guides. In this case, the depth of information varies and the hut description is often not very detailed. Sometimes further information needs to be requested directly (by phone or email).

The Wilderness Trail Eifel National Park

The Wilderness Trail Eifel National Park (opened in 2007) is an 85-km-long hiking trail that winds its way across four sections (18–25 km each) through the Eifel National Park. The routing was designed for hikers to pass all characteristic landforms of the Eifel National Park (forests, plateaus, 11 Eifel viewpoints). When designing the trails, attention was paid to use natural paths instead of forest roads to enhance the wilderness experience. The route is marked with the Eifel National Park's uniform wood panels and it is also possible to use a GPS device. Corresponding data is stored on the website of the Eifel National Park. Since 2009, heritage interpretation has been introduced following the example set by American National Parks. As such, valuable information (about sights, geology, animals and plants) and short stories are available via audio and video files (45 short videos and podcasts in German) and can be downloaded on a smartphone or GPS-device (Mr Michael Lammertz personal communication 2 July 2009; Nationalpark Eifel 2016). Accommodation options primarily include hotels and guest houses in the Eifel National Park. A "low-budget option", with huts and campsites, is also possible. However, hut-to-hut hiking is still in a development stage and is intended to be increased and further improved in the future (Mr Michael Lammertz personal communication 24 April 2016). The Wilderness Trail can be organised individually or booked as a package, including accommodation, transportation, accompanying literature, hiking pass and certificate. Optional offers such as rest days, luggage transport or a ranger can be also added (Nationalpark Eifel 2016).

Between 2008 and 2012, 2,827 package tours with a turnover of 585,000 euros were booked (excluding transport, meals, admission fees and other purchases). In total, the Wilderness Trail added approximately 9,000 additional overnight stays and contributed to an additional turnover of 1.17 million euros between 2008 and 2012. Common calculation models estimate an employment effect of 16.6 additional full-time jobs per year (Landesbetrieb Wald and Holz Nordrhein-Westfalen 2013).

Canada

Canada is known for its vast extent and sparse population. With nearly 9 million km² and about 36 million people, in early 2016, the population density is just under four people per km² (Statistics Canada 2016). In 2014 and 2015 approximately 25 per cent (6,281,852) of adult Canadians went hiking, climbing or paddling while on an out-of-town, overnight trip of one or more nights. This was the fourth-most common outdoor activity type undertaken by Canadian pleasure travellers in those two years. Hiking as a same-day excursion (18.1 per cent) was the most common activity, followed by freshwater kayaking or canoeing (8.9 per cent), and wilderness hiking or backpacking as an overnight trip with camping or lodging (5.6 per cent) (TAMS 2006).

> Hikers, Climbers and Paddlers are evenly divided between males and females. Relative to the average Canadian pleasure traveler, they are more likely to be young (18 to 34 years of age) and they are over-represented among young singles and young couples. This is a well-educated segment with 40.1 per cent having a university degree . . . and above-average household incomes ($77,490).
>
> *(TAMS 2006: 4)*

In total, Canada attracts about 18 million international overnight visitors annually, with the majority (approximately 12.5 million) coming from the United States (Destination Canada 2015). Unfortunately, characteristics of international hikers are not available.

Canada offers more than 278,000 km of managed trails and the vast majority is located in rural regions (95 per cent). Many of these trails are tracks for single use, such as snowmobiling, all-terrain vehicles, hiking, cross-country skiing, cycling, mountain biking or horseback riding. More than 71,000 km of managed trails in Canada are shared-use trails (Norman 2010).

Canada also offers at least 60 huts for hikers, skiers, snowshoers, etc. Most of them are located in British Columbia and some are only accessible by helicopter or skis. Few of these huts are, however, located on or next to the long distance trails (*Backcountry Magazine* 2016). The largest hut operator is the Alpine Club of Canada which runs 36 lodges (ACC 2016a).

Overall, there aren't many hut-to-hut experiences in Canada, since a lot of hikers camp, rather using camp-to-camp trails. This is also found in a study from 2006: 16.4 per cent of the respondents stayed at a campsite in a wilderness setting, but only 2.5 per cent in a remote or fly-in wilderness lodge (TAMS 2006). Since the focus of this chapter is hut-to-hut hiking, a detailed online research on huts and tracks in Canada was conducted. Lecturers and professors from Canadian universities (among others Thompson Rivers University and University of Calgary) also assisted with this research. The results are presented in Table 16.1.

Table 16.1 Overview of hut-to-hut hiking in Canada

Name of the trail	Description	Webpage/s
Tracks		
Esplanade Track, British Columbia	• 6- or 7-day trails with 3 huts in alpine basins • Organisers: West Canada Tours, Yamnuska Mountain Adventures (among others)	• http://canadianrockieshiking.com/hiking-walking-tours/esplanade-track-hut-to-hut-hiking • www.westcanadatours.com/hiking/wells_gray_5.shtml
Sunshine Coast Trail (SCT), British Columbia	• 180-km track from Sarah Point in Desolation Sound to Saltery Bay • 13 huts (for 8–12 people), making it the longest hut-to-hut hiking experience in Canada (and the only free one) • SCT is listed among the 50 best hikes in the world by Explore Magazine	• http://sunshinecoast-trail.com

Name of the trail	Description	Webpage/s
Tracks		
Wapta Ice Hike, Lake Louise, Banff National Park, Alberta	• 3-day traverse: from Bow Lake via the Bow Glacier to the Peyto Glacier with alpine huts en-route • Possible for skiers in winter (e.g. 4- or 6-day tours) • Organisers: Yamnuska Mountain Adventures, OnTop (among others)	• http://ontopmountaineering.com/index.php/trips/trek/canada/little-wapta-glacier-trek • http://canadianrockieshiking.com/hiking-walking-tours/wapta-ice-hike1 • http://yamnuska.com/ski-mountaineering/wapta-traverse
Wells Gray, British Columbia	• 3 comfortable cabins sited a day's hike apart • 3, 4, 5 and 7 days through the Cariboo Mountains • Organiser: Wells Gray Adventures • Rated by *National Geographic* as 'One of the 30 best North American Trails' (http://adventure.nationalgeographic.com/adventure/trips/best-trails/wells-gray-huts-british-columbia)	• http://wellsgraypark.info/hut-to-hut-hiking • www.skihike.com/site/summer/hut_to_hut_hiking.html
Superior associations		
Alpine Club of Canada (ACC)	• 36 huts, mostly in British Columbia and Alberta • The huts are not commercial lodges, and no staff-based services are provided • Individual hut-to-hut treks have to be created by booking the cabins separately	www.alpineclubofcanada.ca/facility/view-all-huts
Backcountry Lodges of BC Association	• Association of 29 privately owned lodge operations (since 2004) • All lodges are located in the mountainous regions of British Columbia • 8–30 beds, an average of 12 beds • Not hut-to-hut, but some huts can be connected • Most of these are lodges to ski out of and back to on a daily basis	http://backcountrylodgesofbc.com

As most of the huts are operated by the Alpine Club of Canada, the ACC will be described in more detail. The ACC hut system integrates facilities operated by the national level of the clubs in Alberta and British Columbia, as well as additional huts operated by other ACC sections across Canada. Huts range from small remote shelters to log cabins which have capacity for six to 40 people in sleeping areas.

Typically, the huts provide propane stoves for cooking, propane lamps for lighting, cooking utensils and dishes, as well as foam mats in the sleeping areas. Many of the huts are also equipped with wood or propane burning stoves for heating. Privy toilets are provided and these most often utilize a fly-out barrel system, where human waste is periodically removed by helicopter for treatment.

(ACC 2016b)

In contrast to Germany, only one cabin category exists and no route suggestions are provided. However, the ACC has a hut classification for four target groups: 24 of the cabins are more suitable for climbers, 11 for hikers, 19 for skiers, and five are provided for the Wapta Traverse (a multi-day hut-to-hut ski traverse in Banff National Park) (Table 16.1).

The hut users need to bring their own sleeping bag, do their own cooking, fetch fresh water from nearby streams or melt snow, keep the huts clean and take the waste back. There is no local staff on site. In addition, hikers are required to plan their own trips, pay attention to the weather conditions (including avalanche risks in winter) and bring all necessary equipment (ACC 2016b). Due to the isolated location of some huts, specific safety information for the winter season has been published (for example for the Bill Putnam Hut). The environment is an important factor and the ACC constantly seeks to introduce new, environmentally responsible energy and waste management systems to reduce the negative environmental impact.

Bookings can be made personally in the Canmore Clubhouse or via phone. Further information is also available via email, brochures or the websites of the ACC and other partners (e.g. the International Climbing and Mountaineering Federation). Huts cost CAN $30 per night for members and CAN $40 for non-members. In addition to the rates per hut, all hikers need to purchase a National Park Wilderness Pass (Overnight Wilderness Pass: CAN $9.80, Annual Wilderness Pass: $68.70). Due to high demand in winter, ski weeks have to be booked through a lottery system for some huts (for example, for the Bill Putnam Hut and Kokanee Glacier Cabin, which are both only accessible by helicopter in winter). As such, groups (minimum four people) can enter the lottery to stay at the respective hut for a week (CAN $1,000 per person, including return flights and accommodation) (ACC 2016c).

New Zealand

New Zealand's climate, diverse geography and beautiful scenery make it a popular hiking destination. There are thousands of kilometres of formed walking tracks in the country that range from highly developed and structured tracks (accessible for wheelchairs) to remote and barely formed trails in wilderness, and from very short walks to those of several days' duration (Walrond 2012). The country's international tourism marketing organisation, Tourism New Zealand (TNZ), actively promotes hiking to showcase New Zealand's diverse landscapes, wildlife and environments (TNZ n.d.b).

In 2013, approximately 230,000 visitors participated in a hiking activity during their visit to NZ (total international visitor arrivals in 2013: 2,717,695). While these figures have been declining slightly (2011: 270,000), hiking remains a key driver of economic growth within NZ's tourism industry. Those visitors travelling to NZ for hiking stay longer and spend more (NZ $3,600 on average) than "normal" holiday visitors (NZ $2,800). Most of them come from Australia, USA, UK, Germany, Japan and the Netherlands, i.e. western markets clearly dominate. Forty-nine per cent of the walking and hiking visitors are aged 15–34 and there is a slight bias toward males (51 per cent). The visitors are also predominantly independent travellers (89 per cent) (TNZ 2014).

Most hiking in NZ takes place in national parks, reserves and other land managed by the Department of Conservation (DoC). The DoC is the government agency in charge of conserving NZ's natural and historical heritage (DoC n.d.a). It manages approximately 14,000 km of tracks, 960 huts and 330 campsites around NZ (DoC 2015). The tracks are usually well developed, maintained and signposted. Hikers can either stay in campsites or huts along the tracks. The huts come in a wide range of forms, shapes and sizes. They usually provide bunk beds (75cm per person) and water supply (from a rainwater- or streamwater-filled tank) but hikers need to bring their own cooking utensils, showers, sheets, blankets, rubbish bags and toilet paper (DoC n.d.b).

Among the tracks managed by the DoC, the nine Great Walks have become the most well known (TNZ n.d.a). The branding of these walks under the banner of the Great Walks was a promotional strategy from DoC in 1993, combining existing well-known tracks in NZ with other newer, lesser-known tracks (NZTB/DoC 1993). The Great Walks are promoted internationally as showcasing some of the best scenery and landscapes in NZ, while being well maintained and easily accessible. All of them are located in national parks and are classified as "easy tramping tracks". Except for the coastal Abel Tasman track, the tracks are located in high country or mountain areas. One of them, the Whanganui Journey, is, however, a river trail that can be explored by canoe or kayak only (TNZ 2016b; Werner et al. 2009). In 2018, a tenth walk is expected to open on the west coast of South Island: the Pike29 Memorial Track, a 45-kilometre walk in the Paparoa National Park to commemorate the 29 men who perished in a 2010 mining disaster in this area (TNZ 2016b).

Each Great Walk (except for the Whanganui Journey) is between 30 and 80 km long, with a completion time between two and five days. The main walking season for the tracks is from October to May ("Great Walks season"), with the most popular time being the summer months (December to March). Accommodation options include either huts or campsites (DoC 2013). Since they are promoted as "iconic" tourism attractions for nature-based tourism, the huts, campsites and tracks on the Great Walks have a higher standard than most other facilities managed by DoC (Werner et al. 2009). The huts have bunks, mattresses, water supplies, toilets, hand washing facilities, heating (with fuel available) and wardens (in peak summer season). The Great Walks have their own website (www.greatwalks.co.nz), which provides general information (such as promotional videos, safety tips) as well as detailed descriptions about each single track (including access information, fees and bookings).

The Great Walks have become very popular and the number of tourists on all nine tracks has increased by 10 per cent a year for the past three years (Cook 2016). In 2012/13, approximately 87,000 tourists hiked the Great Walks (Smith 2013). To deal with this increasing demand, DoC has introduced an online booking system for all huts and campsites on the Great Walks. All huts and campsites require a booking. Five of the Great Walks are managed throughout the year. The remaining four have a Winter/Off-Season, when walkers cannot make bookings, and only need to purchase hut tickets before heading off. These are the Milford, Routeburn, Kepler Tracks and the Tongariro Northern Circuit. They lead through alpine terrain, which can be inaccessible during winter. This is not a cheaper option for the budget traveller – only experienced and skilled walkers should attempt to walk these tracks during the off-season (Ms Anja Kohler personal communication 30 May 2016). Huts cost between NZ $22 and $54 per night. The most popular ones are often fully booked months in advance. The increasing popularity of the tracks in recent years has led to several issues, such as an increase in litter and defecation, vegetation damage, water pollution and noise, as well as a rising number of "illegal" hikers (Cook 2016; Werner et al. 2009). Enhanced visitor management (through the booking system), an increase in the number of volunteers along the tracks, as well as fining "illegal" hikers, are some of the means used by DoC to tackle these issues (Cook 2016).

Japan

While not having the reputation of a hiking destination, Japan offers a wide variety of walking tracks in different climatic regions – from remote multiple-day trips to day-walks that are easily accessible from the big city hubs like Tokyo and Kyoto. Since Japan is a predominantly mountainous country (21 peaks are over 3,000 metres), hiking has become a popular activity. Climbing Mt Fuji (open in July and August only) has become particularly fashionable, especially to enjoy the sunrise (JNTO 2016a). Other hiking areas include UNESCO World Heritage Sites (e.g. Shirakami-Sanchi mountain range, Yakushima National Park), but also pilgrimage routes such as the Shikoku pilgrimage, a 40-day hike to the 88 Buddhist temples of Shikoku island (JNTO 2016a). The country thus provides the opportunity to combine technologically advanced cities, traditional culture and beautiful nature with forested mountains, lakes, volcanoes and abundant wildlife (e.g. bears, foxes, boars, mountain goats and monkeys) (McLachlan et al. 2009; Japan-guide.com 2016a). With regards to cultural experiences, the *onsen* bathing (thermal hot springs) dates back to ancient times. Since *onsen* baths contain a varied content of natural gases and minerals, they serve as relaxation and medical purposes (relieving, for example, skin disorders, rheumatism and arthritis). *Onsen* are found across Japan, with several located at huts in the backcountry. They are very popular with hikers to ease sore feet and tired legs (McLachlan et al. 2009).

In 2015, 19,737,409 foreign visitors came to Japan, of which 16,969,126 were tourists (JNTO 2016b). The majority came from China, South Korea, Taiwan, Hong Kong and the USA. More detailed statistics about hikers or nature-based tourism are not conducted by the Japan National Tourism Organization (JNTO) (Ms B. Leitzbach personal communication 23 May 2016). A guide book on hiking in Japan, published in 2009, described Japanese hikers as follows:

> Although the young do go trekking, the average age of the hiking fraternity is probably close to 60. The feats of endurance that these young-at-heart grandparents complete are a source of constant amazement. Compared to their Western peers they really are fit and have incredible stamina.
>
> (McLachlan et al. 2009: 23)

Characteristics of international hikers are unfortunately not available.

Japan offers a wide variety of tracks of different length and levels of difficulty which can be found across the country, i.e. from Hokkaidō in the north, with subarctic climate, to the southern Okinawa Islands, with subtropical climates (JNTO 2016c). Japanese hiking trails are typically well developed and marked with signs, flags or paint. Signs often display the names and distances but are mostly written in Japanese (Japan-guide.com 2016b). Japan's well-organised and efficient transportation network provides a convenient way to reach most tracks, mostly via rail and bus. Accommodation options range from comfortable lodges, hostels and hotels to camp sites, mountain huts (mostly privately owned) and free unstaffed emergency shelters. On some hikes, traditional Japanese lodgings like inns (*ryokan*), guesthouses (*minshuku*) and temple lodgings (*shukubō*) help to experience traditional Japanese culture (McLachlan et al. 2009). Reservations are recommended for all types of accommodation. Mountain huts are common along most hiking routes. They vary from basic one-room shelters to hostel-like facilities with beds, showers and hot meals (Japan-guide.com 2016b). While some mountain huts can be free, most warden-controlled huts charge a fee of approximately 9,000 yen (75 euros) a night, including futon, dinner and breakfast (or 6,500 yen without meals). The huts can get very crowded at peak times and hikers may have to share a futon with one or more other people. If not staying overnight, climbers are allowed to take a rest inside (around 1,000–2,000 yen/hour). Most huts sell food, water and other climbing provisions (Habington 2013; Japan-guide.com 2016c).

The North Alps include Japan's highest peaks and are the most popular hiking region in Japan (McLachlan *et al.* 2009). Due to the climatic conditions and the harsh winters, most of the tracks in this area can only be hiked between early July and mid-October. Peak season is during summer holidays (approximately 20 July to 20 August) and the huts can become very crowded, sometimes reaching twice their normal capacity (McLachlan *et al.* 2009). Kamikōchi is a highland valley located in the Hida Mountains range, approximately 1,500 m above sea level, offering some of Japan's most spectacular mountain scenery (Japan-guide.com 2016d). The valley is protected as part of the Chūbu-Sangaku National Park, with no access for private vehicles. Kamikōchi's most famous sight is the Kappa-bashi Bridge, a wooden suspension bridge over the Azusa-gawa River (JNTO n.d.). Kamikōchi has plenty of accommodation and is a hiking gateway, as several half-day and day hikes but also some multi-day tracks start from here. The Tate-yama to Kamikōchi Track (from Murodō to Kamikōchi) is a six-day hike (65 km), often referred to as the 'top hike in Japan' (McLachlan *et al.* 2009: 17). While the track is quite long, it is described as not particularly difficult and no technical skills or special gear are required. There are several options for escape routes should the weather turn bad. Several huts line the track, such as Yari-ga-take-sansō at 3,060 m, which has room for 650 people. This hut also offers a free medical clinic run by university teachers and students between mid-July and mid-August – a service that is provided at different huts throughout the Chūbu region (McLachlan *et al.* 2009).

Conclusion

Hiking is no longer an activity for the older generation only. Rather, more and more young people also spend their leisure time and/or holidays going hiking. In this context, hut-to-hut-hiking trails play an important role and have helped to further increase the popularity of hiking activities and their related scope.

Research on hut-to-hut hiking is, however, rather limited to date and only a few studies, articles and statistical data are available. The current chapter helps to close this gap and has provided an overview on hut-to-hut-hiking offerings in four different countries. While the overall hut-to-hut-hiking experience in the four destinations is quite similar, some differences do exist and each of them has some strengths and weaknesses (Table 16.2).

As such, the hut management is organised rather differently, with approaches ranging from central management (through a national department) to privately operated or owned huts. Similarly, the marketing approach is also rather different. Many national tourism organisations (NTOs) still do not collect data about (international) hikers or hiking tourism (e.g. Japan, Canada). However, the examples from Germany and New Zealand demonstrate that hiking can add value, generate employment and can be used to attract younger and/or new target groups. While hiking and hiking tourism is sometimes used strategically to promote the destination internationally (as in the case of New Zealand), other destinations do not carry out international marketing campaigns and only reach a limited international profile as a hiking destination (for example, Japan).

In conclusion, there is high potential in the future to further develop hut-to-hut hiking (including track and hut facilities, market research, marketing, new hut-to-hut-hiking trails, availability and quality of information, sustainability considerations, as well as the use of new technologies) in several of the considered countries, in order to promote the destination, attract new target groups and benefit from increased incomes. At the same time, care has to be taken to

Table 16.2 Strengths and weaknesses analysis of four selected hiking destinations

	Germany	Canada	New Zealand	Japan
Strengths	• The Alps are one of the largest and most important hiking areas in Europe • Three hut categories available in the Alps • Extensive online tour portal • Several hut-to-hut trails and also cross-border hut-to-hut hiking possible • Sustainability becomes more and more important • Eifel: integration of new technological services for hikers (smartphone or GPS device)	• Large variety of hiking tracks • Low population density and therefore plenty of space for hiking activities • Reasonable prices • Huts can be used all year round	• The Great Walks as a brand (strategic international marketing) • Availability of information • Efficient visitor management • The DoC as "owner"/ operator of the Great Walks and point of contact • Ease of the tracks so that most people can do them • Infrastructure of the tracks • Accessibility of the tracks • Network of Great Walks will be extended	• Hiking in Japan still an "insider tip"/not so well known • Variety of tracks in different climatic regions • Accessibility of the tracks • Free medical clinics at huts during high season • Huts provide board/ supplies can be purchased • Onsen experience
Weaknesses	• Often located near to cities rather than in remote areas • Declared hut-to-hut-tracks are rare	• Only a few sole hiking huts available • The tracks are mostly marketed individually, no superior organisation • Mostly guided tours on offer • Camp sites (for hiking) are more common than huts	• Overcrowding and related issues (e.g. impacts on environment) • Apparent ease of the tracks can lead to safety issues due to uninformed hikers • Seasonality of the tracks • Focus on Great Walks, other tracks may be neglected	• Availability of information on hiking • Limited (international) marketing • Huts rather expensive • Seasonality of most tracks

not overdevelop existing, sought-after tracks (e.g. Great Walks in New Zealand), as otherwise feelings and experiences of wilderness and nature, of backcountry and ruggedness, i.e. the main motivations to go hiking, will be compromised. As such, finding the right balance will be a challenge for destination marketing organisations and national, regional and local authorities in the future.

References

ACC (2016a) *The ACC Operates the Largest Network of Backcountry Huts in North America*. Alpine Club Canada. Available at: www.alpineclubofcanada.ca/facility/view-all-huts (accessed 25 May 2016).

ACC (2016b) *Huts and the Environment*. Alpine Club Canada. Available at: www.alpineclubofcanada.ca/facility/huts-and-the-environment (accessed 19 May 2016).

ACC (2016c) *Booking Huts*. Alpine Club Canada. Available at: www.alpineclubofcanada.ca/facility/booking-huts/#how-to-book (accessed 19 May 2016).

AVS/DAV/oeAV (2006) *Die umweltfreundlichsten Schutzhütten der Alpenvereine 2006/2007*. Alpenverein Südtirol, Deutscher Alpenverein and Oesterreichischer Alpenverein, Munich: Bozen.

Backcountry Magazine (2016) *Backcountry Hut, Lodge and Yurt Guide*. Available at: http://backcountrymagazine.com/stories/backcountry-hut-lodge-yurt-guide (accessed 2 June 2016).

Beedie, P. and Hudson, S. (2003) 'Emergence of mountain-based adventure tourism', *Annals of Tourism Research*, 30 (3): 625–643.

Canadian Tourism Commission (2003) *Canadian Soft Outdoor Adventure Enthusiasts – A Special Analysis of the Travel Activities and Motivation Survey (TAMS)*. Available at: http://en.destinationcanada.com/sites/default/files/pdf/Research/Product-knowledge/TAMS/Canadian%20Travellers%20Outdoor%20Activity/tams_Canadian_soft_adventure.pdf.

Chhetri, P., Arrowsmith, C. and Jackson, M. (2004) 'Determining hiking experiences in nature-based tourist destinations', *Tourism Management*, 25(1): 31–43.

Cook, A. (2016) 'Rogue campers "ruining" great walks', *Radio New Zealand*. Available at: www.radionz.co.nz/news/national/294829/rogue-campers-'ruining'-great-walks (accessed 26 May 2016).

DAV (n.d.a) *Hüttenbesuch – Arbeiten wo Andere Urlaub machen*. Deutschen Alpenverband. Available at: www.alpenverein.de/huetten-wege-touren/huetten/huetten-in-den-alpen/huettenwirt-werden-arbeiten-am-berg-saisonkraft_aid_10210.html (accessed 14 April 2016).

DAV (n.d.b) *Hüttenbesuch – Hüttenkategorien, Winterräume und Selbstversorger*. Deutschen Alpenverband. Available at: www.alpenverein.de/huetten-wege-touren/huetten/huetten-in-den-alpen/huetten-huettenbetrieb_aid_30.html (accessed 18 April 2016).

DAV (n.d.c) *Hüttenbesuch – Hütten- und Tarifordnung*. Deutschen Alpenverband. Available at: www.alpenverein.de/huetten-wege-touren/huetten/huetten-in-den-alpen/huettenordnung-tarifordnung-uebernachten-auf-huetten_aid_10214.html (accessed 21 April 2016).

DAV (2016) *Alpenvereinshütten – Selbstversorgung auf Alpenvereinshütten*. Deutschen Alpenverband. Available at: www.alpenverein.de/huetten-wege-touren/alpenvereinshuetten-selbstversorgung-auf-alpenvereinshuetten_aid_16580.html (accessed 14 April 2016).

Destination Canada (2015) *Tourism Snapshot – A Monthly Monitor of the Performance of Canada's Tourism Industry*, December, 11(12).

DoC (n.d.a) *About Us*. Department of Conservation. Available at: www.doc.govt.nz/about-us (accessed 25 May 2016).

DoC (n.d.b) *Backcountry Huts*. Department of Conservation. Available at: www.doc.govt.nz/Documents/parks-and-recreation/places-to-stay/hut-information/backcountry-huts-information.pdf (accessed 27 May 2016).

DoC (2013) *Get Out and Walk: New Zealand's Great Walks*. Department of Conservation. Available at: www.doc.govt.nz/Documents/parks-and-recreation/tracks-and-walks/great-walks-summary.pdf (accessed 26 May 2016).

DoC (2015) *Statement of Intent 2015–2019*. Department of Conservation. Available at: www.doc.govt.nz/about-us/our-role/corporate-publications/statement-of-intent-archive/statement-of-intent-2013-2017 (accessed 25 May 2016).

Dreyer, A. and Menzel, A. (2016) 'Hiking tourism in Germany's low and high mountain regions', in H. Richins and J. Hull (eds), *Mountain Tourism: Experiences, Communities, Environments and Sustainable Futures*, Wallingford, Oxon: CABI International, pp. 184–193.

Dreyer, A., Menzel, A. and Endress, M. (2010) *Wandertourismus: Kundengruppen, Destinationsmarketing, Gesundheitsaspekte,* Munich: Oldenbourg.

Gross, S. and Menzel, A. (2012) 'Innovations in trekking tourism: hut hiking in the Harz region', paper presented at IUFRO Conference on Forest for People, Alpbach, Tyrol/Austria, May.

Habington, W. (2013) *All Day and All Night: A Brief Guide to Spending the Night at Kamikochi.* Available at: www.kamikochi.org/articles/featured-articles/243-all-day-and-all-night-a-brief-guide-to-spending-the-night-at-kamikochi.html (accessed 27 May 2016).

Japan-guide.com (2016a) *Hiking.* Available at: www.japan-guide.com/e/e2427.html (accessed 25 May 2016).

Japan-guide.com (2016b) *How to Hike.* Available at: www.japan-guide.com/e/e2427_how.html (accessed 25 May 2016).

Japan-guide.com (2016c) *Climbing Mount Fuji.* Available at: www.japan-guide.com/e/e6901.html (accessed 25 May 2016).

Japan-guide.com (2016d) *Kamikochi.* Available at: www.japan-guide.com/e/e6040.html (accessed 25 May 2016).

JNTO (n.d.) *Kamikochi.* Japan National Tourism Organization. Available at: www.jnto.go.jp/eng/location/regional/nagano/kamikouchi.html (accessed 26 May 2016).

JNTO (2016a) *Trekking and Hiking.* Japan National Tourism Organization. Available at: www.jnto.org.au/trekking-and-hiking/ (accessed 25 May 2016).

JNTO (2016b) *Foreign Visitors & Japanese Departures.* Japan National Tourism Organization. Available at: www.jnto.go.jp/eng/ttp/sta/PDF/E2015.pdf (accessed 25 May 2016).

JNTO (2016c) *Climate.* Japan National Tourism Organization. Available at: www.jnto.go.jp/eng/arrange/essential/climate.html (accessed 25 May 2016).

Landesbetrieb Wald and Holz Nordrhein-Westfalen (2013) *Gemeinsam für den Wald: Wald und Holz NRW – Nachhaltigkeitsbericht 2013,* Münster.

Lumma, K. and Gross, S. (2010) 'Natur- und Aktivtourismus in deutschen Mittelgebirgsregionen – Produktinnovationen für das Destinationsmanagement', in A. Kagermeier and J. Willms (eds), *Tourism Development in Low Mountain Ranges, Studien zur Freizeit- und Tourismusforschung,* Mannheim: MetaGIS-Fachbuch, pp. 115–134.

McLachlan, C., Ryall, R. and Joll, D. (2009) *Hiking in Japan (Travel Guide),* Footscray, Victoria, Australia: Lonely Planet.

Menzel, A., Endress, M. and Dreyer, A. (2008) *Wandertourismus in deutschen Mittelgebirgen: Produkte – Destinationsmarketing – Gesundheit,* Hamburg: ITD-Verlag.

Musa, G., Thompson-Carr, A. and Higham, J. (eds) (2015) *Mountaineering Tourism,* Abingdon: Taylor & Francis.

Nationalpark Eifel (2016) *Through the Heart of Nature.* Available at: www.nationalpark-eifel.de/go/eifel/english/Under_your_own_steam/Wilderness_Trail.html (accessed 21 April 2016).

Norman, T.J. (2010) *Canadian Trails Study: A Comprehensive Analysis of Managed Trails and Trail Uses,* Halifax, NS: National Trails Coalition.

NZTB/DoC (1993) *New Zealand Conservation Estate and International Visitors,* Wellington: New Zealand Tourism Board and Department of Conservation.

Project M, Ostfalia Hochschule für angewandte Wissenschaften, Institut für Management und Tourismus & Deutscher Wanderverband (2014) *Wanderstudie. Der deutsche Wandermarkt,* Berlin.

Smith, N. (2013) *Record Increase in Great Walk Use.* Available at: www.beehive.govt.nz/release/record-increase-great-walk-use (accessed 29 May 2016).

Statistics Canada (2016) 'Table 051–0005 – Estimates of population, Canada, provinces and territories, quarterly (persons)', *CANSIM (database).* Available at: www5.statcan.gc.ca/cansim/a26?lang=eng&id=510005 (accessed 19 May 2016).

TAMS (2006) *Canadian Activity Profile – Hiking, Climbing and Paddling While on Trips: Of One or More Nights.* Travel Activities and Motivation Survey. Available at: www.mtc.gov.on.ca/en/research/travel_activities/CDN_TAMS_2006_Hiking,_Climbing_and_Paddling_Oct2007.pdf.

Taylor, S. (2015) 'Hiking', in C. Cater, B. Garrod and T. Low (eds), *The Encyclopedia of Sustainable Tourism,* Wallingford, Oxon: CAB International, p. 263.

TNZ (n.d.a) *Great Walks of New Zealand.* Tourism New Zealand. Available at: www.newzealand.com/int/feature/great-walks-of-new-zealand (accessed 29 May 2016).

TNZ (n.d.b) *Walking and Hiking.* Tourism New Zealand. Available at: www.newzealand.com/int/walking-and-hiking (accessed 29 May 2016).

TNZ (2014) *Tourist Special Interest: Walking and Hiking*. Tourism New Zealand. Available at: www.tourismnewzealand.com/media/1768/tourism-profile-walking-and-hiking.pdf (accessed 29 May 2016).

TNZ (2016a) *Special Interest*. Tourism New Zealand. Available at: www.tourismnewzealand.com/markets-stats/sectors/special-interest/walking-and-hiking (accessed 29 May 2016).

TNZ (2016b) *Discovering New Zealand's 'Great Walks'*. Tourism New Zealand. Available at: http://media.newzealand.com/en/story-ideas/new-zealands-nine-great-walks (accessed 25 May 2016).

Walrond, C. (2012) *Tramping – New Zealand Tramping, Clubs and Culture, Te Ara – the Encyclopedia of New Zealand*. Available at: www.TeAra.govt.nz/en/tramping/page-1 (accessed 29 May 2016).

Werner, K., Orams, M., Kibe, N. and Histen, S. (2009) *Hiking/Trekking Tourism in New Zealand and Australia*, Auckland: New Zealand Tourism Research Institute.

17

Taking you home

The Masar Ibrahim Al-Khalil in Palestine

Rami K. Isaac

Introduction

Routes and trails have been under-researched and their importance understated by tourism academics (Timothy and Boyd 2015). Trails are one of the most powerful leisure resources on the globe today. Almost all destinations claim a trail or route, yet attention by scholars to these linear spaces has not been matched by their importance. Trails, hiking routes and other linearly connected tourism and recreation resources may not be considered an exciting, innovative or perhaps challenging research topic, yet they form an integral element of most regions' tourism offer and should be given serious academic attention (Timothy and Boyd 2015).

Hiking is nowadays among the most popular leisure and holiday activities in Europe. According to Kouchener and Lyard 2000 (cited in Kastenholz and Rodrigues 2007), in Italy and France there are more than 3 million hikers, whereas in the UK the number rises to 10 million, while more than 30 per cent of the Swedish population walk in forests and in the countryside, and almost half of the population in England hikes recurrently. Hiking is a leisure activity that may attract tourists to these areas, help to make natural and cultural resources accessible and visible, and may contribute to visitors spending more time and money. Hiking is an interesting field of research, because it interconnects three traditionally distinct, theoretical fields: tourism, recreation and leisure (den Breejen 2007; Butler *et al.* 1998). Hiking is too, a diverse and dynamic activity that is difficult to comprehend and manage (Kay and Moxham 1996), and the various labels and definitions used to describe the concept increase the misunderstanding of it. Thousands of trails exist throughout the world at many different scales and sizes, but only recently have scholars begun to scrutinize their unique characteristics (Cheung 1999; Prideaux 2002; Sevigny 1992).

This chapter seeks to explore the significance of hiking trails in Palestine, focusing on "The Masar Ibrahim Al-Khalil" in Palestine. Using the Masar Ibrahim as a frame, this chapter will also discuss issues associated with governance (or absence thereof), funding, community support, rights of access in the Palestinian context and the implications for trail development. The path is a route following the footsteps of the prophet Ibrahim through the Middle East. Although there is no ultimate historical or archaeological evidence that Abraham actually lived, Christian, Muslim and Jewish traditions all recognize the story of Ibrahim and claim it as a canonical text. Limited research has been carried out in the field of trail development and management (Timothy and Boyd 2006) and it is the author's intention that this research would be useful to trail developers and management.

The Abraham Path (Masar Ibrahim Al-Khalil)

The Abraham Path, also called in Arabic *Masar Ibrahim al Khalil*, is a route following the footsteps of the prophet Ibrahim through the Middle East. The story of Ibrahim is also part of many folktales, village traditions and local mythology. The path links the places which Ibrahim was supposed to have passed during his journey and thus is based, as Dr William Ury, founder of the Abraham Path Initiative (API) and a negotiation expert at Harvard University, describes it, 'on anthropological reality' or 'cultural memory' (API 2009). The first walking sections of the Path opened in 2008 mainly in Jordan, Turkey and Palestine. The path can be called a long-distance walk, because the length of the whole trail is around 1,200 km and the path crosses five different countries in the Middle East: Turkey, Syria, Jordan, Israel and Palestine.

The current path begins in Turkey, where it starts in Sanliurfa (also called Urfa) and from there the 170-km trail leads across different cultural places to Harran. Sanliurfa (ancient Edessa) is a sacred city in South-East Anatolia, where Ibrahim is supposed to have been born, and Harran is the biblical city where Ibrahim lived with Sarah until he received the call from God to leave his home and travel to the promised land of Canaan.

From Turkey the path passes through Syria, where it crosses the main cities of Aleppo, the Forgotten Cities (700 ruins of Romano-Byzantine settlements), Damascus and Bosra (Busra al-Sham, a stopover on the caravan route to Mecca). Aleppo (Haleb), formerly the biggest city of Syria, is the place where Ibrahim gave milk to passing travellers. Later on, the path crosses Damascus, which is one of the world's oldest inhabited cities, where Ibrahim is reputed to have stayed.

From Syria, the path connects with the route in Jordan, where it starts in Tel Mar Elias (supposed birthplace of Elias), followed by Jerash (a ruined city with buildings from the Hellenistic, Roman, Byzantine periods) and Mt Nebo (where Moses/Musa is said to have viewed the land of Canaan, and is reputed to be buried). Then the *Masar Ibrahim* crosses the border with Palestine where the route passes Jenin and the actual path starts in Nablus (where the tomb of Joseph/ Yusef and well of Jacob/Yakub can be found) followed by Duma, Taybeh and at the end crosses Betin (Ramallah). Close to the city of Nablus, Ibrahim received again a call from God and God showed him the Promised Land. In Betin, Ibrahim stopped his journey for a moment to build an altar for God, and it is the site of Jacob's ladder. Then the path enters Jerusalem, the holy (ancient) city to Jews, Christians and Muslims, where Ibrahim asked for blessings and where the story of the binding of Isaac (Akedah) reputedly occurred, on the top of the Moria Mountain. Followed by Bethlehem (the birthplace of Jesus/Issa), and Hebron/Al-Khalil, where Ibrahim and his wife Sarah are buried (also home to the Tomb of Patriarchs). Next, the route continues into the Negev Desert in Israel, visiting Rahat, Beer Sheva, Tel Sheva, Drejat and Tel Arad. According to historic sources, Ibrahim made his covenant in old Beer Sheva. In Tel Sheva, an Abrahamic-era site, the ruins of old Beer Sheva city walls and canals can be found. In addition to the historical aspects of the prophet Ibrahim within all these places, these locations offer a lot of different cultural attractions, such as old buildings, places ranked on the World Heritage List, and different communities and cuisines.

Palestine: Masar Ibrahim Al-Khalil

Masar Ibrahim Al Khalil is a trail of community-based tourism, which follows the footsteps of Ibrahim through the Middle East. The story of Ibrahim's journey, which has been kept alive for around 4,000 years in the landscape and memory of this region, records the origin of a spiritual tradition shared by more than 3 billion people in the world today.

By retracing this journey, *Masar Ibrahim al Khalil* provides a place of meeting and connection for people of all faiths and cultures, inviting us to remember our common origins, to respect our cultural differences, and to recognize our shared humanity. The path too serves as a catalyst for sustainable tourism and economic development; a platform for the energy and idealism of young people; and a focus for positive media highlighting the rich culture and hospitable people of the Middle East.

The *Masar Ibrahim al Khalil* runs from the Mediterranean olive groves of the highlands of the north to the silence of the deserts in the south, from the area west of Jenin to the area south of the Sanctuary of Abraham (known in Arabic as Al-Haram Al-Ibrahimi) in the city of Hebron.

But this is more than just a hiking trail. It is a path that potentially leads deep into the memory and heritage of the Palestinian people, inviting travellers to discover for themselves the family life of the Palestinian villages, the proud ways of the Bedouin, and the age-old traditions of hospitality that lie at the heart of Palestinian life.

Masar Ibrahim Al Khalil (MIAK) is a non-profit community-based tourism initiative to delineate and develop *Masar Ibrahim* in and around the different Palestinian localities. Community-based tourism aims at benefiting the local community in general, and the fragile rural communities in particular, through inviting tourists to visit these communities, hike in their natural landscapes, be exposed to the cultural diversity, be guided through the historical and archaeological sites, experience the taste of the traditional food, and have the privilege of staying overnight in the communities' accommodations. The organization endorses cultural diversity and exchange, safeguards tradition and heritage, inspires storytelling, and encourages friendships based on the advancement of human values and the preservation of the surrounding environment and the people's needs for further growth and education. MIAK works closely with the local communities to cultivate their resources, capacities and the opportunity for a better life.

Masar Ibrahim in the West Bank represents an innovative approach to tackling rural development, employment and women's empowerment in communities normally excluded from tourism and disconnected from one another. Youth play a basic role in *Masar Ibrahim Al-Khalil*, presenting as a pillar of the work, essential to developing a good future of the *Masar* by raising awareness about multiple topics in environment, community service, art and culture.

The World Bank Project *Masar Ibrahim* (Szepesi and Rabineau 2014) has enabled the *Masar Ibrahim* to continue working alongside local partners and local communities in constructing sustainable frameworks for trekking tourism in Palestine. The *Masar Ibrahim* is a whole network of people, communities and businesses that links a series of towns and villages and facilitates tourist movement (Figures 17.1 and 17.2).

Governance

Masar Ibrahim Al Khalil (MIAK) brings together the efforts, work and achievements of three organizations working in union with a close partnership with Bethlehem University:

174

- The Palestine Wildlife Society
- The Rozana Association
- The Siraj Center for Holy Land Studies

MIAK is also a member of the so-called NEPTO, Network for Experiential Palestinian Tourism Organization, which includes virtually all NGOs engaged in developing new community-based tourism projects (Saadeh 2016). Bethlehem University is another local partner involved in training local trekking guides, who will be the first of their kind to be certified by the Palestinian Ministry of Tourism and Antiquities. The *Masar Ibrahim* has nine members on its board of directors (Raed Saadeh, personal communication 2015). The vision of MIAK is a 'vibrant Palestinian communities in a sustainable environment for an enticing experience of Palestine's cultural history along Masar Ibrahim Al-Khalil', and their mission is 'developing and promoting community-based tourism through Masar Ibrahim Al-Khalil'.

Figure 17.1 Logo of Masar Ibrahim

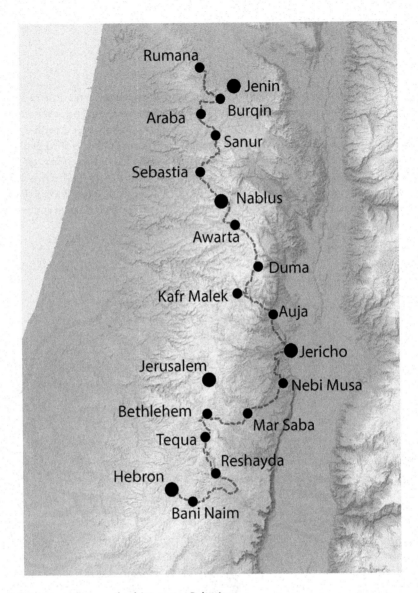

Figure 17.2 Map of Masar Ibrahim route, Palestine

Economic development in the West Bank across fragile communities

There are essentially three types of funding associated with trails: acquisition, development and operations (Fiala 1999). In contemporary society, funding for routes and trails is uncommon and unpredictable (Paine 2001). Autumn 2014 saw a movement of new activities popping up along the *Masar Ibrahim*, between Jenin and Hebron in Palestine. Girl and boy scout clean-up events, university photography competitions, guided weekly walks, homestay training (community-based tourism), trail analysis and educational meetings with Palestinian municipalities are just a few examples of these activities. All of these are largely possible thanks to the two-year, $2.3 million grant from the World Bank and Peace-building Fund for a project entitled Masar

176

Ibrahim: Economic Development Across Fragile Communities. *Masar Ibrahim*, Siraj Center and Rozana Association will utilize the funds to engage more communities in the West Bank, bring more walkers, initiate promotional activities, and increase job creation and income generation on the Path, particularly for women and young people (Dintaman 2014a). The main elements of the grant include:

- investment in people and institutions, including a comprehensive one-year guides' training by Bethlehem University and capacity building for local partner organizations;
- path development, including increasing trail distance in the north and south and improving maps and other practical hiker materials;
- marketing, business development and communication, including outreach to tour operators, profiles on points of interest, market studies and production of marketing materials;
- action research, including the publication of 10 research papers which analyse the impact of the *Masar Ibrahim* and capture lessons about job creation through trail development.

In addition to the World Bank grant, other financial support came from the French government. The French project concerns reaching out to local authorities and building partnerships with them. The project contributes to the renovation of homestays, and the training of all the individuals that are part of the homestays in terms of hospitality training, English-language training, sewing and embroidery training, improving the promotion of the agricultural products, and the marketing of these products. Furthermore, the project focusing on developing the path, which concerns the coordination with local authorities regarding installing information panels and the validation of them, finalizing the technical expertise regarding the accommodations, and signing the accommodations agreement and the convention between *Masar Ibrahim* and the local authorities regarding the maintenance of the path's marking.

Guide training at Bethlehem University

Guides are fundamental to a good experience on the *Masar Ibrahim*. Nevertheless, it is possible to hike many of the sections of the route independently, a guide's ability to contextualize the experience and bridge differences of culture and language makes for a far richer experience. This need for more qualified guides has led to the creation of a training course specifically designed to support the unique needs along the *Masar Ibrahim* Path. The year-long course is held at Bethlehem University and enrols 22 students on average. Graduates receive a guide certificate from the Palestinian Ministry of Tourism. The first cohort, which started 2015, comprised mostly of professionals, men and women in their thirties, many of whom were already working in the tourism industry. Although the programme's primary focus is to provide a comprehensive training that provides graduates with knowledge and skills necessary to share the *Masar Ibrahim* experience with walkers, students were also intentionally selected to be geographically distributed along all the different regions along the trail in Palestine. It is hoped that this will create a tight-knit network of tourism professionals with the expertise to make sure that hikers are fully supported every step of the way (API 2014).

Rozana Association Hospitality Training

In addition to the one-year training programme for guides at Bethlehem University, Rozana Association introduced a one-day hospitality training for women from the local villages along the *Masar Ibrahim* (Dintaman 2014b). The training was hosted at the Arraba Municipality in the northern West Bank, Palestine. Thirty-eight women participated in the training from the Jenin district, gathered to learn about the *Masar Ibrahim*, leadership skills, professionalism, food, safety and housekeeping. The goal of this one-day workshop was preparing the women to operate a homestay for hikers on the *Masar Ibrahim*. The trainer encouraged participants to accentuate the positive and to view their home villages through the eyes of a tourist. George Rishmawi (personal communication 2016), director of *Masar Ibrahim*, introduced the group to the highlights of the *Masar Ibrahim*, and emphasized the way that the path connects the villages to each other, as well as to world-famous historical and cultural sites. In a different room, a group of 14 local men and women participated in a trekking guide training workshop, with the topics of trails in Palestine, history, flora and fauna and community-based tourism. The goal of this workshop was to prepare local trekking guides to lead hikers through their villages and the surrounding landscapes. Raed Saadeh (personal communication 2015), co-founder of Rozana Association and the Network for Experiential Palestinian Tourism Organization (NEPTO) presented about social tourism (see also Saadeh 2016), including other trails in Palestine, such as the Sufi trails in the Birzeit area, near Ramallah. In addition to these trainings, *Masar Ibrahim Al-Khalil* works at activating and empowering the role of women in the women-based organizations, which is considered fragile in Palestinian society. The *Masar* focuses its empowerment in the field of community tourism on the villages that *Masar Ibrahim* passes through. This is through embroidery and sewing trainings, English language skills, and homestay trainings (Masar Ibrahim 2016).

Wilderness First Aid Training

In September 2013, the API led a Wilderness First Aid Training programme for Palestinian guides, co-organized with local partners *Masar Ibrahim*, Siraj Center for Holy Land Studies, Palestinian Wildlife Society and Rozana Association. This three-day course was the first of its kind in the Middle East, with 16 local guides and escorts from all over the West Bank receiving certification. Topics of the course included patient assessment, environmental emergencies, traumatic injuries, medical emergencies, improvising materials and moving patients. Participants practised hands-on skills with a variety of scenarios, from treating simple cuts to splinting broken bones to evacuating patients with suspected spinal injuries (API 2014).

Overview of travellers

Different categories have varying economic impacts on stakeholders. Though high-impact travellers – such as foreign groups spending multiple days and nights in and between West Bank communities in a short time period – are important, they are not the only relevant determinants of impact over the long term. What can be perceived as lower-impact travellers – such as expert independent walkers going out for one day – may be more frequent and recurring, and literally provide the feet on the ground that raises awareness, quality and appeal to other travellers (Pöytäniemi and Szepesi 2015). There are two main categories, organized (A) and independent travellers (B), with several subcategories in each of them.

A) *Organized travel* concerns travel in which one actor organizes travel for an individual or group from start to finish. The actor can be a tour operator, an NGO or an individual providing tour-operator-type services to a client. This category can be subdivided into multi-day and one-day organized trips. Each of those categories can be further subdivided into foreign hikers who travel from abroad, and local hikers who reside in the region.

Table 17.1 Masar Ibrahim travellers' data, 2012–2015

Year	Walkers (West Bank, Palestine)
2012	816
2013	877
2014	1581
2015	3012

Source: Masar Ibrahim, personal communication

B) *Independent travel* concerns travel in which the individual or group organizes parts or all of the journey on their own. Independent travellers may use no services whatsoever, or pay for the services of a guide, hotel or host family individually, but the defining feature is that they initiate the arrangements on their own and not through a third party. This category can be subdivided into multi-day and one-day organized trips. Although separate data on each category has not been kept the overall number of hikers on the Masar Ibrahim has continued to increase (Table 17.1).

The supply chain of trail-based hiking tourism in the West Bank

A study conducted by Rabineau and Pöytäniemi (2015) highlighted the supply chain of the *Masar Ibrahim* hiking tourism in the West Bank, Palestine. They posed the questions: Which links are already in place, and which links are missing? Which links are well-developed and which require further work?

First, the trail must be attractive to hikers; that is, it must possess features that make a large clientele of hikers interested in coming to visit. Second, the trail must be well known: information on the trail should be easily available so that hikers around the world know about it, and thus they can plan trips along it. Third, hiking infrastructure must exist along the trail, such as signs that enable hikers to find their way, and lodging and resupply points that meet their day-to-day needs. Fourth, the trail must be easily accessible by visitors, so that arranging hikes is not so complicated or expensive that it turns away prospective hikers. Each of these points will be addressed below from the perspective of *Masar Ibrahim Al-Khalil* in the West Bank.

Attractiveness

Visitors to the *Masar Ibrahim* consistently cite the beauty surrounding the trail as a key reason for hiking. The trail's historical, religious and cultural assets are also strong incentives for hikers. A number of well-known ancient sites located at or near the route, and other interesting sites can be easily visited before or after hiking the trail. Cities like Bethlehem and Hebron serve as pilgrimage destinations for religious travellers. Contemporary history and politics attract visitors interested in learning more about the modern Middle East and the Israeli–Palestinian conflict. Local culture and gastronomy are also a draw for many hikers who appreciate the potential of a long-distance trail to offer a view of everyday life in small towns and rural villages. However, the perceived security situation in Palestine and Israel presents serious challenges for trail-based hiking tourism. The West Bank itself can be a complex area to navigate, especially for independent travellers who have to sort out logistical details themselves. The boundaries of Areas A, B, and C, for example, are largely unmarked, and their respective security arrangements is confusing. The most important geographic factors to have stemmed from the 1993 and 1995 Oslo Accords were the breakdown of Palestinian lands under Areas A, B and C, denoting the extent of Israeli or Palestinian jurisdiction, and the policy of closures. Closure is meant to deny Palestinians their right to free movement, stemming from a "pass system" first introduced in 1991, which required that every Palestinian had to obtain a colour-coded identification card and apply for a permit to move between and within what would eventually become Areas A, B and C (Tawil-Souri 2011). In the West Bank, Area A, under direct Palestinian control, includes the major populated cities but constitutes no more than 3% of those areas; Area B encompasses 450 Palestinian towns and villages representing 27% of the West Bank, jointly controlled territory in which the Palestinians would exercise civil authority but Israel would retain security control; and Area C, which is still occupied and exclusively controlled by Israel, constitutes the rest of the West Bank (70%), including agricultural land, the Jordan Valley, natural reserves, areas with lower population density, Israeli settlements and military areas (Hanafi 2013). All of these factors contribute to a sense of difficulties for potential visitors, as well as Palestinian guides of the *Masar Ibrahim* and to the West Bank as a whole.

The trail must be well known

The publicity and branding elements of this link are relatively strong. The *Masar Ibrahim* is young, and has not yet attained an iconic worldwide status, but it has succeeded in clearly branding itself and developing a reputation as a world-class hiking trail. It has been mentioned in a number of major media outlets, and was designated as the world's number-one new hiking trail by *National Geographic Traveller* in 2014, CNN, and *Haaretz* Israeli newspaper. Its presence on social media has grown rapidly over the past two years. *The Masar Ibrahim* has mass international appeal and is poised to thrive, if actual and perceived security conditions improve.

Local knowledge of the *Masar Ibrahim* among local hikers in the West Bank is growing, but is limited by the fact that the local hiking community is still relatively small. Outdoor walking is not a traditional mode of recreation and leisure in most Middle Eastern countries, but Palestinians have begun to build a local culture of hiking and backpacking.

During 2014, the majority of hikers hiking the trail in the West Bank are foreign residents of Jerusalem and Ramallah, who spend more money on services than local hikers. Local hikers offer fewer economic benefits to local communities on the front end than foreign hikers do, but they strengthen the trail's infrastructure through sustained use. They also increase local communities' awareness of the trail and create a sense of local ownership. As the volume of local hikers grows, a culture of multi-day hiking and through-hiking may develop, creating a local tourism market that brings economic benefits to rural communities, and which uses the trail even when few foreign visitors come to the West Bank.

Basic infrastructure

The trailheads, signage and way-marking element of the *Masar Ibrahim* are particularly weak compared to other long-distance trails around the world. The trail's physical presence and visibility in the West Bank is minimal, but increasing. Trailheads exist in a virtual sense; stage descriptions and GPS data on the website give starting and ending points for different sections, and enable hikers to find their way between them. Similarly, signage is minimal along the main trail but improving thanks to the financial grants. None of the route is waymarked, which means independent hikers have difficulty following the trail with any confidence.

Lodging and resupply points are available primarily in the framework of tour packages offered by *Masar Ibrahim* local partners. A typical multi-day hike on the *Masar Ibrahim* is characterized by meals and overnight lodging in local communities. A guide leads the way, and handles transportation and any food and water resupply that might be necessary in the course of the day's walk. In regards to accommodation, a first step is furnishing the homestays by delivering and installing the beds and wood crates to the homestays that are located all along the path. Then there are different trainings for the host families to develop their capacities regarding all needs of accommodation. This is so that the guest would feel home, get to know the Palestinian culture, and experience the traditional food of the Palestinians

The current guide- and homestay-based approach to leading travellers along the *Masar Ibrahim* works well focusing on community-based tourism, because this approach spreads trail-related work and income among a number of people. This community-based approach allows destination residents to participate fully in the benefits of tourism. Trail infrastructure and grassroots community involvement are closely connected. Making trails visible on the ground increases their permanence and sends a message that they are worthy investments for nearby entrepreneurs.

Easily accessible

Until recently, the range of services available to hikers, especially in the areas that relate to independent travel, have been somewhat limited, and service providers have been few. Those that have been available have been easy to access through the *Masar Ibrahim* website and through local partners in the West Bank. But nevertheless, this link has begun to improve considerably. It is only since 2015 that tour operators outside the West Bank have been featured in *Masar Ibrahim* tour brochures. Once on the trail, hikers generally must travel with local guides, but movement along the trail within that framework is unhindered by government restrictions. As the *Masar Ibrahim* becomes better known locally, the trail's physical infrastructure becomes better established, private-sector investment in the trail grows, and more diverse budgetary options for lodging become available, then this link in the supply chain should become much stronger.

Land-use rights and community support

Trails are often based on old routes used by humans throughout history; in many cases, however, the actual historical route has been lost or even paved into a modern highway. In order to create a more diverse and pleasant walking experience, the *Masar Ibrahim* seeks out a series of trails that encompass a mixture of hikes. To identify these paths, they turn to those who know the region best and those who owns the land, which in principle are communities living along the path. In coordination with local community members and receiving permission from the local authorities, *Masar Ibrahim* staff walk a multitude of footpaths, dirt roads, shepherds' trails, and paved streets across a region, searching for the best way to travel between communities, historical sites, and cultural points of interest. Nevertheless, the biggest majority of the trail is on public land, which means on agricultural roads (George Rishmawi personal communication 2016). Whenever possible, they coordinate with local communities to waymark the route, making it more navigable for walkers. In addition, the *Masar Ibrahim* developed a land-use study regarding this issue.

The other critical step in ensuring the vitality and sustainability of the trail lies in empowering stakeholders from local communities to both invest in and benefit from the path's presence.

Through partnerships with local organizations and tour operators, *Masar Ibrahim* makes an effort to connect demand for services in the region with supply from path communities: walkers generally seek guides to assist in navigation, and accommodations at the end of each day. The natural hospitality of the communities along the trail renders them fully capable of providing these services.

Conclusion

The aim of this chapter is to explore the significance of hiking trails in Palestine, focusing on "The *Masar Ibrahim*". Using the *Masar* as a frame, this chapter discussed issues associated with governance, funding, community support and training, rights of access in the Palestinian context and the implications for trail development. In recent years, the *Masar Ibrahim* in Palestine has grown in terms of its overall viability as a walking trail. A complete route has been mapped, and an online guidebook has been created, tour packages have been developed and promoted, and the trail has become increasingly well known around the world. Future steps on the agenda are supporting the infrastructure, signage and rehabilitation of historic sites and building along the trail (Raed Saadeh personal communication 2015), in which it can be related to issues regarding community benefits on the protection of shrines, for hosts as well as for guests. In addition, *Masar Ibrahim* would also connect walkers to the various issues that exist in Palestine, which means not only the Palestinian landscape and wildlife, but also water shortages as a result of the occupation and other political issues facing local communities, particularly in Area C. Nevertheless, linkages between agriculture and tourism should be strengthened to promote Palestinian local products in order to create a competitive advantage within the *Masar Ibrahim*, especially in terms of local products and cuisine.

References

API (2009) *The Abraham Path: Application to the Educational Tourism Community, Responsible Tourism Showcase*. Abraham Path Initiative. Available at: http://travelearning.com/filelib/156.pdf (accessed 15 March 2016).

API (2014) *Walking together: Annual Report 2014* Abraham Path Initiative. Available at: http://abrahampath.org/plan/guidebook-downloads/#tab-id-4 (accessed 1 March 2016).

Butler, R.W., Hall, C.M. and Jenkins, J. (eds) (1998) *Tourism and Recreation in Rural Areas*, Chichester: John Wiley & Sons.

Cheung, S.C.H. (1999) 'The meanings of a heritage trail in Hong Kong', *Annals of Tourism Research*, 26(3): 570–588.

den Breejen, L. (2007) 'The experiences of long distance walking: a case study of the West Highland Way in Scotland', *Tourism Management*, 28(6): 1417–1427.

Dintaman, A. (2014a) '$2.3 million grant bolsters economic development on the Abraham Path in the West Bank', Abraham Path Initiative. Available at: http://abrahampath.org/blog/abraham-path-initiative-receives-world-bank-grant (accessed 25 March 2016).

Dintaman, A. (2014b) 'Tourism in their own back yard', Abraham Path Initiative. Available at: http://abrahampath.org/blog/tourism-in-their-own-back-yard (accessed 1 May 2016).

Fiala, S. (1999) 'Happy trails to you: recipes for regional success', *Parks and Recreation*, 34(1): 62–68.

Hanafi, S. (2013) 'Explaining the spacio-cide in the Palestinian territory: colonization, separation, and state of exception', *Current Sociology*, 61(2): 190–205.

Kastenholz, E. and Rodrigues, A. (2007) 'Discussing the potential benefits of hiking tourism in Portugal', *Anatolia: An International Journal of Tourism and Hospitality Research*, 18(1): 5–21.

Kay, G. and Moxham, N. (1996) 'Path for whom? Countryside access for recreational walking', *Leisure Studies*, 15(3): 171–183.

Masar Ibrahim (2016) *Women Development: Women Role in Masar Ibrahim*. Available at: http://masaribrahim. ps/en/local-communities/women-development (accessed 30 May 2016).

Paine, L. P. (2001) 'Blazing the Maine maritime heritage trail: planning and prospects', *Bulletin of the Australian Institute for Maritime Archaeology*, 25: 75–78.

Pöytäniemi, S. and Szepesi, S. (2015) 'The economics of walking in Palestine: a review of existing data and gaps', *Abraham Path/Masar Ibrahim: Economic Development Across Fragile Communities*. Available at: http://abrahampath.org/stories/research/the-economics-of-walking-in-palestine (accessed 30 May 2016).

Prideaux, B. (2002) 'Creating rural heritage visitor attractions: the Queensland Heritage Trails Project', *International Journal of Tourism Research*, 4(4): 313–323.

Rabineau, S. and Pöytäniemi, S. (2015) 'The supply chain of trail-based tourism in the West Bank', *Abraham Path/Masar Ibrahim: Economic Development Across Fragile Communities*. Available at: http://abrahampath. org/stories/research/the-supply-chain-of-trail-based-hiking-tourism-in-the-west-bank (accessed 28 May 2016).

Saadeh, R. (2016) 'Experiential community-based tourism potential in Palestine: challenges and potentials', in R.K. Isaac, C.M. Hall and F. Higgins-Desbiolles (eds), *The Politics and Power of Tourism in Palestine*, London: Routledge, pp. 95–112.

Sevigny, R. (1992) 'Florida's black heritage trail', *Historic Preservation Forum*, 6(4): 6–9.

Szepesi, S. and Rabineau, S. (2014) 'The Abraham Path: experiential tourism across fragile communities in the West Bank', *Abraham Path/Masar Ibrahim: Economic Development Across Fragile Communities*. Available at: http://abrahampath.org/stories/research/experiential-tourism-across-fragile-communities (accessed 20 May 2016).

Tawil-Souri, H. (2011) 'Qalandia checkpoint as space and non-place', *Space and Culture*, 14(1): 4–26.

Timothy, D.J. and Boyd, S.W. (2006) 'Heritage tourism in the 21st century: valued traditions and new perspectives', *Journal of Heritage Tourism*, 1(1): 1–16.

Timothy, D.J. and Boyd, S.W. (2015) *Tourism and Trails: Cultural, Ecological and Management Issues*, Bristol: Channel View.

18

The Wales Coast Path
The world's first national coastal footpath

Stephen Miles

Introduction

On 5 May 2012, the Wales Coast Path (WCP) was officially launched, providing a continuous waymarked route around the coast of Wales from Chepstow in the south-east to Queensferry in the north (Figure 18.1). This 850-mile (1,370-km) route was lauded as the world's first and longest path to follow a nation's perimeter and provided much impetus for other countries to follow suit (England plans to complete its coastal route by 2020). The path soon invited considerable media attention. In 2012, Lonely Planet guidebooks chose Coastal Wales as top of its Best in Travel world destinations because of the coast path, and the route featured prominently in other travel publications, including *National Geographic Traveller* and the US walking magazine *Backpacker*.

In its first year, the WCP attracted 2.8 million visitors and is predicted to bring long-lasting recreational, tourism and economic development opportunities to the peripheral areas of Wales. Although most of the route is aimed at those on foot, there are sections that can be used by cyclists and horseriders; accessibility was central to the design of the path and some sections are suitable for the disabled and families with prams or buggies. The great strength of the WCP is that it caters for both serious and casual participants – from the casual stroller walking only a short distance to the die-hard challenge walker wanting to complete the entire route. The WCP is already emerging as an important challenge route in itself with a "Hall of Fame" on the path's website, listing those who have completed the entire route; this includes some "rounders", walkers who have continued along the Offa's Dyke Path on the Wales–England border to complete a 1,027-mile circumambulation of the bounds of the nation (Natural Resources Wales 2015).

This chapter outlines the development of the WCP and highlights the synergies the project has brought to the peripheries of Wales. It will show how, in addition to clear tangible benefits – as with the stimulation of business activity – there are intangible factors which characterise the route. The WCP has immense symbolic value for Wales, a small nation with a long subaltern history, and often overshadowed by England, its more powerful neighbour. The project reflects the newly found confidence that is the hallmark of a country that has gained renewed national identity since the 1990s. Allied to this is the question of national image, and the way in which the WCP is branded to present a dynamic, forward-looking and engaging message.

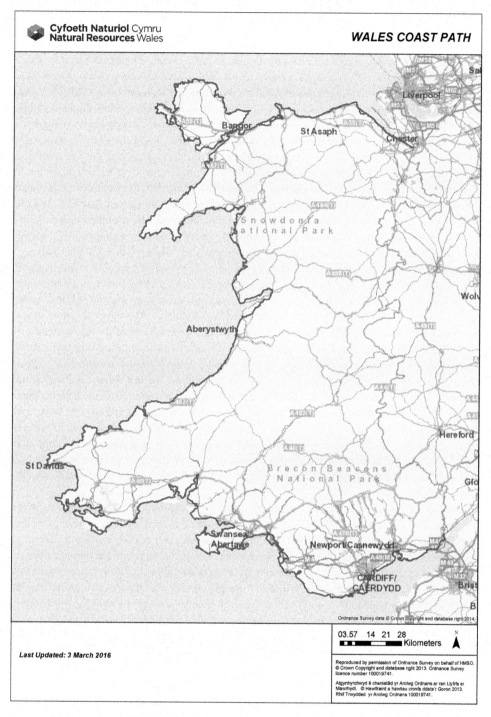

WALES COAST PATH

Liverpool

St Asaph

Bangor

Chester

Snowdonia
National Park

Aberystwyth

Wolv

Hereford

St Davids

Brecon Beacons
National Park

Glo

Swansea
Abertawe

Newport/Casnewydd

CARDIFF/
CAERDYDD

Brist

B

Ordnance Survey data © Crown copyright and database right 2014.

03.57 14 21 28
Kilometers N

Last Updated: 3 March 2016

Figure 18.1 Map of Wales showing the Wales Coast Path (© Natural Resources Wales – used with permission)

The background and context for a Wales Coast Path

Along with England, Scotland and Northern Ireland, Wales is one of the constituent countries that comprise the United Kingdom. It is a small country 8,023 miles^2 (20,779 km^2) in area, with a population of just 3.09 million in 2014. Despite its size, Wales has always been proud of its unique cultural identity reflected through history, folklore, music, sport and, most importantly, language. In the sixteenth century, Wales was legally and constitutionally shoehorned to England and its identity became subsumed into that of its more economically and politically powerful neighbour (Mackay 2010). A development of a Welsh national consciousness and the rise of a nationalist movement in the twentieth century, however, gave the country a new stimulus for achieving greater autonomy from the rest of the UK. A referendum on the issue in 1997 affirmed a desire for devolution (as in Scotland) and the *Government of Wales Act* (1998) established a National Assembly for Wales; in 2007, governance was separated between the elected Assembly and the Welsh Government, which maintains executive functions. The Welsh Government obtained certain powers *devolved* from the UK government in Westminster (Welsh Government 2015); among these were the environment, which allowed a convenient framework for the WCP initiative.

The idea of a WCP began to gain traction from the mid-2000s and the political commitment to the idea was enshrined in the second *Government of Wales Act of 2006*, which made provision for 'the establishment and maintenance of a route . . . for the coast to enable the public to make recreational journeys' (UK Government 2006: Schedule 5, Field 16). The concept gained strong cross-party support in the Welsh Government, since it addressed so many of the major ambitions of the Assembly, in particular, tourism, improving the local environment, sustainability and the need to promote health through physical activity (Welsh Assembly Government 2007). Work started on the WCP in 2007 funded by the Wales Coastal Access Improvement Programme (WCAIP) and with European Union funding secured from 2009. Since 2015, the path has been managed by Natural Resources Wales, the Welsh Government-sponsored body for landscape, environment and wildlife, who fund and co-ordinate the work of the fifteen local authorities and two National Park Authorities through which the path runs. It is important to note that most of the WCP follows pre-existing coastal paths, with just 80 km of new linear access created (although created and improved sections comprise 74% of the total length) (Natural Resources Wales 2014a: xiii).

The case for developing a WCP was strengthened by the evident decline in the level of coastal tourism by the late 2000s. Between 1991 and 2006, the seaside share of the UK holiday market in Wales fell from 61% to 41%, with firm recommendations made that coastal 'towns and resorts . . . seek to strengthen their attractiveness for tourism by developing appropriate opportunities to provide land and water based recreation facilities' (Visit Wales 2008: 4, 26). In tandem with this was the encouraging finding that the number of people visiting the seaside actually partaking in an activity had increased to 80% and of these the most popular activity was walking (69%) (Visit Wales 2008). This is augmented by the dominance of walking in wider physical activity surveys: for example, in the Sport Wales *Active Adults Survey*, walking 2+ miles had come top consistently since 1987. In 2012, this survey showed how in Wales 41.7% of adults had walked more than 2 miles in the previous 4 weeks (an increase from 33.8% in 2008/09) (Sport Wales 2014: 1). The WCP can thus be understood in the context of a revitalisation of the coastal tourism 'product' and the opportunities presented by the growing popularity of walking. Additionally, much of the drive to establish the path developed out of a desire to build on the success of two existing Welsh coastal footpaths – the 186-mile Pembrokeshire Coast National Trail and the 124-mile Isle of Anglesey Coastal Path – both of which had made demonstrable contributions to the economy of Wales.

The impact of the Wales Coast Path

In 2009, a benchmarking study concluded that, judged by a range of evidence, on average Welsh "seaside towns" are not especially disadvantaged or deprived, relative to the rest of Wales. Nevertheless, this masked wide variations between towns, with growth in employment between 2003/04 and 2006/07 ranging from +55% in some places (New Quay) to −15% in others (Tywyn). The average employment rate in Welsh seaside towns is 68%, below the Welsh average of 71%, and in economic output terms the Gross Value Added in those parts of Wales containing seaside towns is below the average for Wales as a whole (Beatty *et al.* 2009). Based on these findings, economic development is of great importance to the coastal region as a whole, and particularly so with regard to the less affluent places along it.

Between October 2012 and September 2013, gross expenditure by adult visitors on or away from the path was estimated at £32.3 million; allowing for leakages, this is £31.7m of additional demand in the Welsh economy; £15.9m of Gross Value Added; and around 715 person-years of employment (Natural Resources Wales 2013a: 8). But how does this transfer to the everyday operational climate of the more than 5,400 tourism-related businesses in a 2-km corridor along the path? Does the route make any difference? Natural Resources Wales have shown how within those areas in receipt of EU funding (the 'Convergence' areas), businesses employed an extra 41 staff as a result of the WCP, the equivalent of 28.2 full-time equivalents. Moreover, four additional enterprises had been created because of the path; 18% of tourism businesses reported that the WCP had a direct effect on their number of customers and 16% having heard of the path had introduced a new service or product to encourage its use among their customers (Natural Resources Wales 2013b). These figures exceeded Welsh European Funding Office (WEFO) targets and demonstrate that the path has the capacity to "add value"; yet the project is still in its infancy and there remains more scope to connect businesses to the path and its users.

A study into the economic value of the health benefits of the route (using the World Health Organization's Health Economic Assessment Tool (HEAT)) has shown how the path prevents seven deaths per year among the walking population compared to those who do not walk regularly; 19% of the sample said that without the path they would not have walked at all, which, in economic terms, transfers into £3.5 m of benefits per year directly attributable to the path (Natural Resources Wales 2014b).

A team effort – encouraging collaboration

The WCP required the successful collaboration of a number of bodies and individuals from the public, private and voluntary sectors. From a public sector viewpoint, the path encouraged joint working between local authorities as, for example, with appointing a single project officer or sharing staff (Natural Resources Wales 2014a). Engagement with a wide array of stakeholders and the involvement of local communities was a pivotal aspect of the project from its inception. Central to this was in the involvement of Local Access Forums (LAFs). The *Countryside and Rights of Way Act* (2000) placed a statutory duty on highway authorities and National Parks in England and Wales to set up LAFs to advise on public access and recreation; these comprise representatives from users, land owners and occupiers and other interests relevant to the land over which access is planned/provided. LAFs have been closely involved with local authorities along the WCP from the development stage and are consulted on work programmes, path alignment, and monitoring and reviewing of progress (Natural Resources Wales 2014a).

The path has also provided excellent opportunities for volunteering among established groups and in encouraging new participants (Natural Resources Wales 2014a). The involvement of

Ramblers Cymru (Wales) – a charity devoted to walking and the protection of public access to the countryside – in supporting the project and providing much-needed voluntary labour in footpath clearance and access improvements is crucial; this continues an enthusiastic British tradition of public respect and activism for the maintenance of countryside access (Shoard 1999).

Perhaps the most innovative and imaginative use of the path for community benefit has been the journey of the academic and IT specialist Professor Alan Dix who walked the entire route in 2013. He described the walk as 'a technological and community [journey], exploring the needs of the walker and the people along the way' (Dix n.d.), and part of the project was to assess the IT problems and needs of rural communities along the path. This examined such issues as poor mobile signals and low capacity broadband. This is an excellent example of an active technological project with benefits to communities and the broader research agenda; it also reflects the dynamism of the WCP, which has the capacity to stimulate wide interests and questions beyond the immediate recreational usage of the path itself.

'Walking the shape of a nation'

Wales entered the new millennium with a renewed sense of vitality and ambition. With increased powers of self-government, there were opportunities to develop a sharper sense of national identity and what it means to be "Welsh". The problem with Wales is that its identity has for long been defined by those who are not Welsh; this is complicated by the heterogeneity of a country where acute contrasts exist between the old industrial south ("Valleys" Wales) and the more traditional Welsh-speaking rural areas to the west and north (known in Welsh as *Y Fro Gymraeg*) (Pritchard and Morgan 2003). The ability of Wales to form an "imagined community" (Anderson 2006), not based upon face-to-face interaction, has been hampered by these powerful and diverse perceptions and exacerbated by the notion that Wales is also a "state of mind" drawn from pictorial and media representations. For the first time in its modern history Wales is now able to challenge a hybrid and often confused collective persona and re-forge a modern identity.

The creation of a WCP is a highly symbolic reflection of this new identity crystallised in the strap-line "walking the shape of a nation". The most significant aspect of this phrase is that it situates the project firmly within the context of the nation. As Jane Davidson, Minister for Environment and Sustainability in the Welsh Government (2007–11), Vice-President of Ramblers Cymru, and instigator of the path, has said:

> You're saying 'we are a nation' – which actually is an incredibly important message for other parts of the UK, as well as elsewhere, for a place that still in many people's organisational terms was a region . . . [It] was very much about Wales saying 'we are confident in our identity'. It's not that we needed to do it, it's that we were ready to do it.
>
> (*Jane Davidson, personal communication, 24 February 2016*)

The last point reinforces the energetic and ambitious ethos of the new administration which didn't create this remarkable recreational resource through necessity but had the opportunity to do so. She continues:

> So it's not just about walking the *shape* of a nation it's also the *shaping* of a nation in the context of being confident enough to create a coast path . . . the most important aspect of that is that walking the shape of a nation and shaping a nation are two different things that go hand-in-hand. There would have been no nation to walk the shape of had Wales not been

shaping a nation in so many other ways – in music, in art, in film, in theatre, in the Assembly, in politics. So all those things, you know, came together.

(Jane Davidson, personal communication, 24 February 2016)

Thus seen, the WCP appears to represent a microcosm of Welsh public and political life; it is a statement of the nation's prowess alongside a range of disparate and seemingly unrelated cultural achievements.

One of the most salient features of the path is that it provides the user an *aperçu* of the different landscapes that Wales has to offer: from the gritty urban and post-industrial terrain of the south and north-east to the pristine coastal and mountainous scenery of the west and north (Morris 2012). This equips the dedicated user with a more complete understanding of the variety of landscapes that Wales has to offer, and also a truer appreciation of the often fraught historical context of the nation's economic development. These contrasts are well appreciated by Davidson, who comments on

its treasures and warts. But what is quite incredible is one person's treasure is somebody else's wart . . . And I say that because the first time I walked Milford Haven I was absolutely amazed by what a wonderful walk it was. And yet you're walking industry the whole time.

(Jane Davidson, personal communication, 24 February 2016)

(Milford Haven is an area in south-west Wales dominated by large oil and gas installations and a port.)

The shape of the nation is multi-faceted and the WCP permits a deeper understanding of the complexities that comprise modern Wales. The path can be seen as a guide to the nation, albeit along a predetermined handrail; it has the potential to shape public opinions of Wales – its scenery, culture, people and contemporary concerns – which many routes are unable to do. It thus has agency and underlines the idea that 'any nation or national identity is not an artefact but a process' (Pritchard and Morgan 2003: 126).

Destination image and brand identity

A 'place' only becomes a 'destination' through the crafting of appealing narratives and the communication of images of place via tourism promotional materials. Central to this is the creation of a strong brand image to achieve positive place reputation and the 'holy grail' of distinctiveness and place competitiveness (Morgan *et al.* 2011). Places are made, not just physically, but perceptually, in the minds of tourists, who make pre-departure decisions based upon messages and images. Morrison (2013) identified four objectives of successful destination branding: differentiation; increased awareness, recognition and memorability; a positive image; and a strong and compelling brand identity. All these are reflected in Wales's continuing endeavour to attract increased market share and, as a small nation, "punch above its weight" as a destination in an international tourist market. I will show here how the WCP is an important contributor to the Welsh tourism "product".

Destination marketers are faced with an increasingly difficult task in making their offerings stand out in a highly competitive and crowded market place; tourists now have a greater range of choices than before utilising ever more sophisticated marketing techniques. It has been calculated that 70% of the world's tourists only visit the top-10 major destinations, so small countries like Wales are chasing a very small relative market share (Morgan *et al.* 2002: 70). Nevertheless, small countries can complete with top destination brands if they concentrate on clearly defined market segments.

The need for Wales to develop as a niche destination with a more dynamic brand is well understood. As Claire Chappell, Head of Brand Performance for Visit Wales (the Welsh Government's tourism division), told the author:

> [Country] brands need to create and retain a desired reputation, one that gives an unassailable advantage over competitors. We're in a very competitive market, but Wales has a number of core, defining strengths: world-standard adventure products; an outstanding natural environment; a distinctive culture; and a rich and ancient heritage. The opportunity is to develop and celebrate these strengths in a way that is at once unique, and deeply rooted, and also international in scale, relevance and appeal. Our vision is to continually develop new products for Wales, and to take these to the market in a way that is 'inherently Welsh, with a global outlook'. The Wales Coast Path is an example of a brand-defining product of this kind – 100% Welsh and internationally outstanding.
>
> *(Claire Chappell, personal communication, 17 March 2016)*

Part of this is to surprise those who thought they knew Wales and to transform how people see the nation through re-inventing and re-imagining old places and introducing dynamic new experiences. Claire continues:

> Visit Wales has recently launched a thematic strategy to promoting Wales as a destination – starting with Year of Adventure in 2016, followed by Year of Legends in 2017. The purpose of this approach is to clarify the Wales brand proposition by bringing our strongest and most competitive products – the great outdoors, activities, culture, heritage – to the fore, in a contemporary and refreshing way based on creating, and celebrating dynamic and defining destinations and attractions.
>
> *(Claire Chappell, personal communication, 17 March 2016)*

A key element of this product positioning is the creation of *brand experiences*, and the WCP is one of these. The path is a perfect opportunity to draw people's attention to the beauties of Wales's coastline and to surprise and delight them; it is an invitation to discover Wales afresh and to encourage positive new perspectives on the nation. It is also a golden opportunity to attract tourists to parts of Wales they might not have considered visiting ("I never thought this was Wales").

Visit Wales is currently developing a checklist – a series of benchmarks for defining experiences, and future campaigns. These are: (1) Does it elevate Wales's status?; (2) Does it surprise and inspire?; (3) Does it reinforce positive perceptions?; (4) Does it do good things?; and (5) Is it unmistakably Wales? (Claire Chappell, personal communication, 22 March 2016). The WCP has the potential to meet all of these objectives – it is "on-brand" – and is a good example of a *demonstrator project*, designed to reinforce people's perceptions of what Wales really is. Moreover, the WCP is well placed to support a number of large-scale themed tourism initiatives that are being planned by the Welsh Government: as mentioned above, 2016 has been declared the Year of Adventure in a bid to promote Wales as the "capital" of UK adventure tourism, and the WCP is an important complement to this describing itself as 'the perfect place to start your own adventure' (Natural Resources Wales 2015). The path also has an important role to play in the 2017 Year of Legends and particularly the planned 2018 Year of the Sea. It is a key component of the new brand approach.

What is most notable about the WCP's own brand identity is the strong visual image that is associated with it. The brand is represented by a striking yellow and blue logo in the shape of a dragon's tail (Figure 18.2) (Welsh Government n.d.); this is a recognised and memorable

Figure 18.2   Sign showing the Wales Coast Path logo (author's own collection)

symbol used on signage all along the route, in local communities as well as by businesses. The logo appears in a variety of guises – as roundel or carved wooden signage, metal street signs and in print form in leaflets and guidebooks. The use of the dragon's tail brings Welsh imagery right back to its roots in the Red Dragon (*Y Ddraig Goch*) – the national emblem of the nation, as represented on its flag. The vivid colours also represent the blue of the sea and the yellow of the daffodil, another national symbol of Wales. The logo provides a coherent and consistent imprimatur for the brand grounded in the nation's culturally symbolic background.

A 'first' for Wales

Prominent among the promotional messages surrounding the opening of the WCP in 2012 was that it was the first continuous walking route along a country's coast. This was given equal value alongside the natural and cultural aspects of the walk in a number of different media reports (e.g. BBC 2012; Morris 2012) and on the website of Visit Wales, where the WCP is described as 'the world's first uninterrupted route along a national coast' (Visit Wales 2016). It is clear that the nature of the "first" is crucial in establishing a positive reputation for those who achieve it; a country first to abandon environmental protection legislation, for example, is not likely to endear itself to the wider global population. But when the achievement is considered of positive value, a "first" provides a measure of kudos and serves to draw attention to a person, organisation, team or nation; it conveys a strong message of success underpinned by diligence, effort, ingenuity and competence. To be first is to be valued. In marketing terms, it is the equivalent of shining a bright spotlight on a product.

In the context of Wales's efforts in refashioning its national image, being first is a useful adjunct to the creation of an attractive brand identity; it reflects a forward-looking dynamic attitude and a willingness to seek out opportunities for creativity and change. Being first can contribute to a nation's positive reputation and, in the case of Wales, demonstrate to the world that a small country can have notable achievements. According to Anholt (2011: 30), apart from close neighbours, people across the world can normally only admire around fourteen or fifteen countries aside from their own. To establish an enhanced level of country reputation, governments often seek opportunities for "symbolic actions", which will attract the attention of a global audience. These are 'especially suggestive, remarkable, memorable, picturesque, newsworthy, topical, poetic, touching, surprising, or dramatic' (Anholt 2011: 26–27) acts, which allow a country to rise above anonymity. Wales has not been slow to seize the potential of such actions: it was the first UK country to vote against smoking in public places (a ban was instituted in 2007) and, in 2011, the first to require retailers to charge for single-use plastic carrier bags to lessen their impact on the environment (Welsh Government 2015: 22). These projects help to put Wales "on the map" and are integral to the concept of "shaping a nation", the precursor to the 'shape of the nation' mentioned above. It is no coincidence that the same Welsh Government Minister for Environment and Sustainability (Jane Davidson) was responsible for both the WCP and the plastic bag charge.

But while being first is a highly positive achievement for a nation, it can also have its downside; in brand-creation terms, emphasising firsts has its limitations. As Claire Chappell comments:

> Wales can be agile and is a creative country – celebrating the way in which this innovation is helping to make Wales distinctive and world-leading is clearly a priority. However, we also need to remember that there's also a need to keep our existing 'firsts' fresh and relevant – so that products like the Wales Coast Path continue to be market-leaders, and continue to attract interest in Wales.
>
> *(Claire Chappell, personal communication, 17 March 2016)*

As a first the WCP offers a perfect 'substantiating message' to reinforce the brand's core values – 'creative, authentic and alive' (Claire Chappell, personal communication, 22 March 2016); and the opportunity lies in ensuring that the WCP and other Welsh products continue to innovate and lead the way, in the long term. This is an opportunity for Wales – and the WCP.

Conclusion

The WCP has been an imaginative and progressive project bringing great benefits to users, the communities at 'the edge' and the wider nation of Wales. People care more about places when they give them value and the path has great potential to stimulate increased respect for the country's environment. But the path faces challenges: the power of being "first" will inevitably decline and the path's stewards will need to maintain its appeal for future generations.

Further issues remain for study beyond the limitations of this chapter: writing mainly from a tourism angle I have not explored the social impact of the path – both good and bad – on communities. Much empirical analysis needs to be undertaken in this area for us to obtain a complete picture of the route and its broader effects. In 2012, the Royal Geographical Society praised the 'transformational change' the path had brought to communities and acknowledged that a 'number of international lessons have been learnt' from creating the path (BBC 2014). The WCP is an exemplar of outstanding good practice, a blueprint for other nations who seek to enhance their coastal landscapes.

Acknowledgments

I am grateful to the following people who were interviewed for this chapter: Jane Davidson and Andrew Campbell, University of Wales Trinity St David; Quentin Grimely, Natural Resources Wales; and Claire Chappell, Visit Wales.

References

Anderson, B. (2006) *Imagined Communities: Reflections on the Origin and Spread of Nationalism*, revised edn, London: Verso.

Anholt, S. (2011) 'Competitive identity', in N. Morgan, A. Pritchard and R. Pride (eds), *Destination Brands: Managing Place Reputation*, London: Routledge, pp. 21–32.

BBC (2012) *Wales Coast Path Officially Opens with Events in Cardiff, Aberystwyth and Flint*. Available at: www.bbc.co.uk/news/uk-wales-17968524 (accessed 11 April 2016).

BBC (2014) '"World can learn" from Wales' coastal path, experts say'. Available at: www.bbc.co.uk/news/uk-wales-28955713 (accessed 12 April 2016).

Beatty, C., Fothergill, S. and Wilson, I. (2009) *Seaside Towns in Wales: A 'Benchmarking' Study*, Sheffield Hallam University: Centre for Regional Economic and Social Research.

Dix, A. (n.d.) *Alan Walks Wales: One Thousand Miles of Poetry, Technology and Community*. Available at: http://alanwalks.wales (accessed 6 April 2016).

Mackay, H. (ed.) (2010) *Understanding Contemporary Wales*, Milton Keynes/Cardiff: Open University/University of Wales Press.

Morgan, N., Pritchard, A. and Pride, R. (2002) 'Marketing to the Welsh diaspora: the appeal of *hiraeth* and homecoming', *Journal of Vacation Marketing*, 9(1): 69–80.

Morgan, N., Pritchard, A. and Pride, R. (2011) 'Tourism places, brands and reputation management', in N. Morgan, A. Pritchard and R. Pride (eds), *Destination Brands: Managing Place Reputation*, London: Routledge, pp. 3–20.

Morris, S. (2012) 'Wales coastal path offers a walk on the wild – and industrial – side', *The Guardian*, 4 May. Available at: www.theguardian.com/uk/2012/may/04/wales-coast-path (accessed 11 April 2016).

Morrison, A.M. (2013) *Marketing and Managing Tourism Destinations*, London: Routledge.

Natural Resources Wales (2013a) *The Wales Coast Path Visitor Survey 2011–13: The Economic Impact of Wales Coast Path Visitor Spending on Wales 2013*, Cardiff: Natural Resources Wales.

Natural Resources Wales (2013b) *Evaluating the Benefits to Business of the Wales Coast Path*, Cardiff. Available at: www.walescoastpath.gov.uk/media/1144/evaluating-the-benefits-to-business-of-the-wales-coast-path.pdf (accessed 11 April 2016).

Natural Resources Wales (2014a) *Wales Coast Path – End of Project Report*, Cardiff: Natural Resources Wales.

Natural Resources Wales (2014b) *Economic Assessment of the Health Benefits of Walking on the Wales Coast Path*, Cardiff: Natural Resources Wales.

Natural Resources Wales (2015) *Wales Coast Path*. Available at: www.walescoastpath.gov.uk/?lang=en (accessed 28 March 2016).

Pritchard, A. and Morgan, N. (2003) 'Mythic geographies of representation and identity: contemporary postcards of Wales', *Tourism and Cultural Change*, 1(2): 111–130.

Shoard, M. (1999) *A Right to Roam*, Oxford: Oxford University Press.

Sport Wales (2014) *Walking and Cycling in Wales*. Available at: http://sport.wales/media/1510933/walking_and_cycling_in_wales.pdf (accessed 29 March 2016).

UK Government (2006) *Government of Wales Act 2006*. Available at: www.legislation.gov.uk/ukpga/2006/32/schedule/5/part/1/paragraph/wrapper1n2 (accessed 11 April 2016).

Visit Wales (2008) *Coastal Tourism Strategy*, Cardiff: Visit Wales.

Visit Wales (2016) *Wales Coast Path Guide*. Available at: www.visitwales.com/things-to-do/activities/walking-hiking/wales-coast-path (accessed 11 April 2016).

Welsh Assembly Government (2007) *One Wales: A Progressive Agenda for the Government of Wales*, Cardiff: Welsh Assembly Government.

Welsh Government (n.d.) *Wales Coast Path: Brand Guidelines*, Cardiff: Welsh Government.

Welsh Government (2015) *Welsh Government: A Quick Guide*. Available at: http://gov.wales/docs/caecd/publications/150917-quick-guide-en.pdf (accessed 11 April 2016).

19

Improving the experience quality of hiking trails

A setting-experience-relationship approach

Diana Müller, Heinz-Dieter Quack, Kathrin Schumacher and Franziska Thiele

Introduction: hiking tourism as research object

While hiking has had an effect on tourism since the beginning of alpinism in approximately 1850, it was not until the 1990s that significant contributions to the relevant literature of tourism science started to be made. In Germany, the professional analysis of the demand for hiking started in the year 2000 by tourism specialists, when quality standards were implemented on a national level (introduced by the German Hiking Association). It was only then that studies on a national basis for recording and finding out different types of the demand for hiking commenced (Brämer 2003; BMWi 2010).

Hiking is now an almost ubiquitous phenomenon in Germany. Around two-thirds of the German population hike during their leisure time, even though around half of these do so less often than 'regularly' or 'occasionally' (PROJECT M 2014: 10). The comparison of studies in 2010 and 2014 illustrates that the number of non-hikers declined and people are more interested in irregular hiking activities (Table 19.1).

Since 2000, the tourism industry has experienced an enormous expansion of trails and infrastructure development. Two competing quality labels for hiking trails have been developed; today, more than 600 trails across Germany are certified. That's why hiking tourism as a market segment plays a prominent role in the marketing of the respective destinations. The positive development of the demand and the resulting competition in the hiking industry led to a new differentiation and change of values in hiking tourism. The visitor can choose between a variety of different hiking destinations and hiking trails in low or high mountain ranges to find individual nature experiences (PROJECT M 2014). The positive impacts of natural environments and moderate outdoor activities on emotional and social wellbeing have been shown in studies from different disciplines (e.g. Abraham *et al.* 2010; Tsunetsugu *et al.* 2010; Hill *et al.* 2009; Kaplan *et al.* 1998). However, individual factors, the relation of setting elements and the psychological response of the hiker during the spatio-temporal hiking experience in different landscapes have only been considered in a few studies (e.g. Dorwart *et al.* 2010). Therefore, it is not surprising that hiking trails are normally planned and designed without any special relationship to such research. Therefore, this chapter provides an experience approach, including the spatial setting

Table 19.1 Frequency of hiking of German population

Frequency of hiking	2010	2014
Regularly	15%	11%
Occasionally	23%	23%
Seldom	18%	35%
Never	44%	29%
Not applicable	–	2%

Source: Derived from Project M 2014

from a visitor's perspective, in order to better understand individual onsite experiences in hiking tourism and recreation environments (Popp 2012; Dorwart *et al.* 2010; Williams 2007). It focuses on a target-oriented, holistic planning and designing of hiking trails, based on the relationship between hikers and their environment (setting-experience-relationship approach). This approach integrates multidisciplinary perspectives of environmental psychology and leisure and tourism geography. The results of a research project will be used to illustrate this new perspective of the hiking experience, measured in situ (i.e. during the walk with the researcher) with the method of "commented walks" (Thibaud 2001). With this method, it is possible to give practical implications to improve the experience quality of hiking trails.

Nature, hiking experience and the setting-experience relationship

Experiencing nature and landscape is the key element of tourism, including visual perception of spectacular landscape scenery, stays in natural areas or activities in natural surroundings (PROJECT M 2014). Hiking as one of the most important activities in leisure, recreation and tourism as it is not only focused on the movement, but it also incorporates nature and landscape into the activity (PROJECT M 2014; BMWi 2010; Dorwart *et al.* 2010; Dreyer *et al.* 2010; den Breejen 2007). The experience of nature and landscape is the primary motive for hiking (cf. PROJECT M 2014; Dreyer *et al.* 2010; Brämer 2003). In comparison to other activities, this motive is much more pronounced. It seems plausible that slow movements rather than other activities of spatial mobility, such as cycling, favour the experience of nature and landscape (Brämer 2003). Schultz (2014: 298; trans. by authors) emphasises that 'since the modern period and especially in Romanticism around 1800 hiking became the epitome of nature experience par excellence'. That's why it is necessary to consider the experience of nature and landscape in connection with the physical activity of hiking.

Previous investigations undertaken to determine the actual experience in natural surroundings were focused mainly on wilderness settings (e.g. Cole and Hall 2009; Borrie and Roggenbuck 2001) or green spaces, such as parks in urban environments (e.g. Kaspar 2012; Tessin 2008). Some research papers also address the topic of walking or hiking (e.g. Dorwart *et al.* 2010; Cole and Hall 2009; den Breejen 2007; Chhetri *et al.* 2004; Hull and Stewart 1995). In these studies, hiking experiences and their influence factors were researched as a phenomenon in itself (e.g. Dorwart *et al.* 2010), or with the objective of 'managing the setting to influence experience opportunities' (Cole 2012: 67).

The focus on the visitors' experience to improve the quality of the hiking trails is challenging. Experience is an elusive and blurred phenomenon, which is diverse and complex (Vespestad and Lindberg 2011; Volo 2009). This becomes particularly obvious when looking at the various

195

meanings of tourist experiences presented by Vespestad and Lindberg (2011) or Volo (2009). Chhetri *et al.* (2004: 34) come to the conclusion that '[t]here is no single theory that defines the meaning and extent of tourist experiences, although a number of authors have made attempts to formulate models by generalising and aggregating information'. With the focus on the onsite experience, there are characteristics that have been investigated: for instance, onsite experience is also seen as dynamic, which means it may vary across time and space. These variations can be observed, for instance, in the increase and decrease of intensity of different emotions, moods, feelings, attention states during the onsite experience (den Breejen 2007; Borrie and Roggenbuck 2001). With this in mind, hiking experiences can operationally be understood as a variety of subjective dimensions, such as sensory experiences, bodily sensations, feelings, imaginations, conscious thoughts or scenic beauty appraisals of hikers moving through natural landscapes (cf. Dorwart *et al.* 2010; Goller 2009; Hull and Stewart 1995). 'These experiences range from the immediate emotional reactions of joy and satisfaction in a setting to the enduring changes in an individual's well-being (what recreation researchers often refer to as benefits)' (Williams 2007: 30). Williams (2007) also notes that the experiences can be positive as well as negative. Therefore, the onsite hiking experience is considered as 'a "bundle" of separate experiences', which forms an overall trip experience – also referred to as an "experience gestalt"' (Cole 2012; cf. Dorwart *et al.* 2010; den Breejen 2007; Roggenbuck and Driver 2000). The quality of this overall trip experience is finally evaluated by the hiker and has again an effect on future experiences (Dorwart *et al.* 2010).

With special emphasis on the hiking experiences, it is important to bear the individual's movement in mind. The physical activity always has an effect on the experiences; every new move or sight can have a changing influence on the experiences (Popp 2011). Popp (2011: 41; trans. by authors) concluded that '[i]f the nature of experiences shall be observed and thereby particular attention be paid on the context of the environment, it seems appropriate to explore the experience both in situ and in motion' (see also Dorwart *et al.* 2010; McIntyre and Roggenbuck 1998; Hull and Stewart 1995).

Currently, the planning of hiking trails in Germany primarily resides with experts using their own knowledge or experiences and/or transferring general research results into practice (expert approach). In addition to that approach, the target-oriented and holistic designing of hiking trails must also consider the relationship between the experiences of hikers and their environment (setting-experience-relationship approach). In following this new perspective as Popp (2012: 82) has suggested, the actual experience should be analysed 'through the eyes' of the hiker.

The setting-experience-relationship approach represents a relatively recent phenomenon in leisure, recreation and tourism studies (Popp 2011; Vespestad and Lindberg 2011; Williams 2007). From the perspective of trail managers the idea is that, by improving and optimising 'the setting (environmental, social and managerial conditions), managers influence the nature and quality of experiences to a substantial degree' (Cole and Hall 2009: 24–25). However, the relationship between the setting and the experience is not only a simple stimulus-response concept, but rather 'something created by the individual or group through active engagement with the setting' (Williams 2007: 30). In this respect, it is possible to consider the setting as 'a frame within which individuals have the power to create their own experiences' (McIntyre and Roggenbuck 1998: 417). Managers can only improve and optimise the framework conditions of a setting in order to encourage experiences (Cole 2012; Popp 2011; Vespestad and Lindberg 2011) Hence the 'challenge for . . . managers is to develop a more comprehensive understanding of the link between setting and experience' (Williams 2007: 31) to enhance the quality of hiking trails.

The quality of hiking experience

Besides experience, quality is a multidimensional and complex construct (Jennings 2010), which is why there is no clear understanding of the concept, and the practical transfer and adoption by managers is difficult. Planners and designers in hiking tourism assume that the trail conditions are crucial for the quality assessment and satisfaction of hikers. This quality assessment is habitually passed for the perceived experience quality. Perceived service quality has been defined as the quality of the attributes of a service that are under the control of a supplier, while perceived experience quality involves not only the attributes provided by a supplier, but also the attributes brought to the opportunity by the visitor (Chen and Chen 2010; Cole and Scott 2004; Otto and Ritchie 1996). Therefore, experience quality is not confined to service performance and functional dimensions, but also refers to the psychological outcomes resulting from customer participation in activities. When aiming at developing a high experience quality of hiking trails, the concept of "aesthetics of pleasure" (Tessin 2008) can be a particularly suitable approach to the subject.

The "aesthetics of pleasure" refers to a place of well-being, i.e. the significance of recreation or relaxation in a natural environment for psychological restoration. Tessin (2008) suggests being mindful of the visitors' need to feel well and comfortable, while pleasure is regarded as a mode of aesthetic experiences, like enjoyment of a beautiful view or appreciation of a waterfall, and situational events like bird watching or encounters with other hikers. The hiking setting thus becomes a place for activities and leisure charged with aesthetic elements and situational events beyond and in contrast to everyday life. According to this approach, the aim for designing spaces and settings for hiking experiences is to create an experience quality where well-being has gained centre stage. Therefore, besides the dimensions of the psychological restoration theory (being away, scope, coherence, fascination and compatibility), the characteristics of pleasure and situational factors should also be taken into account to enhance the quality of hiking experience (Figure 19.1). According to Williams (2007: 30), the quality of an experience is

> the result of three categories of immediate cause: situational influences such as weather and the actions of other people in the setting; individual and group characteristics (e.g., interests, skills and attitudes of the individual and significant companions) as well as the dynamics among group members; and landscape or setting influences that concern resource managers.

Besides these environmental setting conditions, the experience is influenced by personal characteristics as culture, biology, knowledge, motivation and expectations (Williams 2007; Tessin 2008).

As stated above, the experience quality should be analysed in its entirety; from the manager perspective it should be noted, however, that not every factor of the setting (e.g. weather, group dynamics) can potentially be affected by managers (Cole and Hall 2009). There are individual criteria of well-being, which have to be explored, merged in a "right" way, operationalised with individual aspects and simultaneous consideration of the existing social–spatial context (Tessin 2008). So, it should be emphasised that there is no one-size-fits-all solution to improve the experience quality of hiking trails, but an individual tailored treatment for possible improvements of each single trail.

That's why the demand-oriented creation of the requested place of well-being in hiking tourism can not only be found on an expert system. There is a need for an alternative approach to take the individual perspective of hikers into account. Summed up in the words of Otto and

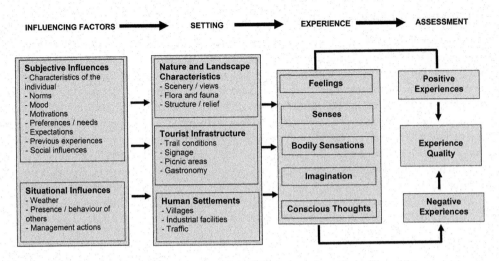

Figure 19.1 Factors affecting the quality of the hiking experience

Ritchie (1996: 167–168), who conclude 'that a measure of the quality of the service experience might be a useful complement – if not an alternative – to traditional quality of service measures'. In the next section, one possible method to measure hiking experience quality will be described.

Methodical approach and exemplary results

With the qualitative survey method of 'commented walks' (French: 'parcours commentés'), it is possible to analyse the relationship between the experiences of hikers and the setting (Thibaud 2001; Kazig and Popp 2011; Popp 2011). The core of this method is characterised by the fact that the experiences are being collected during the hiking 'in situ' (i.e. during the walk with the researcher). After a preparatory discussion, the hiker is encouraged to verbalise his sensory impressions, bodily sensations, feelings, imaginations and conscious thoughts during the walk with this so-called introspection. These comments are recorded with a tie-clip microphone and recording device. After the hike, a structured retrospective interview and a short questionnaire are conducted to collect influencing factors such as motivations and preferred hiking areas (Müller *et al.* 2014; Kazig and Popp 2011; Popp 2011).

The experiences of twenty hikers on two German hiking trails were collected in 2013. The interviews were held during hiking tours on the Hahnenbachtaltour trail and on the Diemelsteig trail. With the help of methods of qualitative content analysis based on the methods of Kuckartz (2014), the transcribed interviews are analysed. This research project works with a computer-based structured-thematic content analysis. Therefore, various categories are inductively formed, based on the material. This system of categories is the centre of the analysis and represents sub-aspects of the hiking experience and the relationship to the setting. To improve the experience quality of hiking trails by increasing the well-being of hikers, it is necessary to know which factors influence the experience during a hiking tour. With the help of the content analyses, it is possible to create a comprehensive overview of the multifaceted nature of hiking experiences and the positive and negative influential factors. The results are summarised and structured in a category system with three levels, as shown in Figure 19.2.

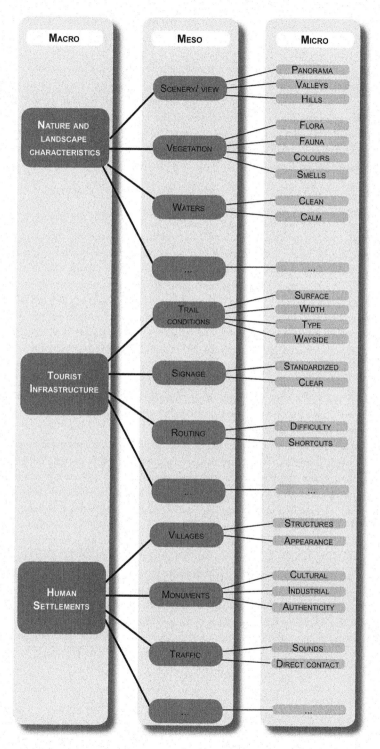

Figure 19.2 Category system to identify elements of hiking experience

The root categories of nature and landscape characteristics, tourist infrastructure and human settlements can be seen as the macro level, which describes the dimensions of the hiking experience in general. The second level differentiates these dimensions in respective subcategories to understand the needs of the hiker and the requirements for the best possible setting-experience relationship. The codings of the micro level contain the individual perception of single elements and the positive and negative experiences regarding the specific setting of the trail. On this level, the individual design of hiking trails is situated. With the whole category system, it is possible to find out how single setting elements of a hiking trail affect the cognitive aspects, emotions and behaviour of the hiker and finally to define implications for the improvement of hiking experience quality. Results are presented below.

Nature and landscape characteristics

Natural and landscape characteristics, such as flora and fauna, mountains, lakes and rivers exert a great influence on the hiking experience. There are some participants who perceive the overall appearance of the countryside, and others who are more interested in various elements and details of the varied landscape. The verbalised constitutive setting elements on the meso level are 'scenery/views', 'vegetation', 'waters', 'structure/relief'. The impressions and the expressed needs of hikers concerning these different setting elements show that the most important nature and landscape characteristics are vast landscape and open views, tranquillity, contrasts, colour shades, variety, cleanliness and closeness to nature. It could be argued that for the design of the route course, it is essential to cater to these needs. On the micro level, even more individual elements become visible. In the interviews of the Diemelsteig, for example, the view on the relief of valleys, forests and fields with different green colours is described: 'A wonderful panorama. Here you overlook lawns, wood and slowly incipient yellow flowering meadows' (interview IP3_1 Diemelsteig; trans. by authors).

The most influential factors of hiking experience quality are the emotional sensations triggered by the setting elements. With the analysed settings on both hiking trails, participants express positive emotions like pleasure, satisfaction, relaxation, well-being or excitement. To stimulate these positive emotions 'it is important to create nature-based experiences that capture the aesthetic qualities' (Breiby and Slatten 2015: 341) of scenery/views, vegetation, water and structure/relief in the design of the hiking trail. The results of this study show that on the micro level of the Diemelsteig, concerning the water, the only opportunity where the hiker can see and hear the water from a little stream is almost invisible. A positive example for the experience design of nature setting elements is the Hahnenbachtaltour. The trail is not only named after the local stream Hahnenbach, but the routing along and across the stream enables a multisensory experience. There are route sections where hikers can hear, see and even touch the stream. Combined with the sound of running water of the Hahnenbach, the twittering of birds and a variety of plants and flowers along the trail cause a deep calmness and relaxation. All these elements together create an overall feeling of untouched nature and nativeness.

Tourist infrastructure

Considering that the experience of natural and cultural environment is very difficult to influence and alter by the manager, it is important to focus on the design of tourist infrastructure and the characteristics of the hiking trail itself, including the impact on the individual hiking experience. The subcategories of this dimension are conditions of the trail, signage, routing and embedding in the landscape, relief of the trail, resting opportunities and accommodation. The needs which are verbalised regarding the infrastructure are a pleasant feeling of walking, safety, cleanliness, challenges and alternatives in routing. On the micro level of the trail, hikers perceive aspects like conditions of the surface, width, type and wayside. In particular, hikers prefer a cultivated, wide, dry and soft hiking trail that bounces while walking, which creates a feeling of relaxation. On the Diemelsteig, one participant tries to explain the experience of the body sensation related to the surface: 'And then this feeling of walking on an unpaved path again. The steps swing more through the body, you feel it's not that solid and it's motivating to walk. Yes' (IP1_3 Diemelsteig; trans. by authors). Whereas muddy and slippery trails are especially uncomfortable, because the hiker has to be on alert all the time while walking, and it is almost impossible to experience the nature and environment in full. Also, the wayside can have an influence on the experience quality. On a specific route section of the Diemelsteig, participants reported that the narrow field border is too monotonous and the use of pesticides is conspicuous. This experience is related to negative emotions like disturbance and discomfort. An implication for this trail section is the establishment of a wider and more diversified field border to enhance the natural feeling of the trail. Furthermore, a clear, understandable and standardised signage system is essential for the orientation on the trail and supports the feeling of security. Thus it is reasonable to install safety advice and facilities that ensure a safe passing of danger trail sections, which can be identified on 'commented walks'.

In addition to these factors, hikers prefer clean and comfortable resting places such as benches along the way, so they can relax in the sun and enjoy the view. The micro level of this study shows places where benches affect a negative experience because of a missing view. Concerning the design of the furniture, natural materials, like tree trunks or new, modern designs are particularly preferred. But also the frequentation of seating areas matters, because of crowding effects. A high frequency of other people can lead to displeasure and sometimes even anger. Participants on the Hahnenbachtaltour explained that in such sections it would be almost impossible to relax, if they had to hear other hikers all the time while walking.

Human settlements

The root category 'human settlements' comprises the cultural and human-made environment of the trail. On the meso level, the needs of the hikers with regard to 'villages', 'cultural and industrial monuments', 'land utilization' of agriculture and forestry, 'wind turbines' and 'traffic' are explored. The participants on both trails emphasised that "civilisation" should be invisible and nature seemingly untouched. That means that they do not like to see or hear engines, traffic and rail networks or industrial areas, if they are not part of the historical appearance. And also wind turbines or agriculture with extensive monoculture can disturb the landscape scenery and the needs of the hiker. It is important that landscape structures are not destroyed, and villages or cultural monuments are harmoniously embedded instead. On the micro level, this harmony on the Diemelsteig is described with genuine structures, well-looked-after and restored timber-framed houses. A village located at the end of the walk has a positive influence on the hiking experience, it is perceived as peaceful and quiet. On the Hahnenbachtaltour, the trail leads along cultural monuments and a Celtic settlement. Cultural monuments and settlements on both trails evoke positive emotions like curiosity and excitement as the following statement shows: 'One sure is a little curious. What are these walls you can see over there?' (interview IP3_9 Hahnenbachtaltour; trans. by authors). Some hikers also imagine how the sights and the environment might have looked in the past, or they describe that they feel as though they have been transported back to ancient times.

Conclusions and recommendations

The content analysis shows a variety of influential factors and their strong connections to each other. Important factors which influence the hiking experience quality on both trails are summarised and exemplary recommendations that can improve the experience quality of the examined hiking trails are given in Figures 19.3 and 19.4.

This chapter contributes to a setting-experience-relationship approach to tourism and recreation research that helps to understand walking experiences from the hiker's point of view. The literature review reveals that when focusing on the onsite experience, the individual and spatial context should be taken into account. With the in-situ method of "commented walks", direct and detailed insight into positive and negative experiences of participants on two German hiking trails has been gained. This methodical approach turns out to be much more precise than simple classical paper-and-pencil studies. In a qualitative data analysis, these experiences

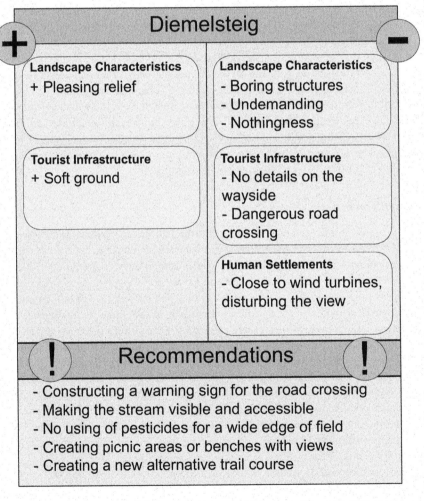

Figure 19.3 Factors influencing hiking experience quality on the Diemelsteig trail

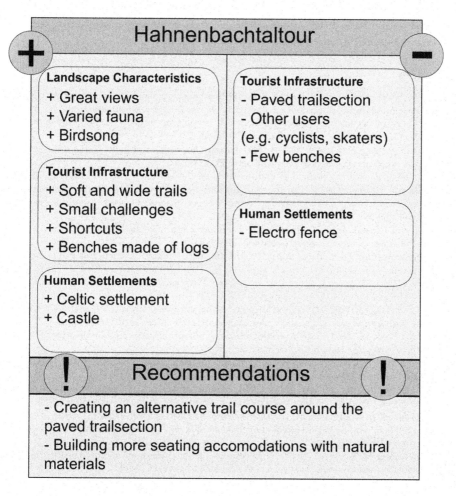

Figure 19.4 Factors influencing hiking experience quality on the Hahnenbachtaltour trail

can be structured and categorised on a macro, meso and micro level. While on the macro and meso level, the needs and preferences of hikers concerning the experiences of landscape, tourist infrastructure and human settlements can be regarded in general, the micro level reveals positive and negative aspects of individual experiences which are unique to the single trails. For the latter, recommendations to enhance the experience quality of the examined hiking trails can be provided for practitioners. It has to be emphasised that the effort of field work, and the analysis of data in particular, are highly intense and time-consuming, so cannot usually be accomplished by locally acting experts. Nonetheless, the use of the method 'commented walks' highlights opportunities for future research on experiences and experience quality in different kinds of recreation and travel. With this method, it is possible to gather visitors' onsite experiences and their individual quality assessments directly in the existing setting and the spatial-temporal context. A further development of in-situ methods and analysis, as well as a wider empirical basis, can be a conceivable aim and contains a great potential for qualitative research to reduce the effort of acquisition and implementation. For instance, a typology construction of common attributes by exploring the individual setting-experience relationship in different environmental surroundings can be a valuable addition to derive implications for target-group segmentation, in order to adjust the experience quality of hiking trails to the particular needs.

References

Abraham, A., Sommerhalder, K. and Abel, T. (2010) 'Landscape and well-being: a scoping study on the health-promoting impact of outdoor environments', *International Journal of Public Health*, 55: 59–69.

BMWi (ed.) (2010) *Grundlagenuntersuchung Freizeit und Urlaubsmarkt Wandern – Forschungsbericht Nr. 591*, Berlin: Bundesministerium für Wirtschaft und Technologie.

Borrie, W.T. and Roggenbuck, J.W. (2001) 'The dynamic, emergent, and multi-phasic nature of on-site wilderness experiences', *Journal of Leisure Research*, 33: 202–228.

Brämer, R. (2003) 'Zurück zur natur? Die wald-und-wiesen-therapie', *Psychologie Heute*, April: 20–28.

Breiby, M.A. and Slatten, T. (2015) 'The effects of aesthetic experiential qualities on tourists' positive emotions and loyalty: a case of a nature-based context in Norway', *Journal of Quality Assurance in Hospitality & Tourism*, 16: 323–46.

Chen, C.-F. and Chen, F.-S. (2010) 'Experience quality, perceived value, satisfaction and behavioral intentions for heritage tourists', *Tourism Management*, 31: 29–35.

Chhetri, P., Arrowsmith, C. and Jackson, M. (2004) 'Determining hiking experiences in nature-based tourist destinations', *Tourism Management*, 25: 31–43.

Cole, D.N. (2012) 'Wilderness visitor experiences: a selective review of 50 years of research', *Park Science*, 28: 66–70.

Cole, D.N. and Hall, T.E. (2009) 'Perceived effects of setting attributes on visitor experiences in wilderness: variation with situational context and visitor characteristics', *Environmental Management*, 44: 24–36.

Cole, S.T. and Scott, D. (2004) 'Examining the mediating role of experience quality in a model of tourist experiences', *Journal of Travel & Tourism Marketing*, 16: 79–90.

den Breejen, L. (2007) 'The experiences of long distance walking: a case study of the West Highland Way in Scotland', *Tourism Management*, 28: 1417–1427.

Dorwart, C.E., Moore, R.L. and Leung, Y.-F. (2010) 'Visitors' perceptions of a trail environment and effects on experiences: a model for nature-based recreation experiences', *Leisure Sciences*, 32: 33–54.

Dreyer, A., Menzel, A. and Endreß, M. (2010) *Wandertourismus*, Munich: Oldenbourg.

Goller, H. (2009) *Erleben, Erinnern, Handeln: Eine Einführung in die Psychologie und ihre philosophischen Grenzfragen*, Stuttgart: Kohlhammer.

Hill, E., Goldenberg M. and Freidt, B. (2009) 'Benefits of hiking: a means-end approach on the Appalachian trail', *Journal of Unconventional Parks, Tourism & Recreation Research*, 2: 19–27.

Hull, R.B. and Stewart, W.P. (1995) 'The landscape encountered and experienced while hiking', *Environment and Behavior*, 27: 404–426.

Jennings, G. (2010) 'Research processes for evaluating quality experiences: reflections from the "experiences" field(s)', in M. Morgan, P. Lugosi and J.R.B. Ritchie (eds), *The Tourism and Leisure Experience: Consumer and Managerial Perspectives*, Bristol: Channel View Publications, pp. 81–98.

Kaplan, R., Kaplan, S. and Ryan, R.L. (1998) *With People in Mind: Design and Management of Everyday Nature*, Washington, DC: Island Press.

Kaspar, H. (2012) *Erlebnis Stadtpark: Nutzung und Wahrnehmung urbaner Grünräume*, Wiesbaden: Springer VS.

Kazig, R. and Popp, M. (2011) 'Unterwegs in fremden Umgebungen. Ein praxeologischer Zugang zum "wayfinding" von Fußgängern', *Raumforschung und Raumordnung*, 69: 3–15.

Kuckartz, U. (2014) *Qualitative Inhaltsanalyse: Methoden, Praxis, Computerunterstützung*, 2nd edn, Weinheim and Basel: Beltz Juventa.

McIntyre, N. and Roggenbuck, J.W. (1998) 'Nature/person transactions during an outdoor adventure experience: a multi-phasic analysis', *Journal of Leisure Research*, 30: 401–422.

Müller, D., Quack, H.-D. and Thiele, F. (2014) 'Praktikabilität des setting-experience-relationship-ansatzes zur verbesserung der erlebnisqualität von wanderwegen', in S. Küblböck and F. Thiele (eds), *Tourismus und Innovation*, Mannheim: MetaGIS-Systems, pp. 183–197.

Otto, J.E. and Ritchie, J.R.B. (1996) 'The service experience in tourism', *Tourism Management*, 17: 165–174.

Popp, M. (2011) '"Was die Leute tatsächlich erleben, darüber wissen wir erstaunlich wenig" – ein Forschungsprojekt zum touristischen Erleben', in A. Kagermeier and T. Reeh (eds), *Trends, Herausforderungen und Perspektiven für die tourismusgeographische Forschung*, Mannheim: MetaGIS-Systems, pp. 37–50.

Popp, M. (2012) 'Erlebnisforschung neu betrachtet – ein Ansatz zu ihrer räumlichen Kontextualisierung', *Zeitschrift für Tourismuswissenschaft*, 4: 81–100.

PROJECT M (ed.) (2014) *Wanderstudie: Der deutsche Wandermarkt 2014*, Berlin: PROJECT M.

Roggenbuck, J.W. and Driver, B.L. (2000) 'Benefits of nonfacilitated uses of wilderness', in S.F. McCool, D.N. Cole, W.T. Borrie and J. O'Loughlin (eds), *Wilderness Science in a Time of Change Conference – Volume 3: Wilderness as a Place for Scientific Inquiry*, Missoula, MT, May 1999, pp. 33–49.

Schultz, H. (2014) *Landschaften auf den Grund gehen: Wandern als Erkenntnismethode beim Großräumigen Landschaftsentwerfen*, Berlin: Jovis.

Tessin, W. (2008) *Ästhetik des Angenehmen: Städtische Freiräume zwischen professioneller Ästhetik und Laiengeschmack*, Wiesbaden: Springer VS.

Thibaud, J.-P. (2001) 'La méthode des parcours commentes', in M. Grosjean and J.-P. Thibaud (eds), *L'espace urbain en méthodes*, Marseille: Parenthèses, pp. 79–99.

Tsunetsugu, Y., Park, B.-J. and Miyazaki, Y. (2010) 'Trends in research related to "Shinrin-yoku" (taking in the forest atmosphere or forest bathing) in Japan', *Environmental Health and Preventive Medicine*, 15: 27–37.

Vespestad, M. and Lindberg, F. (2011) 'Understanding nature-based tourist experiences: an ontological approach', *Current Issues in Tourism*, 14(6): 563–580.

Volo, S. (2009) 'Conceptualizing experience: a tourist based approach', *Journal of Hospitality Marketing & Management*, 18: 111–126.

Williams, D.R. (2007) 'Recreation settings, scenery, and visitor experiences: a research assessment', in L.E. Kruger, R. Mazza and K. Lawrence (eds), *Proceedings: National Workshop on Recreation Research and Management*, Portland: U.S. Department of Agriculture, Forest Service, Pacific Northwest Research Station, pp. 29–41.

20

Hikers' preferences and DMO strategies

Contrasting perspectives and conflicting views?

Ingeborg M. Nordbø

Introduction

In Norway, hiking is a popular leisure activity traceable back to the formation of the Norwegian nation-state. Since then hiking and outdoor life (Norwegian *friluftsliv*) have been essential elements in building national identity and have become an integral part of Norwegian culture (Svarstad 2010; Ween and Abram 2012; Nordbø *et al.* 2014).

The Norwegian Trekking Association (DNT) has been a pioneering organization in this respect. Ween and Abram (2012) argue that the DNT holds a central position in defining preferred ways (for Norwegians) to be in nature, and that the DNT through its technologies of governing has managed

> to place hiking in a dominant position in relation to other rural activities and to stamp their authority and control onto ways of walking. Basic governmental techniques such as map-making, marking and guiding can be seen as technologies of ordering and standardizing Norwegian nature.
>
> *(Ween and Abram 2012: 156).*

The DNT, in its governing and dissemination of hiking and outdoor life, focuses on values and practices related to simplicity (minimal equipment and non-luxury accommodation and food), authenticity (being at one with nature and minimal intervention) and challenge (wilderness skills, hard work, mastery and rewarding of physical efforts) (Nordbø *et al.* 2014). The DNT's version of nature is not uncontested, but given the organization's size and influence in the Norwegian society, it functions as a guiding light and gatekeeper with reference to what has been defined or understood as the 'correct' way to hike in Norway (Nordbø *et al.* 2014). The DNT is the largest environmental organization in Norway with 20,000 members and 50 branch offices. It operates approximately 430 mountain lodges in high mountain areas in Norway (Ween and Abram 2012).

Since 2000 we have seen an increase in an export of the DNT way of hiking and being in nature outside Norway and to other nationalities. Hiking, for example, is promoted as a prime example of how to integrate refugees into Norwegian society and culture, and the Norwegian

Foreign Ministry has supported the DNT in transferring its hiking model to developing countries such as Kyrgyzstan as a way to inspire the Kyrgyz people to grow the love of their country and to promote ecological tourism development.

In terms of tourism, nature always has been promoted as the prime attraction or reason for foreigners to visit Norway. It has been since 2000, however, that the tourism industry in Norway, in close cooperation with the DNT, has started to promote hiking in a more strategic and coordinated way. In 2002, the Norwegian National Tourism Board launched a hiking campaign with the aim of raising awareness of Norway as a hiking destination among their main international markets and invited local and regional destinations to join in. Participation in the campaign provided financial support to the destinations and access to market analyses and local market knowledge to ensure appropriate product development and marketing. A number of local and regional destination management/marketing organizations (DMOs) joined the campaign to work with quality improvements in their hiking products or offerings (Nordbø *et al.* 2014).

When hiking is looked upon from a market perspective, it is relevant to ask whether the DNT way of hiking and being in nature, which seems to find such favour among Norwegian hikers, is also the way to work with hiking in an international context. Adopting the concept of service quality, the aim of the chapter is to identify possible gaps between international hikers' customer needs and the actual services provided at different stages of service delivery. This chapter also will provide suggestions on how identified gaps can be closed.

Theoretical considerations

To deliver superior value to customers is an ongoing concern of those who work with product development. Quality improvements in tourism are deemed essential (Augustyn and Ho 1998) and applies also to the development of nature-based products such as hiking. The rapidly changing tourism industry and the increasing expectations of tourists who travel more frequently makes it increasingly important for tourism destinations and companies to know and provide the right service quality.

In this respect, services in simple terms can be understood as 'deeds, processes, and performances provided or coproduced by one entity or person for another entity or person' (Zeithaml *et al.* 2012: 8). Service quality is a multi-dimensional and many-faceted concept (Kouthouris and Alexandris 2005), and gap analyses are often used to illustrate how (tourism-related) organizations can improve their service quality.

This chapter uses the concept of service quality to shed light on the market orientation and product development of Norwegian DMOs compared with international hikers' needs and preferences in order to identify gaps in service delivery. A number of models to measure service quality have been developed and tested; the SERVQUAL model is perhaps the best known and uses five gaps to understand mismatches in service quality: customer gap, knowledge gap, policy gap, delivery gap and communication gap. Although the study by Kouthouris and Alexandris (2005) found that SERVQUAL is not a good measurement model of service quality in the outdoor industry, the customer gap and knowledge gap with inherent perspectives serve to shed light on the findings presented in this chapter.

The customer gap has to do with the difference between customer expectations and customer perceptions. The customer gap is the most important gap to measure service quality, and, in an ideal world, the customer's expectation would be almost identical to the customer's perception. Customer expectations are what the customer expects according to available resources, and they are influenced by factors such as personality, cultural background, family lifestyle, demographics, advertising, available information online and experience with similar products.

In the literature on service quality and gap analyses, the measurement of perceptions vis a vis expectations is a disputable issue (Kouthouris and Alexandris 2005). Because the aim of the chapter is to look into service quality of more than one organization, "customer expectation" was modified to "customer importance", meaning that instead of measuring expectations toward the delivery of a specific hiking product/experience from one DMO, the focus was put on measuring benefits that hikers in general seek when hiking. Furthermore, of special relevance with reference to the customer gap in terms of the issues studied in this chapter is how cultural background might influence, not only customer importance, but also customer perception.

Customer perception is subjective, as it is based on the individual customer's interaction with a given product or service. Perception is derived from the customer's satisfaction with the specific product or service and the quality of service delivery. In this study, the hikers' experience with the hiking product was measured at four trails in the southeast part of Norway to get a more varied and complete picture of the possible variations of hikers and types of trails.

From a management point of view, identifying the gaps in customers' evaluations is always a very useful task, because strategies can be designed to close these gaps. The theory on customer service quality thus highlights that, in a customer-orientated strategy, delivering quality service for a specific product should be based on a clear understanding of the target market, and thus a clear market-orientated (MO) strategy. Market orientation is regarded as important in order to have the right attention toward latent needs of consumers and to create competitive advantages (Slater and Narver 1998; Kohli and Jaworski 1990). Understanding customer needs and knowing customer expectations and the benefits they seek thus should be the best way to close the gap.

The knowledge gap deals with the difference between customers' expectations of the service provided and the company's provision of the service. Adapted to this study, that means the difference between what hikers deem as important attributes when hiking and the experiences with the same attributes with reference to a specific trail. Management, in this case of the DMOs, is not always aware of, or has not correctly interpreted customers' expectations in relation to the product or services offered. If a knowledge gap exists, it might mean the organizations are trying to meet wrong or non-existing consumer needs. In a customer-orientated business, it is important to have a clear understanding of the consumer's need for service. Comprehensive market research thus is required to close the gap between the consumer's expectations for service and management's perception of service delivery.

Method

The empirical data which is examined in this chapter consists of semi-structured qualitative interviews with local and regional DMOs at 18 hiking destinations spread across the country conducted in 2013 (Nordbø et al. 2014). It also includes data from structured interviews (through questionnaires) of 683 hikers conducted at four trails in southeast Norway during the summer of 2014 (Nordbø and Prebensen 2015). Seventeen of the 18 DMOs in the qualitative study claimed to have started working more strategically with hiking in the wake of the launch of Innovation Norway's hiking campaign. One of the destinations, however, reported that it has worked more or less strategically with hiking for the past 20 years. Two destinations had just started, while the average was 6.5 years (median = 5 years).

As in general for tourism enterprises in rural areas of Norway, the DMOs are small organizations. Referring to the number of employees, the biggest DMO involved in the study had only five employees, while the smallest ones (actually three of the DMOs) had one (Nordbø et al. 2014). The four trails involved in the quantitative research were Gaustatoppen, Venelifjell, Lårdalsstigen and Falkeriset, located in the municipalities of Tinn, Vinje, Tokke and Vrådal, respectively, in the region of Telemark. The trails represent a good variation in terms of the types of Norwegian trails as represented by the DNT and are quite different in terms of length, physical challenge and degree of facilitation; thus they were found suitable to provide access to a broad spectrum of hikers.

In the study, 720 questionnaires were handed out, and 683 valid questionnaires were returned, providing a response rate of about 95 per cent (Nordbø and Prebensen 2015). A trained interviewer handed out, assisted when necessary, and collected the structured questionnaires, consisting of quantitative measures and a few open and qualitative questions. The data were analysed using various quantitative analysing techniques and tested with reference to significance, reliability and validity. Based on Yoon and Uysal's (2005) destination attributes and Williams and Soutar's (2009) perception measures, a total of 20 items were found relevant. After the testing, this number was reduced to 18 (Nordbø and Prebensen 2015).

Results

Kouthoutis and Alexandris (2005) argue that studies that aim to measure service quality in the outdoors should include a separate dimension about the physical environment. In their study, Nordbø and Prebensen (2015) measured the importance and perceptions of hikers, according to four dimensions and 18 items or attributes. The four dimensions were that of the facilitation of trails, information provided, physical benefits and mental benefits related to the hiking. These were measured using a 5-point Likert-type scale ranging from 1 (*Not Important*) to 5 (*Very Important*) and from 1 (*Not at all Satistifed*) to 5 (*Very Satisfied*), according to the dimension measured (Nordbø and Prebensen 2015). Furthermore, the respondents were asked to agree or disagree on a number of statements regarding hiking, where the same 5-point Likert-type scale was used, with responses ranging from 1 (*Totally Disagree*) to 5 (*Totally Agree*).

The results show that when the empirical material is analysed as a totality, the most important factors for the hikers were the mental benefits and the facilitation of the trails, while the least important factor was information. The perception of the mental benefits from the hike were in general rated significantly lower than the importance given to the mental benefits. This is in contrast to the facilitation of the trails, which was rated significantly higher for perception than for importance (Nordbø and Prebensen 2015). In terms of national and international tourists, it is interesting to see that there were significant differences in terms of both demographic characteristics and with reference to a number of factors measured in terms of service quality.

Who are the hikers?

Altogether, 67 per cent of the hikers were tourists (foreign and national), 19 per cent characterized as second-home owners and 10 per cent were locals. Approximately 30 per cent of the respondents were foreign tourists (10 per cent from other Scandinavian countries (Denmark/ Sweden) and 20 per cent from other countries). As noted in Nordbø and Prebensen (2015), the data represent respondents from 14 European countries and 30 tourists from other continents. In terms of gender, 50.8 per cent of the Norwegian hikers were male, and the average age was 44.8 (*SD* = 14.7). For education, 63.9 per cent of the Norwegian hikers had a university degree and 78.7 per cent had a yearly family income greater than 53,500 Euro. Among the international hikers, 50 per cent were female, and the average age was 39.9 (*SD* = 12.7 years). For the international hikers, 54 per cent had a college/university degree and 54 per cent had a family income greater than 53,500 Euro. In terms of hiking with family, 42 per cent of the Norwegian hikers participated as a family, compared to 50.8 per cent for the international hikers.

Facilitation of trails

When it comes to the facilitation of trails, we see that the foreign hikers are not as concerned about general facilitation as the Norwegians. Some of the foreign hikers even commented that they find that the trail is too facilitated, as the following statement indicates: 'You should leave the nature its own way to be, not to build the stairs'. Although marking/signing of trails in general is important for all nationalities, we see from Table 20.1 that the actual evaluation of this attribute is significantly lower among foreign tourists than Norwegians, and a number of the respondents gave more specific comments regarding this issue: 'The paths are difficult to find. I was often lost in space. There are not enough signs. You must improve the way to indicate the hiking ways'.

For the Norwegians, the perception related to the marking/signing of the trails was significantly higher than the importance (4.2 versus 4.8), while for other nationalities the importance was slightly lower than the perception (4.2 versus 4.0). We also see that in terms of other nationalities, the importance given to an easy access to the starting point is somewhat higher (4.2) than the actual evaluation (4.0). This is confirmed through several of the qualitative comments from the international hikers: 'It was a little difficult for me to find the start of this trail and had to ask the tourist office' or 'More info about where to find trails + where it starts'.

Information

When the empirical material was analysed as one, the least important factor was information. When the material is broken down, however, we see that other nationalities put fairly high importance toward good maps and, to a certain degree, toward information provided during the hike (Table 20.2). Furthermore, the perception of these factors is rated significantly lower, especially when it comes to the maps (there is a 20 per cent difference). A number of the qualitative feedback statements from the questionnaires confirm the quantitative evaluations: 'More

Table 20.1 Ratings for facilitation of hiking

Trail facilitation	Norwegians	Scandinavians	Other nationalities
General facilitation	3.9/4.0	3.9/3.8	3.6/3.6
Marking/signing of trails	4.2/4.8	3.9/4.1	4.2/4.0
Maintenance	3.8/4.0	3.9/3.8	3.8/3.8
Easy-to-find starting point	4.1/4.0	4.1/4.1	4.2/4.0

5-point Likert-type scale ranging from 1 (Not Important) to 5 (Very Important) and from 1 (Not At All Satisfied) to 5 (Very Satisfied)

Table 20.2 Ratings for information about hiking

Information	Norwegians	Scandinavians	Other nationalities
Oral information from local tourist office	2.3/2.2	2.6/2.6	3.1/2.9
Good maps	3.3/2.8	3.3/3.0	4.1/3.4
Information during hike	3.2/3.1	3.3/3.3	3.5/3.2

5-point Likert-type scale ranging from 1 (Not Important) to 5 (Very Important) and from 1 (Not At All Satisfied) to 5 (Very Satisfied)

Table 20.3 Ratings for physical benefits of hiking

Physical benefits	Norwegians	Scandinavians	Other nationalities
Good exercise	4.4/4.0	3.8/3.9	3.9/3.7
Improve my health	4.2/3.9	3.7/3.8	3.6/3.5
Physically challenging	4.0/3.6	3.4/3.4	3.5/3.4
Test my physical capabilities	3.5/3.3	3.9/3.9	3.2/3.2
Give energy to my body	4.3/3.9	3.9/3.8	3.9/3.6

5-point Likert-type scale ranging from 1 (Not Important) to 5 (Very Important) and from 1 (Not At All Satisfied) to 5 (Very Satisfied)

information in English', 'A map before you start hiking, some information about the plants and animals along the way' or 'A sign which explains which mountains and lakes you see on top. A sign which explain what animals you can meet'.

We also see that the oral information from the local tourist office is found to be insufficient among the respondents from other nationalities, although the data here shows a great difference between the different trails and related offices. In Dalen (Lårdalsstigen), the local tourist office has put a lot of effort into providing high-quality information regarding the hike, and this is reflected by the fact that the tourists in general were very satisfied with the information from this office. The results show that the international hikers wanted more information during the hike, and the qualitative comments show that this deals with very specific information, such as the name of mountains which are visible from the trail, animals you could expect to meet/see, the local flora and so on.

Physical benefits

For the empirical material in general, there is a high correlation between hiking as a physical activity and mental benefits, as highlighted by Nordbø and Prebensen (2015). We see that when the physical benefits are broken down in terms of nationalities, all of the attributes related to physical benefits are evaluated higher in terms of importance among Norwegians, as compared to other nationalities (Table 20.3). Furthermore, all the items listed also scored significant higher on importance than the actual perception for the Norwegian hikers. Some of the international hikers, on the other hand, commented that the trails were physically more challenging than expected: 'The climb was longer and steeper than we expected from the brochure', and even on the limit of being irresponsible: 'The path is not very good at the end. It's even a bit dangerous'.

Mental benefits

Mental benefits are, as formerly mentioned, the one factor that in general scored the highest in importance among all factors among all hikers when analysed as one, but here also we see significant differences in terms of Norwegian and international tourists (Table 20.4). For the Norwegians, it was more important to get mental energy from hiking than for the foreigners, while peace and quietness was slightly more important for the foreign tourists. We see that on a number of the items related to mental benefits, the score was lower on the actual experience on the trails than the importance given to the attribute. The 'peace and quietness' attribute scored low on perception among all groups, and was especially visible at the Gaustatoppen trail, where there are thousands of hikers every year. Both international and national hikers commented on

Table 20.4 Ratings for mental benefits of hiking

Mental benefits	Norwegians	Scandinavians	Other nationalities
Get mental energy	4.2/3.8	3.9/3.7	3.9/3.7
Get away from the duties of everyday life	4.3/3.8	4.2/3.9	4.2/4.1
Peace and quietness	4.1/3.4	4.2/3.7	4.3/3.8
Enjoy the landscape	4.5/4.1	4.5/4.5	4.6/4.3
Satisfy my curiosity	3.8/3.4	4.0/3.8	4.0/3.7
Learn about local culture and nature	3.4/3.1	3.4/3.2	3.6/3.1

5-point Likert-type scale ranging from 1 (Not Important) to 5 (Very Important) and from 1 (Not At All Satisfied) to 5 (Very Satisfied)

this aspect: 'Alone time. Too many people' or 'It is too crowded'. In general, the material shows that a number of the hikers do not want to meet other hikers when they hike; this is especially true among the Norwegians, although most of them do not hike alone (only 4.7 per cent of the total number of hikers in study). Only 15 per cent of the Norwegians are interested in meeting other hikers, 12 per cent of the Danes and Swedes, and 31 per cent among the other nationalities. We also see that other nationalities are interested in learning more about local culture and nature, which is strongly related to the findings presented in Table 20.2, where other nationalities would like more information about local flora and fauna during the hike. Related to this is also the fact that the international hikers place great importance on the educational aspect of hiking (Norwegians 2.7, Scandinavians 3.1 and other nationalities 4.2).

Discussion and conclusion

Ween and Abram (2012) argue that through the DNT's encouragement of a repertoire of standardized performance, not only does a nation of Norwegians appear, but also a Norwegian sense of nature and being in nature. Clearly, differences exist among the national and international hikers, as described previously, but there also are differences in how hiking is perceived in terms of popularity and whether it is an activity for the general population. When specifically asked, more Norwegians than foreigners agreed that hiking has become very popular, and they strongly disagreed with the statement that hiking is only something that especially interested people do (Norwegians 2.5, Scandinavian 2.8, other nationalities 3.1).

Hiking in Norway is attached with a degree of social prestige, which also is visible through the fact that, when specifically asked, a greater number of Norwegians than foreigners found that the trip undertaken made them feel acceptable to others (Norwegians 3.7, Scandinavian 3.2 and other nationalities 2.5).

We see from the analyses reported in this chapter that, in terms of both the importance and perceptions placed on the different attributes or items, important differences exist between Norwegians and other nationalities. Of special interest is the fact that all factors related to the perceived physical benefits of hiking were given significantly higher importance among Norwegian hikers than those from other nations. This seems to correspond well with the DNT's understanding of the 'challenge' aspect of hiking (e.g. focus on wilderness skills, hard work, mastery and rewarding of physical efforts), as argued by Nordbø et al. (2014).

It also is interesting to see that when it comes to physical benefits, the perception or experience does not live up to the expectations among the Norwegians, because all of the items studied scored significantly lower on the actual evaluation than the benefits sought. There are, however, differences according to trail or path studied, and Lårdalsstigen, which is the most physically challenging of the paths, does seem to deliver on the physical benefits aspect among the Norwegians.

Another interesting note is that the Norwegian hikers, to a greater extent than the foreigners, preferred to hike alone. For Norwegians, the most important when hiking is to be able to mediate and think (weighted 3.9 by Norwegians, 2.8 by Scandinavians and 2.5 by other nationalities), while for the other nationalities, the most important thing was to enjoy the scenery and landscape (weighted 3.8 by Norwegians, 4.0 by Scandinavians and 4.4 by other nationalities). Clearly, in the DNT version of being in nature, we see that man's meeting with wilderness and individual development through solitude, physical challenge, meditation and contemplation frequently figures.

We see from the material that more importance was given to mental benefits than physical benefits among the international hikers, and that the evaluation or perception of the actual experience scored significantly lower than the importance given to all the attributes studied. It is interesting to note, given the high importance that both national and international hikers placed on the perceived physical and mental benefits of hiking, that hiking does not make Norwegian, Scandinavian or international hikers happy (only 10.7 per cent of the Norwegians, 12.2 per cent of the Scandinavians and 11.7 per cent of other nationalities). So one could ask, if hiking does not make them happy, why do they hike?

Furthermore, the international hikers, logically enough, give high importance to a number of attributes that make it easier for them to manage on their own and that facilitate the experience of the mental benefits. This deals with information from the local tourist office before the start, good maps, information provided along the hike, marking and signing of trails, and the ease of finding the starting point of the trail. For all of these items, the evaluation of the attributes were lower than the importance given, and thus they are something the DMOs should work on, in terms of improving the service quality for international hikers. The management of the DMOs does not seem to have interpreted correctly the international customer's expectation in relation to the product or services offered. As argued above, the theory on customer service quality highlights that in a customer-orientated strategy, delivering a quality service for a specific product should be based on a clear understanding of the target market and thus a clear market-orientated (MO) strategy.

The findings presented show that international hikers place importance on a number of benefits other than those placed by Norwegians. For the DMOs to provide the right service quality, they therefore must acknowledge and consider these differences when developing their products, if they want to ensure that the hikers' perceptions match their expectations in relation to the different trails. However, how is the local/regional DMOs understanding or work on this aspect in terms of international hikers?

As argued in Nordbø et al. (2014), local and regional DMOs have little or no knowledge about their target market. When the managers at the DMOs were asked to describe the hikers at their destination, they all found great difficulty with this, and provided very general statements such as 'it depends', it is 'highly variable' and 'difficult to describe'. Nor could the DMOs elaborate on their principal target group(s) in terms of demographic characteristics, and 82 per cent answered that their target group was everybody: 'Everybody: Norwegians, families with children, adults, couples and groups of tourists' or 'old, young – everybody' (Nordbø et al. 2014: 393). Quite a few also admitted that they did not know much about the hikers at their destination and that it would be better to ask the DNT or Innovation Norway.

Nordbø et al. (2014) furthermore highlighted that, in terms of product development and differentiation at the Norwegian hiking destinations, an extensive "copy-and-paste" exercise is taking place. Hiking the DNT way should, as argued, involve a bit of hard work, and good efforts are encouraged. One of the most popular product developments that has taken place at most of the Norwegian hiking destinations are "peak competitions", in which hikers are rewarded according to the number of mountaintops they have climbed at the destination. The peak competition concept was promoted by the DNT and initiated by Destination Hemsedal as an initiative aimed at the local population and the second-home owners in the area. They argue that as the concept grew in popularity, it turned into a type of mantra for product development among the Norwegian hiking destinations. It also was perceived as the best way to work with hiking in terms of marketing and conceptualization toward foreign tourists.

In a 2010 newsletter, the local DMO at Destination Hemsedal wrote: 'The extensive number of nations that attend the Top 20 shows that Hemsedal is a very international destination, and that correct facilitation is the key to success both in the national and international marked' (Hemsedal 2011, cited in Nordbø et al. 2014: 395). Nordbø et al. (2014) go on to question whether the type of product development that takes place at the Norwegian hiking destinations caters for the international hikers' needs and preferences. The findings presented in this chapter would suggest that they do not. Correct facilitation is important, but it is less important for international hikers than for Norwegians, and it is not, as the quote above claims, "the key to success".

References

Augustyn, M. and Ho, S.K. (1998) 'Service quality and tourism', Journal of Travel Research, 37(1): 71–75.
Hemsedal, T. (2011) 'Hemsedal Top 20', press release. Available at: www.hemsedal.com/no/Presse/Aktuelt/Hemsedal-Topp-20.aspx (accessed 29 January 2012).
Kohli, A.K. and Jaworski, B. (1990) 'Market orientation: the construct, research propositions, and managerial implications', Journal of Marketing, 54(2): 1–18.
Kouthouris, C. and Alexandris, K. (2005) 'Can service quality predict customer satisfaction and behavioral intentions in the sport tourism industry? An application of the SERVQUAL model in an outdoors setting', Journal of Sport & Tourism, 10(2): 101–111.
Nordbø, I. and Prebensen, N.K. (2015) 'Hiking as mental and physical experience', in J.S. Chen (ed.), Advances in Hospitality and Leisure, Volume 11. Bingley, UK: Emerald, pp. 169–186.
Nordbø, I., Engilbertsson, H.O. and Vale, S. (2014) 'Market myopia in the development of hiking destinations: the case of Norwegian DMOs', Journal of Hospitality Marketing & Management, 23(4): 380–405.
Slater, S.F. and Narver, J.C. (1998) 'Customer-led and market-oriented: let's not confuse the two', Strategic Management Journal, 19(10): 1001–1006.
Svarstad, H. (2010) 'Why hiking? Rationality and reflexivity within three categories of meaning construction', Journal of Leisure Research, 42(1): 91–110.
Ween, G. and Abram, S. (2012) 'The Norwegian Trekking Association: trekking as constituting the nation', Landscape Research, 37(2): 155–171.
Williams, P. and Soutar, G.N. (2009) 'Value, satisfaction and behavioral intentions in an adventure tourism context', Annals of Tourism Research, 36(3): 413–438.
Yoon, Y. and Uysal, M. (2005) 'An examination of the effects of motivation and satisfaction on destination loyalty: a structural model', Tourism Management, 26(1): 45–56.
Zeithaml, V.A., Bitner, M.J., Gremler, D.D. and Pandit, A. (2012) Service Marketing, 6th edn, New York: McGraw Hill.

21

Re-signifying smuggling

Cross-border walking trails as a tourist experience in the Spanish–Portuguese border

Heriberto Cairo and María Lois

Introduction

In an overview about boundary narratives in Political Geography, Newman and Paasi (1998) identified several topics of discussion on border research. One of them, repeatedly evoked, is the assumption that borders were in process of 'disappearance' (Newman and Paasi 1998: 191). As enforced in interpretations of the processes and rhetoric of globalization, the "borderless world" seems to come, but did not arrive yet. In the meantime, these and other authors (see, for example, Paasi 2005; Newman 2006; van Houtum *et al.* 2005; Agnew 2008; Kuus 2009) propose multidimensionality on border research, and their conceptualization not as permanent and static structures, but as historically contingent processes (Newmann and Paasi 1998). This way, the largely assumed univocal nature of borders may be replaced for their comprehension as paradoxical and non-fixed place, as sites of constant negotiation. As social representations, borders are constantly being reproduced and created, in material, discursive and practical ways, and paradoxes are just one of their characteristics.

Border-crossing as a tourist experience may be also considered as a bordering practice. If borders have been traditionally conceptualized as a barrier or a constraint for tourism, from the seminal paper by Timothy (1995: 527), it is clear that 'one of the most obvious relationships between the two is that of political boundaries as tourist attractions'. Maybe this is because 'when lines are marked on the ground by tangible objects, they have the potential to become tourist attractions' (Gelbman 2008: 195), or for the travellers 'being able to claim, for reasons of prestige, that they have been in a foreign country' (Timothy 1995: 527). But, it is the case that the promotion and managing of border-crossing tourism implies different practices and representations (Timothy 2001; Coles *et al.* 2004) that conform interlinked discourses at several levels, from local to national.

There is a growing literature on the cultural construction of the Spanish–Portuguese border (Amante 2010), and the heritageization and touristification of smuggling in this border (Silva 2009). The aim of this chapter is to analyse the new narratives of smuggling associated to paths that try to represent the old landscape of smuggling in the Spanish–Portuguese border. We understand these narratives and associated practices as part of heritageization of the border (Lois and Cairo 2015), framed – in the European Union cross-border cooperation agendas – as a device for the development of impoverished peripheral regions. We have identified several places, located at different regions and areas of the Spanish–Portuguese border, where smuggling trials are re-made as tourist attractions. These places display artefacts and narratives oriented towards the performance of the border for tourism, with national, local or regional perspectives.

Border-crossing as a tourist experience in Europe

Cross-border paths and trails, institutionalized in several ways, are a common feature in current EU interstate borders. The Council of Europe and the European Commission have launched programs, including specifically cultural paths and routes, as a mean to promote '[the European] cultural identity [that] is, today as yesterday, the result of the existence of a European space laden with collective memory and traversed by roads which overcome distances, borders and a lack of understanding' (Council of Europe 2011: 14). Narratives of regional or even continental unity are also commonly used in relation to them, and they are a device of the never-ending (re)construction of the national and local identities. However, the economic objective of the promotion of these trails and routes, often in deprived and marginalized areas, is patent and explicit:

> Tourism is a major economic activity with a broadly positive impact on economic growth and employment in Europe [. . .] Transnational synergies can ensure better promotion and a higher profile for tourism. This may include the full range of heritage: cultural heritage (including cultural itineraries).
>
> *(European Commission 2010; see also European Commission 2008)*

Paths and trails are designed from continental to local scale in Europe: the E-paths are European long-distance paths that unite national and regional paths, but 'it has been agreed to identify them also with a uniform marking: a blue shield with the yellow stars of Europe, in the middle of which is the letter E and the corresponding number of the E-path' (European Ramblers Association 2014). Some European tourist authorities assert without refrain that cross-border paths are 'a landmark on the path to a united Europe' (German National Tourist Board 2014). 'United in diversity' is another good example. The main idea of this project is to support the sustainable development and promotion of the South Baltic Region (regions of Central Pomerania, Bornholm and Scania), by creating a joint cross-border bicycle thematic route, 'Vikings and Slavs – in search for a common heritage' (SGPPS 2011), following on from the notion that mobility and the infrastructures for mobility seem to be a good way to construct Europe (Jensen and Richardson 2004).

In any case, practising borders in the EU has become something quite different than it was in pre-Schengen context; some common dimensions transcend specific local conditions, but always getting uneven and paradoxical situations. Aside from the blossoming of trails and paths, we find some other practices b/ordering the interstate boundaries. Representations of smuggling in the past and its use as a tourist resort today have shown as a common feature of borders in the EU. That is the case of the border between Sweden and Finland, at Tornio River Valley, north Gulf of Bothnia (Prokkola 2008b). Since 1995, with the entry of both countries in the EU, cooperation in institutional terms, between the municipalities and the Swedish side, the Finnish side has intensified. The European Union initiatives are a source of funding for border activities, in order to 'promote cross-border networks and regional identity', including a subprogram for tourism and cultural initiatives (Interreg Nord n.d.).

In this case, the commodification of smuggling emerged around a cross-border cooperation project in 2004. A theatrical performance called *Smuggling Opera* was staged at municipalities on both sides during the summers of 2004 and 2005 (see Prokkola 2008a). It is an opera that traces the history of the local smuggling in several periods, but with special emphasis on the 1950s and 1960s, when the legislation about smuggling was relatively extensive. This representation becomes a vehicle of local memory and representations of borders in the state and local narratives. The commemoration of the border transgression is encouraged institutionally, and this transgression has become a reference standard of an illegal activity. The local contra-representation of borders came to be shown on Swedish national television (Prokkola 2008a). The celebration of transgression, institutionally sponsored, gives meaning to the difference marked by the border, the state order is contested and the border and their differences are integrated into the everyday spaces available. These (and others) would contest the hegemonic narratives and reconstruct the histories of the border, from archetypes, places with a history of identifying where the reconstruction of border disputes between states as transgression is overcome by constructions based on the memory of a transnational cooperation.

The border between Finland and Russia is about 1,300 kilometres, and of marked importance in geopolitical terms, historical and symbolic. The separation between East and West was formalized in this border during the Cold War era, although the permeability of the border has been changing through the nine treaties in which it has changed its delineation. This boundary, unlike the Swedish–Finnish, exhibits features classically linked to the state boundary: barriers, barbed wire, money exchange offices and an endless routine to cross it. For its strong symbolic dimensions, the most heritageable activity of this border seems to be to cross it. Something that seems obvious if we see tourism firms that reproduce the crossing of the border to Russia without leaving the territory of Finland, through a staging of the attributes considered essential parts of the type of tourist attraction. At least two companies have already built their own 'crossing points' in terms of tourism (Löytynoja 2007). Through experiencing, mainly linked to the rituals of a visually identifiable border, borders become places not just in crossing, but as part of a tourist destination. National memories and local memories play together as spatial stories displayed around the border marking constant reconstruction of representations and narratives.

Old smuggling trials as tourist resources in the Spanish–Portuguese border

Although smuggling forms part of the traditional landscape of the border, in the 1930s, with the Spanish Civil War, basic necessities such as bread, sugar, soap or even salt were scarce in the Spanish side, which gave to the Portuguese that lived near the border the opportunity to make a profit from re-selling in Spain these products that were cheap in Portugal (Freire *et al.* 2009; Godinho 1995). Smuggling can be interpreted in two ways: either as a strategy of subsistence of local people in front of the state impositions, or as "another" kind of work: this is the usual interpretation between old smugglers (Cáceres and Valcuende del Río 1996). That is a dimension that probably has a bearing on the temporal scopes of narration and in the local non-institutional actors in terms of appropriation. Labour relationships are asymmetrical, and those asymmetries in some periods linked to the dictatorships in both countries and shortages, e.g. in the 1960s, where the changing conditions showed that there was partly justifiable trade and partly purely illegal enrichment. There was a shift from smuggling products to cover basic necessities to smuggling tobacco and other illegal products.

Smugglers used lonely and often difficult routes. They went through these difficulties frequently at night trying to avoid the police forces: the Portuguese *guardiñas* or the Spanish *carabineros* or *guardia civil.* Smuggling suffered a drastic reduction in the 1980s, after the accession of both countries to the EU. The trials were not abandoned, but the use was far less frequent. Some of these paths have recently been heritageized as tourist experiences. Without an intention of being exhaustive, and only as examples, we have identified and visited six smuggling paths (*trilhos de contrabando* or *senderos de contrabando*), from north to south: Tourém (Portugal) to Randín (Spain); Vilardevós (S) to Segirei (P); Hinojosa de Duero (S) to Peña la Vela (S); Cedillo (S) to Montalvão (P); Oliva de la Frontera (S) to Barrancos (P); and Santana de Cambas (P) to Mina de São Domingos (P).

The smuggling route known as *Trilho de Tourem* links this Portuguese village with the village of Randín, in the Spanish autonomous community of Galicia. It is a circular path, beginning and ending in Tourem. In 2007, an accompanied walk was organized following the path, associated with a project of creation of cross-border paths financed by Interreg III. Silva (2009) describes this first walk. A private company, Serra Aventura Lda, trying to recreate a smuggling journey at night, organized it. Old smugglers that narrated old days' stories accompanied walkers, and there was a theatrical performance about the apprehension of the smuggled products by the Spanish *guardia civil.* The path is marked from that date, but it is not much used by walkers, particularly from the Spanish side. When asking in a public bar in Randin about where the path continues after the village, the waiter did not know even the existence of it, and some of the marker poles have been knocked down by Portuguese villagers in disagreement with the initiative. Here, we can find the tensions between the locals about the issue of tourism in their lands: some promote the paths, some others ignore them (often when the initiative comes from the other "side" of the border) and still some others try to boycott them.

In Vilardevós, also in Galicia, there is a (Museum) Centre of Interpretation of Smuggling. In it, the smuggling (*estraperlo*, in its local name) is exposed as a post-war survival activity, and also as the marker that opened the possibility of enjoying the smuggling routes (see Lois and Cairo 2015). The reconstruction and heritageization of smuggling routes was sponsored by one of the EU programs, LEADER. On the ground, there is a replica of a border marker, the number 295, located at the municipality. With this introduction, the starting point of the smuggling routes is located for the tourist, and exposes a narration based on their links with other border resources and networks, but also smuggling in the specific municipality. The routes end in different places in Portugal, but the best known ends in Segirei, which is approximately 16 km away. Border markers (*hitos*) are there; when walking the smuggling routes, neighbours mention that the signs are not located at the *real* border. They all seem to know where the limit is, even if they were subverting it for years. But, as pointed out above, the reconstruction of the smuggling practices as a heritageization narrative for tourism consumption is no more than an experience for minor groups of visitors. In that sense, at Vilardevós there is not a hegemonic narrative about smuggling. It is considered as a local non-institutional actors' narrative, but full of heterogeneities, and difficult to capitalize for cultural consumption. Even if the Interpretive Centre is the departure point of an institutionally promoted walking experience of the border, the reconstruction of memories for re-bordering the daily de-bordered border is complex. The daily smuggling stories, the different conceptions between smuggling as work and smuggling as everyday necessity, and the marginal situation of Vilardevós town, in spite of the use of EU funds, indicates that memories of transgression remain as local context narrative, but are not in this case openly exhibited or accepted by local non-institutional actors (Lois and Cairo 2015).

Hinojosa de Duero is a village in the Spanish autonomous community of Castile y León. There we can find a smuggling route (*ruta de contrabando*) from Hinojosa to the River Duero, which actually is not exactly a cross-border path since it ends at the bank of the river, which forms this part of the border. The path strictly begins in a parking area not far away from the village where the old smuggling methods are reproduced in several panels that make also a description of the route. This is 7 km long, and ends in the Peña la Vela viewpoint, from where the Spanish *guardia civil* used to control smugglers. But there are longer scenic routes from Hinojosa, just to the river, organized walking tours by the Hinojosa municipality since 2010. The walking tour ends with a lunch with local products that the tourist can also buy. Narratives of smuggling are not controversial in this area, and the reconstruction of a smuggling route seems to be mainly with economic development objectives.

Another interesting smuggling route goes from Cedillo, in the north of the Spanish autonomous community of Extremadura, to Montalvão, Portugal. Since 1999 every year, an organized walking tour goes the 20 km from one village to another, crossing the River Tajo by boat. The organizers of the walking tour are a local Portuguese youth association, in collaboration with both municipalities. The tour usually ends in Montalvão with a lunch provided by the municipality and music played by local Portuguese groups. There are a lot of participants, from both countries, in the walking tours (in 2013, there were 400 walkers), which makes necessary a relatively large infrastructure and organization. Local development is present here, but also important is the objective of socialization (*convivio*) between the participants from both sides of the border.

In Oliva de la Frontera, a village in south Extremadura, there is an Interpretive Centre of the Border (*Centro de Interpretación de la Frontera*) (see Lois and Cairo 2015) that houses several rooms used for locale leisure associations. One of them is occupied by the Pack-carriers Club (*Club Los Mochileros*), a hiking association founded in 2003, and named after the old Spanish and Portuguese smugglers that used a sack to carry their load. The club, organized around a local narrative of smuggling and to sponsor cultural exchange between both sides of the border, inaugurated the Smuggling Route in 2006, managed jointly by the club and by the municipality of Barrancos (Portugal). In that sense, the municipality of Barrancos is the counterpart for the local smuggling narrative and trails (Simões 2008). The complete route to Barrancos is 26 km long, and it crosses a small river, the River Ardila, which is the "natural" border between the two countries. There is also a shorter circular route 16 km long, which ends at the bank of the river. This is more used by walkers than the other, but when there is an organized walking tour, it used to end in Barrancos. The walking tours are organized, according to the words of the president of the Club 'to honour our ancestors, all those Spanish and Portuguese people who had the need to exercise this activity [smuggling] as their only means of living' (González 2015). The references to smuggling, to the relationships with the other side and, especially, to the Civil War in Spain and the liminality aspect of the borderland are present everywhere in Oliva and Barrancos, which have developed a village brotherhood based on the smuggling connections and the solidarity during the Spanish Civil War (Simões 2013).

Santana de Cambas, located at the Mértola municipality, is a Portuguese *freguesia*, where a Smuggling Museum (*Museu do Contrabando*) was opened in June 2009, in the form of the European LEADER+ program 2007–2013 (Rodrigues 2008). Smuggling in the area is remembered in different panels and books (Lois and Cairo 2015). One of them talks about the geography of the smuggling routes:

> for the smuggler, the walking geographies only have the obstacle of the Fiscal Guard [. . .] everything was made with a strong will of erasing the famine at home [. . .] The 37 Fiscal Guard posts at the border never were enough to stop the smuggler from starting again.
>
> *(Maçarico 2005: 9–10)*

The scope of this geography is again linked to the borderland, and, as in other cases, has also been reflected in a tourist experience, a walking experience, which takes form in the Route of

Smuggling and Mines (from Santana de Cambas to Mina de São Domingos). The trail starts at the museum, and follows the route of the old railway (that made the connection between the mine and the transport of ore at Pomarão), passing by the old São Domingos mining complex and the Chança River, the final stage for the border crossing. In any case, the museum and the trail are a good bet for the *freguesia* development in terms of tourism, in a context surrounded by the strong presence of industrial heritage (Minas de São Domingos), archaeological restorations (Archaeological Camp, and integrated by Roman art, Islamic art and Visigoth art, in the case of Mértola), and the Guadiana Valley Natural Park.

Concluding remarks

Some borders and borderlands have become a tourist attraction and destination. Their crossing has even become a final destination and touristic experience. A transgressive space, classically understood and performed as liminal space, enables part of the tourism landscape to be staged as a place for "intense experiences". These experiences are particularly exciting when they are associated with forbidden activities, such as smuggling, whose practitioners are presented as adventurers, putting aside 'the poverty, privation and sacrifice often associated to smuggling' (Silva 2009: 13). When walking the smugglers paths, the tourists 'are looking for an adventure and recreational experience, because of their amusement or hedonistic [. . .] interests' (Silva 2009: 13).

The smuggling routes are set in both countries. Spatial socialization around the routes does not seem to change the local geographies or imaginaries about the ways that Vilardevós – or other nodal points of the routes – belongs to the national construction of Spain (Lois 2009). It is already and primarily set as a border and a marginal area, something that seems to work with similar historical place making; in this case, decisions about smuggling as a legal or illegal border practice are made elsewhere. The local population will have its own opinion, but smuggling is not lived as a cultural resource. It was a daily situation, linked to social, political and economic marginality; but the presence of tourism has not changed the social and spatial order of the community. In fact, the links between the two sides seem now softer than ever.

Where smuggling is a key part of the new tourist narratives of the border, it plays another role: it opens a *theatre* for other border performance actions. In some ways, they empower the local population through a (re)interpretation of smuggling beyond the central discourse of being a crime. In this context, smugglers become 'normalized' neighbours that smuggled in times of shortages and poverty. Links to borderlands emphasize their peripheral dimension too, but practices of representation of the border read it as place for transgression, resistance and agency against impoverishment and extreme difficult conditions.

This way, all the study cases shed lights on the formation of myths, since they also have the function of founding and articulating spaces (de Certeau 1984), including for walking, with different reference points, but, in smuggling and migration spaces, they open a scenario to unofficial stories and subversive geographies of the border in practice. In addition, in that scenario, the fetishization of products to satisfy basic necessities (coffee, shoes, textiles and floor coverings) becomes a counterpoint of the heritageization of mechanisms of control linked to the border.

The border is politically conceptualized as an experience, but it remains a way to draw social differences and to show the history of dis-encounter between state administrations. The EU re-ordering does not seem to work here, even if intended to be a bottom-up-driven practice. In any case, border regions become part of some institutional network through tourism, linking the tourist destination to other structures and foster the idea of region. This process of becoming tourist places not only affects the economic activities, but also forces the re-creation of the representations of local contexts, in process of *encounter* with the tourist expectations. These specific actions at the national borders open a re-signification of boundary-making, the practices and discourses about limits, and how these are lived and produced daily. In this sense, tourism, as policy and politics of the EU for border areas, becomes a social spatialization intervention, in terms of creation of collective spaces and times. In other words, practising Europe refers to the ways these implementations are parts of social transformation and the way it is working in everyday life recompositions.

How the border is practised through the European policies, and how these practices are lived and experienced in local geographies and communities of fate shows how not only the multiple structures but also the agencies (including non-institutional but social actors) get involved in re-creating (or not) those bordering practices, and their everyday reproduction and constant recreation of a social context.

In smuggling literature, the border is often seen as a material resource. Incorporating peripheries becomes a diverse process, with different views, and individuals as subjects of re-creating memories and practices. As pivotal spaces of integration (Sidaway 2005) and places of constructing geographies of Europeanness by re-ordering socioterritorial markers through tourism, this laboratory is showing the paradoxical elaboration of border as a heritageized object. From the long European Cultural Routes, such as the Santiago Route (Camino de Santiago) or Vía Francígena, to these short smuggling routes on the Spanish–Portuguese border, all these cross-border paths designed for tourists are financed by European funds in order to construct Europe.

Acknowledgments

This paper is the result of the project 'Cooperación transfronteriza y (des)fronterización: actores y discursos geopolíticos transnacionales en la frontera hispano-portuguesa' (CSO2012–34677), financed by the Ministerio de Economía y Competitividad of Spain.

References

Agnew, J. (2008) 'Borders on the mind: re-framing border thinking', *Ethics & Global Politics*, 1(4): 175–191.

Amante, Maria de Fátima (2010) 'Local discursive strategies for the cultural construction of the border: the case of the Portuguese–Spanish border', *Journal of Borderlands Studies*, 25(1): 99–114.

Cáceres, R. and Valcuende del Río, J.M. (1996) 'Hacer la carrera de Portugal, el trasperlo y otras formas de contrabando', in P. Palenzuela (ed.), *Actas del VII Congreso de Antropología del Estado Español*. Zaragoza, Spain: FAEE, pp. 137–149.

Coles, T., Duval, D.T. and Hall, C.M. (2004) 'Tourism, mobility and global communities: new approaches to theorising tourism and tourist spaces', in W. Theobold (ed.), *Global Tourism*, Oxford: Heinemann, pp. 463–481.

Council of Europe (2011) *Impact of European Cultural Routes on SMEs' Innovation and Competitiveness: Provisional Edition*. Available at: www.coe.int/t/dg4/cultureheritage/culture/routes/StudyCR_en.pdf (accessed 13 February 2016).

de Certeau, M. (1984) *The Practice of Everyday Life*, Berkeley: University of California Press.

European Commission. (2008) *Hacia una mayor colaboración en el turismo europeo. Síntesis de la legislación de la UE: acceso directo a la página principal de las síntesis*. Available at: http://europa.eu/legislation_summaries/ enterprise/industry/n26107_es.htm (accessed 25 February 2009).

European Commission (2010) *Communication from the Commission to the European Parliament, the Council, the European Economic and Social Committee and the Committee of the Regions – Europe, the World's No 1 Tourist Destination – A New Political Framework for Tourism in Europe*, COM/2010/0352 Final. Available at: http://eur-lex.europa.eu/legal-content/EN/TXT/?uri=CELEX:52010DC0352 (accessed 25 February 2016).

European Ramblers Association (2014) What Are "E-paths"? Available at: www.era-ewv-ferp.com/walking-in-europe/e-paths (accessed 23 April 2014).

Freire, D., Rovisco, E. and Fonseca, I. (ed.) (2009) *Contrabando na fronteira Luso-española. Práticas, mémorias e patrimónios*, Lisbon: EdiçoesNelson De Matos.

Gelbman, A. (2008) 'Border tourism in Israel: conflict, peace, fear and hope', *Tourism Geographies*, 10(2): 193–213.

German National Tourist Board (2014) *Route Verte – The Green Route: In the Spirit of Franco–German Friendship*. Available at: www.germany.travel/sk-mobile/leisure-and-recreation/scenic-routes/route-verte-green-route.html (accessed 12 March 2016).

Godinho, P. (1995) 'O contrabando como estratégia integrada nas aldeias da raia transmontana', *A Trabe de Ouro*, 22: 209–222.

González, A. (2015) *Interview with Antonio González*. Available at: www.youtube.com/watch?v=9O_e8A6xxPA (accessed 23 April 2016).

Interreg Nord (n.d.) *Gränslösa möjligheter*. Interreg IIIA Nord-European Regional Development Fund. Available at: www.interregnord.com (accessed 26 February 2009).

Jensen, O. and Richardson, T. (2004) *Making European Space. Mobility, Power and Territorial Identity*, London: Routledge.

Kuus, M. (2009) 'Critical Geopolitics', in R. Denemark (ed.), *The International Studies Encyclopedia*, Chichester, Sussex: Wiley-Blackwell, pp. 683–701.

Lois, M. (2009) 'Practicar frontera: turismo, geografías locales y relaciones sociales en las periferias europeas', in H.C. Carou, P. Godinho and X. Pereiro (eds), *Portugal e Espanha. Entre discursos de centro e práticas de fronteira*. Lisbon: Colibri, pp. 199–213.

Lois, M. and Cairo, H. (2015) 'Heritage-ized places and spatial stories: b/ordering practices at the Spanish–Portuguese Raya/Raia', *Territory, Politics, Governance*, 3(3): 321–343.

Löytynoja, T. (2007) 'National boundaries and place-making in tourism: staging the Finnish-Russian border', *Nordia Geographical Publications*, 36(4): 35–45.

Maçarico, L.F. (2005) *Memorias do contrabando em Santana de Cambas*, Beja, Portugal: Junta de Freguesia de Santana de Cambas.

Newman, D. (2006) 'Borders and bordering: towards an interdisciplinary dialogue', *European Journal of Social Theory*, 9(2): 171–186.

Newman, D. and Paasi, A. (1998) 'Fences and neighbours in the postmodern world: boundary narratives in political geography', *Progress in Human Geography*, 22(2): 186–207.

Paasi, A. (2005) 'Generations and the "development" of border studies', *Geopolitics*, 10(4): 663–661.

Prokkola, E. (2008a) 'Border narratives at work: theatrical smuggling and the politics of commemoration', *Geopolitics*, 13(4): 657–675.

Prokkola, E. (2008b) *Making Bridges, Removing Barriers. Cross-Border Cooperation and Identity at the Finnish–Swedish Border*, Nordia Geographical Publications, 37.

Rodrigues, R. (2008) 'Santana de Cambas, uma freguesia da margem esquerda do Guadiana', *Alma Alentejana. Revista Cultural*, 9(21): 12–13.

SGPPS (2011) '"United in diversity" project', *Common Future for Baltic Tourism II Conference*, September 2011, Finland. Stowarzyszenie Gmin i Powiatów Pomorza Środkowego. Available at: http://service.mvnet.de/_php/download.php?datei_id=44782 (accessed 21 April 2016).

Sidaway, J. (2005) 'The poetry of boundaries: reflections from the Portuguese–Spanish borderlands', in H. Van Houtum, O.T. Kramsch and W. Zierhofer (eds), *B/ordering Space*, Aldershot, Hants: Ashgate, pp. 189–206.

Silva, L. (2009) 'A Patrimonialização e a Turistificação do Contrabando', in E. Rovisco, I. Fonseca and D. Freire (eds), *Contrabando na Fronteira Luso-espanhola. Práticas, Memórias e Património*, Lisbon: Nelson de Matos, pp. 255–287.

Simões, D. (2008) 'Fronteras estatales y relaciones sociales en la frontera hispano–portuguesa. El caso de Barrancos y Oliva de la Frontera', *Gazeta de Antropología*, 24(2), articulo 52. Available at: www.ugr.es/~pwlac/G24_52MariaDulce_Antunes_Simoes.html (accessed 11 January 2012).

Simões, D. (2013) *Frontera y Guerra Civil Española: dominación, resistencia y usos de la memoria*, Badajoz, Spain: Departamento de Publicaciones de la Diputación de Badajoz.

Timothy, D.J. (1995) 'Political boundaries and tourism: borders as tourist attractions', *Tourism Management*, 16(7): 525–532.

Timothy, D.J. (2001) *Tourism and Political Boundaries*, London: Routledge.

van Houtum, H., Kramsch O.T. and Zierhofer W. (eds) (2005) *B/ordering Space*, Aldershot, Hants: Ashgate.

22

The solo-hike

A journey of distance and closeness

Hannelene Schilar

Introduction: approaching the solo-hike

First came the idea to hike myself: to walk far and alone in the most remote area I could reach. Images of walking through landscapes devoid of human signs grew in my mind. The prospect of physical challenge and pain drew me; and I was curious about what thought and solitude would do to me. These feelings lasted until the day I finally went. For three months in summer 2014, I hiked different trails in northern Sweden, Norway and Finland, walking about 800 kilometres.

Yet with a background in human geography and particular interest in tourism I was also a researcher – sceptical towards these motivations, observant to the experience and highly interested in what others seek *out there*. So, my planning of the trip became also the preparation of a research project and the hike became also fieldwork. I encountered sixteen other solo-hikers along the way and sought to grasp their aspirations as well as experiences.

The leading questions were: What do they seek out there? What is solo-hiking about? What does it feel like? Purposively open and explorative, they emphasize the phenomenological stance of the project. Drawing from a synthesis of the phenomenological school developed by Max Van Manen in *Lived Experience* (1990), one can apprehend solo-hiking as a complex phenomenon approachable in systematic ways. Phenomenology believes in the essence of a phenomenon – the aspects that are fundamental, making it what it is, but nothing else. Accordingly, my ambition was to understand what essentially constitutes the solo-hiking experience. However, phenomenological work also sets its own limitations: 'lived life is always more complex than any explanation of meaning can reveal. The phenomenological reduction teaches us that complete reduction is impossible, that full or final descriptions are unattainable' (Van Manen 1990: 18). Thus, phenomenology strives towards deeper, richer insight, but cannot provide final conclusion.

Is it then even worth discussing, researching phenomenological topics? I argue, yes it is; and that legitimacy lies within phenomena's nature: they constitute meaningful aspects originating from people's *lifeworld*. It could be experiences such as parenting, driving a car or dancing. They concern people. Thus, it is typical for phenomenological problems not to appear distant or purely theoretical. So, when I speak about solo-hiking within an academic or private context, people easily connect to the topic. Solo-hiking can be something they have done, thought about, admired, disapproved of, etc. Literature and fine arts throughout history have richly documented which mysticism and transformative potential is ascribed to walking experiences in nature, and particularly when done alone. Besides, both the experience of solitude as well as of walking can be seen as fundamentally human. Maybe it is this universality of the topic that led you to read this chapter or book in the first place.

Striving to translate the phenomenological approach into practice, my work has been characterized by *moving forward*, not only on the paths, but interview by interview – building, rebuilding and discarding hypotheses, seeking a deeper understanding of the solo-hiking experience (Gadamer 1975; Giorgi 1994). I have carried out sixteen in-situ, in-depth interviews (in the outdoors in northern Scandinavia; on natural context as source of insight, see: Roberson and Babic 2009). The encounters occurred unplanned along the paths. This way of doing allowed me to meet them as an equal, a solo-hiker, sharing their experiential world and building a trust-based relationship. Also they perceived an abundance in time and were somewhat enthusiastic to share their insights. The people I spoke to hiked for between a week and one month, slept mostly in tents (some in huts or under the sky), carried their 15–20-kg backpacks and their food. Typically, they were either young, single adults or male, married pensioners. They were originally from Sweden, Germany, Austria, Estonia, France and Australia. For most, it was their first longer hike alone. The conversations turned centrally around their motivations to hike, especially to hike alone, their feelings and experiences outdoors, their interpretations of the environment (*wilderness?*) and their personal life stories *that brought them there*.

I have assembled the diversity and depth of their accounts in my thesis 'Out There – A Phenomenological Approach to Solo-Hiking in Northern Scandinavia' (Schilar 2015). For this chapter, I have selected key aspects of particular contribution to the volume. So, first, in the section 'Seeking solitude(?)', the *solo* in solo-hiking is discussed. Further, the sections 'Moving forwards' and 'Turning inwards' embrace the idea that the solo-hike is essentially experienced as an outwards journey, leading to perceived distant places, as well as an inwards journey, bringing people closer to their inner selves.

Since this book addresses walking experiences, attention must be given to the solo-hiker. On renowned trails their number is relevant and growing: 30% on the Appalachian Trail, US, in 1999 (Kyle *et al.* 2003); another 30% on the West Highland Way, Scotland (den Breejen 2007); and around 10% on the Kings Trail, Sweden in 2003 (Wall Reinius 2009). Hence, a deeper understanding of the solo-hiker is of interest from multiple perspectives, whether it is academic-theoretical contributing to tourism studies, or applied in tourism planning, for example, regarding the management of national parks. Further, the chapter illustrates the ways in which phenomenology can be used as methodological framework to deconstruct complex experiences as they typically occur in tourism. Finally, it also problematizes the tensions between expectation and experience, suggesting life-path approaches for tourism studies.

Seeking solitude(?)

Picturing the solo-hiker in the northern Scandinavian landscapes, images of a lone wolf arise: wandering through birch forests, traversing ice-cold streams, exploring green valleys and struggling to mountains tops. Initially, the solo-hike disguises itself as a celebration of solitude and independence. 'Aaah, this is so great . . . I am alone, I love this!!!' exclaims Disa, and glances over the landscapes around her. While we walk, I see her touching the plants with her fingertips. David says: 'It is this wanting to be free, to walk as far as you want . . . just this independence.' People emphasize the importance of following their own pace, putting their tent where they want and simply taking independent decisions. Particularly when they face difficult situations – steep slopes or rapid rivers – solitude is the element that makes the hike an adventure and a possibility to test one's abilities. Solitude is never seen as boring, but in its calm and beautiful moments, it gets lonely at times: 'This one night I had the whole cabin to myself, I am like "oh man", I'd love to have somebody to share this with right now' (Ben).

These insights are very much in line with findings of other researchers, arguing that solitude allows a deeper engagement with and profounder experiences of the natural surroundings (Laing and Crouch 2009; Wylie 2005), as well as that, independence is a major motivation to travel alone in the first place (Mehmetoglu *et al.* 2001). In this way, the material also partly reflects the impressions gained through literature or movies – a somewhat Romantic vision of the solitary walker. However, there is more than the mere being alone, isolation, intensity or independence to the solo experience. One aspect that often gets overlooked is that not every person chooses to hike alone; some might not have a companion and are solo-hikers by default (see also Mehmetoglu *et al.* 2001). Some of the younger people mention feeling somewhat different from their peers; Ben asserts:

> I don't know, it's hard to convince people to come hiking, in like [pause] in the Arctic, for three weeks, alone! All the people that I met on [university] exchange, anyway, most of them were pretty intent on just drinking. I don't know, I don't wanna go with those people anyways.
>
> *(Ben)*

Jan is the youngest interviewee. His parents ask him what he wants for his eighteenth birthday. He decides to take the money he receives and go hiking. His friends are enthusiastic, but do not want to join. When he turns eighteen, he is out walking alone in the Swedish mountains. His story seems to illustrate his character and strong drive to hike at this point of his life. The experience of solitude was something he accepted, but it was not his primary pursuit.

On the other hand, being alone also means meeting (more) people. Thus, it's about 'landscapes and encounters!' (Daniel F) and the solo experience is more of an illusion: 'When my mates at home say: "Wow, you travel alone!" I say: "Fair enough, I start alone, but I am not alone." You meet people from Australia, Norway, Sweden . . . You see, suddenly I am not alone any more!' says Andreas, and points at the scene as we sit, talk and have a coffee. Thus, actual solitude is a much-negotiated attribute of the trip; and what appears a search for solitude can in reality be a search for company.

Finally, the material gives an understanding that the solo-hiker is not a simplistic archetype – a loner or a hard-core adventurer. Rather the solo-hiker is a momentary role people are curious about or long for. This experience is often depicted in contrast to their social/family lives and symbolizes a response to it. Disa says: 'I am a really social person, erm, like super-social . . . but it gets a bit overloaded too . . . It makes me realize how much time I need to spend with myself to be able to be with other people.' Also Janina's way of reasoning is very particular: 'In Germany I often feel very lonely. So I decided, why don't I go where there are few people, than I would feel less lonely . . . Therefore, I was looking forward to solitude.'

Thus, the search for and experience of solitude can have elements of the images of awe and independence that arise so easily; but they are also relative. The search for solitude springs from a particular context/home environment, it is sometimes not a choice or represents even the search for company. In the end, it is appreciated because it is a momentary experience.

Moving forwards

'It's about the walking, it's a lot about the walking, isn't it?!' asserts Disa as we speak. Maybe she is right: to begin with, the hike is very bodily and physical. Simply a forward movement. Moving forward is satisfying and natural (Tuan 1977). There is the body and its only task is the path.

You just go ahead. A hundred, two hundred, three hundred kilometres. Sometimes you stumble. Sometimes it rains. It is exhausting. She says: 'You test your muscles, your abilities and kinda really like that, like arrr [*makes strong noise*], arrr, you can feel it, you are pushing through!'

Describing the physical experience, people speak of challenge, struggle, pain and an encounter with their limits. It should be emphasized that the attraction lies again in the difference to the challenges of everyday life; David states: 'I feel in daily life you never go until your limits, I mean your physical limits, so I wanted to do something physically exhausting, where you meet your natural boundaries.' Strikingly, some people might come in the first place because of an encounter with their *psychic* boundaries (work, family, etc.). So, out there they play with their physicality and test their bodies instead, which seems to establish a different way of proving oneself. Thus, walking is seen as bringing physique and psyche in balance. Inge asserts: 'I love walking in the mountains . . . I recharge my batteries, both physical and psychological ones.' As Andreas points out, it is somewhat contradictory, but the physical exhaustion symbolizes an intake in energies and essentially even relaxation. These recreational aspects have been carefully described by other scholars (e.g. Kaplan 1995; Roberson and Babic 2009) and the interplay between body and mind, as well as the mental/physical health benefits of walking, are covered across different chapters in this volume. Thus, instead of discussing these facets in more detail, I will lift out two aspects more thoroughly: the construction of *adventure* and *awayness* through the forward movement.

Adventure

One can observe that the physical nature of walking and experiences of liminality become exploited in people's storytelling to construct some form of adventurer-identity: *moving forwards, the solo-hiker becomes an adventurer.* Ben's story gives a complex example of how his experiences, adventure storytelling, identity construction and performance interplay. He tells me about hitting his head on a rock on his last solo-hike in Norway, yet enriches his story with laughter and self-irony. 'On the way up the hill, I slipped on this icy rock and then I just felt so sick and I definitely had concussion.' Alone in the mountains there is nobody to help you, no doctors, he considers. You should not fall asleep, better get out of there. 'But that's what I did' – fall asleep or 'pass out', as he says. He laughs. And he laughs even more, speaking in dramatic tones about 'this huuuge black eye' he had gotten. How swollen it was. Anyway, once home, he posts a picture of his violet-bluish eye on Facebook. He comments: 'Thanks for the good times Norway!' He gets seventy likes.

First, this example illustrates how people use humour to turn rather risky experiences into adventure stories where they are heroically pitted against nature. Similarly to Gyimothy and Mykletun (2004: 874), I depict how people flick 'back and forth in their descriptions of extremely playful and extremely serious situations'. Second, it shows how he actively portrays himself as adventurer through his storytelling towards me and the Facebook entry. As other scholars have observed, tourism is the industry of performance par excellence (e.g. Edensor 2000; Hyde and Oleson 2011; Noy 2004). People collect and retell experiences to earn higher status, respect from peers or to establish their personal record of achievement (e.g. Gyimothy and Mykletun 2004; Mehmetoglu *et al.* 2001). Recently, a hotspot has been installed on the Kebnekaise peak (highest mountain in Sweden), so people can now take a selfie, then log on using wifi, and share it. This is just another indication that actual solitude is very constructed and relative. One can ask critically: What is solitude, then, really?

I remember when I walked without seeing anybody for hours or sometimes days. You walk completely alone, unobserved. When you then spot a person on the horizon something strange happens: you become aware of your body through the eyes of the other, how you walk, what you look like; you immediately censor your behaviour. As some interviewees state: hiking alone means to be unmirrored, to be unreflectedly yourself. Controversially, people also sabotage these moments of solitude/unobservedness and introduce elements of performance: taking pictures for social media and even changing behaviour to fulfil a certain motive. The reoccurrence of dramatic selfie-accidents points towards the pronounced importance individuals give to the way they portray themselves: 'I have been there, done that.' Thus, is the solo-hiker ever alone? What is performed? One last evidence in that respect is that nearly all interviewees carry adventure books and repeatedly mention outdoor heroes in their narratives. These different aspects lead to the conclusion that they seek an *adventure aesthetic* and the forward movement is *a becoming*: first, through their physical embodiment, and second, through their narratives (see also Pedersen Gurholt 2008; Repp 2004).

Awayness

Further, the forward movement brings the solo-hiker *away*. Away from *real life*, the *city*, work, technology and society. It is about being somehow close to nature and far away from '*all this*' (Jan). Nature is described as awesome, wild, gentle, green, paradisiac, wide, open and whole. As Tuan (1974: 111–112) observed, it becomes a 'symbol for the orderly processes in nature', in contrast to the 'real and imagined failings of city life'. Accordingly, some interviewees convey a notion of societal critique and frustration:

> Hastiness and speed. And when you turn on the TV in the morning you need to face so many negative things that happened somewhere. It interests me, but I can barely follow what happens everywhere in the world. It overwhelms me and scares me which horrible things happen. So I am happy not to hear these things for some weeks . . . Somehow our society is completely wrong.
>
> *(David)*

David goes on to speak about the destruction of nature, plundering of resources, greed and consumerism. Janina highlights the anonymity and coldness of society. In contrast, people see nature as less harsh, but offering calm, relaxation and peace. Thus, they construct nature as dichotomy to society (Oelschlaeger 1991). There is a *here* and a *there*. 'Life here [in nature] is so different, completely different and very relaxing' (Madis). In this respect, nature is a place that is away and distant, not necessarily in terms of geographical distance, but distant and different in terms of experience. Moving forward, the solo-hiker enters and explores another experiential world, another lifeworld. Time and place are perceived differently: they evaporate (Gelter 2009) or dissolve (Honoré 2004). People speak of following the flow of the day and inner rhythm instead of a schedule or clock. They also describe a different way of place-making that is free and unconstrained. They have the feeling of being able to go anywhere, to make places their own by simply putting up the tent and give them meaning (McIntyre and Roggenbuck 1998). They tell about a deep engagement with place and particularly the path (den Breejen 2007; Terry and Vartabedian 2013).

Other scholars have grasped the notion of a different experiential world through the terms *awayness* (Boller *et al.* 2010) or *out-there-ness* (Elands and Lengkeek 2012). I conclude from the accounts that the interviewees seek 'distance from real life' (Annika) in an awesome, natural world that they believe is out there. They portray that world as free in terms of time and space. Yet again, this world and its construction stand very much in relation to *real life*. The solo-hikers strive to travel and live outdoors, collect new experiences and return. Again the appeal lies in the temporariness of the experience; the interviewees equally acknowledge their appreciation of the home environment with its people, habits and comforts. They clearly portray the solo-hike not as an escape, but rather as an establishment of balance. As Tuan (1974: 248) phrases it, their movement is a search of an 'equilibrium that is not of this world'.

Turning inwards

The equilibrium Tuan speaks of might not only embrace the *here* and *there*, but also the *inner/outer*, *mental/physical*. Solnit (2001: 5) expresses the interrelatedness of these dimensions: 'walking, ideally, is a state in which the mind, the body and the world are aligned, as though they were three characters finally in conversation together, three notes suddenly making a chord'. Hence, while the paragraphs above focus on exploring the physical forward movement and its symbolism, I give now attention to the solo-hike understood as an inwards turn, exploration of the self and its place within the life path. Essentially, the solo-hike is said to give frame for thought; and thoughtfulness is seen as desirable. People say they 'wander in their minds' (Magnus). Some speak of walking themselves into flow-experiences (David; see also Csikszentmihalyi 1975), reaching a state of meditation (Disa) or losing the path while exploring the mind (Jan). Some want to think about specific topics that concern them, others simply seek more insight:

> Sometimes I give myself one question a day to think about: What do I enjoy in life? Which things in life draw energy from me? If I didn't do what I do, what would I do? . . . I don't necessarily need to reach a conclusion because the process of just thinking about it is giving me more insight on who I might be.
>
> *(Magnus)*

Interestingly, how these reflection processes concretely work is quite obscure to people. Occasionally, it is expressed that the simplicity of tasks (walking, eating, camping) liberates the mind. Yet, I remember these also occupy the mind greatly: How far have I walked? What will I cook? Where will I put my tent? And some interviewees express disappointment that finally they did not think as profoundly about certain topics as they expected to. Daniel says:

> When I sat at this beach I thought "Now it would be the perfect moment to think about *the big things in life*." But then nothing came to my mind and you cannot force yourself either. I just thought about stupid stuff, this and that, everything and nothing. Yet, I have the impression that I have learnt a lot, but I cannot really point out what it is.
>
> *(Daniel)*

He is not the only one; also others claim to feel more calm and orderly in their minds, without knowing how. Thus, somehow, without thinking directly about specific topics 'it helps anyways' (Annika). Finally, looking inwards is also interpreted as challenge 'I think . . . some people might be scared of themselves and don't dare to go alone, because they would not be able to deal with their own thoughts' (Andreas).

Exploring the inwards turn reminds me of a stone lying at the beginning of the Kings Trail in northern Sweden; there it is written: 'The longest journey is the journey inwards – Dag Hammarskjöld'. People depart on that journey often with a certain purpose – an inner destination. Hence, I argue that the walking path and the individual life path are closely intertwined. So, some people seek to overcome specific life events (death, separation, loss of job; see also Terry and Vartabedian 2013); for others, the path symbolizes a rite of passage between childhood and maturity (see also Pedersen Gurholt 2008; Turner 1973). Some interviewees report a gain in confidence (Annika, Daniel, Janina).

Popular culture is full of *tales of salvation* through solo-hiking: stories of a daughter losing her mother and overcoming her grief, stories of the drug addict reconnecting to herself, etc. (see also chapter 4, this volume). It raises critical questions: Is that a promise? Does the solo-hike always *function* the way people hope for or expect? Is there always a rewarding inner experience? One of the interviewees, David, expresses this concern:

> I think you cannot expect that it will change you. I am rather sceptical, when it's about people in a difficult phase in life: somebody who got fired, the wife left or somebody died. There are so many similar stories and I doubt if walking really helps. Difficult to say, but at least you should not expect that the trip helps or changes you. And if it does, maybe you don't even notice it. . . . I am really sceptical if you find answers when you might not even know the questions. I think it is true that you learn a lot here, but you don't even know what.
>
> *(Daniel)*

People say "the path is the goal", but maybe they essentially expect something more and lasting? Daniel F tells how he feels overcome with sadness coming home after a hike – feeling still empowered from the nature experience, but then realizing: it is yet the life from before he returns to. Hence, I call for more critical scrutiny of the interplay between path and life path. Ideally, longitudinal approaches should be used to explore the wide range of experiences that individuals gain when turning inwards and when placing the solo-hike within their life paths.

Closing interpretations of the solo-hike

If I were now to draw a picture of the solo-hiking experience I would draw a soup bowl. A soup can have different ingredients and a solo-hike can be the search for different experiences. As there can be carrots, potatoes, leeks, people can seek adventure, awayness, insight, etc. There are different tastes, and solo-hikers put different emphasis/meaning on their trip. People make different soups, yet they are still soups. People motivate, plan and experience the solo-hike differently, but the solo-hike is essentially a forward movement and inward turn that are experienced (to some extent) alone. Solitude takes the role of a spice to that soup: in different doses, it gives taste, makes it special and intensifies the experience.

I would draw a person bending over the soup bowl. She sits at the table, ready to eat, and watches the reflection on the surface of the soup. What she sees would be a natural landscape on that surface that pleases the imagination: rivers, lush valleys and snowy mountains seemingly distant from the well-known room around her, but also a reflection of her own face. She could explore her eyes and face, her cheeks and mouth, maybe even watch profoundly.

She passionately eats up the soup. Maybe it tastes as expected or maybe different. Maybe the pictures on the surface shift slightly while eating – both of her and of the landscape. When she finishes, she puts down the spoon and looks around the well-known room.

If you ask what the solo-hike is about, I would say it is like such soup – she feels for it, prepares it passionately, and while it is still hot she eats it up. What comes next is unclear. Is it satisfaction, disillusion or hunger for more? Whatever the response, the experience stays with her – a temporary journey, essentially directed inwards and outwards.

To conclude, this chapter echoed the understanding of the solo-hike as essentially a journey of distance to common life spaces and closeness to the inner self – an experience appreciated because of its temporariness. While it could at first seem that the solo-hike stands isolated in time and space, seemingly remote and alone, the material emphasized instead the embeddedness of the solo-hiking experience within a specific social, societal context and point in life. These are findings that scholars should take into methodological consideration regarding future walking studies. Longitudinal, life-path approaches, taking possibly different walking experiences of individuals into account (the walk to work, the solo-hike or the family-hike), could deepen the understanding of the situatedness of single experiences and explore the tensions between expectations and experiences – tensions crucial to tourism studies – in more detail. Finally, the project and this chapter illustrated phenomenology as a valuable methodology to address such complex hiking/travel experiences.

Acknowledgements

I thank the Formas Sami project and Carina Keskitalo for giving me the frame and time to work on this chapter. In the original thesis, I go more in detail on my work with phenomenology, the wilderness construction and the complex stories of the individuals, which could be of interest.

References

Boller, F., Hunziker, M., Conedera, M., Elsasser, H. and Krebs, P. (2010) 'Fascinating remoteness: the dilemma of hiking tourism development in peripheral mountain areas', *Mountain Research and Development*, 30(4): 320–331.

Csikszentmihalyi, M. (1975) *Beyond Boredom and Anxiety*, San Francisco: Jossey-Bass.

den Breejen, L. (2007) 'The experiences of long distance walking: a case study of the West Highland Way in Scotland', *Tourism Management*, 28: 1417–1427.

Edensor, T. (2000) 'Staging tourism: tourists as performers', *Annals of Tourism Research*, 27(2): 322–344.

Elands, B. and Lengkeek, J. (2012) 'The tourist experience of out-there-ness: theory and empirical research', *Forest Policy and Economics*, 19: 31–38.

Gadamer, H.G. (1975) *Truth and Method*, London: Sheed and Ward.

Gelter, H. (2009) 'Friluftsliv as slow and peak experiences in the transmodern society', Conference Proceeding at the 150-Year International Dialogue Conference Celebration *Henrik Ibsen: The birth of "Friluftsliv"*, Levanger, Norway, September, 2009.

Giorgi, A. (1994) 'A phenomenological perspective on certain qualitative research methods', *Journal of Phenomenological Psychology*, 25: 190–220.

Gyimothy, S. and Mykletun, R. (2004) 'Play in adventure tourism – the case of Arctic trekking', *Annals of Tourism Research*, 31(4): 855–878.

Honoré, C. (2004) *In Praise of Slow – How a Worldwide Movement is Challenging the Culture of Speed*, London: Orion.

Hyde, K. and Oleson, K. (2011) 'Packing for touristic performances', *Annals of Tourism Research*, 38(3): 900–919.

Kaplan, S. (1995) 'The restorative benefits of nature: toward an integrative framework', *Journal of Environmental Psychology*, 15: 169–182.

Kyle, G., Graefe, A. and Manning, R. (2003) 'Satisfaction derived through leisure involvement and setting attachment', *Leisure/Loisir*, 28(3–4): 277–305.

Laing, J. and Crouch, G. (2009) 'Lone wolves? Isolation and solitude within the frontier travel experience', *Geografika Annaler*, 91(4): 325–342.

McIntyre, N. and Roggenbuck, J. (1998) 'Nature/person transactions during an outdoor adventure experience: a multi-phasic analysis', *Journal of Leisure Research*, 30(4): 410–422.

Mehmetoglu, M., Dann, G. and Larsen, S. (2001) 'Solitary travellers in the Norwegian Lofoten Islands: why do people travel on their own?', *Scandinavian Journal of Hospitality and Tourism*, 1(1): 19–37.

Noy, C. (2004) 'Performing identity: touristic narratives of self-change', *Text and Performance Quarterly*, 24(2): 115–138.

Oelschlaeger, M. (1991) *The Idea of Wilderness*, New Haven, CT: Yale University Press.

Pedersen Gurholt, K. (2008) 'Norwegian friluftsliv and ideals of becoming an "educated man"', *Journal of Adventure Education and Outdoor Learning*, 8(1): 55–70.

Repp, G. (2004) '*Friluftsliv* and adventure: models, heroes and idols in a Nansen perspective', *Journal of Adventure Education and Outdoor Learning*, 4(2): 117–131.

Roberson Jr., D. and Babic, V. (2009) 'Remedy for modernity: experiences of walkers and hikers on Medvednica Mountain', *Leisure Studies*, 28(1): 105–112.

Schilar, H. (2015) 'Out there – a phenomenological approach to solo-hiking in Northern Scandinavia'. Unpublished master's thesis, Umeå University, Diva. Available at: http://umu.diva-portal.org/smash/record.jsf?pid=diva2%3A827919&dswid=popup.

Solnit, R. (2001) *Wanderlust: A History of Walking*, London: Verso.

Terry, D. and Vartabedian, S. (2013) 'Alone but together: eminent performance on the Appalachian Trail', *Text and Performance Quarterly*, 33(4): 344–360.

Tuan, Y.-F. (1974) *Topophilia: A Study of Environmental Perception, Attitudes and Values*, Englewood Cliffs, NJ: Prentice Hall.

Tuan, Y.-F. (1977) *Space and Place: The Perspective of Experience*, Minneapolis: University of Minnesota Press.

Turner, V. (1973) 'The center out there: Pilgrim's goal', *History of Religions*, 12: 191–230.

Van Manen, M. (1990) *Researching Lived Experience*, London, ON: University of Western Ontario.

Wall Reinius, S. (2009) *Protected Attractions – Tourism and Wilderness in the Swedish Mountain Region*, Stockholm: Stockholm University.

Wylie, J. (2005) 'A single day's walking: narrative self and landscape on the South West Coast path', *Royal Geographic Society*, 30: 234–247.

23

Walking to care

Pilgrimage as a slow tourism development – Kumano-kodo pilgrimage, Wakayama, Japan

Kumi Kato

Introduction

This chapter conceptualizes walking tourism as an agent facilitating formation of a community concerned with sustainability, and thus demanding more environmentally aware tourism, through a case study of a World Heritage-listed trail, *Kumano-kodo* (Kumano ancient trail) in Wakayama prefecture, located on the Kii Peninsula, central-eastern Japan. Walkers, although mostly non-religious, attempt the walk for spiritual purposes, and set particular parameters for tourism service, facilities and experience. Using the concept of slow tourism, this chapter identifies the roles played by a range of stakeholders, including walkers (visitors and residents) and the surrounding community, thereby formulating a specific set of standards for tourism development.

Kumano-kodo represents a network of five trails leading to three Grand Shrines, located at the southern end of the Kij peninsula. The trails were established during the twelfth century, as the journey became popular for nobles and civilians in and around the ancient capital of Kyoto. The end of the peninsula was regarded as "the other world" and thus the return journey, taking up to three months, became a "rebirth experience". The shrines and trails were designated as part of UNESCO World Heritage for its cultural landscape values in 2004 (Government of Japan 2003).

Today, walkers (modern pilgrims) attempt various lengths of the trails with non-religious intent – self-fulfillment, health and wellness, attaining a sense of achievement and alternative to a materially dependent and energy-intensive lifestyle, even for a few days. These qualities define today's pilgrimage as "spiritual", in the way it promotes more ethical ways of engaging with a place, attempting a more holistic understanding of social and environmental sustainability. With this idea, various participants in pilgrimage tourism, including walkers (visitors, conservation volunteers), resident walkers (walking and heritage guides, interpreters, restoration workers) and the surrounding community (providing accommodation, transport, local residents providing local products), become stakeholders for sustainability, working collaboratively for "slow tourism". Walking-based tourism can actively promote a "community of care", with walkers and supporters taking part themselves. This idea has an implication for new types of walking tourism, such as the coastal trail being developed along the area of northeast Japan overwhelmed by the 2011 earthquake and tsunami.

Pilgrimage and walking

A pilgrimage is defined as 'a journey resulting from religious causes, externally to a holy site, and internally for spiritual purposes and internal understanding' (Barber 1993: 1). Today, the notion of pilgrimage may be more widely applied to journeys to spiritual sites, festivals, memorial sites, shrines (religious, secular), sporting and event venues, and other experiences in addition to sacred constructions. Visits to sites associated with a negative history, disaster or death, may be included as part of dark tourism (Sharpley and Stone 2009). In the Japanese context, pilgrimage even includes a visit to a site associated with certain anime production (Okamoto 2014; Yamaguchi 2014; Okamoto 2015). The mode of travel may vary, not necessarily on foot, but this chapter gives particular attention to the walking journey along the pilgrimage route with a specific focus on "slowness" as an agent to facilitate more locally engaging, sustainability-oriented tourism development.

Walking provides time and rhythm which allows our senses to awaken and engage with the surroundings spatially and temporally. It is the process of active and dynamic engagement with the place. Walking, for many, is also a reflective practice that enables thinking and writing as well as gaining aesthetic inspiration (Lucas 2008). 'Walking as an aesthetic practice', according to Lucas (2008: 169), 'has the potential of informing our thinking across many disciplines and practices'. The notion of slowness suggests more locally engaged, mindful and lower-impact tourism, which also enables more attention to local places and people that may lead to activities such as volunteer restoration and story-telling. Such "slow tourism" has significant implications for tourism development, setting particular parameters by demanding more intentional, locally engaged and sustainable tourism.

Slow tourism

Slow travel and tourism is closely related to the concepts of both slow food and slow cities (Matos 2004; Dickinson et al. 2011; Hall 2012; Nilsson 2013; Hall et al. 2017; Gardner 2009). Matos (2004) discusses the concept of slow tourism as a potential market development in response to the pressing issue of environmental degradation, in this case, of the Alpine region of Europe. Slow tourism becomes the process of enjoying the destination without bringing heavy environmental impact. Two core principles are proposed: taking time, especially in relation to perception of nature as well as understanding local culture; and encouraging attachment to a place with regard to the special characteristics of the locality, its architecture for example, as a contribution to the sense of place.

Some scholars distinguish between slow tourism, slow travel or soft mobility. Ceron and Dubois (2007) argue that slow tourism describes rail-based tourism and longer stays and has been linked to slow food (Simpson et al. 2008), while soft mobility is described as destination-based travel on foot and by bicycle, as distinguished from slow travel, which describes less travel-intensive tourism, for example, using train, sailing and bus (Dubois and Ceron 2006). No such distinction is made in this chapter, which employs soft tourism as a generic term.

Lumsdon and McGrath (2011: 265) propose that slow tourism is 'about slowing down, travelling shorter distances and enriching the travel experience both en route to and at the destination', and is 'a response to the social dilemma of tourism development, whilst at the same time offering a reduction of carbon emissions'. Slow tourism may, therefore, be used as a specific parameter to enable a shift towards lower environmental impacts and less travel (Ceron and Dubois 2007; Germann Molz 2009; Hall et al. 2017). The different elements of slow tourism as suggested by different authors is indicated in Table 23.1.

Table 23.1 Different elements of slow tourism

Author	Suggested elements
Lumsdon and McGrath (2011)	• Slowness and the value of time • Locality and activities at the destination • Mode of transport and travel experience • Environmental consciousness
Gardner (2009)	• A state of mind • Tourists should travel slowly and avoid aircraft • Locality is important • The journey is intrinsic to the tourism experience • Slowing down to enjoy the city or the landscape is a key element • Culture through language and engagement with local people makes for a better holiday • Tourists should make opportunities by seeking out the unexpected
Caffyn (2009)	• Better tourism experience • Transport as tourism experience • Minimizing travel distance (at least by car/plane) • Maximizing the time available for the trip, relaxing, refreshing the mind and body • Exploring the local area in depth – seeking out distinctiveness • Contact with local people, culture, heritage and community • Eating at local restaurants, buying in local markets or direct from producers, trying local drinks, beer and wine • Creative and unstructured play for children • Learning and skills activity – personal development • A minimum of mechanization, little technology • Limited commercialization, few global brands, local economic multipliers • Quality experiences and authenticity • Relative sustainability and a modest carbon footprint • Good for the visitor and their companions

In essence, slow travel enables a valuing of time, appreciation of locality (nature, culture, people), and reduction of environmental impact, although this may be at a conscious level. Here, appreciation and care for others (human, non-human) is expressed, as in the notion that 'giving back to local communities is integral' (Lumsdon and McGrath 2011: 266) and travel time as a gift and co-production of experience with other travellers en route (Jain and Lyons 2008). Caffyn (2009) applies Honore's (2004) notion of slow to the phenomenon of tourism, which involves making real and meaningful connections with people, places, culture, food, heritage and the environment. Slow tourism, therefore, potentially drives the sustainability agenda like a slow and carefully moving vehicle, also enabling those who participate to express their choices, as 'tourism is one of the mechanisms through which people are able to present their identity to others' (Dickinson et al. 2011: 295).

With slowness allowing more conscious engagement with locality (environment, culture, people) and pilgrimage as a spiritual practice, walking tourism along the pilgrimage routes is seen as a co-creation process with walkers, surrounding communities and the environment advocating a sustainable mode of tourism. This is discussed with a specific example of Kumano-kodo pilgrimage trail in Wakayama Prefecture, Japan.

Heritage sites and conservation: sacred sites and pilgrimage routes in the Kii Mountain Range

The World Heritage site, *Sacred Sites and Pilgrimage Routes in the Kii Mountain Range* is located across three prefectures (Wakayama, Mie and Nara Prefectures) on the Kii Peninsula, central east coast of Japan. The heritage site occupies the central part of the peninsula, and is the largest in Japan with the total area of 9,900 km². The site was designated as the UNESCO World Heritage in 2004, as Japan's twelfth nomination (at the time of writing there were 19 World Heritage sites in Japan, 15 cultural and four natural). Three major sacred sites – Kumano-sanzan, Koyasan and Yoshino-Omine – are linked by pilgrimage routes originating in the ancient capitals of Kyoto and Nara. The central government's sites during 511–518 and 518–526 were within today's Kyoto, where the capital was formally situated during Heian period (794–1180).

Kumano-sanzan refers to three grand shrines of Kumano: *Kumano Hongu, Kumano Hayatama* and *Kumano-Nachi Grand shrines* that were established in the tenth century as a ground where Japan's native aminism developed uniquely into Shintoism blended and developed with Buddhism. Yoshino-Omine refers to a region in the Omine mountain range, where Shugendo (asceticism) practice was established in the tenth century with Yoshino and Omine mountains as sacred mountains with four associated temples and shrines. Koyasan is a mountain town where Shingon Mikkyo Esoteric Buddhism was founded by Kukai in 816 as a monks' training site, One hundred and seventeen temples exist today, with almost half of them offering lodging to worshippers and tourists.

Six pilgrimage routes, totaling a distance of 307.6 km, were included in the World Heritage nomination (Table 23.2). The routes to Kumano-sanzan are collectively referred to as Kumano-kodo (Kumano ancient routes), which receives over 2 million visitors annually, walking various sections of the routes or visiting the main sites by vehicle (Wakayama Prefecture 2011). In this chapter, the visitors to these pilgrim sites are referred to as 'pilgrims', regardless of their religious status, or distance they choose to walk.

Kumano-kodo is part of the two pilgrimage sites nominated in the World Heritage, alongside the *Route of Santiago de Compostela in Spain* (nominated in 1993) (Camino de Santiago n.d.; see also Chapter 37, this volume). Regular exchange takes place between the two properties, including the sister-province relationship between Wakayama Prefecture and the State of Galicia, Spain

Table 23.2 Six routes nominated in the *Sacred Sites and Pilgrimage Routes in the Kii Mountain Ranges*

Routes		Distance (km)	Comments
Omine-Okugake		86.9	Connecting Yoshimo-Omine and Kumano-sanzan
Kumano	Nakahechi	88.8	Mountain, approaching from the west
Sankeimichi	Kohechi	43.7	Mountain, approaching from the north
	Ohechi	10.0	Coastal, approaching from the west
	Iseji	54.2	Coastal, approaching from the east, and one specific for ascetic practice, Omine-Okugake
	Sub-total	196.7	
Koyasan Choishimici		24.0	Starting at the foot of Koyasan
		307.6	

Source: Government of Japan 2003: 2–3

as well as the sister-city relationship between the City of Santiago de Compostela and Tanabe City, Wakayama. Regular exchange of youth groups takes place between Wakayama and Galicia, and Tanabe City is initiating tourism exchanges with the City of Santiago, using the respective city tourism bureaus as the basis of exchange. The exchange between the two routes was initiated in 1988, and the Tanabe–Santiago exchange was formalized in celebrating the tenth anniversary of the Japanese nomination in 2014.

Among the Kumano-kodo, *Nakahechi* is a popular route for a number of reasons, as outlined in Table 23.3. Nakahechi has been successful in developing a variety of public participation opportunities in conservation, guiding and general understanding of its history, involving local residents as well as visitors. These participatory activities are directly and indirectly responding to the need and preferences of visitors (pilgrims), forming a fundamental basis for sustainable tourism. Residents and visitors who play an important role in sustainable management of heritage sites as stakeholders include the following.

1) Participants in conservation projects (e.g. conservation volunteers).
2) Expert leaders who have (intrinsically or through training) historic, geographic and ecological knowledge of the sites and can lead visitors as a guide/instructor or interpreter.
3) Students with a specific aim of learning (formal/informal, domestic/international).
4) Local community that provides various service and facilities.

Table 23.3 Reasons for the popularity of Nakahechi

Distance	Nakahechi (45 km) can be completed in two or three days by walkers with a basic level of physical fitness. It offers the option of walking only part of the way and otherwise using local bus services.
Spiritual beliefs	Shinto, as well as Shingon Esoteric Buddhism, values rituals, practices and training (mental and physical), in which walking is regarded as providing time and space for meditative and humbling experiences.
Landscape	The routes are mostly through forests, with significant sites (Oji) scattered en route, which makes the trail interesting.
Local culture	The route crosses through three villages that can provide food and lodging, but which keeps the walking experience authentic.
Gradient	Terrains are mostly undulating with several steep sections. Trails are well managed.
Signage	The trails are clearly signed in Japanese and English. Roads cross neither trail although there are many "escape" options. In 2012, a section of Nakahechi was closed, due to the damage sustained by the typhoon of September 2011. Although the route itself was not damaged, an alternative route (by bus) was taken for that section as recommended by the authorities.
Cultural significance	The Nakahechi route can be divided into three major sections, each of which has significant shrines and temples that offer highlights for the day. A number of historic interpretations are available.
Accommodation	Traditional guesthouses providing three meals, including packed lunch for the following day.
Luggage transport	Luggage transport service between lodges can be arranged for through walkers for a small charge.
Hot spring	Each accommodation stop has a traditional hot spring, which is welcoming at the end of the day and also offers a unique cultural experience.

These categories may overlap, and participants in each category may play multiple roles. Participation may be through tourism products (heritage, volunteer, conservation) government agencies, participating enterprises, and tourism agents have collaborated to develop products in volunteer tourism, cultural heritage and conservation tourism.

A number of examples of stakeholders involvement can be illustrated using examples from the Wakayama prefecture.

Volunteer conservation programs

Many parts of the pilgrimage trails are subject to erosion, due to steep gradients and high precipitation (average 2,730 mm/year), and inaccessible by vehicles, especially large trucks. Soil therefore needs to be carried in by hand for trail restoration (*Michi-bushin*), and involving walkers was an ideal way, which turned out to be attractive to many walkers who were willing to help conserve the heritage. The "Conservation Walk" program combines short heritage walks and restoration work called *fushin*. *Fushin* traditionally meant requesting support for community members in money and labour for building and restoring houses and infrastructure in the community. The term is now used for volunteer works in building or restoring public facilities (road, canals, disaster recovery). Today, conservation walks attract more than 2,000 participants annually, including corporate groups using opportunities for CSR and staff training, school and community groups. In 2011 there were 44 groups, or 2,159 participants; 2,064 participants in 2012, and 2,138 in 2013. Participants come as individuals, corporate, school and other groups, and the 2013 participation record shows: Individual (via travel agency): 459, Corporate 16 groups: 886, School (primary, secondary, technical school) 9 groups: 425, Other: 11 groups: 368. In this case, soil can also be donated by visiting groups (1 t = ¥15,000 or US$147). Individual participation is also possible through a package tour, which provides transport to and from the restoration site. If participants choose to stay overnight in the area, they pay for the lodging.

Expert leaders

Local training is also taking place in heritage management and conservation (*World Heritage Master* program). This is a three-day guide-training program held annually, to which a Certificate of *World Heritage Master* is issued by the Prefectural governor on completion. Ninety-three Masters have been certified since 2006, who are actively involved in conservation works (e.g. regular trail inspection) and educational activities (e.g. school visits). Master status is voluntary and may be renewed every three years.

There are a number of private organizations facilitating training and works of guides, instructors or interpreters, some in specially trained roles and others in more of a voluntary capacity. An informal network sets a standard fee charged for guiding in the local area, and interpretation of historic incidents, natural flora and fauna. There are two kinds of guides/instructors/interpreters working in the heritage site: *Kumano therapists* who provide various kinds of activities beneficial to health, including walking, hot spring, herbal medicine and organic food. The therapists are trained to accompany walks and provide health advice on general lifestyle, dietary requirement and daily routines. They use various natural elements found to be therapeutic: eating fresh mountain vegetables, using various herbs to stimulate the senses, bathing in hot spas, breathing fresh air, enjoying silence, and walking on various natural surfaces, collectively referred to as *Chikei-Ryoho* (geo- or terrain therapy) (Shuh and Koseki 2012). *Kataribe* are story-tellers or keepers of folktales, myths and legends, but now the term is commonly used as a guide who interprets local places. Most operate for a fee, and some groups provide services in English in internationally popular areas. Currently, twelve private groups train and promote guides with local knowledge, history, conservation principles and interpretation skills. Many World Heritage Masters also work as *Kataribe*.

Students and learners – educational programs for domestic and international students

At Wakayama University, various educational programs are offered in relation to the heritage sites, and an intensive program, *Environment and Spirituality: Walking the Pilgrimage in Wakayama*, is jointly offered with Australian and American universities, which features two pilgrimage walks (Nakahichi, Koyasan) followed by a four-day community contribution program. In heritage walks, students meet priests at the heritage-listed shrines, heritage centre staff and community members who are directly involved in heritage sites on a daily basis. In this program, local residents serve as the host, instructor and facilitator of learning. From 2011 to 2015, 71 international students have participated in the program (Kato 2014).

Local community involvement

A village alongside the Nakahechi pilgrimage trail is now gaining younger new settlers who have moved to the area seeking a more sustainable, safe and healthy environment for their families. Younger generations relocating from urban to rural environments include so-called *I-turns* (those moving to a new place), *U-turns* (those going back to their hometown) or *J-turns* (those relocating to areas near their hometown). This represents a post-development phenomenon that values intangible qualities of life (i.e. family time, healthy environment, safe food and community unity) more than materialistic values, even if their income may be reduced or life becomes less convenient. The phenomenon increased particularly after the East Japan earthquake and tsunami (11 March 2011) that challenged much of the current material-dependent and energy-intensive lifestyle.

The lifestyle of those choosing to live in rural areas tends to be environmentally oriented, interested in locally produced organic food, natural clothing materials, chemical-free products, hand-made products, alternative energy and spiritual wellbeing. Businesses arising from these interests, e.g. shops, restaurants, accommodation or guiding, instructing and teaching (local knowledge, food, exercise, spiritual guidance), create tourism opportunities that also promotes lower-impact lifestyle and sustainability.

Discussion

The various range of people participating in the activities reviewed above – local residents, guides, volunteers, tourists and students – are motivated to contribute to heritage conservation as they are attracted to the spiritual significance of the place that is in line with a more sustainable way of living. Even if they do not use the term sustainability and their involvement is small, they form an important "community of care" to recognize and value natural and cultural integrity of the place. Tourism can nurture and enhance such quality, raising awareness, facilitating ongoing direct and indirect contribution and publicizing widely its significance and outcomes. As a result, several contributing factors to heritage conservation through tourism can be identified (Table 23.4).

The implications from this case study may be relevant to other heritage sites, especially in the Asia-Pacific region, where spiritual heritage has a strong presence in local communities.

Table 23.4 Contributing factors to heritage conservation through tourism in Wakayama

Promotion of spiritual heritage (supported by community cohesion and resilience)	• Promoting spiritual significance of heritage strongly connected to the natural world • Attracting and promoting ethical and responsible tourists and tourist behaviour • Making clear and creative connections between human and nature (nature as living cultural heritage to be cared for)
Facilitating a wide range of public participation	• Creating a wide range of educational and informative programs • A system to participation that generates a sense of ownership, pride, responsibility and connection through conservation projects • Facilitating urban–rural populations (especially urban population seeking "healing" opportunities) • Facilitating inter-generational connections (local elders' knowledge, historic and ecological, offered to local residents, visitors and students) • Promoting the distinct identity of a local place, generating a sense of pride among local residents.
Promoting leadership by experts and trained volunteers	• Investing in training and education in guides/instructors/interpreters, even if they work in volunteer capacities. • Creative interpretation of a place, combining history, mythology, anecdotes or scientific/ecological information can be an effective management tool to minimize the environmental impacts, while providing promotional, educational and management value.
Environmental branding	• Promoting low-impact and beneficial activities with respect for locality, which may be defined as slow travel. • Health, healing and spiritual tourism for sustainable living and volunteer tourism as social contribution.
Students (formal/informal) engaging locally	• Community participation in formal educational programs (as a host, instructor and facilitator) • Acknowledging values of the place (bringing external perspectives) as their identity. • Inter-generational or inter-cultural communication to impart knowledge and stories specific to the area.

Spirituality in heritage places and associated community groups contains knowledge, beliefs and skills originating from living in a specific environment over time and may be critical for disaster prevention and recovery, as well as various strategies for and adaptation to climate change. Management of heritage sites that facilitate a wide range of public participation in educational and informative conservation programs can also be a model of sustainable stakeholder collaboration in tourism development, given the significance of cultural interpretation grounded in community strength.

Conclusion: walking – slow tourism development for sustainability

At the north end of Tohoku, where nearly 500 km of coastal area was devastated by the tsunami of 2011, a 'Sea Breeze Trail (*Shiokaze Trail*)' has been developed as an initiative of the Ministry of the Environment. Approximately 375 km of trail will be completed in 2016. In July 2014, 254 people received a 'completion certificate' through a check-point system, and the total number of registered uses was 2,417. Registration data shows that more than half of the walkers are in their thirties or younger, and over one-third are from the six prefectures in the Tohoku region (Ministry of the Environment 2012). The trail is one of the seven reconstruction project initiated by the Ministry of Environment alongside the establishment of a national park, Sanriku Fukko (Reconstruction) National Park (2013), and the Satoyama/Satoumi Field Museum. Sato-yama and Sato-umi are Japanese terms, meaning the areas of yama (mountains) and umi (ocean) bordering the human living and cultivation area (sato). It is the area where human–nature interactions, both usage and conservation, occur. Promotion of ecotourism projects, ecological research to restore biodiversity of the region, environmental education programs, including leadership development and environmental monitoring of the affected areas, are all part of the initiative (Ministry of the Environment 2012).

At a faster pace, running events are now viewed as tourism, and one inaugurated in Tohoku as part of the reconstruction strategy. *Tohoku Fudo Marathon Festival*, was held in Tome, Miyagi Prefecture (23–24 April 2016), as an event promoting fudo (風土 *local landscape and culture*) and food (*fuudo*, now popular usage in Japanese). Nearly 3,800 people participate in full and half marathons, shorter distances (3, 2 and 1 km) and relay runs. The event was supported by more than 600 volunteers attending aid stations, marshalling and managing the sites. At the aid station every 2 km, various local food and drinks were supplied and, at the end, even local varieties of sake and 64 food stalls entertained 27,000 visitors in total. Funds were also raised for the Kumamoto Earthquake that devastated the central Kyushu region only ten days before (14 April 2016).

Walking (and running) tourism has a 'caring' quality, to the walkers themselves, to the hosting communities and to the surrounding environment. The humble act of walking, being outdoor without technology, equipment or any other assistance, nurtures the capacity to care, for others and for the environment. Walking tourism will be increasingly desired for the healing quality of natural environment, time and pace, as more effort is made to ease tourism's environmental, social and cultural impact. Walking will be a quiet but powerful force for sustainability.

References

Barber, R. (1993) *Pilgrimages*, London: The Boydell Press.

Caffyn, A. (2009) 'The slow route to new markets', *Tourism Insights*, September.

Camino de Santiago (n.d.) *The Pilgrimage Routes to Santiago de Compostela*. Available at: www.santiago-compostela.net.

Ceron, J. P. and Dubois, G. (2007) 'Limits to tourism? A backcasting scenario for sustainable tourism mobility in 2050', *Tourism and Hospitality Planning and Development*, 4(3): 191–209.

Dickinson, J., Lumsdon, L. and Robbins, D. (2011) 'Slow travel: issues for tourism and climate change', *Journal of Sustainable Tourism*, 19(3): 281–300.

Dubois, G. and Ceron, J. P. (2006) 'Tourism/leisure greenhouse gas emissions forecasts for 2050: factors for change in France', *Journal of Sustainable Tourism*, 14(2): 172–191.

Gardner, N. (2009) 'A manifesto for slow travel', *Hidden Europe*, 25: 10–14.

Germann Molz, J.G. (2009) 'Representing pace in tourism mobilities: staycations, slow travel and the amazing race', *Journal of Tourism and Cultural Change*, 7(4): 270–286.

Government of Japan (2003) *World Heritage List Nomination. Japan. Sacred Sites and Pilgrimage Routes in the Kii Mountain Range, and the Cultural Landscape that Surround them*. Agency for Cultural Affairs and

Ministry of the Environment. Available at: http://whc.unesco.org/uploads/nominations/1142.pdf (accessed 15 May 2014).

Hall, C.M. (2012) 'The contradictions and paradoxes of slow food: environmental change, sustainability and the conservation of taste', in S. Fullagar, K. Markwell and E. Wilson (eds), *Slow Tourism: Experiences and Mobilities*, Bristol: Channel View, pp. 53–68.

Hall, C.M., Le-Klähn, D.-T. and Ram, Y. (2017) *Tourism, Public Transport and Sustainable Mobility*, Bristol: Channel View Press.

Honore, C (2004) *In Praise of Slow*, London: Orion.

Jain, J. and Lyons, G. (2008) 'The gift of travel time', *Journal of Transport Geography*, 16(2): 81–89.

Kato, K. (2014) 'Spiritual and sensory engagement with more than human: an ecohumanities approach to sustainability learning'. in D. Selby F. Kagawa (eds), *Sustainability Frontiers*, Berlin: Barbara Budrich Publishers, pp. 221–237.

Lucas, R. (2008) 'Taking a line for a walk. Walking as an aesthetic practice', in T. Ingold and J. Vergunst (eds), *Ways of Walking*, Aldershot, Hants: Ashgate, pp. 169–184.

Lumsdon, L. and McGrath, P. (2011) 'Developing a conceptual framework for slow travel: a grounded theory approach', *Journal of Sustainable Tourism*, 19(3): 265–279.

Matos, W. (2004) 'Can slow travel bring new life to the Alpine regions?', in K. Weiermair and C. Mathies (eds), *The Tourism and Leisure Industry*, New York: Haworth, pp. 93–103.

Ministry of the Environment (2012) 'Green reconstruction: creating a new national park', *Ministry of the Environment, Government of Japan*. Available at: www.env.go.jp/jishin/park-sanriku/green-reconstruction (accessed 20 April 2016).

Nilsson, J.H. (2013) 'Nordic eco-gastronomy', in C.M. Hall and S. Gössling (eds), *Sustainable Culinary Systems: Local Foods, Innovation, and Tourism and Hospitality*, Abingdon, Oxon: Routledge, pp. 189–204.

Okamoto, K. (2014) 'Anime tourism', in S. Ohashi, K. Hashimoto, H. Endo and K. Kanda (eds), *Guidebook for Tourism Studies*, Kyoto: Nakanishiya, pp. 188–191.

Okamoto, R. (2015) *Seichi-junrei: sekai-isan kara anime no butai made* [Pilgrimage to Sacred Places: From World Heritage to Amine Sites], Tokyo: Chuo-koron.

Sharpley, R. and Stone, P. (2009) *The Dark Side of Travel: The Theory and Practice of Dark Tourism*, Bristol: Channel View Publications.

Shuh, A. and Koseki, N. (2012) *Kuaoruto Nyumon (Introduction to Kuaorto, Kurortologie Klimatherapie Klimatische Terrainkur)*, trans. Yuko Horigome-Gotte, Shoshisai.

Simpson, M.C., Gössling, S., Scott, D., Hall, C.M. and Gladin, E. (2008) *Climate Change Adaptation and Mitigation in the Tourism Sector: Frameworks, Tools and Practices*. UNEP, University of Oxford, UNWTO, WMO: Paris, France.

Wakayama Prefecture (2011) *Report on the Wakayama Prefecture Visitation Survey*. (kankokyaku dotai chosa hokokusho). Available at: www.pref.wakayama.lg.jp/prefg/062400/documents/23houkokusho.pdf (accessed 3 December 2014). In Japanese.

Yamaguchi, M. (2014) 'Media', in S. Ohashi, K. Hashimoto, H. Endo and K. Kanda (eds), *Guidebook for Tourism Studies*, Kyoto: Nakanishiya, pp. 126–131.

24

Hindu pilgrimage in India and walkability

Theory and praxis

Subhajit Das and Manirul Islam

Introduction

Hinduism in India dates back to 5000 BCE (Singh 2006) and has systematically organized the sacred space of the country (Bharadwaj 1973). Traditionally, Hindu pilgrimage has been characterized by some sort of austerity and strenuous walking, which became ritualized as part of the spiritual experience of pilgrims. Although the notion of pilgrimage and its practice have evolved over times, walking is still central to Hindu pilgrimage. The conduciveness of environment matters to pilgrims when they walk to the religious sites. Although the concept of walkability has become increasingly significant (Litman 2003; Kemperman *et al.* 2009; Southworth and Ben-Joseph 2013; Ujang and Muslim 2014; see also chapter 30, this volume), no attempt has previously been made to study the walkability issues associated with Hindu pilgrimage.

The purpose of this chapter is to explore the importance of walking and, hence, walkability in the context of Hindu pilgrimage. The aim is to examine the major issues and challenges of pilgrimage walkability. The chapter begins with a brief outline of the concepts of pilgrimage and religious tourism, and is followed by a historical perspective on walking and Hindu pilgrimage. Thereafter, major issues and challenges of walkability are reviewed. The chapter concludes with a case study of Vaishno Devi Yatra, to highlight the walkability issues associated with pilgrimage.

Pilgrimage and religious tourism

Pilgrimage is one of the oldest forms of touristic activity, and understanding pilgrimage as a phenomenon is a necessity in the study of the development of leisure and tourism (Collins-Kreiner 2010). It has been observed that 'a tourist is half a pilgrim, if a pilgrim is half a tourist' (Turner and Turner 1978: 20), and there are fundamental similarities between tourists and pilgrims, as both require time, sufficient financial resources and social sanctions to undertake their journey (Smith 1992). Smith's (1992) continuum of travel places pilgrims and tourists at opposite poles: one is located at the pole of the sacred, the other at the pole of the secular.

There are seemingly endless possibilities of combination of the two, and one of the central combinations is religious tourism. Pilgrimage and tourism are combined in the concept of religious tourism and travel theorists point out that traditional dichotomies between tourism and pilgrimage are no longer justifiable in 'the shifting world of post-modern travel' (Badone and Roseman 2004: 2). Religious tourism encompasses all kinds of travel that is motivated either in part or exclusively by religion and where the destination is normally a religious site (Rinschede 1992; Blackwell 2007). The term pilgrimage has, in recent times, gained secular associations, and meaningful travel to non-religious places is also often referred to as pilgrimage (Digance 2006; Hall 2006). In the context of Hindu pilgrimage in India, religious tourism, however, is not equivalent to pilgrimage. The Hindu concept of pilgrimage as represented by the term *tirtha-yatra,* literally means undertaking a journey to river fords (Bharadwaj 1973), and involves certain elements that are specific to it. It involves notions of obligation, piety, ritual austerity, hardship and suffering. Referring to the *Skandapurana,* Bhardwaj (1973) explains that *tirtha-yatra* not only means the physical act of visiting the holy places, but also implies mental and moral discipline. Simply, '*travelling* to a sacred site is not sufficient to identify the traveller as a pilgrim' (Blackwell 2007: 39), but it may suffice to define him or her as a religious tourist. The journey is as important to the pilgrim as is the sacredscape. The chief difference between tourists and *tirtha-yatris* (pilgrims), therefore, lies in their motivation and in the execution of their journey.

Hindu pilgrimage and walking

Hindu pilgrimage as a cultural phenomenon has a long history. Scholars have traced the earliest reference to the practice of pilgrimage to *Aitareya Brahmana* of the *Rg Veda,* composed between *c.* 1500 and *c.* 1000 BC (Bharadwaj 1973). The *Mahabharata* (*c.* 400 BC to *c.* 200 AD) refers to a number of pilgrimage circuits (Bharadwaj 1973; Singh 2004; Singh 2006) and in the second century BC, *Gautamiya Sastra* speaks of the *tirthas* 'as sin destroying localities' (cited in Bharati 1963: 137).

Pilgrimage, however, emerged as a mass culture in the medieval age, as a result of Brahminical revival and ritualization of Hinduism and 'through its partial absorption into local, non-Brahmanic cults' (Bharati 1963: 135). The *Puranas,* dated at between the eighth to the sixteenth centuries (Singh 2006), bear evidence that Hinduism became a more formalized religion around 1000 AD and the importance of ritualistic elements saw a significant increase in pilgrimage (Bharadwaj 1973). Apart from the *Puranas,* Laksmidhara's *Krityakalpataru* (*c.* 1110 CE), Vachaspati Mishra's *Tirthachintamani* (*c.* 1460 CE), Narayan Bhatta's *Tristhalisetu* (*c.* 1580 CE) and Mitra Mishra's *Tirthaprakasha* (*c.* 1620 CE) are some of the texts that gives us important insights into traditional Hindu pilgrimage.

Pilgrimage in the Sanskritic tradition involves austerity and hardships (Singh 2004), and part of the rigour has been strenuous walking to the pilgrimage sites and performing some form of ritual walk at the sacred site itself. Pilgrimage is also considered to be 'a *way* to heal the body and soul by walking and opening the soul to the spirit inherent in Mother Earth' (Singh 2006: 223), and therefore, it often requires barefoot walking or walking on the knees or rolling the body on the earth. As many common features of traditional Hindu pilgrimage are retained 'through time and space' (Singh 2004: 44), various forms of walking remain integral to it even today. However, with increasing motorization and opening up roads to the pilgrimage locations, the nature of walking has evolved and two basic forms of walking are now seen: walking on the way to the sacredscape and the *parikrama/pradakshina* or circumambulation at the pilgrimage site itself.

As part of their ritual and religious obligation, pilgrims walk long and short distances to the pilgrimage sites. Some of the famous places of pilgrimages in India, where walking is considered obligatory, are Mansarovar Yatra, Pandharpur Yatra, Deoghar Yatra and Char Dham Yatra (Badrinath, Dwarka, Jagannath Puri and Rameshwaram). In some cases, particularly the pilgrimage sites in the northern Himalayas, the only way to reach the shrines is to walk or trek. Interestingly, both pilgrims and non-pilgrim tourists walk the distance to fulfil their quest, religious or otherwise, and there has been an increase in the number of adventure tourists or cultural tourists (Singh 2004). *Parikrama/pradakshina* or circumambulation involves cyclic walking around the shrines. With ever-increasing use of transport to reach the sacred sites, the significance of the *parikramas* has grown (Jacobsen 2013). Clockwise circumambulation normally involves walking around the temple or the deity, but at certain places of pilgrimage, circumambulation routes loop pilgrims around an entire city and the holy places (Davidson and Gitlitz 2002). Circumambulation at Varanasi, for example, involves a walking circuit of 80 kilometres, while the circumambulation at Vraj by the devotees of Krishna involves several days of walking. As walking is a significant element of Hindu pilgrimage, walkability is very relevant to it.

Walkability and Hindu pilgrimage

There is a dearth of literature on walkability in the field of pilgrimage studies and the concept of walkability has primarily been limited to the domains of transportation and urban studies (Hall *et al.* 2017; see also chapter 30, this volume). According to Litman (2003), walking is an activity and walkability is the situation or the condition of walking pursuit. Walkability studies incorporate the factors responsible to make the environment conducive to walking. Walkability is regarded as an important quality of a particular place in terms of major characteristics including foot friendliness, safety and security, utilities (shops and services), the environment and cultural and social diversity (Bradshaw 1993). Southworth (2005) suggested a six-fold strategy for walkability and emphasized connectivity, linkage, land-use pattern, safety, the quality of path and the path context; while Samarasekara *et al.* (2011) considered activity potentials, safety from traffic, comfort and shade as major factors of walkability. Nevertheless, in spite of certain risks encountered while walking, pilgrims generally have not been deterred from visiting the sacred sites (Blackwell 2007). However, along with the strong religious motivation, walkability can be an added impetus to pilgrimage.

The Hindu pilgrimage in India is increasingly inclined towards the promotion of religious tourism. Several Hindu walking trails, especially in the Himalayan regions, are being modified and reoriented to facilitate walking. The trails are being purposefully managed to reduce the extremity of the level of austerity and, at the same time, maintain the authenticity of experience for pilgrims. Walking trails, whether organically evolved or purposively promoted (Ramsay and Truscott 2002), are being gradually commodified (Dickinson and Lumsdon 2010), in order to keep pace with the changing nature of the supply and demand of the tourism market (Murray and Graham 1997). Along with trends in many other religions, the number of pilgrims and non-pilgrim walkers to Hindu sacred sites is increasing day by day (Stausberg 2011; Timothy and Olsen 2006) and the situation is comparable to the Western phenomenon of mass tourism (Mustonen 2006). The involvement of larger numbers of people has also attracted the political class, the government and the policy makers to the pilgrimage trails and there have been attempts to promote and manage the traditional rites, rituals and other forms of activities attached to pilgrimage.

Walkability issues and challenges in Hindu pilgrimage in India

Walking has been theorized as a way to achieve sustainable tourism, as it has multiple benefits on health, society and environment (Southworth 2005; Hall *et al.* 2017). The walking experience enables the walkers to feel the proximity to nature and connectedness with landscapes and streetscapes (Wilson 1996; Mulligan 2007). Walkability also creates more demands for pilgrimage trails along with growth in lodging and other services to the traveller. The promotion of a walkable trail is also considered by many stakeholders as a tool to help conserve traditional cultures and heritage resources and protect the natural environment from being exploited and degraded. Local communities may also get positively involved in such activities to develop an empowered decision-making system for further improvement of walkability conditions. Small and medium (either local or non-local) entrepreneurs also receive economic benefits. This, in turn, improves the quality of life of locals. Moreover, the walkability of a trail leads to the development and improvement of the quality of the resource, which can be further enjoyed and utilized for transport purposes (Timothy and Boyd 2014).

Improvements in walkability facilitate different forms of religious rituals and rites of hardship and austerity other than walking, e.g. walking on knees, scrolling and *dandavata* (performed by standing in one spot, offering obeisances like a stick, or *danda*, by lying prostrate on the ground and then continuing, contiguously, until the entire route is covered), and also helps ensure safety and security, which increases the number of pilgrims. Women may avoid walking mainly because of their fears of being unsafe and insecure (Cloke *et al.* 1996; Foster *et al.* 2004). Therefore, improvements in walkability can be an effective tool to increase participation of women and minimizes the gender gap in pilgrimage. Walking may also help to overcome the barriers of class, caste, religion, and other limitations of social hierarchy. As the pilgrims have similar kinds of motivations and avail themselves of the common facilities along their journey, pilgrimage can lead to feelings of solidarity and 'communitas' (Turner 1969: 96).

Nevertheless, the development of walking trails may negatively affect the environment. The clearance of vegetation while promoting walkability may result in species disturbance and changes in habitat. Introduction of foreign weeds, noise pollution and the problem of solid wastes are other negative dimensions (Hammitt *et al.* 2015). Although it is reported that pilgrimage has less destructive effects on the local culture, society and environment than other forms of tourism development (Gupta 1999), other research has found that religious tourism can have negative impacts on the environment and society (Timothy 1994, 1999). For example, Kuniyal and Jain (1999) pointed out the negative impact of high demand on pilgrimage trails in Himalayan region for religious purposes, with litter and waste disposal recorded as a major problem along such trails. Furthermore, greater emphasis on touristic dimensions for economic benefits 'erodes the potential dimension of pilgrimage' (Preston 1992: 36) and very often limits the authentic experience of pilgrimage. Religious sites are often being visited by people who are half motivated by pilgrimage and half by the immediate areas for educational or holiday-making purposes (Rinschede 1992). The pressure of mass tourism in several cases violets the sanctity of sacred places. Therefore, any failure in management leads to a possibility that the sacred site will be transformed into an "entertaining" religious destination (Timothy and Olsen 2006).

In India, the mass flow of pilgrims attracts crimes against visitors. In addition, religious tourism may become the soft target of national as well as international political violence and terrorism, affecting the image of any tourism site (Hall *et al.* 2004; Alvarez and Campo 2014). Therefore, important Hindu sacred places in India are kept under close surveillance, such as the tightly secured trails of Amarnath yatra and Vaishno Devi yatra. Nevertheless, it is a great challenge to maintain the high level of security round the year, especially in the Himalayan regions which are more susceptible to political and militant violence because of their border locations.

Shri Vaishno Devi Yatra – walkability in praxis

The shrine of Vaishno Devi is located inside a cave where pilgrims do obeisance. The cave is the Trikuta Hills of Siwalik Himalayan ranges at an altitude of 5,200 ft (1,585 m). It is 13 km from the base camp at Katra at an altitude of 2,500 ft (762 m) and 50 km from the town of Jammu. Following the mythology, the pilgrimage journey to Shri Vaishno Devi gets accomplished with an obeisance at the temple of Bhairon at Bhairoghati only after visiting the cave of Vaishno Devi. Bhairoghati is at an altitude of 6,619 ft (2,017 m) and at a distance of 14.5 km from Katra (SMVDSB n.d.).

The sacred cave of Vaishno Devi remained obscure until the sixteenth century, when Maharaja Gulab Singh (1792–1857) and his descendents, such as Ranbir Singh (1830–1885), started promoting the destination by establishing the Dharmarth Council to look after management, fund protection and other issues of the pilgrimage activities undertaken there. The site received publicity and further scope for religious activities when all the temples of the region were made accessible to lower-caste people like Harijans, who were historically considered to be the untouchables, following the 1932 declaration by Maharaja Hari Singh (Chauhan 2010). Since then, the flow of pilgrims has steadily increased. Traditionally, the cave was primarily visited by people from the region (Foster and Stoddard 2010), primarily because of the remoteness and hardship of the trail. Walking up barefoot is one of the major votive rituals of pilgrimage at Vaishno Devi Yatra (Chauhan 2010), although pilgrims do not always walk barefoot. In spite of the development of road and railway links to Katra from all over India, the route to the sacred destinations atop the hills is still kept non-motorized, although facilities are available to assist the pilgrims who cannot walk because of obesity or other physical problems. Pony services, horse riding and being carried by other people are instances of such facilities, while a helicopter service has also been introduced from Katra to Sanjhichhat, which is very close to the sacred cave of Shri Vaishno Devi. These facilities show the increasing commoditization of the trail and it is indicative of the general transformation of the sacredscape to a religious tourism site (Foster and Stoddard 2010).

Walking is the main activity at Vaishno Devi Yatra and has become ritualized over time (Foster and Stoddard 2010; Chauhan 2010). The phenomenological changes in the publicity and arrival of visitors have been recorded after the year 1986, when, in the month of August, the Shri Mata Vaishno Devi Shrine Board (SMVDSB) was set up following the abolition of the Dharmarth Council. Thereafter, the numbers of pilgrims have increased and it has become an important religious destination of the Siwalik range (Erndl 1993). The picturesque landscape of the Siwalik Himalayan range, the spectacular beauty of the forest and the serenity and calmness of the mountains on the way from Katra to sacred destinations have turned Vaishno Devi Yatra into an important religious tourist destination (Chauhan 2010). The major walkability components of the route are detailed below:

Connectivity

Katra, the base camp of the trail, is well connected with all the parts of India by road and rail networks. Katra is well connected with sacred destinations at the hills by trails, some of which have evolved historically and others exist because of anthropogenic interventions.

Foot-friendly environment, path quality and activity potentials

The floor of the whole trekking trail has been covered with smooth walkable tiles to facilitate walking, even for those with bare feet. Lamp posts have been installed to facilitate night-time walking. A separate route (measuring 5.5 km) to the sacred cave has also been constructed with accompanying facilities at a cost of 65 million rupees by SMVDSB to manage the crowd load on the trail and to increase its potentiality for walking.

Traffic, shade, comfort and utility shops

Separate mule routes for the pony and horse services have been constructed and some are still under construction to make the route more comfortable and safe for the pilgrims. Most of the trail is covered with shade to minimize the effect of scorching heat and rain. The trail is kept clean by the SMVDSB. Shady rest stops, water facilities and toilet facilities are available on the walk. The SMVDSB also runs accommodation and food stalls at major important points on the trail, some for free and others at subsidized rates. Seated areas and cafeterias are also available to serve the walkers. Medical and massage services are provided to the pilgrims. Several shops can be found along the trail, selling different kind of products.

Safety and security

For participation in the *yatra* (journey), pilgrims have to collect a *yatra* slip from specific counters of SMVDSB, where the fingerprint and photograph of each pilgrim are recorded, and it is mandatory to start the journey within a stipulated time, failing which the permit gets cancelled. The *yatra* starts at Katra with a very high security when the whole body and each of the personal belongings and the *yatra* slip are thoroughly checked by the security personnel. The procedure is repeated at important points. Cloakrooms are available at major points free of cost, so that the walkers can keep their belongings safe and get refreshed for the next phase of trek. Security persons are deployed throughout the trail.

Conclusions

Since its establishment, the SMVDSB has striven hard to improve facilities to reduce the hardship of trekking. As a result of the rapid development of the pilgrimage infrastructure along the Vaishno Devi trail, the number of pilgrims grew from 1.39 million in 1986 to approximately 11 million in 2012 (SMVDSB n.d.). However, after 2012, the number of pilgrims started decreasing and in 2015 fell to 7.77 million. The decline in visitors is regarded as being primarily due to the Kedarnath disaster at Uttarakhand in 2013, devastating floods in Jammu in 2014 and border disputes and skirmishes in Kashmir and parts of Jammu (Pargal 2015, 2016).

In spite of being well designed for walkability, the Vaishno Devi trail is not free from challenges. The over-modification of the trail has caused significant changes in the local environment. Deforestation, construction of shades and the flooring of the whole trail with tiles has caused some damage to the natural ecosystem. It is observed that, in spite of being continuously monitored, the trail is not free from problems of waste disposal. The trails are also often problematic because of the unmanaged driving of pony and horses. Very often, the drivers do not follow the tracks assigned for ponies and horses, creating issues for those walking. The trail is very congested in some places, because of encroachment of shops. During the peak season, the trail experiences huge pressure from pilgrims on essential services, such as sanitation and crowd management. In addition, the trail attracts people such as thieves, who remain engaged in illegal activities along the trail (Foster and Stoddard 2010). Moreover, the authenticity of the religious and pilgrimage ambience at Vaishno Devi Yatra is under question, as Foster and Stoddard (2010: 120) observe, 'Vaishno Devi is one of the most popular pilgrimage places in India perhaps because here religion validates the currency of consumerism.' These crucial issues may threaten the viability of religious tourism at Vaishno Devi in the long run.

A final issue of pilgrimage walkability in India is the intervention of politics in policy making. Politics is supposed to address religious tourism policy in terms of overall development of the quality of life, sustaining biodiversity, protecting the environment that pilgrims (both traditional and secular) and local people receive benefit from in the long run. However, in most of the cases, economic interest maligns such objectives even when the founding values are religious and/or spiritual (Trono 2015).

References

Alvarez, M.D. and Campo, S. (2014) 'The influence of political conflicts on country image and intention to visit: a study of Israel's image', *Tourism Management*, 40: 70–78.

Badone, E. and Roseman, S.R. (2004) 'Approaches to the anthropology of pilgrimage and tourism', in E. Badone and S.R. Roseman (eds), *Intersecting Journeys: The Anthropology of Pilgrimage and Tourism*, Urbana, IL: University of Illinois Press, pp. 1–23.

Bharadwaj, S.M. (1973) *Hindu Places of Pilgrimage in India*, Berkeley, CA: University of California Press.

Bharati, A. (1963) 'Pilgrimage in the Indian tradition', *History of Religions*, 3(1): 135–167.

Blackwell, R. (2007) 'Motivations for religious tourism, pilgrimage, festivals and events', in R. Raj and N.D. Morpeth (eds), *Religious Tourism and Pilgrimage Management: An International Perspective*, Wallingford, Oxon: CABI Publishing, pp. 35–47.

Bradshaw, C. (1993) 'Creating – and using – a rating system for neighborhood walkability: towards an agenda for "local heroes"'. Paper presented at 14th International Pedestrian Conference, Colorado: The School of Cooperative Individualism. Available at: www.cooperative-individualism.org/bradshaw-chris_creating-and-using-a-rating-system-for-neighborhood-walkability-1993.htm (accessed 23 December 2015).

Chauhan, A. (2010) 'Sacred landscape and pilgrimage: a study of Mata Vaishno Devi', in R.P.B. Singh and R.H. Stoddart (eds), *Holy Places and Pilgrimages: Essays on India*, New Delhi: Shubhi Publications, pp. 105–126.

Cloke, P., Milbourne, P. and Thomas, C. (1996) 'The English national forest: local reactions to plans for renegotiated nature–society relations in the countryside', *Transactions of the Institute of British Geographers*, 21(3): 552–571.

Collins-Kreiner, N. (2010) 'Researching pilgrimage: continuity and transformations', *Annals of Tourism Research*, 37(2): 440–456.

Davidson, L.K. and Gitlitz, D.M. (2002) *Pilgrimage: From the Ganges to Graceland: An Encyclopedia, Volume 1*, Santa Barbara, CA: ABC-Clio.

Dickinson, J.E. and Lumsdon, L. (2010) *Slow Travel and Tourism*, London: Earthscan.

Digance, J. (2006) 'Religious and secular pilgrimage: journeys redolent with meaning', in D.J. Timothy and D.H. Olsen (eds), *Tourism, Religion and Spiritual Journeys*, London: Routledge, pp. 36–48.

Erndl, K.M. (1993) *Victory to the Mother: The Hindu Goddess of Northwest India in Myth, Ritual, and Symbol*, New York: Oxford University Press.

Foster, C., Hillsdon, M. and Thorogood, M. (2004) 'Environmental perceptions and walking in English adults', *Journal of Epidemiology and Community Health*, 58(11): 924–928.

Foster, G. and Stoddard, R. (2010) 'Vaishno Devi, the most famous goddess shrine in the Siwāliks', in R.P.B. Singh and R.S. Singh (eds), *Sacred Feography of Goddesses in South Asia: Essays in Memory of David Kinsley*, New Delhi: Sundeep, pp. 109–124.

Gupta, V. (1999) 'Sustainable tourism: Learning from Indian religious traditions', *International Journal of Contemporary Hospitality Management*, 11(2/3): 91–95.

Hall, C.M. (2006) 'Travel and journeying on the sea of faith: perspectives from religious humanism', in D. Timothy and D. Olsen (eds), *Tourism, Religion and Spiritual Journeys*, London: Routledge, pp. 64–77.

Hall, C.M., Duval, D. and Timothy, D. (eds) (2004) *Safety and Security in Tourism: Relationships, Management and Marketing*, New York: Haworth Press.

Hall, C.M., Le-Klähn, D.-T. and Ram, Y. (2017) *Tourism, Public Transport and Sustainable Mobility*, Bristol: Channel View Publications.

Hammitt, W.E., Cole, D.N. and Monz, C.A. (2015) *Wildland Recreation: Ecology and Management*, New York: John Wiley & Sons.

Jacobsen, K.A. (2013) *Pilgrimage in the Hindu Tradition: Salvific Space*, Abingdon, Oxon: Routledge.

Kemperman, A.D., Borgers, A.W. and Timmermans, H.J. (2009) 'Tourist shopping behavior in a historic downtown area', *Tourism Management*, 30(2): 208–218.

Kuniyal, J. and Jain, A. (1999) 'Public involvement in environmental assessment of solid waste management in UP Himalayan tourists' treks, India', *Environmental & Waste Management*, 2(4): 279–290.

Litman, T. (2003) 'Economic value of walkability', *Transportation Research Record: Journal of the Transportation Research Board*, 1828: 3–11.

Mulligan, J. (2007) 'Centring the visitor: promoting a sense of spirituality in the Caribbean', in R. Raj and N. Morpeth (eds), *Religious Tourism and Pilgrimage Management: An International Perspective*, Wallingford, Oxon: CABI, pp. 113–126.

Murray, M. and Graham, B. (1997) 'Exploring the dialectics of route-based tourism: the Camino de Santiago', *Tourism Management*, 18(8): 513–524.

Mustonen, P. (2006) 'Volunteer tourism: postmodern pilgrimage?', *Journal of Tourism and Cultural Change*, 3(3): 160–177.

Pargal, S. (2015) 'Vaishno Devi yatra may hit all time low of 5 years in 2015', *Daily Excelsior*, 6 November. Available at: www.dailyexcelsior.com/vaishno-devi-yatra-may-hit-all-time-low-of-5-years-in-2015 (accessed 23 December 2015).

Pargal, S. (2016) 'Mata Vaishno Devi ji yatra picks up after two-year slump', *Daily Excelsior*, 2 June. Available at: www.dailyexcelsior.com/mata-vaishno-devi-ji-yatra-picks-two-year-slump (accessed 10 June 2016).

Preston, J.J. (1992) 'Spiritual magnetism: an organizing principle for the study of pilgrimage', in A. Morinis (ed.), *Sacred Journeys: The Anthropology of Pilgrimage*, Westport, CT: Greenwood, pp. 31–46.

Ramsay, J. and Truscott, M.C. (2002) 'Tracking through Australian forests', *Historic Environment*, 16(2): 32–37.

Rinschede, G. (1992) 'Forms of religious tourism', *Annals of Tourism Research*, 19(1): 51–67.

Samarasekara, G.N., Fukahori, K. and Kubota, Y. (2011) 'Environmental correlates that provide walkability cues for tourists: an analysis based on walking decision narrations', *Environment and Behavior*, 43(4): 501–524.

Singh, R.P.B. (2006) 'Pilgrimage in Hinduism: historical context and modern perspectives', in D. Timothy and D. Olsen (eds), *Tourism, Religion, and Spiritual Journeys*, London: Routledge, pp. 220–236.

Singh, S. (2004) 'Religion, heritage and travel: case references from the Indian Himalayas', *Current Issues in Tourism*, 7(1): 44–65.

Smith, V. (1992) 'Introduction. The quest in guest', *Annals of Tourism Research*, 19(1): 1–17.

SMVDSB (n.d.) Shri Mata Vaishno Devi Shrine Board website. Available at: www.maavaishnodevi.org (accessed 6 June 2016).

Southworth, M. (2005) 'Designing the walkable city', *Journal of Urban Planning and Development*, 131(4): 246–257.

Southworth, M. and Ben-Joseph, E. (2013) *Streets and the Shaping of Towns and Cities*, Washington, DC: Island Press.

Stausberg, M. (2011) *Religion and Tourism: Crossroads, Destinations, and Encounters*, London: Routledge.

Timothy, D.J. (1994) 'Environmental impacts of heritage tourism: physical and socio-cultural perspectives', *Manusia dan Lingkungan*, 2(4): 37–39.

Timothy, D.J. (1999) 'Built heritage, tourism and conservation in developing countries: challenges and opportunities', *Journal of Tourism*, 4: 5–17.

Timothy, D.J. and Olsen, D. (eds) (2006) *Tourism, Religion and Spiritual Journeys*, London: Routledge.

Timothy, D.J. and Boyd, S.W. (2014) *Tourism and Trails: Cultural, Ecological and Management Issues*, Bristol: Channel View Publications.

Trono, A. (2015) 'Politics, policy and the practice of religious tourism', in R. Raj and K. Griffin (eds), *Religious Tourism and Pilgrimage Management: An International Perspective,* 2nd edn, Wallingford, Oxon: CABI, pp. 16–36.

Turner, V. (1969) *The Ritual Process: Structure and Anti-structure,* Chicago: Aldine Publishers.

Turner, V. and Turner, E. (1978) *Image and Pilgrimage in Christian Culture,* New York: Columbia University Press.

Ujang, N. and Muslim, Z. (2014) 'Walkability and attachment to tourism places in the city of Kuala Lumpur, Malaysia', *Athens Journal of Tourism,* 2(1): 53–65.

Wilson, C. (1996) *The Atlas of Holy Places & Sacred Sites,* London: Dorling Kindersley.

Part IV

Health, Well-being and Psychology

25

Rambling on

Exploring the complexity of walking as a meaningful activity

Kirsty Finnie, Tania Wiseman and Neil Ravenscroft

Introduction

Walking is the most popular leisure activity in the UK and is considered to be appropriate exercise for maintaining physical health, for both men and women, of all ages (Kay and Moxham 1996; Morris and Hardman 1997; Fox and Rickards 2004; Curry *et al.* 2012). It is a fundamental part of human development (Solnit 2006), and is also felt, by participants, to be highly therapeutic (Robertson and Babic 2009), providing a range of physiological and psychological health benefits (Department of Health 2009; Roe and Aspinall 2011). These benefits are particularly important as people enter older age and their range of leisure pursuits declines (Freysinger and Ray 1994), yet, as a population we tend to walk less than we used to (Department of Health 2009), many healthy walking initiatives have failed (Curry *et al.* 2012), and more than half of the adults in England are not meeting the minimum recommendations for physical activity (HSCIC 2012). This is particularly the case for men, whose relative lack of engagement with walking is likely to be influenced by activity patterns and identities that are formed early in their lives and remain stable across their lives (Liechty and Genoe 2013).

Given the undoubted benefits of walking to men, we want in this chapter to examine the meanings of walking as a way of shifting debates away from instrumental associations with physical health towards a more rounded view of meaning that may resonate more strongly with many men's established leisure activities and identities. The literature that explores walking is diverse, including many disciplines, and focuses on the benefits. What follows is a review of leisure-focused walking literature, in order to explore meanings, rather than outcomes.

The benefits of walking

While the benefits of walking and hiking in extreme environments, such as wilderness, are well established (Russell and Phillips-Miller 2002; Caulkins *et al.* 2006), the multiple benefits of recreational walking are still being articulated. In their paper on walking as a remedy for modernity, for example, Robertson and Babic (2009) found that walkers in a park near Zagreb identified many of the same attributes of walking that are found in more extreme environments, including feeling fitter and more resourceful, experiencing a connection with nature and the outdoors; and enjoying the company of others. This is consistent with the work by Markwell *et al.* (2004), who found that walking through historic areas can raise walkers' awareness of the surroundings. Similarly, in a study of organised outdoor physical activity conducted by Allen-Collinson and Leledaki (2014), both visual and haptic sensory engagement were felt to contribute to participants' self-awareness, which offered heightened feelings of being alive. Other studies, by Hynds and Allibone (2009) and Wensley and Slade (2012), have found that recreational walking is associated with social connectedness, connections to nature and to a sense of well-being.

Much of the research on walking focuses on the health benefits of organised walking groups (Hynds and Allibone 2009; Curry *et al.* 2012; Wensley and Slade 2012). These studies demonstrate that social connection is an important aspect of participating in group walking and, possibly as a result, tend to focus on women, who tend to be more highly represented in such groups (Hynds and Allibone 2009). However, as Curry *et al.* (2012) argued, the broader benefits of such groups must be cast in doubt, given that few of them survive in the long term. Rather, as Wylie (2005) observed, walking is not centrally experienced as a means of achieving physical health gains, but is more about the psychological benefits of aligning self, others and nature.

This raises the question of whether the benefits of activities such as walking are experienced universally, or according to social and cultural divisions such as age and sex. As Liechty and Genoe (2013) noted, while there have been studies that have observed different patterns of leisure behaviours between men and women (e.g. see Freysinger and Ray 1994) – and between men and women at different life stages – there have been few attempts to study the experiences and perspectives of men (for exceptions, see Scraton and Holland 2006; Wiersma and Chesser 2011). Yet, as Nimrod and Janke (2012) have argued, there is considerably complexity in men's leisure lives, particularly as these are bound up with their traditional work identities, and are exacerbated as they move from paid work into retirement.

Leisure activity is generally associated with improved life expectancy in older adults (Agahi *et al.* 2011). However, as Nimrod and Janke (2012) suggest, this masks variations between men and women, in terms of what they do, how they perceive themselves and, consequently, what benefits they gain. A quantitative study of older adults in Sweden found, for example, that men participated later in life in solitary pursuits such as cultural activities, gardening and reading books, while older women tended to be more involved in group activities. In both cases, there is continuity with their earlier phases of life, with men, in particular, seeking to continue to use their work experiences through deployment of the skills that they have learned in new leisure activities (Liechty and Genoe 2013). Because of this emphasis, there is growing concern that men do not benefit from simple physical activities such as walking to the extent that women do, which can impact negatively on men's health and well-being, especially in later life.

A research project was undertaken to explore the leisure experience of walking for men. In recent years, there has been an increased interest in the phenomenological analysis of embodied leisure experience (Allen-Collinson and Leledaki 2014). Walking as a meaningful activity is a topic that has the potential for research bias at every point, in order to remove the bias of the data being generated for a health researcher, by health research participants, alternatives to traditional interviews were explored, including web-based and broadcast materials. A rich source of data was discovered in a series of BBC podcast interviews about rambling (BBC 2011).

Method

A qualitative study using a phenomenological approach to analyse semi-structured interviews was designed. This design allowed the exploration of the participants' experiences of walking as a meaningful activity. Phenomenology has been described as a two-step process: the participant provides a natural description of specific experience or situations; and the researcher seeks to explain the experience (Finlay and Ballinger 2006; Finlay 2014). An existential phenomenological perspective values the importance of the physical body in human experience (Merleau-Ponty 2001). This is the perspective held in this research.

Participants

A BBC radio podcast series about rambling in the UK was explored in order to find personal accounts of the experience of walking for leisure for men (BBC 2011). Ethical approval was granted through the research ethics process of the authors' host institution. Consent was obtained from the producer of the radio programme. Although the data was public in nature, confidentiality was maintained and pseudonyms were used to ensure anonymity in this work.

The sample consisted of eight men aged between 39 and 60 years old, speaking in interviews aired between 2011 and 2013. Due to the nature of this data, it is not possible to establish health status, ethnicity or other identifying characteristics of the participants. This purposive sampling strategy focused on men's experience of walking for leisure. Using eight participants is appropriate to gain a rich description of the meaning of walking outdoors to men (Morse 2000).

Selection procedure

The series of podcasts was selected due to the rich content: 55 interviews were screened for inclusion. The first author selected 18 interviews that indicated discussion of leisure walking, and these were listened to in full, in order to gain context, broaden the researchers' understandings, and choose those that focused on men's experience of walking for leisure. Podcasts with the same professional broadcast interviewer were chosen to ensure consistency of interview technique. A final six podcasts were selected, four with individual men, and two with two men who did not know each other. Interviews took place in rural settings, chosen by the participants, the setting eliciting rich discussion. Each interview lasted 25 to 30 minutes. The interviews were downloaded and transcribed verbatim.

Data analysis

Interview information was transcribed fully, ensuring there was a clear distinction between the opinions and questions of the interviewer and the interviewee. These transcripts were then thematically analysed, following the method outlined by Braun and Clarke (2006). Each transcript was read and reread to highlight major themes before the data were considered as a whole. Initial analytical comments were included on the left of the transcripts, while emerging themes were included in a column to the right (Braun and Clarke 2006). Finally, the data set as a whole was analysed and a table of key findings and supporting quotes from the text was produced.

In order to increase the rigour of the analysis, the first author analysed the data, and the second author reviewed the data, themes and subthemes to ensure that the themes represented the data, using a process of facilitated critical reflection (Finlay 2014). A reflective journal focusing on the first author's position as a committed leisure walker was maintained throughout the research by the first author, enabling researcher preconceptions on the meaning of walking for leisure to be acknowledged and developed using reflexivity in order to become aware of personal meanings that might influence the data analysis (Finlay 2014). This journal was shared with the second author in order to facilitate critical reflection on the generation of themes. This was used to ensure that the data analysis was rigorous, and congruent with the participant's experience of walking, rather than the first author's and therefore reducing researcher bias and increasing dependability of the findings (Finlay 2014).

Findings

Three main themes emerged, each with three subthemes (see Table 25.1). Example quotes from the transcripts are illustrated in the text, using pseudonyms to identify participants.

Appreciation of surroundings

One of the main motivations found was to take the time to notice the setting. Participants made a point of commenting on their surroundings over the course of the walk, which was often linked and intertwined with the past, the place and nature.

Connection to past

Throughout the transcripts, participants commented on how the space in which they were walking had historically been used or changed. They alluded to the present being physically linked to the past by paths which had been created and maintained to access the landscape (Rory) and appreciated that the past has shaped and influenced the experience of the walk in the present (Nigel).

> We're on a local road but we're going to pick up a little field path and the field path will lead us to a Roman road and the Roman road will lead us to the Icknield Way and then that is this immense thoroughfare that joins up with the Ridgeway and all the other famous old track ways.
>
> *(Rory)*

Table 25.1 Key themes

Key themes
Appreciation of surroundings
Connection to past
Connection to place
Connection to nature
Awareness of self
Present self
Past self
Well-being
• Emotional
• Freedom
• Physical
Opportunities
Viewing the world differently
Inspiration
Exploration and discovery

It's the depth, the knowledge that millions of people's feet have walked these islands before us. And they've left traces in various ways. And it's being able to pick up on that . . . All that we're experiencing and what people have done with it.

(Nigel)

Connection to place

Participants discussed how the place can evoke strong emotions and provide motivation to walk (Rory). The location of the walk was often described as holding personal significance for many of the participants.

I'm more interested in the places through which I pass and the people I meet. And, this ongoing puzzle of how landscape shapes us and fascinates us and drives us to risk our lives in the mountains or spend years of our life walking if we're a long term pilgrim or walker.

(Rory)

Connection to nature

Aspects of nature were considered by participants over the course of their interview, attributing specific meaning to the amount of life that exists beyond themselves on the walk (Garry). A number of particpants expressed a sense that walking outdoors in the natural envrionment offered an opportunity to connect to the earth and therefore with life (Mark).

We're coming in amongst the trees; already we're feeling less of the wind and coming into this special quiet space. Which, if you look hard enough you see is teeming with life.

(Garry)

Be connected with the earth. If you're connected with the earth you're connected with life. If you're connected with the earth you're connected with your body. If you're connected with the earth you will become very sensitive and centred. And that's what's needed.

(Mark)

Awareness of self

Participants expressed their sense of self in terms of their present selves, how the walk inspires reminiscence of past self and in terms of the overall well-being experienced while walking.

Present self

From the data, there was a sense that walking offered an opportunity to be mindful and this may be a contributing factor to your physical and psychological health (Jack). Being in the present often evoked strong emotional responses from the participants (Garry).

When you're walking and you're walking within yourself that's the time when I feel at my best.

(Jack)

257

> When I stumbled across this particular tree. And then found that this gorge is actually full of them . . . I feel a sense of rootedness. I feel comfortable here in a way that I didn't out on the bare exposed hills. And it's a sense of being surrounded by this rich warm ecosystem.
>
> *(Garry)*

Past self

Due to the personal nature of the landscape, a number of participants disclosed a strong sense of how walking in that place reminded them of their past (Adrian). This also often inspired participants to reflect on previous walks in the area and, in the case of Garry, how it made him feel primal to engage in the natural environment to the extent that it made him feel "at home".

> I feel right now at this second that I'm standing in a kind of blizzard of visible things coming at me from the past. I see my mother and I see my brother I see the weather in a particular day I see what this little place used to look like.
>
> *(Adrian)*

> I was trying to spear flounders in the local estuary here . . . I was really tuned in and suddenly this other very weird thing happened, I was possessed . . . by this absolute conviction that I had done it before, not just once but a thousand times till I was walking through this with the familiarity with which I might be walking home and again I realised I was tapping into that deeply buried set of vestigial emotions.
>
> *(Garry)*

Well-being

Participants were all aware of their well-being, which was related to experiences of spirituality, liberation, awareness of self and surroundings.

> It's a bit of a drug to me as well as like my gym. And I think also it's a little bit of a church to me as well in the sense that I don't get much spirituality unless I'm, unless I'm out here.
>
> *(Jack)*

Walking generated positive feelings among the participants, who often commented on how much they enjoyed the experience. Walking was a way to counteract the stresses and strains of life (Richard) and to work through problems. Participants described feelings of freedom from walking outdoors and being free from life's constraints; often alluding to savouring the illusion of isolation and independence felt when walking (Bob). A number of participants also discussed the need to keep moving all the time and linked walking with physical health (Adrian).

> You know so much of life involves a need to be somewhere at a certain time or the stress of responsibility and . . . when you walk you don't have any of that you have no guilt, no responsibility you have no stress. But you have maybe a goal which is . . . and a time to do it in which is enough reason for the day really.
>
> *(Richard)*

[W]e should stick to our own two feet. Because it allowed us to strike out on the road amongst mountains and moors. In a manner completely independent.

(Bob)

I do try and make a point of walking as much as I can around town as I possibly can. Partly to stop myself getting too fat but also because you look at things in a way you don't look at them when you're sitting on the bus. You just slow yourself down a bit.

(Adrian)

Opportunities

Participants demonstrated that walking provides opportunities to view the world differently, gaining inspiration from the surroundings and from the rhythm of walking, as well as discovering and exploring new things.

Viewing the world differently

Some participants reflected on accessing the landscape (Rory), and the physical perspective gained when walking (Bob).

The footpath network is the key to this . . . it's the way in. It's a way of walking into a landscape as well as across it and it . . . is a kind of territorial miracle really and it allows you to pick your way across what would otherwise be private land and find your way into nooks and crannies.

(Rory)

We are really high. We're very isolated . . . it takes your breath away. A place like this, a view like this and a day like this.

(Bob)

Inspiration

A number of the participants identified how the rhythmic nature of walking influenced their work (Adrian).

The actual physical business of moving yourself about getting your blood stream going, feeling a certain rhythm establish itself in your body which then in a mysterious way transmits itself into the poems if that's what you're writing. I mean I think that's really fundamental.

(Adrian)

Exploration and discovery

A motivator for a number of participants was the unknown aspect of walking, the opportunity to explore and discover new things (Richard).

It's a fantastic way to see things in the countryside but you're never quite sure what you're going to see, it's always a surprise you know.

(Richard)

259

Discussion

This study illustrates the multifaceted and complex nature of walking as leisure, demonstrated by the three main themes and nine subthemes emerging from the data. Participants discussed similar and different aspects of walking, providing a deeper understanding of the rich complexities of engaging in this activity and the perceived resulting positive benefits (Reed 2011). It is certainly clear from the findings that the benefits of walking go well beyond achieving the recommended weekly activity intake. Indeed, the physical benefits of the activity were routinely lost within a deeper connection with the landscape, nature and a keen sense of the past. This study thus illustrates that there are a number of different meanings for men of walking for leisure, challenging ideas of walking as simply physical exercise and men's leisure as essentially instrumental. Walking, for these participants, provided a platform to connect with themselves and the natural environment, both in the present and the past, and to reap the benefits of these connections.

While tending to support previous studies that suggest that the benefit depends on the individual's experience of walking (Reed 2011) and the environment in which this leisure occupation occurred (Wensley and Slade 2012), these findings offer new insights into the potential value of walking for men. Chief among these insights is that – unlike many of their other activities – walking can introduce sociability into men's lives, as well as giving them an apparently safe space in which to experience themselves. Contrary to current literature, which places significance on walking in a group and values social connectedness (Wensley and Slade 2012; Hynds and Allibone 2009), this study demonstrates the importance of surroundings. This was important to the participants' experiences of meaningfulness; supporting the findings of Hammell's (2004) earlier work on connecting past and present. The surroundings offered participants a sense of homecoming, belonging and familiarity, and were related to the physical environment in terms of history, landscape and nature. Participants disclosed feelings of the past influencing their experience in the present and how in the present there is an opportunity to be a part of history.

Participants described a connection to specific places, which suggests that the landscape provides cultural importance to the individual. This supports the unique value of personal experience and the finding that people access different landscapes for different reasons to meet specific needs. Beyond this, local places matter to people, as they are part of their history or heritage and therefore contribute to the experience of walking as a meaningful activity. The participants considered nature over the course of their walk. The natural environment allowed participants to live in the moment and feel a part of something greater than themselves. Connecting to nature made participants feel alive, which supports the value of outdoors and the natural environment, providing emotional and cognitive restorative benefits to psychological well-being (Roe and Aspinall 2011).

An awareness of self was a strong theme emerging from the participants' experiences of walking. The participants reflected on aspects of themselves as part of their walking experience and these emerged in three subthemes of present, past and well-being. Participants disclosed experiences of being grounded, as well as reminiscing about their past, positive emotional well-being, freedom and physical well-being. Aspects of personal past recurred throughout the interviews, which may indicate that the value and meaning of walking for leisure was created in the formative years of these participants. This supports the work by Lougher and Creek (2008) and Freysinger and Ray (1994), who showed that that activities performed while growing up are carried through men's lives and inform habits and routines that tend to enforce social and gender roles.

Contrary to common discourse about walking, social aspects (Hynds and Allibone 2009) did not appear to be a key element for participants in this study. Masculinity also did not emerge as a main finding within awareness of self, which may be incongruent with the social construction of men portrayed in leisure studies (Connell 2005). This may be due to the type of walking or rambling that the men were discussing, as it could be argued that this level of activity lacks many of the more 'masculine' characteristics, such as competition or stamina. The physical aspects of well-being were not commonly highlighted as a main part of engaging in walking outdoors. Similarly, negative aspects of walking alone, such as vulnerability (Foster *et al.* 2004), were also not raised, which may suggest why the physical benefits of walking were not at the forefront of the discourse; participants may not have considered walking primarily as a form of exercise.

Walking provided a platform to engage in other activities. Participants were able to view the world differently, gain inspiration to feed their creativity and explore and discover new things. This theme is congruent with doing, which values exploring new opportunities as a way of experiencing meaningful occupations (Hammell 2004). A main factor of this theme was being able to experience life without stress, guilt or responsibility, which is congruent with previous research (Wensley and Slade 2012). Walking and the surroundings offered an opportunity to be inspired, building on recent research that suggests that the act of walking itself can improve creativity, separate from the surroundings in which it takes place (Oppezzo and Schwartz 2014). Walking also elicited a sense of adventure, which appeared to motivate many of the participants to engage in it, because they valued the unpredictability of the experience.

Ultimately this study highlights, for men, the complexity of meanings and experiences that can be associated with walking for leisure. Rather than concentrate on the physical benefits that can accrue from such exercise, or the extent to which they can deploy skills learned in other parts of their lives, the participants in this study identified a range of meanings and emotions not conventionally associated with men's leisure.

Conclusions

At the start of this chapter, we commented on the decline in walking being experienced in the UK, and the negative impacts that this may have on people's health. We noted that this is particularly the case for men, who tend not to engage in this type of activity, either alone or in groups, to the extent that women do. While this may be the case, our study demonstrates that men have much to gain from walking, whether alone or in groups. Indeed, the findings indicate that men gain manifold benefits from walking – benefits that they may not routinely get from their other leisure activities. It is clear that this knowledge should be utilised when considering appropriate leisure interventions to encourage men to engage in more physical activity. The complexities and unique aspect of the participants' experience highlights the benefit of meaningful occupation and the need to remain focused on the individual person in context. The work thus offers a contribution to the understanding of the meaning of walking for leisure in a rural setting, and offers an insight into why men walk and may therefore be used to inform practice and health promotion to encourage those who do not.

Strengths and limitations

The unique source of interviews ensured that there was no health bias on data collection. However, there may be researcher bias on interpretation as bracketing personal experiences is thought to be difficult to implement and is therefore acknowledged as a limitation to this methodology (Creswell 2013). While the interviewer was experienced and well prepared, the nature of the questions may have put pressure on the participants to come up with something 'interesting' to say. The participants were also discussing rural areas, which may not be so relevant to walking experienced in urban settings.

K. Finnie, T. Wiseman and N. Ravenscroft

Recommendations and implications

The participants in this study walked with an interviewer and a producer, therefore an alternative strategy to gain information solely about the experience of walking may entail walkers self-recording their responses to a number of exploratory questions. Similarly, investigating the experience of walking in urban areas could be studied, as this may negate the benefits received from the natural environment and reveal other aspects of the walking experience which may be beneficial. Group walking could also be revisited to explore the meaning of walking for the men that do participate in walking-for-health groups, and therefore gain an understanding of the motivations of men in both cases.

Physical health was not a priority when discussing the meaning of walking for these participants. Therefore the occupational benefits discussed, such as the role of outdoors, stress relief and liberation from daily routine, may offer important findings for health promotion policy in encouraging walking as an enjoyable leisure activity. By encouraging alternatives to walking for health groups, such as geocaching or history walks, it may be possible to provide an opportunity to engage with the surroundings while remaining physically active.

References

Agahi, N., Silverstein, M. and Parker, M.G. (2011) 'Late-life and earlier participation in leisure activities: their importance for survival among older persons', *Activities, Adaptation & Aging*, 35(3): 210–222.

Allen-Collinson, J. and Leledaki, A. (2014) 'Sensing the outdoors: a visual and haptic phenomenology of outdoor exercise embodiment', *Leisure Studies*, 33(1): 1–14.

BBC (2011) *Ramblings*, Radio 4, September/October. Available at: www.bbc.co.uk/programmes/b006xrr2/broadcasts/2011/09; www.bbc.co.uk/programmes/b006xrr2/broadcasts/2011/10

Braun, V. and Clarke, V. (2006) 'Using thematic analysis in psychology', *Qualitative Research in Psychology*, 3(2): 77–101.

Caulkins, M.C., White, D.D. and Russell, K.C. (2006) 'The role of physical exercise in wilderness therapy for troubled adolescent women', *Journal of Experiential Education*, 29(1): 18–37.

Connell, R.W. (2005) 'Hegemonic masculinity: rethinking the concept', *Gender & Society*, 19(6): 829–859.

Creswell, J.W. (2013) *Qualitative Inquiry & Research Design: Choosing Among Five Approaches*, 3rd edn, Thousand Oaks, CA: Sage Publications.

Curry, N.R., Crone, D., James, D. and Gidlow, C. (2012) 'Factors influencing participation in outdoor physical activity promotion schemes: the case of South Staffordshire, England', *Leisure Studies*, 31(4): 447–463.

Department of Health (2009) *Be Active, Be Healthy: A Plan for Getting the Nation Moving*, London: Department of Health.

Finlay, L. (2014) 'Engaging phenomenological analysis', *Qualitative Research*, 11: 121–141.

Finlay, L. and Ballinger, C. (2006) *Qualitative Research for Allied Health Professionals*, Hoboken, NJ: John Wiley & Sons.

Foster, C., Hillsdon, M. and Thorogood, M. (2004) 'Environmental perceptions and walking in English adults', *Journal of Epidemiology and Community Health*, 58(11): 924–928.

Fox, K. and Rickards, L. (2004) *Sport and Leisure: Results from the Sport and Leisure Module of the 2002 General Household Survey*, London: The Stationery Office.

Freysinger, V.J. and Ray, R.O. (1994) 'The activity involvement of women and men in young and middle adulthood: a panel study', *Leisure Sciences*, 16(3): 193–217.

Hammell, K.W. (2004) 'Dimensions of meaning in the occupations of daily life', *The Canadian Journal of Occupational Therapy*, 71(5): 296–305.

HSCIC (2012) *Is the Adult Population in England Active Enough? Initial Results*, Leeds: Health and Social Care Information Centre.

Hynds, H. and Allibone, C. (2009) *What Motivates People to Participate in Organised Walking Activity?*, Sheffield: Natural England.

Kay, G. and Moxham, N. (1996) 'Paths for whom? Countryside access for recreational walking', *Leisure Studies*, 15(3): 171–183.

Liechty, T. and Genoe, M.R. (2013) 'Older men's perceptions of leisure and aging', *Leisure Sciences*, 35(5): 438–454.

Lougher, L. and Creek, J. (2008) *Occupational Therapy and Mental Health,* 4th edn, Edinburgh: Churchill Livingstone Elsevier.

Markwell, K., Stevenson, D. and Rowe, D. (2004) 'Footsteps and memories: interpreting an Australian urban landscape through thematic walking tours', *International Journal of Heritage Studies,* 10 (5): 457–473.

Merleau-Ponty, M. (2001) *Phenomenology of Perception,* trans. C. Smith, London: Routledge & Kegan Paul.

Morris, J. and Hardman, A. (1997) 'Walking to health', *Sports Medicine,* 23(5): 306–332.

Morse, J.M. (2000) 'Determining sample size', *Qualitative Health Research,* 10(1): 3–5.

Nimrod, G. and Janke, M.C. (2012) 'Leisure across the later life span', in H. Gibson and J. Singleton (eds), *Leisure and Aging: Theory and Practice,* Champaign, IL: Human Kinetics, pp. 95–106.

Oppezzo, M. and Schwartz, D.L. (2014) 'Give your ideas some legs: the positive effect of walking on creative thinking', *Journal of Experimental Psychology. Learning, Memory, and Cognition,* 40(4): 1142–1152.

Reed, K. (2011) 'Exploring the meaning of occupation: the case for phenomenology', *Canadian Journal of Occupational Therapy,* 78(5): 303–310.

Robertson, D.N. Jr. and Babic, V. (2009) 'Remedy for modernity: experiences of walkers and hikers on Medvednica Mountain', *Leisure Studies,* 28(1): 105–112.

Roe, J. and Aspinall, P. (2011) 'The restorative benefits of walking in urban and rural settings in adults with good and poor mental health', *Health & Place,* 17(1): 103–113.

Russell, K. and Phillips-Miller, D. (2002) 'Perspectives on the wilderness therapy process and its relation to outcome', *Child and Youth Care Forum,* 31(6): 415–437.

Scraton, S. and Holland, S. (2006) 'Grandfatherhood and leisure', *Leisure Sciences,* 25(2): 233–250.

Solnit, R. (2006) *Wanderlust: A History of Walking,* London: Verso Books.

Wensley, R. and Slade, A. (2012) 'Walking as a meaningful leisure occupation: the implications for occupational therapy', *British Journal of Occupational Therapy,* 75(2): 85–92.

Wiersma, E. and Chesser, S. (2011) 'Masculinity, aging bodies, and leisure', *Annals of Leisure Research,* 14(2–3): 242–259.

Wylie, J. (2005) 'A single day's walking: narrative self and landscape on the South West Coast path', *Transactions of the Institute of British Geographers,* 30(2): 234–247.

26

Life-changing walks of mid-life adults

Robert Saunders, Betty Weiler and Jennifer Laing

Introduction

> Travel offers you more opportunities to change your life than almost any other human endeavor.
>
> (Kottler 1997: xi)

> I like walking because it is slow, and I suspect that the mind, like the feet, works at about three miles an hour. If this is so, then modern life is moving faster than the speed of thought, or thoughtfulness.
>
> (Solnit 2000: 10)

Much of the empirical research into personal change through tourism deals with formative effects on young adults, where travel often functions as a rite of passage. These kinds of travel experience have a long history, which, in many ways, reflects the evolution of tourism itself (Adler 1985). Contemporary expressions of travel as a rite of passage include backpacking (e.g. Cohen 2003; Noy 2004), volunteer tourism (e.g. Broad 2003; Matthews 2008), the international student sojourn (e.g. Brown 2009; Milstein 2005) and the 'gap year' (Hall 2007). Such travel is often seen as 'an experience' (Dilthey 1976), as something personally significant in life, and can be linked by participants to developing ideas of the self (Wearing 2002). But beyond the youth to adulthood transition, little research appears to have been undertaken into whether, and how, particular kinds of travel experience generate enduring effects on individuals.

Long-distance walking (LDW) is an increasingly popular and diverse activity, known to attract participants from a wide range of age groups, including mid-life adults. As Solnit (2000) implies above, walking can reduce the perceived pace of life and create opportunities for contemplation and reflection. Reflection is identified by Lean (2009: 18) as 'a key to transformation'. Long-distance walking thus offers a valuable perspective for examining transformative travel.

This chapter outlines the results of a qualitative study of mid-life adults who reported personally significant experiences on long-distance walks. In-depth interviews were used to identify those who portrayed enduring changes in aspects of their lives related to these experiences. The perceived nature and extent of these effects were then explored, along with associated lived experiences and life contexts. Long-distance walking was used as a relatively contained field within which to collect individual stories of personal change. This is consistent with Lean's (2009: 203) suggestion that 'future research [into transformative tourism] . . . needs to be conducted on a smaller scale with a fixed scope, so as to reduce complexity'.

Synopsis of relevant literature

Outcomes and benefits of long-distance walking

Kay and Moxham (1996: 176) characterize walking as 'not so much an end in itself but rather a means to complex ends, to comprehensive experiences'. Walking is of interest in this study as a vehicle for a range of experiences with the potential to alter participants' views of themselves or the world. Extended walking is associated with increased sensory awareness, contemplation and reflection (Edensor 2000; Solnit 2000). In turn, contemplation and reflection have been linked to the construction and recognition of meaning (Kottler 1997), with transformative learning (Mezirow 1991), and with travel-related transformative change (Lean 2009).

An enhanced sense of well-being through walking pilgrimage is reported by Devereux and Carnegie (2006), but a lack of longitudinal data in their study means that the longevity of these effects is unknown. Increased enjoyment, positive emotions and reduced stress have also been reported during and immediately after long-distance walks undertaken without spiritual intent (Crust et al. 2011; den Breejen 2007). These may be short-term biochemical effects, however, because endurance activities such as LDW are known to produce exercise induced analgesia or 'runner's high' (Boecker et al. 2008).

A longitudinal study involving long-distance walking investigated 15 upper-year university students who had trekked the Inca Trail in Peru (Quinlan Cutler et al. 2014). Interviews carried out several months after that trek revealed that more than one-third of participants saw the experience as 'a marker of self-change' (Quinlan Cutler et al. 2014: 160). However, a year later, 'none of the participants specifically credit the Inca Trail or Machu Picchu experience as a catalyst for self change' (Quinlan Cutler et al. 2014: 161).

Another study which touches on aspects of personal change through LDW is Mueser's (1998) survey of people who walked the entire 3,500-km Appalachian Trail in the eastern United States. Mueser (1998) noted that for 18 of the 136 hikers in his sample, the experience of 'closeness with nature, the mountains, the earth and . . . fellow hikers . . . led to a job change to work in ecology and the environment' (Mueser 1998: 152). Other tangible changes recorded include joining conservation organizations and devoting voluntary time to environmental causes. These results seem tantalizing rather than definitive, but endorse the potential of LDW as a vehicle for further research.

Life-changing experiences through travel

Despite widespread popular belief in travel's potential to stimulate personal change, the nature, extent and longevity of its effects on individual tourists are disputed in the literature. Regarding visits to Third World countries, Bruner (1991: 242) contends that 'the tourist self is changed very little by the tour, while the consequences of tourism for the native self are profound.' Nash (1996: 50–51) is also sceptical about the capacity of popular forms of tourism to dramatically alter participants' lives, arguing that 'too many tours are too short, too superficial and have qualities too much like home to result in enduring personal transformations'. In contrast, Lean (2009: 21) identifies a 'wide variety of transformations' in his web-based pilot study, while confirming that 'the more removed a particular experience is from those with which the traveller is familiar . . . the greater the probability of transformation.'

Psychological processes of transformative change are also recognized as under-researched (Heatherton 2011) and, as a result, any antecedent or mediating factors are largely unknown. Encouragingly, the psychology literature provides some analysis of lasting personal change associated with focal events (e.g. Heatherton and Nichols 1994). The identification of key characteristics of epiphanic experiences has illuminated this field (McDonald 2008), although it remains unclear whether many subjects perceive that 'everything changed' (Miller and C'de Baca 1994: 271). In broader terms, it is unknown whether transformative change can be considered a single distinct phenomenon or a cluster of phenomena with related outcomes.

Change is of course a normal part of human life. Kottler (1997) refers to three types of change: developmental, situational and discontinuous change. He suggests that any of these can become problematic in adults, including transitions associated with parenting or retirement, the ups and downs of relationships, job redundancy or relocation, or the sudden shock of a health scare, accident or natural disaster. The current study has been framed to explore positive personal change perceived or portrayed as related to LDW, and to be sensitive to the life context of participants.

Methods

A purposeful sampling strategy recruited adults aged 30 to 65 years who reported a 'personally significant experience' on a walk of at least three nights' duration. Collectively the walks involved a variety of nature-based and cultural settings, different degrees of self-reliance, and lengths up to 1,000 km. The constant comparative method (Boeiji 2002) was used to determine the number of subjects, overlapping data collection and analysis to identify when additional interviews became redundant.

During in-depth semi-structured interviews with the 25 participants, 17 portrayed *enduring* personal changes related to LDWs, and became subjects for more detailed, longitudinal study. Blogs, diaries and other sources provided observations from the time of the walks, and follow-up interviews over one to three years provided insights into the nature and longevity of reported changes and processes of personal change. Interpretive Phenomenological Analysis (IPA) was used because of the study's focus on meaning-making around experiences participants found significant (Smith *et al.* 2009). Interviewees were assigned pseudonyms which are used here to preserve anonymity.

Life domains were used to map the nature and extent of personal change portrayed in participant accounts. Life domains are definable areas of human experience (Rojas 2004) widely used in life satisfaction research and other areas of social science. Ten categories were framed, using terms which could readily be interpreted from the accounts of subjects: working activity, personal relationships, family life, social world, lifestyle, physical health, mental health, leisure, spirituality, and self-perception (Saunders 2014).

A spectrum of significant personal change

A range of deep and lasting effects was evident in the 17 subjects, and ramifications of LDW experiences were perceived in diverse aspects of their lives. Five of these 17 subjects portrayed *extensive* changes, with enduring outcomes portrayed in a majority of life domains. Two examples are presented here.

Susan is a teacher who had suffered clinical depression for almost a decade. Overworked, overweight and unfit, she used medication every day to manage her symptoms. After her husband

Stan retired, Susan took extended leave so they could walk the 1,000-km Bibbulmun Track in Western Australia together over eight weeks. Susan described waking up one morning during the walk, knowing that she had to leave her job:

> I didn't actually need to sort of wrestle with that at all – it just seemed to come to me in not thinking about it for several weeks. It just came to me that that was how it should be.

After the walk, while still on leave, Susan undertook voluntary work at an alternative school before moving to a paid position that she found fulfilling. She also took up daily walking and monitoring of a section of track near her home as a volunteer warden. Susan described enduring positive changes in her mental health, physical health, working activity, personal relationships, leisure, lifestyle and self-perception.

Major changes also occurred in Dianne's life following a two-week guided walk along the 230-km Larapinta Trail in Central Australia. On that walk, she met and began a romantic relationship with David. Meeting David confirmed long-distance walking as a central life interest for Dianne:

> Larapinta was a turning point. It was just so stunning. I thought 'I want more of that. I have to see more' . . . It's always been in the back of my mind – that is what I want to do . . . We're planning a lot of trips. And that's almost consuming our entire life.

At the time of her Larapinta walk, Dianne was in her early forties and lived alone. She later resigned from her job and travelled overseas with David before living with him interstate. Dianne links her Larapinta walk with changes affecting her personal relationships, working activity, family life, social activity, lifestyle, leisure patterns and self-perception.

The depth, extent and longevity of these changes are consistent with effects described elsewhere as transformative (e.g. Miller and C'de Baca 1994). However, subjects of this study generally recognized the stability of some aspects of their lives while embracing change elsewhere. To avoid any implication that suddenly "everything changed", the authors propose a new conceptual framework in this field, which we call *Significant Personal Change* (SPC). While SPC is profound and enduring, it overtly involves differing extents of change (e.g. the number of life domains affected) and variations in character (e.g. different life domains in which change is expressed).

The concept of SPC can also be applied to the *less extensive* effects seen in the other 12 of the 17 subjects, who reported enduring change in a minority of life domains. As with the five extensively affected subjects, these 12 reported they had "changed as a person". We propose that change in the domain of self-perception is a defining characteristic of SPC, and that tangible changes are also expressed in other life domains.

The remaining eight of the 25 original interviewees did not report changes in self-perception and did not perceive or portray enduring changes in any of their other life domains. Some mentioned short-term positive effects, particularly around mental health, physical health and leisure. However, these effects lasted only for a few weeks.

Modes and processes of SPC

Thematic analysis and a consideration of antecedent conditions and change processes portrayed by the 17 subjects suggest that SPC is not a single phenomenon. Three distinctive modes of SPC were discerned in this study. We refer to these as *therapeutic, induced* and *adaptive* modes of SPC. These modes are described and illustrated below, using indicative subjects.

Therapeutic SPC

Kottler (1997: 14) suggests that 'there are two main reasons why people make changes in their lives – because they *need* to, and because they *want* to'. The former is of particular relevance to the therapeutic mode of SPC. In almost half the participants in this study, LDW experiences played a role in transcending negative life events or antecedent conditions. Two examples are considered here.

Despite the sudden epiphany implied in Susan's quote above, close analysis of her story reveals periods of contemplation, preparation and action, which occurred over many months. Susan's overall change process can thus be likened to the 'stages of change model' used in the management of health interventions (Prochaska and Velicer 1997). Before the walk, Susan discussed with her doctor the idea of using the walk as an opportunity to reduce her medication, and she gave it up completely after the walk. Susan later planned and explored alternative options through voluntary work. Finally, she made lifestyle changes to maintain her health and build her resilience.

Courage and confidence were important elements in Susan achieving SPC. An incident during her LDW emerged as a symbol of these characteristics. She had been concerned about a particular river crossing for many days and had not slept well the previous night because of her worries:

> It was a high tide, the waves were surging and the river was going down and [Stan] said 'Well just watch me go across, and you can make up your mind.' So I watched him go across and it was up to his waist . . . Then he came back of course, and I said 'All right, I'll give it a go.' And I did it! You know . . . the absolute *thrill* of actually making it!

In her interview, Susan emphasized how this experience remains relevant to her today: 'It was just so good for me in terms of feeling like I can push through physical difficulties.'

Increased self-confidence, which transferred to other areas of life, was particularly evident in subjects who mentioned negative antecedent conditions. Their narratives often included "self stories" (Denzin 1989), positioning them at the centre of challenging events. Self-stories become memorable symbolic moments, which can be called upon in future situations. Oliver's self-story is particularly symbolic.

For much of his life, Oliver had suffered from a chronic fear of heights. But he was determined not to let it interfere with his love for the outdoors. During an extended trip to New Zealand, Oliver seems to have undergone a form of "systematic desensitization" (Seligman 1993), facilitated by a skilful and understanding guide:

> We were above the clouds . . . And the guide . . . took me aside from everyone else and said . . . 'I'm going to have you walk up and down just this one section of rock five or ten times . . . walk up 20, 30 feet and then come back down' . . . I actually only did it two or three times before I started thinking this isn't so bad . . . it was a good technique for getting me to focus less on . . . my fear.

A few days later, on his own initiative, Oliver successfully completed a bungee jump, which he wrote up in his blog as 'absolutely exhilarating'. Now, whenever he is faced by something challenging in life, Oliver uses his bungee jump as a benchmark and recalls how good it made him feel.

Processes of SPC evident in Susan and Oliver are readily described in terms of known models from the fields of health promotion and psychotherapy. They appear to have been largely self-directed, although apparently not consciously so. Embodied tasks associated with LDW also seem to have enhanced their confidence, and transferred to other areas of their lives.

Induced SPC

A different kind of SPC is evident where the impetus for change originates with other people. With induced SPC, there is no obvious need to change, although there does seem to be an underlying openness to engage and to connect. Two examples are presented here.

Andrew walked the Kokoda Trail in Papua New Guinea, an iconic battlefield of the Pacific theatre of World War II. As he expected, Andrew found the ten-day, 95-km trek physically demanding, but he was surprised by the intensity of his emotional response to ceremonies, poetry readings and incidents during the trek. These deeply engaged Andrew with the cultural meaning of the battlefield setting. His guide encouraged Andrew to reflect on what these experiences meant to him, and to consider what he would do as a result of those reflections. The guide then invited Andrew to share his thoughts with the entire trekking group.

An incident at the significant battlefield site of Brigade Hill created a dilemma for Andrew. Another trekking group spread out their tents to dry over what Andrew had been told were graves of Australian soldiers. While others from his group intervened to move the tents, Andrew observed passively, concerned that conflict might erupt between the groups. To Andrew, that would have been even more disrespectful (Saunders 2014).

On his return from Kokoda, Andrew continued to process his experiences through discussions with relatives, friends and colleagues. He began visiting veterans of the Kokoda Campaign in nursing homes, listening to their reminiscences. He joined one of the Kokoda Battalion Associations as an associate member and began attending commemorative events. Andrew subsequently became influential in the development of a major Kokoda memorial.

Andrew's story evokes Mezirow's (1991) concept of perspective transformation. The Brigade Hill incident created a disorientating dilemma and generated critical self-reflection. The emotional impact of the tour events and the guide's encouragement for Andrew to share his reflections with the group seem to have facilitated this process.

A less dramatic example of induced SPC is evident in Elaine. Before her walk along the 54-km Milford Track in New Zealand, Elaine's life revolved around her husband Frank, her work and achieving a high level of material comfort. Frank had always wanted to walk the Milford Track, but Elaine had never tried pack-carrying and hated the idea of camping.

One night, Frank made a spur-of-the-moment booking for them both to trek to Milford Sound. Elaine was 'absolutely dead scared' about that walk, and the first night she was kept awake by the noise of twenty other people in the bunkroom. But on the track, Elaine met some younger trekkers who made her feel accepted:

> All those youngsters kept on saying we hope we're like you when we're your age . . . So it was great, we made friends with all these kids and we fed a couple of them because some of them didn't bring any food.

Elaine's new friends looked out for her and made sure she could sleep comfortably:

> One of the girls had got there before me and she'd kept a space for us . . . which was
> nice because we'd got friends with all these youngsters and they kept, they wanted us
> with them.

Elaine enjoyed interacting with other walkers and loved the natural environment of the Milford Track. After the walk, Elaine kept in touch with trekkers from other countries; visiting
them and having them visit her. Elaine and Frank also completed other LDWs in Australia
and New Zealand, increasingly enjoying the scenery and the wildlife. Elaine now sees herself
as much less materialistic, and more appreciative of the natural environment, as well as more
adventurous.

Processes of SPC evident in Andrew and Elaine relate to their engagement with the settings of their LDWs and to connections with associated values. People who shared those
values became conduits into new social worlds, where growth and development could occur.
The concept of perspective transformation (Mezirow 1991) appears relevant to this mode
of SPC.

Adaptive SPC

A third style of SPC is evident in Dianne and Roy. We refer to this mode as adaptive SPC.
In these cases, LDW assists in successfully negotiating life-stage transitions. These changes are
essentially occurring in the broader life context of the person concerned. They are potentially
problematic shifts that can generate unpredictable effects.

It appears that Dianne was open to forming a romantic relationship when she chose to walk
the Larapinta Trail. Her previous long-distance walks had all been undertaken through a bushwalking club, but this time Dianne chose a commercial operation as she wanted to 'meet new
people'. Her description of meeting David emphasizes their common interests, and from early
in the trek they walked together:

> We were the only ones that wrote a diary, the only ones that took photos . . . had our maps.
> So . . . we had a lot in common. And it's a very special thing to do a walk together, and
> develop a relationship on that, without having any inkling that that's going to happen . . .
> It was a very special time.

In this case, long-distance walking can be seen as change-inducing, but the new relationship
emerges as the key change agent. Dianne's story can be interpreted as an example of Berger and
Luckmann's (1967) construct of *alternation*, as it demonstrates many of the characteristics they
describe, including the letting-go of previous activities and connections. Her relationship with
David led to her leaving work, ending her previous leisure activities, and disconnecting from
her existing social worlds, including moving away from her parents. LDW was a catalyst in a
major life-stage transition, but also it became an important shared interest, which helped maintain her relationship.

For Roy the life-stage transition of retirement loomed for two years, after a restructure of
his organization was announced. He used the time to plan a three-month walk as a conscious
"rite of passage" for himself and his wife. Reflecting on the walk afterwards, he felt the time
out had been effective:

[O]ur trek was to put some distance between our lives in the workforce and our future lives; a time to walk, a time to reflect and a time to rejuvenate. I think that it has largely succeeded in this goal. There is no better place to reflect than while walking silently down a long isolated stretch of beach, and we passed many of these. Some of the cynicism built up during 30 years of work has been shed and we certainly have no fears for what life now holds.

Since then, Roy and his wife have walked extensively in Australia, New Zealand, Europe and elsewhere. Roy has taught himself web design to help him create an extensive blog about their walks. The blog has become a central life interest, allowing Roy to express a 'slightly artistic side' that was constrained in his previous life. While he sees the changes that have come from walking as 'life-shaping' rather than 'life-shattering', Roy has clearly grown and developed, and has built a new social world through his website.

Renewal and growth are evident in adaptive SPC. For Roy, LDW has played an important role in his adjustment to a major life-stage transition. As with Dianne, it has helped him to restructure his life goals and commitments and to develop new interests and social connections. Extended travel as a ritual of life stage and a path to personal growth, learning and the discovery of new meaning in life has previously been observed in the context of early mid-life (Ateljevic and Doorne 2000) and older travellers (Roberson 2003; White and White 2004). It has also been suggested that a liminal space for reflection is an important element of such journeys (Muller and O'Cass 2001).

Conclusion

Through its focus on long-distance walking experiences of mid-life adults, this study has shed light on the field of transformative travel and has helped to demystify some of its more contentious aspects. The authors suggest that the term "transformation" is imprecise. It is rarely defined in the tourism literature and has been interpreted differently in other fields (Saunders 2014).

We propose an alternative concept of Significant Personal Change (SPC), which overtly recognizes a spectrum of life changes. A defining aspect of SPC is change in the subject's self-perception. Findings suggest that SPC is not a single phenomenon, but rather a cluster of at least three distinct modes, and that change processes may vary between modes. Processes observed in this study correspond to documented theories from health, psychology, education and sociology.

As Solnit (2000) suggests in the quote at the beginning of this chapter, perhaps there is something about the pace of walking which aids reflection and the processing of experience. For many subjects of this study, long-distance walking was found to facilitate moments of insight through which issues were seen more clearly, or placed in a new context. Throughout the world, wild lands and heritage areas are increasingly becoming settings for designated long-distance walking tracks. This study suggests that long-distance walking may offer important experiential opportunities for those in mid-life who are searching for, or at least receptive to, significant personal change.

References

Adler, J. (1985) 'Youth on the road: reflections on the history of tramping', *Annals of Tourism Research*, 12: 335–354.
Ateljevic, I. and Doorne, S. (2000) 'Tourism as an escape: long term travellers in New Zealand', *Tourism Analysis*, 5: 131–136.

Berger, P.L. and Luckmann, T. (1967) *The Social Construction of Reality: A Treatise in the Sociology of Knowledge*, London: Allen Lane.

Boecker, H., Sprenger, T., Spilker, M.E., Henriksen, G., Koppenhoefer, M., Wagner, K.J., Valet, M., Berthele, A. and Thomas, R.T. (2008) 'The runner's high: opioidergic mechanisms in the human brain', *Cerebral Cortex*, 18: 2523–2531.

Boeiji, H. (2002) 'A purposeful approach to the Constant Comparative Method in the analysis of qualitative interviews', *Quality and Quantity*, 36(4): 391–409.

Broad, S. (2003) 'Living the Thai life: a case study of volunteer tourism at the Gibbon Rehabilitation Project, Thailand', *Tourism Recreation Research*, 28(3): 63–72.

Brown, L. (2009) 'The transformative power of the international sojourn. An ethnographic study of the international student experience', *Annals of Tourism Research*, 36(3): 502–521.

Bruner, E.M. (1991) 'Transformation of self in tourism', *Annals of Tourism Research*, 18: 238–250.

Cohen, E. (2003) 'Backpacking: diversity and change', *Journal of Tourism and Cultural Change*, 1(2): 95–110.

Crust, L., Keegan, R., Piggott, D. and Swann, C. (2011) 'Walking the walk: a phenomenological study of long distance walking', *Journal of Applied Sport Psychology*, 23(3): 243–262.

den Breejen, L. (2007) 'The experiences of long distance walking: a case study of the West Highland Way in Scotland', *Tourism Management*, 28: 1417–1427.

Denzin, N.K. (1989) *Interpretive Biography*, Newbury Park, CA: Sage Publications.

Devereux, C. and Carnegie, E. (2006) 'Pilgrimage: journeying beyond self', *Tourism Recreation Research*, 31(1): 47–56.

Dilthey, W. (1976) *Selected Writings* (ed., trans. and introd. H.P. Rickman), Cambridge: Cambridge University Press.

Edensor, T. (2000) 'Walking in the British countryside: reflexivity, embodied practices and ways to escape', *Body and Society*, 6(3–4): 81–106.

Hall, C.M. (2007) *Introduction to Tourism in Australia. Development, Issues and Change*, 5th edn, Frenchs Forest, New South Wales, Australia: Pearson.

Heatherton, T.F. (2011) 'A life-changing paper? That depends on your interpretation', in R. Arkin (ed.), *Most Underappreciated: 50 Prominent Social Psychologists Describe Their Most Unloved Work*, New York: Oxford University Press, pp. 22–26.

Heatherton, T.F. and Nichols, P.A. (1994) 'Personal accounts of successful versus failed attempts at life change', *Personality and Social Psychology Bulletin*, 20: 664–675.

Kay, G. and Moxham, N. (1996) 'Paths for whom? Countryside access for recreational walking', *Leisure Studies*, 15: 171–183.

Kottler, J. (1997) *Travel That Can Change Your Life: How to Create a Transformative Experience*, San Francisco, CA: Jossey-Bass.

Lean, G.L. (2009) 'Transformative travel: inspiring sustainability', in R. Bushell and P. Sheldon (eds), *Wellness Tourism: Mind, Body, Spirit, Place*, New York: Cognizant Publishers, pp. 191–205.

McDonald, M.G. (2008) 'The nature of epiphanic experience', *Journal of Humanistic Psychology*, 48(1): 89–115.

Matthews, A. (2008) 'Negotiated selves: exploring the impact of local–global interactions on young volunteer travellers', in K. Lyons and S. Wearing (eds), *Journeys of Discovery in Volunteer Tourism*, Abingdon, Oxon: CABI, pp. 101–117.

Mezirow, J. (1991) *Transformative Dimensions in Adult Learning*, San Francisco, CA: Jossey-Bass.

Miller, W.R. and C'de Baca, J. (1994) 'Quantum change: toward a psychology of transformation', in T.F. Heatherton and J.L. Weinberger (eds), *Can Personality Change?*, Washington, DC: American Psychological Association, pp. 253–280.

Milstein, T. (2005) 'Transformation abroad: sojourning and the perceived enhancement of self-efficacy', *International Journal of Intercultural Relations*, 29(2): 217–238.

Mueser, R. (1998) *Long-Distance Hiking. Lessons from the Appalachian Trail*, Camden, ME: Ragged Mountain Press.

Muller, T. and O'Cass, A. (2001) 'Targeting the young at heart, seeing senior vacationers the way they see themselves', *Journal of Vacation Marketing*, 7: 285–301.

Nash, D. (1996) *Anthropology of Tourism*, Oxford: Pergamon.

Noy, C. (2004) 'This trip really changed me: backpackers' narratives of self-change', *Annals of Tourism Research*, 31(1): 78–102.

Prochaska, J.O. and Velicer, W.F. (1997) 'Behaviour change: the Transtheoretical Model of health behaviour change', *American Journal of Health Promotion*, 12(1): 38–48.

Quinlan Cutler, S., Carmichael, B. and Doherty, S. (2014) 'The Inca Trail experience: does the journey matter?', *Annals of Tourism Research*, 45(1): 152–166.

Roberson, D.N. Jr (2003) 'Learning experiences of senior travellers', *Studies in Continuing Education*, 25(1): 125–144.

Rojas, M. (2004) 'The complexity of well-being: a life satisfaction conception and a domains-of-life approach', proceedings of the International Workshop on Researching Well-being in Developing Countries, Hanse Institute for Advanced Study, Delmenhorst, near Bremen, Germany, 2–4 July.

Saunders, R.E. (2014) 'Steps towards change: personal transformation through long-distance walking', unpublished PhD thesis, Monash University, Victoria, Australia.

Seligman, M.E.P. (1993) *What You Can Change . . . And What You Can't. The Complete Guide to Successful Self-Improvement*, Columbine, NY: Fawcett.

Smith, J.A., Flowers, P. and Larkin, M. (2009) *Interpretative Phenomenological Analysis*, Los Angeles: Sage Publications.

Solnit, R. (2000) *Wanderlust. A History of Walking*, New York: Penguin.

Wearing, S. (2002) 'Re-centring the self in volunteer tourism', in G. Dann (ed.), *The Tourist as a Metaphor of the Social World*, London: CABI, pp. 237–262.

White, N.R. and White, P.B. (2004) 'Travel as transition: identity and place', *Annals of Tourism Research*, 31(1): 200–218.

27

Walking to promote increased physical activity

Ian Patterson, Shane Pegg and Wan Rabiah Wan Omar

Introduction

Physical inactivity has become an important issue for many developed countries and has grown rapidly among residents in the larger cities in both developed and less-developed countries throughout the world (WHO 2008). More than 30% of adults in 122 countries around the world were found to be physically inactive (Hallal *et al.* 2012). Physical inactivity increases the risk of obesity and studies by the World Health Organization have shown that there are more than 1 billion adults worldwide are classified as overweight, with at least 300 million being clinically obese (Guthold *et al.* 2008). Illnesses that are associated with physical inactivity have been said to be responsible for the deaths of at least 1.9 million people worldwide, with approximately 220,000 cases reported in North America, 320,000 in European countries, and over 13,000 reported cases in Australia (WHO 2008). In mainland China, for example, cardio-vascular disease has recently emerged as the leading cause of death attributed to poor diet and physical inactivity (Tanenbaum *et al.* 2016). It has been predicted that by 2020, the annual death rates of individuals classified as overweight and/or obese will increase to approximately 5 million people worldwide (WHO 2012).

This disturbing situation has become a major problem throughout the world and urgently needs attention (Owen *et al.* 2004). Interventions to increase physical activity are crucial and WHO have recommended that individuals need to engage in at least 30 minutes per day of any form of moderate intensity physical activity (Ekkekakis *et al.* 2008). For the greatest population impact, it has been recommended that activities can be easily integrated into daily routines, and to utilise strategies that can reach the greatest number of individuals in the most cost-effective manner (Merom *et al.* 2007). Among all types of physical activities that are both structured and unstructured, research findings have shown that recreational walking, which promotes relaxed walking behaviour, generates the greatest gains overall for population health. It should be incorporated as a lifestyle component that can be easily integrated into people's daily routines (Fenton 2005; Gobster 2005; Merom *et al.* 2007). Walking has also been found to be the most effective strategy for the promotion of physical activity in sedentary populations (Giles-Corti and Donovan 2003).

Walking can be incorporated into daily routines and is suitable for most people in a community (Humpel *et al.* 2004; Owen *et al.* 2004; Merom *et al.* 2007). Furthermore, walking has been reported to be the most commonly reported physical activity, especially for those who are concerned about their health (Gobster and Westphal 2004; Sugiyama and Thompson 2008). Furthermore, walking is an accessible form of activity and is suitable for all socio-demographic groups (Humpel et al. 2004; Owen et al. 2004). Walking is an activity of choice for most people, because it serves various purposes (recreation, exercise or to reach a destination), can be performed at a moderate intensity, is convenient, inexpensive and has a low risk of skeletal muscular injuries. Importantly, walking activity results in multiple benefits that extend beyond mere physical activity to encompass a range of dimensions that include physical, mental and spiritual health and restoration benefits (Mouden and Lee 2003; Gobster 2005; Cleland et al. 2008). The following section provides an explanation and discussion of walking behaviour and the different motives that encourage people to participate in walking.

Definitions of walking behaviour

Walking refers to any trip made by foot (Dickinson and Lumsdon 2010). Addy et al. (2004) classified walking behaviour into three main categories: regular walkers, who walk more than 150 minutes per week; irregular walkers, who walk 10–150 minutes per week; and non-walkers who walk less than 10 minutes per week. Walking behaviour is also known as pedestrian behaviour, and research has found that it requires various motivations for people to engage in walking. The most commonly cited motives for walking are for recreation, to reach a destination (transport), and to maintain good health (Gobster 2005; Cerin et al. 2007; Hall et al. 2017). The following section discusses the main motivations that encourage individuals to engage in walking activity.

Walking for recreation

Walking for recreation refers to trips made on foot, principally for recreation, relaxation or to explore places (Pralong 2006). Activities which are usually associated with recreation walkers are sightseeing of attractions such as flora and fauna, landscapes, streetscapes, as well as interacting with people such as friends and neighbours (Matos 2004). According to Matos (2004), these interactions with people and places on a deeper level provide rewarding experiences and great satisfaction. This activity allows close contact with landscapes and streetscapes, and the absorption of atmosphere, which enables recreational walkers to enjoy the uniqueness of the surrounding environment (Dickinson and Lumsdon 2010). In addition, the opportunity to interact with people has an important impact on positive social cohesion (Sugiyama and Thompson 2008).

Walking for recreation is one of the most popular walking behaviours and has been found to be related to socio-economic status (SES), as people with a high SES tend to engage more in recreational walking (Wen et al. 2007; Giles-Corti et al. 2008). Research conducted by Shafer et al. (2000) and Gobster (2005) in the USA reported that the majority of walkers utilised trails for recreational walking purposes. Similar findings have been found in Australia (Giles-Corti et al. 2008) and Finland (Neuvonen et al. 2007). In addition, the emphasis on walking facilities located close to residential areas provides easy access and establishes recreational attractions for daily outings (Sugiyama and Thompson 2008). Furthermore, these attractions can help to beautify an area by offering an improved landscape and cleaner surroundings (Baran et al. 2008; Jamrozy and Walsh 2008).

Walking for transport

Although some walkers walk for recreation, others walk to reach a destination (Hall et al. 2017). Walking to catch a bus or train has also been found to be associated with socio-economic status, as the lower the status, the more likely that the individual walks for transport purposes (Wen *et al.* 2007). Research findings have shown that a change in people's preferences from using motor vehicles to walking would help to decrease automobile and motorcycle traffic and, consequently, enhance the local environment, due to a reduction in air pollution (Hall *et al.* 2017).

While walking for transport purposes supports improved quality of life by promoting physical activities as well as reducing pollution levels, relatively few people actually walk for transport purposes (Hall *et al.* 2017; see also chapter 1, this volume). A study conducted in Adelaide, Australia has shown that number of people walking for transport purposes would increase by limiting of the number of parking spaces, and their proximity to commercial destinations, workplaces and schools (Cerin *et al.*, 2007). In addition, the provision of trails that are easy to walk on, with no obstacles, and with the provision of good facilities, such as toilets and shelters, were found to contribute to increased walking for transport purposes (Sugiyama and Thompson 2008).

Walking for health

The main benefits of walking are health-related, where health consciousness plays an important 'push factor' for people to participate in active physical activities, such as walking, running or cycling. Encouraging people to regularly walk is seen as the best way to provide the greatest gains to the health of the general population (Cleland *et al.* 2008). Gobster (2005) found that trail users in America who were more health-motivated, tended to become more frequent trail users than others who were not as health-conscious (Brownson *et al.* 2008). Similarly, in Helsinki, walking for fitness is among the most popular motives (Neuvonen *et al.* 2007). Research has also found that people who live in walkable areas that promote walking behaviour were found to be less likely to be obese (Frank *et al.* 2008; see also chapter 30, this volume). In order to gain certain health benefits, the recommended time that people should walk is at least 30 minutes a day, five days per week (WHO 2005; Darker *et al.* 2007). However, if the 30 minutes of walking at one time is difficult to achieve, 10-minute bouts of brisk walking can provide similar health benefits when they total 30 minutes a day (Brown *et al.* 2007).

The findings from previous studies have shown that regular walking is able to prevent the development of fatal and non-fatal cardiovascular diseases (Boone-Heinonen *et al.* 2008). Regular walking activity can lower blood pressure and, consequently, reduce the risk of cardiovascular disease (Lee *et al.* 2010). Although regular walking is beneficial in reducing the risk of contracting diseases, a faster walking pace has been found to have greater impact on decreasing the risk (Hu *et al.* 1999). In respect of weight gain control, experimental research has shown that walking 15 minutes a day will burn 100 calories and keep off 0.5–1 kilogram per year, which will help prevent weight gain (Brown *et al.* 2007). Generally, research indicates that regular physical activity such as walking surpasses the effectiveness of any drugs or other types of medical treatment (Wittink *et al.* 2011). Besides physical health, the experience of walking helps to provide contact with nature and has been shown to have a positive effect on mental health, which has been referred to as the restorative effects of nature. Walking in an outdoor environment is often associated with more frequent contact with friends and neighbours, and these types of social contacts have also been found to make an important contribution to mental health and well-being for people (Pegg 2001; Sugiyama and Thompson 2008).

Influential determinants of walking behaviour

Despite the multiple purposes and benefits generated by walking activity, participation rates still remain low in most countries (Giles-Corti and Donovan 2003; Merom *et al.* 2007; Wen *et al.* 2007; Hall *et al.* 2017). This suggests that there is an urgent need to persuade people to engage in regular walking to gain its maximum benefits. Conceptually, there are two catego-ries of non-participation; those who do not desire to participate, and those for whom con-straints or barriers exist (Jackson 1988). Constraints refer to limitations or barriers imposed by, and on, individuals, that may lead to decreased or non-participation in an activity. Under-standing the constraints of non-participation enhances the ability of policy makers to design intervention strategies that meet the needs and interests of people (Jackson 2005). Two types of constraints that are commonly found are internal constraints, which are seen as within the individual's control, and external constraints, that refer to those beyond an individual's control (Stemerding *et al.* 1999). Thus, the challenge for policy makers is to identify walking intervention strategies that reduce these constraints, as well as to increase people's motivations to walk regularly.

Previous research has consistently shown that walking behaviour is related to multi-level determinants, which include socio-demographic variables, their social surroundings, as well as trail characteristics (Spence *et al.* 2001; Glanz *et al.* 2005). An understanding of these three fac-tors and how they interact will provide fundamental information to help formulate appropriate interventions.

Individual influences on walking

Socio-demographic characteristics pertinent to walking activity include the person's ethnicity, age, gender, car ownership, education and work status (Lee *et al.* 2007; Giles-Corti *et al.* 2008). The following section will elaborate on these potential factors that influence people's walking behaviour.

Ethnicity and culture

Several studies have found that many Asian-Americans are restricted in their participation in exercise programmes, because of the double burden of working outside and inside their home. Many ethnic minority women do not exercise because of their multiple duties as mothers, work-ers and family caregivers (King *et al.* 2000; Eyler *et al.* 2003). Payne *et al.* (2002) also found that African-Americans preferred man-made amenities that preserved the natural environment (open, well-groomed) that had more structured facilities (such as fields and paved trails); while white Americans mainly favoured wild land for recreation activities.

Seo *et al.* (2009) also argued that physical activity such as walking appears to be more related to specific cultural values. For example, cultural issues such as language barriers, being in an exercise group with others from a different ethnic background, and peer non-acceptance due to cultural beliefs were all found to be barriers to physical activity that are more unique to women from diverse racial or ethnic backgrounds (Eyler *et al.* 2002).

Age

As age increases, participation in physical activity tends to decrease (Malina and Little 2008). This is because participation in physical activity requires physical strength, stamina and good health. Generally, as people grow older, these factors decrease and, consequently, they tend to become physically inactive. For example, Giles-Corti and Donovan (2003) concluded that individuals who were aged over 59 years were found more likely to have medical problems which prevented them from being physically active than younger people. As the majority of them became more physically inactive, they tended to experience poorer health status. However, one of the promising ways of reducing this prevalence of morbidity due to sedentary lifestyle among the ageing population is by engaging in walking activity.

Gender

Looking at walking behaviour from a gender perspective, women of various age categories were generally found to be more likely to be inactive in comparison to their male counterparts (Cooper et al. 2003; Bellows-Riecken and Rhodes 2008; Martinez et al. 2009). The main reason for their reduced involvement in physical activity is attributed to their preoccupation with their daily routine (such as looking after children and doing house chores), which left them with limited time for physical activity (Martinez et al. 2009). Women tended to be more motivated to walk if they had friends to walk with, received family support, could walk with a baby in a stroller, and had a variety of places to walk (Kavanagh and Bentley 2008; Martinez et al. 2009). In contrast, walking activity among men was not found to be associated with people around them who made walking easy or hard, but was more associated with their level of education (Kavanagh and Bentley 2008).

Car ownership

Car ownership has been found to be highly correlated with walking behaviour. A study conducted in California has shown that people with more cars in the household walked less compared to those households with fewer cars (Shores and West 2008). Another study conducted in the Atlanta region concluded that households with no car, or only one car, were four times more likely to walk for transport as those in households with three or more cars (Kerr et al. 2007). Thus, it appears that people tend to walk less if they have greater access to cars.

Education

A person's level of education has been found to be strongly correlated with their income (Bodea et al. 2009). In addition, the levels of education and income have also been shown to have a significant association with physical activity. That is, the higher the educational and income levels, the more likely that these people tend to be more physically active. However, a study by Krizek et al. (2007) reported otherwise; i.e. there were no significant differences between those who reported being regular trail users and the socio-demographic characteristics when income, race and gender were taken into consideration.

Work status

Work status is normally associated with financial ability and the availability of leisure time to participate in recreation activities. For example, unemployed people usually prefer to engage in more close-to-home and less costly recreational activities, such as walking and cycling, due to financial constraints (Krizek et al. 2007). Working people who have fewer constraints on their financial ability have other constraints such as limited time to participate in leisure activity. This situation has made walking and cycling in the local neighbourhood to be the most appropriate form of physical activity for most people, rich or poor. The following sections discuss the modifying factors in relation to walking behaviour.

Intrapersonal influences on walking

The most basic factors that influence individual behaviour occur at the intrapersonal level (Rimer and Glanz 2005; Shores *et al.* 2007). People's behaviour is influenced through the intrapersonal relationships that are reflected by their surroundings (Fisher 2008). Examples of intrapersonal characteristics that influence people's behaviour include knowledge, attitudes, beliefs and personality traits (Robinson 2008). The whole range of intrapersonal factors can influence individual perceptions of health behaviour, including walking (Champion and Skinner 2008). The intrapersonal determinant has been found to be one of the important influential factors; thus, an understanding of this factor is essential for developing intervention strategies to increase walking behaviour (Rimer and Glanz 2005).

Although an intervention at an intrapersonal level can promote walking behaviour, research studies have shown that a single-level approach will only have a short-term impact on behavioural change (Hall 2014). Therefore, in order to sustain a longer impact on the local population, walking intervention strategies should also consider environmental factors (Giles-Corti *et al.* 2005). The following section will discuss how the social environment influences people's walking behaviour.

Social influences

One type of interpersonal factor is termed the social environment, which is basically derived from the structure, process and functions of social relationships (Heaney and Israel 2008). Social relationships exist within the social network where individuals interact through the specific relationships between individuals and other people in the network, and the general relationship of networks as a whole. According to Heaney and Israel (2008) a social network gives rise to various social functions: social influence, social control, social understanding, social comparison and social support.

Social support has been recognised as one of the important influential determinants on walking activity (Burton *et al.* 2005; Cleland *et al.* 2008; Sugiyama and Thompson 2008). Social support usually comes from both informal and formal social networks. Examples of informal networks are family members, friends and co-workers, while more formal social networks include health care professionals and human service workers (Heaney and Israel 2008). In addition, the findings from previous research have shown that social support from health care professionals (medical doctors), friends/peers and support from spouse/family are positively associated with participation in physical activities (Bauman *et al.* 2002; Sallis *et al.* 2008).

Support from social relationships have been found to influence a person's behaviour through providing: (a) emotional support that involves the expressions of empathy, love, trust and caring; (b) informational support that involves the provision of advice, suggestions, and information; and (c) appraisal support that involves the provision of information that is useful for self-evaluation (Heaney and Israel 2008). In addition, people's behaviour can also be influenced through mediation in social norms, expectations from a person's culture, tradition, family and friends (Robinson 2008). Generally, these social influences are dynamic and vary according to individual characteristics (Phongsavan *et al.* 2007). This is because people from different social demographic backgrounds are found to behave differently in response to their social surroundings (Payne *et al.* 2002).

Although intervention strategies to promote walking behaviour through modifying the social factors have been found to be important, the strategies have to be supported with other physical interventions, such as providing suitable facilities in order to make walking convenient

(Giles-Corti and Donovan 2003; Reynolds *et al.* 2007). Thus, this last section will discuss how to help increase walking behaviour through the provision of walking trails.

The provision of walking trails

Walking has also been found to be related to the availability of walking trails in local neighbourhood areas (Cohen *et al.* 2007; Henderson 2006; Vojnovic *et al.* 2006). Studies have shown that people living near to walking trails and having appropriate physical environmental settings become more involved in walking activity (Pierce *et al.* 2006). Walking trails provide an ideal setting to engage in physical activity, such as walking and jogging, and for many, it is the mental well-being resulting from relaxation that is considered the most important (Davies *et al.* 2012).

The cost of trail provision has been found to be reasonable and sensible, compared to the expanding health costs associated with physical inactivity (Mouden and Lee 2003; Shores and West 2008). For example, a study in the USA (Lincoln, Nebraska) has shown that every $1 investment in trails for physical activity has led to $2.94 in direct medical benefits, indicating that building trails is cost beneficial from a public health perspective (Wang *et al.* 2005). In addition, this strategy of physical activity promotion benefits all people exposed to an environment, rather than focusing on improving one person's health at a time. Furthermore, the benefits generated from trails are not merely the provision of a venue for walking, they also help to cater for recreation and exercise demand, serve as a transport mode, assist in the conservation of the environment, promote the social integration of people, thereby enabling them to get together, and also facilitate economic activities (Ravenscroft and Markwell 2000; Henderson 2006; Khalid Zakaria 2006; Baran *et al.* 2008). In a study of walkers in the Paris metropolitan area, Perchoux *et al.* (2015) also found that creating supportive built environments such as sport and cultural facilities around residences could stimulate recreational walking.

The model of physical environmental factors audit tool developed by Pikora *et al.* (2006), the Irvine–Minnesota Inventory developed by Day *et al.* (2006) and the SPACES model by Reynolds *et al.* (2007) provide a fundamental list of potential trail characteristics that are important in influencing people's walking behaviour. These include safety from crime and traffic, a suitable trail surface, accessibility, scenic views, trailside facilities and regular maintenance; each of these trail characteristics will be discussed below.

Safety from crime

Walking is affected by psychological characteristics, such as their perception of safety (Tan *et al.* 2007). A study of 11 neighbourhoods in California examined the relationship between urban design features and adult walking, and found that safety had the greatest impact on people walking in a neighbourhood (Shores and West 2008). With regards to trail safety, there are two categories of safety: safety from crime and safety from traffic (Pikora *et al.* 2003; Day *et al.* 2006; Pikora *et al.* 2006; Hall *et al.* 2017). Walking behaviour has been found to be strongly influenced by crime and fear of crime, and when walking trails are perceived as safe they are able to draw a greater number of users (Vojnovic *et al.* 2006). The most vulnerable trail users are women, older people, children and people with disabilities (Luymes and Tamminga 1995). Therefore, it is important to ensure that safety requirements for these groups are considered as important in walking trail design, so as to encourage increased walking behaviour.

The basic principle for increasing safety from crime for trail users can be achieved by having regular trail patrols (Vojnovic *et al.* 2006), minimising hiding places (Reynolds *et al.* 2007), cutting down vegetation and tall shrubs (Reynolds *et al.* 2007), ensuring well-lit paths (Pikora *et al.* 2006;

Brown *et al.* 2007), installing surveillance devices (e.g. CCTV) and emergency call box places at regular intervals (Day *et al.* 2006; Pikora *et al.* 2006), and not permitting dogs without leashes (Troped *et al.* 2006).

Safety from traffic

Traffic safety for trail users can be improved by creating barriers to separate trails and motor vehicles (through the presence of a shoulder between trails and roads), safe street crossings (pedestrian crossings, traffic lights) and the separation of walkers from cyclists (Day *et al.* 2006; Brown *et al.* 2007). Safe trails have been found to be important for walking, but the combination with other characteristics, such as a good walking surface, together with accessibility to parks and schools, and the presence of scenic views, creates an overall composite environment which is supportive of people's walking behaviour.

Surface features

Walking surfaces mainly consist of surface materials, with the width and slope being important. Trail surfaces can be unpaved or paved. Unpaved surfaces normally refer to natural trails that are not covered with additional material. Conversely, paved surfaces refer to trails that are covered with certain types of materials. Different surface materials suit different types of trail activity and will affect people's participation in walking (Reynolds *et al.* 2007). A fine-grained surface creates an efficient environment for pedestrian travel and, more importantly, it enables wheelchair users, as well as families with babies in strollers, to use walking trails (Vojnovic *et al.* 2006). In addition, the surface width of trails contributes to enhance the convenience level of users. The identification of the correct width of trails is important, because if trails are too narrow, they will cause inconvenience to trail users, and if too wide, they will be a waste of resources. The slope of the gradient is also part of the trail surface design. Walking on undulating trails is more challenging compared to flat trails, because walking on hilly terrain requires extra leg strength and consumes more energy. The absence of hilly terrains has been found to be associated with higher levels of trail use (Troped *et al.* 2006).

Accessibility

The accessible location of trails is important to encourage people's interest in utilising them. Those who participate in non-vigorous (walking) activity generally travel for a shorter amount of time than for vigorous activity (McCormack *et al.* 2006). The close proximity of recreation facilities in the community offers greater opportunities for participation in physical activities for the purpose of enjoyment, healthy activity or as a transport mode (Henderson 2006).

Studies of the environmental and individual determinants of physical activity has shown that facilities located close to home are used more often than facilities that are located elsewhere (Wendel-Vos *et al.* 2004, 2007; McCormack *et al.* 2006; Neuvonen *et al.* 2007). Kaczynski and Henderson (2007) also found that trails are more accessible to people if they are located within close proximity to people's workplace. The proximity of walking trails to home is important to attract trail users, although the definition of 'close to home' is different for different people. Neuvonen *et al.* (2007) suggested that the average distance to an area that was suitable for walking, jogging or cycling to be less than half a kilometre.

Apart from being close to home, walking trails that are accessible to facilities such as schools, shops, schools, bus/taxi ranks and open spaces are more likely to attract greater walking activity, especially for transport purposes (Pikora *et al.* 2003). Walking trails that are close to community facilities provide a further attraction for local residents to walk, because trails can be utilised not only for leisure and exercise, but also for visits (Vojnovic *et al.* 2006). Furthermore, a continuous accessible trail with an uninterrupted path of travel is important to increase accessibility for people with disabilities (Darcy and Cashman 2008; Darcy *et al.* 2010). An accessible trail encourages people with disabilities to be part of wider community and helps to break down the traditional barriers between "the able" and "the disabled" members in the community, as well as to foster social interaction (Patterson 2007).

Scenic views

Trail characteristics that have scenic views offer special attraction to users, which will influence their walking behaviour. Research in the USA has found that the majority of regular trail users place scenic beauty as one of the important attractions (Gobster 2005). McGinn *et al.* (2007) also concluded that scenic views of the surrounding environment play an important role in an individual's decision to walk on trails.

Trailside facilities

The presence of trailside facilities is likely to enhance the convenience of users and has often been associated with higher trail usage (Reynolds *et al.* 2007). Trailside facilities cover many types of structures, such as telephones, toilets, benches, picnic tables, drinking fountains, garbage bins, signage (cautionary, directive, interpretive, objective and regulatory signs), parking, bike racks, fitness equipment, play equipment, kiosks, public transit stations/stops, and facilities for people with disabilities (Troped *et al.* 2006; Reynolds *et al.* 2007). Additional trailside facilities for people with disabilities include handrails to assist in weight-bearing, accessible toilets, and seats to provide resting areas (Darcy and Cashman 2008; Darcy *et al.* 2010).

Maintenance

Studies of trail usage in the USA suggest that well-maintained trails attract more walkers (Reynolds *et al.* 2007; Sugiyama and Thompson 2008). The potential attributes of trail maintenance include the need for cleanliness (rubbish collection, bins provided, free from animal droppings), tidiness (grass cutting, tree trimming and graffiti cleaned off walls) and the restoration of broken items (Day *et al.* 2006; Troped *et al.* 2006; Sugiyama and Thompson 2008). In addition, the most effective trails are usually generated from community input that emphasises community interest (Gauvin *et al.* 2005; Day *et al.* 2007; Tan *et al.* 2007). Therefore, it is important to consider a range of people's perspectives in the design of trails, in order to encourage greater interest in walking.

Conclusion

The general findings of this review of walking behaviour propose that a multi-level intervention is the most desirable option to achieve increased walking activity. This chapter advocates for a multi-level investigation targeted at individuals, the social environment and the provision of suitable walking trails in a local neighbourhood community. An understanding of these three factors provides fundamental information to help formulate appropriate interventions (Spence *et al.* 2001; Glanz *et al.* 2005) (Figure 27.1).

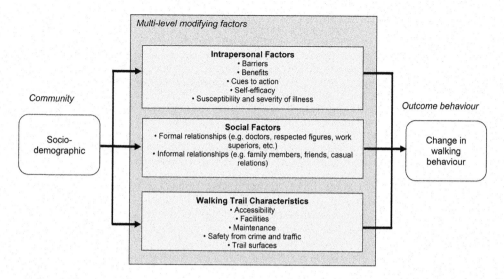

Figure 27.1 Conceptual framework based on the Social Ecological Model for walking behaviour. *Source*: adapted from Hutzler (2007) and Pikora *et al.* (2003) (see also Figure 30.1, this volume)

Figure 27.1 provides a conceptual framework that helps explain the relationship between socio-demographic, multi-level factors (intrapersonal, social and trail characteristics) and expected outcomes of walking behaviour. Socio-demographic characteristics provide basic input for interventions, because previous studies have shown that behaviour preferences are strongly related to socio-demographic characteristics (Champion and Skinner 2008). Socio-demographic characteristics pertinent to walking activity include age, gender, ethnicity, car ownership, education and work status (Lee *et al.* 2007; Giles-Corti *et al.* 2008). The socio-demographic characteristics are internal to the individual, and are generally not modifiable, but are useful in guiding the tailoring of intervention strategies. Therefore, intervention to increase walking behaviour should target influential factors that can be modified.

The first and most basic factor that influences individual behaviour occurs at the intrapersonal level. Examples include knowledge, attitudes, beliefs and personality traits. Because the intrapersonal factor is one of the important influential factors that is internal to people and is often within their personal control, mediating this factor will result in changing their behaviour (Glanz *et al.* 2005). Thus, an understanding of this factor is essential for walking behaviour intervention strategy (Giles-Corti and Donovan 2003; Rimer and Glanz 2005). The second modifiable factor that influences walking behaviour is individual social support. Although this factor is generally beyond an individual's control, some interventions that focus on social support are able to change people's behaviour (Sallis *et al.* 2008). This form of social factor is basically derived from the structure, process and functions of social relationships. The third modifiable factor that has been found to influence walking behaviour is walking trails, which have the capacity to either obstruct or facilitate walking activity.

References

Addy, C.L., Wilson, D.K., Kirtland, K.A., Ainsworth, B.E., Sharpe, P. and Kimsey, D. (2004) 'Associations of perceived social and physical environmental supports with physical activity and walking behaviour', *American Journal of Public Health*, 94(3): 440–443.

Baran, P.K., Rodriguez, D.A. and Khattak, A.J. (2008) 'Space syntax and walking in a new urbanist and suburban neighbourhoods', *Journal of Urban Design*, 13(1): 5–28.

Bauman, A.E., Sallis, J.F., Dzewaltowski, D.A. and Owen, N. (2002) 'Toward a better understanding of the influences on physical activity: the role of determinants, correlates, causal variables, mediators, moderators, and confounders', *American Journal of Preventive Medicine*, 23(2): 5–14.

Bellows-Riecken, K.H. and Rhodes, R.E. (2008) 'A birth of inactivity? A review of physical activity and parenthood', *Preventive Medicine*, 46(2): 99–110.

Bodea, T.D., Garrow, L.A., Meyer, M.D. and Ross, C.L. (2009) 'Socio-demographic and built environment influences on the odds of being overweight or obese: the Atlanta experience', *Transportation Research Part A: Policy and Practice*, 43(4): 430–444.

Boone-Heinonen, J., Evenson, K.R., Taber, D.R. and Gordon-Larsen, P. (2008) 'Walking for prevention of cardiovascular disease in men and women: a systematic review of observational studies', *Obesity Reviews*, 10(2): 204–217.

Brown, B.B., Werner, C.M., Amburgey, J.W. and Szalay, C. (2007) 'Walkable route perceptions and physical features: converging evidence for en route walking experiences', *Environment and Behavior*, 39(1): 34–61.

Brownson, R.C., Housemann, R.A., Brown, D.R., Jackson-Thompson, J., King, A.C., Malone, B.R. and Sallis, J.F. (2000) 'Promoting physical activity in rural communities: walking trail access, use, and effects', *American Journal of Preventive Medicine*, 18(3): 235–241.

Burton, N.W., Turrell, G., Oldenburg, B. and Sallis, J.F. (2005) 'The relative contributions of psychological, social, and environmental variables to explain participation in walking, moderate-, and vigorous-intensity leisure-time physical activity', *Journal of Physical Activity and Health*, 2(2): 181–196.

Cerin, E., Leslie, E., Toit, L. Owen, N. and Frank, L.D. (2007) 'Destinations that matter: associations with walking for transport', *Health & Place*, 13(3): 713–724.

Champion, V.L. and Skinner, C.S. (2008) 'The health belief model', in K. Glanz, B.K. Rimer and K. Viswanath (eds), *Health Behavior and Health Education: Theory, Research, and Practice*, 4th edn, San Francisco: Jossey-Bass, pp. 45–65.

Cleland, V.J., Timperio, A. and Crawford, D. (2008) 'Are perceptions of the physical and social environment associated with mothers' walking for leisure and for transport? A longitudinal study', *Preventive Medicine*, 47(2): 188–193.

Cohen, D.A., McKenzie, T.L., Sehgal, A. and Williamson, S. (2007) 'Contribution of public parks to physical activity', *American Journal of Public Health*, 97(3): 509–514.

Cooper, A.R., Page, A.S., Foster, L.J. and Qahwaji, D. (2003) 'Commuting to school: are children who walk more physically active?', *American Journal of Preventive Medicine*, 25(4): 273–276.

Darcy, S. and Cashman, R. (2008) *Benchmark Games: The Sydney 2000 Paralympic Games*, Petersham, New South Wales, Australia: Walla Walla Press, in conjunction with the Australian Centre for Olympic Studies, University of Technology, Sydney.

Darcy, S., Cameron, B. and Pegg, S. (2010) 'Accessible tourism and sustainability: a discussion and case study', *Journal of Sustainable Tourism*, 18(4): 515–537.

Darker, C.D., Larkin, M. and French, D.P. (2007) 'An exploration of walking behaviour: an interpretative phenomenological approach', *Social Science and Medicine*, 65(10): 2172–2183.

Davies, N., Lumsdon, L. and Weston, R. (2012) 'Developing recreational trails: motivations for recreational walking', *Tourism Planning and Development*, 9(1): 77–88.

Day, K., Boarnet, M., Alfonzo, M. and Forsyth, A. (2006) 'The Irvine–Minnesota Inventory to measure built environments', *American Journal of Preventive Medicine*, 30(2): 144–152.

Dickinson, J. and Lumsdon, L. (2010) *Slow Travel and Tourism*, London: Earthscan.

Ekkekakis, P., Backhouse, S.H., Gray, C. and Lind, E. (2008) 'Walking is popular among adults but is it pleasant? A framework for clarifying the link between walking and affect as illustrated in two studies', *Psychology of Sport and Exercise*, 9(3): 246–264.

Eyler A., Wilcox S., Matson-Koffman D., Evenson K., Sanderson B., Thompson J., Wilbur J. and Young D. (2002) 'Correlates of physical activity among women from diverse racial/ethnic groups: a review', *Journal of Womens Health and Gender-based Medicine*, 11(3): 239–253.

Eyler, A., Matson-Koffman, D., Young, D., Wilcox, S., Wilbur, J., Thompson, J., Sanderson, B. and Evenson, K. (2003) 'Quantitative study of correlates of physical activity among women from diverse racial/ethnic groups: the women's cardiovascular health network project – introduction and methodology', *American Journal of Preventive Medicine*, 25(3): 93–103.

Fenton, M. (2005) 'Battling America's epidemic of physical inactivity: building more walkable, livable communities', *Journal of Nutrition Education and Behavior*, 37(2): 115–120.

Fisher, E. (2008) 'The importance of context in understanding behavior and promoting health', *Annals of Behavioral Medicine,* 35(1): 3–18.

Frank, L.D., Kerr, J., Sallis, J.F., Miles, R. and Chapman, J. (2008) 'A hierarchy of sociodemographic and environmental correlates of walking and obesity', *Preventive Medicine,* 47(2): 172–178.

Gauvin, L., Richard, L., Craig, C. L., Spivock, M., Riva, M., Forster, M., Laforest, S., Laberge, S., Fournel, M.-C., Gagnon, H., Gagne, S. and Potvin, L. (2005) 'From walkability to active living potential: an "ecometric" validation study', *American Journal of Preventive Medicine,* 28(2): 126–133.

Giles-Corti, B.and Donovan R.J. (2003) 'Relative influences of individual, social environmental, and physical environmental correlates of walking', *American Journal of Public Health,* 93(9): 1583–1589.

Giles-Corti, B., Timperio A., Bull F. and Pikora T. (2005) 'Understanding physical activity environmental correlates: increased specificity for ecological models', *Exercise and Sport Sciences Reviews,* 33(4): 175–181.

Giles-Corti, B., Knuiman, M., Timperio, A., Van Niel, K., Pikora, T.J., Bull, F., Shilton T. and Bulsara M. (2008) 'Evaluation of the implementation of a state government community design policy aimed at increasing local walking: design issues and baseline results from RESIDE, Perth Western Australia', *Preventive Medicine,* 46(1): 46–54.

Glanz, K., Sallis, J.F., Saelens, B.E., and Frank, L.D. (2005) 'Healthy nutrition environments: concepts and measures', *American Journal of Health Promotion,* 19(5): 330–333.

Gobster, P.H. (2005) 'Recreation and leisure research from an active living perspective: taking a second look at urban trail use data', *Leisure Sciences,* 27(5): 367–383.

Gobster, P.H. and Westphal, L.M. (2004) 'The human dimensions of urban greenways: planning for recreation and related experiences', *Landscape and Urban Planning,* 68(2–3): 147–165.

Guthold, R., Ono T., Strong, K., Chatterji, S. and Morabia, A. (2008) 'Worldwide variability in physical inactivity: a 51-country survey', *American Journal of Preventive Medicine,* 34(6): 486–494.

Hall, C.M. (2014) *Tourism and Social Marketing.* Abingdon, Oxon: Routledge.

Hall, C.M., Le-Klähn, D.-T. and Ram, Y. (2017) *Tourism, Public Transport and Sustainable Mobility,* Bristol: Channel View.

Hallal, P., Anderson, L., Bull, F., Guthold, R., Haskell, W. and Ekelund, U. (2012) 'Global physical activity levels: surveillance progress, pitfalls and prospects', *Lancet,* 380(9838): 247–257.

Heaney, C.A. and Israel, B.A. (2008) 'Social networks and social support', in K. Glanz, B.K. Rimer and K. Viswanath (eds), *Health Behavior and Health Education: Theory, Research and Practice,* 4th edn, San Francisco: Jossey-Bass, pp. 189–200.

Henderson, K.A. (2006) 'Urban parks and trails and physical activity', *Annals of Leisure Research,* 9(4): 201–213.

Hu, F.B., Sigal, R.J., Rich-Edwards, J.W., Colditz, G.A., Solomon, C.G., Willett, W.C., Speizer, F.E. and Manson, J.E. (1999) 'Walking compared with vigorous physical activity and risk of type 2 diabetes in women', *Journal of the American Medical Association,* 282(15): 1433–1439.

Humpel, N., Owen, N., Iverson, D., Leslie, E. and Bauman, A. (2004) 'Perceived environment attributes, residential location, and walking for particular purposes', *American Journal of Preventive Medicine,* 26(2): 119–125.

Hutzler, Y. (2007) 'A systematic ecological model for adapting physical activities: theoretical foundations and practical examples', *Adapted Physical Activity Quarterly,* 24(4): 287–304.

Jackson, E.L. (1988) 'Leisure constraints: a survey of past research', *Leisure Sciences,* 10(3): 203–215.

Jackson, E.L. (2005) 'Leisure constraints research: overview of a developing theme in leisure studies', in E.L. Jackson and T.L. Burton (eds), *Constraints to Leisure,* State College, PA: Venture Publishing, pp. 3–19.

Jamrozy, U. and Walsh, J.A. (2008) 'Destination and place branding: a lost sense of place', in S.F. McCool and R.N. Moisey (eds), *Tourism, Recreation and Sustainability: Linking Culture and the Environment,* 2nd edn, Wallingford, Oxon: CABI, pp. 131–141.

Kaczynski, A.T. and Henderson, K.A. (2007) 'Environmental correlates of physical activity: a review of evidence about parks and recreation', *Leisure Sciences,* 29(4): 315–354.

Kavanagh, A.M. and Bentley, R. (2008) 'Walking: a gender issue?', *Australian Journal of Social Issues,* 43(1): 45–64.

Kerr, J., Frank, L., Sallis, J.F. and Chapman, J. (2007) 'Urban form correlates of pedestrian travel in youth: differences by gender, race-ethnicity and household attributes', *Transportation Research Part D: Transport and Environment,* 12(3): 177–182.

Khalid Zakaria, E.A.I. (2006) 'Role of urban greenway systems in planning residential communities: a case study from Egypt', *Landscape and Urban Planning,* 76(1–4): 192–209.

King, A., Castro, C., Wilcox, S., Eyler, A., Sallis, J. and Brownson, R. (2000) 'Personal and environmental factors associated with physical inactivity among different racial/ethnic groups of US middle-and older-aged women', *Health Psychology*, 19(4): 354–364.

Krizek, K.J., El-Geneidy, A. and Thompson, K. (2007) 'A detailed analysis of how an urban trail system affects cyclists' travel', *Transportation*, 34(5): 611–624.

Lee, J.S., Kawakubo, K., Kohri, S., Tsujii, H., Mori, K. and Akabayashi, A. (2007) 'Association between residents' perception of the neighborhood's environments and walking time in objectively different regions', *Environmental Health and Preventive Medicine*, 12(1): 3–10.

Lee, L.-L., Watson, M.C., Mulvaney, C.A., Tsai, C.-C. and Lo, S.-F. (2010) 'The effect of walking intervention on blood pressure control: a systematic review', *International Journal of Nursing Studies*, 47(12): 1545–1561.

Luymes, D.T. and Tamminga, K. (1995) 'Integrating public safety and use into planning urban greenways', *Landscape and Urban Planning*, 33(1–3): 391–400.

Malina, R. and Little, B. (2008) 'Physical activity: the present in the context of the past', *American Journal of Human Biology*, 20(4): 373–391.

Martinez, S.M., Arredondo, E.M., Perez, G. and Baquero, B. (2009) 'Individual, social, and environmental barriers to and facilitators of physical activity among Latinas living in San Diego county: focus group results', *Family and Community Health*, 32(1): 22–33.

Matos, R. (2004) 'Can slow tourism bring new life to alpine regions?', in K. Weiermair and C. Mathies (eds), *Tourism and Tourism Industry: Shaping the Future*, New York: Haworth Hospitality Press, pp. 93–103.

McCormack, G.R., Giles-Corti, B., Bulsara, M. and Pikora, T.J. (2006) 'Correlates of distances traveled to use recreational facilities for physical activity behaviors', *The International Journal of Behavioral Nutrition and Physical Activity*, 3(18). DOI: 10.1186/1479-5868-3-18.

McGinn, A.P., Evenson, K.R., Herring, A.H. and Huston, S.L. (2007) 'The relationship between leisure, walking, and transportation activity with the natural environment', *Health & Place*, 13(3): 588–602.

Merom, D., Rissel C., Phongsavan, P., Smith, B.J., Van Kemenade, C., Brown, W.J. and Bauman, A.E. (2007) 'Promoting walking with pedometers in the community: the step-by-step trial', *American Journal of Preventive Medicine*, 32(4): 290–297.

Mouden, A.V. and Lee, C. (2003) 'Walking and bycling: An evaluation of environmental audit instruments', *American Journal of Health Promotion*, 18(1): 21–37.

Neuvonen, M., Sievanen, T., Tonnes, S. and Koskela, T. (2007) 'Access to green areas and the frequency of visits – a case study in Helsinki', *Urban Forestry & Urban Greening*, 6(4): 235–247.

Owen, N., Humpel, N., Leslie, E., Bauman, A. and Sallis, J.F. (2004) 'Understanding environmental influences on walking: review and research agenda', *American Journal of Preventive Medicine*, 27(1): 67–76.

Patterson, I. (2007) 'Changes in the provision of leisure services for people with disabilities in Australia', *Therapeutic Recreation Journal*, 41(2): 108–118.

Payne, L.L., Mowen, A.J. and Orsega-Smith, E. (2002) 'An examination of park preferences and behaviors among urban residents: the role of residential location, race, and age', *Leisure Sciences*, 24(2): 181–198.

Pegg, S. (2001) 'The importance of leisure in the lives of individuals with a mental illness', in I. Patterson and T. Taylor (eds), *Celebrating Inclusion and Diversity in Leisure*, Williamstown, Victoria, Australia: HM Leisure Planning, pp. 93–102.

Perchoux, C., Kestens, Y., Brondeel, R. and Chaix, B. (2015) 'Accounting for the daily locations visited in the study of the built environment correlates of recreational walking (the RECORD Cohort study)', *Preventive Medicine*, 81: 142–149.

Phongsavan, P., McLean, G. and Bauman, A. (2007) 'Gender differences in influences of perceived environmental and psychosocial correlates on recommended level of physical activity among New Zealanders', *Psychology of Sport and Exercise*, 8(6): 939–950.

Pierce Jr, J.R., Denison, A.V., Arif, A.A. and Rohrer, J.E. (2006) 'Living near a trail is associated with increased odds of walking among patients using community clinics', *Journal of Community Health*, 31(4): 289–302.

Pikora, T., Giles-Corti, B., Bull, F., Jamrozik, K. and Donovan R. (2003) 'Developing a framework for assessment of the environmental determinants of walking and cycling', *Social Science & Medicine*, 56(8): 1693–1703.

Pikora, T., Giles-Corti, B., Knuiman, M., Bull, F., Jamrozik, K. and Donovan, R. (2006) 'Neighborhood environmental factors correlated with walking near home: using spaces', *Medicine and Science in Sports and Exercise*, 38(4): 708–714.

Pralong, J.-P. (2006) 'Geotourism: a new form of tourism utilising natural landscapes and based on imagination and emotion', *Tourism Review*, 61(3): 20–25.

Ravenscroft, N. and Markwell, S. (2000) 'Ethnicity and the integration and exclusion of young people through urban park and recreation provision', *Managing Leisure*, 5(3): 135–150.

Reynolds, K.D., Wolch, J., Byrne, J., Chou, C.P., Feng, G.J., Weaver, S. and Jerrett, M. (2007) 'Trail characteristics as correlates of urban trail use', *American Journal of Health Promotion*, 21(4): 335–345.

Rimer, B.K. and Glanz, K. (2005) *Theory at Glance: A Guide for Health Promotion Practice*, Washington, DC: US Department of Health and Human Services.

Robinson, T. (2008) 'Applying the socio-ecological model to improving fruit and vegetable intake among low-income African Americans', *Journal of Community Health*, 33(6): 395–406.

Sallis, J., Owen, N. and Fisher, E.B. (2008) 'Ecological models of health behaviour', in K. Glanz, B.K. Rimer and K. Viswanath (eds), *Health Behavior and Health Education: Theory, Research and Practice*, 4th edn, San Francisco: Jossey-Bass, pp. 465–485.

Seo, D.C., Torabi, M.R., Jiang, N., Fernandez-Rojas, X. and Park, B.H. (2009) 'Cross-cultural comparison of lack of regular physical activity among college students: universal versus transversal', *International Journal of Behavioral Medicine*, 16(4): 355–359.

Shafer, C.S., Lee, B.K. and Turner, S. (2000) 'A tale of three greenway trails: user perceptions related to quality of life', *Landscape and Urban Planning*, 49(3–4): 163–178.

Shores, K.A. and West, S.T. (2008) 'The relationship between built park environments and physical activity in four park locations', *Journal of Public Health Management and Practice*, 14(3): 9–16.

Shores, K.A., Scott, D. and Floyd, M.F. (2007) 'Constraints to outdoor recreation: a multiple hierarchy stratification perspective', *Leisure Sciences*, 29(3): 227–246.

Spence, J., Shephard, R., Craig, C. and McGannon, K. (2001) *Compilation of Evidence of Effective Active Living Interventions: A Case Study Approach*. Available at: www.utoronto.ca/chp/CCHPR/activelivingcasestudy.pdf.

Stemerding, M., Oppewal, H. and Timmermans, H. (1999) 'A constraints-induced model of park choice', *Leisure Sciences*, 21(2): 145–158.

Sugiyama, T. and Thompson, C.W. (2008) 'Associations between characteristics of neighbourhood open space and older people's walking', *Urban Forestry & Urban Greening*, 7(1): 41–51.

Tan, D., Wang, W., Lu, J. and Bian, Y. (2007) 'Research on methods of assessing pedestrian level of service for sidewalk', *Journal of Transportation Systems Engineering and Information Technology*, 7(5): 74–79.

Tanenbaum, H., Felicitas, J., Yamen, L., Malaika, T., Chih-Ping, C., Palmer, P., Spruijt-Metz, D., Reynolds, K. and Johnson, C. (2016) 'Overweight perception: associations with weight control goals, attempts, and practices among Chinese female college students', *Journal of the Academy of Nutrition and Dietetics*, 116(3): 458–465.

Troped, P.J., Cromley, E.K., Fragala, M.S., Melly, S.J., Hasbrouck, H.H., Gortmaker, S.L. and Brownson, R.C. (2006) 'Development and reliability and validity testing of an audit tool for trail/path characteristics: the path environment audit tool (peat)', *Journal of Physical Activity & Health*, 3(1): 158–175.

Vojnovic, I., Jackson-Elmoore, C., Holtrop, J. and Bruch, S. (2006) 'The renewed interest in urban form and public health: promoting increased physical activity in Michigan', *Cities*, 23(1): 1–17.

Wang, G., Macera, C.A., Scudder-Soucie, B., Schmid, T., Pratt, M. and Buchner, D. (2005) 'A cost–benefit analysis of physical activity using bike/pedestrian trails', *Health Promote Practice*, 6(2): 174–179.

Wen, M., Kandula, N.R. and Lauderdale, D.S. (2007) 'Walking for transportation or leisure: what difference does the neighborhood make?', *Journal of General Internal Medicine*, 22(12): 1674–1680.

Wendel-Vos, G.C.W., Schuit, A.J., De Niet, R., Boshuizen, H.C., Saris, W.H.M. and Kromhout, D. (2004) 'Factors of the physical environment associated with walking and bicycling', *Medicine and Science in Sports and Exercise*, 36(4): 725–730.

Wendel-Vos, W., Droomers, M., Kremers, S., Brug, J. and Van Lenthe, F. (2007) 'Potential environmental determinants of physical activity in adults: a systematic review', *Obesity Reviews*, 8(5): 425–440.

WHO (2005) *Review of Best Practice in Interventions to Promote Physical Activity in Developing Countries*, Beijing: World Health Organization.

WHO (2008) *Physical Inactivity: A Global Public Health Problem*. World Health Organization. Available at: www.who.int/dietphysicalactivity/factsheet_inactivity/en.

WHO (2012) *Obesity and Overweight: Fact Sheet Number 311*. World Health Organization, Available at: www.who.int/mediacentre/factsheets/fs311/en/index.html.

Wittink, H., Engelbert, R. and Takken, T. (2011) 'The dangers of inactivity: exercise and inactivity physiology for the manual therapist', *Manual Therapy*, 16(3): 209–216.

28

Taking the first step

From physical inactivity towards a healthier lifestyle through leisure walking

Miia Grénman and Juulia Räikkönen

> I have two doctors, my left leg and my right.
>
> (Trevelyan 1913: 56)

Introduction

This chapter discusses physical activity, namely leisure walking, in relation to the wellness lifestyle, which has become one of the most recognized lifestyles in the Western consumer societies. The wellness lifestyle can be considered as a by-product of the current consumer culture, in which health and physical appearance are highly valued and expressed through consumption (Smith Maguire 2008). Furthermore, it represents a form of transformative consumption, in which value emerges from the enhancement of health and well-being (Rosenbaum 2015). Wellness emphasizes self-responsibility and proactive behaviour in achieving holistic well-being, i.e. the balance of physical, mental, and social well-being (e.g. Müller and Lanz Kauffman 2001; Travis 1972). In reference to the sociological discussions, wellness relates to the interior and the exterior of the body, which is seen as a consumer object that constantly needs to be improved, managed, and displayed through self-work (Smith Maguire 2008). Moreover, wellness relates to identity and lifestyle construction (e.g. Giddens 1991), which is manifested through the consumption of various health-related products, services, and experiences (Bauman 2007; Featherstone 2007; Sassatelli 2010, 2012).

Paradoxically, while the valuation of health and physical appearance is at its highest ever, obesity and physical inactivity have simultaneously increased significantly (WHO 2008). Physical activity can be defined as '*any bodily movement produced by the contraction of skeletal muscle that increases energy expenditure above the basal level*' (WHO 2016). Leisure walking, in turn, can be considered as the nearest to perfect form of physical activity as it is possible for everyone, except for the seriously disabled or very frail (Morris and Hardman 1997).

Physical activity is a significant part of the wellness lifestyle and has become an important public health issue that is widely addressed in societal and academic discussions (US DHHS 2008; Van Tuyckom and Scheerder 2010). Previous research on physical activity has, however, been dominated by the psychological, physiological, and biomedical perspectives, while the socio-cultural aspects have been largely ignored (Goodsel *et al.* 2013). In particular, socio–cultural contexts that involve everyday situations and lifestyle choices offer new insights and are crucial for understanding physical activity as a part of everyday life (cf. Goodsel *et al.* 2013; Koski 2008).

Further, physical activity has rarely been examined in relation to individuals' overall ensemble of life, acknowledging that all individuals have some kind of relationship with physical activity, regardless of whether they are physically active or inactive (Koski 2008). Accordingly, there is a need for further research on the meanings and social embeddedness of physical activity among different groups, such as young people (Marks *et al.* 2011). In order to broaden the established understanding of the socio-cultural aspects of physical activity, this chapter discusses leisure walking in relation to consumer culture and the wellness lifestyle, and empirically examines how perceived well-being, valuation of different life domains, and meanings of physical activity differ in relation to the level of physical activity.

From illness to wellness

The growing interest in health and physical appearance can be found in the convergence of several social, economic, and political factors. In addition to the rise of the consumer culture and the image-driven service economy, the wellness trend has been fuelled by the popular cultural interest in self-enhancement and the societal emphasis on individual responsibility, demedicalization and the commercialization of health, as well as the increasing sedentariness both in leisure and work (e.g. Crawford 1980; Smith Maguire 2008).

The roots of the wellness ideology can be traced back to the 1950s, when health scientists in the United States related wellness to health promotion through lifestyle change (Dunn 1959; Travis 1972). Notably, the current understanding on wellness is largely based on the ideas of John Travis (1972), who developed the Illness–Wellness Continuum as a response to the traditional medical view that considered an individual healthy if no symptoms of illness were present. He also emphasized personal self-responsibility, and highlighted that reaching wellness is an ongoing process moving from disability, symptoms, and signs of illness towards higher-level wellness through awareness, education, and growth (SRI International 2010; Travis 1972).

Today, wellness is considered as a lifestyle of self-discovery that originates from an individual. Instead of being reactive and focusing on treating diseases and curing illnesses, wellness emphasizes proactive behaviour in achieving holistic well-being and a balanced life (e.g. Müller and Lanz Kaufmann 2001). When basic needs are fulfilled, it is possible to concentrate on higher-level needs, such as self-actualization or a better quality of life (Maslow 1954). Along this path, lifestyle choices not only support the pursuit of a balanced and meaningful life, but they also signal social status through the ability and willingness to make permanent lifestyle changes (e.g. Smith Maguire 2008; cf. Bourdieu 1984).

The wellness lifestyle is tightly intertwined with consumption and identity creation, following the principles of consumer culture (cf. Arnould and Thompson 2005). The wellness lifestyle is, indeed, expressed through the consumption of, e.g. healthy food, vitamins and supplements, physical exercise, fitness clothing and equipment, and beauty care (cf. Müller and Lanz Kaufmann 2001). During recent years, wellness has moved from a grassroots, niche movement to the mainstream, creating a global multi-trillion-dollar wellness market (Pilzer 2007).

From products to transformations

Leisure walking is an integrated part of everyday life and, in essence, it does not require a substantial investment of time and money, nor specific skills or equipment (Morris and Hardman 1997). Yet, a large number of people still remain physically inactive. Marketing has the potential to make the physical culture more appealing and commercialized (e.g. Smith Maguire 2008), by adding value through the experiential and symbolic aspects of consumption (cf. Arnould and Thompson 2005; Pine and Gilmore 1999). Indeed, a large consumer industry has emerged around leisure walking, offering consumers various traditional and specialized products (e.g. footwear, clothing, pedometers, Nordic Walking poles), services (e.g. training programs for walking and jogging), as well as physical and emotional experiences (e.g. hiking, walking tourism, pilgrimage).

Leisure time physical activity is connected to a wider societal and economic change – the experience and transformation economy – in which consumers are not looking for mere products and services but, instead, emotional experiences and permanent transformations (Pine and Gilmore 1999). According to the 'experience economy logic', experience is a further development of service; it is subjective in nature and takes place in the mind of a consumer, thus requiring commitment and active participation (e.g. Alsos et al. 2014; Pine and Gilmore 1999). Consumers have become active co-creators of their own experiences and, through personalized interaction, co-create unique value for themselves (Prahalad and Ramaswamy 2004; Vargo and Lusch 2004).

Previous research has, however, been criticized for over-emphasizing the service provider perspective, while ignoring the real consumer focus (e.g. Heinonen et al. 2010). This is especially essential in regard to personal transformations that revolve around meaning and interaction (cf. Arnould and Thompson 2005), placing the consumer at the centre of the value creation process. Consumers do not only choose a product or service based on preferences or experiential aspects, but, more importantly, based on how products and services transform them, their lives, and their ways of thinking (e.g. Mermiri 2009; cf. Sassatelli 2012). Noteworthy, personal transformations can only be 'guided' or 'coached' and they take place only if the products and services are meaningful and resonate with a consumer (cf. Gilmore and Pine 2007). Recently, increasing interest has been placed on consumer centricity and empowerment by arguing that consumers themselves interpret their own experiences and reconstruct the consumer reality in which value is embedded (Heinonen et al. 2010, 2013). This is particularly evident in relation to the wellness lifestyle, which emphasizes the central and proactive role of the consumer.

While the consumer culture reinforces material consumption as a part of everyday life and a culturally accepted means of seeking happiness, well-being, and a better quality of life, currently these value outcomes are increasingly pursued through non-material consumption (Rosenbaum 2015). Similarly, value is increasingly evaluated with non-economic measures, emphasizing the desire for holistic well-being and a meaningful life (Uysal et al. 2016). The wellness movement is one of the most visible forms of this shift and, thus, examining the meanings and motivations of wellness-related behaviour, such as leisure walking, is important in order to understand what 'wellness value' is and how it emerges.

Data and methods

Drawing on the theoretical discussions on physical activity as a part of the wellness lifestyle, we compare the physically active and the inactive Finnish university students to analyze: 1) how engagement in leisure walking influences the various aspects of perceived well-being; 2) how different life domains are valued; and 3) how the meanings of physical activity differ between the levels of physical activity. The data is derived from the nationally representative *University Student Health Survey*, collected in Finland in 2012 (Kunttu and Pesonen 2013). The target population consisted of Finnish university students, aged 18–34 years. The self-report survey was implemented as a postal and online questionnaire and 4,403 useable responses were received, yielding a response rate of 44%.

The broad survey on students' physical, mental, and social well-being has been carried out every four years in cooperation with various health professionals. In 2012, the health-centricity of the survey was broadened with a more sociological perspective on the role of physical activity in students' everyday life. In the current study, we analyzed variables related to physical well-being (four variables), mental well-being (two variables), social well-being (four variables), value perceptions and personal life goals (10 variables), as well as the meanings of physical activity (54 variables). The operationalization of the measures and variables followed the traditions of previous health surveys (e.g. Kunttu and Pesonen 2013) and similar studies of physical activity (Koski and Tähtinen 2005; Zacheus 2010).

In the analysis, we first identified three categories: the physically inactive; the moderately active leisure walkers; and the highly active leisure walkers. Then, we conducted various cross tabulations and analyses of variance (ANOVA) to trace the differences between these categories in relation to perceived well-being, as well as value perceptions and personal life goals. Furthermore, we conducted a principal component analysis (PCA) with the original 54 meanings of physical activity to reveal the higher order meanings, which were then analyzed with ANOVA.

Results

Physically inactive, moderately active leisure walkers, and highly active leisure walkers

In order to identify the level of physical activity in general, we analyzed the question: 'How often do you engage in leisure time physical activity for a minimum of half an hour so that you sweat and become at least slightly short of breath?' The analysis revealed that 22% (n = 975) of the respondents were physically inactive, exercising fewer than three times per month. The majority, 52% (n = 2254), were moderately active, exercising 1–3 times a week, while 26% (n = 1139) were highly active, exercising more than four times a week.

To identify the leisure walkers, we analyzed the open-ended question: 'What types of physical activity do you engage in and how frequently? Give max. three of your favourites.' For the further analysis, we included the following types of physical activity: walking, Nordic walking, walking with a dog/pram, and hiking. Additionally, jogging was included if it appeared on its own or together with walking, but excluded, when combined with running. As a result, we identified 1,680 leisure walkers (38%) who, on average, practised leisure walking 6.3 times a week (SD = 3.47) and 6.9 hours a week (SD = 4.00). By combining the identified leisure walkers with the level of physical activity, three categories were formed: the physically inactive (n = 975); the moderately active leisure walkers (n = 976); and the highly active leisure walkers (n = 441). Notably, the first category also included some respondents who engaged in leisure walking but, based on their activity level, fell into the physically inactive.

Perceived well-being

As wellness lifestyle centres on holistic well-being, leisure walking was examined in relation to physical, mental, and social well-being (Table 28.1). Physical well-being was analyzed with the questions: 'How would you rate your physical well-being?', 'When buying food, do you consider its healthiness?', and 'Have you ever dieted and lost a lot of weight?' Additionally, the Body Mass Index (BMI) was calculated, based on each respondent's height and weight. The analysis showed that the perceived physical well-being and the consciousness of healthy eating increased with the level of physical activity. Furthermore, physical activity had a positive effect on weight

Table 28.1 Perceived well-being in relation to the level of physical activity

	Physically inactive	Moderately active	Highly active
Physical well-being			
Perceived physical well-being (1 = very poor, 5= very good) n = 2346; F = 166.926***	M = 3.39 (SD = 0.86)	M = 3.74 (SD = 0.78)	M = 4.23 (SD = 0.68)
Healthy eating (seldom–sometimes–often) n = 2386; X^2 = 168.058***	8.3%–42.35–49.4%	1.7%–28.4%–69.9%	0.5%–21.6%–77.9%
Weight loss (yes–no) n = 2381; X^2 = 18.397***	25.9%–74.1%	27.1%–72.9%	36.6%–63.4
BMI (kg/m²) n = 2376; F = 10.177***	M = 24.30 (SD = 5.00)	M = 23.64 (SD = 4.21)	M = 23.24 (SD = 3.52)
Mental well-being			
Perceived mental well-being (1 = very poor, 5 = very good) n = 2347; F = 33.354***	M = 3.46 (SD = 0.99)	M = 3.74 (SD = 0.86)	M = 3.84 (SD = 0.88)
Feeling stressed (yes–no) n=2382; X^2=17.123***	85.5%–14.5%	81.6%–18.4%	76.5%–23.5%
Feeling unhappy and depressed (yes–no) n = 2386; X^2 = 29.992***	71.8%–28.2%	64.6%–35.4%	57.4%–42.6%
Feeling worthless (yes–no) n = 2381; X^2 = 29.580***	54.3%–45.7%	44.9%–55.1%	40.2%–59.8%
Social well-being			
Perceived social well-being (1 = very poor, 5 = very good) n=2345; F = 29.204***	M = 3.57 (SD = 0.97)	M = 3.84 (SD = 0.84)	M = 3.89 (SD = 0.85)
Leisure time with friends (fewer than 3 times per month–once a week– more than 2 times a week) n = 2375; X^2 = 70.741***	38.2%–27.8%–34.0%	25.6%–28.2%–46.2%	20.6%–27.2%–52.2%
Belonging to a group (yes–no) n = 2378; F = 31,767***	54.3%–45.7%	62.6%–37.4%	68.7%–31.3%
Loneliness (yes–no) n = 2374; X^2 = 15.604***	50.3%–49.7%	43.4%–56.6%	40.3%–59.7%
Holistic well-being (1 = very poor, 5 = very good) n = 2344; F = 66.951***	M = 3.57 (SD = 0.81)	M = 3.84 (SD = 0.72)	M = 4.05 (SD = 0.69)

*** p>0.001; **p>0.01; *p>0.5

management, as the highly active had controlled their weight the most and had the lowest BMI. More precisely, the share of overweight respondents (BMI>25 kg/m^2) decreased from 34% to 28% and obese (BMI>30 kg/m^2) from 12% to 3% when comparing the inactive with highly active leisure walkers.

Mental well-being was assessed with the questions: 'How would you rate your mental well-being?', 'Have you recently felt constantly under strain?', 'Have you recently been feeling unhappy and depressed?', and 'Have you recently been thinking of yourself as a worthless person?' Similarly to physical well-being, the perceived mental well-being increased gradually. Accordingly, the higher the level of physical activity, the lower the levels of feeling stress, depression, and worthlessness.

Social well-being, in turn, was examined with the questions: 'How would you rate your social well-being?', 'How often you spend leisure time together with friend/s?', 'Do you feel that you belong to any study-related group?', and 'Do you feel that you are lonely?' The analysis revealed that perceived social well-being increased with the level of physical activity in general, as well as in relation to leisure and work. The more physically active spent more leisure time with friends and expressed belonging to a study-related group. They also felt less lonely than the physically inactive.

Finally, we analyzed the question: 'How would you rate your holistic well-being?' With regards to holistic well-being – as well as all domains of well-being – the results indicated a similar tendency; the differences between the inactive and the moderately active leisure walkers were substantial, while the differences between the moderately and the highly active were modest. Interestingly, the perceived physical well-being of the highly active leisure walkers was clearly higher than their social and mental well-being. By contrast, the physically inactive and the moderately active leisure walkers considered their social well-being to be the highest.

Value perceptions and personal goals

To assess what the respondents valued in life, we analyzed two questions. First, the respondents answered the question: 'How well do the following statements describe you in general?' with the statements: 'I am happy' and 'I am satisfied with my life'. Second, they evaluated 'How important are the following life domains for you at the moment?' in relation to study, leisure time, hobbies, friendship, standard of living/material well-being, health, social status in the study/work community, self-improvement, mental balance, and quality of life. In general, all respondents considered themselves fairly happy and satisfied, with a progressive increase in relation to their level of physical activity (Table 28.2). The same applied to other value perceptions and life domains; they were all valued above the average and their significance rose with the level of physical activity. Across all categories, the most important aspects were health, friendship, quality of life, and mental balance. Again, the differences between the physically inactive and the moderately active leisure walkers exceeded the differences between the moderately and the highly active, indicating that even a small increase in physical activity matters.

Meanings of physical activity

The meanings of physical activity were examined with the question: 'How important are the following variables for you when engaging in physical activity?', which comprised 54 variables. To summarize the information of the original variables into higher-order meanings, a PCA was conducted (Table 28.3). All variables with loadings greater than 0.40 were included (four variables excluded), and all components with an eigenvalue greater than 1 were retained in the solution. As a result, ten components were identified, accounting for 62% of the explained variance, and named 1) sociability, 2) recreation and relaxation, 3) physicality and excitement, 4) trendiness,

Table 28.2 Value perceptions and personal goals in relation to the level of physical activity

Value perceptions (1 = totally disagree, 5 = totally agree)	Physically inactive	Moderately active	Highly active
I am happy n = 2370; F = 30.167***	M = 3.59 (SD = 1.06)	M = 3.89 (SD = 0.93)	M = 3.96 (SD = 0.94)
I am satisfied with my life n = 2358; F = 29.665***	M=3.54 (SD=1.04)	M = 3.84 (SD = 0.94)	M = 3.89 (SD = 0.92)

Personal goals (1 = totally insignificant, 5 = very important)			
Study n = 2361; F = 4.445*	M = 3.86 (SD = 1.00)	M = 3.94 (SD = 0.92)	M = 4.02 (SD = 0.90)
Leisure time n = 2361; F = 24.421***	M = 4.11 (SD = 0.87)	M = 4.31 (SD = 0.72)	M = 4.37 (SD = 0.70)
Hobbies n = 2361; F = 229.846***	M = 3.24 (SD = 1.07)	M = 3.86 (SD = 0.83)	M = 4.31 (SD = 0.76)
Friendship n = 2359; F = 2359	M = 4.15 (SD = 0.91)	M=4.37 (SD=0.74)	M=4.43 (SD=0.75)
Standard of living/ material well-being n = 2358; F = 3.028*	M = 3.49 (SD = 0.99)	M = 3.58 (SD = 0.83)	M = 3.58 (SD = 0.85)
Health n = 2363; F = 129.363***	M = 4.08 (SD = 0.87)	M = 4.53 (SD = 0.64)	M = 4.66 (SD = 0.57)
Social status in study/ work community n = 2360; F = 4.208*	M = 3.38 (SD = 1.07)	M = 3.48 (SD = 0.96)	M = 3.53 (SD = 0.99)
Self-improvement n = 2363; F = 28.555***	M = 3.88 (SD = 0.85)	M = 4.08 (SD = 0.75)	M = 4.19 (SD = 0.74)
Mental balance n = 2359; F = 33.110***	M = 4.02 (SD = 0.88)	M = 4.30 (SD = 0.74)	M = 4.28 (SD = 0.73)
Quality of life n = 2359; F = 35.541***	M = 4.13 (SD = 0.77)	M = 4.39 (SD = 0.64)	M = 4.36 (SD = 0.67)

*** p>0.001; **p>0.01; *p>0.5

Table 28.3 Results of the Principal Component Analysis on the meanings of physical activity

Principal components	Loading	Eigenvalue	Variance explained	Cronbach's alpha
Sociability		15.44	28.58%	0.90
Sense of belonging	0.77			
Group exercising	0.76			
Cooperation and/or encouragement	0.75			
Same-spirited exercisers	0.70			
Instruction from others	0.60			
Creating social contacts	0.58			
Indulging in a different role	0.55			
Being together with family and/or friends	0.52			
The feeling of being good at something	0.44			
Fun and/or play	0.42			

Principal components	Loading	Eigenvalue	Variance explained	Cronbach's alpha
Recreation and relaxation		4.65	8.61%	0.87
Recreation	0.74			
Relaxation	0.71			
Sense of well-being	0.71			
Escaping from the everyday life	0.68			
Joy	0.64			
'Me-time'	0.63			
Pressure and/or stress relief	0.63			
Being in nature	0.55			
Achieving balance	0.53			
Physicality and excitement		3.28	6.60	0.83
Extreme efforts	0.73			
Physical strain	0.62			
Striving for better performance	0.60			
Following up on one's own progress	0.58			
Gaining muscle mass and/or power	0.56			
Speed	0.53			
Danger/risks/excitement	0.45			
Trendiness		2.01	3.72	0.86
Trendy and/or famous exercising facility	0.80			
Trendy outfit and/or gear	0.76			
Achieving a trendy image	0.75			
Trendy sports	0.72			
Technical outfit and/or gear	0.64			
Self-development		1.85	3.42	0.75
Improving self-control	0.69			
Improving self-confidence	0.64			
Minimizing failure	0.58			
Mental growth	0.55			
Appearance and fitness		1.58	2.93	0.72
Improving appearance	0.77			
Controlling and/or losing weight	0.67			
Improving physical fitness	0.49			
Pursuing and/or maintaining health	0.45			
Competition		1.38	2.56	0.87
Success and/or winning	0.74			
Competition	0.70			
Convenience		1.20	2.22	0.60
Affordability	0.76			
Accessibility	0.72			
Familiar sports	0.44			
Regularity		1.08	2.00	0.77
Regularity of exercise	0.65			
Regular exercise program	0.62			
Experientiality		1.04	1.92	0.80
Learning new skills	0.58			
New experiences	0.56			
Variety	0.46			
Intellectual stimulus	0.42			

PCA. Varimax Rotation with Kaiser Normalization; n=2135; KMO=0.953; X^2=61106.346; Bartlett's test of sphericity p<0.001

Table 28.4 Meanings of physical activity in relation to the level of physical activity

Meanings of physical activity (1 = totally insignificant, 5 = very important)	Physically inactive	Moderately active	Highly active
Sociability n = 2339; F = 39.381***	M = 2.73 (SD = 0.87)	M = 2.98 (SD = 0.81)	M = 3.13 (SD = 0.81)
Recreation and relaxation n = 2339; F = 171.112***	M = 3.53 (SD = 0.76)	M = 3.99 (SD = 0.57)	M = 4.13 (SD = 0.57)
Physicality and excitement n = 2339; F = 222.190***	M = 2.68 (SD = 0,80)	M = 3.06 (SD = 0.72)	M = 3.59 (SD = 0.69)
Trendiness n = 2338; F = 83.341***	M = 1.87 (SD = 0.69)	M = 2.12 (SD = 0.72)	M = 2.40 (SD = 0.81)
Self-development n = 2337; F = 40.913***	M = 2.76 (SD = 0.91)	M = 2.97 (SD = 0.80)	M = 3.19 (SD = 0.81)
Appearance and fitness n = 2339; F = 103.034***	M = 3.61 (SD = 0.85)	M = 4.01 (SD = 0.62)	M = 4.13 (SD = 0.65)
Competition n = 2338; F = 51.815***	M = 1.82 (SD = 0.95)	M = 1.91 (SD = 1.02)	M = 2.41 (SD = 1.16)
Convenience n = 2335; F = 7.630***	M = 3.53 (SD = 1.04)	M = 3.70 (SD = 0.85)	M = 3.62 (SD = 0.87)
Regularity n = 2339; F = 327.403***	M = 2.56 (SD = 1.03)	M = 3.22 (SD = 0.88)	M = 3.92 (SD = 0.87)
Experientiality n = 2338; F = 77.330***	M = 2.91 (SD = 0.91)	M = 3.23 (SD = 0.82)	M = 3.50 (SD = 0.81)

*** p > 0.001; **p > 0.01; *p > 0.5

5) self-development, 6) appearance and fitness, 7) competition, 8) convenience, 9) regularity, and 10) experientiality. Finally, the mean values of the 10 meanings were calculated and used in the ANOVA to trace the differences between the levels of physical activity.

The results of ANOVA (Table 28.4) showed that the most important meanings of physical activity for all categories were 'appearance and fitness' and 'recreation and relaxation'. Interestingly, the physically inactive valued the former over the latter, while the more active considered both meanings equally important. Convenience was also an important aspect of physical activity, yet the highly active valued 'regularity' over 'convenience'. They also perceived 'physicality and excitement' substantially more important than the other categories. Additionally, the 'experientiality' of physical activity was considered fairly important, especially among the highly active leisure walkers. By contrast, 'sociability' and 'self-development' were not considered essential, and 'trendiness' and 'competition' were the most insignificant meanings for all categories.

Conclusions and discussion

In the current chapter, we discussed leisure walking in relation to consumer culture and the wellness lifestyle. Through the large survey data, we analyzed how the perceived well-being, valuation of different life domains, and meanings of physical activity of Finnish university students' differed according to their level of physical activity. The results can be further elaborated in relation to the positive effects of physical activity on personal well-being, the changing nature of value and value creation, and, finally, the wider societal implications on health promotion.

This study reinforced the previous understanding on the various benefits of physical activity. The engagement in leisure walking clearly increased the perceived physical, mental, and social well-being of the respondents. Additionally, the valuation of different life domains and the meanings of physical activity were seen as more important among the physically active than the inactive. Remarkably, the differences between the inactive and the moderately active leisure walkers were larger that the differences between the moderately and the highly active. This indicates that even a small increase in the level of physical activity has considerable effects on health and well-being, but also on happiness, life satisfaction, and quality of life, which, on the personal level, may be even more significant for individuals. Indeed, on the path from total physical inactivity towards a healthier lifestyle, leisure walking is an excellent first step.

However, from the perspective of the wellness lifestyle, this 'first step' is not enough. Only the 'second step', from moderately active to highly active leisure walkers, began to represent an assimilation of the wellness lifestyle. The data revealed that, in addition to the amount of physical activity, other practices of everyday life, such as the consumption of healthy food and weight management, illustrated awareness and willingness to invest in a healthy lifestyle. Furthermore, the tightly intertwined entities of leisure time, hobbies, and self-improvement were valued more than the traditional economic measures of well-being, i.e. the standard of living and material well-being. This supports the current discussion on the importance of the enhanced value outcomes, such as health, well-being, quality of life, and happiness (Rosenbaum 2015; Uysal et al. 2016), in pursuing a meaningful and a good life.

The experiential and transformational aspects of the wellness lifestyle were accentuated, especially in the meanings of physical activity. The valuation of the exterior of the body was signified through the importance of "appearance and fitness" and "physicality and excitement". "Recreation and relaxation" and the "experientiality" of physical activity, in turn, represented the interior of the body, placing emphasis on self-enhancement, learning, and inner growth. Additionally, the importance of "regularity" among the highly active leisure walkers denoted that physical activity is, indeed, a part of their lifestyle; it does not necessarily have to be convenient, but rather, a meaningful and desirable part of their everyday life.

This brings us to the discussion on *wellness value*, which we define as *"value that originates from the personal transformation towards a healthier lifestyle". It influences both behaviour and a person's way of thinking, aims at achieving a meaningful and a good life, and is evaluated mainly by non-economic measures.* As this process evidently goes beyond the experience economy logic, we suggest that the concept *transformation economy logic* would better illustrate this changing nature of value and value creation. Personal transformation, such as adopting the wellness lifestyle, cannot occur if it is not truly meaningful for the individual. This places consumer centricity, empowerment, and commitment in the spotlight, and, accordingly, also changes the role of the service provider (see Heinonen et al. 2010, 2013). A lifestyle change can only be initiated and supported, but not maintained by the service provider, as it originates from the individual and is influenced by all everyday choices.

On the societal level, physical activity – and especially physical inactivity – is an important public health issue, due to the growing number of lifestyle diseases and the increasing health-care costs. As the results indicated, health is definitely one the most valued assets of life, but health *per se* is not sufficient in motivating individuals to engage in physical activity and adopt a healthier lifestyle. Thus, understanding of the rational and, more importantly, the emotional moving forces that create value in physical activity, needs to be acknowledged in health promotion by both public and private sectors. Notably, besides the traditional managerial implications, marketing can also be harnessed to serve societal purposes by enhancing the well-being of individuals, communities, and ecosystems in a wider sense (Rosenbaum 2015).

In closing, we address the main limitations and suggest directions for future research. Our data set was large, but concentrated on a rather homogeneous group in terms of age, life course stage, and economic position. However, students in higher education are likely to represent the healthy and the wealthy future consumers, forming an interesting target group for the proactive wellness market. The data also represented a Finnish perspective, which challenges the generalization of the results. Further, the methods of analysis were fairly basic, yet serving the aim of the study and shedding light on the scarcely researched social-cultural aspects of physical activity. Evidently, more cross-national multi-method research in this area is needed. In particular, we call for research addressing value and value creation in relation to the wellness lifestyle and the wider context of transformation economy.

References

Alsos, G.A., Eide, D. and Madsen, E.L. (2014) 'Introduction: innovation in tourism industries', in G.A. Alsos, D. Eide and E.L. Madsen (eds), *Handbook of Research on Innovation in Tourism Industries,* Cheltenham, Glos: Edward Elgar, pp. 1–24.

Arnould, E.J. and Thompson, C.J. (2005) 'Consumer Culture Theory (CCT): twenty years of research', *Journal of Consumer Research,* 31(4): 868–882.

Bauman, S. (2007) *Consuming Life,* Cambridge, UK: Polity Press.

Bourdieu, P. (1984) *Distinction: A Social Critique of the Judgment of Taste,* Cambridge, MA: Harvard University Press.

Crawford, R. (1980) 'Healthism and the medicalization of everyday life', *International Journal of Health Services,* 10(3): 365–388.

Dunn, H. (1959) 'High-level wellness for man and society', *American Journal of Public Health,* 49(6): 786–792.

Featherstone, M. (2007) *Consumer Culture and Postmodernism,* 2nd edn, London: Sage Publications.

Giddens, A. (1991) *Modernity and Self-identity: Self and Society in the Late Modern Age,* Stanford, CA: Stanford University Press.

Gilmore, J.H. and Pine, B.J. (2007) *Authenticity: What Consumers Really Want,* Boston, MA: Harvard Business School Press.

Goodsell, T.L., Harris, B.D. and Bailey, B.W. (2013) 'Family status and motivations to run: a qualitative study of marathon runners', *Leisure Sciences,* 35(4): 337–352.

Heinonen, K., Strandvik, T., Mickelsson, K.-J., Edvarsson, B., Sundström, E. and Andersson, P. (2010) 'A customer dominant logic of service', *Journal of Service Management,* 21(4): 531–548.

Heinonen, K., Strandvik, T. and Voima, P. (2013) 'Customer dominant value formation in service', *European Business Review,* 25(2): 104–123.

Koski, P. (2008) 'Physical Activity Relationship (PAR)', *International Review of the Sociology of Sport,* 43(2): 151–163.

Koski, P. and Tähtinen, J. (2005) 'Liikunnan merkitykset nuoruudessa [The meanings of sport and physical activities in youth]', *Nuorisotutkimus,* 23(1): 3–21.

Kunttu, K. and Pesonen, T. (2013) *Korkeakouluopiskelijoiden terveystutkimus 2012 [Student Health Survey 2012: A national survey among Finnish university students],* Helsinki: Ylioppilaiden terveydenhoitosäätiö.

Marks, D.F., Murray, M., Evans, B. and Vida Estacio, E. (2011) *Health Psychology: Theory, Research and Practice,* 3rd edn, London: Sage Publications.

Maslow, A.H. (1954) *Motivation and Personality,* New York: Harper.

Mermiri, T. (2009) *The Transformation Economy. Arts and Business: Beyond Experience, Culture, Consumer and Brand,* London: Arts and Business Organization.

Morris, J.N. and Hardman, A.E. (1997) 'Walking to health', *Sports Medicine,* 23(5): 306–332.

Müller, H. and Lanz Kaufmann, E. (2001) 'Wellness tourism: market analysis of a special health tourism segment and implications for the hotel industry', *Journal of Vacation Marketing,* 7(1): 5–17.

Pilzer, P. (2007) *The New Wellness Revolution,* 2nd edn, Hoboken, NJ: Wiley & Sons.

Pine, J. and Gilmore, J. (1999) *The Experience Economy: Work is Theatre Every Business a Stage,* Boston, MA: Harvard Business School Press.

Prahalad, C.K. and Ramaswamy, V. (2004) *The Future of Competition: Co-creating Unique Value with Customers,* Boston, MA: Harvard Business School Press.

Rosenbaum, M.S. (2015) 'Transformative service research: focus on well-being', *The Service Industries Journal*, 35(7–8): 363–367.

Sassatelli, R. (2010) *Fitness Culture: Gyms and the Commercialisation of Discipline and Fun*, Basingstoke: Palgrave Macmillan.

Sassatelli, R. (2012) 'Self and body', in F. Trentmann (ed.), *The Oxford Handbook of the History of Consumption*, Oxford: Oxford University Press, pp. 633–652.

Smith Maguire, J. (2008) *Fit for Consumption: Sociology and the Business of Fitness*, London: Routledge.

SRI International (2010) *Spas and the Global Wellness Market: Synergies and Opportunities*. Global Spa Summit. Available at: www.globalspasummit.org/images/stories/pdf/gss_sri_spasandwellnessreport_rev_82010.pdf (accessed 4 October 2010).

Travis, J. (1972) The Illness-Wellness Continuum. Available at: www.thewellspring.com/wellspring/introduction-to-wellness/357/key-concept-1-the-illnesswellness-continuum.cfm (accessed 4 October 2010).

Trevelyan, G.M. (1913) 'Walking', in *Clio, a Muse and Other Essays*, London: Green and Co.

US DHSS (2008) *Physical Activity Guidelines for Americans*. Department of Health and Human Services. Available at: http://health.gov/paguidelines/guidelines/pdf/paguide.pdf (accessed 16 January 2016).

Uysal, M., Sirgy, M.J., Woo, E. and Kim, H.L. (2016) 'Quality of life (QOL) and well-being research in tourism', *Tourism Management*, 53: 244–261.

Van Tuyckom, C. and Scheerder, J. (2010) 'Sport for all? Insight into stratification and compensation mechanisms of sporting activity in the 27 European Union member states', *Sport, Education and Society*, 15(4): 495–512.

Vargo, S. and Lusch, R. (2004) 'Evolving to a new dominant logic for marketing', *Journal of Marketing*, 68(1): 1–17.

WHO (2008) *Mean Body Mass Index (BMI)*. World Health Organization. Available at: www.who.int/gho/ncd/risk_factors/bmi_text/en (accessed 9 May 2016).

WHO (2016) *Physical Activity*. World Health Organization. Available at: www.who.int/topics/physical_activity/en (accessed 9 May 2016).

Zacheus, T. (2010) 'Liikuntaan ja urheiluun liittyvät merkitykset suomalaisten elämän aikana [The significance of exercise and sport for Finns during their life span]', *Kasvatus & Aika*, 4(2): 55–68.

29

Dog walking in urban greenspaces

Giovanna Bertella

Introduction

Urban greenspaces are very important for residents' physical and mental health (Sugiyama and Ward Thompson 2008; Maas *et al.* 2006; van den Berg *et al.* 2010; Roy *et al.* 2012; Buchecker and Degenhardt 2015; Strandell and Hall 2015). Walking in such areas can be described by the term "soft fascination". This may be defined as a combination of light physical activity, effortless concentration and aesthetic pleasure. Soft fascination is often described by the pleasure deriving from various sources, such as, for example, the observation of vegetation and animals, at a distance removed from urban landscapes, typically studded with offices and shops (Kuo *et al.* 1998; Kaplan 1995; Herzog *et al.* 1997; Hartig *et al.* 2003; van den Berg *et al.* 2010).

The companionship of a dog usually motivates people to use urban greenspaces for daily walks (Brown and Rhodes 2006; Wood *et al.* 2007). However, certain studies highlight that simple ownership of a dog does not necessarily lead to performance of daily walks (Cutt *et al.* 2008; McCormack *et al.* 2011). The willingness of people to walk dogs depends also on their perception of their dogs as a source of motivation and social support, and on dog-specific factors, such as breed and temperament. Nonetheless, it can be said that urban greenspaces provide a leisure-oriented landscape to which many dog guardians daily bring their canine companions to play, exercise and socialise with other dogs and humans.

Despite the possibility of conflicts deriving from dog fights and from the different needs and behaviours of the various users of public greenspace, dog walking is a particularly beneficial urban walking experience. This can be explained by the strong bond between the guardians and their pets and the social benefits resulting from bonding among dog walkers (Beck and Meyers 1997; Wood *et al.* 2005; Crawford *et al.* 2006; Cutt *et al.* 2007; Walsh 2009; Urbanik and Morgan 2013; Graham and Glover 2014).

This study aims to contribute to a deep understanding of the dog walking experience in urban greenspace, so that such activity can be promoted and managed through public health and life quality programmes (Bauman *et al.* 2001; Coleman *et al.* 2008; Salmon *et al.* 2010). The focus is on those aspects related to the dog guardian's mental well-being, understood as an experience of pleasure, happiness, sense of meaning and self-realisation (Ryan and Deci 2001).

Theoretical background

Dog ownership and companionship

The manner in which dogs are viewed by their guardians depends on the socio-cultural context, on the guardian's personality and on his or her inclination towards animals and "different others" (Bagley and Gonsman 2005; Brown 2007). Dogs are sometimes understood in relation to the role they play in the context of a job or sport; alternatively, they may be viewed as status symbols (Hirschman 1994). This utilitarian view can be related to the conceptualisation of dogs as objects, necessarily meaning that they can be used by virtue of their being the subject of ownership. The case of dogs motivating their guardians to be more active can, to a certain degree, be viewed in this perspective.

Alternatively, dogs can be perceived as non-human persons, who, although legally owned, are conceptualised, not as objects of property, but as significant others. Such a view is quite diffuse in many Western countries. In this regard, dogs tend to be socially constructed as loyal companions with whom meaningful relationships can be easily established (Beck and Madresh 2008; DeMello 2012).

The guardian–dog relationships are often very intense and complex. Dogs tend to make their guardians feel treasured and desirable, and some guardians view their dogs as friends, partners, substitutes for children, replicas of themselves or as individuals to look up to (Hirschman 1994; Holbrook *et al.* 2001; Brown 2007).

The dog walking experience

Dog walking is among the daily routines through which the guardian–dog relationship manifests itself (DeMello 2012). As with other practices performed by humans and their pets, dog walking can be described as a daily ritual shaped by a combination of the guardians' conceptualisation of their dogs and other more practical considerations, such as, for example, the time available for the activity, and the physical conditions and characteristics of the dog (Holbrook *et al.* 2001; Holak 2008).

According to Wharf Higgins *et al.* (2013), the dog walking experience can be described in terms of four main themes. Three of these themes, already mentioned in the introduction, relate to the different roles that the dog may fulfil: as health promoter, walking buddy and social conduit. The fourth and more dominant theme identified by Wharf Higgins *et al.* (2013) is the transcending of the separation between human and animal. This aspect is strictly related to the idea, already mentioned, of the conceptualisation of dogs. According to Wharf Higgins *et al.* (2013), dog walks tend to be performed because dogs are perceived as family members to whom the guardians owe a duty of care. The dog guardians' motivation to walk daily with their dogs is influenced by their inclination and desire to be good human companions. In this sense, the walks can be inspired by a desire to comply with the ethics of care (Donovan and Adams 2007; Gruen 2015). Walks are thus motivated by a strong sense of responsibility as a result of interspecies love and respect, and are designed to satisfy the dogs' physical and mental needs to be active.

Based on these considerations, dog walking can be described as a leisure-friendly obligation (Shaw 1985; Stebbins 2000; Lepp 2009). Dog walking is about commitment and responsibility, as well as enjoyment and relaxation. Thus, the dog walking experience can be situated between the obligation the person feels towards the animal and the pleasant aspect of the activity that, from the perspective of the human, is centred on a strong emotional attachment to the dog as well as personal positive output in the form of soft fascination.

Method

The empirical investigation of this study draws upon analytical auto-ethnographic techniques comprising full integration of the researcher into the subject of study, her commitment to theoretical analysis and her dialogue with relevant informants (Anderson 2006; Anderson and Austin 2012). With regard to the first feature, it is pertinent that the author presents her personal experience in terms of urban dog walking. Having engaged in the practice only occasionally for a few years during her adolescence, by way of volunteering for a local pound, urban dog walking has now been part of the author's daily routine for the past nine years.

With regard to thematic analysis and dialogue with relevant informants, the data were collected while performing dog walks, engaging in dialogue with other dog walkers, and reporting such experiences in a diary. The narrative relative to the diary entries are analysed on the basis of the relevant topics identified in the literature, grouped into two broad categories.

1) Conceptualisation of the dog: dogs as health promoters and motivators, dogs as social conduits, dogs as significant others.
2) The experience of the walk: obligation and leisure, soft fascination, ritual, transcendence of interspecies differences.

Emerging themes that do not fit into any of the categories or into any of the category specifications uncover hitherto unexposed aspects of the dog walking experience. Table 29.1 shows two examples.

Table 29.1 Dog walking

Diary entries	Theme
20 April 2015 Tromsø. [. . .] To avoid the deep snow we have walked partly under the trees, in the forest. The spring vegetation is appearing. Just before the lake we saw a couple of ducks! Dina run after them and stopped after a couple of meters: too much snow. Probably, she remembered that she has no chance to catch any flying animal! It is possible to see some parts of the lake free of ice, and many seagulls that, I suppose, will soon nest. We walked around the lake, Dina on the leash and me stopping every five meters to take pictures of the amazing dark-blue sky.	Soft fascination
7 July 2015 Florence. [. . .] we were 10 people, each of us with a dog. Standing or sitting on the grass, enjoying the morning temperature. We chatted about our dogs: how old they are and how they have entered our lives, their health problems, funny episodes, stories of dog escapes, dog-sittering [sic] and the usual dog-stuff. Somebody mentioned dogs who have passed away, dogs who used to come here regularly. A lady told about the beauty of having the beach all for herself and her dog, when she is on holiday at the seaside, just when the sun rises and the other people have not arrived yet. Similarly, several others shared their stories about early morning walks during the summer time.	Dogs as social conduits. Dogs as significant others. Dog-walkers as a specific type of people.

In order to uncover possible cultural differences and differences derived from the time of the walks, data were collected over a period of four weeks, including weekdays and weekends, during both winter and summer months, from two locations. One location is a quite extensive public park in a densely populated neighbourhood in Florence (Italy). This includes walking paths, a well-equipped children's area, numerous benches and tables, a couple of historical buildings and some statues, large lawns and a small dog area. The second location is a relatively vast and sparsely frequented greenspace in Tromsø (Norway) characterised by a broad path (used by pedestrians, joggers, skiers and bikers), numerous narrow paths (used mainly by joggers and dog walkers), a not-particularly-well-equipped children's area, and a few benches and tables. The author is quite familiar with the physical and cultural environment in both locations, and is relatively well known among the local dog walkers. The walks were undertaken early in the morning and in the afternoon.

Findings and discussion

A shared ritual experience: interspecies couples and communitas

The data show that dog walking was performed usually at fixed times (morning, lunchtime, afternoon and evening), following specific routines (specific paths, stops and games) and using specific objects (leash and collars/harness), with some minor variations due mainly to time constraints and weather conditions. Dog walking was performed by what appeared to be well-matched couples: humans and their dogs. This pattern was observed especially during the early morning walks. Also when the dog was part of a family, it was quite usual for these walks to be performed by the same person. These human–dog couples seemed to be fairly constant and characterised by a strong sense of mutual attachment and loyalty. Most guardians seemed to view themselves as members of these dog–human couples, and they used the pronoun 'we', for example in the expressions: 'We come usually in the morning, just after breakfast' or 'We like the upper part of the park because there are more bushes'. In the Italian greenspace, it was also noted that many dog guardians tended to use nicknames for their dogs such as 'love'.

These findings confirm that the dog walking experience could be viewed as a sort of an interspecies ritual (Holbrook et al. 2001; Holak 2008; Wharf Higgins et al. 2013). In this regard, the repetitive aspect of the dog walking ritual emerged as an important element: those who performed regular dog walks seemed to gain a sort of sense of security from it. For example, when asked about his walking habits, one man answered: 'The afternoon, after work, is for us [him and his dog], no matter what. We come and finish the day as we started'.

Although the dog walking experience appeared to be quite exclusive, involving dog–human couples, the findings suggest that, to a certain extent, the dog walking experience is also shared with other people, more precisely with other dog–human couples. This aspect emerged quite clearly during the walks in Florence. During all these walks, dog guardians met other dog–human couples, and, during the morning walks, the same couples met regularly. Most, if not all, of the dog guardians usually greeted each other and often stopped to chat for a while. It happened that several dog–human couples regularly joined common walks, whereas others did it only occasionally. The park in Florence is clearly a meeting point for the dog guardians living nearby and, as highlighted in the literature, dogs act as social conduits (Wood et al. 2005; Walsh 2009; Graham and Glover 2014; Wharf Higgins et al. 2013).

With regard to this social dimension of the dog walking experience, some data suggest that the dog guardians perceived themselves not only as a specific type of public garden users but also as a group of like-minded people. For example, during a conversation in which six dog guardians participated, a man complained about another type of public gardens users, referred to by the expression 'the moms'. These were described as mothers of young children who tended to overreact in response to off-leash dogs. According to this dog guardian, these women did not teach their children how to behave in the presence of dogs. Talking about a specific episode, this person commented:

> I told her: 'If you scream, the dog barks. If you move fast, the dog barks and runs'. She didn't get it and got angry. We [dog guardians] know it [how to behave in the presence of dogs] but do they [the moms] know it?
>
> *(Diary entry, 5 July 2015)*

During two conversations carried on during walks in Tromsø, the term 'lifestyle' was explicitly used to describe the way of living of people who have dogs and, more specifically, the daily practices related to having a dog, especially the walks at times of the day when people were usually busy with other activities.

A sort of complicity was observed among the dog guardians. For example, people gave each other tips on how to find places suitable for off-the-leash walks, both in nearby popular holiday places and in town, including public as well as private but easily accessible areas. In Florence, such complicity was also observed in the case of early morning walks, when the dog guardians entered the park using a not well-known entrance among the bushes, as the main gate did not open until 8.00 a.m.

Most of the social-related aspects of dog walking were quite often observed in Florence, probably due to the characteristics of the physical environment (relatively limited area designated as a dog park) and the cultural context. Nonetheless, some of the elements presented above were noted in the case of early weekend morning walks in Tromsø. The episode described below, which concerns a Sunday morning walk, illustrates this.

> I saw two other people approaching. One I had seen before, also with the dog he used to have until a couple of years ago. The other was on his skis and had his dog running close to him, as I do sometimes with Dina [the researcher's dog]. 'Dog people' . . . who else is out at this time on a Sunday morning! We stopped: all went well, the dogs were friendly with each other, we chatted a bit about the weather and our dogs, and continued to enjoy the snow and the freedom of a sunny Sunday morning.
>
> *(Diary entry, 12 April 2015)*

Based on these considerations, it may be posited that the social aspect of dog walking can be conceptualised in a way that includes dogs. Drawing on the concept of communitas (Turner *et al.* 1983), it may be further posited that dog walking in urban greenspaces promotes the emergence of spontaneous interspecies communitas. These are social entities which include people and dogs – the latter viewed as significant others – that emerge as temporary states of affectual bonding created through direct mutual interaction and the recognition of similar lifestyles.

Being in-between: dog walking as a liminoid experience

Several aspects of the dog walking experience as emerged from the data can be related to the concept of soft fascination. Dog walking was described or mentioned by the dog walkers as moments of relax and reflection. Moreover, the data suggest that dog walking was also about being away from people to whom the person owed certain obligations, in particular family members and colleagues. The absence of any other obligation apart from that of walking the dog seemed to be experienced with a certain relief. In line with this, it can be stated that, although the findings showed that dog walking was a practice shared with the dog and sometimes with other dog guardians, dog walking was also about spending time alone.

The dog in particular seemed to be perceived as a special significant other with whom the person could be entirely her- or himself. This could be noted in the following diary entry:

> She [the dog] started rolling over, in the snow, throwing the ball in the air and then digging in the snow trying to find it again. It was impossible to resist and I started playing with her, joining one of her puppy-moments, and getting lots of snow inside my boots!
>
> *(Diary entry, 15 April 2015)*

The data suggest also that dog walking was perceived as experiencing a sort of domesticated nature, characterised by vegetation and animals, as well as by human built objects, such as benches and – in the case of Florence – monuments. In this sense, it was an experience somewhere in between being in nature and being in a human-built environment. This double aspect of dog walking was commented on positively in several conversations as an example of both the practical advantages of dog walking and the experience of contrasting realities. This is evident in the following diary entry.

> I had to take a picture showing the monuments of the town centre seen from the park: everything looked so peaceful, although I'm sure that down there it was already full of cars and noises.
>
> *(Diary entry, 1 July 2015)*

A similar entry refers to the view of the airport from the forest of the Tromsø greenspace. Similar comments were made also during the conversations with the dog walkers in both locations, and concerned in particular the pleasure of having the possibility of being in nature, but also in town.

In relation to dog walking as a way to be in a natural environment and, at the same time, to be in town, dog walking was sometimes described as an alternative way to see and live in the town. In this regard, a dog walker noted that, since he had start to walk his dog, he had realised how differently the town could be perceived by an animal: 'I realised the amount of noises and smells that we [humans] tend to ignore or get used to'. Similarly, a diary entry reported:

> The neighborhood has not so many secrets for me now, especially when it comes to things that can be scary or exciting in the perspective of an animal. We can't go to the northern part of the park until they have finished building the new houses: too many noises, and also explosions. I might not hear them but Dina [the dog] does and just refuses to go there.
>
> *(Diary entry, 5 July 2015)*

To a certain extent, the dog guardians' perceptions and experiences of the urban environment seemed to be mediated by the companionship of the dog; more precisely, by the way the guardians interpreted the animals' perception of the environment. This can again be related to the transcendence of interspecies differences, and, more specifically, to empathy, a concept that plays a central role in care-based ethics (Donovan and Adams 2007; Gruen 2015).

Thus, dog walking can be described as a sort of in-between experience – an experience between an obligation and a leisure, an experience of being together and being alone, being in nature and being in town, being a human and being an animal. This twofold aspect can be related to the concept of liminoid experiences as described by Victor Turner, already mentioned above in relation to the concept of communitas. The term liminoid experience is used in leisure contexts to describe experiences sought, not only as means for escaping from the realities everyday responsibilities, but also as opportunities for individual movement and expression (Varley 2011). Differently from pre-industrial liminoid experiences that are usually related to rituals that tend to mark a specific and unique passage from one life phase to another, for dog walking, the liminoid aspect refers to the possibility of sustaining a lifestyle that reconciles different perspectives and realities of today's post-modern society. The adoption of the concept of liminoid experience in the case of viewing dog walking as an in-between experience is in line with what was noted above concerning interspecies communitas, and is also corroborated by certain studies reporting that participants in liminoid leisure activities become members of communitas (Lugosi 2007).

The ethical dimension of dog walking

A theme that has emerged from the data, and which is only partially present in the literature, relates to the ethical dimension of the dog walking experience. As noted above, the dog walking experience depends, among other factors, on the conceptualisation that the guardian has of his or her dog and, presumably, of dogs in general. As noted above, this issue is clearly related to animal ethics and in particular certain aspects of the ethics of care (Donovan and Adams 2007; Gruen 2015).

In addition to this, the findings show that dog walking can also promote reflections on animals in general, and in particular on the usually practised – but seldom discussed – discrimination between the various species. The data concerning the walks during springtime are particularly significant in this sense. Several dog guardians seemed to be aware of the damages that dogs can cause to birds, especially during the nesting time and when the small birds are born. Dog guardians then faced a dilemma: either to follow the usual rules applicable to public areas requiring compulsory use of leashes at specific times of the year, or to ignore such rules, giving absolute priority to the well-being of the pet.

In some cases, such situations could make dog guardians reflect on both their attitudes towards, and beliefs about, different animal species, and also about the value of each animal, viewed as a unique individual and not just as a member of a specific species. During one of the conversations, a man reported about his numerous attempts to save young blackbirds from his dog. He seemed particularly passionate about the welfare of the birds. He also noted that his behaviour was somehow inconsistent, given that he himself was a hunter and followed an omnivorous diet. The springtime diary entries also showed almost constant and sometimes frustrating attempts to find compromises between giving freedom to the dog and not harming other animals.

Conclusion

The findings of this study provide some insights into the complexity of the urban dog walking experience. In addition, to confirm certain previously conducted studies indicating the main themes of dog walking, this study suggests that dog walking in urban greenspaces can be conceptualised using the concepts of communitas and liminoid experience. In this sense, this specific type of dog walking experience can be viewed as a liminoid experience, performed by interspecies couples and sometimes shared within spontaneous interspecies communitas.

With regard to its contribution to the dog guardians' well-being, this study suggests that urban dog walking can be important in terms of soft fascination, and can also be a meaningful experience in terms of security and freedom. This can derive from the possibility of dog guardians' expressing themselves when alone with their canine companions and also in the safe social environment of the interspecies communitas, as described above. Moreover, dog walking imparts to people the possibility of finding harmony in the contrasting aspects of everyday urban life. Finally, dog walking can encourage reflection on the way we experience the physical environment and animal ethical issues, and, consequently, it can be relevant in terms of self-realisation, contributing to personal growth.

This study has also shown that some aspects of urban dog walking can vary, according to the physical and cultural environment. This is particularly true for the social dimension of the experience. With regard to practical implications and if the emergence of communitas is desirable, it is important to design urban greenspaces purposefully, for example, by creating dog parks, yet respecting the local cultural approaches to socialising and living within nature.

References

Anderson, L. (2006) 'Analytic authoethnography', *Journal of Contemporary Ethnography*, 35(4): 373–395.

Anderson, L. and Austin, M. (2012) 'Auto-ethnography in leisure studies', *Leisure Studies*, 31(2): 131–146.

Bagley, D.K. and Gonsman, V.L. (2005) 'Pet attachment and personality type', *Anthrozoös*, 18(1): 28–42.

Bauman, A.E., Schroeder, J.R., Furber, S.E. and Dobson, A.J. (2001) 'The epidemiology of dog walking: an unmet need for human and canine health', *Medical Journal of Australia*, 175(11–12): 632–634.

Beck, A.M. and Meyers, N.M. (1997) 'Health enhancement and animal companion ownership', *Annual Review of Public Health*, 17: 247–257.

Beck, L. and Madresh, E.A. (2008) 'Romantic partners and four-legged friends: an extension of attachment theory to relationships with pets', *Anthrozoös*, 21(1): 43–56.

Brown, S.E. (2007) 'Companion animals as selfobjects', *Anthrozoös*, 20(4): 329–343.

Brown, S.G. and Rhodes, R.E. (2006) 'Relationships among dog ownership and leisure-time walking in Western Canadian adults', *American Journal of Preventive Medicine*, 30(2): 131–136.

Buchecker, M. and Degenhardt, B. (2015) 'The effects of urban inhabitants' nearby outdoor recreation on their well-being and their psychological resilience', *Journal of Outdoor Recreation and Tourism*, 10: 55–62.

Coleman, K.J., Rosenberg, D.E., Conway, T.L., Sallis, J.F., Saelens, B.E., Frank, L.D. and Cain, K. (2008) 'Physical activity, weight status, and neighbourhood characteristics of dog walkers', *Preventive Medicine*, 47: 309–312.

Crawford, E.K., Worsham, N.L. and Swinehart, E.R. (2006) 'Benefits derived from companion animals, and the use of the term "attachment"', *Anthrozoös*, 19(2): 98–112.

Cutt, H., Giles-Corti, B., Knuiman, M. and Burke, V. (2007) 'Dog ownership, health and physical activity: a critical review of the literature', *Health & Place*, 13: 261–272.

Cutt, H., Giles-Corti, B. and Knuiman, M. (2008) 'Encouraging physical activity through dog walking: why don't some owners walk with their dog?' *Preventive Medicine*, 46: 120–126.

DeMello, M. (2012) *Animals and Society: An Introduction to Human–Animal Studies*, New York: Columbia University Press.

Donovan, J. and Adams, C.J. (2007) *The Feminist Care Tradition in Animal Ethics*, New York: Columbia University Press.

Graham, T.M. and Glover, T.D. (2014) 'On the fence: dog parks in the (un)leashing of community and social capital', *Leisure Sciences*, 36(3): 217–234.

Gruen, L. (2015) *Entangled Empathy: An Alternative Ethic for our Relationships with Animals*, New York: Lantern Books.

Hartig, T., Evans, G.W., Jamner, L.D., Davis, D.S. and Garling, T. (2003) 'Tracking restoration in natural and urban field settings', *Journal of Environmental Psychology*, 23: 109–123.

Herzog, T.R., Black, A.M., Fountaine, K.A. and Knotts, D.J. (1997) 'Reflection and attentional recovery as distinctive benefits of restorative environments', *Journal of Environmental Psychology*, 17: 165–170.

Hirschman, E.C. (1994) 'Consumers and their animal companions', *Journal of Consumer Research*, 20: 616–632.

Holak, S.L. (2008) 'Ritual blessings with companion animals', *Journal of Business Research,* 61: 534–541.

Holbrook, M., Stephens, D.L., Day, E., Holbrook, S.M. and Strazar, G. (2001) 'A collective stereographic photo essay on key aspects of animal companionship: the truth about dogs and cats', *Academy of Marketing Science Review,* 1. Available at: http://citeseerx.ist.psu.edu/viewdoc/download?doi=10.1.1.470.7981&rep=rep1&type=pdf

Kaplan, S. (1995) 'The restorative benefits of nature: toward an integrative framework', *Journal of Environmental Psychology,* 16: 169–182.

Kuo, F.E., Sullivan, W.C., Coley, R.L. and Brunson, L. (1998) 'Fertile ground for community: inner-city neighbourhood common spaces', *American Journal of Community Psychology,* 26(6): 823–851.

Lepp, A. (2009) 'Leisure and obligation: an investigation of volunteer tourists' experience at Kenya's Taita Discovery Center', *Journal of Leisure Research,* 41(2): 253–260.

Lugosi, P. (2007) 'Queer consumption and commercial hospitality: communitas, myths and the production of liminoid space', *International Journal of Sociology and Social Policy,* 27(3/4): 163–174.

Maas, J., Verheij, R.A., Groenewegen, P.P., De Vries, S. and Spreeuwenberg, P. (2006) 'Green space, urbanity, and health; how strong is the relation?', *Journal of Epidemiology and Community Health,* 60(7): 587–592.

McCormack, G.R., Rock, M., Sandalack, B. and Uribe, F.A. (2011) 'Access to off-leash parks, street pattern and dog walking among adults', *Public Health,* 125: 540–546.

Roy, S., Byrne, J. and Pickering, C. (2012) 'A systematic quantitative review of urban tree benefits, costs, and assessment methods across cities in different climatic zones', *Urban Forestry and Urban Greening,* 4(11): 351–363.

Ryan, R.M. and Deci, E. (2001) 'On happiness and human potentials: a review of research on hedonic and eudaimonic well-being', *Annual Review of Psychology,* 52: 141–166.

Salmon, J., Timperio, A., Chu, B. and Veitch, J. (2010) 'Dog ownership, dog walking, and children's and parents' physical activity', *Research Quarterly for Exercise and Sport,* 81(3): 264–271.

Shaw, S.M. (1985) 'The meaning of leisure in everyday life', *Leisure Sciences: An Interdisciplinary Journal,* 7(1): 1–24.

Stebbins, R.A. (2000) 'Obligation as an aspect of leisure experience', *Journal of Leisure Research,* 32 (1): 152–155.

Strandell, A. and Hall, C.M. (2015) 'Impact of the residential environment on second home use in Finland – testing the compensation hypothesis', *Landscape and Urban Planning,* 133, 12–23.

Sugiyama, T. and Ward Thompson, C. (2008) 'Associations between characteristics of neighbourhood open space and older people's walking', *Urban Forestry & Urban Greening,* 7(1): 41–51.

Turner, V., Harris, J.C. and Park, R.J. (1983) 'Liminal to liminoid in play, flow, and ritual: an essay in comparative symbology', in J.C. Harris and R.J. Park (eds), *Play, Games and Sports in Cultural Contexts,* Champaign, IL: Human Kinetics Publishers, pp. 123–164.

Urbanik, J. and Morgan, M. (2013) 'A tale of tails: the place of dog parks in the urban imaginary', *Geoforum,* 44: 292–302.

van den Berg, A., Maas, J., Verheij, R.A. and Groenewegen, P.P. (2010) 'Green space as a buffer between stressful life events and health', *Social Science & Medicine,* 70: 1203–1210.

Varley, P.J. (2011) 'Sea kayakers at the margins: the liminoid character of contemporary adventures', *Leisure Studies,* 30(1): 85–98.

Walsh, F. (2009) 'Human–animal bonds I: the relational significance of companion animals', *Family Process,* 48(4): 462–480.

Wharf Higgins, J., Temple, V., Murray, H., Kumm, E. and Rhodes, R. (2013) 'Walking sole mates: dogs motivating, enabling and supporting guardians' physical activity', *Anthrozoös,* 26(2): 237–252.

Wood, L.J., Giles-Corti, B. and Bulsara, M. (2005) 'The pet connection: pets as a conduit for social capital?', *Social Science & Medicine,* 61: 1159–1173.

Wood, L.J., Giles-Corti, B., Bulsara, M.K. and Bosch, D.A. (2007) 'More than a furry companion: the ripple effect of companion animals on neighbourhood interactions and sense of community', *Society and Animals,* 15: 43–56.

Part V
Method, Planning and Design

30

Walkable places for visitors

Assessing and designing for walkability

Yael Ram and C. Michael Hall

Introduction

Walkable places are often considered as an attraction for locals, visitors and tourists and as a measure of urban quality (Talen 2002). Cities, as walking spaces, were developed for their citizens around two forms of walking facilities – streets and what Solnit (2000: 177) described as, 'anti-streets', which refers to public spaces such as parks, gardens and promenades. While the 'streets' reflect everyday life and, before the eighteenth century were seldom used for pleasure, the 'anti-streets' were often built solely for the pleasure of citizens, and especially the emerging middle classes of the industrial revolution (Walker and Duffield 1983; Jordan 1994; Harding 1999; Hickman 2013), and were initially designated to convey or resemble high-class aesthetics (Solnit 2000). In recent years, the streets, as well as the parks, have become foci of research, reflecting the understanding that walking facilitates the pedestrian's mental and physical health (Frank *et al.* 2006; Wanner *et al.* 2012), and can provide environmental benefits as a mode of green mobility (Southworth 2005), as well as encourage the development and maintenance of social capital through engagement and familiarity with the neighborhood and local people (Leyden 2003; Alfonzo 2005; Mehta 2008; Buckley *et al.* 2016).

One of the outputs of the interest in walking streets is the concept of walkability, which is broadly defined as the extent to which a built environment enables walking (Kelly *et al.* 2011), i.e. is pedestrian friendly (Moura *et al.* 2017). Walkability is achieved when the streets and other walking spaces provide pedestrians a secure network of connections to varied destinations, within a reasonable amount of time and effort, and offering a pleasant and interesting context (Southworth 2005). However, Forsyth (2015) notes that the concept is relatively broad and encompasses different approaches and definitions, which may lead to different design outcomes. For example, she notes that some research focuses on environmental features or means of making walkable environments, including areas being traversable, compact, physically enticing and safe, while others deal with the outcomes potentially fostered by such environments, such as making places lively, enhancing sustainable transportation options and inducing exercise. Finally, she notes that some use the term as a proxy for better urban design (see also Talen and Koschinsky 2013). Forsyth and Southworth (2008), for example, suggests that the idea of walkable can be equated to: encouraging physical activity; close; barrier-free; safe; full of pedestrian infrastructure and destinations; and upscale, leafy, or cosmopolitan.

Proximity and access are usually regarded as two of the key factors in walkable built environments (Southworth 2005; Lo 2009). 'Walkable' trips are usually considered by urban planners as trips that take no longer than five minutes (equivalent to 400 meters) for each direction (Bartlett 2003). Previous studies show that for longer trips, people will often prefer to drive to their destinations (Azmi et al. 2013). Other factors that are often mentioned as central to walkability are: connectivity and continuation of the sidewalks and absence of barriers for walking; linkage to other transport modes; safety from traffic, crime and falls; the physical conditions and the quality of the path and contextual values, such as aesthetic and historic interest (Southworth 2005; Vale et al. 2016). However, substantial differences exist with respect to the focus of walkability studies, as well as the measures that should be used, including the significance of qualitative assessments (Riggs 2015), and how the various measures relate to actual motivations to walk (Alfonzo 2005; Mehta 2008; Buckley et al. 2016). Some of these issues are summarized in Table 30.1.

Figure 30.1 presents some of the main dimensions of walkability and the different focal points for research and assessment. There is substantial research on the different demographic, socio-economic, health and psychological dimensions of walkers, although, as discussed further on in

Table 30.1 Issues in measures of walkability

Specification issue	Summary of issue
Spatial	Which spatial and territorial units are being used? i.e. spatial resolution, territorial definition, governance boundaries
Demographic/socio-economic	Are different socio-economic groups and variables being distinguished, reflecting different attributes, needs and constraints, i.e. income levels, nature of employment, age, gender, ethnic identity, dog ownership, club membership
Health	Given the specific focus on walking and health what health measures are being employed?
Trip purpose	Work and/or non-work trips, i.e. commuting, leisure
Transportation mode	Walking alone or walking in conjunction with other modes, i.e. active modes (walk and cycle), public transport, private transport
Temporal	Different times of the day, week or year, i.e. seasonality, peak versus off-peak travel / availability of opportunities
Places of reference (origins and destinations)	Origin-based and/or destination-based measures? Which places are considered origins, i.e. home, work, or a specific location such as a park or attraction? Which places (related to trip purpose) are considered destinations, what opportunities and activities are being considered?
Attractiveness of opportunities	How should opportunities (markets, shopping, cafés, parks, treed spaces, public space, attractions) be measured, i.e. binary, count number for aggregate destination, spatial, distance, time, or a combination or aggregate weighting of measures? How should qualitative attractiveness be measured?

Specification issue	Summary of issue
Walking barriers and impedance	How should travel impedance as a function of distance be measured, i.e. Euclidean, Manhattan, network, economic, cultural, perceptual? Which impedance function should be used, i.e. inverse power, negative exponential, modified Gaussian, cumulative opportunities and how should the parameters be calibrated?
	Topography, weather and path surfaces, either separately or in combination can also act as barriers to walking
	Barriers can also be measured by other variables, i.e. type of primary dwelling, perceived safety, perceived and objective measures of crowding, weather and climate
Land-use mix	How are the various land uses in a defined spatial area to be categorized?
Density	Measures of density may vary, i.e. population density for a given spatial area, the number of floors of primary residential building, workplace density, gross floor area/land area
Infrastructure characteristics	A range of walking infrastructure measures may be employed, i.e. intersection density or count, node/link ratio, block length, sidewalk continuity and quality, pedestrian crossings. Although quality may be measured in objective terms there are also many perceptual measures
Perceived qualities of walkable spaces	The perceived qualities of specific spaces and routes may be major factors in influencing walkability, i.e. perceived safety, cover, aesthetics, interest

Sources: Giles-Conti and Donovan 2003; Handy 2005; Ewing et al. 2006; Forsyth et al. 2008; Mehta 2008; Ewing and Handy 2009; Larsen et al. 2010; Lwin and Murayama 2011; Maghelal and Capp 2011; Adkins et al. 2012; Horacek et al. 2012; Talen and Koschinsky 2013; Riggs 2015; Strandell and Hall 2015; Pafka and Dovey 2016; Vale et al. 2016; Hall et al. 2017

this chapter and elsewhere (Hall *et al.* 2017), there is surprisingly little written about walkers from a tourist perspective. Every walking trip has an origin and a destination, but these do not occur in abstract space. Instead, Figure 30.1 highlights the importance of the behavioral environment within which walking and personal decisions about walking occur. The characteristics of the built environment and the physical geography of a location, e.g. weather, steepness, together with the people who use and inhabit a location create the design and place qualities that walkers experience. These are also affected at the micro-level by decisions with respect to routes, distance, purpose of trip, as well as the time at which walking occurs; and at the macro-level by the governance of walking in a particular location. In an immediate sense, this includes such things as street cleanliness and garbage collection, but over longer time scales it includes path maintenance and design, public space provision, public transport availability, and the planning laws that affect urban design, density, roading and pedestrian friendliness. The combination of these objective

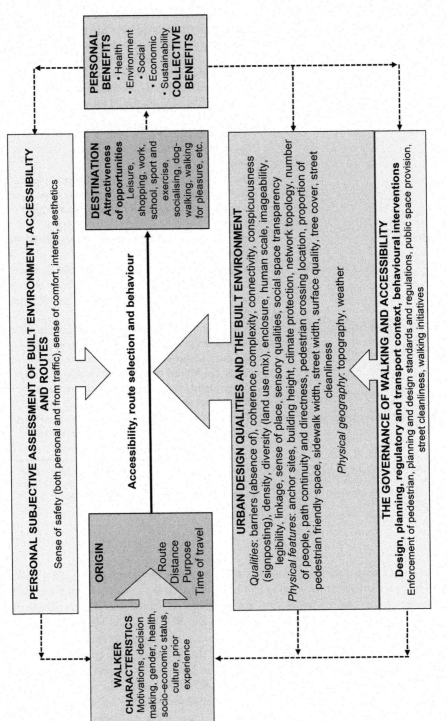

Figure 30.1 Key elements of walkability

and subjective factors provide the environment that determines perceived accessibility, as well as the behavior of walkers (Talen and Koschinsky 2013; Forsyth 2015; Gebel *et al.* 2009; Lee and Talen 2014). Related to this observation is the recognition that the benefits of high levels of walkability in a location and increases in walking accrue at both an individual and a collective level. Improvements in health, for example, benefit both individual well-being as well as the costs of health provision (Doyle 2006; Frank *et al.* 2006). Similarly, reductions in car use can help provide reductions in emissions leading to improvements in air quality, having both individual and public benefits, while overall improvements in walkability have implications for real-estate values, as well as the creation of a consumer habitat that encourages local and visitor expenditure (Wolf 2003, 2004; Yüksel 2013).

However, it is important to note that the vast majority of research addresses local pedestrians. In other words, other users of the streets, such as visitors and tourists, are not a significant focus, even though they may be important constituents of the actual walking environments of many locations, as well as being a significant temporary walking population for many cities. It is important to note that cities host millions of tourists per year, which are added to the crowd in the streets. In several cities, the number of tourists may exceed the number of locals (in an annual calculation), as shown in Table 30.2. Spatially, the number of tourists may also exceed the number of locals in certain districts, such as locations with a concentration of attractions and accommodation, at certain times as well. Hence, research and understanding of tourists' walkability can be perceived as an additional important aspect of walkable places, as well as urban walkability.

Walkable places for tourists and visitors

Walking potentially relates to a more personally meaningful tourist experience than passive traveling by motorized transportation means (Hall *et al.* 2017). Hamid (2014) mentioned three different senses that are activated while walking: sight, hearing and touch. Smell, and in some cases, taste, should be added to these senses. As a result of these sensory encounters, walking can be viewed as providing an alternative to the appreciable 'tourist gaze' (Urry 2002) or 'tourism bubble' (Schmidt 1979), creating an engaged tourist that "gets" the destination firsthand.

Table 30.2 Proportions of locals and tourists in the top ten urban tourist destinations

City	Number of tourists per year (000s) (2013)	Local populations (000s)	% Tourists to locals	Number of tourists per day (000s)	% Tourists per day of local permanent population
Hong Kong	25 587	7188	355.97%	70.10	0.97%
Singapore	22 455	5399	415.92%	61.52	1.14%
Bangkok	17 468	6355	274.87%	47.86	0.75%
London	16 784	8674	193.50%	45.98	0.53%
Paris	15 200	2244	677.36%	41.64	2.85%
Macau	14 269	566	2520.94%	39.09	14.48%
New York City	11 850	8406	140.98%	32.47	0.39%
Shenzhen	11 703	7009	166.96%	32.06	0.46%
Kuala Lumpur	11 182	1589	703.74%	30.64	1.93%
Antalya	11 121	1978	562.22%	30.47	1.54%

Sources: Number of tourists data from: http://blog.euromonitor.com/2015/01/top-100-city-destinations-ranking.html retrieved 1 August 2016. Local populations data from: World Bank and UN data

Accordingly, Ujang and Muslim (2014) found that engaged walking urban tourists developed a sense of place attachment to the visited destination.

In their study of Kuala Lumpur, Malaysia, Ujang and Muslim (2014) identified accessibility, connectivity, comfort, safety, attractiveness and pleasantness as leading criteria for a walkable tourist city, while in the same location, Mansouri and Ujang (2016b) found that spatial features such as accessibility, connectivity and continuity strongly determine tourists' expectation and satisfaction while walking. Connectivity refers to the continuation of the sidewalks and proximity to transit points and public transportation. Comfort is defined as the minimization of effort needed to perform walking. In the context of urban tourism, it refers to pedestrian facilities (such as benches and shades), the physical condition of pavements, walking routes signage and the ability to walk freely without obstruction. The pleasantness of walking and attractiveness refer to aspects of touristic appeal, such as atmosphere, vibrant surroundings, attractive visual appearance, cultural heritage and diversity of people and activities. In a related study, Mansouri and Ujang (2016a) found that the two historical districts in their study, in spite of their proximity to each other, differed considerably in terms of local and tourist pedestrian movement. They suggested that the findings of the pedestrian movement observation and network integration analysis indicate that the presence of certain attractions and land uses in the study area plays a significant role in improving the association between the two historical areas, and indicates that pedestrian movement in Kuala Lumpur is oriented more to the diversity of land use and attractors than to the connectivity of walkways.

Similar criteria to Ujang and Muslim (2014) and Mansouri and Muslim (2016a) were found in an experimental study that identified predictors for walkability decisions based on the analysis of participant narratives, who walked along one of 19 routes, and participant assessment of streetscape images (Samarasekara et al. 2011). Based on the findings of this study, safety, comfort, shades and visual appearance can be perceived as positive cues for walking decisions. The experiment yields two more variables that positively predict walking decisions: the potential for activity; and the potential for exploration. However, these two predictors are intangible and thus cannot be directly included as physical dimensions of walkability. However, it should be noted that, although described as providing cues for walkability assessments by tourists, the participants were 'virtual tourists' (Samarasekara et al. 2011: 505), i.e. university students from the authors' university. Table 30.3 compares the criteria for the walkable tourist city as were found by Ujang and Muslim (2014) as well as Samarasekara et al. (2011) to the walkability dimensions of Southworth (2005). An additional criterion was found in a GIS study that was conducted by the Government of the Sultan of Oman. In this study, Langer and Car (2014) showed how public toilets facilitate urban tourism.

Table 30.3 Comparison of Southworth's walkability characteristics and tourist walkability characteristics

Walkability Characteristics	Tourist Walkability Characteristics	
Southworth (2005)	Ujang and Muslim (2014)	Samarasekara et al. (2011)
Connectivity	Connectivity	x
Linkage with other transport networks	x	x
Land use patterns/access	x	Activity potential
Safety (traffic and crime)	Safety	Safety from traffic
Path quality	Comfort	Comfort, shade
Path context	Touristic appeal	Exploration

There is a suggestion that a walkable city should be a 'magnet for tourists' (Ujang and Muslim 2014: 54), and many tourists believe that the best way to experience a city is to walk it (Thompson 2003). A study in Manchester, England, showed that about 30 percent of tourists walk in the city while staying in the destination (Thompson and Schofield 2007). When the analysis was combined with use of public transport, the percentage of walking (and public transportation use) rose to 60 percent of visitors to Munich, Germany (Le-Klähn et al. 2015).

Four decades ago, Arbel and Pizam (1977) suggested that tourists would prefer accommodations within a convenient walking distance to the main tourist attractions (see also Page and Hall 2003). In a more recent work, Shoval et al. (2011) found that top urban attractions draw tourists, regardless of the hotel location. Still, less popular attractions may depend on accessibility factors and proximity to the location of the hotels. Despite the understanding of the importance of walking to the tourism industry and urban tourism, there is little research on tourist walking behaviors and the relationship to the success of urban attractions and destinations. This chapter therefore aims to bridge this gap and explore the extent to which there is a link between the walkability of an urban tourism destination and: 1) likability of places, as perceived by tourists; 2) the number of visitors to tourist attractions.

As noted above, there are significant challenges with respect to the specificity of walkability concepts and measures (see Table 30.1). In terms of appropriate spatial scale, there is a dearth of secondary data that provides information on tourist visitation and flows. Many destinations only have data on tourists at the destination level rather than for specific locations within a destination. One exception to this is the VisitBritain Visitor Attractions Survey (VisitEngland 2015). The chapter therefore uses London as a case study for examining walking within an urban destination. In 2014, London hosted almost 30 million overnight visits of inbound and domestic travelers and more than 250 million day visits (London and Partners 2014). London accounts for 54 percent of all inbound visitor spent in the UK (VisitBritain 2016), offering numerous different public and private tourist attractions, both charged and free entry. Another source of information on attractions and destinations is the TripAdvisor website, which provides information on the relative favorability of an attraction, as well as numeric value of the number of 'likes' it receives. Information on visitor numbers can, therefore, be compared with TripAdvisor assessments, while the final element of the case study, a value for walkability, can be derived from Walk Score a website and app that provides a value for the relative walkability of any given location.

The VisitBritain Visitor Attractions Survey

The VisitBritain/VisitEngland agency, a public body funded by the Department for Culture, Media and Sport, publishes an annual report regarding the number of visitors to English attractions. This database provides an opportunity to learn about the popularity of attractions, both free and paid (VisitEngland 2015). However, the data on attractions may include all categories of visitors, including school trips, private events and special occasions, and thus offers limited information regarding the number of visiting tourists. Regardless of these limitations, this open source was used to detect the number of visitors to London attractions in 2014.

TripAdvisor

Another source of information regarding London is freely provided by the TripAdvisor website. TripAdvisor is the world's largest travel site, reaching 350 million unique monthly visitors, and reached 385 million reviews and opinions, covering more than 6.6 million accommodations, restaurants and attractions (TripAdvisor 2016a). For August 2016, the London section in

TripAdvisor included 4,488 things to do, supported by 866, 347 reviews. The total number of reviews for London hotels, rentals, restaurants, attractions and other posts was more than 3.5 million (TripAdvisor 2016b).

For each attraction in the current study, two types of information were collected: first, the ordinal ranking of the attraction, compared to other London's attractions; and second, the numbers of reviews received by each attraction. Each attraction in the TripAdvisor website gets a rating score that is based on the average value of the reviews. The reviews on the TripAdvisor website range from 1 = Terrible to 5 = Excellent, and the ranking is based on them, with the first being the best attraction and the last the worst attraction. While the ranking can be utilized as an indicator for likability, the number of reviews can be used as a proxy for the number of tourists that visited a given attraction.

Walk Score

The Walk Score website measures the walkability of any address, using a patented system. For each address, a Walk Score was calculated, based on the distance to different amenities (such as shops, school, parks and bus stops). The given score (Walk Score) is a number between 0 and 100 that measures the walkability of any address. Places with a Walk Score above 90 are considered as 'Walker's Paradise' because all daily errands are accessible by walking. Places with Walk Scores between 70 and 89 points are referred to as 'Very Walkable', meaning that most daily errands can be accomplished on foot. When the scores drop to the 50–69 range, only some errands can be accomplished on foot. People who live in places with Walk Scores of 25–49 are 'Car Dependent', because most errands need cars, and when the Walk Scores are below 24 all of the daily errands need cars. The Walk Score website mission is to help people to decide where to live, and it is owned by a real estate company (Redfin). The data sources include Google, Education.com, Open Street Map, the US Census, and users (Walk Score 2016). The Walk Score refers, among other things, to access to parks, restaurants, public transport and shopping and is aimed at addressing daily needs and not tourist requirements. Therefore, the Walk Score of each attraction was calculated to learn about its walkability, as perceived by urban planners and real-estate specialists and not necessarily by tourists.

Walk Score has previously been applied in a number of studies on walkability. Carr et al. (2011) objectively measured 4,194 walkable amenities in the 13 Walk Score categories for 379 residential and non-residential addresses in Rhode Island, USA. Significant correlations were identified between Walk Score and all categories of aggregated walkable destinations within a 1-mile buffer of the addresses. Test–retest reliability correlation coefficients for a subsample of 100 addresses were 1.0, leading them to conclude that Walk Score may be a convenient and inexpensive research option for exploring the relationship between access to walkable amenities and physical activity. Hirsh et al. (2013) in a US study of 4,552 people found that after adjustment for site, key socio-demographic and health variables, a higher Walk Score was associated with lower odds of not walking for transport and more minutes/week of transport walking. Compared to those in a 'Walker's Paradise', lower categories of Walk Score were associated with a linear increase in odds of no transport walking and a decline in minutes of leisure walking. Studies by Duncan et al. (2011, 2013) also confirm and extend the generalizability of previous findings demonstrating that Walk Score is a useful proxy of neighborhood density and access to nearby amenities and therefore a valid measure of estimating neighborhood walkability in multiple geographic locations and especially at larger spatial scales (800 m street network buffer). However, Carr et al. (2011) also suggested some caution after finding positive associations between Walk Score and reported crime.

Duncan *et al.* (2016) also note that the vast majority of research that has utilized Walk Score in examining walkability has also been conducted in North American geographies, while also often relying on self-reported potentially recall-biased physical activity outcomes. Nevertheless, their research at the trip level on the associations between Walk Score, transportation mode choice, and walking among Paris adults who were tracked with GPS receivers and accelerometers did conclude that walkable neighborhoods were positively associated with increases in walking among adults in Paris, as documented at the trip level.

The case study

All attractions that received more than 5,000 reviews (a proxy for popularity) in the list of "what to do" section for London on the TripAdvisor in the record date of 30 July 2016 were detected in the first stage of the process. For each attraction, the ranking was taken, together with the number of reviews and the exact address. Based on the number of reviews criteria (5,000), 24 attractions were chosen, ranking from 1st place (British Museum, with 38,545 reviews) to 80th place (Madame Tussauds, with 17,905 reviews). Then, the number of visitors in 2014, as listed in the VisitEngland records was checked for each attraction. However, only 11 attractions were listed in the VisitEngland database. For the other attractions, the official sites were studied, and the numbers of visitors of eight more attractions were added to the records as an exact number or estimation. In total, 19 of the 24 attractions had an official number of visitors (89 percent). The last stage in the process included the Walk Score calculation, which was established for each of the attractions, and ranged from 100 (St Paul's Cathedral and Covent Garden) to 91 (the London Eye). All the popular attractions in London were included in the range of 'Walker's Paradise', according to the Walk Score terminology. Additional information that was gathered from VisitEngland list, TripAdvisor and official sites considered the entrance fee. Half of the attractions were free (including museums and parks), while the other half required some entrance fee (cathedrals, exhibitions and historic buildings). However, a preliminary three t-tests found that the numbers of reviews, the number of visitors and the ranking were not related to the existence of an entrance fee (p>.05). Table 30.4 presents the full base of data regarding the 24 attractions.

Results

The potential relationships between the Walk Scores of attractions and TripAdvisor ranking and number of reviews and visitors were tested using a Spearman correlation with the IBM SPSS Statistics (v.22) software. The Spearman correlation is a non-parametric test for testing a correlation when at least one of the variables is ordinal, or when one of the variables failed to meet the normality distribution conditions. In the current case, the TripAdvisor ranking variable was an ordinal variable, and the variables of number of reviews and number of visitors were found as highly skewed (the skewness measurement was larger than 1). The matrix of the bivariate correlations is presented in Table 30.5. The bivariate non-parametric correlation between the TripAdvisor ranking Walk Score yields a non-significant result ($\rho = 0.094$, p = 0.664), indicating that there is no linear ratio between the Walk Score and the ranking. The non-parametric correlation between the number of visitors and the Walk Score was found as positive and significant ($\rho = 0.575$, p = 0.003), and the non-correlation between the number of reviews and Walk Score was found as positive but non-significant ($\rho = 0.365$ p = 0.124).

The results of the Spearman correlations suggested that Walk Score and the number of visitors are monotonically related, even if not linearly related, i.e. when the Walk Score increases, the number of visitors increases as well. However, the non-significant Spearman correlation between

Table 30.4 Ranking, number of reviews, number of visitors and Walk Score of attractions in London

TripAdvisor Ranking*	Attraction	TripAdvisor #Reviews*	Address	Number of visitors (2014)	Walk Score	Entrance fee (0 = no, 1 = yes)	Comments regarding number of visitors
1	British Museum	38 545	Great Russell Street, London WC1B 3DG	6 695 213	99	0	
2	National Gallery	21 994	Trafalgar Square, London WC2N 5DN	6 416 724	98	0	
3	V&A (Victoria and Albert Museum)	17 054	Cromwell Road, South Kensington, London SW7 2RL	3 651 450	98	0	
4	Tower of London	34 116	Tower Hill, London EC3N 4AB	3 081 939	97	1	
5	Big Ben	16 699	Elizabeth Tower, Houses of Parliament, Westminster, London SW1A 0AA	NA	92	0	
6	Churchill War Rooms	12 312	Clive Steps, King Charles Street, London SW1A 2AQ	472 744	95	1	
7	Houses of Parliament	10 600	Westminster, London SW1A 0AA	1 253 326	92	1	
9	St James's Park	9 893	Horse Guards Road, The Storeyard, London SW1A 2BJ	NA	97	0	
11	Tower Bridge	15 700	Tower Bridge Road, London SE1 2UP	NA	98	1	
12	Natural History Museum	17 321	Cromwell Road, South Kensington, London SW7 5BD	5 388 295	98	0	
13	Hyde Park	9 447	Rangers Lodge, London W2 2UH	NA	98	0	Estimation (60 mn in 15 years)
16	Westminster Abbey	11 563	Broad Sanctuary, London SW1P 3PA	1 786 106	95	1	Estimation (100k per weekend)
17	Borough Market	6 526	8 Southwark Street, London SE1 1TL	NA	99	0	For 2012
18	The London Eye	44 727	South Bank of the River Thames, London SE1 7PB	4 000 000	91	1	From official site
23	Camden Lock Market	13 010	Chalk Farm Road, Unit 215–216, London NW1 8AB	5 200 000	99	0	
30	St Paul's Cathedral	8 166	London EC4M 8AD	1 782 741	100	1	

33	Covent Garden	9 382	Covent Garden, London WC2E 9DD	44 000 000	100	0	Estimation (based on london.net)
35	Shakespeare's Globe Theatre	5 043	21 New Globe Walk, London SE1 9DT	357 886	96	1	
40	Buckingham Palace	13 462	Buckingham Palace Road, London SW1A 1AA	558 000	94	1	Estimation (based on official information)
41	The View from The Shard	9 434	Joiner Street, London SE1	900 000	92	1	
45	Imperial War Museum	6 261	Lambeth Road, London SE1 6HZ	914 774	96	1	For the first year of operation (Feb 2013–Jan 2014)
71	Science Museum	5 360	Exhibition Road, South Kensington, London SW7 2DD	3 356 072	96	0	
79	Harrods	9 256	87135 Brompton Road, London SW1X 7XL	15 000 000	98	0	
80	Madame Tussauds London	17 905	Marylebone Road, London NW1 5LR	2 500 000	99	1	Estimation (based on official information)

*Date of record: 30 July 2016

Table 30.5 Matrix of non-parametric bivariate correlations

Spearman correlation (ρ)	Walk Score (n = 24)	TripAdvisor Reviews (n = 24)	Number of visitors (n = 19)	TripAdvisor Ranking (n = 24)
Walk Score (n = 24)	1	–0.041	0.575*	0.018
TripAdvisor Reviews (n = 24)	–0.041	1	0.365	–0.575**
Number of visitors (n = 19)	0.575*	0.365	1	–0.212
TripAdvisor Ranking (n = 24)	0.018	–0.575**	–0.212	1

* Spearman correlation is significant at 0.05 level (two-tailed)
** Spearman correlation is significant at 0.01 level (two-tailed)

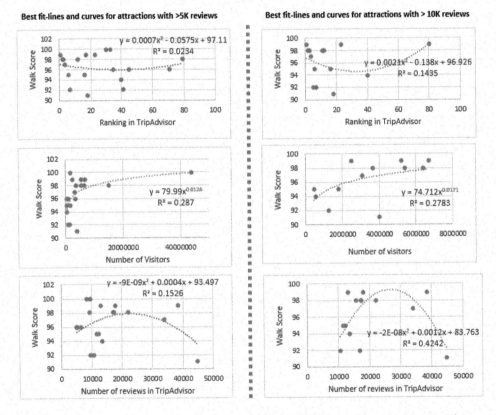

Figure 30.2 Scatterplots and best fit-lines and curves of Walk Score with ranking in TripAdvisor, number of visitors and numbers of reviews in TripAdvisor

Walk Score and number of reviews and rankings indicated non–monotonic relations. Figure 30.2 presents the scatterplots of the data, and enables learning more about the patterns of relations between the study variables. The scatterplots were made twice, first with the 19 attractions that had all the three types of information: TripAdvisor ranking, more than 5,000 reviews in TripAdvisor and information regarding the number of visitors. Second, with the 15 attractions that fulfilled all the above conditions, but were also considered to be very popular, with more than 10,000 reviews. The scatterplots and the best-fit lines in Figure 30.2 reveals that, when addressing the population of 19 attractions, the TripAdvisor rating is not related to the Walk Score measure. On the other hand, there is a power trend line between Walk Score and number of visitors, and an upside-down U-curve (an Order 2 polynomial trend line) relationship between Walk Score and the number of reviews. However, the R-squared values, which represents the goodness of fit, were found as moderated regarding the power trendline, and weak regarding the order 2 polynomial ($R^2 = 0.287$ and $R^2 = 0.153$, respectively).

After limiting the analysis to those attractions that received more than 10,000 reviews, the R-squared value of the upside-down U-curve was increased to $R^2 = 0.424$, implying that the relationship between Walk Score and number of visitors has one peak and two slopes. The R-squared value of the power trendline between Walk Score and number of visitors was not much changed ($R^2 = 0.278$) but a U-curve pattern, with a weak R-squared value ($R^2 = 0.144$) was revealed when the relation between the Walk Score and the ranking of the TripAdisor was studied. These findings suggest that the relationships between Walk Score and Ranking, number of visitors and number of reviews are complicated, and provide no certain conclusions with respect to the relationship between the attendance at visitor attractions and walkability.

Discussion

The current chapter aims to explore the benefits of walkable places, especially for urban tourism. Walkability is a key concept in urban planning and design (Southworth 2005; Lo 2009; Talen and Koschinsky 2013), and provides multiple benefits to people, communities and the environment (Leyden 2003; Southworth 2005; Forsyth et al. 2008). The benefits of walkability to urban tourism were described in previous works (e.g. Southworth 2005; Ujang and Muslim 2014), but were not empirically tested. The current work bridges this gap and provides exploratory empirical evidence to the importance of walkable places.

Using London attractions as a case study, and basing the analysis on popular websites (TripAdvisor and Walk Score), along with official numbers, the work demonstrates how walkability is a key factor for urban tourism and planning. All the popular attractions of London that were studied were located in areas described as 'Walker's Paradise', according to the rating scale of the Walk Score application. It is not clear whether their excellent walkability attracts the visitors, or whether their attractiveness made them so accessible, or whether the level of attendance is an implicit function of density and accessibility (including via public transport). The output of the situation is the same – walkability is positively related to the popularity of attractions. Hence, walkability, likability and popularity go hand-in-hand in the context of walkable places and top tourist attractions. However, a closer look at the results reveals that walkability also has some surprising effects on top attractions that should be noted as well.

Walkability for whom? Tourists vs locals

The Walk Score measurement aims to describe the positive walking attributes of a location from the perspective of a permanent resident, including daily errands as a key factor in determining walkability. However, top attractions are magnets for non-locals. The total numbers of visitors to top attractions, as was reported by VisitEngland records and the official websites refers to a combination of both locals and tourists. The visitors can be part of school trip activities, afternoon classes or special events. They can also be tourists. For this mixed population of visitors, the more walkable a place is, the more visited it is: this suggests that Walk Score may be a valid tool to estimate the number of visitors to top attractions. However, finer data would be obtained if there were a better breakdown in visitor categories to attractions.

When addressing the population of tourists, two further problems arose. First, the Walk Score measurement does not include tourist walkability aspects such as walking route signage, aspects of touristic appeal, cultural heritage (Ujang and Muslim 2014), activities (Samarasekara *et al.* 2011; Ujang and Muslim 2014) and toilets (Langer and Car 2014). In other words, its validation as a walkability measure for tourists requires further examination. Second, the TripAdvisor reviews indicator is not confirmed to be a proxy measure of the actual number of tourists. When the number of attractions was limited (to those that attracted more than 10,000 reviews) the results were changed, raising questions about the reliability of this indicator. Figure 30.2, as well as the results of the correlation matrix, suggests that the walkability factors for tourists, while overlapping, are different from those of locals, and should be tested using different tools and methods. Furthermore, the positive relations that were observed when studying the walkability of visitors were absent when studying tourist walkability. Tourists will visit places that are considered to be less attractive if they are accessible (intervening opportunities), producing a U-curve pattern when addressing the relations between walkability and TripAdvisor ranking. Additionally, tourists may scatter between the more walkable places, in a way that resembles cannibalization, with one attraction drawing from another in a finite market, producing a situation when a more walkable place could receive fewer reviews than a less walkable place. In part, this is because tourists have a limited time budget and therefore a particular space–time prism for mobility and accessibility (Hall 2005). Permanent residents are not assumed to have such constraints in the generation of Walk Scores.

Does walkability have a downside?

The results of the current work indicate that the popular assumption that walkability is always good for places is simplistic and neglects issues of design and assessment. For the urban destination as a whole, walkability is probably an advantage, but there is a lack of reliable and valid measurement tools to confirm it. At the level of the single attraction, walkability may create a cannibalization effect, when tourists prefer other walkable places nearby as a result of intervening opportunities on walking routes. This means that urban planners should pay special attention to the planning of walking facilities in touristic areas, in a way that will support the single attraction level as well. In addition, attractions in walkable places must retain high-quality services and facades, because they are exposed to more tourists and passing pedestrian traffic, even if they are not directly visited, and with the wide use of online reviews, can be punished with negative reviews if their facades are not perceived favorably by observers.

Box 30.1 Is the case of the walkability of London representative enough?

The current chapter sheds light on the walkability of the touristic London, but is London, as a world-leading touristic city, a representative case? In order to test how representative the findings of London are, a similar assessment was conducted for Montreal, Quebec (Canada). According to 2012 data, Montreal attracted more than 26 million visitors, of which almost 9 million stays were 24 hours or longer (Tourisme Montreal 2015). The analysis of walkable tourism in Montreal used three sources: official numbers of

---

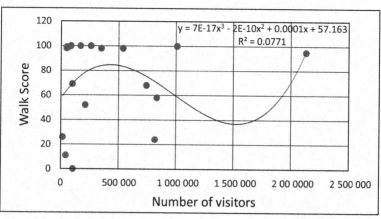

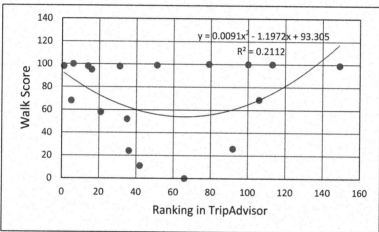

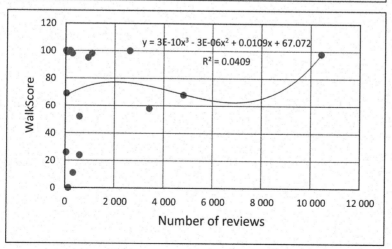

Figure 30.3 Scatterplots and best fit-lines and curves of Walk Score with number of visitors, ranking in TripAdvisor and numbers of reviews in TripAdvisor for Montreal, Canada

visitors (2014), taken from the website of Tourisme Montreal (www.tourisme-montreal. org/Montreal-Tourism/Toolkit), TripAdvisor and Walk Score. The database of Montreal includes 23 attractions, but TripAdvisor information was available for 18 attractions only. The median of TripAdvisor ranking was 39 (range 1–149). The mean number of visitors was 420,000, and the mean number of reviews was 1,430. These two figures were found to be highly skewed, with a small number of attractions pushing up the scales (standard deviations were 520,000 and 2,500, respectively). Montreal's attractions were also checked for their Walk Score and were found as walkable with a mean Walk Score of 72 (SD 34.24).

Figure 30.3 shows the scatterplots and the best-fit lines. TripAdvisor rating was found as related to the Walk Score measure. The power trend line formed a U-curve (An Order 2 polynomial trend line) relation and the R–squared value, which represents the goodness of fit, was found as weak to moderate ($R^2 = 0.211$). The two other scatterplots, addressing the number of visitors and reviews, did not produce clear trend lines. The U-shape trend line between ranking in TripAdvisor and Walk Score was also found in the London analysis (in the >10,000 case), suggesting that the trend line pattern with two peaks (with high and low ranking attractions) deserves more attention and further research. The unclear relations between Walk Score measures and number of visitors/reviews in the case of Montreal indicates, as it was in the London case, that basic assumptions about walkable tourism have to be studied further, with appropriate tools and exact numbers.

Conclusion: designing and planning of walkable places

Walkable places are considered as preferable for locals, visitors and tourists. However, the available tools are primarily directed at locals. When addressing visitors, and especially tourists, the assessing tools are inadequate, overlooking important aspects to tourists such as heritage, atmosphere, toilets and Wi-Fi. Walkable places for tourists should be planned with attention to tourists' special needs. Additionally, they should consider the connectivity between attractions, hotels, restaurants and shopping areas. In designing walkable places, destination managers should pay attention, not only to the destination as a whole, but also to each attraction to avoid an under-optimization of performance in the single attraction level, for reasons such as congestion and cannibalization. However, it should also be noted that people walk for different reasons and motivations (Buckley et al. 2016). Even when a favorable urban design has been created, people may still not walk unless higher-order communal and personal needs have also been attended to (Alfonzo 2005; Mehta 2008; Buckley et al. 2016). Such needs do not just apply to local inhabitants; for example, Mansouri and Ujang (2016b: 52) found walkability for tourists in Kuala Lumpur to be 'based on what could be socially experienced and offered as attractions. These are more significant than the mobility and urban design qualities that support walking. Social aspect of place experience strongly defines pedestrian experience within tourism locations.' Therefore, behavioral interventions and social marketing campaigns may serve to encourage visitors to "get out and walk" in the same way that they may be encouraged to use public transport and behave in an environmentally or culturally responsible manner (Hall 2013; Le-Klähn and Hall 2015).

Future studies should focus on developing assessing tools to tourist walkability at a single attraction level as well as in a destination level. Additionally, interdisciplinary teams of urban planners, GIS specialists, destinations' managers and tourism researchers should address the issue of walkability. Finally, the environmental benefits of walking should be highlighted in future research, as well as in the implementation of walking as the preferable mobility mode of urban tourism.

References

Adkins, A., Dill, J., Luhr, G. and Neal, M. (2012) 'Unpacking walkability: testing the influence of urban design features on perceptions of walking environment attractiveness', *Journal of Urban Design*, 17(4): 499–510.

Alfonzo, M. (2005) 'To walk or not to walk? The hierarchy of needs', *Environment and Behavior*, 37(6): 808–836.

Arbel, A. and Pizam, A. (1977) 'Some determinants of urban hotel location: the tourists' inclinations', *Journal of Travel Research*, 15(3): 18–22.

Azmi, D.I., Karim, H.A. and Ahmad, P. (2013) 'Comparative study of neighbourhood walkability to community facilities between two precincts in Putrajaya', *Procedia – Social and Behavioral Sciences*, 105: 513–524.

Bartlett, R. (2003) 'Testing the "popsicle test": realities of retail shopping in new "traditional neighbourhood developments"', *Urban Studies*, 40(8): 1471–1485.

Buckley, P., Stangl, P. and Guinn, J. (2016) 'Why people walk: modeling foundational and higher order needs based on latent structure', *Journal of Urbanism: International Research on Placemaking and Urban Sustainability*. DOI:10.1080/17549175.2016.1223738.

Carr, L.J., Dunsiger, S.I. and Marcus, B.H. (2011) 'Validation of Walk Score for estimating access to walkable amenities', *British Journal of Sports Medicine* 45: 1144–1148.

Doyle, S., Kelly-Schwartz, A., Schlossberg, M. and Stockard, J. (2006) 'Active community environments and health: the relationship of walkable and safe communities to individual health', *Journal of the American Planning Association*, 72(1): 19–31.

Duncan, D. T., Aldstadt, J., Whalen, J., Melly, S.J. and Gortmaker, S.L. (2011) 'Validation of Walk Score for estimating neighborhood walkability: an analysis of four US metropolitan areas', *International Journal of Environmental Research and Public Health*, 8(11): 4160–4179.

Duncan, D.T., Aldstadt, J., Whalen, J. and Melly, S.J. (2013) 'Validation of Walk Scores and Transit Scores for estimating neighborhood walkability and transit availability: a small-area analysis', *GeoJournal*, 78(2): 407–416.

Duncan, D. T., Méline, J., Kestens, Y., Day, K., Elbel, B., Trasande, L. and Chaix, B. (2016) 'Walk score, transportation mode choice, and walking among French adults: a GPS, accelerometer, and mobility survey study', *International Journal of Environmental Research and Public Health*, 13(6): 611.

Ewing, R. and Handy, S. (2009) 'Measuring the unmeasurable: urban design qualities related to walkability', *Journal of Urban Design*, 14(1), 65–84.

Ewing, R., Handy, S., Brownson, R.C., Clemente, O. and Winston, E. (2006) 'Identifying and measuring urban design qualities related to walkability', *Journal of Physical Activity and Health*, 3(Suppl 1): S223–S240.

Forsyth, A. (2015) 'What is a walkable place? The walkability debate in urban design', *Urban Design International*, 20(4): 274–292.

Forsyth, A. and Southworth, M. (2008) 'Guest editorial: cities afoot – pedestrians, walkability and urban design', *Journal of Urban Design*, 13(1): 1–3.

Forsyth, A., Hearst, M., Oakes, J. and Schmitz, K. (2008) 'Design and destinations: factors influencing walking and total physical activity', *Urban Studies*, 45, 1973–1996.

Frank, L.D., Sallis, J.F., Conway, T.L., Chapman, J.E., Saelens, B.E. and Bachman, W. (2006) 'Many pathways from land use to health: associations between neighborhood walkability and active transportation, body mass index, and air quality', *Journal of the American Planning Association*, 72(1): 75–87.

Gebel, K., Bauman, A. and Owen, N. (2009) 'Correlates of non-concordance between perceived and objective measures of walkability', *Annals of Behavioral Medicine*, 37(2): 228–238.

Giles-Conti, B. and Donovan, R. (2003) 'Relative influences of individual, social environmental, and physical environmental correlates of walking', *American Journal of Public Health*, 93(9): 1583–1589.

Hall, C.M. (2005) *Tourism: Rethinking the Social Science of Mobility*. London: Person.

Hall, C.M. (2013) *Tourism and Social Marketing*, Abingdon, Oxon: Routledge.

Hall, C.M., Le-Klähn, D.-T. and Ram, Y. (2017) *Tourism, Public Transport and Sustainable Mobility*. Bristol: Channel View.

Hamid, S.A. (2014) 'Walking in the city of signs: tracking pedestrians in Glasgow', *Current Urban Studies*, 2(3): 263–278.

Handy, S. (2005) 'Planning for accessibility: in theory and in practice', in D.M. Levinson and K.J. Krizek (eds), *Access to Destinations*, Oxford: Elsevier, pp. 131–147.

Harding, S. (1999) 'Towards a renaissance in urban parks', *Cultural Trends*, 9(35): 1–20.

Hickman, C. (2013). '"To brighten the aspect of our streets and increase the health and enjoyment of our city": the National Health Society and urban green space in late-nineteenth century London', *Landscape and Urban Planning*, 118: 112–119.

Hirsch, J.A., Moore, K.A., Evenson, K.R., Rodriguez, D.A. and Roux, A.V.D. (2013) 'Walk Score and transit score and walking in the multi-ethnic study of atherosclerosis', *American Journal of Preventive Medicine*, 45(2): 158–166.

Horacek, T.M., White, A.A., Greene, G.W., Reznar, M.M., Quick, V.M., Morrell, J.S., Colby, S.M., Kattel-mann, K.K., Herrick, M.S., Shelnutt, K.P. and Mathews, A. (2012) 'Sneakers and spokes: an assessment of the walkability and bikeability of US postsecondary institutions', *Journal of Environmental Health*, 74(7): 8–15.

Jordan, H. (1994) 'Public parks, 1885–1914', *Garden History*, 22(1): 85–113.

Kelly, C.E., Tight, M.R., Hodgson, F.C. and Page, M.W. (2011) 'A comparison of three methods for assessing the walkability of the pedestrian environment', *Journal of Transport Geography*, 19(6): 1500–1508.

Langer, S. and Car, A. (2014) 'GIS-based decision support for public toilet site selection: a case study of South Batinah Region in Oman', in R. Vogler, A. Car, J. Strobl and G. Griesebner (eds), *GI_Forum 2014. Geospatial Innovation for Society*, Berlin: Herbert Wichmann Verlag, pp. 135–139.

Larsen, J., El-Geneidy, A. and Yasmin, F. (2010) 'Beyond the quarter mile: re-examining travel distances by active transportation', *Canadian Journal of Urban Research: Canadian Planning and Policy* (supplement), 19(1): 70–88.

Lee, S. and Talen, E. (2014) 'Measuring walkability: a note on auditing methods', *Journal of Urban Design*, 19(3): 368–388.

Le-Klähn, D.-T. and Hall, C.M. (2015) 'Tourist use of public transport at destinations – a review', *Current Issues in Tourism*, 18(8): 785–803.

Le-Klähn, D.-T., Roosen, J., Gerike, R. and Hall, C.M. (2015), 'Factors affecting tourists' public transport use and areas visited at destinations', *Tourism Geographies*, 17(5): 738–757.

Leyden, K.M. (2003) 'Social capital and the built environment: the importance of walkable neighborhoods', *American Journal of Public Health*, 93(9): 1546–1551.

Lo, R.H. (2009) 'Walkability: what is it?', *Journal of Urbanism: International Research on Placemaking and Urban Sustainability*, 2(2): 145–166.

London and Partners (2014) *Tourism Report 2014–2015*. Available at: http://files.londonandpartners.com/l-and-p/assets/our-insight-london-tourism-review-2014-15.pdf (accessed 9 August 2016).

Lwin, K.K. and Murayama, Y. (2011) 'Modelling of urban green space walkability: eco-friendly Walk Score calculator', *Computers, Environment and Urban Systems*, 35: 408–420.

Maghelal, P.K. and Capp, C.J. (2011) 'Walkability: a review of existing pedestrian indices', *Journal of the Urban & Regional Information Systems Association*, 23(2): 5–20.

Mansouri, M. and Ujang, N. (2016a) 'Space syntax analysis of tourists' movement patterns in the historical district of Kuala Lumpur, Malaysia', *Journal of Urbanism: International Research on Placemaking and Urban Sustainability*. DOI:10.1080/17549175.2016.1213309.

Mansouri, M. and Ujang, N. (2016b) 'Tourist expectation and satisfaction towards pedestrian networks in the historical district of Kuala Lumpur, Malaysia', *Asian Geographer*, 33(1): 35–55.

Mehta, V. (2008) 'Walkable streets: pedestrian behavior, perceptions and attitudes', *Journal of Urbanism: International Research on Placemaking and Urban Sustainability*, 1(3): 217–245.

Moura, F., Cambra, P. and Gonçalves, A.B. (2017) 'Measuring walkability for distinct pedestrian groups with a participatory assessment method: a case study in Lisbon', *Landscape and Urban Planning*, 187: 282–296.

Pafka, E. and Dovey, K. (2016) 'Permeability and interface catchment: measuring and mapping walkable access', *Journal of Urbanism: International Research on Placemaking and Urban Sustainability*. DOI: 10.1080/17549175.2016.1220413.

Page, S.J. and Hall, C.M. (2003) *Managing Urban Tourism*, London: Pearson.

Riggs, W. (2015) 'Walkability: to quantify or not to quantify', *Journal of Urbanism: International Research on Placemaking and Urban Sustainability*. DOI: 10.1080/17549175.2015.1111926.

Samarasekara, G.N., Fukahori, K. and Kubota, Y. (2011) 'Environmental correlates that provide walkability cues for tourists: an analysis based on walking decision narrations', *Environment and Behavior*, 43(4): 501–524.

Schmidt, C.J. (1979) 'The guided tour: "insulated adventure",' *Journal of Contemporary Ethnography*, 7(4): 441–467.

Shoval, N., McKercher, B., Ng, E. and Birenboim, A. (2011) 'Hotel location and tourist activity in cities', *Annals of Tourism Research*, 38(4): 1594–1612.

Solnit, R. (2000) *Wanderlust: A History of Walking.* London: Penguin Books.

Southworth, M. (2005) 'Designing the walkable city', *Journal of Urban Planning and Development,* 131(4): 246–257.

Strandell, A. and Hall, C.M. (2015) 'Impact of the residential environment on second home use in Finland – testing the compensation hypothesis', *Landscape and Urban Planning*, 133: 12–23.

Talen, E. (2002) 'Pedestrian access as a measure of urban quality', *Planning Practice and Research*, 17(3): 257–278.

Talen, E. and Koschinsky, J. (2013) 'The walkable neighborhood: a literature review', *International Journal of Sustainable Land Use and Urban Planning*, 1(1): 42–63.

Thompson, K.J. (2003) 'Urban transport networks and overseas visitors: analysis of the factors affecting usage and the implications for destination management'. Doctoral dissertation, University of Salford, Manchester, UK.

Thompson, K.J. and Schofield, P. (2007) 'An investigation of the relationship between public transport performance and destination satisfaction', *Journal of Transport Geography*, 15(2): 136–144.

Tourism Montreal (2015) 'Database, Tourisme Montreal Research Department'. Available at: www. tourisme-montreal.org/Montreal-Tourism/Toolkit (accessed 15 March 2016.)

TripAdvisor (2016a) 'About TripAdvisor'. Available at: www.tripadvisor.com/PressCenter-c6-About_Us (accessed 9 August 2016).

TripAdvisor (2016b) London. Available at: www.tripadvisor.co.uk/Tourism-g186338-London_England-Vacations.html (accessed 9 August 2016).

Ujang, N. and Muslim, Z. (2014) 'Walkability and attachment to tourism places in the city of Kuala Lumpur, Malaysia'. *Athens Journal of Tourism*, 2(1): 53–65.

Urry, J. (2002) *The Tourist Gaze.* London: Sage Publications.

Vale, D.S., Saraiva, M. and Pereira, M. (2016) 'Active accessibility: a review of operational measures of walking and cycling accessibility', *The Journal of Transport and Land Use*, 9(1): 209–235.

VisitBritain (2016) *Britain's Visitor Economy Facts*, available at: www.visitbritain.org/visitor-economy-facts (accessed 9 August 2016).

VisitEngland (2015) *Visitor Attraction Trends in England 2014: Full Report.* Available at: www.visitbritain. org/sites/default/files/vb-corporate/Documents-Library/documents/England-documents/va_2015_ trends_in_england-full_report_version_for_publication_v3.pdf (accessed 9 August 2016).

Walker, S.E. and Duffield, B.S. (1983) 'Urban parks and open spaces – an overview', *Landscape Research*, 8(2): 2–12.

Walkscore.com (2016) Walk Score Methodology. Available at: www.walkscore.com/methodology.shtml (accessed 9 August 2016).

Wanner, M., Götschi, T., Martin-Diener, E., Kahlmeier, S. and Martin, B.W. (2012) 'Active transport, physical activity, and body weight in adults: a systematic review', *American Journal of Preventive Medicine*, 42(5): 493–502.

Wolf, K.L. (2003) 'Retail and urban nature: creating a consumer habitat', *Population and Environmental Psychology Bulletin*, 29(1): 1–6.

Wolf, K.L. (2004) 'Trees and business district preferences: a case study of Athens, Georgia, US', *Journal of Arboriculture*, 30(6): 336–346.

Yüksel, F. (2013) 'The streetscape: effects on shopping tourists' product/service quality inferences and their approach behaviors', *Journal of Quality Assurance in Hospitality & Tourism*, 14(2): 101–122.

31

Walking on the shoulders of giants

Historical mountain trails as management tools?

Daniel Svensson, Sverker Sörlin, Annika Dahlberg,
Peter Fredman and Sandra Wall-Reinius

Introduction – pathways, trails and multifunctional land use

Most walking in mountain areas takes place on paths or trails. Paths often emerge spontaneously as people and animals move between points in the landscape in activities related to, for example, agriculture, herding, or trade. Some walking paths grow into trails, although the distinction between paths and trails is not easy to draw. Especially since the 19th century, trails for walking have been groomed and increasingly designed to attract and assist walkers, to steer larger numbers of them, minimize degradation, enhance safety and local work tasks, and for a range of other motives (e.g. Timothy and Boyd 2015; Clius *et al.* 2012; Houston 2012). Some trails are based on historical roads and/or walking practices (cultural, religious, military), some have become famous and their names are widely known. Trails for walking are very common in most parts of the world and the total distance of trails, while unknown, is enormous. Many walking trails are increasingly used also for other purposes, such as running, skiing, snowmobiling, horseback riding, biking, and transportation of goods and people. With their omnipresence, accessibility and multifunctionality, trails engage multiple interests and may be a useful tool to minimize conflicts between different users, while aiming to enhance the experiences and landscape values for all. Trails for walking are thus a phenomenon worthy of serious reflection.

Mountains in the Swedish north have historically been depicted as "sleeping giants", with huge potential as reserves for minerals in an industrial economy, a strong tradition in the Swedish mountain region (Sörlin 1988). However, Sweden's mountain landscapes also have a long history of human use and mobility, which together with biophysical processes have continuously reshaped the environment. These landscapes are thus cultural as well as natural landscapes, although they are often perceived and marketed as "wilderness" (see Cronon 1996; Wall-Reinius 2012). Typical for most landscapes, including the mountains region in Jämtland, are the shifts and variations in the meanings ascribed to them, how they are accessed and used, the material outcomes of their use, and in some cases how various uses are reconciled with conservation interests (see Head 2012; although there has also been relevant critique of how the protective role of conservation may be undermined by increasing human presence, see Crist 2013; Wuerthner *et al.* 2014). In the Swedish mountain region, including its national parks, trails are common and have become a key infrastructure in a comprehensive walking tourism. This started to grow in the 19th century, and albeit that trails today are more used than ever, they make up part of what can be called a *movement or mobility heritage* (Svensson *et al.* 2016). This heritage also comprises other landscape elements used when walking (such as bridges, huts, resting places, markers, signs) that may reflect the multicultural origins of paths and trails. Many trails are, at least to some extent, historical remains of long time periods of mobility in the mountains, by the Sami people, mountain farmers and other local communities, tourists, scientists, priests, civil servants, reindeer, and other domesticated or wild animals. The trails themselves thus have a value as cultural heritage. In addition, several of the Swedish Environmental Goals, adopted by Parliament, are relevant for in the landscapes traversed by trails. Relevant goals concern biodiversity and landscape types such as marshes and forests, and there is also a special goal for the mountain region (*fjäll*) (Miljödepartementet 2012). How trails are laid out in the landscape and how they are managed and used is an important factor for achieving these goals.

It is a challenge to enable and balance multifunctional use of mountain environments, including mountain trails, in ways that combine sustainable livelihoods for local populations, local recreational use, tourism, regional business development, as well as national goals related to both the natural and cultural environment; the last, for example, in the form of protected areas and through heritage conservation. Examples of tensions and conflicts are found in areas where stakeholders have different interests, goals and landscape perceptions, for example, due to historical legacies brought through to the present. In the Jämtland case, this can be exemplified with popular tourism trails traversing land where reindeer graze during seasons when they are very susceptible to disturbance, or local fear of potential changes in allowed trail use, e.g. for snowmobiles, if the suggested new national park is established, or how the increase in biking on trails historically intended for walking may affect the environment, as well as cause friction between users. It is, however, important to highlight that trails are definitely not seen only as problems, but also as potential solutions to present conflicts – which will be discussed further on.

In this chapter, we underline the importance of walking trails as management tools in areas where different interest groups co-exist. More specifically, we show that the history and understanding of trails can and should be more clearly articulated. We start by theorizing walking on trails and paths in a more general sense, and frame it in a historical context, highlighting the role of trails as heritage. Thereafter, we use the case of the mountain region of Jämtland, based on individual interviews, group discussions and surveys conducted within an ongoing research project, to analyse how walking trails have been used, and present potential conflicts including new trends and user needs. We also explore different suggestions concerning management of trails in the area. Finally, we bring the previous sections together and discuss trails as a mobility heritage in relation to future sustainable management.

Theorizing mobility and trails – historical, cultural and more-than-human approaches

Paths, by definition, have a history; sometimes short but more often long and shifting. They are established through repetitive use, and connect places in the landscape that thus can be more easily reached. As such, they may signal use by some groups while excluding others. A pathway is often also a forceful metaphor for connecting the past, present and future. Walking specific paths, thereby connecting specific places in historical cultural landscapes, is an embodied experience of past connections; for example, overgrown paths can be restored and be part of memory work. The recent focus on paths for pilgrimage, e.g. the recently started Norwegian-Spanish-American project, Heritage Routes, about value creation linked to pilgrimage routes, is a good example of this. This is similarly true for the ongoing re-discoveries in Sweden of traditional church paths (*kyrkstigar*), charcoal burners' paths (*kolarstigar*), school paths (*skolstigar*), pasture paths (*fäbodstigar*) and other historically significant landscapes of mobility. Studies of civic initiatives to re-establish historical paths in many parts of the world have revealed the importance of new ideas stemming from more sustainable notions of the good life, including physical exercise and excellent food and landscape experiences, which, in turn, speaks to how cultural elements can affect commodity preferences and consumer behavior, but also the desire among local communities to regain control over their rural livelihoods (Syse and Mueller 2015). Pathways thus provide, at the same time, cultural heritage and a venue, or space, where new lifestyles and approaches to landscape experiences have been, and continue to be, negotiated. As such, paths and trails may be regarded as everyday heterotopias (Foucault 1986), where people inscribe themselves in a continuum of movement through time and space.

There have been several attempts to theorize mobility in the landscape, of which walking is a central part. The cultural history of walking with famous names in the Western tradition, such as Jean-Jacques Rousseau, Jane Austen, Henry David Thoreau and others (climbers, alpinists, political ideologists, moralists, outdoor life protagonists, environmentalists) has been studied (e.g. Schama 1996; Solnit 2001; Ingold and Vergunst 2008). Here walking is understood as an element in the forming of the modern individual, of gender properties, and of temporalities linked to social class and culture. The theoretical understanding of landscape monuments, often tied to nationalism (e.g. Lowenthal 1998, 2008), has led to an underestimation of the more subtle and small-scale infrastructures of mobility, of which trails form a part. Trails belong in a more holistic and democratic perspective of landscape use and have been linked to bodily practices of knowing and wayfaring (Ingold 2000, 2011; Tsing 2005; Hastrup 2009).

Mobility that takes form in pathways is also closely linked to domestication and co-existence between humans and various other life-forms, including animals for use and comfort. This relationship reflects different types of nurturing as well as domination enacted by more than one species (Ingold 1994; Oma 2010), in an interactive process (Leach 2003; Haraway 2008). By focusing on paths and trails as remains of multispecies mobility in the mountain landscape, temporal and spatial scales of mobility can be merged. Paths are often examples of co-evolution (van Dooren 2014) between humans and different kinds of animals and, as such, they are useful tools for analysing both conflicting and common interests and uses in the mountains. They are inherited, both as physical remains in the landscape and as local knowledge. Acknowledging this more-than-human inheritance, as well as new forms of interaction through trails, is a way to deepen the discussion about intrinsic and instrumental values. This may open up a more holistic perspective and a broader understanding of the different ways that trails have been and are used – and how this affects the landscape.

Pathways as agents and arenas of change

Walking in mountains is a way of transport in varied terrain and a means to enhance nature experiences and deepen landscape relations. It is also one of the most popular activities in Swedish outdoor life and attracts international tourism (Fredman *et al.* 2014). Walking, and more generally the movement heritage, has had an important part in shaping the understanding and identity of mountain landscapes. Current use depends on this heritage, but not as something static but as part of continuously changing landscapes. Landscapes are dynamic – due to biophysical processes as well as changes in society. The use of land and resources by local inhabitants changes over time, and the demand among tourists and other visitors for places suitable for movement, exploration, solitude, training and events continues to grow. Consequently, questions about how landscapes change, why, for whom and by whom, are now key issues in landscape research and landscape planning, and include questions about protected areas and biodiversity conservation (Wylie 2007).

Pathways could be used in an extended way as kinds of complex experience corridors, where energies, ambitions and possibilities for economic development are increasingly channelled. Many actors, local as well as more removed from the landscape in question, can claim links to the historical creators of the mountain trails, and many more have an interest in using and framing them today. However, despite the multiple users and uses of trails, they are commonly small-scale and have had only marginal direct effects on local ecology and landscape. At the same time, their indirect effect on landscape perception and use of land, water and other resources, through the channelling of various user groups, is massive. The long history of landscape use along these trails, combined with the multitude of voices and interests involved in maintaining them, deserves further attention when efforts of nature conservation, e.g. through protected areas, cause tension and conflict (Dahlberg *et al.* 2010).

Landscapes of mobility are complex and combine natural features with memory, local practice, knowledge and visual representation. Local residents, including Sami, environmentalists, actors in the tourism industry, representatives of nature protection and cultural heritage agencies agree that it is useful to regard trails and pathways as a useful dimension in the mountain landscape. Trails are functional, deeply rooted in tradition, and serve as useful tools of governance and management by steering local inhabitants, as well as visitors, and thus limiting stress on ecologies and heritage. Many respondents in Jämtland have, however, expressed concern with the current status of mountain trails and sense a certain untapped potential. In areas where this potential has already been "tapped", innovative co-existence between sports, tourism, heritage, nature protection and traditional livelihood (be it reindeer husbandry, small-scale farming or small-scale forestry) have emerged during the 20th century. The nature reserve of Vålådalen has been claimed by some to be such an example (Svensson 2014; Svensson and Sörlin 2015). However, our research indicates that if present and future conflicts are to be avoided, there is still much that needs to be negotiated and agreed upon. One aspect raised by respondents is how different user groups, such as hikers and the increasing numbers of bikers, make use of the same trail, whether this is sustainable or not. Others have raised concerns on how to channel visitors so as to minimize negative environmental effects, and, at the same time, maintain costs for maintenance at a reasonable level, and how to combine increasing number of tourists with needs and traditions among local inhabitants.

Another example where multiple user groups have used trails as a means to combine different recreational interests in the same landscape is the Vasalopp Arena in the county of Dalarna in Sweden (Svensson 2014). This trail is based on historical paths of forestry workers, farmers, charcoal burners, and even the 16th-century king Gustav Vasa, who fled from Danish troops along roughly the same trail. The Vasaloppet ski race has successfully built on these traditions, while also offering a multitude of sportified landscape experiences, like skiing, running, biking, and walking (Svensson 2014). These practices, dating back to the early 1920s, in turn reinforce and deepen the articulation of these landscapes as places for sport and outdoor life. Similar events in Norway, like Birkebeinerrennet, have used similar strategies and have produced a similar kind of "national trail" (Sörlin 2011).

Current use of mountain trails – a tourism perspective

Trails have become more and more associated with tourism and outdoor recreation. Nowadays, it is hard to find a tourist region that does not boast trails or routes that are included in a broader package of tourism experiences, but the contribution they have brought to tourism and recreation has been understated. Most outdoor recreation-oriented definitions of trails have emphasized corridors in protected areas and other natural or cultural settings meant for non-motorized foot, bicycle or horse traffic (Timothy and Boyd 2015).

Among the many different types of nature-based recreation settings around the world, mountain areas are often characterized by particularly extensive trail networks for reasons related to safety, navigation and experiences. Many mountain areas are important sites for tourism, and hiking is recognized as one of the most important activities in a number of Swedish studies (Fredman and Tyrväinen 2010; Wall-Reinius and Bäck 2011; Fredman *et al.* 2016; Garms *et al.* 2016). In these studies, landscape beauty, natural scenery, peacefulness and solitude are typical reasons to engage in hiking. Such participation could also be a response to the idea of living more active and healthy lives, and to a wish to be in closer contact with nature and landscapes. Backcountry hiking is one example of what Varley and Semple (2015) label as "slow adventure", with an emphasis on uncertainty, unpredictability, transience and emotions in the context of the outdoors. Hiking is thus not only scenery, and walkers do more than gaze; bodies are multi-sensually engaged, involved and interwoven with the landscape, and, as this "slow adventure" moves along, it incorporates and forms the landscape (Ingold 2000). Which and what kind of trail the hikers follow structures their experience, where broad and well-groomed trails are perceived as less compatible with a sense of adventure and unpredictability. To continue with Ingold (2000), modern constructed trails are close to the building perspective (plan first, then construct, then use/dwell) (Ingold 2000), while traditional trails with a long history are results of continuous "dwelling" in an area. Trails are ideally, to take a "dwelling" perspective, results not of an architectural master plan, but rather of the lived experience of landscape in the place where the trails are found (Ingold 2000).

Hiking in the Swedish mountain landscape for recreational purposes goes back to the 19th century. However, well into the 20th century, only a few hiking tourists travelled to the mountains and to the newly (1909) established national parks; these landscapes were more significant as a tourist icon or dream than as a realistic tourist destination (Wall-Reinius 2009). Today, however, the mountain landscape is a key tourist area (Heberlein *et al.* 2002), and mountain trails play a significant role for contemporary visitors. Hiking, leisure walks and cross-country skiing are among the most popular recreation activities in the Swedish mountain region (Fredman *et al.* 2014), and more than three-quarters of the adult Swedish population think it is positive or very positive that there are marked trails in the mountains (less than 1% have a negative attitude to trails). In terms of motivation, backpackers in the Swedish mountains are just as committed to the activity as backpackers elsewhere, but they have a much higher level of place attachment (Fredman and Heberlein 2005). When people are asked about what activities they believe will increase in the future, mountain biking, hiking and backpacking, all typical "trail activities", are among the top five. Swedish mountain visitors, given the opportunity to express their views about the trail system in an open-ended question format, confirmed the manifold roles of trails in multifunctional landscapes:

> Incredibly good and important that there are trails for people with different experiences so that the mountains are accessible for all! Because spending time in the mountain is very wonderful.

> Last time I hiked in the mountains there were tensions between hikers and bikers. The bikes destroy the trails so they become rocky and bumpy. They were also ahead of us to the cabins and occupied the best rooms.

On-site visitor studies in different mountain areas support the significance of trails to tourists. For example, a visitor survey from 2013 among summer visitors in the Jämtland mountains showed that hiking is the most important activity and 65% of the visitors follow marked hiking trails during their stay (Wall-Reinius *et al.* 2015). However, only 9% of the Swedish visitors, and 4% of the international visitors, state that they carry out their activities outside of marked trails (Wall-Reinius *et al.* 2015). Similar figures are reported from Fulufjället National Park in the southern part of the mountain region, although off-trail hiking appears to increase slightly (Fredman and Wikström 2015). Indeed, twice as many visitors in 2014, as in 2001 and 2003, said there are not enough trails in the area. Similar views were reflected in a study by the Swedish Tourist Association (STF) in 2014, when 278 people aged 17–25 did a number of "experimental hikes" to evaluate the trail and hut system in the Jämtland mountain region (Svenska Turistföreningen 2015). Results from this study show that the young regard mountain hiking as a "back to nature" experience, appreciating the genuine, simple accommodation (huts and tents), and without access to the internet. At the same time, they wanted trails to be better marked, and asked for information about hiking distances and detours to interesting places or mountain peaks. These views may give some hints about what future mountain visitors will desire.

Trails in the future – governance tools

So far, we have established that trails have deep historical roots, represent a key cultural heritage, and are under-theorized. We have also found that their importance is on the rise, especially for tourists and recreational use. They grow in length and presence and serve as embedded elements in a growing tourism, with various forms of walking as a core activity. This means that if they are supposed to serve a function for conservation and management, while continuing to fulfill additional functions such as security and access routes for local inhabitants, new governance issues will arise.

One aspect on this is cost: how much and who pays? A review of the public trail system in the mountain region by the Swedish Environmental Protection Agency (SEPA 2014) concluded that present funding is not enough to maintain the current system of trails, let alone extend it further. A major challenge for the future is to design a trail system and a management organization which meets the demands of contemporary recreational users as well as other users, such as local people and the Sami. As a thought-provoking note on this topic, we observe that in 2014 the Swedish Tourist Association launched a fundraising project among the public, asking for money to support the "King's Trail" in the northern part of the Swedish mountain region (see www.stottakungsleden.se). At the time of writing, 117 km of the trail has been supported, at a rate of 25 SEK/metre, about one-quarter of the total length.

Timothy and Boyd (2015) suggest that trails can function as salient tools for conserving rural landscapes through policy and building awareness through interpretation. Trail management can also be used to control visitor numbers to preserve a rural or wilderness image, which is often the case in protected areas such as national parks. However, it is important to stress here that landscapes with walking trails are much more than landscapes for tourists and conservationists – they are the working and recreational landscapes for different groups within local communities. As such, they should be allowed to remain dynamic, and use of resources and changes to the landscape should not automatically be perceived as negative (Dahlberg *et al.* 2010). Thus terms like "conservation" or "preservation" should be clarified and made specific, to avoid maintaining or creating perceptions of static landscapes reserved for the use of incoming visitors.

Trails represent lines of information in the landscape and, as such, can, if wisely managed, constitute arenas for conflict management (Manning 2011). In the Swedish mountain region, e.g. in Jämtland, semi-domesticated reindeers represent a significant aspect of trail use and management. Also, many types of wildlife follow certain frequent routes and stretches – creating their own network of trails and paths that need to be considered to minimize disturbance. Interpretive signage has for a long time been closely connected with trails, and nowadays physical information in the landscape (signs, maps, information boards) is augmented by information provided online through the internet – taking trails into the virtual reality domain of the landscape. Through information directed to visitors with different interests and previous mountain experience, knowledge about the landscape could be shared and directed to increase awareness of for e.g. history, present uses, and domestic and wild life-forms and their needs. Instruments like these may, it is hoped, decrease disturbance and conflict, which has also been advocated by many, not least the reindeer-herding Sami and the conservation authorities.

Given the above-described multifunctionality of trails, both in terms of utility and functionality, it is easy to see the complexity involved in trail management. To design and maintain high-quality trails requires systematic assessment programmes and monitoring (Mende and Newsome 2006), and to make efficient financial priorities net economic values and impacts are essential (Bowker *et al.* 2007). Analysing future uses and using trails to manage conflicts requires extensive knowledge about the different stakeholders involved (Manning 2011). In Sweden, the state, through delegation to the County Administrative Boards, presently has management responsibility for mountain trails. In discussions with different actors, we have observed that the issue of best future management was approached in a very open manner, with various solutions suggested. These included, but were not limited to, private actors, tourism bodies of different kinds, local authorities (e.g. municipalities) and state agencies. Already there are alternatives to state control and responsibility, since private actors and NGOs shoulder the main responsibility when preparing trails for specific events.

Conclusion

Despite the rich heritage that are embodied in them, the existing trail/path systems, through maps and other information, privilege relatively recent walking and skiing paths and touristic infrastructures. This tends to obscure other forms of mobility landscapes and their context in cultures, ecologies and history. The current trail infrastructure is to some extent a missed opportunity for a number of reasons, many of which were confirmed by stakeholder representatives in the Jämtland mountains: a) it misrepresents local residents and their use and knowledge of landscape; b) it does not adequately articulate the richness of cultural and environmental histories; c) it is underused in the building of local and regional identities; d) its poor articulation reduces the region's potential to attract visitors; e) it has almost no web presence, which means that visibility and usefulness are hampered; f) for all these reasons, its capacity to steer visitors through the landscape in ways that minimizes unwanted disturbance, tension and conflict is underused. Thus, we think it is fair to say that the existing trail system in the Jämtland mountains, and most likely in many other parts of the Swedish mountain region is unfair, ineffective, uneconomical and unsustainable, and holds considerable potential for development and improvement.

What is true for the Swedish mountain regions may possibly be relevant for other parts of the world although, of course, conditions on the ground as well as historical circumstances differ hugely. Trails and pathways are tools for managing different interests and stakeholders, to channel walkers and other users, to minimize unwanted disturbance and degradation, and to enhance positive experiences for all who use them.

Furthermore, trails do and should become even more important for conveying information and knowledge about landscapes – past and present. Here, it is important to discuss which trails and which types of trails are visible, physically in the landscape or as well-remembered legacies of past uses. Why are some trails more well known and well used than others, how have these been "selected", and where lies the power to articulate the importance of certain trails and not others? Where does the social articulation of landscape take place (Sörlin 1998, 1999)? This is obviously not an issue only related to trails, but trails, especially those that are groomed and provided with major infrastructures, are manifest representations of who and what influence landscape presence and perception.

Finally, we should manage trails and pathways because they are important from a social, cultural, historical, economic and ecological perspective. The existence and use of trails have an impact on local identity as well as on visitor identity and landscape experiences, and they are part of the individual and collective memory, which is an often-neglected aspect of landscapes perceived in a holistic manner that includes all living and non-living entities within them. Practice and power shape trails and pathways and, in turn, trails and pathways influence and reinforce values of users and society at large. They also are an integral part of a growing tourism sector. At some very basic level, trails exist because they are needed. They are there, and therefore an informed and flexible governance of trails is essential.

As we stated in the opening section of this chapter, mountains have been seen as "sleeping giants", and perhaps they still are, but in a different sense. Today, not only the mountains themselves, and their content of extractive resources remain of importance, but increasingly also traces of their historical use by different user groups, including non-humans, as they provide a base for current and future tourism, management and governance, much of it performed through walking. Understanding the way we walk, literally on the shoulder of these giants, may prove to be a useful tool to minimize conflicts and social and ecological disturbances in areas where sensitive wildlife, traditional practices and tourism must co-exist.

References

Bowker, J.M., Bergstrom, J.C. and Gill, J. (2007) 'Estimating the economic value and impacts of recreational trails: a case study of the Virginia Creeper Rail Trail', *Tourism Economics*, 13(2): 241–260.

Clius, M., Teleucă, A., David, O. and Moroşanu, A. (2012) 'Trail Accessibility as a tool for sustainable management of protected areas: case study Ceahlău National Park, Romania', *Procedia Environmental Sciences*, 14: 267–278.

Crist, E. (2013) 'On the poverty of our nomenclature', *Environmental Humanities*, 3(1): 129–147.

Cronon, W. (1996) 'The trouble with wilderness; or, getting back to the wrong nature', in W. Cronon (ed.), *Uncommon Ground: Rethinking the Human Place in Nature*, New York: Norton, pp. 69–90.

Dahlberg, A., Rohde, R. and Sandell, K. (2010) 'National parks and environmental justice: comparing access rights and ideological legacies in three countries', *Conservation and Society*, 8(3): 209–224.

Foucault, M. (1986) 'Of other spaces', *Diacritics*, 16(1): 22–27.

Fredman, P. and Heberlein, T. (2005) 'Visits to the Swedish mountains: constraints and motivations', *Scandinavian Journal of Hospitality and Tourism*, 5(3): 177–192.

Fredman, P. and Tyrväinen, L. (2010) 'Frontiers in nature-based tourism: editorial', *Scandinavian Journal of Hospitality and Tourism*, 10(3): 177–189.

Fredman, P. and Wikström, D. (2015) *Besök och besökare i Fulufjällets nationalpark sommaren 2014 (med jämförelser åren 2001 och 2003)*, Mid-Sweden University, ETOUR, rapport 2015: 5.

Fredman, P., Wall Reinius, S., Sandell, K. Lundberg C., Lexhagen, M., Bodén, B. and Dahlberg, A. (2014) *Besök och besökare i fjällen – Resultat från en undersökning avseende svenskarnas fritidsaktiviteter i fjällen, besök i olika fjällområden, landskapsrelationer, fjällen i sociala medier, upplevelser av vindkraft och attityder till skyddad natur*, Mid-Sweden University, ETOUR, Report 2014: 3.

Fredman, P., Wolf-Watz, D., Sandell, K., Wall-Reinius, S., Lexhagen, M., Lundberg, C. and Ankre, R. (2016) *Dagens miljömål och framtidens fjällupplevelser – Iakttagelser av aktivitetsmönster, landskaps- relationer och kommunikationsformer*, Mittuniversitetet, ETOUR, rapport 2016: 3.

Garms, M., Fredman, P. and Mose, I. (2016) 'Travel motives of German tourists in the Scandinavian mountains: the case of Fulufjället National Park', *Scandinavian Journal of Hospitality and Tourism*. DOI: 10.1080/15022250.2016.1176598.

Haraway, D. (2008) *When Species Meet*, Minneapolis, MN: University of Minnesota Press.

Hastrup, K. (2009) 'Taking the life world seriously in environmental history', in S. Sörlin and P. Warde (eds), *Nature's End: History and the Environment*, London: Palgrave Macmillan, pp. 331–348.

Head, L. (2012) 'Conceptualising the human in cultural landscapes and resilience thinking', in T. Plieninger and C. Bieling (eds), *Resilience and the Cultural Landscape: Understanding and Managing Change in Human-shaped Environments*, Cambridge: Cambridge University Press, pp. 65–79.

Heberlein, T.A., Fredman, P. and Vuorio, T. (2002) 'Current tourism patterns in the Swedish mountain region', *Mountain Research and Development*, 22(2): 142–149.

Houston, R. (2012) 'Evaluation of trail impact assessments for use at Oregon Parks and Recreation Department'. Unpublished project, Hatfield School of Government, Public Administration Division Center for Public Service, Portland State University, Oregon.

Ingold, T. (1994) 'From trust to domination: an alternative history of human–animal relations', in A. Manning and J. Serpell (eds), *Animals and Society: Changing Perspectives*, London: Routledge, pp. 1–22.

Ingold, T. (2000) *The Perception of the Environment: Essays in Livelihood, Dwelling and Skill*, London: Routledge.

Ingold, T. (2011) *Being Alive: Essays on Movement, Knowledge and Description*, London: Routledge.

Ingold, T. and Vergunst, J.L. (eds) (2008) *Ways of Walking: Ethnography and Practice on Foot*, Cheltenham, Glos: Ashgate.

Leach, H.M. (2003) 'Human domestication reconsidered', *Current Anthropology*, 44(3): 349–368.

Lowenthal, D. (1998) *The Heritage Crusade and the Spoils of History*, Cambridge: Cambridge University Press.

Lowenthal, D. (2008) 'Authenticities past and present', *CRM: The Journal of Heritage Stewardship*, 5(1): 6–17.

Manning R. (2011) *Studies in Outdoor Recreation: Search and Research for Satisfaction*, 3rd edn, Corvallis, OR: Oregon University Press.

Mende, P. and Newsome, D. (2006) 'The assessment, monitoring and management of hiking trails: a case study from the Stirling Range National Park, Western Australia', *Conservation Science*, 5(3): 285–295.

Miljödepartementet (2012) *Svenska miljömål – preciseringar av miljökvalitetsmålen och en första uppsättning etappmål*. Ds 2012:23, Regeringskansliet, Miljödepartementet, Stockholm.

Oma, K.A. (2010) 'Between trust and domination: social contracts between humans and animals', *World Archaeology*, 42(2): 175–187.

Schama, S. (1996) *Landscape and Memory*, New York: Vintage Books.

SEPA (2014) *Nulägesbeskrivning av det statliga ledsystemet i fjällen. Beskrivning av nuvarande omfattning och skick samt beskrivning av resursbehov och möjligheter för utveckling av ledsystemet*, Stockholm: Swedish Environmental Protection Agency, Sektionen för skydd och förvaltning (Gfs), PM 2014–09–12.

Solnit, R. (2001) *Wanderlust*, London: Verso.

Sörlin, S. (1988) *Framtidslandet: Debatten om Norrland och naturresurserna under det industriella genombrottet*. [With a summary in English: 'Land of the Future: the debate on Norrland and its natural resources at the time of the industrial breakthrough']. Stockholm: Carlsson bokförlag.

Sörlin, S. (1998) 'Monument and memory: landscape imagery and the articulation of territory', *Worldviews: Environment, Culture, Religion*, 2(3): 269–279.

Sörlin, S. (1999) 'The articulation of territory: landscape and the constitution of regional and national identity', *Norsk Geografisk Tidsskrift*, 53(2–3): 103–112.

Sörlin, S. (2011) *Kroppens geni: Marit, Petter och skidåkning som lidelse* [The Wisdom of the Body: Marit, Petter and Skiing as a Passion]. Stockholm: Weyler.

Svenska Tursitföreningen (2015) *Get Real! Summer 2014: 1521 dagar på fjället: Get Real ger vägledning till framtida planering*. Available at: www.svenskaturistforeningen.se (accessed 24 January 2015).

Svensson, D. (2014) 'I fäders spår? Längdskidåkningens landskap som kulturarv', *RIG – kulturhistorisk tidskrift*, 96(4): 193–212.

Svensson, D. and Sörlin, S. (2015) 'Science, Sport et Environnement: le développement des techniques d'entraînement en altitude depuis 1945' [Science, sport and environment: the development of high-altitude training methods after 1945], in G. Quin and A. Bohuon (eds), *Les liaisons dangereuses de la médecine et le sport*, Paris: Editions Glyphe, pp. 193–211.

Svensson, D., Sörlin, S. and Wormbs, N. (2016) 'The movement heritage – scale, place, and pathscapes in Anthropocene tourism', in M. Gren and E.H. Huijbens (eds), *Tourism and the Anthropocene*, London: Routledge, pp. 131–151.

Syse, K.L. and Mueller, M.L. (eds) (2015) *Sustainable Consumption and the Good Life: Interdisciplinary Perspectives*, Abingdon, Oxon: Routledge.

Timothy, D.J. and Boyd, S.W. (2015) *Tourism and Trails: Cultural, Ecological and Management Issues*, Bristol: Channel View Publications.

Tsing, A.L. (2005) *Friction: An Ethnography of Global Connection*, Princeton, NJ and Oxford: Princeton University Press.

van Dooren. T. (2014) *Flight Ways: Life and Loss at the Edge of Extinction*, New York: Columbia University Press.

Varley, P. and Semple, T. (2015) 'Nordic slow adventure: explorations in time and nature', *Scandinavian Journal of Hospitality and Tourism*, 15(1–2): 73–90.

Wall-Reinius, S. (2009) 'A ticket to national parks? Tourism, railways and the establishment of national parks in Sweden', in W. Frost and C.M. Hall (eds), *Tourism and National Parks: International Perspectives on Development, Histories and Change*, London: Routledge, pp. 184–196.

Wall-Reinius, S. (2012) 'Wilderness and culture: tourist views and experiences in the Laponian World Heritage Area', *Society and Natural Resources*, 25(7): 621–632.

Wall-Reinius, S. and Bäck, L. (2011) 'Changes in visitor demand: interyear comparisons of Swedish hikers' characteristics, preferences and experiences', *Scandinavian Journal of Hospitality and Tourism*, 11(1): 38–53.

Wall-Reinius, S., Olausson, F., Ankre, R., Dahlberg, A., Lexhagen, M., Lundberg, C., Sandell, K. and Bodén, B. (2015) *Undersökning bland besökare i södra Jämtlandsfjällen sommaren 2013*, Rapportserien European Tourism Research Institute 2015: 2. Östersund, Sweden: Mittuniversitetet.

Wuerthner, G., Crist, E. and Butler, T. (2014) *Keeping the Wild: Against the Domestication of Earth*, Washington, DC: Island Press.

Wylie, J. (2007) *Landscape*, New York: Routledge.

32

Wayfinding design for rural flânerie in France

Hélène Ducros

Introduction: walking as constitutive of place and human beings

The reasons people walk are varied. People walk as necessity, or for leisure and recreation, often with a pedagogical purpose, as sport, for spiritual purposes (pilgrimages or processions) or survival (transborder migrations), to surpass themselves and as self-actualisation (extreme walking, strenuous treks), as contestation and protest, to express support and solidarity, for health, to connect to others and to connect to place. Ultimately, walking is 'constitutive of human beings' (de Baecque 2016), and a fundamental human activity and means of interacting with the environment (Bassett 2004). One reason is that walking allows for a multi-sensory experience of place and time–space (Edensor 2010). This aspect of our 'lifeworld routine' (Wunderlich 2008) gives meaning to place, shapes our engagement with place and triggers an affective relationship with it. But this should not be taken for granted as something that just happens without planning or design. Since walking is also 'constitutive of place' (Lee 2004), it may be recruited to shape place, especially in heritage sites. Indeed, as walking allows place periodicity to come to light, it reveals the layers of history in that place, the 'incessant stomping' that occurred there over time, and the 'superposed fossil itineraries [that are] unconsciously reactivated by walkers or flâneurs who come *after*' (de Baecque 2016; author's translation). This study thus brings together heritage-making, place attachment and walkability design to highlight the ways in which heritage sites in rural France endeavour to organise and design space to foster an engagement with place and with the past on the part of temporary visitors and permanent residents alike.

Recent publications and conferences have shown walking to gather momentum as an interdisciplinary research axis worthy of attention to better understand socio-cultural relations, as well as our relationship with the lived space. Walking-based literature is on the rise in multiple disciplines. This volume attests to the wide range of scholarly interest in walking. Researchers delving into the processes of walking in order to get a deeper understanding of individual and societal behaviours emerge out of multiple disciplines: planning, psychogeography, urban studies, tourism and leisure, health and wellness, history or religious studies. While a great share of the walking literature is centred on urban walking (Middleton 2010), rural walking has not been completely ignored. However, much of rural walking research focuses on so-called natural spaces (trails, hikes and other greenways) rather than the built environment, and often on physical or bodily activity rather than its all-encompassing phenomenological dimension. This chapter aims at filling this gap by bringing to the fore the experience of small rural municipalities in France (*communes* of up to 2,000 inhabitants) that have opted for a development trajectory based on heritage preservation and valorisation. By joining the associative network of Les Plus Beaux Villages de France – the Most Beautiful Villages of France (MBVF), they agree to abide to the label's demands in terms of spatial organisation. Through this association, they hope to bring new breath into the life of the village and trigger economic opportunities, while also reinforcing local identity and sense of place, as well as share their local history with others. This study finds that walking is an important factor within their strategy of place-making and heritage-making, and highlights how the creation of walkable pathways and pedestrian spaces contributes to valorising their place capital, realising their potential as heritage attractions, and sometimes even renewing residents' engagement with the place they inhabit.

This chapter first gives a brief overview of the aspects of the relationship between walking and place attachment that are particularly relevant to heritage sites in the rural milieu. It then focuses on the Association of the MBVF as an illustration of the ways in which rural heritage-making relies on the implementation of walkability, through norms transforming places in ways not always consensual. It concludes with remarks highlighting how the practice of walking transforms the relationship of people with place and contributes to place attachment in heritage sites in rural France. Based on ethnographic work conducted in villages that are members of the MBVF network in different regions, and time spent shadowing the Association in its activities through participation observation, the study inquires into how residents, mayors and heritage-making actors envisage walkability and how spaces are shaped into places of walking for an enhanced sense of place.

Walking and place attachment

The 17th and 18th centuries saw the emergence of urban promenades in Europe, culminating in the 19th and early 20th centuries with the flâneur as symbol of urban modernity (de Baecque 2016). This is an essentially urban character described by many as an aimless observer and anonymous, invisible and undetected spectator of the ever-changing city (Ferguson 1987; Benjamin 2002; Bassett 2004), albeit the fact that the aimlessness of the flâneur is not met with consensus (Jenks and Neves 2000). In the 20th and 21st centuries, this consumer of urban landscapes may have found its rural counterpart at a time in which the rural landscape wanderer emerges in multiple forms, from the natural world observer to the athletic Nordic walking aficionado, the emblematic trails' trekker, or the cultural heritage tourist. All those have in common that they seek particular experiences, among them emotional and visual experiences. In the context of place-making and consumption of heritage spaces, the concept of spectacle as constituting 'the visual convention and fixity of contemporary imagery' (Jenks and Neves 2000: 9) is particularly relevant. Moreover, Edensor (2010), focusing on mobility, underlines the polyrhythmic quality of place which intersects with people's walking modes, expressing the ways in which immersion in place through movement produces a mobile sense of place as 'place is experienced as the predictable passing of familiar fixtures' (Edensor 2010: 70). Building on Sheller and Urry's (2006) concept of 'dwelling-in-motion', Edensor (2010) highlights the ways in which the deliberate production of specific walking spaces creates a sense of 'mobile belonging' reinforced by multisensory experiences, while putting pressures on identities and walking practices themselves. For Tuan (1977), kinesthesia is also one important way we can access and experience place and is part of a sensory system that allows us to construct a bond with place. Place attachment relies on the five senses that together guide how we engage with the world. Perception is based on experience of place, which can be direct (when we know a place) or indirect (what we know about a place).

The analysis of the MBVF, as a model of place-branding in the rural environment, draws on these connections between walking and place attachment. In the Association's strategy to create a unique sense of place in its member villages, walking spaces and walkability take on an important role in fostering place attachment. Indeed, in numerous interviews with residents, mayors and heritage-making actors, walkability recurrently came up spontaneously, emerging in conversations as it was envisaged as a necessary medium to access the place in fundamental ways that implicated a multi-sensory connection. Concrete examples given included the smells of lavender along the path, familiar or novel sights, the feel of stones under the feet, or the sound of running water on slate on a raining day. Walking was also mentioned as providing a conduit for an emotional connection with place, when it elicits feelings of home and connection with the past, as well as an intellectual and strictly cerebral engagement with place; for example, when it enables learning and understanding what was before.

Walking in the Most Beautiful Villages of France: *piétonnisation* and pedagogy

'Walking is an experience in exploration. Not only of a landscape, of a world that offers itself to being deciphered. But of course of ourselves' (de Baecque 2016: 16; translated by author). This approach to walking is reflected in the Association's motto, which encompasses its threefold mission: 'To know ourselves, to make ourselves known, to make ourselves acknowledged' (translated by author). This shows that its endeavour is driven not only by a desire to revive deserted villages socially and economically and to make them noticed as significant actors, but also to preserve rural vernacular heritage and educate residents and visitors alike. It is about discovery (from without) and introspection (from within).

The MBVF emerged in 1982 in a context of rural waning and neglect. In particular, rural mayors felt isolated in their efforts to valorise their territories and limited in the development opportunities available to their *communes* (municipalities). The Association is a non-governmental organisation that is supported by its members, which are the localities that request inclusion in the network and undergo an evaluation of their heritage value. The selection criteria used go beyond built structures to include local political will to commit to the project over time, and the implementation of planning actions conducive to making each village a successful destination. Although it may appear like a purely touristic endeavour, it is fundamentally concerned with using heritage to bring meaningful life back to rural communes, including by attracting permanent residents who can make a living locally. The heritage tourism sector provides an opportunity. As a consequence, the label of the MBVF has become a well-known brand across the French landscape, sprinkling its aesthetic and development ideology across the countryside, one village at a time. At the time of writing there are 154 members. The Association's influence has also expanded through advisory functions to ten other countries, who have formally solicited it to accompany them in creating similar associations locally, adopt its principles of heritage preservation, place-making and pedagogy, while adapting them to local particularities.

The walking motif is an important and explicit part of landscape preservation and landscape design in member villages. It is part of the rhetoric regularly used by Association's officers to explain their selection of villages. Indeed, walking reinforces their central focus on pedagogy because it assists in the deciphering of place:

One must be able to get lost in a Most Beautiful Village . . . The potential for pedestrian exploration is evaluated. It is an important way to experience place. We like to see paths created that foster interest in the place at the same time as they guarantee people will stay a while, have access to aesthetic resources which are made legible through signage that must be non-intrusive, yet available. If you can't get to it or if you can't understand it, it might as well not be there as far as the label is concerned.

(Interview with MBVF Officer 2012)

The Association recognises that they have privileged villages that offer a latticed network of pathways and that this has become an unspoken norm in MBVs.

It does not mean that there is no patrimonial value in main street villages, but for the members of the Quality Commission [that makes decisions on membership], many feel that those don't invite discovery. You just traverse them, and you may not even get out of the car for that.

(Interview with rural mayor member of the Quality Commission 2012)

Consequently, *piétonnisation*, or "pedestrianisation", has become a key element in place development under the label.

The pivotal instrument standing at the heart of the organisation's work is the *Charte de Qualité*, upon which the *Commission Qualité* rests to appreciate patrimonial value and valorisation efforts made by the communes that approach the Association to obtain the coveted label (at the time of writing, 81 per cent of applications have been turned down since the Charte's creation in 1991). The Charte's 27 criteria dictate place specifications under the label, as they encapsulate the aesthetic and practical requirements that in effect give a definition of the 'beautiful' in the rural setting.

Charte de qualité and sense of place by walkable *cheminements*

By validating certain aspects of patrimonial landscape, the *Charte de Qualité* also assumes an important role in concrete place design. Its multifaceted selection criteria lead to a rigorous evaluation of villages in their physical reality, but also of the experience it offers. One of the main challenges in the quest to create 'places of emotion' (interview with Plus Beaux Villages de France (PBVF) Officer 2012) and to carry out the mission of 'dream-making' (PBVF 2016) is to transform automobilists into walkers, the paradox being that many of the 154 member villages are only accessible by car, since they are isolated from public transport networks. It is precisely their isolation that has preserved their heritage quality. Several mayors of branded villages, as well as officers of the MBVF, concur in assessing that it is neglect and out-of-reachness that made possible the line of development chosen today.

It would be outside the realm of this chapter to explicate all 27 criteria contained in the *Charte*. However, a few diagnostic points used in the field by the expert-delegate to compile the report that is submitted to the Commission are particularly and explicitly pertinent for the construction of walkable spaces, permitting access to heritage places and making them intelligible.

- Diversity of pathways (*cheminements*)
- Control of automobile traffic
- Spatial organisation for parking
- Public lighting
- Organisation and availability of guided tours
- Implementation of directional and informational signage.

Making people walk is not easy. One way in which heritage places are transformed is by the allocation of space to parking, to segregate cars from walking paths. Villages are assessed on their ability to control traffic flows and their parking amenities, which can result in the creation of non-places, as lamented by some long-time residents:

> Where you have the main parking lot now is where we used to play *boules* when I was a kid; now there is no longer a central spot for us, the older folks, to meet, it's all for the tourists.

> [T]hat big field at the edge of the village is now for parking, it's full in the summer, but gosh we used to hang out there and invent all sorts of games there, all the village kids together a long time ago.
>
> *(MBVF resident interviews 2013)*

This tension between customarily engrained uses of space or local memory of place and dedicated space for visitors' use can make it difficult for mayors to allocate municipal space to visitor parking and away from other uses for local residents. Traffic flows remain problematic in places in which the narrowness of streets is part of the aesthetic expectation. Many communes struggle with directing traffic away from the historic centre, in spite of obvious signs posted at the entrances of the village.

> Even with our clear parking signs, you still have people . . . driving caravans and coming through the village. I am in the front row for when they get wedged here between my house and the one across, it's too narrow, we tell them, they come anyway. I take photos of it each time, one day someone will get stuck there between two walls of stone.
>
> *(MBVF resident 2013)*

Once people walk, deciphering place for them is key in triggering place attachment. The design of walkability spaces in MBVs aims at prompting meaningful discovery and embodied experiences. In designing legible walkable spaces, villages often draw on the use of maps, repeat photography, and, increasingly, technology to assist in discovery. Several communes have designed thematic *chemins* (paths) around local heritage, whether natural or built. The *sentier des ocres* in Roussillon (the Ochre path/trail) or the *chemin de la brique et du torchis* in Parfondeval (Path of brick, wattle and daub) are among the themed pathways that interpret the cultural landscape for walkers in MBVs and centre their attention and senses on particular features of local history.

> A[n] MBV, it has to be discovered on foot, so we encourage our villages to make that possible by all means available.
>
> *(MBVF Officer 2012)*

> Walking is feeling the place physically. Connecting to its beauty, its imperfections too . . . For example our streets are not always easy to navigate with the cobblestones. It's a whole: body, mind, past, present. And you can be alone or with other people, your family, your kids.
>
> *(Tourism Office in MBVF 2012)*

> We want people to wander. And you can't wander in a straight line.
>
> *(Commission Qualité Officer 2012)*

> Walking the place is key. You can't get to the essence of a place by a drive-by. I want people to feel the stones under their feet, at the same time as they will smell the smells, hear the

sounds, like the river down below, and be moved by the stories of the local past they read about on the information signs.

(Mayor of an MBVF 2013)

These quotes highlight the views supported by the Association about the role of walking in labelled villages. Walking provides a physical, visceral contact with place that is also necessary in the intellectual discovery and understanding of place. As a result, tangled pathways are often privileged in selection criteria and have become a topographic expectation (Figure 32.1).

Informative signage along the way is meant to guide, inform and connect people to place. Walkable spaces are assessed not only in their physical reality, but also in how they allow an emotional and intellectual engagement with place, by making it more intelligible. Landscape must be legible and organised for viewers. An itinerary will often be suggested, with the help of numbered place-markers for self-guided tours. In one village, some residents actually

Figure 32.1 Wandering in tangled pathways of a Most Beautiful Village

345

participated in the sequencing and placing of those markers and were invited to contribute to the audio self-guided tour. Participants reported learning much about their village and feeling proud of the place as a result. Signage connects people to the place and connects places within the place, geographically and temporally. In many MBVs, maps are made available to visitors who are invited to walk in multiple forms. For example, in Balazuc, visitors can partake in a treasure hunt; in Pradelles or Vogüe, as in many other villages, numbers posted on remarkable buildings refer visitors to an itinerary map that they can obtain from the tourism office or information points. Technology is increasingly enrolled in the process (smart codes, apps or interactive terminals).

Signage is not only directional, but also pedagogical. It helps walking visitors to "see" place and connect to historical and aesthetic narratives of place. Signage puts place on display for walkers, echoing Jenks and Neves (2000: 9) notion of spectacle as 'rules of what to see and how to see it, it is the "see-ness", the (re)presentational aspects of phenomena that are promoted'. In many MBVs, posted repeat or archival photography of place (sometimes provided by residents themselves) reveals the evolution of the cultural landscape through time and informs on past livelihoods, while detailed architectural explanations convey the particularities that give place its regional identity, as, for example, the half-timbered houses in Alsace. Interviews with mayors revealed that the type of signage can result from imitation of practices seen in other MBVs which they have visited. For example, plexiglass is recurrent, leading to a certain uniformity across member villages as far as display styles. This also helps the walker know what signage to look for and expect from place to place and village to village within the network.

However, walkers are not limited to the category of visitors. Pathways are also appreciated by residents and contribute to reconnecting them with their surroundings and transmitting knowledge of place to future generations. The following comments by village residents suggest that public signage acts like a walkable history book of which pages are turned one by one with each step taken:

> I learned a lot from the signs. I bring my grand-children, they live in the big city, I bring them to do the village tour and we read the stories together . . . It's important they know where they come from, the history of the village and the people there, so they keep on preserving it.

> I like to walk with my grand-father, it's hard sometimes, we stop a lot, the ground is not easy, but we stop and we sit on the bench over there.

(MBVF resident interviews)

In MBVs, aesthetic value is also enhanced through the creation of walking nightscapes, to make walking possible at all times of day and night (although often lights do not remain on throughout the night, for energy economy). Residents report that they appreciate the street lighting and that it sometimes encourages them to visit each other at night instead of watching TV. But they also report being worried about the financial burden for the locality of such extravagance. Residents often believe that public lighting is a direct consequence of the MBV label, and report that it is a positive aspect that, although intended to enhance the touristic experience, also makes everyday walking safer for them and their families.

In place-making, walking goes hand in hand with pausing. 'Each pause in movement makes it possible for location to be transformed into place' (Tuan 1977: 6). Movement and immobility are both necessary for reflection in place. Hence, in many MBVs, the design of walkable spaces incorporates spaces of rest. Benches are also where residents may meet up and engage in conversation with each other or take time to connect with the many layers of place, past and present, tangible and intangible.

> I like it, to walk here with Madame . . . Especially now that they built that sidewalk for us. We stop a lot, we sit on the bench over there and we admire the view. We wait for the church bells to ring, it's really loud when you get close, same bells and same sounds since she and I were born.
>
> *(MBVF resident interview)*

Conclusions: rural flânerie and transmission

Through its *Charte de Qualité*, the Association of the Most Beautiful Villages of France takes on a pedagogical approach to landscape and encourages the development of walking pathways that give opportunities to connect emotionally and intellectually to aesthetic and architectural local heritage. This chapter showed that walking lies at the heart of place-making and rural renewal in MBVs and that municipal decisions over place development take walkability and pedestrianisation as key factors in place design. It is telling that one disgruntled mayor, whose village was recently sanctioned upon re-inspection and threatened with expulsion from the network, contested this decision by invoking the many efforts he had made to ensure that new and interesting pathways were created. He regretted that, in spite of the village becoming much more walkable than when it was first instated within the Association, the village would probably be losing the label. Successful *piétonnisation* and access to new walking pathways around the medieval walls were the only concrete arguments he made for why he felt the decision was unjustified.

In MBVs, whether old paths are restored or reinvented or new paths are created, walking spaces are deliberately designed to provide a multiplicity of encounters with place and its many layers. These spaces contribute to place attachment even for residents, although the marked preference for tangled pathways results in normative pressures on the design of walking spaces in heritage landscapes, which in turn shape expectations and aesthetic tastes about what the rural should look like. Indeed, linear plans such as main street villages stand a limited chance to be accepted under the label, unless they can make up for their unlucky topography with outstanding heritage value, such as UNESCO recognition or other types of highly valued natural or built features.

Walkability contributes to enhancing social capital in MBVF by reinforcing the connection between people (residents) and the place, by making them aware of their surroundings in a physical and emotional way, and by triggering care for the place. Through the creation of walking spaces and the enhancement of walkability, the MBVF also succeeds in enhancing place resilience and the passing on of a sensibility to place to future generations.

> Before, in the old times, I don't think anyone walked here just for walking, we had things to do, fields to check on, animals to tend to, things to care for, and anyway the streets were dirty and muddy and at night it was very dark. Now we walk just because it's possible, and just because. We don't have to have any particular reason really. It simply feels nice and for me it makes me proud of who I am and where I am. It makes this place even more home and makes you realize that we should take care of it. Walking puts us in touch with our bond with the place and also our responsibility to it. For example when we notice things that should not be there or should not be happening here, things that are damaging to our image. We are like ambassadors now that we have the label, it's important people keep

that in mind all the time. And that way we can stay proud of everything that happened before we were here.

(MBVF resident interview)

Could it be that in the 21st century, at a time when urbanites increasingly leave cities to get away from their fast-paced lives, and when the changing relation between the rural and the urban gives rise to ambiguous, blurred spaces, the flâneur emerges now as a rural character? In post-agricultural rurality, the Association of the Most Beautiful Villages of France makes is possible for residents to reappropriate their living space through new means, at the same time as it allows visitors to connect with its past meanings.

This study reveals that, by implementing walkability amenities that render the cultural land-scape legible and emotionally and physically accessible in their spatial planning, localities con-struct the conditions for place attachment as they elicit or reinforce a bond between place and visitors or inhabitants. Findings highlight that walking is conceptualised as a means to a multi-sensorial experience of place and envisaged as the conduit to place attachment through access to memorial and aesthetic narratives. The resulting normative effect of walkability "place quality" criteria on heritage place-making – where certain topographies are less prone to recognition – shows that processes of place-making and heritage-making are co-constitutive of place attach-ment in "touristification" and that they contribute to the reinforcement of identity in place for residents, especially through the practice of walking, no longer for the purpose of agrarian works as their ancestors, but more akin to the flâneur's aimless wandering characterised in the past as an urban subject. A sign posted in Turenne (Figure 32.2) indeed suggests that flânerie is no longer

Figure 32.2 Rural flânerie in Turenne

the prerogative of the urban, but that the rural has become the locus for the development of a flâneur's sensibility and relationship with place.

The wanderings of the urban *promeneur* of the 17th century now have a parallel in the rural. The 19th-century flâneur is no longer restricted to the urban character described by Walter Benjamin, and Paris no longer holds the monopoly as the ultimate place for flâneries. Through walkability, the rural is positioned and reinvented as a place of spectacle and where the observer, whether transient visitor or permanent dweller, connects with history as well as intimate emotions, which results not only in a shifting vision of the rural, but also a transformation of place itself, reminding us that 'pedestrian circulation makes humanity' (de Baecque 2016; translated by author).

Acknowledgment

This study was supported by the National Science Foundation (grant #1202703)

References

Bassett, K. (2004) 'Walking as an aesthetic practice and a critical tool: some psychogeographic experiments', *Journal of Geography in Higher Education*, 28(3): 397–410.

Benjamin, W. (2002) *The Arcades Project*, trans. H. Eiland and K. McLaughlin, Cambridge, MA: Harvard University Press.

de Baecque, A. (2016) *Une histoire de la marche*, Paris: Perrin.

Edensor, T. (2010) 'Walking in rhythms: place, regulation, style and the flow of experience', *Visual Studies*, 25(1): 69–79.

Ferguson, P. (1987) 'The *flâneur* on and off the streets of Paris', in K. Tester (ed.), *The Flâneur*, London: Routledge, pp. 22–41.

Jenks, C. and Neves, T. (2000) 'A walk on the wild side: urban ethnography meets the *Flâneur*', *Cultural Values*, 4(1): 1–17.

Lee, J. (2004) 'Culture from the ground: walking, movement and placemaking', paper presented at the Association of Social Anthropologists Conference, Durham, UK, March 2004.

Middleton J. (2010) 'Sense and the city: exploring the embodied geographies or urban walking', *Social and Cultural Geography*, 11(6): 575–596.

PBVF (2016) *Point.com La lettre des Plus Beaux Villages de France*, N°42. Plus Beaux Villages de France.

Sheller, M. and Urry, J. (2006) 'The new mobility paradigm', *Environment and Planning A*, 38(2): 207–226.

Tuan, Y.-F. (1977) *Space and Place: The Perspective of Experience*, Minneapolis, MN: University of Minnesota Press.

Wunderlich, F.M. (2008) 'Walking and rhythmicity: sensing urban space', *Journal of Urban Design*, 13(1): 125–139.

33

Community benefits from walking tourism in Western Norway

Merete Kvamme Fabritius

Introduction

In Norway, tourism emerged in the first half of the eighteenth century. The European aristocracy targeted the wild and pristine landscape of the north and, from the 1850s, nature was highly targeted as an arena for physical activity. Scientists, anglers and mountaineers had formerly explored the unfamiliar areas, and they were followed by the gradually increasing number of travellers with the aim of hiking in Norwegian landscapes (Fabritius 2010). However, walking tourism in Western Norway revealed a need for transportation to desirable, remote hiking destinations and magnificent viewpoints. Tourism therefore appeared as a source of income to the poor Norwegian peasantry, settled far away from central areas.

This case study is the community of Oldedalen in the municipality of Stryn, a river valley enclosed by the Jostedal Glacier, and its glacier arms. One of these is the glacier in Briksdal, a narrow tributary valley at the end of Oldedalen, and an internationally well-known nature-based attraction. Today, there are more than 300,000 tourist visits to Briksdal Glacier (Briksdalsbreen) annually. Approximately 40,000 individuals use the famous and captivating shuttle transport for the 2-kilometre distance, on the steep, curvy and narrow road, to the walking path into the Jostedal National Park and the glacier area. This shuttle business has been collectively organized and conducted by the local farmers for more than 90 years. This chapter will show that the current shuttle business in Briksdal is the result of individual and collective choices and actions undertaken as an interaction between formal and informal rules, the biophysical/material world and characteristics of the community (Ostrom 2005).

Institutions

In order to understand the longstanding collective solution in this community, it is useful to look at the institutional development related to this. All social sciences have assumptions about human behaviour and the relationship between individuals and society. New institutionalism considers individuals' motivation for action to be complex, assuming individuals to act with a purpose, under conditions of limited information, imperfect mental models and transaction costs (North 1990; Brinton and Nee 2001). Based on this approach, individuals make choices within constraints, i.e. make choices and act within various types of constraints, but with the ability to learn, and adapt according to experiences.

The constraints or societal limitations for individual behaviour and action are largely constituted by different institutions. These institutions can be created, such as formal laws, or they may evolve over time as prescriptions, customs or more informal rules. The formal institutions include both legal political and economic rules. The legal institutions are constitutional law, written and customary law, regulations, statutes, and more individual contracts, and all these rules entail restrictions on individuals' freedom of action. Policy rules define the hierarchical structure of political activities, and basic structures for decisions, while economic rules are rules of ownership, such as property rights regimes and rules for assignment or disposal of property.

Informal laws are unwritten rules and include various forms of norms and values that are important for individuals. Institutions are not designed to be socially effective, and, in particular, the formal institutions are designed to serve the interests of those who have the power to create new rules (North 1990). The main point in an institutional analysis is that it is based on "rules in use", which is the set of rules used and known by everyone (Ostrom 2005).

Transformation and transaction costs

Within economic disciplines, the importance of institutions for economic development were long-neglected and disregarded as independent variables. Economic disciplines based their theories on individual choices made under perfect conditions. This neoclassical paradigm was challenged by Coase (1960) and North (1990) by their studies of the significance of institutions for exchange (Brinton and Nee 2001). The conclusion was that institutions matter. They explained the relationship between transformational and transactional costs of exchange and institutional genesis and development, and also the significance of institutions for transformation and transaction. In the 90-year history of tourism development in Briksdal, the question of transaction costs for the community has played a significant role.

Transformation costs are the resources required for the work and the forms of capital that must be used in the process of transforming, for example, natural resources into marketable commodities. Transaction costs include those resources which are used to measure or calculate the value of what is being exchanged, to protect the rights and the negotiations, to monitor and enforce contracts, and to sanction possible violations.

According to North (1990), such costs are mainly related to information, and these costs are sources to the origin of social, political and economic institutions. Institutions affect further all economic activities, by their effect on cost of production and cost of exchange (North 1990). Or, put another way, institutions and institutional change create structures for various forms of exchange which again has direct impact on transformation – and transaction costs.

Institutional enforcement includes both what individuals are prevented from doing, and what the individual is allowed to do. Such limitations make human interaction more predictable, and thereby reduce the cost of interactions. The important role of institutions in society is to reduce uncertainty by establishing predictable structures around human interaction. Sometimes, however, the rules are violated. An important part of the function of institutions is therefore the costs of the violation, and the seriousness of the sanctions. As a consequence, institutions are a form of social capital that contribute to the function of society (Coleman 1994; Ostrom 2000).

Social capital

In this context, social capital is an agent which can be used for obtaining physical, human and social capital. These forms of capital are significant for a society's development, and none of these forms of capital work without the other (Ostrom 2000). While some conceptualizations of social capital regard it as an individual resource, others perceive social capital as a collective resource that individuals can benefit from (Norges forskningsråd 2005). In this chapter, social capital is regarded as structural elements in society, like different features and elements of social life that makes it easier for players to act to accomplish specific objectives. Social capital is, therefore, the adhesive that makes society's various parts hang or work together.

Institutions, credible commitments or reliability, stable social connections or networks characterized by reciprocity, and commitment to participation in activities for the common good, are forms of social capital that promote cooperation and the achievement of important goals. According to Coleman (1994) society's stock of social capital explains why people succeed in cooperating.

Social capital exists on an individual level, community level and a national or international level, and the individuals make choices within a context of various forms of social capital. One aspect of social capital is particularly important; unlike other forms of capital, social capital must be created, maintained and renewed through use; otherwise it will erode or deteriorate (Coleman 1994; Ostrom 2005). Social capital is, therefore, an important resource to the community, which makes it easier to achieve rational exchanges between actors, and a means to reduce transaction costs.

Method

This case study covers more than 100 years of institutional development. The data collection was therefore challenging. To ensure reliability and validity in the study, method and data triangulation has been used, by combinations of interviews and document analyses, from oral and written sources (Silverman 2000). Validity has also been sought by using respondent validation to obtain feedback from the participants during the period of data collection about the accuracy of the data they have given, and the researcher's interpretation of that data.

The written sources in this study are the business protocols, notes and writings, as well as official documents, laws and policy strategies on multiple levels. In addition, a considerable number of local historical sources, such as genealogy books and local historical writings and documents have been used. These local data might be dominated by the perception and context of the narrator, and have therefore been subjected to a critical evaluation and compared with data from other sources. Moreover, scientific historical literature with local, national and international perspectives has been extensively used in this study.

The participants in this study are descendants of the founders of the organization and the current owners of the business, and are therefore sources of important data for the study. As a method, conversational interviews with a narrative approach were chosen. The interviews were guided by a carefully prepared interview guide, which ensured that the informants described relevant thematic areas for the study. In addition, data from both older and recent written sources were brought into the interviews. The aim was to freshen up the informant's memory, and if possible, get supplementary or complementary information relevant to this study.

Early tourism, potential for profit

The Norwegian public transport system originated in the Middle Ages, when transport consisted of horses, boats and horse-drawn carriages. The Norwegian peasantry, with ownership of land, was obliged to perform the practical work of transport. This form of infrastructure lowered the transaction costs of travel for centuries (Coase 1960), and laid the foundations for later tourism development. The transport system made remote areas accessible, and tourism arose as a new source of revenue for the peasantry, especially in parts of the country where transport demand was not particularly exigent.

The remote Briksdalsbreen in Oldedalen became a desired walking destination in the middle of the nineteenth century, because of its location and beauty. Tourists arrived in Oldedalen by crossing the Olden Lake by boat, and then could request a horse equipage for the 5-kilometre distance to Briksdal farm at the end of the valley. From this farm, they started the hike to the glacier.

The potential for cash earnings from transporting foreigners heading for a walk caused frictions and transaction costs to the community. Disputes and competition among inhabitants occurred. Fortune hunters from neighbouring communities appeared and increased the conflicts. Initially, this was handled by organizing the local farmers in a traditional shift system. However, the lack of an accurate information system made both the arrivals and the number of tourists impossible to anticipate. This sometimes caused overcapacity, sometimes shortage of transport and underselling and outbidding as a result. In addition, there was a risk that all the waiting on the pier was futile, and that valuable time that could have been spent on farm chores had been lost.

In 1922, the installation of a phone for trunk calls with the local merchant made a huge improvement in the flow of information. This made it possible to plan the equipages needed for transport, but it did not eliminate contenders from other communities. The protracted and controversial law of the peasantry's obligation to provide public transport was abolished in 1924. This created an opportunity for collective action and 23 farmers in Oldedalen established a formal shuttle business, called Oldedalen Skysslag (OS) in 1923. This was legitimized by the departing institutional framework, and was recommended by the authorities (Rogan 1986). The transportation obligations covered a confined area in the valley (the 5-kilometre distance from the south end of Olden Lake to the farm in Briksdal) and excluded stakeholders with no land.

Building the Kleiva road as a collective action

Oldedalen is located in Nordfjord, which, by the 1880s, was already frequently visited by cruise ships, including those with members of European royal families. As a result of the celebrity visits, Nordfjord became an attractive destination (Jacobsen 1989), although this caused transaction costs, due to an increased and unregulated competition between Briksdalsbreen and other accessible valleys and glacial areas around the fjord.

In Briksdal, there was only one permanently settled farm. The infields and outfields of the farm were located on the moraine plateau in front of the glacier, and a narrow and steep path, carved out by the farm animals and agricultural activities, was the only access to the attractive area for tourists, as well as for the farmer. Due to the competition in this region, stakeholders in Olden and the farmers in OS agreed upon building a new and improved road suitable for walking or riding. The purpose was to make the glacier more accessible, enhance the competitive advantage of the area and increase their revenues. The farmer in Briksdal agreed to this positive intervention of his property, and the OS got the right to work up and maintain the road in the valley.

In 1926, the building of the new road was made possible by collective contributions of local farmers, through physical labour and, rarely, by cash. The Kleiva road was completed in 1928. This collective effort was not done without compensation; in return for the work, the OS awarded their members the right to transport tourists by horse on the road to Briksdal farm. Depending on the extent of physical labour or amount of money, the farmers were compensated by one, two or three rights, but most of them achieved one right. This collective institutional innovation done by the OS took care of the local interests and, for the most part, excluded individuals from neighbouring areas, as they were not allowed to participate.

The post-war period, and need for institutional change

Norway was occupied in 1940, tourism declined and the war put a temporary end to the shuttle business. After the First World War, tourism slowly increased, but for years the flow of tourists was irregular and the enthusiasm for shuttle work was low. The local merchant managed to keep some of the members in the business through the 1950s and 1960s, but grievances increased, especially because the maintenance of the Kleiva road was costly, time-consuming and challenging. In the 1950s, the OS tried to persuade the municipality to take public responsibility for the upkeep of the road, but they considered it private property and refused the request. In addition, in the 1960s, the local youth started to move to the cities for industrial employment or to go to college. Many farmers were anxious about shortage of labour on the farms, and also about the consequences for the local shuttle business.

For the local society in Oldedalen an awareness of new kinds of transaction costs appeared.

- The need of outsiders to participate in the shuttle business, due to lack of labour.
- The risk of rights to the shuttle business to be owned by individuals living outside the valley, due to sale or closure of the farm
- The risk of some locals to monopolize the business if they purchased the neighbouring farm, including the farmer's rights.
- The risk of selling the rights, isolated from the farm.

To handle these challenges, the farmers in OS collectively adjusted the regulations of their organization to the new societal context.

- Individuals from farms in neighbouring communities were allowed to make a profit from the shuttle business, but without membership or rights in the organization.
- The use of the shuttle right only applied to those who lived permanently in the valley.
- By transfer of property between farmers in Oldedalen, the heir or the buyer was allowed to keep the rights of only one of the farms, with remaining rights returned to the OS.
- Rights could not be sold out, or detached from the farm that they were part of.

In the 1990s, the number of active members increased, as younger generations of farmers decided to resume and utilize their rights of transport to increase their income. This made OS update the regulations in 1996, and formalize long-established practices.

The change in infrastructure

A new challenge that occurred was the change in infrastructure. In the late 1950s, the community was connected to the regional transport infrastructure by a 30-kilometre road that ran from the center of Olden to the end of the lake in Oldedalen. This lowered the costs of transport in tourism and daily activities, and the use of buses and private cars increased, both in public and private travel. For the shuttle business, this caused severe competition and therefore created a new kind of transaction costs.

As the transport of locals and tourists to Oldedalen was made more efficient by buses and cars, the demands for shuttle across Olden Lake gradually decreased and finally ended in 1982. This also ended the need for horse shuttle to Briksdal. In Briksdal, however, the shuttle demands on the 2-kilometre steep and curvy road from the farm to the path to the glacier had gradually increased from the 1960s. As a result, the main activity in OS therefore moved to shuttle business on the Kleiva road in Briksdal.

The accidents

In the 1980s and 1990s, tourism increased rapidly in the area. In the 1990s, the general advance of glaciers, and Briksdalsbreen especially, attracted both national and international tourists. The need for shuttle services escalated, and many of the young farmers in Oldedalen invested in horses and transport equipment and revived the shuttle activity. At its height of popularity, 44 equipages formed a cortège on the Kleiva road and approximately 40,000 tourists were transported for a walk to the glacier, in addition to 260,000 walking tourists. In 1999 and 2004, there were fatal and severe accidents involving unruly horses. The shuttle business suffered from negative publicity in the media, complaints from tourists and the stress on the individual coachman. This can be interpreted as a form of new transaction costs that demanded a radical transformation in order to maintain the community benefits from tourism.

From horse to "Trollcars"

The increasing demands for transport, and accidents, made some of the farmers develop ideas for an alternative transport to the glacier. A technical collaboration with a contractor of agricultural machinery resulted in a prototype of a diesel-powered transport vehicle with seating for seven passengers. This vehicle was not accepted by all OS members, as they believed the traditional horse shuttle to be an attraction in itself. They therefore feared that an alternative shuttle would put an end to the business. Disagreements and quarrelling caused transaction costs and influenced the working environment and the collaboration in the OS. In 2003, however, the OS made a collective decision to test this new vehicle. This demonstrated that several tourists preferred the new vehicle over a horse equipage, but the severe accident in 2004 put an end to all disagreements. The farmers agreed to end the traditional shuttle and, since the 2005 season, the shuttle business has been conducted by the new diesel-powered vehicles. This has been a success and still more than 300,000 tourists annually visit Briksdalsbreen, and generate 8 million NOK a year to the OS.

Right of access

The public right of access is a highly important institutional framework for the rise of walking tourism in Norway. This public right, which dates back to ancient times, allows everyone, regardless of nationality, ownership or class, the right of access and stays, experiences and activity in nature (Fedreheim and Sandberg 2008). When the first tourists came to Western Norway, their walks were based on this customary law (now formal law). But how can "this right to roam" become a basis for commercial activity with community benefits? In this case, the nature of the landscape and the topography in this area "forced" the tourists to move along certain networks of paths and roads, established in the interests of the farming and the daily activities. The path and road networks comprised a significant physical capital in the community and in turn helped to facilitate tourists' walking. Lower transaction costs were, therefore, not only associated with a greater degree of mobility, but also less conflict between visitors and locals, and more secure access to beautiful and challenging mountain and glacial areas.

The founding of the shuttle organization

The founding of the OS and its restructuring through 90 years shows that a community like Oldedalen has the capability to secure the benefits from an open-access landscape resource for the members of the community. Thus, the 100 years of walking tourism development has remained a community benefit. As the resurgence of tourism caused competition and disagreements, the community tried from the very beginning to organize this activity collectively. People tried to create order and predictability by using institutionalized rules for distribution of benefits, which gave legitimacy to this organizing model, and were part of the community's social capital. These rules entailed equal distribution of the work and also a system for compulsory attendance by members at the pier (a meeting point) on set days. This also reduced transaction costs by enabling a more predictable and efficient use of time in a legitimate way, and was important for freeing up individuals' time for farm work. Nevertheless, the lack of information still caused transaction costs. There was still uncertainty about the scale of the shuttle contracts and to which extent the horses were needed. The farmers needed to balance the activity between the shuttle and the farm work as the horse was an important daily resource on the farm.

When farmers founded the organization Oldedalen Skyss (OS) early in 1923, this was obviously commercially motivated, but the purpose was also to decrease transaction costs, envy and disagreements in the community. The first paragraph in the OS's regulations confirms that the aim of OS is for the members to stand together on agreements on common tariffs in shuttle contracts (Fabritius 2010). The founding of OS was anchored in the institutional framework of the public transport system and the transport obligation of farmers with land ownership. These laws allowed the obliged farmers with land property to form associations and allocate the work of transport within the area for transport obligation. This made it possible to exclude the unwanted neighbouring actors, as they had no registered land in the area.

The installation of the phone in 1922 transformed the flow of information to the farmers in Oldedalen. Information about arrivals and numbers of tourists gradually became available from the nearby hotels and travel companies, and increased the potential for cooperation, decreased the transaction costs of information, and strengthened the social capital in this Olden area. The phone thus became an important resource to the OS in the shuttle business.

The transformation of obligations in to rights

The farmer's right to shuttle is central to the explanation of how this shuttle business is still maintained in Oldedalen. It is related to the fact that the transport obligations were not felt to be so demanding in this community, and that transport demands therefore were a blessing rather than a burden on the farm. It was, therefore, a source of income that it was important to retain.

In the 1920s, the individual costs of the major economic crisis, both nationally and internationally, also affected Norway's West Coast agriculture. It is therefore natural to believe that the economic crisis caused transaction costs due to competition in tourism in this area. New rules for tax payments and other new expenses created a need for more cash income and economic capital and the transition to a monetary household was especially slow in isolated communities in Western Norway. Tourism, therefore, became of great importance as a source of cash income (Rogan 1986). The competition sharpened when the farmers' transport obligations were abolished in

1924. The obligations to shuttle, legitimized by ancient laws, now ceased and caused transaction costs and a risk of deterioration of the social capital, due to the lack of an institutional framework for the shuttle activity. Therefore, stakeholders in Olden and Oldedalen started negotiations and cooperation. The distribution of areas for shuttle obligations, and later shuttle rights, were institutionalized by the former laws, and became an important part of the social capital in the community. Even if it is not documented in writing, the stakeholders ensured that this distribution was maintained, and thus maintained order and predictability and reduced the transaction costs of competition, quarrelling and changing structures (North 1990).

The stakeholders' verbal agreements must be seen in the context of the institutionalized rules of agreements. Hegstad (2003) points out that as long as stakeholders agreed on a distribution of various rights of use, so they would persist, regardless of formal institutions. Credible commitments and reliability was an important form of social capital in Norwegian communities, so verbal agreements were a widespread and fully acceptable form of contract, which explains the lack of written contract documents from this period (Hegstad 2003). The idea of the road to the glacier in Briksdal, and the agreements with the Briksdal farmers, was not about property sales. It was about usufruct of land, to strengthen the tourism business, and generate more income for the OS. This did not change the structure of ownership, but it did change the structures of usufruct in the area. In modern legal terminology, the OS got what is called a special or partial usufruct to the property. How was this possible?

Robberstad (1963) calls this a 'purpose bound property right' where he claims that 'what sensible people care about in daily life, is the utilization, and not about the theoretical property rights regimes' (author's own translation). It was therefore not unusual that a piece of land had several owners, where each owner had different, but virtually equal, rights. This "split" ownership must be seen in the context of the limited resources. By optimizing the resource utilization in Briksdal, by defining different usufruct of the same land, this generated a decrease in both transaction and transformation costs and strengthened the social capital. The usufruct was often linked to the farm and therefore was an important part of its resource base.

The transformation cost of lack of public subsidy meant that the members of the OS constructed the Kleiva road as a form of voluntary work project or compulsory labour. This was an institutionalized form of cooperation, frequently used in Norwegian rural communities, and an important form of social capital. Low mechanization and limited finances made many tasks very laborious, so neighbours depended on mobilizing each other's help. The voluntary work scheme came into force for heavy tasks of short duration and more irregular character, and it was risky to exclude oneself from the community reciprocity. This could have major consequences with high transaction costs, as social exclusion or lack of inclusion in a working partnership (Klepp 2001).

At the foundation of OS in 1923, each member assigned themselves a shuttle right with one horse. As tourism and the need for transportation were growing, the members therefore collectively allowed themselves to increase and strengthen their shuttle right by participating in the work on the road. By conducting a work session for 14 days of ten hours, the individual farmer earned one right, as the vast majority of the farmers did. When the Kleiva road was completed, the total number of such rights was 52, divided between 23 members (Fabritius 2010).

Handing societal changes and protecting rights

The institutional basis for the shuttle business is a shuttle right, but a right without the tools to enforce it will not act as a right (Ostrom 2005). Therefore, the efforts to maintain the OS have been crucial to the function of the right, and an organization will always attempt to maintain and develop the rules that safeguard their own interests and existence (North 1990). At the founding of the OS, only landowners were allowed, as the ancient transport obligation only applied to those who had ownership of land along a transport route. The official law of transport, therefore, initially gave legitimacy to the exclusion of external actors. Since then, the OS has protected its rights by maintaining this provision and has not admitted members without ownership in the valley.

In the revised OS regulations (1996), the rule that states that an active membership requires permanent settlement on the farm formalized a customary practice that had developed earlier (Fabritius 2010). In this way, the OS secured both their own and the community's interests and strengthened the social capital of the community, by maintaining the local network and the local control, thus eliminating the risk of the rights and revenues to be taken out of the community. The OS also formalized another longstanding practice which prohibited individual assignment of rights, in terms of selling, renting or mortgaging. This also prevented individualization of rights and preserved these as collective rights, exclusive for the farmers in Oldedalen, and thus the basis for OS existence and activities. The regulations of 1996 also stated that the shuttle was to be conducted to Briksdalsbreen; this was a formalization of a well-established practice as the OS had gradually adapted to focusing the transport on the Kleiva road. The increasing tourism and the potential for accidents with horses in Briksdal were prohibitive transaction costs that necessitated fundamental transformation of the tourist operations. The needs for alternative transport awakened entrepreneurial and innovative capabilities in the OS members, who developed a new innovative vehicle for transport, by means of their human capital, such as agro-technological experience and knowledge and their social capital, networks and contacts. This maintained the continuity of the shuttle business, and secured further revenue.

Conclusion

This article demonstrates how one community, the Oldedalen community, was able to benefit economically from the growing tourism in Western Norway. This was done by transforming the ancient and abolished institutional framework of transport obligations into "shuttle rights", and to create a new institutional framework for the transport of tourists by founding of the OS and carving out its regulations. It shows how the members of the OS through 90 years have been safeguarding their own interests by numerous institutional changes and adaptations (Ostrom 2005). These changes are the result of the shuttle organization's efforts to preserve the shuttle rights and reduce transaction costs as the society has evolved and created new opportunities and new conditions for shuttle operations. In the larger picture, it demonstrates how a robust local community collectively can handle the transformation and transaction costs of societal development by the use of its social capital like the framework of property rights regimes, rules for mutual cooperation and resource user networks.

References

Brinton, M.C. and Nee, V. (2001) *The New Institutionalism in Sociology*, Stanford, CA: Stanford University Press.
Coase, R.H. (1960) 'The problem of social cost', *The Journal of Law & Economics*, 3: 1–43.
Coleman, J.S. (1994) *Foundations of Social Theory*, London: The Belknap Press of Harvard University Press.
Fabritius, M.K. (2010) 'Skyssvirksomheten i Briksdal. En institusjonell analyse', unpublished Masters thesis, University of Nordland.
Fedreheim, E. and Sandberg, A. (2008) 'Friluftsloven og allemannsretten i et samfunn i utvikling', *Utmark – tidsskrift for utmarksforvaltning*. Available at: www.utmark.org/utgivelser/pub/2008–1/art/Fedreheim_Sandberg_Utmark_1_2008.html.
Hegstad, E. (2003) 'Om eiendomsregistrering: med hovedvekt på norske forhold', unpublished PhD thesis, Norwegian University of Life Sciences.

Jacobsen, J.K.S. (1989) 'Før reisen fantes oppdagelsen, etter reisen finnes turismen', *I OTTAR – Populærvitenskapelig tidsskrift fra Tromsø Museum*, 175: 35–48.

Klepp, A. (2001) 'Fra nabohjelp til nasjonal floskel, om dugnadsbegrepets skiftende betydninger', *Tidsskrift for etnologi, DUGNAD*, 3/4: 113–128.

Norges forskningsråd (2005) *Sosial Kapital, Innstilling fra et utredningsu tvalg oppnevnt av Norges forskningsråd* [Social Capital. Recommendations from a committee, appointed by the Norwegian Research Council], Oslo: Norges forskningsråd.

North, D.C. (1990) *Institutions, Institutional Change and Economic Performance*, Cambridge: Cambridge University Press.

Ostrom, E. (2000) 'Social capital: a fad or a fundamental concept?', in P. Dasgupta and I. Serageldin (eds), *Social Capital: A Multifaceted Perspective*, Washington, DC: The International Bank for Reconstruction and Development/The World Bank, pp. 172–214.

Ostrom, E. (2005) *Understanding Institutional Diversity*, Princeton, NJ: Princeton University Press.

Robberstad, K. (1963) 'Kløyvd Eigedomsrett', *Lov og Rett, Norsk Juridisk Tidsskrift*, 4: 162–166.

Rogan, B. (1986) *Det gamle skysstellet: Reiseliv i Noreg frå mellomalderen til førre hundreåret*, Oslo: Det Norske Samlaget.

Silverman, D. (2000) *Doing Qualitative Research: A Practical Handbook*, Thousand Oaks, CA: Sage Publications.

34

When walking is no longer possible

Investigating crowding and coping practices in urban tourism using commented walks

Monika Popp

Introduction

Urban tourism has been booming since the 1980s (UNWTO 2012) and this growth is continuing in many cities around the world. While high tourist arrivals are welcomed by many cities, mainly for economic reasons, others, which have seen an enormous increase in tourist numbers, not least due to their 'place luck' (Fainstein and Judd 1999: 11), are often confronted with massive problems. Their carrying capacity is exceeded in many ways. This is not only true for the physical, ecological, economic and social carrying capacity, but also for the so-called perceptual carrying capacity, which relates to the 'number of people a place can welcome before the quality of the tourist experience begins to be adversely affected' (Swarbrooke 1999: 30). Overcrowding is an important aspect of this perceptual carrying capacity and has been recognized as a major problem in many cities (Hall and Page 2014). In some cities, the use density has become so high that even walking – the most-used traffic mode between destinations in dense city centres (Lew and McKercher 2006, cited in Kádár 2015) – has become difficult, causing stress and diminishing the overall quality of experience. Cities, then, not only risk diminishing tourist satisfaction, but might also attract lower numbers of tourists in the future. Furthermore, they also risk harming the quality of life for the locals at the same time.

Problems connected with high use densities are thus quite evident. Accordingly, a growing need for a more sustainable urban design that focuses on the capacity to move around on foot and 'can create a positive consumer habitat valued by locals and tourists alike' (Hall *et al.* 2015: 89) has already been recognized in many cities. Managing tourist flows differently is an important aspect in this context (Riganti and Nijkamp 2008). However, the way tourists as well as locals experience high use densities and how they cope with crowding is still a neglected topic in urban (tourism) research (Popp 2012).

Drawing on crowding research which investigates the effects of high use numbers with a strong focus on outdoor recreation, we find that the actual use numbers are however only one cause of stress related to high use numbers – and often not the decisive one! The phenomenon of crowding perception is much more complex and a number of influencing factors are discussed. The fact that 'the same number of tourists causes overcrowding and conflicts with the locals in some cities while in others there are no visible problems' (Kádár 2015) further emphasizes that use numbers are not the only cause of crowding perception in cities.

Compared to natural environments, cities typically show a greater degree of multifunctionality and are visited by a much broader range of user groups, with a much broader range of different motives, expectations and needs. This co-presence of different material and non–material circumstances results in a much more complex situation, which is also relevant to crowding perception. Urban crowding perception thus appears to be even more complex in cities compared to natural environments. If we want to manage high use densities better, to reduce crowding and to facilitate the use of strategies to avoid or reduce the feeling of stress, we need a better understanding of its effects on walking and on the experience quality in general for tourists and locals alike. In this contribution, a qualitative approach to crowding research is introduced that allows better understanding of the phenomenon.

Crowding research

The feeling of stress related to high use densities within a given area is referred to in the literature as 'crowding' (Graefe *et al.* 1984; Manning *et al.* 2000; Vaske and Shelby 2008). Tourist cities are particularly associated with crowds of tourists moving from one attraction to another and locals being present at the same time, and this causes stress for both groups. However, to date, studies have mainly focused on outdoor recreation, looking at various outdoor activities in remote and lightly-used national parks and wilderness areas in the USA. Although some studies have already transferred the concept to the frontcountry, e.g. festival settings (e.g. Lee and Graefe 2003), very few studies have been undertaken in cities (e.g. Popp 2012; Bryon and Neuts 2008).

Whereas early studies in nature-based contexts assumed that it is predominantly the number of visitors that influences the perception of crowding, it soon became clear that this was a "simplistic assumption" (Ryan and Cessford 2003), as there is only 'a consistent but weak relationship between actual use levels and crowding-related measures of experiential quality' (Mowen *et al.* 2003: 64). The phenomenon is much more complex, and mediating variables such as norms, the behaviour of other visitors, the place and the intensity of contact, the degree to which others are perceived to be like oneself, the number of people encountered compared to the number of people expected, and previous travel experience were found to affect the perception of crowding (e.g. Donnelly *et al.* 2000; Vaske and Donnelly 2002). Reducing use numbers is therefore neither the only, nor – in many cases – the best, possibility to reduce crowding, and perhaps may not even yield the expected effects (see also Manning *et al.* 2000).

In a study by Popp (2012), it was shown that the crowding concept can, in principle, be transferred to urban tourism. However, some modifications are suggested, depending on the aim of research, for two reasons. To begin with, urban tourists are not looking for solitude in the first place. In fact, the exact opposite can be also found. Referring to the concept of tourist gazes, the collective gaze needs the crowd: 'Other people also viewing the site are necessary to give liveliness or a sense of carnival or movement. Large numbers of people that are present can indicate that this is the place to be' (Urry 2002: 78). This is referred to in the crowding literature as "good" or "positive" crowding (e.g. Wickham and Kerstetter 2000; Mowen *et al.* 2003; Bryon and Neuts 2008; Popp 2012). We shall not discuss this further here, however, as the focus of this chapter is on negative aspects of crowding. Second, cities are more complex systems than national parks, for example, with regard to the environment as well as the composition of users.

Coping with crowding

Tourists and locals alike try to avoid (negative) crowding. A range of coping strategies is known, especially from outdoor recreation, that can be employed to obtain overall satisfaction or multiple satisfactions despite the perception of crowding (e.g. Johnson and Dawson 2004; Hall and Shelby 2000). The crowding literature basically differentiates between behavioural (spatial and temporal) and cognitive mechanisms (product shift and rationalization) (e.g. Johnson and Dawson 2004). Spatial strategies are employed when visitors shift their use to other locations within (intraspatially) or outside (interspatially) the area visited, and temporal strategies when visitors change the time of their visit. In contrast, cognitive mechanisms are employed by tourists when they are directly in the crowding situation. Such product shift, sometimes referred to as displacement (Becker 1981; Hall and Page 2014), suggests that visitors who experience higher use levels than preferred or expected may alter their definition of the experience they were seeking (Arnberger and Brandenburg 2007), or shift elsewhere. Rationalization is also used to reduce stress, in that they report higher levels of satisfaction than they actually felt, because of the high investment involved in coming to a destination. As learning about coping strategies in more complex situations, such as cities, can provide a good starting point for action, the approach presented here also includes coping strategies.

Commented walks as an alternative way to investigate crowding

Traditional crowding research has mainly used questionnaire surveys to learn about crowding perception and coping mechanisms (Vaske and Shelby 2008). As a consequence, findings refer to various activities and places without further specification. For example, crowding research shows that motor-boaters contribute more to crowding than canoers, or that the presence of other people disturbs many people more along the route than at picnic areas. Due to the generally lower use numbers, this focus is adequate in many cases. However, cities experience much higher use densities and the co-presence of a broad range of functions and different user types within a small area of the city. Therefore, a closer look – i.e. a more detailed picture of the phenomenon on the micro-scale – is needed to understand how people act, influence each other and are influenced by the setting at the same time.

To achieve this "closer look" at crowding, the commented walks proposed in this chapter build on the one hand on the ambience studies of the Francophone urban and architectural studies (Thibaud 2001), and, on the other, on principles of practice-oriented approaches (Reckwitz 2006). The Francophone atmosphere and ambience research focuses on "how places feel". The so-called atmospheres may change continuously and often within short distances when people walk or stroll through the city (Kazig 2007), which again indicates a need for research at the micro-level, as well as for research in motion, in order to enable a grasp of those changes and the circumstances responsible for them. With its basis in architecture, this strand of research puts a special focus on the interplay of the individual and the (architectural) setting, which is understood as a sensory environment. Thibaud and colleagues developed the *parcours commentés* (Thibaud 2001, 2013) as a thinking-aloud method to capture the sensitivities of people moving through certain places, including all the senses. A special feature of these interviews is the "return-to-the-field observations", which are integrated in the approach presented here too, and which enable us to elicit even those influencing factors that are less obvious at first sight (see also next section).

In the last decade, a broad strand of practice-oriented approaches has also evolved, which directed the focus of research towards practices and their performance (Reckwitz 2006). Various aspects of practices are highlighted, drawing on different theoretical backgrounds, depending on the specific research interest (Kazig and Popp 2011). In the context of crowding, the approaches that are of special interest are those which: (i) focus on the circumstances under which crowding and related practices evolve; and (ii) stress the plurality of practices. Related mobile methods are based on ethnological approaches such as "hanging out". Kusenbach (2003), for example, uses "go-alongs" to elicit the meanings of everyday practices by asking questions, listening and observing. Furthermore, Kazig and Popp (2011) used mobile interviews in unknown environments to elicit perceptions and practices in wayfinding processes. In general, mobile interviewing techniques have increased in importance with the mobility turn that has evolved in the social sciences in the last decade (Sheller and Urry 2006; Büscher and Urry 2009). Surprisingly, spatial location is often dealt with rather crudely in many studies (Evans and Jones 2011). In combining the approach with the Francophone ambience research which stresses the influence of the setting, we try to overcome this deficiency.

The focus on practices and performances in the context of urban tourism also takes account of the fact that the distinction between locals and tourists seems to be increasingly blurred (Bock 2015), as both often pursue the same activities. A tourist, for example, going to the bus station as he did on previous mornings, may be considered and consider himself at this moment less a tourist than a local sitting in a café at the place to be. Rather than looking at tourists and locals as two clearly distinct groups, though, a practice-oriented perspective allows us to take the continuum between touristic and everyday practices into account.

Doing the commented walk

Both research strands presented above combine interviewing with elements of observation in different ways. The commented walks introduced in the following section can also be considered a hybrid form of mobile interview and observation. Observation is thus twofold: participant observation during the interview and 'returning to the field' observations. The whole interviewing process can thus be divided into several steps (Figure 34.1) (Thibaud 2013).

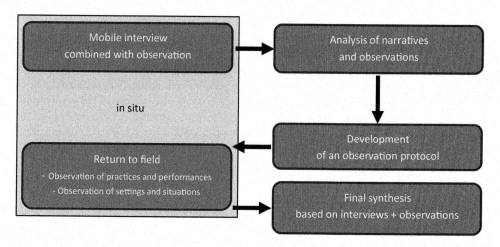

Figure 34.1 Steps in the commented walk

In fact, the individual steps which are presented in a clearly separated way for analytical reasons here are employed in a more flexible way. Doing research using commented walks is rather an iterative process.

Mobile interview combined with observation

As for all types of mobile interviews, the commented walks take place on the move, i.e. the interviewer and the interviewee walk through the city together and interviewees comment on the situation, i.e. the setting, the presence of other people and their behaviour, the weather, sound, etc., at the very moment of being there. This way, it is possible to capture both crowding perceptions and coping strategies in detail and in direct connection with the situation when and where they occur, in the sense of a radical contextualization. It is furthermore possible to include all senses in the narrative.

The commented walks' main principle is that interviews are not so much organized by questions as by settings and situations. This means that the interviewer intervenes as little as possible and primarily keeps the participant talking by being a friendly listener (see also Thibaud 2013). Whenever the interviewee stops talking, the interviewer may ask questions like: 'How do you feel here?', 'What is walking like here?' or, more specifically, 'What do you think about people in this place?' Furthermore, the interviewees are asked for possible ways of avoiding crowding whenever deficiencies are reported. If the interviewee has been to certain places before, he is also asked to talk about past experiences and ways of coping he has used before. The narrative is recorded by clip-on microphones and transcribed verbatim.

The interviews take place along a predefined route. The route is set following a preliminary site observation and should contain different situations. After explaining the mode of the interview, the interviewer and the interviewee walk along the route together. Even though the basic route is fixed, the interviewees can and should decide themselves where exactly they walk along the route, how fast they walk, and whether they stop somewhere. The precise route taken by the interviewee is plotted on a map, allowing even small variations in performance to be captured.

During the interview, the interviewer also observes the interviewees' performance of walking as well as the performance of practices employed to avoid crowding. This reveals further details of crowding and coping, and deepens overall understanding. Finally, the interviewer also takes photos of situations that participants are commenting on, or where they show specific behaviour. This allows a radically contextualized analysis of crowding and coping strategies afterwards, which can be considered a main advantage of this method.

While the first part of the interview focuses on the in-situ perception, the walking performance and possible strategies to avoid crowding, the perspective is changed in the second part of the interview immediately after the walk. Its main aim is a reflexive analysis of the whole walk. At first, participants are asked to divide the route into sections which they perceive as units, to give reasons for this division and to describe a section's specific characteristics in comparison to other sections. Situations that are especially distinctive or problematic should be highlighted. This way, it is possible to comprehend what settings and situations are outstanding and have a lasting effect on the tourists' or locals' experience of them. A map can be used to facilitate this task (Kazig and Popp 2011).

At the end of the interview, the interviewees are asked for some personal information (such as age, sex, where they live, travel experience, and familiarity with the places visited during the interview), using a standardized questionnaire with closed and open-ended questions. This information helps in the interpretation process, as it allows framing of the content of the conversation and the practices observed.

Typical interviews take 20–30 minutes, or even longer. Sometimes tourists in particular are not happy to spend so much time being interviewed. In this case, it is also possible to divide the route into several parts and to do the interviews for individual parts. However, analysis and interpretation are more comprehensive when each participant comments on different settings and situations.

Analysis of narratives and observations

The analysis of the commented walks takes place in two steps. First, paragraphs related to crowding and coping are selected, and codes describing the type of crowding perception or coping strategy are attributed to the relevant paragraphs. This way, an overview of the relevant aspects is achieved. Second, the relevant paragraphs are analysed in more detail, looking at the wording, and the emphasis of the narrative, and are compared between interviewees. The comments of different interviewees, as well as observed practices and performances, are superimposed, and shared perceptions and practices can be identified (Kazig 2007). A special focus is directed at the interplay of settings and situations and the perceptions and performances of the interviewees. This enables the spatial and situational contextualization of perceptions and strategies. Finally, a preliminary typology of crowding perception and influencing factors, as well as a typology of coping strategies, is developed. Programs like MAXQDA are very helpful in this process.

Development of an observation protocol and return to the field

In this step, the researcher returns to the field in order to further specify the elements of the settings and situations that cause crowding, and that enable strategies to reduce crowding. The aim of this step is to recontextualize the perceptions and strategies and thus to learn more about the elements influencing them. Places of special interest in this step are those where crowding is perceived by (nearly) all interviewees, or where perceptions vary from heavily crowded to not crowded (at all). Returning to the field and comparing those situations enables reconstruction of further elements that were not mentioned or not systematically commented on by the interviewees. By doing this, even elements which do not have an obvious effect, but rather influence perception unconsciously, can be elicited.

For this step, an observation protocol is developed based on the preliminary crowding and coping typology. Aspects included in this protocol may encompass certain elements of the material setting, sound levels and type of sound, light conditions, temperature, number of people at the setting and their behaviour. When returning to the field, it is important to choose a point in time with circumstances that are equivalent to the relevant commented walk(s) in terms of the day of the week, time of day and weather. Findings are noted in the protocol and photographs are taken to illustrate them.

Final synthesis

In this step, the preliminary typology is refined and the "final" typology of situations which foster crowding, as well as a typology of strategies to cope with crowding, is set up. The researcher therefore rereads the texts as well as the observation protocols and photos once more, and compares the texts with the return-to-the-field protocols. Whenever certain findings do not fit the picture so far, the researcher will have to go back to the field again and try to clarify the discrepancies.

Crowding and coping strategies in urban tourism – the example of Florence, Italy

To illustrate the potential of the commented walks, some examples from a study undertaken with tourists in Florence, Italy, will be presented. Florence is one of the main destinations in culturally oriented urban tourism in Europe. The city has a long history of tourism, dating back to the Grand Tour undertaken by British aristocrats from the late sixteenth century (Freytag and Popp 2009). Due to its cultural richness, the entire old town was included in the UNESCO list of World Heritage sites in 1982. The city, without doubt, experiences very high tourist densities in the tourist area, which causes diverse problems for tourists and locals alike, including the perception of crowding. In our study, all interviewees reported feeling crowded, especially along the beaten track, albeit in different ways and intensities. Furthermore, they employed different strategies and were to different degrees successful in reducing crowding.

Using commented walks, a deeper understanding of the emergence of crowding and its context was achieved for Florence. As is known from crowding research, use numbers are not the only reason for the perception of crowding, and this is the case for Florence too. Factors underpinning the feeling can be grouped into material and non-material factors of the situation as well as personal factors. Concerning the specific situation, these factors include the street architecture (e.g. length, symmetry, width, surface), the cleanliness of the streets and the kind of rubbish, practices and performances of the other people (e.g. taking photos and the way of taking photos), the kind of 'decoration' (e.g. the promotion of special tourist menus in front of restaurants *vs* washing on the line), whether other tourists appear alone or in groups, the soundscape, including languages spoken by the people around them, texts in languages other than Italian as a sign of also being 'not authentic', light conditions and temperature, to name a few. Often, these elements show people the dominance of tourism in the city centre, aside from the fact of tourists being there. Personal factors include the length of stay (the longer they stay, the worse crowding is perceived in general), use densities in their home town, and thus whether they are used to high use levels or not, the overall travel experience, the motives for the visit and the expectations and norms of the interviewee, to name the most prominent ones. All in all, the emergence and way of perceiving crowding is a complex phenomenon influenced by a combination of the factors mentioned above.

Looking at the strategies employed to avoid crowding, micro-spatial practices which are not at the centre of traditional crowding research proved to be very helpful for tourists in Florence, next to strategies from the other categories. By employing those micro-spatial strategies, interviewees separate themselves from the crowd spatially, even if they are in the midst of it, by creating a private sphere around themselves.

A good example of a micro-scale strategy is looking at an attraction or simply on street life from a spatially separated position, e.g. sitting in a café, on steps, a low wall or on the edge of a flower pot, especially when pleasant walking is no longer possible. This helps people to separate themselves from the bustling people around, not joining their mode of locomotion, while passers-by can proceed easily. A possible way to defuse situations where walking is no longer possible is thus to separate those who wish not only to pass through, by providing seating opportunities – preferably next to the sight or behind the flow of passers-by in an elevated position. Platforms that allow watching from above are often especially welcomed, as they provide even more distance from the crowd and an additional perspective on the sight.

Conclusion

Crowding is a complex phenomenon that is closely linked to specific situations and personal preconditions. As is known from traditional crowding research, use densities are only one factor causing stress, and often not the decisive one. While crowding is one of the most frequently studied subjects in outdoor recreation, research in urban contexts is still in its infancy. Commented walks as a qualitative and highly contextualized form of interviews have proved to be a useful method of gaining detailed insights into tourists' and locals' perceptions of crowding and the strategies they employ.

The ongoing boom in urban tourism and the growing number of initiatives against mass tourism encourage further research. Studies including different city user groups, as well as different cities, could enrich the typology developed for Florence and allow the construction of a more general typology. This would be applicable to other cities as well, and could provide a good starting point for developing suitable action policies, which facilitate not only pleasant walking, but take a broader look at facilitating an overall enjoyable experience that city users are looking for. While it has to be borne in mind that all these strategies are 'a move away from an unacceptable situation, rather than a move toward an optimal one' (Becker 1981: 262), both locals and tourists would however benefit from such systematic crowding management.

References

Arnberger, A. and Brandenburg, C. (2007) 'Past on-site experience, crowding perceptions, and use displacement of visitor groups to a peri-urban national park', *Environmental Management*, 40(1): 34–45.

Becker, R.H. (1981) 'Displacement of recreational users between the Lower St. Croix and Upper Mississippi Rivers', *Journal of Environmental Management*, 13(3): 259–267.

Bock, K. (2015) 'The changing nature of city tourism and its possible implications for the future of cities', *European Journal of Futures Research*. Available at: http://link.springer.com/article/10.1007/s40309–015–0078–5 (accessed 10 June 2016).

Bryon, J. and Neuts, B. (2008) *Crowding and the Tourist Experience in an Urban Environment: A Structural Equation Modeling Approach*. Available at: www.steunpunttoerisme.be/main/files/nieuwsbrief/oktober_2008/paperNVVS_bart_neuts.pdf (accessed 7 June 2016).

Büscher, M. and Urry, J. (2009) 'Mobile methods and the empirical', *European Journal of Social Theory*, 12(1): 99–116.

Donnelly, M.P., Vaske, J.J., Whittaker, D. and Shelby, B. (2000) 'Toward an understanding of norm prevalence: a comparative analysis of 20 years of research', *Environmental Management*, 25(4): 403–414.

Evans J. and Jones P. (2011) 'The walking interview: methodology, mobility and place', *Applied Geography*, 31(2): 849–858.

Fainstein, S.S. and Judd, D.R. (1999) 'Global forces, local strategies, and urban tourism', in D.R. Judd and S.S. Fainstein (eds), *The Tourist City*, New Haven, CT: Yale University Press, pp. 1–20.

Freytag, T. and Popp, M. (2009) 'Der Erfolg des europäischen Städtetourismus. Grundlagen, Entwicklungen, Wirkungen', *Geographische Rundschau*, 61(2): 4–11.

Graefe, A.R., Vaske, J.J. and Kuss, F.R. (1984) 'Social carrying capacity: an integration and synthesis of twenty years of research', *Leisure Sciences*, 6(4): 395–431.

Hall, C.M. and Page, S.J. (2014) *Geography of Tourism and Recreation: Environment, Place and Space*, 4th edn, London: Routledge.

Hall, C.M., Finsterwalder, J. and Ram, Y. (2015) 'Shaping, experiencing, and escaping the tourist city', *LAPlus*, 2: 84–90.

Hall, T. and Shelby, B. (2000) 'Temporal and spatial displacement: evidence from a high-use reservoir and alternate sites', *Journal of Leisure Research*, 32(4): 435–456.

Johnson, A.K. and Dawson, C.P. (2004) 'An exploratory study of the complexities of coping behavior in Adirondack wilderness', *Leisure Sciences*, 26(3): 281–293.

Kádár, B. (2015) 'A network-based spatial planning method for sustainable urban tourism', paper presented at Metropolitan Tourism Experience Development Workshop in Budapest. Available at: www.researchgate.net/publication/290378427_A_network-based_spatial_planning_method_for_sustainable_urban_tourism (accessed 14 March 2016).

Kazig, R. (2007) 'Atmosphären – Konzept für einen nicht repräsentationellen Zugang zum Raum', in C. Berndt and R. Pütz (eds), *Kulturelle Geographien. Zur Beschäftigung mit Raum und Ort nach dem Cultural Turn*, Bielefeld, Germany: Transcript, pp. 167–187.

Kazig, R. and Popp, M. (2011) 'Unterwegs in fremden Umgebungen. Ein praxeologischer Zugang zum Wayfinding von Fußgängern', Raumforschung und Raumordnung, 69(1): 3–15.

Kusenbach, M. (2003) 'Street phenomenology: the go-along as ethnographic research tool', *Ethnography*, 4(3): 455–485.

Lee, H. and Graefe, A.R. (2003) 'Crowding at an arts festival: extending crowding models to the front-country', *Tourism Management*, 24(1): 1–11.

Lew, A.A. and McKercher, B. (2006) 'Modeling tourist movements: a local destination analysis', *Annals of Tourism Research*, 33(2): 403–423.

Manning, R., Valliere, W., Minteer, B., Wang, B. and Jacobi, C. (2000) 'Crowding in parks and outdoor recreation: a theoretical, empirical, and managerial analysis', *Journal of Park and Recreation Administration*, 18(4): 57–72.

Mowen, A.J., Vogelsong, H.G. and Graefe, A.R. (2003) 'Perceived crowding and its relationship to crowd management practices at park and recreation events', *Event Management*, 8(2): 63–72.

Popp, M. (2012) 'Positive and negative urban tourist crowding: Florence, Italy', *Tourism Geographies*, 14(1): 50–72.

Reckwitz, A. (2006) *Die Transformation der Kulturtheorien. Zur Entwicklung eines Theorieprogramms,* Weilerswist, Germany: Velbrück Wissenschaft.

Riganti, P. and Nijkamp, P. (2008) 'Congestion in popular tourist areas: a multi-attribute experimental choice analysis of willingness-to-wait in Amsterdam', *Tourism Economics*, 14(1): 25–44.

Ryan, C. and Cessford, G. (2003) 'Developing a visitor satisfaction monitoring methodology: quality gaps, crowding and some results', *Current Issues in Tourism*, 6(6): 457–507.

Sheller, M. and Urry, J. (2006) 'The new mobilities paradigm', *Environment and Planning A*, 38(2): 207–226.

Swarbrooke, J. (1999) *Sustainable Tourism Management*, Wallingford, Oxon: CABI Publishing.

Thibaud, J.-P. (2001) 'La méthode des parcours commentés', in M. Grosjean and J.-P. Thibaud (eds), *L'espace urbain en méthodes,* Marseille: Parenthèses.

Thibaud, J.-P. (2013) 'Commented city walks', *Journal of Mobile Culture*, 7(1): 2–32.

UNWTO (ed) (2012) Global Report on City Tourism: Cities 2012 Project. United Nations World Tourism Organization. Available at: http://cf.cdn.unwto.org/sites/all/files/pdf/am6_city_platma.pdf (accessed 23 February 2016).

Urry, J. (2002). *The Tourist Gaze*, 2nd edn, Thousand Oaks, CA: Sage Publications.

Vaske, J.J. and Donnelly, M.P. (2002) 'Generalizing the encounter-norm-crowding relationship', *Leisure Sciences*, 24(3–4): 255–269.

Vaske, J.J. and Shelby, L.B. (2008) 'Crowding as a descriptive indicator and an evaluative standard: results from 30 years of research', *Leisure Sciences*, 30(2): 111–126.

Wickham, T. and Kerstetter, D. (2000) 'The relationship between place attachment and crowding in an event setting', *Event Management*, 6(3): 167–174.

35

Assessing the walkability of urban public space with GIS technology

The hidden dimensions of security and community heritage

Peter Schofield, Adele Doran and Ray Nolan

Introduction

This chapter assesses the methodological design, process and results from an Engineering and Physical Sciences Research Council (EPSRC)-funded public health walk consultation in 2006, and evaluates the project's outcomes in 2016 after ten years in operation. The consultation used an innovative application of Geographic Information Systems for Participation (GIS-P) to capture the views of local residents in the planning of the health walk in the Lower Kersal area of the city of Salford in Greater Manchester, one of the most socially and economically deprived areas in the UK. GIS-P was employed to engage stakeholders, including 'hard-to-reach' groups, within established decision-making procedures relating to the planning and implementation of the first of three health walks in an effort to address the area's significant lifestyle-related health problems. More specifically, GIS-P was employed to assess, from the local user perspective, the walkability of the proposed health walk route in terms of its suitability and attractiveness, including attributes relating to accessibility, technical design, walking facilities and perceptions of safety from crime (see Moudon and Lee 2003; Brown *et al.* 2007).

The project was driven by the UK policy agenda to create a safe, inclusive and attractive public realm and improve public health. The public realm was defined as the spaces to which people have unrestricted access (Walpole and Greenhalgh 1996). It is only recently in the UK that urban design has been acknowledged as an important area of practice by the existing built environment professions, and even more recently that it has been recognised by central and local government (Carmona *et al.* 2010). Local authorities throughout the UK have accepted the need to improve the public realm to bring greater community pride and cohesion, and encourage more active lifestyles, through both recreational walking and walking for transport. While walkability has become one of the important concepts for sustainable urban development (Yoshi 2016; Hall *et al.* 2017; see also Chapter 30, this volume), the feasibility of this vision has been questioned because of the fragmented nature of urban society and the assumption of public awareness that these are shared spaces. In reality, they are far from being negotiated; instead, they tend either to be territorialised by particular groups or spaces of transit, and with minimal contact between strangers (Sandercock 2003).

In the UK, research has highlighted significant spatial inequalities in access to health-promoting physical environments, urban parks and, in turn, poor health induced by neighbourhood deprivation (CABE 2010; Shortt et al. 2014). On average, people in the city of Salford have poorer health than in the rest of the country and mortality rates are twice the national average. Not surprisingly, social inequality and lifestyle-related health problems have been key issues for Salford City Council (2005). A further challenge is the engagement of residents in the design and delivery of strategies to improve the urban environment, particularly those who are typically underrepresented in public participation (IPPR 2004; Bickerstaff and Walker 2005). In principle, there has been a strong commitment to increasing public participation in the process, but in practice it has declined, not least because of the growing distrust of authority. As such, the engagement of community groups in upgrading their local environment has been far from adequate. Therefore, the key challenge that the study discussed here attempted to address was how to widen the engagement of diverse "publics" in the design and delivery of improvements to the public realm, in order to significantly enhance people's quality of life. More specifically, given the unhealthy lifestyles and lack of trust of authority in this particular community, and consequently, their lack of interest and unlikely participation in "traditional" forms of consultation, the project was directly concerned with facilitating community participation at "street level" through action research.

The importance of walkable public realm environments

Accumulated epidemiological evidence has highlighted that active travel in the forms of walking and cycling can minimise or offset health costs of sedentary lifestyles via increments in individual energy expenditures (Flint et al. 2014). Increasing emphasis is therefore being placed on walking in both urban design as a sustainable form of mobility and in public health as a means of achieving recommended physical activity and better health outcomes (Tribby et al. 2016). Government policy and planning initiatives define the way cities, towns and neighbourhoods are developed and configured, and are also inextricably linked to all aspects of human health and health-related behaviours (Hooper et al. 2015); more specifically, they can support or undermine residents' ability to be safely and conveniently physically active (Giles-Corti et al. 2014; Knuiman et al. 2014; Witten et al. 2008).

Constituent components of the built environment have been found to promote physical activity behaviour, including walking (Nagel et al. 2008; Saelens et al. 2003). Among these features, urban green spaces constitute one of the most important elements in influencing walking, physical activity, health and mortality. Sarkar et al.'s (2015) study of the direct associations between urban greenery and individual-level active travel behaviour found that urban design and landscaping is associated with both the propensity to walk and the distance walked. However, they also note that it is not greenness alone which induces walking; these environments also need to be suitably configured. While street greening helps to create walkability by connecting individuals to places and nurturing social capital and a sense of belonging, Sarkar et al. (2015) argue that streets also need to be connected by a topological and geometric pattern that raises the chance of through movement from other streets within walking distance.

There is growing evidence to show that higher-density, mixed-use, pedestrian-friendly neighbourhoods encourage walking, which in turn reduces social isolation, traffic congestion and the risk of chronic disease (Giles-Corti et al. 2010; Rissel 2009; Woodcock et al. 2009). However, despite the widespread recognition of these benefits, Giles-Corti et al. (2014) argue that there remains a gap between the rhetoric of the need for walkability and the creation of walkable neighbourhoods. In response, they developed a 'Walkability Index Tool' based on three environmental characteristics: street connectivity, residential density and land use mix. Moreover, a later study by Hooper *et al.* (2015) highlighted the importance of prioritising specific design features that support and encourage walking in mixed-use, pedestrian-oriented, compact developments, namely open spaces and connected footpaths. They found that 'community design', in terms of walkable community hubs that provide for residents' daily needs and a variety of activities, was the most important factor in supporting walking for transport. Koohsari *et al.* (2013a, 2013b) also found that street network design underpins local walking; people living in areas with highly integrated streets are more likely to walk more often for transport because these areas tend to have more local destinations, such as shops and services. This supports the results of research by Leslie *et al.* (2007), which found that increasing the number of direct routes and network intersection can increase walking for transport. Moreover, from a health perspective, Oliver *et al.*'s (2015) research on the relationship between obesity, various built environment features and physical activity behaviours found that street connectivity and neighbourhood destination accessibility were important predictors of body size, together with streetscape and dwelling density as influencing factors.

In contrast to the aforementioned studies, which have focused on cities in developed countries such as Australia, Mateo-Babiano (2016) examined pedestrian needs in the walking environment of Manila in the Philippines. The study found that, while traditional pedestrian facilities, e.g. footpaths, are designed around the need to move, the most important criterion for the pedestrians in this survey was their safety, rather than mobility. Pedestrians, particularly women, are deterred from walking due to feeling unsafe in their residential neighbourhood, particularly in relation to the perceived danger from motorists and strangers. For the residents of Manila, the need for mobility is less critical than protection, ease and equitable access. Yoshi's (2016) research on the walkability of Kyoto's historic alleyways also found resident safety, in this case relating to traffic, to be an important issue, together with health and social cohesion through increased connectivity. Improvements in safety and connectivity were seen to be critical for both increasing residents' quality of life and building a better community; however, they had been neglected during the modernisation of the area's built environment. Li *et al.* (2005) and Sarkar *et al.* (2015) also found that crime and road safety were inversely associated with distance walked. This reflects the psychosocial stress associated with crime, neighbourhood decay and close proximity to road traffic (Koohsari *et al.* 2013a, 2013b).

Action research to widen engagement in public realm improvements

Research on urban walkability has reported that the decision to walk depends largely on three key groups of variables: (i) pedestrian circumstances and characteristics, including their social, cultural and demographic attributes; (ii) individual trip preference and characteristics; and (iii) attributes of the external walking environment (Mateo-Babiano 2016). While socioeconomic characteristics and individual preferences are significant influences, the built environment characteristics often represent a more tractable intervention than changing attitudes (Cerin *et al.* 2007). InSITU (Inclusive and Sustainable Infrastructure for Tourism and Urban regeneration) was developed in response to these challenges. The overarching aim was to provide tools and resources for practitioners and organisations with a strong commitment to widen engagement in the design and delivery of improvements to the public realm. The study was undertaken over a 15-month period by a cross-disciplinary research team based at the Universities of Salford and York, and London Metropolitan University. The Kersal public health walk was one of four case studies undertaken during the period of the study and the researchers worked closely with partners, including Salford City Council, the Groundwork Trust and Sustrans to test and refine the GIS-P methodology, in order to widen user participation and improve public engagement processes. It was envisaged that this could enable 'lay' participants with in-depth local knowledge, particularly members of 'hard-to-reach' groups, to voice their opinions and influence decision making on an equal footing, with each other, and with practitioners who could deliver significant improvements to the public realm. As such, this could enable participants, regardless of their level of expertise, to contribute to the design of the health walk by framing issues and problems in their own terms, and thereby participate in the reshaping of their own local environment (Carmona *et al.* 2010).

GIS-P facilitates this approach to engagement and to gathering local knowledge i.e. non-expert, experience-based data, alongside other forms of knowledge and information about environment and development issues. This allows for comparisons between different spatial datasets to be investigated. As a result, similarities and differences between the expert evidence-based data and the local experience-based data, and perceptions of the same issue in the same place at the same time can be examined. It also feeds this data into the policy and planning process in a more direct way than is often possible with other public participation and engagement tools (Cinderby and Forrester 2005). The attractiveness of GIS maps draws people to engage in a two-way dialogue, and potential confrontation is reduced because participants address points to the map rather than to each other; the map is therefore used as a debating tool to illustrate and support points they make. Data can be recorded spatially on the map or as words to further illustrate an issue relating to a particular point or area; perceptions, feelings and attitudes can therefore be recorded in depth and may also be quantified to facilitate subsequent discussion with other stakeholders (Forrester and Cinderby 2005; Cinderby *et al.* 2007).

Given the features and benefits of GIS-P, the InSITU team considered the tool to be suitable for facilitating a meaningful dialogue with individuals and groups in the local community about the design of the public health walk. The design, implementation and evaluation of the health walk were overseen by a steering group of relevant stakeholders, including experienced practitioners in urban design, architecture and planning. For example, Groundwork, a national body seeking to build sustainable communities and healthier neighbourhoods in areas of need, through community involvement, practical action and partnership with local people (Groundwork 2006), which was active in Lower Kersal at the time of the InSITU project. The sustainable transport group, Sustrans, was also actively involved in the steering process. Sustrans was already engaged at the local level in the area to promote walking and cycling and reduce the negative aspects of motorised transport; their work included infrastructure development, such as creating routes or making improvements to streets, and soft measures such as providing information about how and where to walk and cycle and supporting people to become more physically active (Sustrans 2006).

Using GIS-P to evaluate the walkability of the Lower Kersal public health walk

The team's objectives were, first, to test the tool's application in engaging members of the community; second, to evaluate its utility in securing an accessible, well-designed, safe and attractive route for the walk; and third, to ensure that the public realm improvements would benefit local people and other visitors to the area. The stages of the project were as follows.

1   Steering Group discussion to agree the procedure for the methodology.
2   Public engagement in participatory mapping exercise.
3   Digitisation of data and production of maps.

4   Analysis of participatory and complimentary spatial data.
5   Verification of results with participants.
6   Utilisation of findings in the design process.
7   Evaluation of the GIS-P procedure and outputs.

In order to facilitate access to residents of the Lower Kersal area, where local communities are extremely discrete and self-contained, despite their close proximity, the team identified six geographically dispersed locations in which to interact with the public. At each site, a large-scale map of the area, including the proposed route of the health walk, was set out on six 18" x 18" polystyrene boards, covered in acetate and laid on a table. Key landmarks and prominent features were represented and photographs of various map locations were also displayed to facilitate participant orientation and to increase the attractiveness of the display to encourage on-street interaction (Figure 35.1). At each location, residents, many of whom could not read or write, were asked for their opinions about the health walk, the route, issues relating to particular points and/or sections, their current and past use of the space, its personal and historical associations, concerns about using it and suggestions for improving the route.

Comments were placed on flags and stickers to accurately pinpoint sites and highlight opinions and issues associated with particular places on the map or marked directly on the acetate to denote linear features or the locations and spatial extent of areas. Current and previous use of the area and residents' stories about its history were also recorded. Responses were colour co-ordinated to distinguish between consultation sites and resident characteristics. Facilitators

Figure 35.1   GIS-P map for "on-street" engagement

assisted individuals with writing difficulties to add comments to flags before asking the participants to place the markers on the map in the appropriate locations. By the end of the consultation process, many of the issues were repeatedly raised by different respondents, with little or no new issues being mentioned, indicating that an "information isomorph" had been reached. At this stage, the data were digitised, including speech bubbles to represent issues (see Figure 35.1). Representatives from the local community were then asked to verify that the maps were a true and accurate representation of the comments before they were presented to relevant decision makers, who evaluated the utility of the tool.

The advantages of the map over more conventional approaches were its attractiveness, novelty value (including flags and stickers to encourage participation), visual display (reducing the effects of poor literacy and language skills) and its potential for reducing conflict (because participants address points to the map rather than to each other). Moreover, the "on-street" application of GIS-P had the following advantages: it facilitated interaction with a wider range of subjects (n=120), including many older and younger residents, than would have been possible through invitations to meetings; subjects were able to orientate themselves more easily; individual consultation time was reduced (5–15 minutes); it was less intimidating than discussing issues in a conventional meeting. However, the data may not represent the opinions of all residents, the discussion was limited compared to what would be expected in a meeting, and it is difficult to provide feedback with on-street consultation. A small number of residents refused to participate, and many had to be cajoled into taking part in the mapping exercise; the relatively high levels of illiteracy and innumeracy in Salford may have contributed to their reluctance to become involved.

Subjects' comments focused mainly on security: no-go areas and exclusive sections of the local area; personal safety issues relating to the physical environment (trees and other environmental features); joy riding; remoteness of parts of the proposed route; lack of lighting. But comments also covered litter and fly tipping; the lack of facilities such as toilets, seats, lighting, litter bins; distrust and loss of faith in the Council; poor pathway surfaces; inaccessibility of proposed route for certain users, e.g. those with wheelchairs or prams. This supports the findings of research by Li et al. (2005), Sarkar et al. (2015) and Mateo-Babiano (2016) and highlights residents' psychosocial stress associated with these issues (Koohsari et al. 2013a, 2013b). Most suggestions for improvements related to blocking car access to nearby fields and the banks of the river Irwell; this related to the current practice of setting fire to stolen cars on the proposed health walk route after joy riding. Other suggestions related to increasing the attractiveness of the flood banking, and resurfacing paths. By superimposing the comments of different groups of participants, points of consensus as well as potential conflict were able to be mapped. It is also interesting to note that a comparison of the official crime statistics and local perceptions of high risk spaces showed significant discrepancies which had important implications for the health walk route.

The consultation also highlighted local knowledge about the area's historical features, such as Kersal Cell, formerly an 11th-century monastic site with tunnels beneath the river Irwell to Charlestown, a Tudor building, where John Byrom wrote *Christians Awake* in 1749. It also teased out a number of less widely known heritage features, such as the graves of a Zulu Prince and those of Black Douglas, a notorious 19th-century mill owner, and the children who worked and died in his mill. The remains of a Lancaster bomber that crashed into the river Irwell in 1944, and childhood memories relating to the area's industrial heritage, were also significant features of residents' perceptual maps. These aspects of valued local history were considered to have significant potential for enhancing the attractiveness of the health walk route through heritage interpretation, in order to create a sense of belonging among community residents and to increase their connection with the space (Sarkar et al. 2015).

Evaluation of the findings and their implementation in the short and long term

The steering group's evaluation of the tool's initial assessment of the public health walk route found that the digitised GIS-P maps were clear, easy to interpret and informative. They also incorporated valuable local insights and preferences and showed 'the hotspots of interest as well as the features that did not engage them', and provided 'a very good understanding of how people relate to particular points and areas in the local community'. Additionally, the integration of a variety of themed data in a visual display, which highlights the linkages between related issues, facilities and resources, meant that the maps were an effective aid to stakeholder decision making. The project was also evaluated favourably in a later EPSRC-funded study by Heriot Watt and Cambridge Universities (2010), in terms of yielding significant benefits for practitioners and promoting environmental sustainability.

The methodological tool was also effective in identifying important user accessibility and personal security issues, which were subsequently addressed in the initial technical design of the health walk. For example, one place in particular was identified as an unofficial crime black spot and was circumnavigated. Another, perceived as a high-risk site because of its remoteness and specific features, which provided cover for potential assailants, was appropriately landscaped to open up the area and provide "escape" routes in the event of an assault. In another section of the walk, which was considered to be a "no-go area" at night (Figure 35.2), lighting was installed to encourage access to the health walk during the evenings; however, this was vandalised within one month of installation. To address other concerns about crime, access to the river bank by

Figure 35.2 "No-go area" during the evenings between the river bank and main road

joy riders was further restricted and vandal-proof rest-points were installed in line with residents' recommendations; it was hoped that this would enhance the quality of the user experience and encourage participation from a broader cross-section of the public.

In 2016, a survey of the features and condition of the health walk and consultation with both its users and representatives from the area's "active lifestyles" team was undertaken to assess the long-term impact of the walkability consultation at the ten-year mark. The lighting installed on part of the route, to encourage walking during the evenings, had continued to be only intermittently operational, due to repeated vandalism. By comparison, the restricted river-bank access and rest-points had remained in place, showing that certain improvements resulting from the original project have stood the test of time. Immediately after the consultation in 2006, it was planned to incorporate aspects of the valued local history into heritage interpretation panels along the riverside section of the route, to increase the area's attractiveness. However, this proposal was not implemented. Instead, five Environment Agency interpretation panels, featuring more general aspects of the area's history, were installed in 2010 under the 'New Deal for Charlestown and Lower Kersal' (Figure 35.3), one of which has recently been burned. Perhaps this represents an opportunity to interpret the area's folk heritage to nurture a sense of belonging and promote local community ownership of this space, although the findings of recent research suggest that improvements in safety and connectivity should be prioritised.

Today, the health walk is used primarily by dog walkers and some joggers, groups which would arguably stay active without this particular initiative, while its potential for use by a broader cross-section of the community continues to be constrained by both "inactive lifestyle issues" and "fear of crime". Recent research suggests that green spaces are important features of walkable routes; however, in this particular context, these areas represent some of the more

Figure 35.3 Interpretation along the riverside section of the walk

secluded parts of the walk, which are considered to be unsafe by many residents. Despite the project addressing some of the issues around personal safety, fear of crime is still the key constraint on walking both in this space and in the area more generally, particularly for women. Consequently, health walk usage rates over the past decade have been disappointing, despite the active promotion of 'walking for health' in the city. Therefore, while the consultation facilitated public engagement in the planning process, a key pillar of existing Council policy, and was instrumental in reducing some of the barriers to participation in walking, the area's persistent socioeconomic deprivation has continued to undermine residents' opportunities to be conveniently and safely active and to achieve healthier lifestyles.

References

Bickerstaff, K. and Walker, G. (2005) 'Shared visions, unholy alliances: power, governance and deliberative processes in local transport planning', *Urban Studies,* 42(12): 2123–2144.

Brown, B.B., Werner, C.M., Amburgey, J.W. and Szalay, C. (2007) 'Walkable route perceptions and physical features converging evidence for en route walking experiences', *Environment and Behavior,* 39(1): 34–61.

CABE (2010) *Urban Green Nation: Building the Evidence Base,* London: Commission for Architecture and the Built Environment.

Carmona, T., Tiesdell, S., Heath, T. and Oc, T. (2010) *Public Places – Urban Spaces: The Dimensions of Urban Design,* 2nd edn, Oxford: Elsevier.

Cerin, E., Leslie, E., Owen, N. and Bauman, A. (2007) 'Applying GIS in physical activity research: community "walkability" and walking behaviors', in P.C. Lai and A.S.H. Mak (eds), *GIS for Health and the Environment,* Berlin: Springer, pp. 72–89.

Cinderby, S. and Forrester, J. (2005) 'Facilitating the local governance of air pollution using GIS for participation', *Applied Geography,* 25(2): 143–158.

Cinderby, S., Forrester, J., Jones, M., Schofield, P., Shaw, S., Snell, C. and Owen, A. (2007) 'Leisure and tourism spaces: initiatives for inclusive design in post-industrial cities', *InSITU: Leisure and Tourism Spaces: Facilitating Inclusive Design Using GIS-P,* York: SEI. Available at: www.sei-international. org/mediamanager/documents/ Publications/Future/facilitatinginclusivedesignusinggisp.pdf (accessed 1 June 2016).

Flint, E., Cummins, S. and Sacker, A. (2014) 'Associations between active commuting, body fat, and body mass index: population based, cross sectional study in the United Kingdom', *British Medical Journal,* 349: 4887.

Forrester, J. and Cinderby S. (2005) 'Geographic information systems for participation', in M. Leach, I. Scoones and B. Wynne (eds), *Science and Citizens: Globalization & the Challenge of Engagement,* London: Zed Press, pp. 232–236.

Giles-Corti, B., Foster, S., Shilton, T. and Falconer, R. (2010) 'The co-benefits for health of investing in active transportation', *NSW Public Health Bulletin,* 21: 122–127.

Giles-Corti, B., Macaulay, G., Middleton, N., Boruff, B., Bull, F., Butterworth, I, Badland, H. Mavoa, S., Roberts, R. and Christian, H. (2014) 'Developing a research and practice tool to measure walkability: a demonstration project', *Health Promotion Journal of Australia,* 25: 160–166.

Groundwork (2006) *Landscape Design.* Groundwork Manchester, Salford and Trafford. Available at: http:// manchester.groundworknw.org.uk/page.asp?id=1987 (accessed 1 June 2016).

Hall, C.M., Le-Klähn, D.-T. and Ram, Y. (2017) *Tourism, Public Transport and Sustainable Mobility,* Bristol: Channel View.

Heriot Watt and Cambridge Universities (2010) *Implementation Strategies for Sustainable Urban Environment Systems (ISSUES).* Available at: www.urbansustainabilityexchange.org.uk/ISSUESOutputInSITU.html (accessed 1 June 2016).

Hooper, P., Knuiman, M., Bull, F., Jones, E. and Giles-Corti, B. (2015) 'Are we developing walkable suburbs through urban planning policy? Identifying the mix of design requirements to optimise walking outcomes from the "Liveable Neighbourhoods" planning policy in Perth, Western Australia,' *International Journal of Behavioral Nutrition and Physical Activity,* 12: 1–11.

IPPR (2004) *Lonely Citizens: Report of the Working Party on Active Citizenship,* London: Institute for Public Policy Research.

Knuiman, M.W., Christian, H.E., Divitini, M.L., Foster, S.A., Bull, F.C., Badland, H.M. and Giles-Corti, B. (2014) 'A longitudinal analysis of the influence of the neighbourhood built environment on walking for transportation: the RESIDE study', *American Journal of Epidemiology*, 180(5): 453–461.

Koohsari, M.J., Karakiewicz, J.A. and Kaczynski, A.T. (2013a) 'Public open space and walking the role of proximity, perceptual qualities of the surrounding built environment, and street configuration', *Environment and Behavior*, 45(6): 706–736.

Koohsari, M.J., Badland, H. and Giles-Corti, B. (2013b) '(Re)Designing the built environment to support physical activity: bringing public health back into urban design and Planning', *Cities*, 35: 294–298.

Leslie, E., Coffee, N., Frank, L., Owen, N., Bauman, A. and Hugo, G. (2007) 'Walkability of local communities using geographic information systems to objectively assess relevant environmental attributes', *Health Place*, 13(1): 111–122.

Li, F., Fisher, K.J., Brownson, R.C. and Bosworth, M. (2005) 'Multilevel modelling of built environment characteristics related to neighbourhood walking activity in older adults', *Journal of Epidemiology and Community Health*, 59(7): 558–564.

Mateo-Babiano, I. (2016) 'Pedestrian's needs matter: examining Manila's walking environment', *Transport Policy*, 45: 107–115.

Moudon, A.V. and Lee, C. (2003) 'Walking and bicycling: an evaluation of environmental audit instruments', *American Journal of Health Promotion* 18(1): 21–37.

Nagel, C.L., Carlson, N.E., Bosworth, M. and Michael, Y.L. (2008) 'The relation between neighbourhood built environment and walking activity among older adults', *American Journal of Epidemiology*, 168(4): 461–468.

Oliver, M., Witten, K., Blakely, T., Parker, K., Badland, H., Schofield, G., Ivory, V., Pearce, J., Mavoa, S., Hinckson, E., Sweetsur, P. and Kearns, R. (2015) 'Neighbourhood built environment associations with body size in adults: mediating effects of activity and sedentariness in a cross-sectional study of New Zealand adults', *BMC Public Health*, 15: 1–11.

Rissel, C.E. (2009) 'Active travel: a climate change mitigation strategy with co-benefits for health', *NSW Public Health Bulletin*, 20: 10–13.

Saelens, B.E., Sallis, J.F. and Frank, L.D. (2003) 'Environmental correlates of walking and cycling: findings from the transportation, urban design, and planning literatures', *Annals of Behavioral Medicine*, 25(2): 80–91.

Salford City Council (2005) *Best Value Performance Plan 2005/2006*, Salford, Salford City Council. Available at: www.salford.gov.uk/council/perform/bv-reports/ bvpp200506.htm (accessed 1 June 2016).

Sandercock, L. (2003) *Cosmopolis ll: Mongrel Cities in the 21st Century*, London: Continuum.

Sarkar, C., Webster, C., Pryor, M., Tang, D., Melbourne, S., Zhang, X. and Jianzheng, L. (2015) 'Exploring associations between urban green, street design and walking: results from the Greater London boroughs', *Landscape and Urban Planning*, 143: 112–125.

Shortt, N.K., Rind, E., Pearce, J. and Mitchell, R. (2014) 'Integrating environmental justice and socioecological models of health to understand population-level physical activity', *Environment and Planning A*, 46(6): 1479–1495.

Sustrans (2006) *Liveable Neighbourhoods*. Available at: www.sustrans.org.uk/default.asp?sID=1090834683408 (accessed 1 June 2016).

Tribby, C.P., Miller, H.J., Brown, B.B., Werner, C.M. and Smith, K.R. (2016) 'Assessing built environment walkability using activity-space summary measures', *The Journal of Transport and Land Use*, 9(1): 1–21.

Walpole, K. and Greenhalgh, L. (1996) *Freedom of the City*, London: Demos.

Witten, K., Hiscock, R., Pearce, J. and Blakely, T. (2008) 'Neighbourhood access to open spaces and physical activity of residents: a national study', *Preventative Medicine*, 7(3): 299–303.

Woodcock, J., Edwards, P., Tonne, C., Armstrong, B.G., Ashiru, O., Banister, D., Beevers, S., Chalabi, Z., Chowdhury, Z., Cohen, A., Franco, O.H., Haines, A., Hickman, R., Lindsay, G., Mittal, I., Mohan, D., Tiwari, G., Woodward, A. and Roberts, I. (2009) 'Public health benefits of strategies to reduce greenhouse-gas emissions: urban land transport', *Lancet*, 374: 1930–1943.

Yoshi, Y. (2016) 'Preserving alleyways to increase walkability of historical Japanese cities', *Procedia – Social and Behavioral Sciences*, 216: 603–609.

36

Developing a spatial pattern analysis method for evaluating trails in the mountains

The case of Beban Pass in Tierra del Fuego, Argentina

Marisol Vereda and María Laura Borla

Introduction

> Finding it nearly hopeless to push my way through the wood, I followed the course of a mountain torrent. At first, from the waterfalls and number of dead trees, I could hardly crawl along; but the bed of the stream soon became a little more open, from the floods having swept the sides. I continued slowly to advance for an hour along the broken and rocky banks, and I was amply repaid by the grandeur of the scene.
>
> (Darwin 1909: 225)

Despite the time that has passed since Darwin's remarks about Tierra del Fuego in 1839, the words still apply to the Fuegian landscape from the modern traveller's perspective. Hiking and trekking in Tierra del Fuego, Argentina, are activities becoming increasingly important for visitors who want to experience the wilderness in remote destinations. Ushuaia is the southernmost city of Argentina that hosts visitors. These arrive mostly by plane, followed by cruise ships and, to a lesser extent, car or bus. In this chapter, a model for measuring tourist potential of trails in natural areas is developed, taking into account the different components of the landscape, as well as other aspects such as access, facilities, communications and impacts. This contribution is based on a literature review, fieldwork and in-depth interviews with trekking experts.

The method developed is applied to a mountain trail called Beban Pass, which crosses the Andes mountain range connecting Ushuaia with the southern bank of Lake Fagnano, a very attractive option for trekkers in Tierra del Fuego. As a result of the evaluation methodology, it should be highlighted that the Beban Pass turned out to be valued among the most attractive trails in the region showing a high potential for active tourism based on natural assets.

Recreation and tourism in the wilderness

The development of recent recreational and tourist practices, such as ecotourism, requires places where nature becomes the necessary setting to take up different activities. A quest for practices that may offer a direct experience of authentic natural and cultural assets attracts the attention of particular markets with very specific demands, based on environmental issues. In this respect, hiking and trekking in natural areas have a special meaning, since they can allow the development of "first hand" experiences in scenic areas with high ecological values (Hall and Page 2014).

There are preferences for activities based on ecological, social and economic resources, promoted by the relationship between leisure and the necessity of psychological satisfaction. Preferences for more active practices are also encouraged by the more remote, exotic destinations with natural attributes that are often generally associated with a high degree of participant involvement, with participants who may also be regarded as "explorers" in quest of personal challenges (Tran and Ralston 2006). The way the terms "hiking" and "trekking" are used require a review of some definitions given by experts.

On the one hand, hiking can be defined as a recreational activity, sporty and non-competitive, which is carried out along trails located in natural areas; this activity promotes an approach of people to wilderness and to the knowledge of the place through the landscape components that characterise the area (Rodríguez Aller 2006). Iram-Sectur (2008) refers to hiking as a kind of active tourism, the aim of which is to travel through places with a moderate difficulty level, with recreative and sporty purposes. Bateman *et al.* (2006) define hiking as an energetic walk, which usually takes place in natural areas. It involves the use of certain technical gear such as hiking boots, backpacks and specific clothes according to the area weather conditions, and is often regarded as an activity undertaken in a single day. In contrast, trekking is identified as an activity that comprises longer and more difficult journeys; it involves camping overnight most of the time and it requires the trekker to be in shape and with certain training in orientation (Bateman *et al.* 2006; Colorado 2010). Since, in many cases, trekking is associated with the mountains (Zorrilla 2000), some authors refer to the importance of mountains as vulnerable and high-valued places giving support to recreational and active tourist practices (Antón Clavé and González Reverté 2007; Beedie and Hudson 2003; Dyck *et al.* 2003; Moscoso and Moyano 2006; Zorrilla 2000).

Both hiking and trekking may also be described from double dialectics that involve the individual and the environment as well as the individual and the social-contructed norms, which helps explain the individual's behaviour in undertaking the activity (Borrie and Roggenbuck 2001; Chhetri *et al.* 2004; Chen and Tsai 2007; Galí and Donaire 2004; Lepp and Gibson 2008). The possibility of taking up this kind of activity in natural areas promotes leisure experiences that can be related to 'emerging states of mind, as a sequence of transactions between individuals and their environment, as personal stories with temporal and spatial qualities, and as a lived experience' (Borrie and Roggenbuck 2001: 202).

Every way to go through a trail represents a mental construction, material and/or symbolic, that creates and recreates different aspects of a natural area for each individual, making their own decisions on the way the landscape is understood. As Donaire and Galí (2008) point out, individuals' behaviour in the wilderness can be interpreted as the result of two dialectics: on one hand, the relationship of the person (mental construction) with the place (physical space) and, on the other hand, the relationship of the person (mental construction) with socially constructed rules. In fact, the place is not only important because of its inventory of resources, but for the social value assigned to it. In this respect, nature has been given different attributes, specially taking into account those features already lost due to industrialisation; people are eager to find exotic, pristine environments in wild areas that contain indigenous species and may lead to an emotional state of mind, in which the trekker can feel in harmony with nature, freed from civilisation, inspired, invigorated and spiritually fulfilled (Wynn 2002).

The study area

Tierra del Fuego is an island located in the south of South America, which is shared between Chile (west) and Argentina (east), Ushuaia (54° 48' S / 68° 19' W) is the capital city of the Argentine province. The particular area of study is known as Paso Beban (Beban Pass). This trail was first crossed by three inhabitants of Ushuaia, led by Thomas Beban, who were looking for a way through the mountains to Lake Fagnano in order to find places for Mr Beban to expand cattle grazing in summer. The pass bears his name and links the area around Ushuaia to Lake Fagnano, in the north. This part of the Andes, called the Alvear mountain range, forms one the most picturesque landscapes on the island, running parallel to the southern bank of Lake Fagnano. It constitutes one of the best examples of exposure of the geological Alvear formation bedrock, shaped and eroded by glaciers: horns, glacial deposits, hanging valleys, cirques. The peaks range from 1,100 to 1,500 m high, being among the highest peaks in Argentine Tierra del Fuego. Nevertheless, due to the high latitude, the conditions above the tree line are equivalent to a "high mountain" environment in other parts of the world. It is a two-day-long trail, covering aproximately 19 km (one way), without any kind of signs or facilities, and is in an extremely aesthetic wild area. There are two passes (Beban 1 and Beban 2) to cross the mountains. The trail is not practically marked and trekkers need to follow a topographic map and may also need to use a GPS or a compass to find their way through.

Spatial pattern design

Since there is not enough information available to help systematise data on trails in Tierra del Fuego, and considering the importance of these practices particularly for a destination whose image lies in wilderness attributes, a methodology to inventory and assess the different components present in a trail is developed. Different methodologies for site inventories have been extensively developed (CICATUR/OEA 1983; Domínguez 1994; Boullón 1992; Bote Gómez 1999; Gutiérrez Roa et al. 1986; Álvarez Cuervo 1987; Smith 1992; Muñoz Pedreros 2004; Marzuki 2016), being particularly focused on tourist destinations and natural areas, taking into account large scales of analysis. Others have focused on trails working on methods to evaluate their physical condition (Luque Gil 2003; Tudela Serrano and Giménez Alarte 2008, Galacho Jiménez and Arrebola Castaño 2010), often based on the works by Borla (1998) and Salemme et al. (1999).

Much attention has been given to the study of natural landscapes with regard to visitors and their perceptions of wilderness. Nevertheless, less attention is often given to social values in policy and decision making concerning wilderness (Schuster et al. 2003). In this respect, the works by Ortega Valcárcel (2000) and González Bernaldez (1981) give insight into the idea of landscape as a mental construct, where each individual will have a different view according to one's background, experience and culture. Furthermore, Santos (1996, 2000) reinforces this idea, conceptualising landscape as the portion of a territory, which could be visually covered, existing through its shapes, which were created in different historical moments, but which coexist with the present. It should be also noted that landscape is related to perception: what is gained through the senses. Accordingly, not only is the "material" natural heritage relevant but also those intangible "especially visible" components, more related to the specific knowledge of the area.

The word "landscape" has been closely associated to tourism, turning it into an attraction in terms of being the aim of a trip, the main focus of the tourist experience. Therefore, landscapes are also the result of different social practices, which contribute to build representations of the place (Troncoso 2009). In fact, what makes a place "attractive" for a visitor not only refers to the intrinsic value of its components, but it is also given by those representations and images generated by the demand (Chadefaud 1987; Bertoncello 2002, 2008). Nevertheless, the way a place is viewed and therefore assessed will always depend on the background of those tourists, tourist agents, residents and communicators whose assessment on the attractiveness of places reaches different audiences.

In order to develop a spatial pattern design for trails, a methodology that allows identifying different sections was developed. This inventory divides the trail in smaller units, according to the type of vegetation crossed: primary or secondary woods, scrub, peatbog, Andine vegetation and Andean desert (Borla and Vereda 2005). Within each of these units, called sections, several ítems are listed: name and number of the sector, degree of conservation (protection tools), use degree, facilities, use impact, viewpoints, facilities, seasonal access, communication, length and slope, estimated trekking time, landscape components account (abiotic, biotic and anthropic) and topographic profile. The section limits coincide with nodes (fixed points) where trekkers find a reason to make a stop, which could be viewpoints or a scenic open area, for example. For each section, a filecard that summarises the contents of each unit of analysis is filled in.

In this case study, five sectors located within the Alvear mountain range were identified; a summary for each is presented below. In general terms, access is limited to summer due to the presence of snow and the occurrence of storms with blizzards from May to October. In terms of legal conservation, only the first section lies under the Provincial Decree No. 2,256/94 that protects it as part of a natural reserve for recreational and tourist purposes only. With respect to past uses, logging was important and grazing has occasionally taken place.

Section 1: The trail crosses a portion of secondary southern beech-tree forest (logged-*lenga*), a small river and a peatbog. Flora and birdlife are highlights. There are remarkable viewpoints while crossing the valley in the open areas.

Section 2: The node is a small mountain shelter, in a scenic open area and the trail starts crossing primary southern beech-tree forest (mixed *lenga* and evergreen forest) along a stream. Flora and birdlife are similar to those in Section 1.

Section 3: The node is the treeline. Andine vegetation, which diminishes as the trail goes up, is one of the highlights; nude pink bedrock of the two passes (Beban 1 and Beban 2). There are remarkable viewpoints all along this section.

Section 4: The node is the line where Andine vegetation grows again, coinciding with the source of a narrow stream. The vegetation becomes denser to turn into mixed forest. The highlight in this section is the succession of beaver dams.

Section 5: The node is the magnificent view onto a portion of Lake Fagnano, surrounded by trees. Although this section used to be across primary beech tree forest, this area is of a high impact to the trekker as it was burnt out by an anthropogenic forest fire.

Using the information from the inventory of this spatial study, a map was prepared (Figure 36.1), where the 19-km trail with the different sections can be recognised.

Experts' point of view

In order to gather information from the trekker's perspective, a group of trekking experts was consulted, covering a total of 15 interviews. They were asked about an overall assessment, their preferences for the best two sections, the different components, and the hazards they could cope with, among other questions.

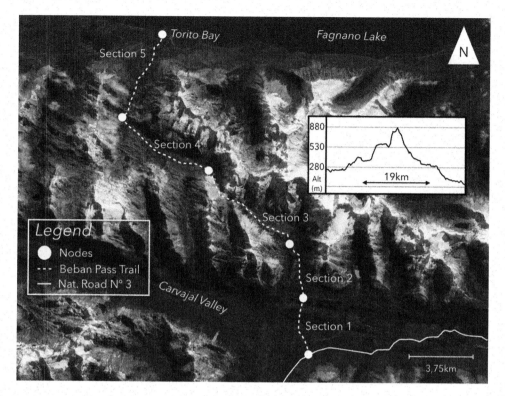

Figure 36.1   Map of Beban Pass trail

Values were assigned to the trail on a 1–5 scale (where 5 means highest value): the mean resulted in 3.57, which places the trail in a good position. When asked why they gave that value, the ones who chose a high value pointed out that the trail gives the chance to encounter a good variety of components and that it is well preserved. Those experts who marked the lowest remarked that even though the trail crosses the Andes, it is a relatively easy area for an experienced trekker. The experts also highlighted different components that justify the decision to trek the Beban Pass; in Figure 36.2 the weighting of each component can be seen (each person marked up to three components).

Likewise, they were asked to highlight the two sections they considered the most important or attractive. In this respect, Section 3 (which includes the two mountain passes up to the beginning of De Las Yeguas river) was chosen by all the experts, who said it represented the most difficult part of the trek. Section 4 (from the beginning of De Las Yeguas river to the point where Lake Fagnano can be seen) was selected because of the views.

It was particularly important to describe the profile of the visitor who was not only fit enough to do the trail but would enjoy it. All the experts agreed on the same characteristics: to be physically capable; to be able to carry a heavy load; and to be knowledgeable in orientation skills. They added that the main motivation would be related to mountaineering. Experts were also asked to point out hazards a visitor might encounter when trekking this area. A few objective hazards were identified and these mainly related to crossing rivers and beaver dams, and poor visibility at the moment of going through the mountain pass. In case of an accident, there are some areas without any possible means of communication, and an evacuation would need to be done on foot, which

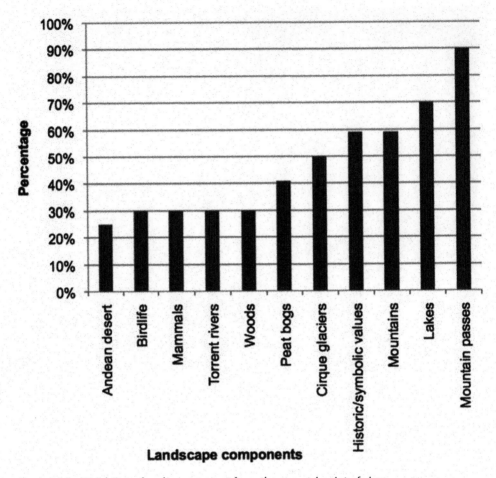

Figure 36.2 Weighting of each component from the experts' point of view

could take several hours. Subjective hazards may appear if there is a mistaken calculation on the time–effort relationship by trekkers.

In order to get acquainted with other aspects related to this trail, 11 statements were made where respondents' answers varied from 1 (strongly disagree) to 5 (strongly agree). The results are presented in Table 36.1. As regards what changes they would consider necessary to improve trekkers' security, as well as getting benefits for the experience, all the participants agreed on having a total coverage of VHF signal would provide more security as well as the distribution of printed material with a detailed map, information and recommendations among trekkers. Almost everyone thought that it would be wise to have staff monitoring the area and low-visual-impact indicators in strategic points.

Hierarchy given to the trail

Taking the above into account, the methodology designed for the evaluation and potential of trails from a nature-based perspective was applied to the Beban Pass. It consists of a system

Table 36.1 Opinions of experts about different aspects of the trails

Statements	Mean
The relatively easy access to the starting point makes the trail attractive to walkers	3.33
Its lack of facilities and dwellings contributes to experience a really pristine environment	4.55
Flora and fauna can be observed in the wild	4.22
Since the area has not been occupied, it shows wilderness values	3.66
The few possibilities of an encounter with other trekkers add value to the experience	4.33
The Beban Pass allows trekkers to be immersed in a wild mountain landscape of singular beauty	4.11
A feeling of "being with oneself", in harmony with nature, can be perceived	4.44
The lack of a clearly marked path or signals can lead to some dangerous situations, making this place available only for people with a certain orientation knowledge	4.11
The trekker has the feeling of being in a remote and isolated place	3.33
Certain landscape features/values make this place distinctive	4.33
The possibility of returning by boat adds value to this trekking experience	4.22

to rank the different components of the trail through the evaluation of each element, based on subjective and objective weighed indicators, assigning numerical values selected for each component within each unit (see Table 36.2). This methodology was developed for the Tierra del Fuego area, based on a series of selected indicators. It assesses the trail at component scale, section scale and trail scale, allowing for comparisons of different components (abiotic, biotic and anthropic) along any given trail, sections along the same trail and trails of the whole area which can assist in ranking all the existing trails in Tierra del Fuego. It is important to point out that the components, which represent the basis of the evaluation, keep the same value in every trail of Tierra del Fuego (Vereda *et al.* 2010). Once the indicators and components are evaluated, the final value of a section is obtained. It may vary from 1 to 8 points, the higher being the better qualified. Finally, there is an addition of 1 point for each type of environment the trail crosses – different from the one at the beginning of the first section – leading to a maximum of 10 points. Three possible trail categories are considered: Category I (over 7 points) reflects the best-ranked trails; Category II (5–7 points) shows the trail may need some improvement, such as the re-tracing of a section and incorporation of facilities; and Category III (under 5 points) may be interpreted as a need for a change, including the possibility of closing the trail.

Once the evaluation methodology was applied to the Beban Pass, it was concluded that the trail is worth 9 points in the 1–10 scale, as the result of the average of the final value sections (7 points) and an addition of 2 points, as the trail crosses two varied environments different from the one at the beginning (the trail starts in the forest and then crosses peatland and Andean desert). The trail is then included in the highest value options in Tierra del Fuego (Category I), as defined by the method. However, an unexpected anthropogenic forest fire destroyed an area estimated at around 500 hectares in 2012, which reduced steadily the value of Section 5 of the Beban Pass trail. Although it is expected that the forest will grow back again, this work reflects the present value of the trail, because the final section was changed so dramatically. This is the reason why the final value of the trail decreased from 9 to 7, as shown in Table 36.2.

Table 36.2 Hierarchy of sections along Beban trail

Section	Indicator and Weight Factor																				Final Value (before 2012)	Final Value (at present)
	CD 0.07		SV 0.08		WE 0.05		AbC 0.16		BC 0.16		AnC 0.16		DU 0.08		UI 0.06		F 0.08		LO 0.1			
1	2	0.14	1	0.08	2	0.1	10	1.6	30	4.8	6	0.96	0	0	0	0	1	0.08	3	0.3	8.06	8.06
2	3	0.21	2	0.16	1	0.05	10	1.6	25	4	4	0.64	2	0.16	2	0.12	1	0.08	2	0.2	7.22	7.22
3	2	0.14	2	0.16	0	0	9	1.44	20	3.2	4	0.64	2	0.16	2	0.12	1	0.08	2	0.2	6.14	6.14
4	3	0.21	2	0.16	1	0.05	5	0.8	27	4.32	4	0.64	2	0.16	2	0.12	1	0.08	2	0.2	6.74	6.74
5	2	0.14	2	0.16	2	0.1	7	1.12	31	4.96	5	0.8	1	0.08	1	0.06	1	0.08	2	0.2	7.7	–
5	**1**	**0.07**	**2**	**0.16**	**2**	**0.1**	**7**	**1.12**	**0**	**0**	**2**	**0.32**	**0**	**0**	**0**	**0**	**0**	**0**	**2**	**0.2**	**–**	**1.97**

	Final Value (before 2012)	Final Value (at present)
Total score of the trail before and after the forest fire	35.86	30.13
Final addition of the value sectors before and after the forest fire	7	6
3 environments before 2012 = 2 points; 2 environments after forest fire = 1 point	2	1
Final value of the trail before and after the forest fire	9 points	7 points

Notes: CD = Landscape Chromatic Diversity; SV = Scenic Viewpoints; WE = Wind Effect; AbC = Abiotic Components; BC = Biotic Components; AnC = Anthropic Components; DU = Degree of Use; UI = Use Impact; F = Facilities; LO = Land Ownership. Shaded cells show the values after the forest fire.

Conclusion

This method described in this chapter allows the construction of inventories and the hiercarchical organisation of different landscape components at a scale that may be adapted to the requirements of each particular trail. To be able to measure the potential of trails is a very useful tool in the decision-making process related to the planning of natural areas. In addition, it provides basic information that may be helpful in the preparation of maps, brochures, field guides, signs and interpretation.

Nevertheless, the design of the method demonstated here can be improved, via the addition of new indicators or values that allows for different variations that may arise during monitoring tasks, an issue that has long been recognised as significant in heritage management (e.g. Hall and McArthur 1993). It should be highlighted that, after the application of this methodology, the Beban Pass turned out to be among the most attractive trails in the region and should be considered a real option for trekkers because of its high potential, but the way it could be presented should take into account a number of issues. First, there are choices with respect to promotion. Should it be promoted to reach all possible users, since its potential is combined with a low degree of difficulty for walkers? Or should it be promoted as an option for more experienced trekkers, who are always eager to try new challenges and usually do not look for information in sources as the Tourist Board or local hikers and trekking organisations? Second, with respect to security and facilities, should the trail be better marked (small signposts, campsites) so that the safety for users may be improved, or should it be designed for "experts only", with the knowledge that it is a relatively "easy-to-guard" trail?

As a final reflection, it must be remarked that the forest fire that burned out the primary forest in this trail was started by a trekker who assumed him or herself to be experienced, which should make all of us raise awareness on what we understand by "experienced" trekker. Whatever the authorities' decision, it must be made under the premise of guaranteeing the preservation of the natural landscape involved and highlighting principles for low-impact tourism. Finally, it is obvious that clear policies for the improvement of Tierra del Fuego as a nature-based tourist and recreational place still need further discussion among local actors, who should take into account the trail users' interests.

References

Álvarez Cuervo, R. (1987) 'Jerarquización de los recursos turísticos', *Estudios Turísticos,* 94: 77–100.
Antón Clavé, S. and González Reverté, F. (2007) *A propósito del turismo,* Barcelona: UOC Editorial.
Bateman, H., Harris, E. and McAdam, K. (eds) (2006) *Dictionary of Leisure, Travel and Tourism,* London: A&C Black Publishers.
Beedie, P. and Hudson, S. (2003) 'Emergence of mountain-based adventure tourism', *Annals of Tourism Research,* 30(3): 625–643.
Bertoncello, R. (2002) 'Turismo y territorio. Otras prácticas, otras miradas', *Aportes y transferencias,* 6(2): 31–50.
Bertoncello, R. (ed.) (2008) *Turismo y Geografía,* Buenos Aires: Ciccus.
Borla, M.L. (1998) 'Tierra del Fuego: a case for the development of a new methodology for the inventory and evaluation of nature-oriented tourist assets', unpublished thesis, Somerset University SA, Brussels, Belgium.
Borla, M.L. and Vereda, M. (2005) *Exploring Tierra del Fuego: A Handbook for the Traveller at the End of the World,* Ushuaia, Argentina: Utopías.
Borrie, W.T. and Roggenbuck, J.W. (2001) 'The dynamic, emergent and multi-phasic nature of on-site wilderness experiences', *Journal of Leisure Research,* 33(2): 202–228.
Bote Gómez, V. (1999) *Planificación Económica del Turismo,* Mexico: Trillas.
Boullón, R. (1992) *Las actividades turísticas y recreacionales,* Mexico: Trillas.

Chadefaud, M. (1987) *Aux origines du tourisme dans les pays de l'Adour. (Du mythe el l'espaee: un essai de géographie historique)*, Pau, France: Université de Pau et des Pays de l'Adour.

Chen, C.F. and Tsai, D.C. (2007) 'How do destination image and evaluative factors affect behavioral intentions?', *Tourism Management*, 28(4): 1115–1122.

Chhetri, P., Arrowsmith, C. and Jackson, M. (2004) 'Determining hiking experiences in nature-based tourist destinations', *Tourism Management*, 25(1): 31–43.

CICATUR/OEA (1983) 'Primer curso interamericano de planificación del desarrollo turístico', *Document No. 3/005*, Mexico.

Colorado, J. (2010) *Montañismo y trekking*, Madrid: Desnivel.

Darwin, C. (1909) *Voyage of the Beagle* (orig. 1839), The Harvard Classics, New York: P.F. Collier & Son; London: Penguin Classics.

Dominguez, L. (1994) *Relevamiento turístico*, Santa Fe, NM: Centro de Estudios Turísticos.

Donaire, J.A. and Galí, N. (2008) 'Modeling tourist itineraries in Heritage cities: routes around the Old District of Girona', *Revista Pasos*, 6(3): 435–449.

Dyck, C., Schneider, I., Thompson, M. and Virden, R. (2003) 'Specialization among mountaineers and its relationship to environmental attitudes', *Journal of Park and Recreation Administration*, 21(2): 44–62.

Galacho Jiménez, F.B. and Arrébola Castaño, J.A. (2010) 'Metodología aplicada para la evaluación con SIG y EMC de senderos según las condiciones físicas del terreno', in J. Ojeda, M.F. Pita and I. Vallejo (eds), *Tecnologías de la Información Geográfica: La Información Geográfica al servicio de los ciudadanos*, Seville: University of Seville, pp. 466–481.

Galí, N. and Donaire, J.A. (2004) 'El análisis del comportamiento de visitantes en los espacios naturales a partir del diseño de un grafo valorizado', *Actas IX Congreso AECIT*, Logroño, Spain.

González Bernáldez, F. (1981) *Ecología y paisaje*, Madrid: Blume Ediciones.

Gutiérrez Roa, J., Castillo, R., Castañeda, J. and Sánchez, J. (1986) *Recursos naturales y turismo*, Mexico: Limusa.

Hall, C.M. and McArthur, S. (eds) (1993) *Heritage Management in New Zealand and Australia: Visitor Management, Interpretation and Marketing*. Auckland: Oxford University Press.

Hall, C.M. and Page, S. (2014) *The Geography of Tourism and Recreation*, 4th edn, Abingdon, Oxon: Routledge.

Iram-Sectur (2008) *Servicios turísticos de senderismo y travesías*, Buenos Aires: Instituto Argentino de Normalización y Certificación y Secretaría de Turismo de la Nación.

Lepp, A. and Gibson, H. (2008) 'Sensation seeking and tourism: tourist role, perception of risk and destination choice', *Tourism Management*, 29(4): 740–750.

Luque Gil, A.M. (2003) 'La evaluación del medio para la práctica de actividades turístico-deportivas en la naturaleza', *Cuadernos de Turismo*, 12: 131–149.

Marzuki, A. (2016) 'A proposed framework for nature-based tourism destinations evaluation', *Jurnal Teknologi*, 78(5): 127–134.

Moscoso, D. and Moyano, E. (2006) *Deporte y Desarrollo Rural*, Madrid: Consejería de Turismo, Comercio y Deporte.

Muñoz Pedreros, A. (2004) 'La evaluación del paisaje: una herramienta de gestión ambiental', *Revista Chilena de Historia Natural*, 77: 139–156.

Ortega Valcarcel, J. (2000) *Los horizontes de la geografía. Teoría de la geografía*, Barcelona: Ariel Geografía.

Rodríguez Aller, J. (2006) *Manual de Senderos*, Valladolid, Spain: FDMESCyL.

Salemme, M., Canale, G., Daverio, M.E. and Vereda, M. (1999) 'Revalorización del patrimonio arqueológico-histórico como recurso turístico. Circuitos alternativos en la Provincia de Tierra del Fuego, Antártida e Islas del Atlántico Sur', unpublished final research report, Ushuaia, Argentina: Universidad Nacional de la Patagonia SJB.

Santos, M. (1996) *Metamorfosis del espacio habitado*, Madrid: Oikos Tau.

Santos, M. (2000) *La naturaleza del espacio*, Madrid: Ariel.

Schuster, R.M., Tarrant, M.A. and Watson, A.E. (2003) 'The social values of wilderness', in J.J. Murdy (ed.), *Proceedings 2003 Northeastern Recreation Research Symposium*, New York: USDA, pp. 356–365.

Smith, S. (1992) *Geografía recreativa. Investigación de potenciales turísticos*, Mexico City: Trillas.

Tran, X. and Ralston, L. (2006) 'Tourist preferences: influence of unconscious needs', *Annals of Tourism Research*, 33(2): 424–441.

Troncoso, C.A. (2009) 'El retrato cambiante de la Quebrada de Humahuaca. Transformaciones y permanencias de sus atractivos turísticos', in R. Bertoncello (ed.), *Turismo y geografía: Lugares y patrimonio natural-cultural de la Argentina*, Buenos Aires: Ciccus, pp. 17–42.

Tudela Serrano, M.L. and Giménez Alarte, A.I. (2008) 'La determinación de la capacidad de carga turística en tres senderos de pequeño recorrido en el municipio de Cehegín (Murcia)', *Cuadernos de Turismo*, 22: 211–229.

Vereda, M., Borla, M.L., Gigli, S.M., Collado, L., Galdames, M. and Cárdenas, S. (2010) 'Evaluación del potencial turístico de senderos en Tierra del Fuego a partir de la creación de un sistema de indicadores. Estudios de caso desde la representatividad de ambientes', unpublished final research report, Ushuaia, Argentina: Universidad Nacional de la Patagonia SJB.

Wynn, S. (2002) 'The Zambeyi river. Wilderness and tourism', *International Journal of Wilderness*, 8(1): 34–39.

Zorrilla, J. (2000) *Enciclopedia de la montaña*, Madrid: Desnivel.

37

Improving the walkability of the Camino

Xosé Somoza-Medina and Rubén Camilo Lois González

Introduction

The last few years of the 20th century witnessed the return of pilgrimages to Santiago de Compostela. An ancient medieval Christian route used by contemporary men and women who wanted to walk to this historical Galician city, a World Heritage site, with motivations as diverse as those that move the complex contemporary society to which we belong (Roseman 2004; Lois-González 2013; Greenia 2014). For some, the Camino remains essentially a religious route, but for most, spiritual motivations (with the multiple interpretations that this expression may include), the landscape, heritage or the simple desire to return to slow mobility constitute the fundamental drive to go to Santiago (Maddrell 2013; Santos-Solla and Pena-Cabrera 2014). As highlighted in several recent works, walking over several days (at least four, as the genuine pilgrim must walk at least 100 kilometres), is linked to several aspects of contemporary culture; the notion that continued exercise is a healthy practice that allows you to interact with others (the idea of *communitas*); to contemplate the scenery in all its dimensions at a slow pace; and to reconnect with your own self (the goal of having enough time to think, to feel, which often leads to *liminal* practices) (Frey 1998; Coleman and Eade 2004; Lois-González *et al.* 2015). It is about returning, at least for a short while, to the time of our grandparents, when the world was perceived at a speed of six, ten or, at most, 40 kilometres per hour.

The recovery of the Camino as a successful international destination: the role of institutional action

For the recovery process, or the contemporary invention, of the Camino to take place and allow an increase from only a few tens of walkers in the 1950s or 1960s to the approximately 300,000 pilgrims in 2014 or 2015, a series of factors have been combined that explain the successful revitalisation of this old medieval route. In an initial period (between the Holy Years of 1965 and 1976), the action of a series of route-recovering enthusiasts, such as researchers interested in promoting the memory of the pilgrimage to Santiago (including historians, philologists and archivists), or clergy encouraged by the idea of walking the Camino, or both (Santos-Solla and Lois-González 2011; López 2012), began to revitalise the route and they narrated their experience in chronicles and articles.

During this period, the first associations of friends of Santiago, which have always maintained the traditional concept of pilgrimage (religious or not), were created, and in doing so exerted great popular influence (Barreiro 2009; Collins-Kreiner 2010). This societal movement was quickly adopted by successive public administrations (from 1976 to the present day), starting with the Spanish Government, which saw the possibility of justifying the historical Europeanness of Spain at the time of the country's integration into the European Community (the first public exhibition organised by the Spanish Ministry of Culture to coincide with the accession Treaty to the EEC was about the legacy of the Camino). Later the Autonomous Regions, which were created in the Spanish democratic transition and are crossed by the route, have built part of their identity and tourism strategy on the promotion of the Camino, while cities and municipalities of the route have built various networks of cultural and urban tourism that appeal to visitors (Caucci 1993; Soria y Puig 1991; Santos-Solla 1999). For decades, these public institutions have competed to restore monuments, paving and planting trees along the Camino to facilitate walking, and building hostels or various facilities aimed at pilgrims in order to improve the route and to make it more convenient (Lois-González and Somoza-Medina 2003; Pichel-Pichel 2004). Such actions were not solely spiritual and were also connected to the cultural and spatial dimensions of governance. For example, the Franco regime used the restoration of monuments along the Camino as part of its strategy of claiming the Catholic and conservative memory of the Spain of that time (Castro-Fernández 2010).

All of these actions carried out on the Camino have resulted in an increase in the number of people that head to Santiago for at least 100 kilometres on foot or 200 kilometres if travelling by bike or on horseback (Figure 37.1). This minimum distance was previously established by the Santiago de Compostela Church Authority in its attempt to single out the traditional pilgrim and, in recent years, it has instigated a consensus to define the phenomenon (with public administrations, associations of friends of Santiago and specialists on the route all agreeing with this threshold) (Herrero-Pérez 2008; Santos-Solla and Lois-González 2011). The number of pilgrims has continued to increase since 1970, when there was a total of 68, until 2015, when the total reached 262,516; from the 1,868 of the Holy Year of 1982 to the 179,944 of the Holy Year of 2004 (Oficina del Peregrino 2015). In this regard, it should be noted that the values normally used come from the Pilgrim's Office managed by the Compostela canonry; that is, it is a private source taken from a place where walkers will receive a certificate of completion of the route (known as the *Compostela*) (Xunta de Galicia and University of Santiago 2007–2010). There is a small underestimation of the flow in this register (there are pilgrims not interested in collecting the certificate) and a certain religious bias in the reasons listed. However, this source notes how in the Holy Years (when the festivity of Santiago falls on a Sunday and there are major campaigns for the promotion of the route), there is a considerable increase of walkers and this increase coincides almost exclusively with the Spanish market. It also shows the dynamic followed by the pilgrimage to Santiago to become a global product; the first ten non-Spanish nationalities that did the Camino in 2015 were Italy, Germany (both around 20,000 pilgrims), United States, Portugal and France (approximately 10,000), United Kingdom, Ireland, Canada, South Korea and Brazil (over 4,000) (Lois-González and Santos-Solla 2015; Oficina del Peregrino 2015).

As for the current situation and future forecasts of the Camino, three points should be noted, which we will develop further below. The first is that the route seems to reinforce its global projection, with an increasing number of users from outside Europe, where Catholics are a minority. The second is that the consensus on the traditional pilgrimage will require the creation of promotional policies for secondary routes, especially the Northern Camino (Camino del Norte), the Primitive (Camino Primitivo) (both World Heritage-listed) and the Portuguese (Camino

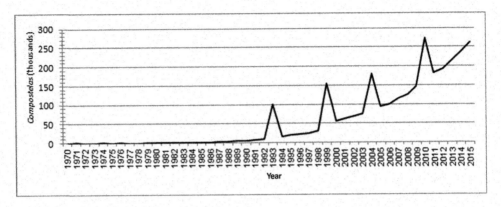

Figure 37.1 Number of pilgrims to Santiago who receive the *Compostela*, 1970–2015.
Source: Derived from Oficina del Peregrino 1970–2015.

Portugués). Finally, that the number of pilgrims will continue to increase moderately until 2021, when a new Holy Year may cause the route to overflow and pose serious saturation problems.

The importance of non-institutional action

Institutions in power have supported the promotion and popularisation of the route to Santiago from its medieval beginnings. In this sense, the attempts of the Santiago de Compostela bishops and archbishops to obtain the recognition of the sanctuary city as an Apostolic Tomb between the 9th and the 13th centuries were consistent with this theme (Villares 1984; López-Alsina 1993). In the middle of the 20th century, Franco's regime used the route and the monumental character of Santiago for its own propaganda purposes (Castro-Fernández 2010). Such instrumental actions were continued by the Spanish democratic government in the 1980s and 1990s, as well as by the Autonomous Regions and cities crossed by the Camino (Barreiro 2009; Lois-González 2013). However, the success of the contemporary pilgrimage is not just due to institutional interest. Various interested parties and stakeholders have played a great part in its recovery, with both religious and non-religious walking associations, writers and film directors and, increasingly, tourism companies that have seen its promotion as a good way of doing business (Santos-Solla 1999; Santomil 2011).

The rediscovery (or reinvention) of the Camino was connected to the actions of scholars of this medieval route and some clergy. At the end of the 19th century, Santiago de Compostela was only a Catholic pilgrimage centre where priests in the vicinity sent their parishioners. However, the monumental book (in three volumes) *Las peregrinaciones a Santiago de Compostela* by Vázquez de Parga et al. (1948/1949) provided major impetus to the route. In writing the book, all three authors walked the route to Santiago in the hard years of the Spanish Civil War and, upon arriving at the Cathedral, the canons were surprised to see the pilgrim authors in old-fashioned dress, not usually seen at that time. The book laid a foundation for modern Camino scholarship (Moralejo 1993), and also proved complementary to the actions of clergy who wished to encourage walking of the Camino or its sections (such as the parish priest of O Cebreiro, E. Valiña) (Lois-González et al. 2015).

Clerical and scholarly enthusiasts constituted the initial nucleus of contemporary pilgrims to Santiago and encouraged the creation of friends of the Camino associations, which held their first convention in the city of Jaca in 1987. The scholars of the route (who in this period, were mainly medieval historians and philologists), some clergy and simply lovers of the walk (Catholic or not), built the first network of promotion of the Camino, following the medieval formula of marching on foot or horseback (to which the bike would be later added) for at least 100 kilometres, staying in modest places and befriending other pilgrims or local people (Lois-González 2013). The network of friends' associations created today expands all over the world, and boasts thousands of members regularly connected in Italy, Germany, Netherlands, United Kingdom, the United States, Poland and Canada, to name a few of the most prominent examples.

The interest of scholars, clergy and walkers in the Camino has also been accompanied by more commercial interests in the development of the image of the Camino. Lyricist and novelist Paulo Coelho, the world's best-selling Portuguese-language novelist, and actress Shirley MacLaine each wrote a book about their pilgrimage experience; works of little interest to the real walkers, but which sold very well, helping to build the profile of the Camino as a global product (Coelho 1987; MacLaine 2001). Slightly more serious and also the most successful in sales of the Camino literature (approximately 5 million books have been sold) is the work of Hape Kerkeling, a comedian and entertainer on German television, which turned the Camino into a popular cultural reference point (Kerkeling 2006) and has been translated into English and adapted for a 2015 film. More rigorous, deep and interesting are the works of Cees Nooteboom (1996) and the Korean Kim Hyosun (2011), who recount with precision their experience of walking to Santiago from the perspective of a devoted writer, or a well-known South Korean journalist. The production of written texts, in the form of books and, increasingly, digital formats, promote the popularity of the pilgrimage in a contemporary context; to the point that the significance of such works on the markets of Brazilian, German and Korean walkers is, in itself, beginning to be studied (Torres-Feijó 2012).

The experience of the Camino has also been treated lavishly by the cinema (see López *et al.* 2015) in various films, among them: *The Way* (Estevez 2010), by Emilio Estevez and his father Martin Sheen, an actor of Galician origin from a village not far from Santiago; *Saint Jacques . . . La Mecque* (Serreau 2005), the main French contribution to the genre; and, to some extent, the Oscar-winning Spanish film *The Sea Inside* (Amenábar 2004), which does not address the issue of the pilgrimage (it is about euthanasia), but spectacularly captures the landscapes of the Atlantic *finisterre* (end of the world) close to Santiago and inspiring visits to the region (see also Chapter 4).

Other private actors who encourage the promotion of the route to Santiago include tourism companies and travel agents of very different sizes and nationalities, who have joined bloggers and groups of pilgrims on social media platforms. Promotional brochures have been studied by Santomil (2011), who notes that, in addition to the common idea of walking, each national market reinforces an attribute according to their own preferences. In this sense, countries such as Germany, Italy and the United States reinforce the message of pilgrimage with an idea of nature, landscape and ecology (in German brochures and websites, greenery dominates when portraying the Camino); of a religious place and of worship in Italy (red tones are prominent in the designs); and the voluntary and solidarity spirit of the route in the United States (a country that, along with the United Kingdom, has led to the institution of the *hospitaleros*, people who work in hostels several weeks or months of the year, and tend to be physiotherapists who aid with foot or muscle injuries caused by walking).

Planning action at different levels: institutional measures to improve the walkability of the Caminos

The Camino de Santiago passes through natural areas, rural communities and towns of different sizes along its way. It is an historical axis of communication that has had an impact on the population of the territory and has focused attention on the different sections with their rich architectural and cultural heritage. Heritage was the object of the first planning initiatives taken with respect to the pilgrimage route, with unique elements and architectural sites being listed as Sites of Cultural Interest, as has happened with many of the villages along the Camino. The heritage planning strategies and, above all, the interior rehabilitation plans allowed for the promotion of the historic-artistic heritage, encouraging residential rehabilitation, boosting the economic revitalisation and improving walkability for the pilgrims, with the pedestrianisation of major public spaces. The urban planning of the populated areas that the Camino crosses has established strict rules that protect these places (López-Trigal 1993).

Something similar happened some years later with natural spaces along the Camino. The planning action on nature also began with the cataloguing of the territory to be maintained through a certain amount of protection, which is followed by the adoption of a planning instrument that allows for the use of the space, path maintenance and spatial governance from the perspective of sustainable development and tourism use (Somoza-Medina 2009). Subsequent landscape legislation after the 2000 European Convention of Florence, led to the specific treatment of this element, which is important for the Camino, with specific rules required on landscape conservation in all future planning documents. Finally, the rural communities that make up much of the area that the pilgrim passes through have benefited in recent decades from European rural development policies. The LEADER initiative, the PRODER programme in its different periods, as well as other institutions of regional rural development (e.g. AGADER in Galicia) have financed the initiatives of local groups (Sánchez-Muñoz et al. 2000). In those areas crossed by the Camino, such policies have become a means of integrating a variety of different interventions, including road maintenance, architectural and cultural heritage conservation, building new public facilities, promoting hospitality and tourism, and improving the walkability of the route. Measures for the latter include tree planting and woodland conservation, changing walking surfaces, creating new rest areas, improving street furniture, and ensuring all routes are properly signposted.

At the end of the 1990s, the first comprehensive management examples of the Camino de Santiago arose with specific planning instruments, at both a regional (in Spain the Autonomous Regions have competencies in territory and planning management) and a local level. Individual actions on the improvement of walkability have been carried out in most of the European network of Caminos de Santiago, but it is in UNESCO World Heritage-listed stages where the most comprehensive intervention plans can be found.

Regional planning

UNESCO granted the Santiago de Compostela French Camino the status of World Heritage in 1993, and in 2015 extended this distinction to what is commonly called the Northern Caminos (the Primitive, and the Northern or Coastal). These routes go through eight Autonomous Regions: Aragon, Basque country, Navarre, Cantabria, La Rioja, Castile and León, Asturias and Galicia, and more than 300 municipalities (Figure 37.2).

UNESCO (2006) noted the difficulty in preserving a route of such length, therefore recommending a precise delimitation of the listed site and an integral action plan. In addition, Spanish legislation, and, in particular, the 1985 Historical Heritage Law, established the obligation of a precise delimitation of the Cultural Interest Assets. Following these decisions, the Autonomous Regions carried out surveys to outline the extension of the Camino and define different levels of protection. This work was arduous, requiring preliminary studies, phases of public consultation, reception of claims and new delimitation proposals so that the definitive delimitations have been delayed since the initial processing of the register. La Rioja made its initial delimitation in 1988 and its final delimitation was the groundwork for the first Special Plan for the Protection,

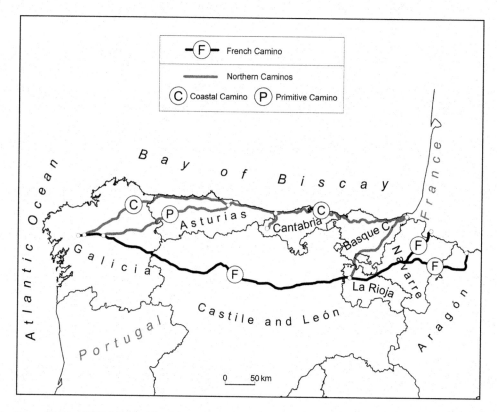

Figure 37.2 UNESCO World Heritage Caminos

Recovery and Revitalization of the Camino de Santiago, passing through this region. Navarre approved the provisional delimitation in 1988 and the final one in 1993. Aragon made their provisional delimitation in 1993 and the final in 2002, while Castile and León began the register in 1993 and proposed the definitive delimitation in 1999. Galicia established its provisional delimitation in 1992 (collecting the boundaries of parishes along the Camino) and the final in 2011. In all these cases, we refer to the French Camino, which had been declared a BIC (Cultural Asset of Interest) Historic-Artistic Site in 1962. In the case of the Northern Caminos, the process started afterwards. Euskadi (the Basque country) declared the stages of the Northern Camino as a BIC in 2000, and Asturias did the same in 2006; Cantabria followed suit in 2007 and in 2015 delimited its layout. In these documents, virtually all the same categories in the delimitation of the road are established: an easement area of 3 metres on each side of the Camino, a protected strip of 30 metres on each side, and a buffer zone which varies between the 100-m delimitation established by Castile and León, the 100 m and 200 m depending on the area in Galicia and 250 m of environmental protection in La Rioja. This delimitation is the preliminary step for the establishment of a comprehensive regional action that has developed slightly differently in each Autonomous Region.

In La Rioja, as already mentioned, the Special Plan was approved in 1998, due in part to its shorter length (65.5 kilometres) with respect to other regions crossed by the French Camino. This Special Plan, in addition to the protected strips, included other specific delimitations, protected areas where there is a risk of undesirable urbanisation near the most populated towns, areas of protection where the Camino runs parallel to roads with a protection area of 50 m, and landscape protection areas to prevent the consolidation of undesirable visual and environmental activities in the vicinity of the Camino. The plan also included specific details from the unique sites catalogue for 11 municipalities and plans of actions designed with the criteria of ensuring the comfortable movement of pedestrians, looking at the continuity of the pedestrian route, improving the location and characteristics of the rest areas, increasing monument routes of interest in urban areas, reordering public squares and looking for the integration of certain areas of particular environmental value (Gobierno de La Rioja 1997).

In Aragon, a Cooperation Agreement was signed in 2008 between the Autonomous Region and the Ministry of Public Works to plan for the restoration, recovery and conditioning of the Camino de Santiago, which included an extensive series of actions. The philosophy behind this plan was to conceive the Camino as a linear archaeological site. Successive archaeological field surveys were undertaken, which allowed the many vestiges of ancient walkways to be recovered. Perimeter walls were consolidated, slopes were levelled, pilgrims were protected with wooden railings in more dangerous locations, pedestrian bridges were built to walk over valleys and small canals, new sheltered rest areas were created, and the Camino signposting was improved to include information on the different areas and attractions of interest and signposts at crossroads indicating the path to take and the kilometres left to Santiago (Méndez de Juan 2011).

Castile and León developed an initial Protection Special Plan between 1989 and 1991 that failed to be approved (López-Trigal 1993). In 2000, a new document was processed but only in the provinces of Burgos and Palencia, as the Leon Province government was already making a similar plan which it left in 2005 to consolidate into a single Regional Plan of the Camino de Santiago, which was approved on a provisional basis in 2010 (Andrés-Mateo and Masiá-González 2011).

In Galicia, the subsidiary rules of provincial planning adopted in 1991 established a field of protection of 100 metres on each side of the Camino. In 1996, the Caminos Protection Law laid down, as in the other regions, the protection strips of the Camino (3 metres) and the surrounding area (30 metres), as well as a system of sanctions and generic regulations while the regional Special Plan was not implemented (Xunta de Galicia 1996). In 2011, the Land Planning Guidelines determined the need to adopt a Special Plan for the Camino (Xunta de Galicia 2011), and finally, the new Galician Cultural Heritage Law from 2016 established a new two-year deadline to approve an Integrated Land Plan of the Caminos de Santiago (Xunta de Galicia 2016). However, 20 years have passed and, despite the obligation to develop the plan, it has still not been approved.

The reality that justifies this delay is complex. On the one hand, the work for the delimitation of the French Camino carried out between 2009 and 2012 discovered a large number of documented variants of the path that were perceived by the local populations as being part of the Camino de Santiago. This generated serious difficulty in implementing different protection strips and also to determine the areas eligible to receive public aid for the rehabilitation of private assets. On the other hand, the increase in the influx of pilgrims was seen by the administrations as a risk that should be strategically addressed, diversifying the routes and arrival paths into Santiago de Compostela to counteract possible saturation. For this reason, other historical routes as well as new branches of existing ones were promoted. The 1996 Protection Law recognised the French Camino, the Portuguese (Camino Portugués), the English (Camino Inglés), the Northern and the Fisterra Caminos, as well as the Silver and the Sea routes of Ulla and Arousa (Ruta de la Plata and Rutas del mar de Ulla y Arousa). The new Cultural Heritage Law (Xunta de Galicia 2016) incorporated the Primitive Camino and the Winter Camino (Camino de Invierno), leaving open the possibility of cataloguing new routes (e.g. sea routes). In addition, the law specifically mentioned that the routes could be of three types: main routes: historical paths that remain in use with traditional characteristics; historical routes: documented historical sections that were lost physically or functionally; and functional routes: alternative paths of cultural, environmental or safer passages for the path users (Figure 37.3). For this reason, pilgrims who headed to Santiago de Compostela via the French Camino in 2016 could find multiple crossings with a 'double Jacobean' signage that offered the possibility to follow complementary paths, either to wander through documented historical ruins or paths to visit places of interest, moving away from the traditional and more congested route. In terms of the improvement of walkability, the key concept in Galicia is the safety of pilgrims, especially in relation to intersections with busy roads, articulating paths that keep pilgrims away from danger.

The other three Autonomous Regions that the Northern, Coastal and Primitive Caminos pass through initiated the processes of cataloguing, delimitation and protection more recently. In the Basque country, the cataloguing and delimitation stages were carried out in 2000 and, in 2009, a Master Plan was approved for the cultural and tourist development and promotion of the Caminos de Santiago. In Cantabria, the delimitation of the paths was approved in October 2015. In Asturias, the Government of the Principality announced the approval of a Special Plan of the Camino de Santiago in 2016, which established measures for the protection and management of the Asturian paths, highlighting among the proposed measures the incorporation of wifi along the length of the entire Camino. The change of motivation in these three cases, which are more oriented to tourism than to the protection of a cultural asset, were explicitly documented in the cataloguing of the Camino in the Basque country, far from the restoration objectives of the Camino in Aragon (Agencia Vasca de Turismo 2009).

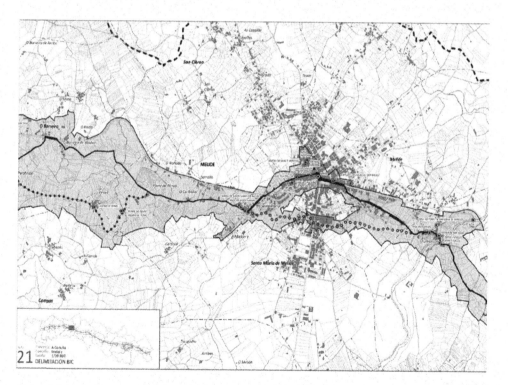

Figure 37.3 Delimitation of the French Camino in the town of Melide (Galicia) *Source*: Xunta de Galicia 2016, used with permission.

Apart from Navarre, where a significant level of Camino protection area is not accompanied by plans or specific regulations for its protection and that of its surroundings, the actions of the Autonomous Regions can generally be seen to have been directed to encouraging the walking of the ancient route to Santiago. For this reason, there has always been a special interest in delimiting the historical route, although this can also be interpreted as the pursuit of historicity in a largely reinvented tradition. Second, it seeks to improve the Camino to facilitate walking. In the third instance, it seeks to act on its surroundings, initially very narrow, just several metres, but later moving towards the concept of a visual valley, as demanded by a landscape approach. Ultimately, everything for the contemporary pilgrims, from the preparation of the place they are going through to the introduction of elements that will facilitate the walking (such as planting trees to give shade), and the landscape, have become subject to the planning process.

Local planning

Local planning is the level that really conserves the Camino, where data of all the properties is kept, and also detailed catalogues of Special Plans, where each small segment of this network of hundreds of kilometres has its specific regulatory and management approach. Together with the Autonomous Regions, the French Camino runs through 169 municipalities in Spain, of which 39 lacked their own planning process in 2016, 13 had a basic document (Delimitation of Urban Land), 54 were regulated by Subsidiary Planning Regulations and 63 had Municipal General Planning Plans, the main general planning mechanism. Spanish municipalities are responsible for creating urban and territorial plans at a local level (with different names as we have indicated). There, approval is mandatory, but many rural municipalities never do this, or approve summarised plans, claiming not to have the money or capacity to undertake detailed planning. In the majority of cases, with the existence of plans, both the Subsidiary Planning Regulations and the General Plans have a detailed catalogue of the historic-artistic heritage of the place where different protection levels of public and private buildings of interest are specified. This is due to the Camino de Santiago being considered a BIC. In this way, almost 70% of the municipalities along the French Camino have protected their historical urban spaces thanks to local planning mechanisms.

With respect to the protection of historical monument settings, the Special Plans for the Interior Protection and Renovation (PEPRI in Spanish), take on fundamental importance. This is a type of development planning aimed at preserving the aesthetic and heritage values of a site, one that standardises the interior catalogues of all built space, listing the possible actions in each building to conserve the urban scene and, at the same time, prevent its degradation. In the case of the French Camino, a total of 11 municipalities had this Special Planning mechanism in 2016. Leon was the first town to have a PEPRI in 1993, followed by Santo Domingo de la Calzada (1994), Mansilla de las Mulas (1995), Jaca (1996), Santiago de Compostela (1997), Melide (1999), Canfranc (1999), Pamplona (2001), Viana (2001), Ponferrada (2001) and Puente la Reina (2005).

At a local level, the instruments for the comprehensive and specific planning and development for the protection of the Camino de Santiago are the Special Plans for the Protection of the Historical Site of the Camino de Santiago. Of the total number of municipalities analysed, only ten had this type of plan, all of them in Castile and León, as they are part of a regional strategy. In fact, the government of this region has established as a rule that all small municipalities through which the Camino runs must have this type of special plan to authorise new construction licences, following the example of the city of Burgos which has had this type of Special Plan since 1999. The Junta (administrative council) supports the creation of such plans, as has happened in several

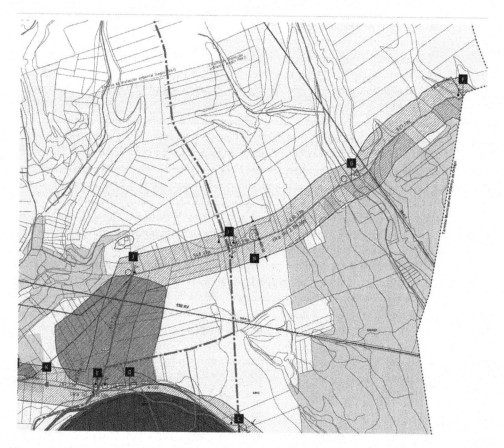

Figure 37.4 Alternative outline proposed in the Special Plan of San Justo de la Vega (Castile and Leon) to separate the Camino from the N-120 road. *Source*: Ayuntamiento San Justo de la Vega, used with permission

municipalities (Carrión de los Condes, Valverde de la Virgen, San Justo de la Vega (Figure 37.4), Sahagún, and Molinaseca, among others).

As noted above, the autonomous regions hold the competences on territorial planning and, in the case of the Camino de Santiago, as set out in each region's protection regulations, the respective Directorate General of Heritage is in charge of approving any significant work that is carried out within the territory affected by the BIC. This, in effect, is the biggest problem perceived by the local population, the difficulties imposed by "heritage" in order to make any changes to their properties. To try to solve this difficulty the Galician Directorate General of Cultural Heritage released a complex guide for the protection of the Camino de Santiago in 2012, which states the rules and criteria that apply when issuing a report on any plan, programme or project on the Camino (Xunta de Galicia 2012).

Conclusions

The Camino de Santiago is increasingly a modern "designed" path on a historical physical base. The Camino is marked by the reinvention of a medieval hiking route with contemporary attributes and the comfort and safety required by the 21st-century pilgrim. It is a complex territorial phenomenon that has sometimes required the combined action of various public institutions, individuals (academic, famous and anonymous) and civil associations of different types to achieve international success. The different visions which constitute the Aragon (linear archaeological site) and the Basque country (contemporary tourist path) plans are, in principle, opposed and represent the constant competition between different strategic visions faced in all the sections of the route. For this, the Camino is more than a spiritual pilgrimage, more than the history of European culture, more than walking tourism and more than the three of them combined.

The initial preparation and promotion of recent decades has given way to a stage of improvement of walkability through planning. The built heritage, public and private, the natural heritage and also the cultural heritage has been preserved. Now it is time to improve the route itself. As this chapter has detailed, the regional planning threat is to break the path into segments which compete among themselves, leading to the development of eight "unique" regional products. Local planning is the basic level for the improvement, section by section, of the Camino, but it can multiply the heterogeneity of the setting. This is why the supervisory work of the regional authorities is so important, although they are often perceived negatively by local populations. Nevertheless, the future of the Camino is positive, as long as the planning strategies are properly implemented. Alternative routes to the French Camino have seen their usage increase and have improved their network of hostels and complementary services, preventing the excessive saturation of the traditional path. This is indeed the great threat; that the Camino may succumb to its own success. The great tool to prevent this from happening is the territorial planning and management of a complex tourist product – one that needs to maintain the perfect alliance between institutional action, the individual promotion of the pilgrims and the active support of the local population.

References

Agencia Vasca de Turismo (2009) *Plan Director para el desarrollo y promoción cultural y turística de los dos caminos de Santiago a su paso por Euskadi*, Agencia Vasca de Turismo [Basque Tourism Agency], Vitoria, Spain: Gobierno Vasco.

Amenábar, Alejandro (dir.) (2004) *The Sea Inside* (motion picture), prod. A. Amenábar, Spain.

Andrés-Mateo, C. and Masiá-González, L. (2011) *Estrategias de planificación territorial. El Plan Regional del Camino en Castilla y León*, Urban-e, Madrid: UPM. Available at: http://urban-e.aq.upm.es (accessed 5 May 2016).

Barreiro, X.M. (2009) *La Fundación de Occidente. El Camino de Santiago en Perspectiva Política*, Madrid: Ed. Tecnos.

Castro-Fernández, B. (2010) *O redescubrimento do Camiño de Santiago por Francisco Pons Sorolla*, Santiago de Compostela: Ed. Xunta de Galicia.

Caucci, P. (1993) *L'Europa del pellegrinaggio*, Milan: Jaca Book.

Coelho, P. (1987) *The Pilgrimage*, New York: HarperTorch.

Coleman, S. and Eade, J. (2004) *Reframing Pilgrimage: Cultures in Motion*, London: Routledge.

Collins-Kreiner, N. (2010) 'The geography of pilgrimage and tourism: transformations and implications for applied geography', *Applied Geography*, 20(1): 153–164.

Estevez, Emilio (dir.) (2010) *The Way* (motion picture), prod. D. Alexanian and E. Estevez, USA: Icon Entertainment International.

Frey, N. (1998) *Pilgrim Stories: On and Off the Road to Santiago*, Berkeley, CA: University of California Press.

Gobierno de La Rioja (1997) *Plan Especial de Protección, Recuperación y Revitalización del Camino de Santiago a su paso por La Rioja*, Logroño: Gobierno de La Rioja [Government of La Rioja].

Greenia, G. (2014) 'What is pilgrimage?', in L. Harman (ed.), *A Sociology of Pilgrimage: Embodiment, Identity, Transformation*. London, Ontario: Ursus Press, pp. 8–28.

Herrero-Pérez, N. (2008) 'Reaching land's end: new social practices in the pilgrimage to Santiago de Compostela', *International Journal of Iberian Studies*, 21(2): 131–149.

Hyosun, K. (2011) Camino de Santiago de Compostela: Camino Francés, Vía de la Plata, Camino Portugués.

Kerkeling, H. (2006) *Ich bin dann mal weg – Meine Reise auf dem Jakobsweg*, Munich: Malik.

Lois-González, R.C. (2013) 'The Camino de Santiago and its contemporary renewal: pilgrims, tourists and territorial identities', *Culture and Religion, An Interdisciplinary Journal*, 14(1): 8–23.

Lois-González, R.C. and Santos-Solla, X.M. (2015) 'Tourist and pilgrims on their way to Santiago: motives, Caminos and final destinations', *Journal of Tourism and Cultural Change*, 13(2): 149–165.

Lois-González, R.C. and Somoza-Medina, J. (2003) 'Cultural tourism and urban management in northwestern Spain: the pilgrimage to Santiago de Compostela', *Tourism Geographies*, 5(4): 446–461.

Lois-González, R.C., Castro-Fernández, B. and Lopez, L. (2015) 'From sacred place to monumental space: mobility along the way to St. James', *Mobilities*. DOI: 10.1080/17450101. 2015. 1080528.

Lopez, L. (2012) 'La imagen de Santiago de Compostela y del Camino en Italia. Una aproximación desde la Geografía cultural', unpublished doctoral thesis, Department of Geography, University of Santiago de Compostela.

Lopez, L., Santomil, D. and Lois-González, R.C. (2015) 'Film-induced tourism in the way of Saint-James', *AlmaTourism – Journal of Tourism, Culture and Territorial Development*, 6(4): 18–35.

López-Alsina, F. (1993) 'La sede compostelana y la catedral de Santiago en la Edad Media', in J.T. Seoane-Prieto and J.M. García-Iglesias (eds), *La catedral de Santiago de Compostela*. A Coruña: Xuntanza, pp. 13–45.

López-Trigal, L. (1993) 'Políticas de rehabilitación das cidades e vilas camiñeras de León', in M. P. Torres-Luna, A. Pérez Alberti and R.C. Lois-González (eds), *Os Camiños de Santiago e o territorio*. Santiago de Compostela: Xunta de Galicia, pp. 793–805.

MacLaine, S. (2001) *The Camino: A Journey of the Spirit*, Atria Books: New York.

Maddrell, A. (2013) 'Moving and being moved: more-than-walking and talking on pilgrimage walks in the Manx landscape', *Culture and Religion*, 14(1): 63–78.

Méndez de Juan, J.F. (2011) *El tramo aragonés del Camino de Santiago (Camino Francés)*. Urban-e. Madrid: UPM. Available at: http://urban-e.aq.upm.es (accessed 5 May 2016).

Moralejo, S. (ed.) (1993) *Santiago, Camino de Europa. Culto y cultura en la peregrinación a Compostela*, Santiago de Compostela: Xunta de Galicia.

Nooteboom, C. (1996) *El desvío a Santiago*, Madrid: Siruela.

Oficina del Peregrino (2015) *Estadísticas de Peregrinación a Santiago de Compostela 1970–2015*, Santiago de Compostela: Archicofradía del Apóstol.

Pichel-Pichel, J.M. (2004) *Arquitectura en el Camino, 1994–2004*, Santiago de Compostela: Xunta de Galicia.

Roseman, S. (2004) 'Santiago de Compostela in the year 2000: from the religious center to European city of culture', in E. Badone and S. Roseman (eds), *Intersecting Journeys. The Anthropology of Pilgrimage and Tourism*, Chicago: University of Chicago Press, pp. 68–79.

Sánchez-Muñoz, M.J., Somoza-Medina, J. and Maya Frades, A. (2000) 'Valoración de los programas de desarrollo rural en las áreas periféricas de Castilla y León', in F. García-Pascual (ed.), *Actas del X Coloquio de Geografía Rural*, Lleida: Universitat de Lleida, pp. 714–723.

Santomil, D. (2011) 'A imaxe exterior de Galicia no século XXI', unpublished doctoral thesis, Department of Geography, University of Santiago de Compostela.

Santos-Solla, X.M. (1999) 'Mitos y realidades del Xacobeo', *Boletín de la AGE*, 28: 103–119.

Santos-Solla, X.M. and Lois-González, R.C. (2011) 'El Camino de Santiago en el nuevo contexto de los turismos', *Estudios Turísticos*, 189: 95–117.

Santos-Solla, X.M. and Pena-Cabrera, L. (2014) 'Management of tourist flows: the Cathedral of Santiago de Compostela', *Pasos: Revista de turismo y patrimonio cultural*, 12(4): 719–735.

Serreau, Coline (dir.) (2005) *Saint Jacques . . . La Mecque* (motion picture), prod. Charles Gassot, France: Téléma.

Somoza-Medina, J. (2009) 'The national park concept in Spain', in W. Frost and C.M. Hall (eds), *Tourism and National Parks*, Abingdon, Oxon: Routledge, pp. 143–154.

Soria y Puig, A. (1991) *El Camino de Santiago: I. Vías, viajes y viajeros de antaño*, Madrid: Ministerio de Obras Públicas y Transportes (MOPT).

Torres-Feijó, E. (2012) 'Interesses culturais e âmbitos receptivos em dous romances sobre o Caminho de Santiago: "Frechas de ouro" e "O enigma de Compostela"', *Romance Notes*, 52(2): 135–150.

UNESCO (2006) *Periodic Reporting 'Route of Santiago de Compostela'*. Available at: http://whc.unesco.org/archive/periodicreporting/EUR/cycle01/section2/669-summary.pdf (accessed 5 May 2016).

Vázquez de Parga, L., Lacarra, J.M. and Uría Ríu, J. (1948/1949) *Las peregrinaciones a Santiago de Compostela* [The pilgrimages to Santiago de Compostela], 3 vols, Madrid: Consejo Superior de Investigaciones Científicas (CSIC).

Villares, R. (1984) *A Historia*, Vigo: Galaxia and Biblioteca Básica da Cultura Galega.

Xunta de Galicia (1996) *Lei de protección dos camiños de Santiago*, Santiago de Compostela: Xunta de Galicia.

Xunta de Galicia (2011) *Directrices de Ordenación Territorial*, Santiago de Compostela: Xunta de Galicia.

Xunta de Galicia (2012) *Guía para a protección do Camiño de Santiago*, Santiago de Compostela: Xunta de Galicia.

Xunta de Galicia (2016) *Lei de Patrimonio de Galicia (Anteproxecto)*, Santiago de Compostela: Diario do Parlamento de Galicia.

Xunta de Galicia and Universidade de Santiago (2007–2010) *Observatorio estatístico do Camiño de Santiago 2007, 2008, 2009 e 2010*, Santiago de Compostela: Universidade de Santiago de Compostela-CETUR and Xunta de Galicia.

38

Walk on

Conclusions and the future

C. Michael Hall and Yael Ram

Overview of this volume

As the various chapters in this volume illustrate, the subject of walking covers a wide range of issues and perspectives. Part I primarily covered cultural and historical context of walking. Bieri (Chapter 2) highlighted the links between walking and contemporary capitalism in the contemporary city, but also noted the historical relationships that contribute to the use and valorisation of urban space. The same patterns of conspicuous consumption noted by Bieri also provide opportunities for oppositional perspectives, an issue raised by Smith in Chapter 3. Smith, building on authors such as Solnit (2000), highlighted that walking is not always a Romantic or a calm practice, but can also used be as an expression for radical ideas (see also Smith 2015). Although some of the observations made by Smith arguably stand in contrast to some of the findings of Reiser and Jansen-Meinen (Chapter 6), who highlighted the way that walking was utilised for more reactionary purposes in Germany in the inter-war period. Nevertheless, it is interesting that they also regarded changes in German walking culture as expressive of the changing nature of political systems and ideologies. Cultural expression was also a theme of Frost and Laing's (Chapter 4) discussion of long-distance walking in films, where walking is presented as an activity that prompts healing and redemption. A similar positive portrayal of walking was found in Goertz's discussion of walking as a means of pedagogy that noted that becoming a college student coincides with becoming a daily walker out of necessity (Chapter 5). Interestingly, she argued that generation Y is the 'walking generation' although, as noted in several other chapters in this volume, the extent to which different generations adopt walking as an activity varies between cultures and locations. The final chapter in Part I, by Boland and Wheeller, also highlights the role that walking plays in learning, and emphasises, among other things, that the combination of walking and dialogue has been an ongoing feature of philosophy and literature. As with other chapters in this volume, Boland and Wheeller emphasise that walking is a dynamic social practice, so that even if one starts travelling alone, one always meets and walks with others.

Part II, consisting of Chapters 8 to 15, emphasised social practices, behaviours and perceptions. Chapter 8, by Iwasaki, focused on the importance of dogs for walking practices. Looking beyond the often-stated health benefits of walking the dog (Hoerster *et al.* 2011;

Utz 2014), the chapter addressed the personal, social and environmental factors that contextualise dog walking, including the effects of socio-demographic factors and urban design. The social dimension of walking also contributed to a sense of attachment to dogs as companions, and of social support for dog walkers (Netting *et al.* 2013). Although not a major focus of the chapter, the significance of dogs for walking behaviour raises substantial questions about the friendliness of places for dog walking and the provision of recreational areas for dogs and their owners. In contrast, Chapter 9, which presents the results of a quantitative study of walking activity in Switzerland, found that walking from A to B is far more important than walking for leisure, while, even in terms of leisure, dogs play only a minor role. Chapter 10 focused on a very specific type of walking behaviour, walking to school, and stressed that walking to school is more than 'only' walking and, instead, acts both an objective space to travel between home and school, and as a leisure space for individual reflection and socialising. The theme of walking having an active social space was also explored in Chapter 14, by Mondschein, who noted the changing ways in which cities are being walked for social purposes and the interaction of such walking with ICT.

Several chapters also examined various dimensions of hiking. Chapter 11, by McCarville and Pilon, examined spiking – the combination of sport and hiking – as well as the growing significance of the internet to tell the story of hiking adventures, even when people are walking alone. The sharing of experiences was also a theme in Chapter 12, by Rantala and Tuulentie, who examined online narratives of hiking in Lapland. They found that hiking in a group was generally a sociable experience and that 'lonely wolves' were usually rare, especially due to security reasons, and, even if someone does hike alone, they usually meet other people, since the wilderness in Lapland is not empty. However, the emphasis on the possibility of solitude for walkers was strong. Chapter 15 by Witte and Hannan also looked at online hiking communities in China and the tension that existed between collectivity and individuality. Chapter 13 also looked at different forms of interaction with the environment, though in this case in Iceland, and found that hikers perceived and understood the landscape in a different way from non-hikers, with their willingness to tolerate certain infrastructure or evidence of environmental disturbance being more limited than non-hikers. Nevertheless, the findings raise questions about the differential acceptability of infrastructure, given that in some highly scenic wilderness locations on walking trails wifi is being made available, to enable people to send photographs on social media and thus encourage further tourism visitation (Foxe 2016).

Part III of the book further extended discussion of long-distance hiking, but also engaged with walking for reasons of pilgrimage. Chapter 16, by Gross and Werner, provided an overview of long-distance 'hut-to-hut' hiking trails in Germany, Canada, New Zealand and Japan. The chapter is complemented by detailed discussion of the Masar Ibrahim Al-Khalil /Abraham Trail in Chapter 17, the Wales Coast Path in Chapter 18, and cross-border walking trails on the Spain–Portugal Border in Chapter 21. These chapters highlighted the way in which trails and long-distance walking are becoming an increasingly commoditised activity, and becoming regarded as a means of regional development, particularly in rural areas (Timothy and Boyd 2015). This being the case, substantial attention is therefore being given to the visitor and service experience to improve the quality of the hiking trails and products (Chapters 19 and 20). Interestingly, the results of the Norwegian research of Nordbø in Chapter 20 illustrate that international hikers place importance on a different set of benefits than those placed by local Norwegians. For the DMOs to provide the right service quality, they therefore must acknowledge and consider these differences when developing their products, as well as face significant strategic decisions with respect to positioning and the markets they wish to focus on. The last three chapters of Part III attend to both the secular and spiritual dimensions of walking. Chapter 22, by Schilar, discusses the experience of the solo-hike, noting that it is essentially a journey of distance to common life spaces and closeness to the inner self, an experience which is appreciated because of its temporary nature. Chapter 23 by Kato discusses the Kumano-kodo pilgrimage in Wakayama, Japan in terms of concepts of 'slow' development, and provides an interesting contrast to the following chapter, by Das and Islam, which discusses Hindu pilgrimage, noting that the structures that develop around such activities can often have a substantial political dimension.

Part IV of the book examines a major theme in contemporary research on walking, that of health and well-being. Chapter 25 (Finnie, Wiseman and Ravenscroft) explored some of the complexities that surround the meaningful nature of leisure walking for British men. The study challenged ideas of walking just being about physical exercise, and men's leisure as essentially instrumental in nature. Instead, for the participants, walking was found to provide a platform with which to connect with themselves and the natural environment, both in the past and the present. Chapter 26, by Saunders, Weiler and Laing, focused on a theme that arose in a number of chapters, namely the way in which walking can provide life-changing experiences. For many subjects of this study, long-distance walking was found to facilitate moments of insight through which issues were seen more clearly, or placed in a new context, and therefore contributed to significant personal change. Chapter 27 (Patterson, Pegg and Omar) provides a review of much of the literature, particularly from the first decade of the century, on reasons for engaging in walking to increase levels of physical activity. This theme was also picked up by Grénman and Räikkönen in Chapter 28, who report on walking and other differences between physically active and inactive Finnish university students and the contribution that engagement in leisure walking clearly made to the perceived physical, mental and social well-being of respondents. The final chapter in Part IV, by Bertella (Chapter 29), reports on the contribution that dog walking can make to human and animal well-being, and noted, as would be appreciated by any dog walker, that the dog walking experience can be viewed as a shared liminoid experience performed by interspecies couples.

Part V discusses issues of planning and design. Chapter 30 by Ram and Hall examined issues of urban walkability from the perspective of tourists, which is an understudied area of walkability research. They noted that, from a destination perspective, walkability is probably an advantage but present measurement tools have been developed from the perspectives of permanent inhabitants rather than of visitors. Chapter 31 (Svensson, Sörlin, Dahlberg, Fredman and Wall-Reinius) looked at the importance of walking trails as management tools in areas where different interest groups co-exist, while the role of walking in placemaking and economic development were discussed in France by Ducros (Chapter 32), and in Western Norway by Fabritius (Chapter 33). The remaining four chapters in Part V all focused on different aspects of management and planning. Popp (Chapter 34) discussed mechanisms of coping with crowded locations, while Chapter 35 (Schofield, Doran and Nolan) examined GIS applications in improving the walkability of urban space in Salford in the UK: this valuable study provides a rare longitudinal perspective on the success of interventions to improve walkability. Chapter 36 (Vereda and Borla) also utilised spatial analysis in improving policy making and management for walking trails, while the final chapter in Part V (Somoza-Medina and Lois González) discussed the problems that arise with the multi-level planning and management of probably the most famous pilgrimage and walking trail in the world, the Camino de Santiago in Spain.

The themes identified in the chapters will undoubtedly be important into the future. However, there are some additional areas that will likely become even more significant for future research. These include such concerns as obesity, an ageing population, the provision of toilets, access to public space, walking inside and privacy issues.

Health, wellness and obesity

More adults in the world are now obese than are underweight. The prevalence of adult obesity ranges from over 60 per cent in some Pacific Island nations to less than 2 per cent in Bangladesh (Ng et al. 2014). Individuals who walk or cycle to work are 13 per cent less likely to be overweight compared to individuals who don't (Azevedo and Vartanian 2015). Increasing rates of obesity, and the overwhelming evidence that active travel, such as walking and cycling, is a significant contributor to reducing obesity, means that walking will continue to be a significant area of public health and well-being research (Haskell et al. 2007; Karnik and Kanekar 2012; Gatrell 2013). However, interventions to encourage walking have major implications for environmental justice, public space provision and urban design (Koohsari et al. 2013; Wolch et al. 2014; Chaufan et al. 2015; Witten 2016), as well as potential health co-benefits for climate change adaptation strategies (Cheng and Berry 2013; Hall, et al. 2017).

Ageing

A related dimension of walking and health and well-being is the rapid ageing of the world's population. The percentage of the population aged 65 or older is expected to double between 2015 and 2050, from 8.5 per cent (617 million) in 2015 to 16.7 per cent (1,600 million) by 2050 (He et al. 2016). Nevertheless, growth in ageing is geographically uneven. In 2015, one in six people in the world live in a developed country, but more than one-third of the world population aged 65 and older, and over half of the world population aged 85 and older, live in these countries. However, by 2050, less than one-fifth of the world's older population will reside in developed countries, with almost two-thirds of the world's older people living in Asia (He et al. 2016). The ageing of the population will undoubtedly lead to various initiatives to encourage greater physical exercise as a means of prolonging health and well-being throughout the older years, while at the same time, there will be more people who will require support structures and appropriately designed infrastructure to maintain walking activity (Capistrant et al. 2014; Fitzgerald and Caro 2014; Hörder et al. 2013; Bauman et al. 2016; Jeste et al. 2016; Müller et al. 2016). Yet these issues will also be bound up within wider policy debates over the economics of ageing and population growth, and the capacity of places to manage the effects of older populations on retirement incomes and aged services, especially at a time of increased upheaval in the workforce because of automisation (Bloom et al. 2015).

Toilets

One specific dimension of an ageing population is growth in incontinence and the need for appropriate toilet facilities to encourage leisure walking (Bichard et al. 2012; Vine et al. 2012; Cerin et al. 2013). However, even though the provision of appropriate public toilet facilities is an incredibly important public health and planning aspect of the capacity of individuals to engage in walking, the subject of toilets is seemingly almost taboo in literature on walking, mobility and tourism (Greed 2003). As Greed (2016) comments:

> If the government wants people to leave their cars at home and travel by public transport, cycle or walk, then the provision of public toilets is essential, especially at transport termini. Public transport passengers, pedestrians and cyclists – unlike car drivers – cannot speed to the nearest motorway service station to use the toilet when they find the local public toilets

have been closed. It should not be assumed that only a minority will need on-street public toilets, because alternative off-street toilet options are readily available.

(Greed 2016: 506)

Cities and regions that are looking to enhance their attractiveness for walking, cycling and public transport need to address public toilet availability as a way of improving the pedestrian environment (Sugiyama *et al.* 2015). In addition, there is a need to ensure the availability of public toilets in rural areas and attractions as well, so as to avoid undesirable disposal of human waste. The availability of toilets can have economic and public health benefits because of their contribution to place satisfaction and increase in likelihood of repeat visitation (Speck 2012; Washington 2014; Afacan and Gurel 2015; Hall *et al.* 2017).

Access to public space

Concerns over access to toilets are part of a bigger issue of access to public space in order to engage in walking activity. Public open spaces, such as parks, green spaces and urban common areas, are key built environment settings that provide opportunities for a variety of physical activity behaviours, such as recreational walking (Koohsari *et al.* 2013, 2015). The enclosure of public space, whether by selling off for private redevelopment, introduction of charging regimes, or other changes with respect to access, can substantially affect walking opportunities. Also detrimental can be a lack of maintenance or provision of infrastructure that encourages people to use public space (Wolch *et al.* 2014).

Walking inside

Although the focus of this book has been on walking outside, the growing urbanisation of society, and the size of cities itself, means that more attention needs to be given to the role of walking in the internal environments of cities: malls; large integrated retail, leisure and housing complexes; and the links between complexes. Although urbanisation and its accompanying dependence on the car is often a negative influence on walking practices and health levels, in some circumstances, whether because of health, cultural reasons, or concerns over the safety of the external environment, walking inside malls or large recreation complexes may constitute a major component of daily exercise (Carpenter 2008; Vincent 2009; Riley-Jacome 2010; Correa-de-Araujo 2015; Lu *et al.* 2015). Walking inside may be particularly appropriate for some groups during winter or summer temperature extremes, and where the inclement conditions preclude walking outdoors (Rothe *et al.* 2010). In some cases, specific behavioural interventions may be appropriate to encourage walking for migrant and refugee communities, and particularly for women (Murray *et al.* 2016), with indoor environments providing the best setting.

The provision of large indoor retail and leisure space is integral to the attraction of shopping malls as walkable spaces (Heitmeyer and Kind 2007), and mall walking has attracted its own body of research (Schacht and Unnithan 1991; Warin *et al.* 2008; King *et al.* 2016). Farren *et al.* (2015), for example, found that, from a public health perspective, 'malls provided safe, accessible, and affordable exercise environments for middle-aged and older adults', although they did also note that research is limited and characterised by poor study designs. However, many cities have extensive covered and underground pedestrian spaces (CUPS) that can provide considerable opportunities for utilitarian (travel to work or shopping) and leisure walking. Both natural and cultural factors influence the development of CUPS. In cities with severe seasonal weather conditions, such as Montréal (Canada), a cold winter city, and Oklahoma City (United States), a windy city, CUPS have provided a climate-controlled environment for social, entertainment, retail and commercial activities. In dense urban settings such as Tokyo, Japan and Shanghai, China, CUPS provide opportunities for much more comprehensive and intensive usage of urban spaces, by accommodating multiple urban functions, comparable to that which occurs at street level. In a review of CUPS, Cui *et al.* (2013) found that the four major influencing factors in the development of CUPS were climate, subway construction, land usage and the economic environment, with the role of CUPS in the built urban structure strongly driven by the level of economic development. Nevertheless, while CUPS are recognised as increasingly important for urban development (Li *et al.* 2013a, 2013b; Broere 2016; Doyle 2016; Li *et al.* 2016), there is relative paucity of research on their use for walking and their walkability (Zacharias 2015). In a study of individual pedestrian itineraries in the Montréal underground, Zacharias (2015) found that location had a major effect, the availability of services had a mixed effect and weather had no effect on trip length or the length of the underground trip portion. Therefore, given the growth in CUPS environments in many cities and their focal point for walking as an activity, far greater attention needs to be given to indoor walking by a much wider range of disciplines than has hitherto been the case.

Technologies, privacy and public surveillance

Changes in technology are also leading to new ways in which the public and private spaces are encountered while walking (Liao 2015; Liao and Humphreys 2015; see Chapter 1, this volume). While augmented technologies will undoubted add value to some, the long-term impacts of such technologies on walking experiences remains to be adequately studied. The growth in mobile and wearable technologies is likely to increase in the light of diminishing costs, ease of wear and ease of use. The growth in mobile technologies also opens up new opportunities for tracking and data gathering by both public and private agencies in the development of 'smart cities' (Albino *et al.* 2015). However, at the same time new issues of privacy and data confidentiality are also created, given that while so-called 'civic hacking' (Townsend 2013) may contribute to managing urban problems, such systems are also open to illegal hacking, as well as private use of public data. The growth of the smart city also creates wilder ethical and political debates over in whose interest data is used, and as to whether it is used for a wider public good or further consolidation of private wealth and a growing divide between the haves and the have-nots. As Sadowski and Pasquale (2015) note:

> There is a certain allure to the idea that cities allow a person to both feel at home and like a stranger in the same place. That one can know the streets and shops, avenues and alleys, while also going days without being recognized. But as government and corporate actors, often in close partnership with each other, fill cities with 'smart' . . . technologies – turning them into platforms for the 'Internet of Things' (IoT): sensors and computation embedded within physical objects that then connect, communicate, and/or transmit information with or between each other through the Internet – there is little escape from a seamless web of surveillance.

Conclusions

Although inherent to the human condition, walking has always been an act with many consequences. As this volume has shown, there are a wide range of perspectives and understandings of something that is much more than getting from A to B. Walking can be understood as much as a political and economic act as something that contributes to health and psychological well-being. Importantly walking can also be an inherently social activity, whether it be with human or animal companions, and, for some people, walking is an act that connects them with place and nature as well as themselves. Walking is therefore a profoundly educational tool, providing opportunities to learn both with and about others, with the very pace of walking being conducive to seeing the world in particular ways. Nevertheless, like all aspects of personal life, the broader social context of walking is changing, affected by technologies, economies and the very right to engage in walking in certain places and times. These issues provide opportunities to draw together a range of different social scientific, medical, cultural and other perspectives on a subject that requires an inter-disciplinary approach to develop better understandings and contributions to enable better walking opportunities. The majority of the world's population now live in an urbanised environment, while public and common spaces are increasingly under threat. At no previous time, therefore, has there been more of a need for the opening-up of academic and physical spaces for walking. We hope that this volume contributes to such openings.

References

Afacan, Y. and Gurel, M.O. (2015) 'Public toilets: an exploratory study on the demands, needs, and expectations in Turkey', *Environment and Planning B: Planning and Design*, 42(2): 242–262.

Albino, V., Berardi, U. and Dangelico, R.M. (2015) 'Smart cities: definitions, dimensions, performance, and initiatives', *Journal of Urban Technology*, 22(1), 3–21.

Azevedo, S.M. and Vartanian, L.R. (2015) 'Ethical issues for public health approaches to obesity', *Current Obesity Reports*, 4(3): 324–329.

Bauman, A., Merom, D., Bull, F.C., Buchner, D.M. and Singh, M.A.F. (2016) 'Updating the evidence for physical activity: summative reviews of the epidemiological evidence, prevalence, and interventions to promote "Active Aging"', *The Gerontologist*, 56(Suppl 2): S268–S280.

Bichard, J., van den Heuvel, E., Gilhooly, M. and Parker, S.G. (2012) 'Tackling ageing continence through theory, tools & technology (TACT3)', *International Journal of Aging in Society*, 1(2): 83–98.

Bloom, D.E., Chatterji, S., Kowal, P., Lloyd-Sherlock, P., McKee, M., Rechel, B., Rosenberg, L. and Smith, J.P. (2015) 'Macroeconomic implications of population ageing and selected policy responses', *The Lancet*, 385(9968): 649–657.

Broere, W. (2016) 'Urban underground space: solving the problems of today's cities', *Tunnelling and Underground Space Technology*, 55: 245–248.

Capistrant, B.D., Glymour, M.M. and Berkman, L.F. (2014) 'Assessing mobility difficulties for cross-national comparisons: results from the World Health Organization study on global ageing and adult health', *Journal of the American Geriatrics Society*, 62(2): 329–335.

Carpenter, C.L. (2008) 'Motivation to exercise: translating our best intentions into action', *Obesity Management*, 4(6): 329–332.

Cerin, E., Lee, K.Y., Barnett, A., Sit, C.H., Cheung, M.C. and Chan, W.M. (2013) 'Objectively-measured neighborhood environments and leisure-time physical activity in Chinese urban elders', *Preventive Medicine*, 56(1): 86–89.

Chaufan, C., Yeh, J., Ross, L. and Fox, P. (2015) 'You can't walk or bike yourself out of the health effects of poverty: active school transport, child obesity, and blind spots in the public health literature', *Critical Public Health*, 25(1): 32–47.

Cheng, J.J. and Berry, P. (2013) 'Health co-benefits and risks of public health adaptation strategies to climate change: a review of current literature', *International Journal of Public Health*, 58(2): 305–311.

Correa-de-Araujo, R. (2015) 'Cultural considerations for exercise in older adults', in G.M. Sullivan and A.K. Pornidor (eds), *Exercise for Aging Adults: A Guide for Practitioners*. Cham, Switzerland: Springer International Publishing, pp. 85–96.

Cui, J., Allan, A., Taylor, M.A.P. and Lin, D. (2013) 'Underground pedestrian systems development in cities: influencing factors and implications', *Tunnelling and Underground Space Technology*, 35: 152–160.

Doyle, M.R. (2016) 'From hydro/geology to the streetscape: evaluating urban underground resource potential', *Tunnelling and Underground Space Technology*, 55: 83–95.

Farren, L., Belza, B., Allen, P., Brolliar, S., Brown, D.R., Cormier, M.L., Janicek, S., Jones, L., King, D.K., Marquez, D.X. and Rosenberg, D. (2015) 'Mall walking program environments, features, and participants: a scoping review', *Preventing Chronic Disease*, 12: 150027. DOI: http://dx.doi.org/10.5888/pcd12.150027

Fitzgerald, K.G. and Caro, F.G. (2014) 'An overview of age-friendly cities and communities around the world', *Journal of Aging & Social Policy*, 26(1–2): 1–18.

Foxe, K. (2016) 'Ireland brings Wi-Fi to wilderness for photos', Lonely Planet Travel News, 12 February. Available at: www.lonelyplanet.com/news/2016/02/12/ireland-brings-wi-fi-to-the-wilderness-for-tourist-photos

Gatrell, A.C. (2013) 'Therapeutic mobilities: walking and "steps" to wellbeing and health', *Health & Place*, 22: 98–106.

Greed, C. (2003) *Inclusive Urban Design: Public Toilets*, Oxford: Architectural Press.

Greed, C. (2016) 'Taking women's bodily functions into account in urban planning and policy: public toilets and menstruation', *Town Planning Review*, 87(5): 505–524.

Hall, C.M., Le-Klähn, D.-T. and Ram, Y. (2017) *Tourism, Public Transport and Sustainable Mobility*. Bristol: Channel View.

Haskell, W.L., Lee, I.M., Pate, R.R., Powell, K.E., Blair, S.N., Franklin, B.A., Macera, C.A. Heath, G.W., Thompson, P.D. and Bauman, A. (2007) 'Physical activity and public health: updated recommendation for adults from the American College of Sports Medicine and the American Heart Association', *Circulation*, 116(9): 1081–1093.

He, W., Goodkind, D. and Kowal, P. (2016) *An Aging World: 2015*. International Population Reports P95/16–1, Washington, DC: United States Census Bureau.

Heitmeyer, J. and Kind, K. (2007) 'Consumer acceptance of urban open-air mixed-use centers: a cross-generational comparison', *Journal of Shopping Center Research*, 14(1): 57–78.

Hoerster, K.D., Mayer, J.A., Sallis, J.F., Pizzi, N., Talley, S., Pichon, L.C. and Butler, D.A. (2011) 'Dog walking: its association with physical activity guideline adherence and its correlates', *Preventive Medicine*, 52: 33–38.

Hörder, H., Skoog, I. and Frändin, K. (2013) 'Health-related quality of life in relation to walking habits and fitness: a population-based study of 75-year-olds', *Quality of Life Research*, 22(6): 1213–1223.

Jeste, D.V., Blazer, D.G., Buckwalter, K.C., Cassidy, K.L.K., Fishman, L., Gwyther, L.P., Levin, S.M., Phillipson, C., Rao, R.R., Schmeding, E. and Vega, W.A. (2016) 'Age-friendly communities initiative: public health approach to promoting successful aging', *The American Journal of Geriatric Psychiatry*, 24(12): 1158–1170.

Karnik, S. and Kanekar, A. (2012) 'Childhood obesity: a global public health crisis', *International Journal of Preventative Medicine*, 3(1): 1–7.

King, D.K., Allen, P., Jones, D.L., Marquez, D.X., Brown, D.R., Rosenberg, D., Janicek, S., Allen, L. and Belza, B. (2016) 'Safe, affordable, convenient: environmental features of malls and other public spaces used by older adults for walking', *Journal of Physical Activity and Health*, 13(3): 289–295.

Koohsari, M.J., Badland, H. and Giles-Corti, B. (2013) '(Re)Designing the built environment to support physical activity: bringing public health back into urban design and planning', *Cities*, 35: 294–298.

Koohsari, M.J., Mavoa, S., Villanueva, K., Sugiyama, T., Badland, H., Kaczynski, A.T., Owen, N. and Giles-Corti, B. (2015) 'Public open space, physical activity, urban design and public health: concepts, methods and research agenda', *Health & Place*, 33: 75–82.

Li, H.Q., Parriaux, A., Thalmann, P. and Li, X.Z. (2013a) 'An integrated planning concept for the emerging underground urbanism: Deep City Method Part 1 concept, process and application', *Tunnelling and Underground Space Technology*, 38: 559–568.

Li, H., Li, X., Parriaux, A. and Thalmann, P. (2013b) 'An integrated planning concept for the emerging underground urbanism: Deep City Method Part 2 case study for resource supply and project valuation', *Tunnelling and Underground Space Technology*, 38, 569–580.

Li, X., Xu, H., Li, C., Sun, L. and Wang, R. (2016) 'Study on the demand and driving factors of urban underground space use', *Tunnelling and Underground Space Technology*, 55, 52–58.

Liao, T. (2015) 'Augmented or admented reality? The influence of marketing on augmented reality technologies', *Information, Communication & Society*, 18(3): 310–326.

Liao, T. and Humphreys, L. (2015) 'Layar-ed places: using mobile augmented reality to tactically reengage, reproduce, and reappropriate public space', *New Media & Society*, 17(9): 1418–1435.

Lu, Z., Rodiek, S., Shepley, M.M. and Tassinary, L.G. (2015) 'Environmental influences on indoor walking behaviours of assisted living residents', *Building Research & Information*, 43(5): 602–615.

Müller, A.M., Ansari, P., Ebrahim, N.A. and Khoo, S. (2016) 'Physical activity and aging research: a bibliometric analysis', *Journal of Aging and Physical Activity*, 24(3): 476–483.

Murray, K.E., Ermias, A., Lung, A., Mohamed, A.S., Ellis, B.H., Linke, S., Kerr, J., Bowen, D.J. and Marcus, B.H. (2016) 'Culturally adapting a physical activity intervention for Somali women: the need for theory and innovation to promote equity', *Translational Behavioral Medicine*, 24 August. DOI:10.1007/s13142–016–0436–2.

Netting, F.E., Wilson, C.C., Goodie, J.L., Stephens, M.B., Byers, C.G. and Olsen, C.H. (2013) 'Attachment, social support, and perceived mental health of adult dog walkers: what does age have to do with it?', *Journal of Sociology and Social Welfare*, 40(4): 261–283.

Ng, M., Fleming, T., Robinson, M., Thomson, B., Graetz, N., Margono, C., Mullany, E.C., Biryukov, S., Abbafati, C., Abera, S.F. and Abraham, J.P. (2014) 'Global, regional, and national prevalence of overweight and obesity in children and adults during 1980–2013: a systematic analysis for the global burden of disease study 2013', *The Lancet* 38(9945): 776–781.

Riley-Jacome, M., Gallant, M.P., Fisher, B.D., Gotcsik, F.S. and Strogatz, D.S. (2010) 'Enhancing community capacity to support physical activity: the development of a community-based indoor–outdoor walking program', *The Journal of Primary Prevention*, 31(1–2): 85–95.

Rothe, E., Holt, C., Kuhn, C., McAteer, T., Askari, I., O'Meara, M., Sharif, A. and Dexter, W. (2010) 'Barriers to outdoor physical activity in wintertime among Somali youth', *Journal of Immigrant and Minority Health*, 12(5): 726–736.

Sadowski, J. and Pasquale, F.A. (2015) 'The spectrum of control: a social theory of the smart city', *First Monday*, 20(7). Available at: http://firstmonday.org/ojs/index.php/fm/article/view/5903/4660

Schacht, S.P. and Unnithan, N.P. (1991) 'Mall walking and urban sociability', *Sociological Spectrum*, 11(4): 351–367.

Smith, P. (2015) *Walking's New Movement*, Axminster, Devon: Triarchy.

Solnit, R. (2000) *Wanderlust: A History of Walking*, New York: Viking.

Speck, J. (2012) *Walkable City: How Downtown Can Save America, One Step at a Time*. New York: Farrar, Straus, and Giroux.

Sugiyama, T., Gunn, L.D., Christian, H., Francis, J., Foster, S., Hooper, P., Owen, N. and Giles-Corti, B. (2015) 'Quality of public open spaces and recreational walking', *American Journal of Public Health*, 105(12): 2490–2495.

Timothy, D.J. and Boyd, S.W. (2015) *Tourism and Trails: Cultural, Ecological and Management Issues*, Bristol: Channel View.

Townsend, A.M. (2013) *Smart Cities: Big data, civic hackers, and the quest for a new utopia*. New York: W.W. Norton & Company.

Utz, R.L. (2014) 'Walking the dog: the effect of pet ownership on human health and health behaviors', *Social Indicators Research,* 116(2): 327–339.

Vincent, D. (2009) 'Culturally tailored education to promote lifestyle change in Mexican Americans with type 2 diabetes', *Journal of the American Academy of Nurse Practitioners*, 21(9): 520–527.

Vine, D., Buys, L. and Aird, R. (2012) 'Experiences of neighbourhood walkability among older Australians living in high density inner-city areas', *Planning Theory & Practice*, 13(3): 421–444.

Warin, M., Moore, V., Davies, M. and Turner, K. (2008) 'Consuming bodies: mall walking and the possibilities of consumption', *Health Sociology Review*, 17(2): 187–198.

Washington, K.M. (2014) 'Go before you go: how public toilets impact public transit usage', *PSU McNair Scholars Online Journal*, 8(1): Article 5.

Witten, K. (2016) *Geographies of Obesity: Environmental Understandings of the Obesity Epidemic*, New York: Routledge.

Wolch, J.R., Byrne, J. and Newell, J.P. (2014) 'Urban green space, public health, and environmental justice: the challenge of making cities "just green enough"', *Landscape and Urban Planning*, 125: 234–244.

Zacharias, J. (2015) 'Underground pedestrian trips – trip generation, spatial distribution and activities in the Montréal underground', *Tunnelling and Underground Space Technology*, 46: 46–51.

Index

Index

tracking technologies 15–19; *see also* GPS, privacy, smartphone, technology
tractivism 37
traffic 140, 201, 371; congestion 1, 370; constraint to walking 42, 52, 280–1; control 343–4; and pedestrian road safety 7–8, 280–1, 312; psychosocial stress 371; speed 101
transformation *see* personal transformation
transformative tourism 265
Trevelyan, G. M. 58
TripAdvisor 142; and walkability 317–25
Tuan, Y-F. 228
Turkey 8; Antalya **315**

Ulysses 76–7
United Arab Emirates **9**
United Kingdom **5**, **8**, 393; *see also* England, Northern Ireland, Scotland, Wales
United States **5**, 6, **8**, 10, 51, 68, 265, 393; Canadian border 51; Death Valley 111; Washington DC 3; New York City **315**; Oklahoma 407
Uruguay **9**
urbanization 10, 68, 395; re-urbanization 32; suburbanization 32
urban design 2, 6, 27–8, 30–31, 83, 280, 311; New Urbanism 34; politics 30; qualities 6–7; *see also* walkability
urban tourism 316–18, 323, 360–3; crowding and coping strategies in 366–7, 391

vandalism 376
Vasaloppet ski race 333
volunteer tourism 237, 264, 267
volunteering 165, 187, 232, 233, 236–8; *see also* volunteer tourism

Wales 184–93
Walk Score 34, 318; and walkability measures 3, 318–25
walkability 6, 7, 55–6, 137, 139, 242, 369; and built environment 20, 31–4, 311–15, 340–1, 370–1, 393–400; of colleges and universities 55–6; design for 31–4, 315–16, 340–1, 343, 372–6; economic implications 2–3; and ICT usage 144; measures of 318–25, 372–3; pilgrimage routes and sites 244–8, 393–400; to school 103; for tourists and visitors 315–27, 393–400
walkable urbanism 27–34; defined 28; images of urbanity 30–1
walking: as art 37–45; commodification 27–35; cross-disciplinary nature 1; design and planning for 27–36, 194–205, 242–50, 311–29, 360–8,

369–78, 390–401; in education 55–64; in film 46–54, 74–9; for health 1, 74, 92, 144, 148, 187, 237; interventions and encouragement for 274–86; 288–99; 300–9; in literature 65–6, 74–9; leisure walking 7, 68, 150, 255, 318; long distance 37, 46–54, 264–72, 404; marketization of 29; as meaning making activity 253–62, 264–72; mode share 94, 96–8, 100; for physical activity 58, 92, 100, 186, 196, 211, 274–83, 288–90, 297; to school 100–101; social practices 1, 6, 12, 86, 101, 147, 382; for spiritual and religious purposes 47–54, 223–9, 242–50; sustainability 7, 66, 71, 245, 370, 394; to work 6, 75, 92; *see also* dog walking, hiking, leisure walking; pilgrimage, walkability
walking behaviour 274–5, 404; conceptual framework *283*; determinants 276–83; significance of dogs for 404
walking clubs 71
walking tourism 232–4, 240, 290, 331, 350–8, 400; community benefits 350–8; *see also* hiking, pilgrimage
walking trails 280
Walkonomics 33
weather 6, 7, 58, 111, 164, 303, 313; narratives of 123, 124, 304; and walking experience 197, 258
Wells Gray trail 163
Wapta Ice Hike 163
The Way 48–51
wayfinding 122–3, 140, 363
well-being 194, 254, 258–9; contribution of walking to 194, 254, 256–9; emotional 194; importance of natural environments 194, 260; mental 291, 293; physical 260–1, 291; social 194, 291; *see also* health
West Highland Way 47, 154, 224
Wild 51–3
wilderness 51, 109, 147, 149, 154, 213, 224, 335, 380–1; Argentina 381–7; Canada 162; Finland 119–25; Germany 161; Iceland 128–35; settings 129, 195; skills 206; Sweden 330; United States 51, 361; values 128–9
wilderness tourism 128, 380–1
Wookie 10
World Bank 174. 176, 177
World Heritage 166, 232, 235, 366, 390, 391, 394–5, *395*; *see also* heritage
World Health Organisation (WHO) 92, 274; Health Economic Assessment Tool (HEAT) 187

Yelp 142

Zeno 58